The Crossroads of Poverty and Prosperity

The Impact of Religious Beliefs and Worldviews on Economic Outcomes

John R Visser

Printing: Druckhaus Berlin-Mitte
Binding: Buchbinderei Stein & Lehmann, Berlin

Dedication

This book is dedicated to my wife, Linda - whose strengths have always wonderfully compensated for my weaknesses – in appreciation of her constant love, her support on this project, and especially her patient proofreading. I would also like to recognize my parents, Eli and Jeanette Visser, whose principled living and sacrificial investment in my nurture and education could not help but lead me to investigate the big questions this book attempts to address.

Acknowledgements

I would also like to thank the many students who, in the process of working to complete their college education, contributed to the research, documenting of sources, and/or proofreading of one or more chapters. Gina (Bonnema) Popma, Melinda (Sybesma) Segaar, Rachel Kobes, Ben Visser, Kayla Gesink and Ashley Hoekstra are some of the ones called upon for significant work, but there are many others who helped with smaller details who must remain unnamed because of my failure to keep a careful log. Thanks also to Erica Vonk for her help with the manuscript, and freeing me from many tasks that could easily have kept this book from reaching final form; and to Josh Visser for applying his creative skills to the cover. Finally, I would like to thank the many people who neither assisted me in my writing nor are part of my family – but who nevertheless supported and/or inspired me over the years. It is my sincere hope that some of them, as they read these words, will know that I recognize my debt to them, even though they shall remain unnamed here.

Table of Contents

Foreword

Genesis

The desire to write this book stems from three events of the late 20th and early 21st centuries, each separated from the previous by about a decade, that framed and in many ways helped me clarify one of the defining struggles of this and many other centuries. The first, which planted the seed in my mind, took place on August 19, 1991, as I rode through the streets of Moscow on a two-colors-fit-all red and white Soviet-era bus en route to the opening ceremonies of a seminar series where American professors, including myself, would teach market-based business principles to Russian university professors and prospective business people. With varying degrees of discomfort, being in the charge of our vodka-toting charter bus driver, my fellow travelers and I, both Russian and American, passed endless rows of camouflage tanks, some strung out like beads around the necklace of the city's "ring roads," others backed strategically on to the sidewalks between the curbs and shop fronts so as to menace those of us glimpsing through rain-streaked windows down the barrels of their turrets. Little did I know at the time that the soon-to-fail coup I was witnessing would, along with other key developments at the end of the 20th century, open the world to an unprecedented experiment in market economics, offering people like me a once-in-a-lifetime opportunity to investigate the impact of history, culture, government, civil society and belief systems on the dynamics of economic development and wealth creation. Before I left for home that September, some of my Russian friends asked me how long I thought it would take for their economy to become healthy, assuming that anticipated political and economic freedoms were not quickly retracted. Naively, in retrospect, I guessed "about ten years," after which I tried to envision the end of religious oppression and evolution of a civil society in Russia and how this might nurture the growth of a private sector and the Russian economy. During the decade of my prediction, a steady supply (some would say a revolving door) of Western business persons, consultants and politicians entered and exited Russia. Nevertheless, at the end of this period Russia was still very much teetering on the brink of bankruptcy. Meanwhile, its neighbor, China, where I started a routine of teaching summer short courses in 1996, in spite of its continued embrace of a communist political system, developed at a pace that made it the envy of the developing (and in some ways the entire) world.

It is not surprising then that, nearly a decade after I watched history unfold on the streets of Moscow, it took a second event to remind me of the need to renew my search for the roots of economic development. On July 23, 1999, I strolled the elevated walkway that circles the statue of the beloved Dr. Sun Yat-Sen in Nanjing, China, which had been China's capital city prior to its destruction by Japanese invaders. Fresh from repelling some aggressive boy-beggars whose tactics included everything short of sticking their hands in my pockets, I was confronted with the haunting image of a young girl, burned almost beyond recognition, rigid, except for her eyes, in front of a small dish with a few coins in it. While I rationalized why I should pass her by (e.g., helping beggars just encourages them to sit on the street all day; surely a small contribution couldn't begin to help someone with such severe problems; besides, perhaps those aggressive boys, or an unscrupulous adult, had placed her there and would be confiscating her money) her eyes met mine and followed me until I was well past her. It wasn't until I was back in my four-star hotel room that the well-known words of Christ, "whatever you did not do for one of the least of these, you did not do for me" worked their way into my mind. Mentally extending her plight to millions of others, I began to wonder how useful the economic statistics kept by the Chinese government actually were for measuring the quality of life of the average Chinese citizen. How many other people, like her, found themselves sadly hidden in the cracks of the cities or behind hedges in the countryside in places where economic development was just a distant rumor?

But time and distance have a way of eroding our sensibilities and passion, so it took the global financial and economic crises that began in 2008 to force me to do the hard work of sorting out my thoughts and writing them down in a way that would make them intelligible to others. How was it that so few people, and outwardly respectable people, could do so much damage to so many across the globe in such a short time? How was it, that in spite of all that we have learned and institutionalized about economics in well-developed economies, like those of the U.S and Europe, we were still so susceptible to these problems?

Purpose

The answers to these questions are of course multifaceted, but my experience in Russia had already convinced me that one important contributor to economic development, and one that I had spoken about a number of times in speeches and seminars, was that no democracy or market economy could thrive without a civil society. But had my reaction to the little burned girl been civil? Had the mortgage and investment bankers who were at the heart of the financial crisis been civil with their clients? What evidence was there that we Westerners were so civil with each other or more civil than non-westerners? And, if civil society was the key, was this both necessary and sufficient for our economies to keep humming along? The U.S.'s test would come soon enough; in fact it had already started with the dot.com crash, and would soon include the 9/11 World Trade Center attacks and several other serious economic difficulties. And although by most measurements the U.S. weathered these events fairly well, it became increasingly clear to me during these years that our economic success (and that of others) depended very much on how we decided to define success. And shortly thereafter, upon concluding that our success (and therefore economic development) measures were deeply flawed, I set out on a quest to find out why nations and people measure economic progress and development the way they do. During this quest I discovered two important things: that measurements of success reflect people's core beliefs and values; and that the things that lead to sustainable economic development (or its antithesis) have their tap roots in a not widely studied and even unlikely place – people's religious beliefs. Because of this, I became increasingly convinced that understanding and incorporating religious beliefs into economic development policies is not only the key to freeing people and nations that have known little other than poverty for centuries, but also the path by which people in so-called developed nations can find real joy and lasting satisfaction in their prosperity.

This is not to say that I want to denigrate the role that either markets or democracy have played in development, but it is fair to say that I can no longer be a card-carrying member of the large and growing crowd that has elevated one or both of these to the status of miracle workers. Nor would I say I don't appreciate, for example, the freedoms I enjoy as a U.S. citizen, the inroads that democracy is making around the world, or the ascendancy of market economies to a prominent position in the global economy. But what my experiences in countries like Russia and China, and more recently on the continent of Africa make clear is that democracy and markets, although important, are certainly not sufficient to usher in a good life. Of course the antithesis of these things, the possibility of efficiently centrally planning every detail of a complex modern economy, has been thoroughly discredited, so I am not arguing that some kind of "big brother" will make all well in an economy. Capitalism comes in many stripes, but we need to better understand the role that religious beliefs play in shaping its various forms, from a purely secular Darwinian survival of the fittest on one end, to some more humane (and I would argue, better functioning) religiously-tempered versions on the other.

My primary goal is not to write about how culture affects economic outcomes from a broad sociological or political perspective. Lawrence Harrison in his books *Underdevelopment is a State of Mind*, and *Who Prospers*, and Francis Fukuyama in his book *Trust*, among many others, have already done a good job of making those connections. Rather, as a person with training and experience in business and finance, I hope to extend their work by fleshing out in more detail on how value is created in an economy (including, for example, the kinder, gentler things that help businesses succeed or stock prices to rise), and in the process bring to light some of the hidden connections between wealth, culture, and religion. This accomplished, I hope to build a case to convince business people and government officials that it is a critical part of their mission (and perhaps essential to a company or nation's competitiveness in the long run) to nurture both civil society and the kind of values that are foundational to wealth-creating activities and a good society. This in turn requires an informed perspective on the role that religion plays in nurturing a civil society and healthy economy, and what freedom of religion needs to look like in private organizations or the public square for religious beliefs to spur rather than impede the wealth creation process.

Audience

At the broadest level this book is for what I contend are the hundreds of millions of people around the world from a variety of backgrounds, cultures, educational and socioeconomic levels, who know instinctively that healthy economies ultimately rest on moral and ethical commitments (and who know there is a big difference between personally-beneficial economic activities and unmitigated greed). Committed to basic freedoms and fully aware of how important markets are, most of these people are nevertheless uncomfortable with the idea that free markets by themselves can usher in the good life. They have a nagging feeling that people's excesses may come back to haunt them or their children, or are already haunting the "have-nots" and their children around the world. On the other hand, most of these people have absolutely no use for violence or revolution as tools for effecting change, or simplistic "knee-jerk" laws and regulations that so often produce the kinds of counterintuitive results that have frustrated economists, business people and policy makers throughout the history of free societies.

Within "developing" countries this group includes many who have little or no voice in the political process, or whose choices have been routinely frustrated by endemic corruption. They may have dropped out of the political process (or never entered) because they view it as disconnected from their daily lives, biased, elitist or hopelessly adversarial or preferential. But this large group, although composed mostly of so-called "ordinary people," also includes many who are politically involved, economically wealthy and in positions of authority. Nevertheless, most of the people in this target audience have not had the luxury of reading authors like Hobbes, Locke, or Rousseau, and may not know Western history well. They may not know the shades of meaning associated with expressions like "Neo-classical economics," "The Enlightenment," "modernism," or the transformation in the meaning of the word "liberal" that took place between the 17th and 21st centuries. And since these terms do not lend themselves to easy translation, I have chosen to avoid them as much as possible and write in plain English. Doing so means I must at times give up the standard academic practice of giving credit to the first Western thinker to make a particular point. This is not to imply that history is not important; however, the average person doesn't need to know whose ideas she has picked up as much as she needs to pick up good ideas, connect them with her experience, and make a commitment to use them when looking forward to find "a better way." By doing this, I hope to make this book accessible to a relatively large number of people with diverse backgrounds and interests, so they can translate the lessons of the book into their daily lives and make a large, collective contribution to economic development in the future.

Included in this group, I believe, are tens of millions of business people who are primarily motivated by the challenge of managing talent and technology to transform resources into useful products and services. As such, they are often much more interested in using their talents and serving people than in the prospect of getting rich (although most of them will gladly accept their share of the surplus created by a well-run, wealth-creating business). Some in this group are already rich (by any global standard) and may find riches curiously unsatisfying, or in a few cases, uncomfortable. Their interest in this book may be an attempt to achieve a broader understanding of the confluence of factors that enabled them to get where they are, or to reach more clarity on the responsibilities that accompany accumulation. But I also hope that those who are by necessity still preoccupied with "making it" will be equally curious about the fundamentals of how wealth is created and economic development takes place.

Also in this group, I believe, are some who have chafed at the fragmentation and tunnel vision of an excessively specialized higher education system; who clearly see the connectedness between the many dimensions of life, and know that problems often cannot and should not be defined one-dimensionally as narrowly economic, psychological, scientific, spiritual, or political. Generally speaking these readers will be looking for (and hopefully find) this writing integrative and cooperative rather than narrowly specialized or adversarial.

Finally, this book is designed to be accessible to people of all ages and education levels, from all socioeconomic groups, religious and cultural backgrounds, and especially to those who run and/or work in both businesses and not-for-profit organizations (since not-for-profits are far more important to the wealth creation/economic development process than they may realize), investors, political representatives and policy makers, and economic development specialists. Many academic books, although important, are not accessible or interesting to non-specialists, meaning those without advanced education in a certain discipline, or schooled in a certain way of thinking. And, in the same way that a good product can fail to be a commercial success because its value is not effectively communicated to the market, good ideas often fail to make the impact that they should because of the delivery system chosen. It is my desire, therefore, to play the role of an academic middleman, a sort of bridge between other professors and writers who are comfortable being more specialized and having their heads a little closer to the clouds than I and the people in the work-a-day world who want and need to know where wealth, well-being, and economic development ultimately come from. I choose this role because in my heart I am not the kind of scholar who can stay locked up in a library for days at a time, all but salivating at the idea of uncovering a few additional nuggets of highly specialized information. I also choose this role because I believe that there are many, complex, interrelated and important "ways of knowing" that go beyond the widely embraced methods of empirical verification, and which, unfortunately, are both severely undervalued in higher education and, therefore, less understood than they need to be. So, I prefer to play the role of a sort of puzzle piece assembler, using my gifts to assimilate a large volume of information from such diverse places as philosophy, sociology, psychology, theology, business, and economics, and boil it down to something that makes sense and is useful to the average person. Hopefully the picture that emerges from the pieces will tell a convincing (and true) story about economic development and the role that religious beliefs play in it, and one that ends up having more impact than a room full of dusty dissertations (including mine, wherever it is).

Apology

Having decided this book should be written, I then had to come to the begrudging conclusion that I should be the one to write it. It is sometimes said that fools rush in where angels fear to tread, and that's perhaps where this book comes into the picture. With no Ivy League degrees behind my name (although I do have a PhD), and living in Iowa, a state whose motto when I started writing was "you make me smile" (dare I say smirk?), I realized that generating interest in and enthusiasm for the book on this subject in urban centers of power and influence might be difficult. Having moved from Chicago to a small town more than thirty years ago, I knew better than most the obstacles I would face. Most of my life I had been conditioned to think, for example, that big was better than small, urban superior to rural, commercial better than agricultural, etc. But, then I reflected on the fact that a man named Adam Smith from a predominantly rural coal mining and salt panning area of Kirkcaldy in the little sub-country of Scotland had written a remarkable book in 1776 which has come to be referred to simply as *The Wealth of Nations*. This is not to say that I had any delusions about my ideas having anything near the impact of Smith's; rather I was convinced that in the "information age," ideas are one of the critical engines of wealth creation, and since they have the potential to spread, for better or worse, more quickly than ever before, I should toss mine into the fray. Besides, I have learned that wisdom often resides in unexpected places and people, and my research has already taken me to some of these places and people, to my great delight. Because of this, I trust the reader will find this journey was worthwhile.

Caveat

One final comment: As some readers may already suspect, true post modernists may find this book upsetting, since it will become clear that it is intellectually irresponsible to pretend that everyone's beliefs, ideas, tastes, or preferences are equally valid (even though I am a strong proponent of the value of diversity). One of my most deeply-held values is that all people are worthy of respect, but, to me, this means respecting them enough to take their most deeply held beliefs and ideas seriously enough to disagree with them. So, I hope it would become clear as the book unfolds, civil society and economic development are both seriously harmed by moral and ethical relativism, in part because these things too often imply that the pursuit of truth is optional. This means that although tolerance should always govern how we treat others, it should never go so far as to cause us to lie to them or to turn an uncaring or deaf ear to those who persist in beliefs and practices that are damaging to them (and in some cases the rest of us). Likewise tolerance should never stop us from one of the most important of all human activities (and one which, I will argue adds immensely to the creation of wealth and economic development) – the hard work of distinguishing between right and wrong, and doggedly attempting to pass on what we've discovered to be right until we've "passed on" and can no longer do so. Unfortunately, this perspective does not allow us to continue to treat the variety of religious beliefs that people hold with kid gloves. Rather, we need to admit that religious beliefs will always play a central role in all human activity, and make this the beginning point of our conversations, rather than doing an "end run" around them by pretending that their proper place must be confined to the dark corner of a mosque or cathedral. Of course, this should always be done realizing that, in our attempts to "pass on" what we know, we need to be open to the likelihood that we may be wrong and need to be on the receiving end of what others can teach us about these things.

Regardless of whatever else this book accomplishes or whether it is commercially successful, if it proves helpful to even a small number of the billions of people who have been looked down upon, or marginalized from the halls of our academies and government buildings because of their religious beliefs, it will have enriched the cultures it touches and made my efforts worthwhile. More importantly, if it accelerates development by opening up faith-based paths to development, thereby improving the lives of millions of people more rapidly that they would have otherwise improved, my efforts will have been more than worthwhile.

Chapter 1: The Global Economic Meltdown

In spite of our PhDs, politicians, and pundits, between 2008 and 2010, the world experienced a financial market meltdown and economic contraction unlike anything seen since The Great Depression. From peak to trough, asset value declines approached ten trillion dollars in the U.S. and as much as fifty trillion globally. As the crisis deepened, lenders greatly curtailed lending to all but the most creditworthy borrowers, consumers severely cut back their purchases, and thousands of businesses laid off millions of workers and/or closed their doors for good. Modern speed-of-light communication systems allowed fear and contagion to spread around the world in unprecedented ways. Governments everywhere pulled out their heavy monetary and fiscal policy stimulus artillery with limited success. For those who had paid little attention to financial markets and economic policies prior this time, two things became painfully obvious. One is that money and financial markets are a cornerstone of economic health and development. The second is that the health of the financial markets and the economy are themselves dependent on truthfulness, trustworthiness, and a number of other critical values which can too often erode during good times.

Conventional wisdom has come to lay much of the blame for the crisis on the excessive use of debt in the years preceding the crisis, primarily because in the twenty five years leading up to the crisis, debt of all types increased about 45 trillion in the U.S., or about four times faster than GDP increased (11 trillion), and similar trends were seen in many other countries. And it cannot be denied that excessive debt has caused serious problems for individuals, companies and countries at various times and places. But debt in and of itself is not a bad thing, since it has the potential to funnel excess funds from those who have limited productive uses for them to those with innovative ideas and the ambition to employ them productively. In fact, many of the poorest countries around the world are stuck in poverty precisely because this flow of funds does not take place – i.e. their people, governments or businesses may do too little lending and borrowing. So it stands to reason that the crisis was about more than the inherent danger associated with debt. In fact it laid bare something much more important, something that has been painfully obvious to people in poor countries for decades: without widespread honesty, or integrity, or a commitment to stewardship or justice, borrowing and lending, like business, government, and so many other good things, can go horribly awry.

A brief look at the events leading up to this most recent global financial meltdown is instructive in this regard. As it turns out, a plethora of questionable values at the governmental, institutional, and individual levels was necessary to create a problem of this magnitude. Let's start with government, and for simplicity, we will focus on the U.S. Federal Government. Although, a strongly growing world economy had boosted savings around the globe - which had been supplying greater liquidity to the global economy, and especially to the U.S. - the U.S. Central Bank, the Federal Reserve, added significant quantities of "easy money" to this supply in its fight to ward off a recession, either major or minor. True to form, this kept real interest rates at historic lows, but a steady dose of this made it far too easy for homebuilders to build and buyers, including speculators, to purchase too many expensive and often unaffordable homes and for investment banks and others to purchase the mortgages financing these assets with massive amounts of low-cost debt. These bargain interest rates, made even lower by tax breaks associated with mortgage loans, also encouraged people to finance unaffordable lifestyles by taking out second and sometimes third mortgages against their property. But while borrowers and spenders prospered, savers watched their savings stagnate, and even shrink, in real terms, because of these low interest rates.

Good intentions aside, since the goal of widespread home ownership is by itself laudable, the roots of this recession lay not as much in low interest rates as in the fundamental assumption that it is government's job to actively manipulate interest rates and its assumptions about when and how it is legitimate to do this. The fundamental question, then, is one of justice – is it right for government to redistribute funds from non-homeowners to homeowners by using monetary policy and tax breaks to increase home affordability? Such incentives encourage middle and upper-class taxpayers to become homeowners, allowing them to disproportionately benefit from rapidly increasing home prices. Likewise, is it the government's role to redistribute funds from savers to borrowers over long periods of time? (Penalizing U.S. savers in this way surely contributed to a drop in the personal savings rate to near zero at the time the crisis unfolded.) To further grease the home ownership wheels and keep cheap credit flowing, the government created two agencies (whose names, Fannie Mae and Freddie Mac are now familiar to many people around the world), eventually privatizing them and encouraging them to purchase large numbers of risky subprime mortgages. (These mortgage loans were risky because home buyers had not been required to put much, if any, of their own money down, or even verify that their incomes were truthfully stated or adequate to afford the mortgage payments they were assuming.)

To make matters worse, the government allowed Fannie and Freddie to purchase these mortgages with massive amounts of debt, so that even relatively minor decreases in home prices, and subsequent decreases in the value of the mortgage loans on Fannie and Freddie's balance sheets that rely on these home prices, could put their investors at risk. Then, to ensure that this would not damage Fannie and Freddie's ability to sell their securities to investors, the government left buyers of these mortgages-backed securities with the distinct impression that the government would guarantee the payment of principal and interest on the underlying mortgages if the home buyers defaulted. In doing so, they obligated American taxpayers to foot the bill for both the foolishness of mortgage lenders and excesses of subprime home buyers. Finally, as if the aforementioned mistakes were not enough, government (often state governments in this case) made it easier for homebuyers who bought unaffordable homes to simply walk away from their loans, leaving taxpayers, as it turns out, to pick up the loss. This is because "non-recourse" laws in many states limit homeowners' liabilities to the collateral value of their homes. This allows them, when times get tough, to save themselves tens or hundreds of thousands of dollars by "giving" the devalued home back to the bank, rather than continuing to make payments on a debt that exceeds the market value of the home.

Government also forced investment banks to value their mortgage-backed securities at market prices (so-called "mark to market" accounting) and required them (through government imposed capital[1] requirements) to sell assets or bring fresh money into the company whenever the value of these securities fell. This would be similar to telling homeowners that they would have to sell their house or give the bank more cash when the market value of their home decreased – even if they were gainfully employed and current on their monthly payments. These rules forced the banks to sell mortgage-backed securities that were already rapidly dropping in value for the purpose of raising levels of capital, which further accelerated the decline in the value of these assets. Eventually no one wanted to buy these "toxic" declining-value assets, and banks that had previously accepted them as valid collateral for loans had little choice but to cease this method of financing, causing their values to drop even more. A vicious cycle set in, causing an increase in worldwide risk aversion, interest rates on private loans to rise, a rapid slowdown in spending, the evaporation of business profits, and sharp increases in layoffs and unemployment - all related in part to government's good intentions but murky understanding of the limits of its competence or its appropriate role.

But government's inability to understand its appropriate role would not by itself have been enough to damage the world economy at the level it was damaged. Serious moral and ethical cracks also revealed themselves at the individual and business levels. For whatever reason, people routinely started buying homes they couldn't afford, and living their lives as if debt did not pose real risks. Many lived beyond their incomes in other ways as well, saving almost nothing from their incomes and borrowing against appreciating assets (especially their homes) to finance various types of consumption; often continuing to spend even as energy and food prices soared; even increasing their purchases of non-necessities as the recession intensified and jobs disappeared. On the other side of the ledger, many investors gobbled up risky mortgaged-backed securities with no questions asked in order to increase their anticipated yields by a couple of percentage points. Others lent their life savings to people they had never even met, or succumbed to the siren song of "too good to be true" promised returns. In short, many adults lived almost like children who believed that mom, dad, or Uncle Sam (now revealed as Uncle Taxpayer) would always be there to pick them up when they fell.

Greed also got the best of many in the banking and investments industries. Gradually, financial institutions that once made it their business to lower risk for their customers began to design assets that shifted risk to their customers, leaving them vulnerable to changes in the global economy. Fraudsters misdirected people's life savings, unbeknownst to them, into inappropriate investments, or worse yet, directly stole money from them through Ponzi schemes[2] that funded lavish live-a-lie lifestyles. To juice their profits, investment banks operated with as little owner money as regulations allowed (made easier by asleep-at-the-switch regulators) which contributed to the need to rapidly sell their assets to raise capital when things started to go sour. They also paid out unconscionable bonuses for a decade or more before the crisis, rather than leave some of the money in their banks for the inevitable rainy day. Commercial banks too kept as little money on hand as possible, while also increasing the riskiness of their loans and off-balance sheet activities (thus allowing increasing amounts of risk to fall to those who were insuring the deposits – i.e. government agencies, and ultimately the taxpayers). They and their mortgage brokers found untold creative ways to bask in lucrative fee-based income by making the kind of foolish loans they wouldn't have been caught dead with on their own balance sheets, and passing them on others who were too detached from the original transaction to know how ill-advised these loans were. In addition, investment banks and other financial companies jumped into the business of selling credit default insurance, only too happy to accept up front easy-money insurance premiums for promises to take over distant, hard-to-value financial obligations of companies they knew very little about. Other companies gladly paid them for this "service" and usually did far too-little "due diligence" into the size and safety of these future promises (so-called counterparty risk). To complete the circle, ratings agencies content to sell sometimes outdated and overly optimistic credit reports for their own lucrative fees gave everybody the peace of mind they were looking for as they moved closer and closer to the edge of the cliff. In short, like frogs in a pot, a surprisingly large number of people were willing to turn a blind eye to the big-picture, long-term vulnerability of an economy characterized by extremely low savings rates, massive government and trade deficits, high and growing consumer debt burdens, rapidly rising food and energy prices, and a lemming-like trust in high and continually increasing financial asset prices (including not only homeowners but a mass of baby boomers planning on using income from financial asset interest, dividends, and capital gains to power their retirement lifestyles).

But misunderstandings of the appropriate role of government, misguided ethics, and outright foolishness are ultimately rooted in more fundamental values and assumptions about life. What made people feel entitled to use massive amounts of leverage to get a big house and three nice cars, or so willing to enslave themselves to high debt payments? What made it so easy for large numbers of individuals to lie on their mortgage application forms? How is it that people came to routinely make life-changing financial decisions outside of any kind of accountability structure or authentic community? How is it that fear and greed have the power to become self-fulfilling prophecies in financial markets? What are the roots of the "bandwagon effect," causing people to accelerate their purchases of houses and stocks when their prices are already high and accelerate their sales of the same when their prices are already low? How is it that autonomy and privacy, and a little additional interest, became so important to investors that they became willing to risk their life savings in opaque investments and securities that they did not understand? Is it as simple as the Old Testament writer of the book of Proverbs seems to indicate when he said that "one who chases fantasies will have his fill of poverty,"[3] or, as the Apostle Paul said in his New Testament letter to Timothy, that "People who want to get rich fall into temptation and a trap and into many foolish and harmful desires that plunge [them] into ruin and destruction?"[4] Certainly not, but this latest and deepest financial crisis makes it clearer than ever that economic outcomes are inextricably tied up with assumptions, beliefs, and values that need to be better understood in order to reduce the likelihood of a reoccurrence of this kind of global meltdown.

It is also clear that these assumptions, beliefs, and values circle outward and affect institutions and societal structures as well. For example, what was it, besides lack of government oversight, which led banks and investment banks, originally formed to bring borrowers and lenders together and shelter them from some of the uncertainties of financial life, to instead separate borrowers from lenders and increase their risk? What in the character or structure of these institutions permitted them to so confidently sell exotic securities, that they did not themselves fully understand, to unsuspecting buyers? Why did so many mortgage companies and commercial bankers turn a blind eye to falsehoods on mortgage applications and the obvious danger of zero-down-payment loans? What led investment banking companies to routinely pay massive bonuses to employees rather than keep an equity cushion in the business for the inevitable downturn? How did these organizations come to the point that they believed they could predict the likelihood of default without any personal contact with the borrower? Was it that they came to see the purpose of a business as something "secular," such as "making money," rather than something moral, like service, honesty, or loving one's neighbor? And if so, where in turn did the tap roots of these beliefs draw their sustenance?

Similar questions need to be asked about the government's role in this massively destructive series of events. Is it the proper role of government to favor homeowners over renters, or borrowers over savers? Is it within the boundaries of its legitimate authority when it creates companies and orders them to buy subprime mortgages with massive amounts of debt? How does a government go decades without correcting regulatory oversights, and why would it risk the entire financial system looking for a sneaky way to get poor people into homes without paying the true price of this social policy? Why would they set up a limited liability structure that allows companies to payout millions in bonuses and dividends to employees and stockholders with no possibility of recovering this money for their clients/creditors when their greed and deception are eventually revealed? Or why would a government be so willing to deny a lender "recourse" for the full amount borrowed? And, perhaps most importantly in the present situation, how does a government determine the appropriate limits of its powers when trying to stabilize the economy or when dealing with economic crises?

In the aftermath of the crisis that began in 2008, the U.S. Government's response was to rescue some companies (but not others), to create massive amounts of money and encourage central banks (globally) to do the same, to keep interest rates low, to temporarily prevent markets from expressing their lack of confidence in financial institutions (e.g., by preventing the "short selling" of financial stocks), to expand deposit insurance promises, to temporarily make short term loans directly to businesses (by buying their commercial paper), to take over mortgage-packaging companies (and order them to buy more mortgages than they otherwise would), to take over the biggest insurance company (and biggest credit default insurer/gambler) in the world, to pump trillions into the biggest banks to shore up their capital and buy their "troubled assets," and pump trillions more in "stimulus" money into the economy in the hope of stabilizing the financial system and jumpstarting consumer spending and job creation.

Many supported these government actions, while others would agree that much of this amounts to a massive redistribution from savers to borrowers and from present and future taxpayers to *selected* present and future corporate and individual beneficiaries. What are the roots of the idea that what we make on the way up is ours to spend or invest as we see fit, but on the way down we are entitled to put our hands in other people's pockets? Do we put blind faith in individual freedom and markets on the way up and government on the way down? Have we come to value freedom and autonomy more than knowledge of right and wrong? Have we come to see the government's role as protecting people from their own foolishness as opposed to maintaining justice, or as a savior rather than a servant? Was this latest economic crisis (and the others before it) related to people on both sides of the political spectrum pushing morality and ethics out of the marketplace and public square? Regardless of how we answer these questions, it seems clear that the roots of our economic decisions and actions are as much moral and ethical as they are economic.

This book, however, is not primarily intended to explain temporary crises in the global economy. Rather, as noted in the *Foreword*, it will take us on a journey through the economic development/wealth creation process,[5] attempting along the way to distinguish the kinds of activities that significantly improve people's lives from those activities that only masquerade as development, and will be quite different than other books on this subject. In the process, it will require the reader to consider the relationship between two things that people do not often think about at the same time, religious beliefs, on the one hand, and the processes by which wealth is created and economic development takes place on the other. It will investigate the role that beliefs and values, and particularly religious beliefs play in causing and perpetuating poverty, on the one hand, or preventing and providing an escape from it, on the other, and the implications of this for development. It is our hope to trace underdevelopment back to its roots, even if doing so opens up the need to rethink much of what has to be accepted about the world, its major problems, and/or religion. It may seem at times like we are opening up a can of worms that would be best left unopened because of its complexity. But it is often these kinds of things that must be done to take us from where we are to where we need to go.

Chapter 2: The Bigger View

Just before the 2008 global economic meltdown, after decades of fits and stops, government helps and hindrances, and steady valiant efforts by a small army of devoted but mostly obscure development workers laboring to improve the lot of the poorest of the poor, the fields of economic and community development finally showed up on the radar screen of global opinion leaders, including rich celebrities (like Oprah Winfrey and Angelina Jolie) and the mass media. This was good news, of course, since the prospect of wealthier countries turning their focus away from their own problems gives hope to those who have long hoped against hope that the plight of the world's least comfortable would become the concern of the world's most comfortable. Nevertheless, despite of the publicity associated with activities such as micro-credit lending, international celebrity adoptions, and "the lost boys of Sudan," the conversation in the wealthy world remains very much focused on putting a face on poverty, encouraging charity and making the best of bad situations, and far less on the root causes of poverty, injustice and brokenness.

In stark contrast to the dizzying media attention given to celebrities is the relative obscurity of a small group of people who devote a large percentage of their time, talents or money to what has traditionally been termed "economic development," or more broadly, "community development." Most of these folks have a very different perspective on wealth than many others of their societies. While economists and business people are often preoccupied with economic growth, development workers (and those working in relief agencies) are usually less concerned with making people wealthy than with making life livable. They typically live in a world where poverty and disease are rampant. They've witnessed, at times, their organizations spending millions of dollars to build communities only to see the fruits of their labors swept away by injustice. They've also witnessed governments and international organizations spending hundreds of millions of dollars in development funds attempting to plant markets and democracies in political and economic soil that lacked the necessary nutrients (such as civil society[1], moral political/economic leadership, or appropriate religious beliefs) for any real or lasting change to take place. They've felt that wretched feeling in their stomach that comes from seeing innocent children die for no good reason. The stories that follow, which happen to focus on Russia, India and several African countries - but represent of the kinds of things that occur every day all around the world, are the kind of thing they witness day after day.

Some Stories

Sergei's father committed suicide at the age of 42, after a tough life and some tough living, leaving Sergei with no assets and the responsibility of supplementing his mother' meager income and filling the void left in his younger brother's life resulting from their father's death. Although his father had been hopeful for a time after the breakup of the Soviet Union, his skills were little in demand in the new Russian economy, and his excessive smoking and drinking had not only exacerbated his tuberculosis and worsened his heart disease, but had also helped impoverish the family. At one point, Sergei went to talk to a doctor about his father's situation but quickly discovered that not only would the official prices for medical care be out of the family's reach, but the doctor would need an "additional" payment to ensure that his father would actually be put in a safe environment and get the care that he needed.

At the same time, Sergei's uncle had an idea for a small business in St. Petersburg and had wanted to offer Sergei a job. Unfortunately, after spending all of his savings to rent a building, he had been unable after several months to obtain the necessary permissions to use the electricity or water in the building. Although he was told by the permit officials in both the water and electricity offices that there was a "special office" that he could go to "expedite" his request, each charged a 5000 ruble "fee" which he was unable to pay. Besides, he knew that he would need at least ten other "permissions," to start his business. His acquaintance, who was already in business, had told him that he should also expect "health," "fire" and a host of other "inspections" where it would be difficult to know if the inspectors were legitimate or not. Overall, he estimated that he would have to pay about 10% of his revenues in bribes - better than what the criminal gangs were demanding in the mid-1990s but still a large expense item. What was even more worrisome, though, was that he had heard of several other firms losing their property or having been forcibly taken over by criminals, sometimes working with security or "justice" officers. After evaluating all of these extra costs, Sergei's uncle concluded that his business would not even be profitable enough to support his own family, much less Sergei and his family.

While these things were happening to Sergei, Yuri's Moscow-based pornography business was thriving in the new Russian economy, especially because he found it easy to demand that his customers pay him in cash. In the past, he reported about 20% of his revenues to the government, but because his revenues were growing so rapidly, he recently made a decision to cut this down to 10%. Unfortunately, Yuri's failure to pay his fair share of the taxes to the government encouraged, via revenue shortfalls and the need to underpay government employees, precisely the kind of corruption that grounded Sergei's uncle's business plans, leaving Sergei and his family with little opportunity or hope.

Half a world away about this same time, a man in Botswana contracted AIDS and spread it to his wife and several other sexual partners. He believed he had the right to force them to have unprotected sex and to reject an AIDS test that might bring him both bad news and the personal stigma that goes with being HIV positive. He, his wife, and several other victims of his misguided views are all now too ill to work productively, and a number of their children are at risk of having to grow up without their parents.

Across the continent, in the horn of Africa, specifically in Eritrea, a severely malnourished child was brought by a well-fed father into a health clinic during a severe drought. An investigation revealed that the crop had failed in part because, although the field that the family farmed was near a lake, it had not been irrigated; and the child was malnourished in part because it was the custom in that part of the country for the man to eat first and the women and children to eat what was left. It also turned out that the Eritrean government had expelled the U.N and a variety of aid organizations, as a way of expressing its disapproval of the U.N's handling of its border dispute with Ethiopia, which had also resulted in significant quantities of food aid rotting in warehouses. Unsurprisingly, in this environment, the Eritrean economy was making little progress.

In most of the countries between Botswana and Eritrea, and throughout much of Sub-Saharan Africa, people continue to suffer for other reasons, and particularly from the carnage perpetrated in recent decades by the so-called "big men" who managed to seize and hold power, authority, and resources that they were not morally or ethically equipped to have. In Uganda (and Sudan and Congo), for example, Joseph Kony, the witchdoctor leader of the Lord's Resistance Army trained child soldiers to raid and kill innocent villages for nearly two decades. In Sudan, the Khartoum government armed Musa Hilal and other Jangaweed (Arabic-speaking tribes in Southern Sudan and Chad) to counter an insurgency (involving the Sudan Liberation and Justice and Equality Movements). These groups proceeded to kill and rape hundreds of thousands of Darfurians and drive more than a million others from their homes— and continued to do so even after many of the perpetrators were absorbed into the Sudanese Armed Forces.

In spite of this, in the early years of the raids much of what happened in Darfur was not even considered newsworthy, following as it had in the footsteps of even more repulsive acts in other countries. In 1993 and 1994 in Rwanda, for example, Hutus[2] maimed and killed nearly a million Tutsis with machetes and raped hundreds of thousands of women and girls. When the carnage ceased, many Hutus were driven into the Eastern Congo, where vast mineral wealth had long served as a catalyst for ethnic conflict, and horrific injustices, including thirty years of human rights abuses under Joseph Mubuto. The confluence of these and a number of other conflicts culminated in a civil war between 1998 and 2003 that resulted in the murder of at least four million people, many of whom were innocent victims of the diverse warring parties and the corrupt and violent government of Laurent Kabila and his son Joseph Kabila.

Further to the north and west, between 1990 and 2003, militia groups in Liberia killed an estimated 150,000 people and drove more than a million others from their homes. The roots of this crisis can be traced back to 1980, when Samuel Doe and his rebels seized power in a coup by killing the president and other key officials. In 1989, Charles Taylor invaded the country and, together with several other warring parties, committed untold numbers of war crimes in a vicious civil war that destabilized much of the region. This included the Liberia's next door neighbor, Sierra Leone, where roving bands of child soldiers (of the same sort that had contributed to the atrocities in Rwanda, The Democratic Republic of the Congo and Liberia) routinely hacked their victims hands off, sometimes smiling when asking if their victims preferred "long or short sleeves." And far too often, as innocent, displaced people attempted to survive by congregating in safe havens and refugee camps, so-called "peacekeeping" soldiers from neighboring countries exploited them, spreading AIDS or fathering children they gave no thought to caring for.

In other places across the African continent where fighting has not killed thousands of innocent people, many women are still not being given adequate educational opportunities; spousal abuse and forced sex are common; genital mutilation, although rare, is still practiced; rape often goes unpunished; and polygamy is still widespread. In some locations (like Nigeria) people continue to suffer from the rampant infiltration of counterfeit drugs that did untold damage to unknowing victims while their distributors protected themselves by paying off unscrupulous government officials and judges. But in many ways it would be unfair to single these countries out. For many decades, across the African continent, hundreds of billions of dollars were stolen annually by unscrupulous leaders and other kinds of gangsters.

It would also be unfair to dwell too long on Africa. Further north, in Iraq, Sunni Muslims regularly detonated car bombs and IEDs in places filled with civilians, while their Shiite victims retaliated by sending out assassination squads. And along Iran's border with Pakistan and Afghanistan, Abdolmalek Riga and his Jundullah (Soldiers of God) killed indiscriminately in the name of Sunni Islam and Balochi nationalism. Unfortunately, similar examples could be drawn from almost any continent.

Whole books have been written about the complex historical, political, economic and cultural dimensions of some of the problems cited above and provide useful reading for those interested in a fuller understanding of (and potential solutions to) these problems. But in the countries where the suffering is taking place, victims would prefer that the world not wait for slow, complicated ethical analyses of history, politics, systems, organizations, and/or structures before taking serious steps toward solutions to these problems. Although important and useful, these kinds of analyses can be done even as small steps are taken and known causes are addressed. One such step involves addressing the moral and ethical issues that have often times been pushed (often inappropriately) from the limelight in so-called developed countries; these include simple issues that still have a major influence on development, such as peaceful conflict resolution, the importance of showing up for work every day, not stealing, not lying, not drinking excessively, not smoking or doing other drugs, not killing, and not being sexually promiscuous or using force to get one's way or take advantage of others. These of course, are the kinds of things that religious traditions have talked about for decades or millennia. And it needs to be acknowledged once again that progress toward adhering to these kinds of moral laws is an essential part of taking countries (and even continents) down the path of development.

Digging a little deeper

Nevertheless, stopping here would leave the impression that religious beliefs are only about prohibiting immoral and unethical behavior. Religious beliefs do address moral behavior, but unfortunately *some* religious beliefs also have the potential to *encourage* immoral and unethical behavior. Equally damaging, *some* also have a history of restraining people from doing the good that they should do. But thankfully, *some* religious beliefs also have a long history of spurring amazingly positive contributions to development that have been far more influential than the good they have done by deterring negative, development-inhibiting behaviors. We limit ourselves, in the following paragraphs, to a few recent stories to make the point.

Narayana Murthy founded *Infosys* with six colleagues in 1981, which had become one of India's largest companies just 20 years later. A devout Hindu, Murthy continues to live a relatively simple lifestyle in spite of the enormous amount of wealth he has been instrumental in creating. His religious beliefs have also contributed to his strong desire to break with Indian business traditions and create wealth legally and ethically. His challenge was how to do this in a country where 1) a relatively small percentage of young people went to college (so turnover rates and salaries were high among the educated workers he needed, 2) where a key law prevented firms with more than 100 employees from firing anyone (so while the best employees had an incentive to leave, the worst had an incentive to stay), 3) where high government deficits made corporate borrowing expensive, and 4) where unreliable power supplies and counterproductive government regulations made his business operations and cash flows unpredictable.

In explaining the success of his company in an interview recorded in the June 2006 issue of *YaleGlobal*, Murthy starts out by saying that "God has been very kind to us." He then notes that he and the other founders were unanimous, when founding the company

"that we would seek respect. We would seek respect from customers, from
our employees, from our investors, from our lender departments, from the
government and from the society. And we said, if we seek respect from each
of these stakeholders, we will do the right thing for them. And if we do the
right thing for them, then everything will fall into place." [3]

In the same way that strong religious beliefs allowed Murthy to imagine a company built on respect, another set of equally strong religious beliefs opened the door for some of his countrymen at the bottom of the socio-economic pyramid to envision the possibility of escaping what can only be described as subhuman status. Bharat Jayaraman was born a Dalit and although the Indian Constitution had long ago outlawed discrimination based on caste, many other Indians thought of him as so unworthy that he was not permitted to enter temples, own land, or drive a vehicle, and could hope for little more than the most menial work accompanied by long hours, pay that was subsistence level at best, and no job security. (At times Dalits were even beaten and stripped in public as a warning to others not to overstep the boundaries of their caste.) In spite of this, Bharat was given an opportunity to attend a Christian university in Hyderabad, which changed everything. Not only did he receive an education, but this enabled him to obtain a good job, recognition, and, for the first time in his life, a real sense of hope. More importantly, his transformed worldview enabled him to forgive those who had mistreated him, and to change the way his siblings, parents, and eventually his children understood themselves, enabling them to raise their standards of living as well. It also contributed to his strong desire to start a business, creating jobs and hope for many others.

Half a world away, in Western Africa, Nigeria's president Olusegun Obasanjo appointed Dora Akunyili to head up the NAFDAC (National Agency for Food and Drug Administration and Control), in part because as a devout Catholic (and eventual recipient of the Christian Integrity Award), she was committed to rid her country of the immoral and unethical behavior that kept many of her fellow citizens in poverty. She fearlessly confronted the criminal elements in her country, so much so that assassins opened fire on her car with AK-47s as she rode to work in December 2003, and arsonist gangs torched four floors of her Lagos Island office building in 2004. Undeterred, she successfully led her staff in reducing the level of counterfeit drug distribution in Nigeria by 80% during her tenure.[4]

South and east of where Dora was bravely confronting criminal gangs, Aloysius Kongoli's life changed radically when, at sixteen, both his parents died within a year and he became one of millions of AIDS orphans. Fortunately, around the same time, Timothy Jokkene moved to Aloysisus' town (Kampala, Uganda) to rebuild his business, and his religious faith led him to volunteer to find homes for AIDS orphans. Timothy helped Aloysius find an apprenticeship with a tailor, gave him a sewing machine as a gift, and mentored him as he started his own business. Eight years later, Aloysius was earning enough to help eleven employees support their families and was also paying for the education of his three younger siblings.

Finally, a CEO of a major Chinese company who had been taught from childhood that "only rural grandmas believe in God," became a committed Christian. His new-found faith invigorated him to keep only one set of books, pay his taxes honestly, treat his employees with "love" and always pay them promptly. He gently encouraged his employees to consider his new faith, and reported that when employees left their atheism behind to follow Christ they often increased in optimism, tolerance, integrity and customer service.[5]

But to stop only after balancing some of the negative effects of belief systems on developing countries with some of the positive effects would also be ill advised. Stopping at this point could leave at least two other mistaken impressions: that religious beliefs are primarily about prohibiting or encouraging immoral and unethical behavior, and that they may not be as important to economic outcomes in wealthier countries as they are to "developing" countries. In fact, as we noted briefly when discussing the global economic meltdown that started in 2008, and shall see in much more detail in the remainder of this book, the things people believe, including what those who might label themselves as "secularists"[6] believe, are integrally related to economic practices, policies, institutions and outcomes in all countries, including those countries that do everything within their power to maintain the "separation of church and state." To illustrate we turn to a rural North American economic beehive.

Chapter 3: Lessons from Flyover Country (and some questions that need asking)

Introduction

It is the kind of place that most people from the Big Apple or The Land of Fruits and Nuts would characterize as a great place to fly over. It is a place that most government officials, academic researchers, urban power brokers— in fact just about anyone who assume that bigger things (whether farms, factories, schools, or cities) are better than small ones— will likely never see. Tucked in the flatlands of Northwest Iowa, it is not well situated for a quick stop off an interstate (none go through it), or as a tourist destination (no mountains, lakes or "must see" cultural attractions), and one would have to drive more than 200 miles from it to see a professional sporting event. To the best of anyone's knowledge, it has never made anyone's list of the "best places to live." Nevertheless, it's a perfect place to illustrate the religious roots of economic development, because it is full of people who take their religious beliefs seriously, and it is also an economic beehive. Such beehives exist all over the world, in big cities and small towns, in rich countries and poor. Their distinguishing features are that they thrive economically and that their positive economic outcomes are quite obviously related to religious beliefs and practice.

This particular beehive is a county, Sioux by name, after the proud Native Americans who roamed the land before being overwhelmed by homesteaders, and the U.S. Cavalry that backed them up. Settled primarily by people of Dutch and German extraction, it has only recently become home to a growing Hispanic population. Although remarkably diverse in terms of the size, shape, creativity, personality, and education of its people, it is not particularly diverse in most of the ways valued by those who fly over it, for example, religiously, ethnically, racially or in terms of sexual preference. Chances are the people of Sioux County would be pretty uniform in their opinions about people like Donald Trump, Paris Hilton, or Rue Paul: Love them, and perhaps pity them, but for heaven's sake don't act like them! Without a single city with more than 7500 people, it is a certifiably rural place. It looks pretty much the way political pundits would expect a "red state" county to look, but doesn't quite fit the stereotype. Even a quick glance reveals fewer than expected bars, mobile homes, bass fishermen and NASCAR fans, and perhaps a bit too much interest in politics and appreciation for government-at least at the local level. But this non-descript county in a not-particularly-sought-after geographic location is anything but the stereotypical "laid back" and sit-for-hours-in-small-cafes-talking-about-the-crops-and-weather place that urban elites might expect it to be. In fact, labeling this county (and others like it) as anything other than an economically healthy beehive would be inaccurate.

Economic Leadership

This is not necessarily to say that Sioux County amounts to a slice of urban culture spliced onto the cornfields. For the most part, it is a reflective place, where the tyranny of the urgent does not really have a grip on people, and one doesn't hear much talk about the "rat race." But with a surprisingly young (median age of 32.8 years) and growing population (both of which buck the trends for other rural Iowa counties), two private colleges, modern growing industrial parks (with a long history of healthy numbers of manufacturing jobs - in contrast to national concerns about outsourcing of manufacturing jobs to places like China), any number of highly (and sometimes globally) competitive companies, its economic base is both diverse and, based on decades of low unemployment, resilient. And although this economic base makes it less agricultural than many other rural Midwestern counties, industrial growth has clearly not been at the expense of agriculture since, according to the Des Moines Register, Sioux County has more farms than just about any of the other 98 counties in Iowa, was either first or right near the top in the state in the sale of cattle, calves, hogs, sheep, corn and soybean production.[1] All this economic activity gives the county considerably higher per capita bank deposits and household net worth than comparable counties. But it would be a mistake to assume that the entire economic impact can be measured in dollars. Several towns in the county note on their web sites that large investments have been made in libraries, graduates from the local schools have standardized test scores that far exceed state and national averages, that they have a highly motivated and educated workforce, low crime rates, affordable housing, and even a symphony orchestra. Public library book circulation rates in the largest towns in the county are twice what they are in some neighboring counties. Large numbers of educated and ethical young people are "exported" to other parts of the country and world to make their impact there.

The Importance of Looking Carefully

But this is only half of the story (actually less than half). According to another Des Moines Register article, Sioux County also has the dubious distinction of being one of the most traditionally religious counties in the state.[2] Not only did it have (at the time of the article) thirteen private Christian schools (in addition to its public school districts), but on paper it looks almost puritanical. Quoting the Register article, it had, relative to other counties in Iowa, "the lowest percentage of Playboy readership (0.6%), and highest percentage of church members (96.4%)." The article also notes that Sioux County "ranks 91st of 99 counties in the number of bars per capita", is "83rd in divorces and 77th in crime" (in a state that, overall, is one of the safest in the nation, according to Morgan Quitno's *Most Dangerous and Safest States*" rankings). On top of this, Sioux County is, according to the County Health Rankings compiled by the Robert Wood Johnson Foundation and the University of Wisconsin Population Health Institute, the healthiest county in Iowa, [3] and, according to The Harvard School of Public Health's longevity rankings, is tied with several other counties for the highest life expectancy in the U.S.[4]

Of course it would be easy to jump to conclusions about Sioux County. What fun is it to become wealthy if all the fun has to be squeezed out of life in the process? The Ten Commandments may have been good for the Old Testament Israelites, but most people today would prefer that the number be cut down a little, or at least that they be turned into the ten suggestions. And, who wants to live in a place where many of the businesses are closed on Sundays, where there is a limited selection of hard liquor, and where some, if not most of the inhabitants believe in encouraging each other to avoid the kind of behaviors that, in spite of being a bit seedy, would, in most places, would fall staunchly in category of "it's none of your business?"

But the purpose of this book is to bring to light the nuances of religious beliefs and their impact on economic outcomes. Sioux County certainly has these nuances but finding them requires that we take the major theme of this book seriously, and look more closely at the specific beliefs of the people, which requires spending time and talking with the people who live there. As long as Sioux County (and places like it) remains buried in a database where its economic statistics are averaged in with lots of other counties that also happen to have large numbers of "religious" people, much of what is important will remain hidden. Uncovering this hidden information requires first of all that we first remove our stereotyping glasses. No doubt there are some bigoted and judgmental people in Sioux County (like in most places), but this is certainly not the reason for their economic success. More likely it is the many caring and friendly occupants for whom a work ethic is more important than country of origin, and compassion and community is more important than autonomy and privacy. Even a modicum of research indicates that the people themselves identify that it is their religious beliefs that are the primary motivator for them to work together to solve the kinds of community problems that often confounded people with more individualistic or secular belief systems. For example, by working in community, and according to agreed-upon ethical principles, less goes to waste. People routinely share valuable information with each other or help friends and neighbors accomplish tasks, which makes an increase in efficiency, knowledge, and skills (for example, in gardening, auto repair, or home improvement) a byproduct of the process of building healthy social relationships. If a customer brings an item to the checkout counter at the local hardware store, the store employee might ask what he plans to use the item for. If the item is not the appropriate fix for the problem, the store employee might suggest that the customer not make the purchase (even though it means a lost sale) and send him on to another store that carries the needed item. Throughout the county, local businesses generously support both the public and Christian schools without worrying that they could be inadvertently "advancing religion" when supporting Christian school students. The local colleges attract excellent students, not because they can compete on a name recognition basis with large secular universities, but because they tap into other communities with similar values who have cultivated students who want an education that goes well beyond a path to individual fame and fortune.

The motto of the town in the center of the county, appropriately named Sioux Center, is "Progress through cooperation" which hints as to how some of these efficiencies accrue to the county's institutions. One example is the way in which a private religious college (Dordt College), the public school district, and the city itself jointly fund many public works projects in order to both reduce the monetary burden on any one entity and to promote more efficient use of the facilities constructed. Another is how, when one of the grain elevators suffered a fire, other elevators in town ("competitors") volunteered to help store its grain and service its customers, until they were able to rebuild. In short, although far from perfect, many of the people in the county seem more concerned with making life better for everyone than they are about accumulating personal riches. Wealth, in such a situation, becomes more of a by-product of people's values than an end in itself.

Tocqueville[5] Would Have Liked This Place

Most of the people in Sioux County have probably not heard of Tocqueville, and few use academic words, like civil society, to describe what goes on there. But the religious commitments of the people and their sense of communal responsibility have spawned a host of not-for-profit and volunteer organizations aimed at accomplishing whatever needs to be done. Examples include organizations that provide community education, distribute food and clothing, train diaconal workers, tutor people in financial management, strengthen marriages, prevent and deal with family crises, provide housing to those unable to afford it, assist those with alcohol or drug problems, provide assistance to the aged and handicapped (including one organization that has distributed more than 50,000 wheelchairs in 100 countries around the world), assimilate newcomers (including ESL tutoring), provide legal aid, provide crisis pregnancy counseling, assist at-risk pre-schoolers, provide school tuition to people inside and outside the community who can't afford it, provide fire protection, and stimulate recreation and the arts. External outreach programs includes a farmer-to-farmer mentor program, a business mentoring program, and interchurch organizations that send work teams to areas plagued by poverty or natural disasters, to name a few. In addition to these community ventures, individual churches (of which there are many) also have a host of education and outreach programs. Furthermore, charitable contributions far exceed national averages.

Hidden Efficiencies Found

To paraphrase the famous British pastor, John Wesley, it is difficult to keep wealth from accumulating where large numbers of people believe it is their religious duty to work hard, be thrifty, limit waste, share their resources with each other, and solve problems communally. Wealth accumulation is also spurred in these situations by the efficiencies that go along with an emphasis on honesty, integrity, and other moral virtues. Banks, for example, can offer people better rates, or lower closing costs, or be more profitable because they don't need to waste money on bank guards, or fight through lots of title problems. Insurance rates are low because most people obey the law, insurance fraud is low, people tend not to file lawsuits, jury awards are sensible, and repair shop operators are both skilled and honest. Housing prices are reasonable, because politics don't distort zoning rules, builders put in a good day's work for a day's pay, and the larger-than-average number of intact families allow for more occupants to share a dwelling and results in less demand for the available housing.

A handful of rural historians and sociologists have given some attention to these things. In fact, the religious roots of Sioux County's economy were studied by Janel Curry-Roper, a rural geographer whose paper formed the basis for one of the Des Moines Register articles cited earlier. Her research covered eight religious subgroups in seven Iowa communities. To measure how people's beliefs differed, she developed a questionnaire-based scale which uncovered differences in two dimensions of people's worldviews: the degree of their individualism (vs. communal orientation) and the degree of their utilitarianism (meaning the degree to which they will be swayed by what works, or what benefits them, rather than just by moral and ethical principles). She then assessed the impact of these differing worldview elements on economic outcomes. In the process, she found, for example, a strong communal character to the Sioux County farmers which allowed them to work together to achieve efficiencies without having to consolidate farms as quickly during the farm crisis of the 1980s as was occurring in some other parts of the state. She also noted the tendency of the Sioux County inhabitants to view their work as a sacred calling from God, which raised their view of the importance of the work of the farmer, business person, or kindergarten teacher to the same level as that of a doctor or pastor. She further pointed out that this "community worldview has meant people stayed and were in turn taught how to invest in institutions," resulting in a steady accumulation of social capital. Over all, she found that, even though the seven of her eight groups would be classified as "Protestant Christian," there were noticeable differences in land use, animal husbandry, and farm inheritance practices among the groups she interviewed, which were tied to differences in their religiously-based worldviews.

The community mindedness of the Sioux County residents may also help explain some of their longevity. Although we are not aware of any research study that has tried to explain the reason for the longevity of Sioux County inhabitants, it does not take a great leap of faith to surmise that when people are enfolded in community, and feel safe enough to leave their houses unlocked and their keys in their cars, they might also live a little longer (although fresh rural air - ignoring the animal odors, peace and quiet, minimal traffic, and being able to see thousands of stars at night may also have something to do with this). Such a conclusion also fits well with the research cited earlier suggesting a positive relationship between strong religious beliefs/regular religious practice and better health and longevity.

Other rural sociologists have also found significant correlations between religious beliefs and economic outcomes.[6] Of course, most people know that the Amish resist the use of certain technologies because of their religiously-based concepts of stewardship. But much more has been uncovered. Rice, for example, identified a conservative group of Swedish Lutherans in Minnesota who were more economically prosperous than their neighbors. McQuillan concluded that the German Mennonites in Kansas were able to better withstand the many challenges of central Kansas agriculture than other groups, in part because of the communal nature of their religious beliefs. Pederson concluded that a group of Norwegian Lutherans in Wisconsin was successful, in part because, like the Sioux County Dutch, they were convinced that work was a sacred calling from God and approached their tasks communally. Dilly found that adoption of technological change, land ownership patterns, and inheritance practices all varied based on religious beliefs that determined whether groups remained separate from the economic "world," straddled the worlds of religion and economics, or attempted to integrate their beliefs and economic activity into a seamless whole (or refrain from separating them, as the case may be).[7]

Conclusion

An important point to draw from all of this is that people trying to understand a place like Sioux County, or some of the other economic beehives mentioned, from a secular point of view, have few options beyond trying to explain its high life expectancy or economic prosperity by pointing to the genetic makeup, ethnicity or racial homogeneity of most of its citizens. But most members of these communities would militate against such an analysis, and for good reason. They are well aware that they have no particular advantage over, nor are they more deserving than, any of the rest of the earth's inhabitants. In fact, if survey data among the college students in the area is to be believed, they often think less highly of themselves than students in other parts of the U.S., even as they outperform them. In short, one does not have to talk to very many residents of the county to learn that most of them attribute any differences in economic outcomes between them and others, not to themselves but to the benefits of Biblical wisdom regularly received in their families, schools and churches, and the grace of a benevolent God.

As noted earlier, these religiously and economically distinct enclaves are not just in the agricultural heartland of the U.S. People anchored by their religious beliefs are present in U.S. inner cities, cultural centers and suburbs and in surprising oases all over the globe; in most cases distinguished by their core beliefs and lifestyle, rather than by the usual demographic markers. In some cases they live in geographical proximity to their spiritual kin, and in some cases they are separated geographically and connected only by shared beliefs or institutions. And, of course, none of these places is perfect. Proving so is not the purpose of this writing, and attempting it would be an impossible task. Some of these folks may use the earth's resources too intensively, give favored treatment to those most like themselves, struggle to find the optimal balance between work and rest, or mistakenly try to substitute conformity for more essential things like community or unity. Nor are they static. As a familiar Southwest Airlines commercial notes, the people of Sioux County "are free to move about the country" (and many do), and for those who tend to stay put, competing belief systems seep in through TV cables, DSL lines, movie theatres and DVD machines. And seep may be the wrong word to use; continued technological changes show every sign of turning trickles into streams and streams into rushing rivers. Ten year old research reports may be only partially valid today. Nevertheless, these "economic beehives stand as a testimony to the importance of religious beliefs to economic outcomes, and ought to be valued, at the very least, for their efficient production of the goods and services, made available for our benefit and enjoyment. The least we owe them, it would seem, for their efforts, is an honest acceptance of the importance of what they believe, and a willingness to allow them to remain free to practice their religion. How much better is this than attempting, in some well-meaning but misguided way, to force them to adopt a secular worldview, so that those who do not worship the same God that they do can be "protected" *from* their religious beliefs.

Questions to Set the Stage

The story of Sioux County all but begs us to examine the myriad ways, beyond morality and ethics, that religious beliefs impact economic outcomes. Perhaps the best way to pursue this (toward the beginning of a book) is to ask a number of other questions that will make us more curious about the subject. Not only will this lay the groundwork for future chapters, but it may also make readers more interested in reading them. There are of course an infinite number of questions that could be asked, and we present only a small sample here, arranged somewhat arbitrarily in fifteen categories; but the ones we ask are of two main types: 1) How does what people believe affect development (pro or con), and 2) How do religions (or non-theistic belief systems) differ with respect to their perspective on these things?

Beliefs about the World

Does believing that the world is stained by sin and needs to be renewed lead to different development strategies than believing it is sacred, and object of worship, to be accepted as it is? Does believing that it is a dark and frightening competitive "jungle" lead to different actions than the belief that it is a "garden" to be tilled, planted and cared for? Does believing that the world will eventually be destroyed lead to different development strategies than the belief that it is our permanent home?

Beliefs about People

Does believing that all people are brothers and sisters lead to different approaches to development than the belief that people are fundamentally in competition with each other and only the fittest survive? Does the belief that some people are inherently superior or that "to the victor belongs the spoils" lead to a different development plan than the belief that "all people are created equal" or that "the meek shall inherit the earth?"

Values

Do widespread expectations of truthfulness, humility, self-control, respect, trustworthiness, love or charity, or a work ethic lead to different development outcomes than the toleration or acceptance of deception, arrogance, self-indulgence, revenge, selfishness, mistrust, violence or laziness?

Change

How important is it to development that some belief systems embrace change while others seriously impede new ideas and important precursors to development such as novel ideas, agricultural or technological improvements?

Education

Do religious beliefs affect people's commitment to universal education, the number and quality of the educational institutions they establish, or levels of educational achievement?

Authority

Is development better served by authorities who feel morally and ethically bound to be accountable, transparent, and "public servants" than by those who their authority to dominate other sectors of society (e.g. the family, church or businesses), enrich themselves by extorting money from those desiring to start a business, register property, or obtain financing?

Wealth and Poverty

How do belief systems affect the accumulation of wealth via their influence on attitudes toward wealth, poverty, inequality, envy, property, savings rates, bequests, willingness to take risks, consumption habits, etc?

Chapter 3

Relationships and Social Progress

How do religious beliefs or participation affect economically relevant social variables like family stability, child rearing practices, school attendance, social deviance, teen pregnancy, substance abuse, physical and mental health? Do they affect the number of broken families that need to be mended or the number of addictions that need to be cured?

Efficiency and Stewardship

Do all belief systems lead companies to do what is most needed and sustainable, rather than anything/everything that is possible? To accomplish needed tasks with the fewest resources possible? Reduce the depreciation and depletion of their assets or protect the environment? Or try to solve fundamental problems rather than just addressing symptoms?

Products and Services

Does time spent producing locks, surveillance systems or antivirus software, or the training of police, soldiers, security guards or airport screeners or other activities necessitated by the moral failings of individuals leave less time to produce food, teach children, build computers, discover life-saving drugs, or engage in development work? Are resources wasted when people are made to feel insecure and later offered a host of products to reduce their insecurity (e.g. diet pills, plastic surgery or anti-anxiety drugs)?

Structures and Processes

Are some support structures, processes or behaviors more conducive to economic development (such as private property, the rule of law, the development of civil society, and/or entrepreneurial activity) than others, and are some belief systems more conducive to their development?

Justice

How important is the promotion of justice to development? Do all belief systems focus equally on promoting justice? It is possible that some belief systems stifle incentives because they either ignore or tolerate injustice and corruption and fail to demand effective structures and processes for dealing with them?

Business Practices

Do certain religious beliefs affect the efficiency, profitability and ethics of businesses through their impact on employee honesty, commitment, work attitudes, conduct or trust levels? Have religious beliefs influenced the development (or lack thereof) of laws that provide the framework for dealing with things as diverse as property rights, liability, usury, creditor rights, or bankruptcy? Do they affect the formation and effectiveness of large working communities through their influence the values of objectivity, concern for others, forgiveness or tolerance?

Economic Habits

How might religious beliefs affect the values that affect the risk preferences, spending, saving, borrowing and investing habits of people, or the other things that affect the value of financial and real assets, and indirectly, the stability of the financial systems and economies of which they are a part?

Political Structures and Activity

To what degree do religious beliefs affect political participation or political and economic stability because they influence attitudes toward war and peace, tolerance and inclusiveness, or ideas about acceptable methods of achieving change, agreement or social order?

Chapter 4: Wealth Creation and Economic Development

Before we can complete the circle connecting religious roots and economic development/wealth creation, we need to briefly consider what wealth is and why it is important, particularly since there is so much confusion surrounding it. When most people use the word "wealth," they are referring to material wealth, and people around the world seem transfixed on this when they think about wealth. From China, where Deng Xiao Ping launched China's remarkably long growth period with his astonishing 1977 proclamation that "to get rich is glorious," to the U.S., where entertainment programs following the lives of the rich and famous, and reality shows where people will do almost anything for the possibility of winning large prizes, seem to multiply faster than maggots in a hot summer garbage pile, it now seems that nearly everyone is preoccupied with material wealth and money. In the U.S. alone, the Federal Reserve Bank reports that the total accumulated wealth of individuals hovered around sixty *trillion* dollars, depending on which end of the recession we are on. Approximately forty percent of all Americans own stocks, either directly or indirectly, down from its pre-recession peak but up from less than one-third just twenty-five years earlier.

Brand new stock markets have sprung up in the remotest parts of the earth as people of nearly every language, ethnicity, and religious persuasion clamor to get a piece of the action in the new global economy. But at the same time that these markets for commodities, stocks and bonds, and goods and services, in both traditionally and newly rich countries, create new millionaires (and billionaires), many hard working members of the middle and lower economic classes, particularly those with little or no savings or investments, are left feeling like the train has left the station without them.

Of course, no one feels this way more than the citizens of the poorest countries around the world who are trying to lift themselves out of poverty, and those who have made it their life's work to help them in these efforts. Big numbers, like those cited above, mean little to many of these people, other than evoking some vague understanding of how much potential that much money could have if redirected, wonderment on why such things happen elsewhere but not in their neighborhoods and countries, and/or perhaps a degree of resignation. It is not our goal to help these folks figure out how, "by hook or by crook," to get on the same train that those in the wealthiest countries of the world are riding. That train, at the very least, needs a tune up, and, without some serious overhaul work, is not capable of having the rest of the world climb on board. But stopping the train is not the solution either.

Of course, getting a handle on poverty, or helping countries develop requires that we start with some idea, statistically, about the wealth status of various countries. But throughout most of history, the idea of measuring global wealth was little more than a pipe dream. Although a few countries, like Britain and the U.S., have been measuring some forms of wealth for more than a century, most countries in the world still don't measure it at all. But at the beginning of the 21st Century the World Institute for Development Economics Research (WIDER) took on the task, at least for personal wealth.[1] Although their initial report required them to "impute" data for most of the countries in the world, their methods seem reasonable. Interestingly, they found a median global net worth of $2,161 in the year 2000, which means that anyone fortunate enough to have that much was in the wealthier half of the human race. More importantly, they found that wealth is much *less* equitably distributed than income, with more than 50% of wealth owned by just 2% of the world's population in the year 2000. One might think that this matters a lot, but it may not because personal wealth is just one part of the picture. For example, they found that the poorest 50% of Swedes had a collective net worth of less than zero (and most consider Sweden a wealthy country). And Finland's per capita wealth was unremarkable at $39,000 (compared to a U.S. average of around $140,000, and in spite of the fact that Finland boasted one of the highest per capita incomes in the world at the time). The reason for this is that governments play such a significant role in the income security in these countries that the true wealth of Swedes and Fins may be masked. Since government is such an immense player in their economies, the only way to get an accurate picture of the true wealth of Swedes or Fins (or people from any other country for that matter) would be to measure the wealth held by the various government entities and recognize that this wealth is just as real as the personal wealth that the researchers measured. Foundations and not-for-profits may also hold significant amounts of land, shares of stock and other forms of wealth in some countries. These examples point out the tenuous nature of the statistics that researchers and governments use to determine the relative well-being of people around the world. Cross-country comparisons of income and wealth are difficult enough, but because wealth and income are related, the independent use of measures of personal income, without regard to people's wealth, is likely less useful than most people realize. And since both income and wealth are difficult to measure, and have sometimes been measured inconsistently, studies that purport to demonstrate differences in standards of living may not be as accurate as we think.

The Nature of Wealth

We must make the case for how economic development is related to the accumulation of wealth, which in turn requires that we distinguish briefly between income and wealth. We will limit our initial discussion to conventional (material) measures of wealth and look at the case of a single individual. Personal wealth is usually measured as the difference between the market value of one's assets minus the market value of one's liabilities, the mathematical remainder of which is most commonly known as one's "net worth" (or wealth). In some places markets are not well developed for certain assets, and in some parts of the world, large numbers of people are not able to secure ownership rights to assets. Such situations do not mean that these assets do not have value; only that their value may be difficult to measure or may be concentrated in the hands of a government or a small number of people. Likewise, there is a lot of important work for which people are not monetarily compensated (such as child rearing), but which adds to the stock of wealth in a country. Nevertheless, governments usually only measure wealth and income that is tangible; hence we will start our discussion at this level.

Wealth and Income Defined, and the Importance of Distinguishing Between Them

Many U.S. and Canadian farm families are wealthy if we measure the value of their assets (land, equipment, animals, crops, etc.), but may be relatively poor if we measure their net income, since they may have been receiving low prices for many years for the product of their labor (e.g., corn, soybeans, beef or pork) - so low in fact, that on occasion their income is negative. Negative income *by definition* means their expenses exceeded their revenues for the year, and that in order to pay all of their expenses, they must liquidate some of their wealth. This can involve selling off their assets or taking on debt, either of which has the same negative impact on their net worth (or wealth). If this continues long enough, of course, the farmers will no longer be wealthy since the value of whatever assets they have managed to hang on to has been largely offset by the money they owe to others (usually a bank). High levels of income, on the other hand, can lead to an accumulation of wealth over time, but only if the spending of that income is both wise and restrained.

Since there is an active market for land, crops, meat, machines, etc., these aspects of a farmer's, business person's or family's wealth can be and are routinely measured. But things like the value of the farmer's education, the joy experienced in his or her marriage and family, the peace associated with watching the sun rise and set each day, the skill and character development associated with running a farm, or the pride of ownership are not priced in the market, and therefore do not show up in official or unofficial wealth statistics. The same could be said for liabilities that aren't market-priced. The farmer may be unknowingly farming in an area prone to floods or tornados which would make his property less valuable than he thinks. Or he could have poor organization skills, an obnoxious personality, or poor communication skills, and these would also not detract from his measured wealth directly. The important point once again, is that the measurement of wealth is more complicated than meets the eye, a topic we will return to later, before we begin to discuss how religious beliefs impact wealth creation and economic development.

The preceding example indicates that income is an important contributor to the creation of wealth. But it is also not possible to generate income without wealth in the form of assets. People need homes to sleep in, tools, and money to generate income. Measures of wealth have the potential to capture the benefits of income in ways that people seldom think about. For example, in the same way that a farmer loses financial ground if his expenses exceed his revenues, his employee will also lose ground if her expenses (meals clothing, shelter) consistently exceed her income. Only if she is able to shift her expenditures from things that are used up (like rent payments, interest payments, shoes, and burritos) to things that last, or, better yet, appreciate (like the purchase of a home, savings account, or ownership in a shoe store or restaurant) will she make real economic progress. Each time she purchases or invests in something that has lasting value, she increases her net worth, or wealth. Thus, measures of wealth are more comprehensive than measures of income; they have the potential to capture the benefits of various kinds of income (e.g. past, present and future) as well as the impact of, for example, wise and foolish uses of that income.

It is not a great leap from understanding the previous example to the realization that little or nothing could be produced in the future if we were unwilling to accumulate some surplus (wealth) in the present. A young couple accumulates wealth in the form of a down payment in order to purchase their first house. The farmer depends on accumulating wealth in the form of seed, equipment, and money to sow next year's crop. The factory accumulates profit (or more correctly, "retained earnings") to purchase new equipment or production facilities. Wealth in the form of real assets, like houses, buildings or machines, also serves as collateral for loans, which can in turn be used to finance new companies or innovative ideas. Wealth in the form of secure homes and comfortable beds can make people more rested or joyful, and therefore, more productive. Wealth in the form of accumulated savings serves as a cushion that allows people to weather economic downturns, and allows them to time their expenditures to their advantage. In fact, it can be safely said that nearly all of the things that an economy produces for our enjoyment, other than what springs spontaneously from the ground, requires the prior accumulation of wealth.

In summary, a person's wealth (or net worth), can increase in only five ways: by receiving a gift, receiving compensation for work, restraining spending, caring for existing assets so they don't depreciate too much, and finding ways make current and previous savings grow. Surpluses that come from these five sources can in turn be used to purchase new assets, improve existing assets, or pay down debt. When less is spent on consumption (things that don't last) or on assets that tend to depreciate, and more on assets that have the potential to produce income or appreciate, or when better investment decisions are made, wealth increases more quickly. Companies, nonprofit organizations, and governments are all subject to these same principles. In companies we call savings "retained earnings" and in nonprofit organizations and governments we call them "surpluses." But the "bottom line" is this: the trillions and trillions of dollar, yen, yuan, or rouble-denominated wealth in existence, everything over and above the initial store of minerals, plants, animals given to us as part of an "undeveloped" earth, all comes from these five humble sources.

But before moving on, we should briefly note that these five humble sources can also be used to accumulate other equally important forms of wealth (but this requires us to see that wealth can be defined far more broadly than it usually is by those who have adopted secular and materialistic ways of looking at the world). Psychiatrists must accumulate a wealth of knowledge to properly diagnose their patients and meet their needs. Priests, pastors, and rabbis must accumulate spiritual insights to be a blessing to their parishes or congregations. People, companies, and governments need to accumulate good values, attitudes, habits, and reputations. In fact, it can be safely said that nearly all of the things that take people beyond the subsistence level, including both products made to meet our needs and for our enjoyment, and services that we perform for each other, require the prior accumulation of a variety of kinds of wealth/capital. And as we shall see, many of these are intangible and have their roots in belief systems.

The Importance of Starting at the Beginning

Hopefully the discussion above has whetted our appetites for a much more detailed look at how wealth should be defined, how it is created and the role that religious beliefs and worldviews play in that process. Before doing this, we will review the misconceptions that people have about wealth creation and the role of beliefs, and particularly religious beliefs in that process. We will do this by reviewing the "wealth" of knowledge about these subjects that was already available to the global community around the time the U.S. came into existence. As noted in the Foreword, a moral philosopher/economist named Adam Smith wrote an influential series of books in 1776 that has come to be referred to as *The Wealth of Nations*.[2] Unfortunately, there are few people in the world, including most Westerners, who have read his books - or those of other influential "enlightenment thinkers" like Hobbes, Locke, Rousseau or Ricardo, and even fewer who have understood them. The average person has also not been schooled at distinguishing the shades of meaning associated with terms like "neo-classical economics," "modernism," or the confusing evolution in the meaning of the word "liberal" as it applies to economics. Fortunately, these are theoretical battles we do not need to fight to improve the economic wellbeing of large numbers of people around the world. We may choose instead to spend less time studying "Enlightenment" thinkers and more time understanding and evaluating ideas, recognizing their power, connecting them with our experiences, and culling out the good ones for the purpose of finding "a better way." There is some efficiency in this since, like all intellectuals, Western thinkers have had lots of bad ideas as well as good ones.   Our goal, here, then will be to focus on uncovering the truth about the wealth creation process, since it is ultimately by discovering, understanding, and applying the truth that we (meaning, in this case, large numbers of people from diverse places and with diverse backgrounds) will succeed in doing a better job creating and distributing wealth than our ancestors did.

We are not trying here to depreciate the importance of intellectual leadership. But we are admitting our reluctance to place too much trust in academic elites. Although good leadership is essential to economic development, it needs to be of a certain type, and elitist is not generally what comes to mind when we picture ideal leaders. More importantly, we are convinced that the long term viability of an economy, indeed any society, requires that large numbers of people (rather than a select group of elites) need to not only know what must be done and how to do it, but also *why* things are done the way they are, and *why* they are worth doing. In the context of the present problem, this means that economies will be healthier when more people understand the real reasons why some nations are rich and others poor, why some people in every nation are rich while others are poor, what the role of trade is in economic development, why China grew faster than Russia even though it has not embraced democracy, or even something as mundane as why some stock markets languish while others flourish. To reach this point, we first need to look deeper into the "mystery of wealth."

Chapter 5: Explaining the Mystery of Wealth: Adam Smith's contribution

Seven Sources of Wealth

Regardless of culture or country, the total value of the aggregate amount of wealth in existence appears to have seven primary sources:

- Our common endowment (land, mineral, water, etc.)

- Savings handed down to us because previous generations limited their consumption and made wise investments with their surplus.

- New wealth we create by limiting our own consumption to something less than the value of what we earn or produce.

- Investing our wealth prudently, regardless of its source, so that it increases our income or the productivity and the value of what we produce in the future.

- Taking appropriate steps to keep existing assets from unnecessary depreciation and depletion.

- The existence of a moral, political and economic atmosphere in which productive activity is encouraged and the (real) market values of assets rise.

- The belief systems to which people adhere and their congruence with wealth-creating ideas and behaviors.

The first five of these, which were introduced briefly in the previous chapter, could be considered *conventional* components of wealth creation and have been understood, at least by some, for more than two hundred years - but a brief explanation of each is in order. The final two are less well understood, but are not entirely new. To introduce them in a little more depth, we will refer initially to Smith's *Wealth of Nations*, which was so instrumental in exposing the evils of Mercantilism[1] and laying the intellectual groundwork for much of the economic change that the world has experienced since Mercantilism's demise, supplementing it, when appropriate, with recent insights from development research.

Unfortunately, what most people think about when they hear Smith's name are the concepts of "self-interest" and laissez faire capitalism, neither of which, was a focal point of his writings. In fact, Smith never even used the term "laissez faire" in *Wealth of Nations*, and his lengthy discussions about government and morality indicate he would have had little in common with modern libertarians or radical individualists. What he did say was that widespread commercial activity, even if self-interested, was valuable because it prompted people to be thoughtful, industrious, dependable, prudent, temperate, and attentive to the needs of their customers. These virtues, he insisted, even if only a by-product of the search for gain, were nevertheless good for society as a whole. But he also knew that an appropriate political and economic environment was necessary for this to happen.

"Self-interest," Smith assumed, would motivate people to make things and trade them for other things they needed (and he assumed some of these interests would be altruistic). In such a world, Smith noted, the products and services that we use will be produced by thousands or even millions of people whom we don't know and will never meet. Therefore, although we can't necessarily depend on their benevolence toward us, we can depend on them working and trading based on their self-interest (meaning, more broadly, working to further the things they know and care about). And rather than focus narrowly on individualism, he tried hard to describe how greater and greater benefits accrued as people cooperated at increasingly complex levels. Thus, rather than laissez faire capitalism, Smith's main contribution to our knowledge of the creation of wealth was his careful description of the benefits that accrue to social cooperation and the development and maintenance of institutions that promote moral behavior. Without intentionally focusing on it, his pursuit of the truth regarding the creation of wealth took him straight into the study of belief systems (as is evident from his first book, *The Theory of Moral Sentiments*).

Smith's writings highlight many different components of wealth creation. For the benefits of specialization and trade to be able to continue to be benefits today, we need not only the right social and political environment and the beliefs needed to nurture them, but we also need to have this knowledge passed from generation to generation, stewardship of resources, and a host of other things which beg for as broad as possible a view of wealth. So before moving on, it seems appropriate to give Smith the credit that is due him by using some of what he did say about these things as we discuss and explore these seven "sources of wealth" in more detail.

Our common endowment:

Smith said little about this component of wealth, probably because the ratio of available resources to people was so high at the time he wrote, and the long-term impact of the exploitation of natural resources was not of major concern at the time. He did discuss how resources such as land were wasted and underutilized because of the political, legal and economic structures of the day. But our understanding of the critical role that the natural world plays in wealth creation and economic development is considerably greater today.

Some scholars, such as Jared Diamond, a geography professor and author of *Guns, Germs and Steel* (1997), and *Collapse: How Societies Choose to Fail or Succeed* (2005), have elaborated on the importance of differing endowments to the economic development process. Diamond and others have noted the tendency for more economic development to take place in temperate climates. Although the exact mechanism for this effect is not known, one could speculate that this could be related to the particular challenges that a temperate climate brings, or the increased incentive for reflection when people are cooped up (with cooler or cold weather), or because people's bodies and minds are more productive at moderate temperatures. Diamond also points out how native plants like taro and bananas in places like Papua New Guinea were inferior to European or North American grains in proteins and in their suitability for agricultural specialization and mass storage, and how the biggest animals in Papua New Guinea (pigs) were not big enough to pull plows. Similarly, wheat and barley did not grow well in places in Africa where there were only two seasons, dry and rainy. In his opinion, most of the animals with the best potential for domestication were native to the Middle East (e.g., cows, sheep, goats), and it was these endowments that drove agricultural specialization and surpluses, which were in turn largely responsible for higher rates of development in this area and Europe.

Regardless of variations in endowments that Diamond addresses, the critical point remains that a good chunk of our wealth can best be described as a gift: an earth weighing approximately six sextillion tons, filled with hundreds of different elements which have millions of potential uses. Its surface contains a variety of soils, minerals, liquids, plants, and animals which function according to complex cycles and rhythms in communities which form the basic building blocks for all other wealth, not to mention life itself. By conservative estimates, there are probably at least 10 million different species of plants and animals, less than two million of which have already been identified.[2] Surrounded by an immensely useful atmosphere, the earth and its inhabitants receive a steady supply of energy from an amazing ball of fire 93 million miles away called the sun, which is little more than a minor player in a universe filled with far more magnificent things. However, since all of this is an endowment, the gift of which is in no way related to anything that people have done, we can say little more than we should be thankful for it, care for it, and move on to other components of wealth.

Savings handed down from previous generations:

Once again, this is a gift to us, from people throughout history and from all over the world who worked individually and collectively to transform their time and material resources into living quarters, work places, places of worship, material objects, aesthetic creations, services, and perhaps most importantly, into ideas, technologies, principles, and codes of conduct which enable wealth to be created, preserved, and renewed. Smith and many others since him have noted clearly the role of savings in the process of wealth creation, so we could easily assess the market value of public and private assets or the store of knowledge bequeathed to us by our ancestors and tie these benefits to the concept of "savings." But as we shall see, it is perhaps more important to ask why some of our ancestors did more of this than others, and secondly, what it is those of us who have been blessed with productive and thrifty ancestors should do to make ourselves more thankful and accountable for the gifts they gave us, so that we might continue in the their footsteps for the sake of generations yet unborn. Perhaps it is sufficient to say, before moving on, that those of us who are not prisoners of poverty are much more indebted to those who have gone before us than we realize.

New wealth from limitations to consumption.

Smith was very clear about the importance of self-control and self-denial to the creation of wealth. In the eighth chapter of his first book, he notes that real wages cannot increase without additional investments in facilities, equipment, or tools to equip and support laborers so they can become more productive. In his second book, which focuses on "capital," (by which he means assets available for use in the production of further assets), he notes that increases in capital depend on increased saving (or parsimony, as he preferred to call it). Savers, he reasoned, since they were frugal by nature, would naturally try to lend their hard-earned money only to productive ventures. In doing this they would be putting an increasingly larger share of society's wealth in the hands of people who would use it productively, and a smaller share in the hands of those who would use it foolishly. Although inequality would result from this, so would increased wealth creation.[3] Smith's ideas notwithstanding, it should be obvious that the more we produce and the less we consume, the more we will accumulate. But having said this, we do not want to give the impression that all work and no play is the best path to follow. It is also costly to succumb to stoicism or to produce and accumulate too many of the wrong kinds of things. Denying ourselves the basic necessities of life can leave us with too little energy to be productive. Likewise, having things we don't need or use can also make us poorer than we would be otherwise, since these things are costly to produce, store and maintain but yield us very little benefit. But pursuing this discussion requires that we first address the concept of stewardship.[4]

Investing wealth productively:

Smith is perhaps best known for his careful delineation of this principle of wealth creation, that of investing wealth to increase productivity, because of the way he illustrated, in the first chapter of his first book, the critical importance of specialization and division of labor. Using the now famous example of a pin factory, he described how dividing up the work involved in pin making into eighteen separate tasks allowed ten well-trained and well-equipped people to produce 48,000 pins per day - compared to "certainly not more than twenty" pins per day for a single individual working alone. He further noted that people could only take advantage of these tremendous efficiencies if they were free to expand their businesses to the point where they benefited from significant economies of scale, and were free to trade their surplus output with others who were specializing in the production of other things.

In a related perspective on investment, Smith, in the second chapter of his third book, notes how Europe wallowed in poverty for years, partly because laws of *primogeniture and entails*[5] kept massive chunks of land in the same family for generations, regardless of whether the land was being used efficiently. More recently, we note both Russia's pre-Soviet concentration of wealth and Soviet state owned "cooperative" farms as examples of how notoriously unproductive land can be when ownership problems keep it from being worked efficiently. North Korea may be the best recent example of this, with the per hectare or per acre output of the large collective farms being one-fourth to one-third of the output of "private" garden plots,[6] but similar problems plague many developing countries, especially in Latin America and Africa.

On a larger scale, countless wars around the globe have not only halted the normal productivity of assets, but have destroyed massive quantities of assets and kept people from realizing positive "returns on investment" for long periods of time. But even in peacetime, there are scores of ways individuals, organizations, and governments can use savings in unproductive ways. Heirs to large fortunes squander wealth bequeathed to them under the maxim of "easy come, easy go." Companies make poor decisions and end up in bankruptcy, destroying the wealth of their owners, creditors, and employees. Governments and international organizations throw taxpayer money down veritable "black holes," particularly when their actions are not open or subject to public scrutiny. All such actions at best generate no additional wealth and at worst (either inadvertently or intentionally) deplete or destroy the hard-earned wealth of others and/or previous generations.

Unfortunately, when Smith wrote, stock markets were in their infancy, and their role in wealth creation and development is still neglected to this day. To partially fill this gap we will briefly address their importance in the next chapter.

Minimizing depletion and depreciation:

In Smith's second book, dealing with capital, he focuses on the importance of using capital efficiently. He notes that countries which devote a larger percentage of their "revenues" to capital are wealthier. He also notes that using capital efficiently includes finding ways to reduce the costs of maintaining it and to minimize its depreciation. His discussion immediately spills over into a discussion of "human capital" since Smith seemed to view capital as a form of "stored labor." He notes that the proportion of money going to capital as opposed to that going to government revenue collectors or consumption seems to "regulate the proportion between industry and idleness." Since the time of Smith's writings, businesses and industries in the Western world have been on a relentless crusade, albeit unevenly, to provide "more for less." Contrary to much of the conventional wisdom that assumes businesses plan obsolescence into their products in order to guarantee future sales, successful businesses know that to survive in a competitive marketplace, they have to be on a relentless march to make their products last longer and perform better. True enough, they don't try to make things that last forever. Doing so, aside from being impossible from an engineering perspective, would also make many products unaffordable to the people who need and want them. It would also be wasteful, since, for example, it doesn't make sense to put components which are designed to last a thousand years into a car which will, for a variety of reasons, such as advancing knowledge and technology, changing consumer tastes, or changing government emissions standards, likely be obsolete in twenty years.

Development researchers have also given a lot of attention to the importance of minimizing depletion and depreciation. For example, Diamond describes how germs have depleted the human contribution to development in many parts of the world. He notes that Europeans may have accumulated special immunities because of their proximity to certain animals. This allowed them to prosper in Europe, and in the more temperate areas of Africa (such as South Africa), although he notes that they didn't do as well farther north in Africa, especially in places where they were ill prepared to deal with scourges such as malaria. Similarly, Africans inside of the Tropic of Capricorn did fairly well because of their immunities, but changing life patterns resulting from colonialism sometimes worked to their detriment. For example, Diamond describes how the Banta in the Congo were often moved out of their homelands in the high and dry areas by the Belgians to places where they were more vulnerable to malaria.

Diamond's research is particularly helpful in seeing that depreciation and depletion can be applied to more than just natural resources or machinery. His research also points, albeit indirectly, to the fact that self-interest, although often good for one party, may cause depreciation or depletion elsewhere, with a net loss in economic progress.

Creating an atmosphere where the market value of assets will rise:

Adam Smith had a surprising amount to say about the importance of creating and maintaining an atmosphere conducive to healthy asset prices because he often wrote and in detail about the importance of moral conduct and responsible government to the creation of wealth. He argued that people needed to create institutions that encourage citizens to act in morally and socially responsible ways. He considered the market to be one of the institutions that would do this and wrote about how self-interest could serve the public good. But he also noted that markets alone were not guaranteed to do so without other institutions that fostered respect for life and property, a concern for the common good, and a host of virtues like self-control, prudence, and farsightedness.

Despite the perception that people have of him today, he believed government would naturally get larger as civilization advanced, and wrote *Wealth of Nations* in part to convince politicians and officials to recognize their responsibility to seek the public good and to create an atmosphere where people would have incentives to do what was in the best interest of all people. His desire for limited government reflected, more than anything else, his beliefs that other institutions in society were better qualified than government to provide the moral and ethical training that under-girded the creation of wealth, and that government officials were often neither in a good position to micro-manage economic exchanges nor necessarily inclined to promote the public good. In making this latter point, he denounced companies like the East India Company and their European government "allies" that allowed them to profit at the expense of both the nations they were trading with and their own nations, and especially at the expense of the European taxpayers who were forced not only to pay high prices because of these companies' monopoly positions, but to finance the armadas that were necessary to protect them. Markets, he believed, had the potential to pit admittedly imperfect and sometimes selfish competitors against each other, forcing them to promote the public good. This, he believed, would result in better products and services and greater wealth overall.[7] Government, acting properly within its sphere of authority, would improve people's material well-being primarily by promoting justice and fostering institutions that would encourage moral decency and other wealth-creating behaviors.

Much early research into economic development focused inordinately on government's role in alleviating poverty. In many cases poverty was considered as much a cause as it was a result of underdevelopment. Poverty was also thought of primarily in terms of lack of income and the problems associated with this, the assumption being that lack of resources (including financial capital) as the root cause of underdevelopment. Fortunately, this emphasis on government's role in filling resource gaps eventually led to more detailed study of non-monetary resource-related issues, including, for example, the need for infrastructure to smooth geographic, climate, agricultural and other natural resource uncertainties; reducing the polluted water and poor sanitation practice at the root of many health problems; and dealing with educational deficiencies. Early on, the discussions about educational deficiencies focused on the "brain drain," and much attention was given to how to stem the long-term migration of the "best and brightest" from poor to wealthy countries. Significant attention was also given to the importance of population growth and other demographic factors. Excessive population growth, it was often assumed, would require that the resource pie be sliced into smaller and smaller pieces, with the result that countries with the highest population growth were likely to find themselves severely restricted in their ability to increase incomes per capita. Eventually scholars saw the need to broaden their "indicators" of development to reflect more than income, and in 1975 the Human Development Index was created to combine educational achievement, life expectancy, and per capita income into a single indicator of development.

The economic development literature also extended Smith's work on the importance of markets and democracy to development. Interest in the subject heightened at the time that colonial ties were loosened or cut, and greatly accelerated after the Eastern Block began to crumble. One thread of this discussion called particular attention to the relationship between the problems in developing countries and their lack of property rights, noting the importance of land reform and property rights improvements to successful development. In the midst of this discussion, the development spotlight turned for a while to the serious external debt problems of developing countries, with special attention paid to the relationship between trade and development and in particular to the importance of and problems associated with capital mobility and government exchange rate policies and controls. This discussion eventually encompassed the role that government mismanagement and corruption had played in contributing to the impoverishment of both people and countries, and eventually, when the spotlight was turned directly to the problem of corruption, attention was given to the need to measure it and reduce it through codes of conduct and pressure from international agencies.

Recent research, led by scholars Amartya Sen and Hernando de Soto, extended this conversation to the general importance of ethics to development, and of equipping governments to govern better by improving their capacity and institutions, as well as removing barriers to markets. In light of this research, the World Bank in particular commissioned a host of studies into the economic development effects of corruption, bureaucracy, and regulatory obstacles to land ownership, business startups, dispute resolution, contract enforcement, credit extension, lender recourse, and bankruptcy. An undercurrent of this research focused on the critical roles that freedom and empowerment play in development. The importance of privatization and other ways of forcing government to be more responsive and efficient also received a lot of ink, as have the roles of both civil society and democracy. Finally, as people became more environmentally conscious toward the end of the twentieth century, earlier discussions about resource problems broadened to include discussions about environmental risks and the damage caused by environmental degradation in general.

The beliefs of people:

This last category of wealth creation is the one that Smith clearly understood - that ideas and beliefs were the foundation of wealth creation. He was a student of the nature of man, who saw man as a "weak and imperfect creature," and mentioned frequently how character problems such as pride, avarice, or injustice hampered the creation of wealth. But he also believed a "benevolent Creator" had planted in people the ability and desire to see themselves as potentially praiseworthy. He wrote extensively about how government needed to create institutions that would channel people's natural inclinations toward self-interest, insecurity, passion, and power toward productive ends. In fact, a major theme of the first book that he published, *The Theory of Moral Sentiments*, was the need for people to create institutions and structures which would transform their natural inclination toward self-love and self-interest into altruistic and benevolent behavior. He believed, and was missionary-like in his promotion of the idea, that people and nations should pursue economic activity out of "the love of mankind" rather than by attempting to obstruct the development of their neighbors. He also revealed his fears that excessive attention to commerce could result in the neglect of other important aspects of culture, and that excessive dependence on reason had the potential to create a moral vacuum. He believed the very existence of society depended on virtues like politeness, truth, fidelity, chastity, dependability, and justice. Interestingly, the man so often associated with acquisitive capitalism did not die with a large accumulation of material wealth. Oriented by a Calvinist religious heritage, he quietly gave away much of the wealth he had been instrumental in creating during his lifetime. A religious man, he was nevertheless opposed to religious monopoly and the idea that any one group of clerics could corner the truth; rather, he felt that moral teaching aimed at inculcating proper beliefs about what constituted moral behavior to be at the core of the wealth creation process. Unfortunately, many who castigate him in recent decades have done a decided "end run" around this part of his legacy.

Today Smith's ideas on this would be considered part of a broader discussion on the impact of worldview on economic outcomes/development. Unfortunately, this remains an "underdeveloped area" in the literature and one of the motivating factors for this work. Neglecting the role of worldview on development has also contributed to two other notable tendencies in the literature – the tendency to focus almost exclusively on what we can learn from empirical studies to the detriment of many of the other "ways of knowing," and a general unwillingness to recognize the role of differing spiritual/moral/ethical perspectives on the more widely-recognized contributors to development. To fill in this gap, we will, in subsequent chapters, go beyond the pragmatic empirical studies dealing with development and "peel the layers off the onion" to uncover and summarize the *attitudes* that underlie pro-development activities, in particular those attitudes which are influenced by religious beliefs. But prior to this we need to address common misconceptions about where wealth comes from.

Chapter 6: The Importance of Intangible Wealth to Development

In our previous discussion we noted, among other things, the importance to development of wise investing and maintaining a political and economic climate where the market value of assets can increase. But increasingly, the assets that contribute to wealth creation and development are intangible, and where these kinds of assets are not well understood, development suffers. Stocks and bonds are two of most important of these, and part of a class of intangible assets that we refer to as financial assets, and a basic understanding of them is required before we begin to put together the puzzle pieces that make up the wealth creation and economic development processes.

Company Wealth Creation

An understanding of how companies create wealth requires a brief introduction to what shares of stock are and how they are valued. A share of stock is legal evidence of a small piece of the ownership in a corporation in the form of either a paper stock certificate or its electronic equivalent. It gives the owner a pro rata share in the "net worth" or accumulated wealth that resides in the company, as well as the right to a share of the profits (or net income). So if the company ceased doing business, for whatever reason, and its assets could be sold and its creditors repaid, the shareholder would be entitled to a pro rata share of whatever is left (the *liquidation value* of the shares). Of course most owners prefer that the company continue to operate, because the shareholders have a perpetual claim on the company's earnings (or, more technically, they have a right to receive dividends, which are that portion of the company's profits that do not need to be plowed back into the company to either replace depreciating assets or purchase new assets). If a company is functioning as intended, the value of what it sells will be higher than the cost of all its inputs, and it will be "creating value" for its customers and "earning" a profit as it goes about its business.

Stock prices have value primarily because they entitle the owner to a share of these profits. Their collective value (based on market prices) can be thought of as a best guess of the worth to society of the work that business people have done in putting together money, real estate, machines, and people in organizations for the purpose of providing products and services to the public. The value of these companies, although abstract, has real consequences as people can use this wealth to educate their children, provide gifts to foundations and not-for-profit organizations, fund their retirements, or secure loans. And, perhaps most importantly, increases in stock prices represent additional value (or new wealth) to stock owners, without concurrent losses to others.

Shares of stock vary significantly in what they give investors. If a company is growing rapidly it will usually pay small or no dividends, but if it has little internal need to fund growth, most of the profits will be paid to owners. If the company retains most of its earnings, it makes sense that its value will increase relative to what it would have been if more of the profits had been paid out as dividends. But in some cases this may not be true because the owners may prefer to receive the money rather than have it reinvested in the company. In this case they may show their displeasure with the company's retention policy by selling their shares (and thereby lowering the value of the company). But either way, the profits belong to the shareholders and, generally, they will prefer that the money be kept in the company if the company can use/invest it more productively than they can on their own. The stock price, then, will be the greater of the current "net worth" of the market value of the company's net assets (assets minus liabilities) and its value as a money-earning, dividend-paying entity. This later value is often referred to as the "present value" of the money that the company is expected to earn and eventually pay out to the owners in the future.

A Stock Market Primer: Basics of Stock Valuation

How much will a company be worth if it is valued on the basis of future earnings and dividends? It depends on how much the promise of future money is worth at the present time. When a saver puts $100 in the bank at 6% interest, he will receive $106 back at the end of the year, and he has received a 6% return on his investment. Likewise, if a company is likely to pay a dividend of $1.06 per share at the end of the year, and the investor wants to earn 6% on the money he has invested in the company, he will be willing to pay $1.00 at the present time for the right to receive that piece of the company's future profit (the present value of the dividend). But if financial analysts, who research this company or the investor himself, see that the company is growing and will likely pay an even larger dividend two years from now, say $1.17 per share, the investor should be willing to pay approximately $1.04 for this second piece of the company's future profits. This is because, returning to our savings account analogy, she would have to put $1.04 into the bank (at an annual interest rate of 6%) *today* in order to withdraw $1.17 after two years. Extending this process we can see how the current price of a share of stock reflects the sum of the "present values" of many dividends that the investor expects to receive from the company in the foreseeable future. If we looked at this company's prospects over, say, a twenty year period, and added up the present value of all twenty expected dividends we might conclude that it is worth paying $25 now for the privilege of receiving (or "withdrawing") the twenty dividends from the company over the next two decades.

But what if the company isn't paying any dividends? We can also see that a company that doesn't currently pay any dividends (like many high tech companies), but reinvests all of its earnings in the company at a high rate of return, could put its owners in a position to receive an exceptionally large amount of money at a distant point in time, rather than small amounts of money each year in the near future. This company could still have a very high stock price because the company's assets and future earnings will grow more rapidly as they retain and reinvest each year's earnings, easily accumulating enough to compensate the investor in the distant future for the dividends he is foregoing at the present time. And as long as a *financial market* exists, any investor who can't wait for this to happen can sell her shares and receive cash now from another investor who is willing and able to wait for the future payoff.

A stock's price, then, is determined first by what happens in the company: the quality of its investment decisions and operations as reflected in the surplus (profits) it generates.[1] But we can also see that conditions in the financial markets and the society will affect stock prices (regardless of the quality of the company's management). If, for example, interest rates rise from 6% to 8%, a saver would only have to put approximately $98 in the bank today in order to accumulate $106 by the end of the year. Similarly, a dividend of $1.06 to be received from a company in a year would only command a price of $.98 today (as opposed to $1.00 above). And since the "present value" of the company's dividends would decrease if interest rates rise, so would its stock price. On the other hand, if interest rates drop, money received in the future is worth more at the present time. For example, if interest rates dropped to zero, a dividend payment of $1.06 in the future would be worth $1.06 today, since that is how much one would have to put in the bank at 0% to be able to withdraw $1.06 in the future. Clearly then, low interest rates (other things held constant), and economic conditions or government policies that bring them about are good for stock prices.

But future payments from companies are almost always riskier than future payments from banks. Therefore, in order to entice a saver to put her money into shares of stock, the company will have to offer a higher return than a bank. So, if the bank is paying 6% interest, the company may have to offer 12% to attract the investor's money, which means our investor would only be willing to pay about $.95 for the uncertain possibility of receiving the $1.06 dividend that the company is promising to pay next year (and correspondingly less for all the other dividends the investor hopes to receive in the future). It should be clear from this that anything, including a host of "non-economic" factors, that increases the risk associated with a company's operations (assuming that this doesn't simultaneously increase profits) will lower the value of the company's stock.

In summary, *shares of stock create wealth by creating a vehicle for investors to put their money to work in companies that use it to meet people's ongoing needs or wants well into the future.* This enables the institutions employing these funds to create goods and services that people value more than what it costs the companies to provide them, which makes the companies profitable. If legal and ethical structures make it easy for ownership rights in these institutions to be easily bought and sold, thereby reducing risks to investors, they add even more value. In this way companies, their owners and their societies are able to create new wealth by "capitalizing" *today* on the expected future benefits of their ingenuity and labors.

This also means that decreases in earnings, higher interest rates, and higher risk generally lower the value of companies, while sustained earnings increases, lower interest rates and lower risk generally raise the value of companies. Likewise, other things that *affect* earnings, interest rates or risk will indirectly affect the value of companies. For example, a declining societal work ethic will lower earnings, while widespread dishonesty will increase risks. Fears that increased inflation will lower the purchasing power of money received in the future has the potential to raise interest rates and depress stock prices.[2] Political uncertainty, corruption, social unrest, or excessive regulation will depress stock prices because they tend to both depress earnings and increase the uncertainty (risk) associated with future earnings and dividends. The important point here is that things as far ranging as personal habits, government integrity - as expressed in its fiscal or monetary policy, or government's ability to govern will routinely create or destroy wealth by affecting the companies' profits, cost of funds, and stock prices.[3]

Faith and Wealth: Asset Prices as Harbingers of Things to Come

The financial capital evidenced by stock ownership is only one of many essential inputs for economic activity. Doing business *requires the gathering and coordination of a wide variety of other assets*, such as money, raw materials, technological know-how and infrastructure, but also managerial prowess, positive attitudes and ethical systems, into an integrated whole. Much of the capital that is essential to the creation of wealth is not material in nature. A company could retain all of its material capital (e.g., land, money, machines, or technology), but if its people found it difficult to work together, or routinely lied or stole things, the value of both the company and its material capital would plummet. Remove any one of these inputs and the value of the others drops as well.

This reminds us once again of subtle but important relationship between beliefs and economic outcomes. There is no denying that even something as technical as stock valuation is to some degree couched in faith. This is perhaps most obvious when markets are being moved more by emotion than rationality. For example, the vast majority of the stock-price increases at the end of the second millennium was caused by the emergence of a new kind of believer: not a believer in God, or reason, or science, but one who believed that that prosperity, high company earnings, low interest rates, and low risk were likely to persist as far out into the future as the eye could see, and that the American economic juggernaut would take her or him to the "promised land."

The object of this faith proved unworthy, as, in the years following, a dot com crash, the horrendous events which took place on September 11, 2001, and other events caused stocks and the U.S. economy as a whole to languish for the better part of a decade, as increased security concerns, heightened uncertainty, pessimism and recession lowered profit expectations and raised risks. When the faith of investors falters, they may sell their shares for another asset, often cash, provided they can find other investors who believe the company's shares are worth buying at the asking price. When there is *widespread* pessimism, as was the case globally in 2008, the value of measured wealth could drop precipitously. If investors subsequently lose faith in the currency that they exchanged their shares of stock for (perhaps because they expect its value to decline as inflation increases) they are also free to exchange their currency for anything else they want, including "hard assets" like land, cars, houses or art. But the values of these things are also dependent on people's beliefs about the future.

An example from the world of baseball may be particularly useful to drive this point home. A number of years ago a person paid $3 million for the baseball that marked the 70th home run that baseball star Mark McGuire hit in the 1999 season. One could legitimately ask why a baseball was worth millions while a cup of pure water, was priced in the same country at less than a penny. Part of this is due to scarcity. There is only one such baseball, whereas there is a large and steady supply of clean water. But clearly the value of the baseball was also significantly affected by emotions and beliefs, a situation that is increasingly common, particularly in wealthy societies. The purchaser may have claimed that the baseball was purchased as an investment, but this does not negate the fact that a baseball is still relatively useless for sustaining life. Clearly the purchaser had a strong faith that things would continue as they were, that someone else wouldn't hit 71 home runs the following year, that it would always be possible to distinguish this baseball from fraudulent contenders, that the value of the ball would not be compromised by allegations that Mr. McGuire took steroids, that the owner would continue to be wealthy enough not to have to sell the baseball under duress, or if he had to sell it, that there will be at least one other wealthy person who would be willing to pay even more for the ball. But far more common items also depend on faith for their value, and, more particularly *what people have faith in*. RVs, cars, hotels, and even land could lose their value quickly if there were severe oil shortages (unless land becomes critical to producing an oil substitute), and even houses could drop in price if for example, people widely *expect* them to (as they did, for good reason, in 2008), or people began to *believe* that living simply and communally is more fulfilling than living in well-appointed isolation.

The Importance of Embracing Uncertainty: the Role of Financial Markets

It follows from what we have been saying that the ability to embrace uncertainty is essential for economic development. This value, which is related to both an orientation toward the future and a willingness to take risks, is often in short supply in underdeveloped countries. Some of this is due to the fact that it takes more faith to personally risk a small surplus than a small piece of a large surplus, but there are other reasons as well. If one *believes* time is short, or that he has only one shot at making it big, he is more likely to take risks. If the rewards associated with the risk taking will have to be shared with lots of others (for cultural or religious reasons), the risk is less likely to be taken. If one's self image is tied to not making mistakes and taking a risk introduces the possibility of public humiliation, less risk will be taken. Some of these risks will be lessened with the development of efficient financial markets, which allow investors to discretely take risks and, if necessary, discretely swallow their losses, or to transfer the risk to someone else who is more favorably disposed to living with uncertainty. The development of efficient financial markets, however, requires a high degree of trust, which in turn requires both a high degree of personal integrity among the participants and a strong system for administering justice in the event that the trust relationship between creditor, debtor and/or middleman is violated. The latter requires an additional peculiar mix of values that encourages people to think long term and to build institutions that promote justice, a subject that we shall return to later.

The Importance of Debt

Before moving on, one other major intangible financial asset must be discussed – debt. One reason debt is essential to development is because in most cases the people who have money to invest and the people who need it are not the same. In nations with efficient financial markets, (often younger) people with lots of energy and good ideas will be looking for creative ways to obtain and employ the money that (often older) people with less energy and more wealth have. Although they could start companies and allow the people with the money to own and profit from them, they would often be better off borrowing the money, thereby limiting their legal obligations to capital providers to fixed interest payments, and reaping more of the benefits from their entrepreneurial instincts and hard work themselves. So the possibility of borrowing encourages economic creativity and therefore development.

Looking at debt this way is in stark contrast to public outcries claiming the developing countries are necessarily crushed by debt burdens. The truth is that borrowing and lending affect the wealth creation process only indirectly, and affect it *positively* only when the borrower finds ways to use the money more productively than the lender could. It is not wise to say that a lot of debt is either a good or bad thing. If borrowers, including borrowing countries, use debt for projects that generate greater returns than the cost of the debt, their wealth will increase. Of course wealth can easily be destroyed by imprudent borrowers. This is obvious when we look at a very simple example. If Pedro lends his money to George, but George spends it all on vodka, so that he is unable to pay back the loan, Pedro's wealth is decreased with no corresponding increase in George's wealth. Of course the vodka seller may benefit from George's choices, but the small profit he makes on a few bottles will in no way offset Pedro's loss of the entire amount, not to mention the impact of the vodka on George's health and productivity. Wealth will have been destroyed. On the other hand if George uses the money to start a business which ends up being valued by its customers, employees and owners at millions or even billions of dollars, Pedro will receive both principal and interest and many others will be enriched as well. Once again, values matter.

Chapter 7: Incorrect and Incomplete Thinking about the Origins/Creation of Wealth

Resource Issues

If people do not think correctly about the processes by which wealth is created, economic development will suffer. One incorrect way of thinking is to view wealth as *little more than* an endowment. As we noted earlier, although receiving an endowment of natural resources is *one* source of wealth, most of the wealth in the world today is the result of what people have done and do with that original endowment. This dynamic view of the wealth creation process is in stark contrast to the traditional "wealth as endowment" thinking, which generally assumes that the quantity of wealth is basically fixed - so if one person ends up with more of it, someone else will end up with less. This kind of thinking underlies a variety of conflicts. For example, businesses as a group create wealth (which we will better understand shortly), but it is not uncommon for union leaders and environmentalists to accuse them of earning profits at the expense of laborers, or robbing future generations of their rightful share of the earth's resources. Of course some businesses do exploit workers or the environment, but the assumption that one's gain is another's loss is extremely dangerous to economic development. The easiest way to expose the fallacy in this belief system is to give a person a small plot of ground and watch the wealth creation process proceed, as she works the ground, plants some vegetable seeds, channels the water, harvests the produce, stores some seed, sells the surplus, and composts the ground to prepare the soil for the next cycle. If she does this well, not only can she sell the produce for more than the cost of the inputs, but the value of her land will increase as well. Wealth has been created by this person, and most people can also quickly see that she and her neighbor will also benefit from trading both inputs and outputs with each other, since, for example, her neighbor may have ground ideally suited for fruit trees rather than vegetables. Perhaps a better example is when a company creates a personal finance software program that sells for $50. It ends up saving the average customer hundreds of dollars a year in time and money and making its owners into millionaires.

But somewhere between these simple examples and the complex modern global economy, people lose confidence in these relationships. Some politicians tell their countrymen that foreign investment will greatly benefit them while others insist that foreign investors are really "invaders" who will drive their country into dependence and bankruptcy. Many people believe that a business owner's profit must be at the expense of employees' salary or wages, or that when a business buys goods from another country, the foreign country is usually being exploited.[1] Of course part of the reason for this is that *sometimes* one person's gain is another person's loss. This is most obvious in the case of outright stealing, imperialism, war or pillage, but it also happens when workers refuse to give a good day's work for a good day's pay, when corrupt government officials refuse to carry out their duties, or greedy company owners live lavish personal lives while their companies suffer neglect, falter or fail. However, if these activities were the norm, we would not observe near-continuous increases in household net worth that we do in countries with vibrant business sectors. The bottom line is that a company's business will not increase over time if it doesn't continuously find ways to provide useful products and services. When its business increases it will need to hire more workers, or pay its existing workers more, or both. So for global incomes and wealth levels to rise almost continuously (which they have, dramatically, in recent decades), companies, on balance, must be providing goods and services that people value, and the citizens of the global community, including workers as a group, should be sharing the economic benefits of this.[2]

Unfortunately, when these principles are not well understood, entire nations can go hundreds of years engaging in less-than-optimal behaviors. European powers established colonies and exploited their resources even though the global economy would have been better served in the long run if they had worked to set up a system of fair exchanges. Pre-WWII Japan exploited their neighbors, only to learn after the war (and beyond the shadow of a doubt) that a nation does not need to be endowed with great supplies of natural resources or use imperialism to dominate another's natural resources in order to thrive. Around the globe, many resource-rich countries continue to struggle economically, while relatively natural-resource-poor islands like Hong Kong, Japan, and Taiwan long ago escaped poverty by engaging in productive activity and trade.

The picture emerging from this is that resource endowments can either help or hurt a nation, depending on the beliefs and actions of the people and their leaders. Many resource-rich African nations, like Nigeria, Sierra Leone, the Democratic Republic of the Congo, and Angola, have seen far more political upheaval than wealth accumulation from their oil, gold, or diamonds. In fact, recent research by Michael Woolcock (2001) of the World Bank seems to make a good case that in the absence of certain moral and ethical beliefs, natural resource windfalls may hurt real progress by trapping nations in the lure of easy money and by inviting corruption and financing political conflict. Size of country doesn't seem to be the key to the creation of wealth either, although it is widely believed that the presence of large markets in advanced countries gives them a distinct advantage. Many relatively small countries around the world are quite wealthy, while some larger countries continue to struggle. For example, when we look at Africa, some small countries like Botswana, Ghana, Uganda, Equatorial Guinea and Mozambique have made good strides relative to some of their resource-rich and larger neighbors, like Nigeria, The Democratic Republic of the Congo, Kenya, and Sudan.

Of course endowments and diseases can only explain so much. Singapore and parts of Malaysia, where vast tracts of land were once little more than malaria-infested swampland, have been successful in controlling malaria and have become quite wealthy. And many nations with poor resource endowments have, in spite of this fact, become quite wealthy. So we need to recognize that to some extent, even careful researchers may not find what they are not looking for. If we believe that the most likely explanation for wealth is luck, we may overlook a host of attitudes and actions which others, who believe "there is no such thing as luck", would focus on.

Markets and Democracy

This understanding of the relatively unimportant role that resource endowments and country size play in development has emboldened some to urge that the most important ingredients in economic development are free markets and democracy. Clearly their importance is hard to dispute, but it doesn't take long to realize that Asian nations like Korea, Thailand, Indonesia, and Malaysia experienced phenomenal wealth increases for decades even though their markets were distorted by tariffs, other import barriers, cartels, and government interference. Experiences in Russia and other countries of the former Soviet-Block also hint that economic development requires much more than a theoretical acquaintance with the benefits of free markets. Many Eastern European countries liberalized their markets but suffered through seriously unstable periods in the process. This was due in part to the fact that markets developed ahead of needed belief paradigms and the kinds of institutions that flow from them, which gave a powerful advantage to insiders and opportunists. They in turn too often used their power to gain an unfair advantage - politically, economically or socially, to exploit customers or employees, or to hide their wealth from tax authorities.

Democracy may also be less necessary to development than is commonly believed, or it may flow logically from other factors that spur development, rather being an essential requirement for it. A number of economically successful countries (including most of the Asian nations mentioned above), have had or continue to have ideas about democracy that vary widely from Western ideals. Even more notably, China has grown remarkably for nearly four decades despite a lack of democracy, whereas many countries in Africa, where hundreds of millions of dollars have been spent on democratization, have made little or no economic progress during the same time period.[3] One historically-supported reason for this is that democracy, absent of appropriate beliefs and values, can lead to the exploitation of the powerless by the rich and powerful, or the exploitation of the rich by the poor and powerful (majority), or the abuse of minority (racial or ethnic) groups by the majority, or even to chaos.

On the other hand, a belief system that spurs economic productivity can not only lead to economic growth in the absence of democracy and completely free markets, but can eventually lead to democracy and freer markets when people see that these things are healthy for economic development. Institutions, too, will function only as well as their leaders' and employees' ethics allow. For example, monetary and fiscal authorities can steal from the populace (by bringing on inflation, high interest rates and declining asset prices) if not committed to integrity. Employees can seriously damage their companies through their incompetence or unethical practices. Companies can seriously damage their communities through unethical environmental practices. The likelihood that any of these problems, or a host of others, will surface may depend more on the foundational beliefs of the participants than on the presence of completely free markets or democracy.

Exploitation and Ideology

Other bits of conventional wisdom about wealth creation also take a beating when examined carefully. It is thought by many that Spain became rich via the gold it accumulated by exploiting other nations during the colonization period. It is true that colonizing Spaniards lugged gold to Spain from all over the world and did a number of other despicable things in the process. When the gold was unloaded, however, they found that even gold was little more than one limited kind of wealth. It was not edible, for example, and couldn't cure diseases. It was useful as money, but they soon found out that even too much money is not always good because it tends to cause inflation. As it turns out, the Spaniards and their colonial rivals, who were preoccupied with exporting more than they imported, thereby gaining a "favorable balance of trade" and becoming rich by accumulating precious metals, were largely wrong about the wealth creation process. Gold and other precious metals are not necessarily more useful, and in some cases were considerably less useful than what had been exported in exchange for them, things like clothing, furniture, tools, and books, many of which had the potential to actually sustain or improve life.

Marx, on the other hand, noted that since imports were coming into a country and exports were leaving, it might be better to get "more for less" by having the value of imports exceed exports. Piggy-backing on these ideas, some economists have even argued that the U.S. prosperity of the last few decades of the 20th century and early 21st century was directly related to its massive imports of low priced foreign products (as evidenced by its large and persistent balance of trade deficits). Nevertheless, although imports can be useful, especially when they are low priced, neither the performance of Marxist-based economies nor the increasing debts that the U.S. accumulated in the process of financing its import binge make this strategy look any better than Mercantilist (or Chinese, for that matter) ideas about *exporting* their way to wealth.

Soviet Russia also had strong beliefs about the role of exploitation and ideology on wealth creation. They operated for seven decades on the assumption that wealth was created primarily by labor, which in their minds had too often been exploited for the benefit of capitalists. Marketing, finance, and many administrative activities were thought to be relatively useless activities that allowed capitalists to raise prices and take large and undeserved shares of the revenues for themselves. Unfortunately this kind of thinking led them to neglect many modern "value-based" management and marketing techniques, and their financial markets and institutions to wither, until the economy finally imploded due to lack of incentives, moral and political corruption, and widespread shortages.

Social Organization

Even within a single country, most people have trouble answering the question "Where does wealth come from?" Some people assume religious and not-for-profit institutions are a drag on the economy, but in the U.S. and many of the most competitive and wealthy countries in the world, a healthy percentage of citizens aren't even working in economically-oriented for-profit institutions. In the U.S. (according to the Urban Institute Center on Non-profits and Philanthropy), there were more than 1.5 million churches and non-profit organizations reporting to the IRS (but not earning profit or paying taxes) at the beginning of the twenty-first century, and a host of others that are either not well organized enough or required to report.[4] Additionally, the U.S. economy supports a massive legal infrastructure and more high-priced lawyers than most of the other countries in the world combined, which at first glance would seem to make it less competitive than other less argumentative and diverse societies. It is also plagued by high crime rates and deteriorating families, is home to a widely criticized K-12 public education system, and has governments that take at least a third of its citizens' hard-earned money. Its labor is high priced, and judging from its TV talk shows and tabloid journalism, much of its population is preoccupied with things not at all related to productivity activity. How can a nation compete so effectively in the international economy and build unprecedented wealth under these circumstances? Democratic and free market values may tell part of the story, but clearly much more needs to be said.

Smokescreen Wealth

Even if we abstract from these academic complexities, there is still much confusion among individuals, even in apparently well-developed countries, about how their personal and family decisions tie into the wealth creation process. Much of what people do can rightfully be classified as economic activity but has little or nothing to do with the creation of wealth. For example, people line up to buy lottery tickets from cunning state governments, which promise the possibility of unfathomable riches while discreetly neglecting to tell ticket purchasers how many more times likely it is that they will be struck by lightning than become a winner. Get-rich-quick programs seem to be proliferating throughout the "developed" world, and many people speak openly about wanting to be wealthy enough to buy whatever they want and not have to work. But such statements reveal more than a modicum of ignorance about the creation of wealth. What these people should be saying is "I'd like to be a leech" since they want to produce nothing, and serve no one, preferring in turn to be pampered by consuming large quantities of what other people are laboring to make.

The reasoning behind attempts to justify such comments is, of course, convoluted, and varies from culture to culture. In some cultures it takes the form of assuming that the right to engage in an opulent lifestyle attaches to a position of privilege related to inheritance or blood lines. In the U.S., people are more likely to argue that they have the right to spend whatever they have because it is "theirs," or that by spending money, even on exotic non-necessities, they are creating jobs. But such lines of reasoning reflect a highly individualistic, and we would argue, in the long run, a very unproductive belief system, or make the incorrect assumption that if money wasn't being used to gamble or buy these luxury goods it would be out of circulation. This is very seldom the case, since most people do not keep all of their wealth under a mattress or live their lives without interacting economically with the outside world. In most situations unspent money would be deposited in a bank or be invested in some other way and would be used by another party to make investments or to purchase goods and services. So it would be better to say that one who wants to consume a lot and work only a little is choosing to deplete wealth. For starters, this kind of behavior reduces the flow of funds into the financial markets, which makes interest rates higher than they would otherwise be and deprives others from borrowing and productively investing. This behavior also deprives the poor of a host of benefits that would be theirs if the wealth was shared rather than wasted. And clearly, if everyone adopted this kind of "all play and no work" orientation, nothing would be produced, wealth (initially financial capital and eventually other forms of wealth as well) would dwindle. In the end the citizens of the world would be left with the ugly spectacle of people fighting over decreasing stockpiles of necessities.

These examples are included to warn poorer countries of the potential inefficiencies associated with emulating current Western country economic practices when attempting to pull themselves out of poverty. It should be clear that many things can masquerade as economic activity but not really improve people's lives. The best strategy for developing countries, then, is to identify the beliefs, values and attitudes that lead to widespread pro-development behaviors and policy choices, and concentrate on the most effective way to inculcate these into people's minds and hearts. This requires as much attention to culture and religion as to politics and markets.

Misconceptions about Wealth at the Global Macroeconomic Level

One other important component of the wealth creation puzzle needs to be addressed - that of the role of trade in development - because one vigorous and persistent belief that merits some discussion is that trade between countries hurts some while helping others. It is particularly common for people in wealthier countries to believe that freer trade will cause jobs to migrate from higher wage to lower wage countries. Ross Perot, a 1992 independent candidate for the U.S. presidency, famously captured this sentiment when he claimed that the free trade legislation then being proposed would create "a gigantic sucking sound" of jobs being pulled across the southern border of the U.S. toward Mexico. Indeed, the movement toward freer trade faces formidable opposition from an unlikely coalition of special interest groups, particularly in the richer countries of the world.

Cries for protectionism come from many places. Nationalism, in both the industrialized and the developing nations, leads to the exploration of ways to prevent "foreign competition" from "taking away" domestic jobs. New businesses claim they cannot get a toehold in the domestic market when foreign competitors are underpricing them. Existing businesses claim that they cannot compete with low-cost foreign labor. Trade unions claim that buying foreign products puts their people out of work. Others claim that it is immoral to buy foreign products because the producer of these products exploits his workers or the environment in order to undercut sellers in other countries. Unfortunately, there is an element of truth to each of these claims, which is why clear thinking on this issue is so difficult to find. But a little knowledge can be a dangerous thing. The long term detrimental effects of restricting people's rights to sell their products across borders are surely far greater than the short term disruptions associated with permitting them to do so. Likewise, allowing people to despoil the environment and slapping their hands with trade restrictions is surely more costly in the long run than making environmental stewardship a priority while simultaneously encouraging trade. In fact, restricting trade was a primary response of the U.S. and Europe to the economic difficulties they faced on the cusp of the Great Depression of the 1930s and this is now widely believed by economists to have been one of the major contributors to its severity.[5] Therefore, it is imperative for anyone interested in development to be able to think clearly about this issue rather than allow repeated episodes of escalating protectionism to cause regular troughs in economic progress.

The main problem with the thinking of the various groups who routinely lobby for restricted trade is that they tend to see the negatives associated with foreign competition, without seeing the benefits to others or to themselves. The underlying reality is that trade allows specialization, which allows increasingly specialized knowledge and skills, which leads, in turn, to massive increases in productivity. Ideas, too, can be traded, leading to even more substantial gains.[6] And as long as trade remains voluntary, and mechanisms are in place to combat fraud and enforce contracts, both parties (and countries) will gain from these transactions. Some may be quick to complain that government subsidies or other types of privileges may distort prices, or bribes will be paid to people who have the power to prevent their countrymen from free and voluntary exchanges, so that one country will in fact lose from trade; however, it must be remembered that these are domestic problems and should not be blamed on trade. Restricting trade would only make it easier to hide these poor domestic policies or moral failings, causing more damage to the country over a longer period of time. Gains from trade are also backed up empirically. Since World War II, there has been a long and remarkable increase in the real standards of living of nations who have embraced trade and "cleaned up" their domestic markets and institutions so that trade could be as fair as possible. It is not a stretch to say that every nation that has lifted itself out of poverty since WW II has done so, at least in part, by embracing trade.

The Role of Exports and Imports

We noted earlier that there has been some confusion historically about the benefits of both importing and exporting. But the lessons of history are not always accepted, and this is certainly true of the idea that export-driven growth is a tried and true path to wealth. This is likely because people in all cultures seem to know instinctively that exports create jobs. But they also need to understand the impact that importing has on a country. Imports create jobs in a country because they commonly drive exports of domestically produced technology and/or subcomponents (which become part of the imported product), and demand for local marketing, management and financial services. Also, low-priced imports give citizens more disposable income to spend on other domestic products, which stimulates demand in other domestic sectors. Perhaps most important, however, it is only a country's willingness to import that makes it possible for them to export to other countries. In order for other countries to buy a country's products, the foreign countries need to pay in the local currency, and their primary means for obtaining this currency is by selling their products to that same country. Thus, whatever jobs have been lost because of the increased importation of some products that could otherwise have been produced at home will be replaced (albeit often in different sectors of the economy) by export-related jobs or services. A U.S. Federal Reserve Bank study backed up this line of thinking by stating that jobs created to handle imports, produce exports, and produce additional domestically-consumed products which can be purchased with the extra money people have from buying lower priced imports, exceed the number of hypothetical jobs lost to foreign producers. Simple observation (in the U.S. and other counties) also backs this up. The U.S. has had both massive trade deficits and exceptionally low unemployment rates for long stretches, and other countries have experienced this as well.

These same benefits are of course also available to the people in the trading partner country. They too benefit from import- and export-related jobs, the economies of scale that go along with specialization and the additional spending power that comes from buying products from another country at less than their local cost of production. It is nearly impossible to imagine that we would erect barriers preventing families from ordering pizzas because doing so will put mothers out of work. It is equally hard to imagine erecting barriers that make it difficult or impossible for Iowans to sell their corn in Arizona or enjoy a good meal that includes gulf shrimp or Florida oranges. Relatively open country borders do nothing more than extend this common sense wisdom across national borders. No one will be forced to buy foreign products or sell to foreign buyers. But all will be free to do so if it serves them. And we should not ignore one other substantial benefit of trade. It gives all people, regardless of their language, skin color, educational level, or religion, a fair opportunity to work and enjoy the fruits of their labor.

Foreign competition, like other forms of competition, also creates wealth by forcing domestic companies to better serve their customers. Innovation and productivity are spurred; quality is improved; workers will have to give a good day's work for a good day's pay.[7] In fact, it can be persuasively argued that no nation will be able to persist in a highly consumptive, low productivity lifestyle for any significant amount of time in an open trading world, without experiencing real decreases in wealth. In addition, the citizens of both countries will develop cross-national friendships, as well as an appreciation for and the adoption of some of the best aspects of each other's culture. This is not to say that people and even nations cannot pick up bad habits from trading partners. But to blame this on trade is a mistake. We would not stop educating our children because some of them accept and act on bad ideas or values, and we should not restrict trade for the same reason. In all areas of life involving social contact, there are some risks associated with exchanging ideas and thinking patterns, but this is a price worth paying for something that is at the core of worldwide economic and social development.

In the long run, this increased interaction could even lead to increased chances for world peace and cooperation. Free exchange, it would seem, should be accepted as an infinitely better way of exchanging goods and property than going to war.[8] In spite of this, the misconception that war is good for an economy continues to persist. But it is not! Books have been written about the cost of nearly every major war, and they include everything from the salaries paid to soldiers, the ongoing medical costs of physically or psychologically injured soldiers and civilians, the cost to the families of lost loved ones, the cost of replacing damaged military equipment and civilian infrastructure and private property, environmental damage, and much, much more. Some change resulting from wars can be positive (particularly when destructive or psychotic tyrants are stopped), but the destruction of property and life is never better economically than the peaceful resolution of problems or peaceful changes of government.

Our discussion of the value of relatively open trade reminds us yet again how beliefs and values are at the foundation of the creation of wealth. But before we move to an in-depth discussion of the importance of belief systems, we should clarify that a world without rules is not the same thing as relatively unrestricted trade. The same people who value equal access to markets for all nations will also want to make sure that those who are potentially harmed in the short run by open trading do not unfairly or disproportionately bear the costs associated with changing patterns of trade. Just governments (cooperatively at all levels) must stand in the gap and offer, for example, temporary income assistance, job retraining, incentives which attract substitute employers, or something else which allows others to share the costs of these economic adjustments. Since the businesses participating in trade, consumers, and producers of complementary products[9] all benefit from trade, a well-run government should easily be able to generate enough revenue to provide such temporary assistance to those whose lives have been disrupted by trade. But, they must be interested enough in justice and have the political courage to do so. This brings us back, once again, to the importance of belief systems.

Chapter 8: Religious Beliefs – Extent, Importance and Paths of Influence

Introduction

We now return to one of the central tenets of this book, that religious beliefs are critical to development. The reasons for this are myriad, but we will attempt to address them in an organized fashion in this and the following three chapters as follows. In the present chapter we will look at 1) the extent of religious belief, 2) the inherent complexity involved in connecting religious beliefs with economic outcomes, and 3) how religious beliefs affect some of the catalysts for development highlighted in Chapters four through seven. In Chapter nine we will make some connections that go beyond what we discussed in Chapters four through seven and focus briefly on the economics of good and evil and why it is the substance, rather than the religious nature, of people's beliefs that merit our attention. In Chapter 10 we assemble a sizeable mass of anecdotal evidence on the impact of religious beliefs by citing examples of how they have changed people's lives, and altered the course of nations and history. Finally, in Chapter 11 we will summarize some of the writing and empirical research on the relationship between religious beliefs and economic outcomes, concluding with why a responsible treatment of the subject requires that we refrain from making artificial distinctions between religious and non-religious beliefs.

The Extent of Belief

One reason religious beliefs have so much impact is because they are so widespread. Statistically, according to the *World Christian Encyclopedia*,[1] most of the people in the world, certainly at least 80% of its population, would answer yes if asked if they are religious.[2] The vast majority of them would also readily admit that their religious beliefs infiltrate other aspects of their lives, and it is likely that they are correct about this - because evidence indicates that people who subscribe to the same expression of a particular religion (or non-theologically-based belief system) often have great similarities in how they see and interpret the world even when they have different ethnic or cultural backgrounds. If we add to this group those who hold the <u>strong belief</u> that there is no God, or that there may be a God, but he is not particularly relevant to day-to-day living, this percentage quickly rises to 100%.

It is widely published that citizens of the United States are among the most religious in the world (when religion is looked at narrowly as a belief in a Divine Being). If recent polls are to be believed, 78% of U.S. citizens "believe in God" and another 15% believe in a "higher power" they might prefer not to refer to as "God," and 42% the population regularly attends a house of worship.[3] But it would be more accurate to say that the religiosity of U.S. citizens is similar to that of most of people in the world, recognizing that those who see the U.S. as unusually religious tend to rely on research that compares it only to other Western/wealthy economies which are farther down the secularization path than the U.S.[4]

There are in fact more identifiable belief systems today in both rich and poor countries than ever before, and this number continues to increase. Perhaps most notably, religious participation is increasing in places where it was previously repressed, including most recently in Africa, Eastern Europe and China. Interestingly, this is part of a bigger picture where people in the countries classified by International NGOs like Freedom House as "most free" tend to be more religious than those in countries classified as "not free," with emigrants from "un-free" to "free" countries often *increasing* in religiosity, with notable numbers converting to Christianity.[5] It appears then that religious commitments have a tendency to *increase* where they are not restricted by a state, official church or legal constraints.

From an economic perspective, it could be said that in the same way that new products, services, businesses and NGOs spring up on a continuous basis when the barriers to entry are low, and total economic activity increases as a result, so too churches, synagogues, temples and mosques appear to increase in number when they are allowed to do so. Some of these, of course, simply represent existing religious groups moving to new locations. But others are, in one form or another, new religious movements, even when they may have been birthed by existing religious denominations. This should not, however, necessarily be thought of as unhealthy evidence of the balkanization[6] of religion, or as being in opposition to existing/traditional belief systems and structures. Often they offer what is perceived as a significant improvement on, or something that was perceived as missing or lost in the more established congregations.

In addition to the growing number of religious expressions, major world belief systems are also undergoing both significant change and significant migration, altering the religious landscape of the world in the process. Marxist belief systems are in decline; Islam is expanding from its Middle Eastern roots, with large and growing Muslim populations in, e.g., Northern Africa and Asia. Overall, Islam is growing faster than global population, at a rate estimated at 1.84% per year, primarily through high birth rates in Asia, the Middle East and Europe.[7]   The epicenter of Christianity is shifting from the North and West to the South and East, so that now the "typical" Christian is a person of color in the Southern Hemisphere. According to B.J. Vander Walt,[8] the number of Christians in Africa increased by 350 million in the twentieth century, and Christians are now reported to comprise nearly 60% of the African population. He estimated that more than 150,000 people become Christians *daily*, and nearly three million new churches were established between 2000 and 2010 in Africa, Asia and Latin America.[9] It is now the case that more Christian missionaries are being sent out *from* recently Christianized countries like Korea and the developing countries of the Global South than from Western countries. And this spread of religious belief (at least where it is not tightly controlled by autocratic clerics) is also characterized by an amazing amount of diversity. This is also true in developed Western countries where secular elites have been reasonably successful in keeping traditional religious beliefs from playing any significant role in the public education or political systems. Even in these environments resistance to secularism is alive and well: traditional religions have often strongly resisted marginalization and an interesting variety of "spirituality" movements have risen to fill what they perceive to be a religious void. The result of all this, according to David B. Barrett, the primary author of the *World Christian Encyclopedia*, is that at the turn of the beginning of the 3rd millennium (Gregorian calendar) there were around 10,000 distinguishable belief systems in the world, with the number increasing by two or three per day.[10] So, at the very least, it seems fair to say, in opposition to predictions made by Weber, Marx, Freud, Nietzsche and other well-known writers, that religious beliefs, and their effects on development, are here to stay. Shut the door, and religious beliefs will come through the window.

The Complexity of the Connections between Belief and Development

Because there are so many paths of influence connecting beliefs with economic outcomes, our goals at this point must necessarily be modest: to make enough connections between beliefs and values that people largely agree to be religiously-based religious beliefs and the catalysts for development that we have already identified. In the process of doing this, we must also decide whether to concentrate here on how the beliefs and values associated with *different religions* lead to different economic outcomes **or** more generically how a *particular belief or value* (rather than a particular religion) will influence people's economic choices (and outcomes). We have chosen *at this point* to focus on the latter of these, sampling the positive and negative impacts of values plucked from a variety of belief systems as needed, and will wait until Chapter 14 to establish and organize what differentiates one belief system from another in economically-influential ways. To complete the circle, we will still need to address in detail some of the central tenets of *specific* belief systems and evaluate the paths between the teachings of these belief systems and economic outcomes. But because there are so many belief systems and because they impact wealth creation and economic development in so many ways, we will have to choose a small subset of belief systems to illustrate the impact of a belief system in depth. Our choice is to devote ten chapters toward the end of the book to the two specific belief systems (Christianity and Secular Materialism) that have arguably had more influence on wealth creation and economic development than any others.

An analogy for the relationship between religious beliefs and economic outcomes

Admittedly, we are getting to a point where things get very difficult. As the broader discussions in earlier chapters make clear, underlying beliefs (both those traditionally viewed as religious and those traditionally viewed as ideological or secular) at the very least color, and in many cases, influence or even drive many of the most important aspects of human thought and activity. And it is both assumptions that underlie particular belief as well the nature and content of those beliefs that are important. More precisely, people's beliefs about the nature of God, the universe, people, relationships, truth, or right and wrong can have both direct and indirect influences on their economic outcomes. Beyond these foundational commitments, most belief systems also have sacred texts or oral traditions that specify a significant number of attitudes, priorities and behaviors as appropriate (or inappropriate) for its adherents. But, since life is composed of an almost infinite number of attitudes, values, goals, or priorities, many of which have multiple and blended causes, sources or impacts, there is no simple way to isolate (or empirically measure) how a particular set of these things will contribute to economic development or impede it.

Perhaps the best analogy for how religious beliefs affect economic outcomes is the neural network operating in the human brain. As we process information for decision making, data comes to the brain from various sensory organs and electronic pulses follow a variety of paths to different parts of the brain. Synapses occur in various locations which send pulses to other locations which jointly contribute to both voluntary and involuntary responses/decisions, which in turn lead to messages being sent from the brain to various organs of the body, resulting in specific responses and outcomes. No combination of paths or synapses is ever quite the same, but the inputs are clearly affecting the outcomes, even if it is difficult to explain just how this happens. In the present work, religious beliefs affect a host of other things that in turn affect economic outcomes, but the paths are too numerous and too complicated to easily describe. But just because something can't be done easily is no reason not to take a stab at it. (As a familiar saying goes…"Fools rush in where angels fear to tread.")

Chapter 8

Channels of impact

We will start by organizing our thoughts around things we already learned to be important to development in Chapters 5-8. To summarize, we noted that wealth/asset accumulations are essential to the kind of investments (private for-profit and not-for profit, and government) that can fund innovation and productivity increases, and that these wealth increases come from people's incomes, savings habits (current or past generations), stewardship of assets, and ability to make wise investment choices. These in turn depend on secure property rights, appropriate economic incentives, the freedom to pursue appropriate business strategies, and well-functioning markets (and especially financial markets). They also require the taking of significant financial risks, which requires confidence in the future. Confidence, in turn, increases when we have well-run ethical companies, wise, predictable government policies, and sustainable economic practices. And, the more people in a society who understand why these things are essential and what is required to achieve them, the better.

For now, we will refer to these as "routine economic understandings," and concentrate on making some of the connections between them and underlying beliefs a little more obvious — even as we continue to wish they were widely-enough understood to deserve to the adjective "routine."

Wealth and poverty

Beliefs regarding wealth and money range from outright worship and joyful accumulation, on one end of the spectrum, to assumptions at the other end that, since the economic world is "zero-sum,[11]" that all wealth accumulations are harmful to the poor, and therefore those who accumulate wealth are morally reprehensible and should be coerced to give it to those less fortunate ones who demand it. For some, wealth arouses feelings like envy and resentment, while for others it evokes admiration, emulation or industry, and for yet others, something in the middle. Although not all of these beliefs are exclusively religious, they are all nevertheless to some degree affected by religious commitments.

Both Catholicism and Eastern Orthodoxy have traditionally been and continue to be more suspicious of wealth accumulation than Protestantism, in part because of their experience that wealth has the potential to undermine justice or exacerbate laziness or selfishness. Protestants were and are more likely to view wealth as a blessing, albeit a blessing that entails significant responsibility. Coupled with an emphasis on Biblical teachings about self-restraint or stewardship this could lead to the accumulation of large amounts of wealth. But some Christians who emphasize Jesus' detachment from material things, or Biblical warnings about the problems that can accompany wealth, may save little or nothing for the future. This latter group may view wealth not all that differently from many expressions of Buddhism, that aspire to *The Four Noble Truths*, one of which notes that "life is suffering" and another that "the root of suffering is desire/attachment." Most expressions of

Buddhism also prescribe a path (*Nirodha*) which can lead to the cessation of suffering (sometimes described as the Noble Eightfold Path), one important part of which calls for the cessation of desire. But different expressions of Buddhism interpret this differently, and those that emphasize the root of suffering as the desire or aspiration to escape suffering, will experience very different economic outcomes than an expression that emphasizes the root of suffering to be the attachment to craving, self-indulgence, or ignorance. Clearly these differing perspectives can lead to radically different consumption habits, with long-lasting impacts on wealth creation. Wealth is unlikely to accumulate unless people *believe* that wealth is a good thing, and poverty a bad thing; they also need to *believe* that wealth can be created, rather than just shuffled around from one (losing) party to another (winning) party.

But different religious expressions also have different ideas about *the nature and causes* of the problem of poverty, the eradication of which is undoubtedly a high priority for anyone reading this book. Many traditional African religions, for example, would associate poverty with things like not being married, not having a family, or not being socially accepted. To Western secular materialists, poverty is primarily a lack of income and wealth, which is why increasing people's incomes was a centerpiece of the U.S. war on poverty that started in the 1960s. To most Christians, however, poverty has a broader connotation: being poor could mean a shortage of material wealth or money, but it could also mean a life without meaning and purpose, lived irresponsibly, in isolation from, or in rebellion to God and outside of the kind of relationships he intended for people.

Religious traditions also tend to steer people into accumulating particular *forms* of wealth, which is perhaps most obvious if we observe people who tend to wear much of their wealth, or those from traditions that tend to avoid all investments except the safest. If people hold their wealth in relatively unproductive forms like stored commodities, gold, silver or jewelry, not only will they prevent these commodities from potentially beneficial uses, but they will need to devote scarce resources to storing and protecting them. Likewise, when they hold these, or even hold paper money, they will not experience the same kind of increases in living standards as they would if they invested their wealth in value-adding ventures like new business startups, real estate, shares of stock, or bank deposits.

Property and credit

These influences of religion on views of wealth also spill over into differing perspectives on private property and credit, two particularly important building blocks of economic development. If we go back far enough, in many ancient traditions, things that didn't owe their existence to any particular person (e.g. air, water, land) couldn't be owned.[12] But already at the time the Pentateuch (the first five books of the Bible) was being written, Jewish teaching had affirmed both God's ownership of everything and how that overarching claim was to be translated into individual and family property rights, with particular attention to limitations on the king/government's ability to infringe on these rights. In addition, Sabbatical Laws and laws associated with "Jubilee" both limited what people could do with their land and protected family succession rights to land

The Christian tradition, at least early on, although respecting private property, was less supportive of the idea of individuals accumulating wealth. As early as the 3rd century AD, the church began acquiring large amounts of property as some Christians, convicted that large accumulations of wealth were unjust or spiritually perilous, donated large trusts to the church. A more formal clergy emerged around this same time, sometimes becoming landowners, and often (by Church law) passed their estates to the church upon death. Overtime, the land holdings of the Catholic Church became significant. In general, the early church fathers (prior to the split between the Catholic and Eastern Orthodox churches) were quite vocal in their criticism of *private* (i.e. non-church and non-government) property ownership. Clement, for example, noted that exclusive possession ran somewhat contrary to the fellowship God desired for his people, and Basil insisted that one who loves his neighbor as himself will possess no more than his neighbor.[13] Ambrose added to this understanding by focusing on how excessive concentration of property robs the poor of their birthright, how excessive possessiveness impoverishes everyone by greatly restricting everyone's access, and how trust in wealth and property can be deleterious to trust in God. And Augustine wrote about how excessive attachment to private ownership could contribute to jealousy, idolatry, pride, crime, and war. Nevertheless, some of these Christian philosophers also seemed to understand that common ownership (at least outside of the church) was somewhat utopian and that private property/ownership could serve some useful functions.

The Reformers, like Martin Luther and John Calvin, were considerably more sympathetic to private property, perhaps because they were keenly aware that some of the Catholic Church's power was related to property ownership. Generally their writings indicated that they believed that private property was sanctioned by Holy Scripture. Luther in particular noted that the communal ownership practiced in the early church was not compulsory, that private property provided incentives to be productive, and that it was important for the preservation of the family. He even went so far as to draw an analogy between communal ownership and "putting sheep and the wolves in the same pen." Calvin added that private property was implied, if not mandated, by commandments such as "you shall not steal," that ownership is one of the rightful rewards of labor, and that God in his providence chooses to bless some with property and wealth for purposes of enjoyment, stewardship and the benefit of others. These teachings were influential in the gradual move over many centuries toward private property in Europe, and particularly in England where some land was taken away from the Catholic Church and redistributed to favored individuals, and steadily increasing amounts of common property were enclosed to facilitate sheep-raising.[14] Of course, countries with very different religious traditions have had very different experiences with private property. Atheistic communism, for example, forced communal property ownership on people throughout Eastern Europe. Most secular materialists (and particularly staunch individualists), on the other hand, assume individual private property rights to be completely natural outgrowths of freedom and competition, with little of the kind of baggage that Christians or communists may bring to the subject.

Religious beliefs have also influenced the development of both credit and investment. Both the medieval Catholic Church and modern day Muslims oppose(d) the charging of interest (*raja*). In addition, according to Guison, et al., the Sunnah[15] prohibits "the formation and conclusion of aleatory contracts based on chance,"[16] which not only affects loans with uncertain interest payments but also other kinds of riskier investments. Adequate levels of investment are also influenced by religious beliefs because they depend on both limits to selfishness and people's ability to cooperate in the creation and running of productive businesses. Healthy development requires that companies create value and supply people with "goods and services" rather than with "bads and disservices," and this is much more likely to happen when businesses have a higher purpose than just enriching owners. The global financial crisis of 2008-2011 made it abundantly clear that when company managers and owners paid themselves too much and otherwise removed excessive quantities of capital from their companies, they put both their companies and the entire economy at risk. Likewise, markets sent strong signals that they cannot function well in the absence of honesty and integrity, and the trust that depends on them. (A shortage of these undermined confidence and the willingness to take risks, which in turn roiled the credit markets and the ability of companies to create jobs.) These and other moral failures harm productive activity in a host of other ways as well. Customers and companies lose faith in each other when promises are not kept. Efficiency declines when management lacks the humility to admit mistakes, or as it becomes riskier to delegate authority. Productivity drops as the work ethic deteriorates or as employees become more suspicious of each other. Waste and pilferage increase when employees have little regard for stewardship. Indeed, many things that underlie business activity, from customer service, to accounting practices, to clock watching, to the very notion of a "limited-liability corporation" owe their origins and health to religiously-rooted moral and ethical concepts.

Freedom

We also noted in Chapters 5-8 that a healthy amount of freedom is essential for economic actors to make wise, value-creating business decisions. It is also spurs business development and job creation, as there is nothing that fuels entrepreneurial passion more than the freedom to do what one feels in her heart-of-hearts must be done to change things for the better. Freedom also spurs economic activity because it allows a broader range of individual preferences to be expressed by both producers and consumers. But economic freedom is inextricably tangled up with *religious* freedom, since religious beliefs cannot help but express themselves in people's economic preferences (production, consumption, savings, and investment). Not only do people work harder for companies that respect their beliefs, and produce products and services that are congruent with their beliefs, but many of their purchases are also influenced by these beliefs.

But *unrestrained* freedom also allows for significant inefficiencies to enter the economic system if the values of people are such that they are not tuned in to the need for stewardship, or the efficiencies associated with moral and ethical behavior, or the impact of their choices on others (present and future), or the need to work communally to solve joint economic problems. Of course, freedom has always elevated the importance of moral and ethical consciousness (since non-free people are usually restricted to some degree in their ability to act on their nobler or baser instincts anyway). But the importance of moral conscience is especially important at this point in history since an unprecedented awakening desire for freedom is gradually sweeping across the globe.[17]

It is perilous, then, to ignore the strikingly different perspectives on freedom that exist among religions. For example, many of the core "doctrines" of atheism, agnosticism and secular humanism flow out of the belief that man should be free from the constraints so often associated with traditional religious teachings. In many cases their assumption has been that the only way to achieve the desired level of freedom is to remove God (or gods) from the picture and elevate man to god-like status. And many of the differences *between* religions are about what people are free or not free to do. Some of these effects are relatively insignificant: Orthodox Muslims and Jews are not permitted to eat pork, or Hindus beef. Amish people are not particularly free to use every new technology that comes along. More broadly, religiously-based watchdog groups have on occasion created some (relatively minor) difficulties for certain companies. For example, many Christians and secular humanists pushed for trade restrictions with South Africa during the apartheid period; church groups sometimes monitor companies' treatment of employees (and especially sweatshops); many Christian and Muslim groups frown on business activity that is associated with immoral activity (the sex trade, alcohol, gambling, cigarettes, etc.); many religious groups also frown on commercial activity that unfairly takes advantage of people.

But perhaps the larger freedom-related effects of religious beliefs on economic outcomes involve perspectives on what is permitted or not permitted. May interest be charged, and if so, how much? May women fully participate in the economy? Should people be free to own their own property? May religious beliefs and values be taught in school and if so, which ones? Or which moral and ethical principles should be ensconced in law?

Personal values and economic decisions of individuals and families

The questions at the end of the previous paragraph lead naturally into the connection between religious beliefs and the values and choices of individuals and families. This could include something as seemingly benign as whether a mother chooses to spend her money on cosmetics and expensive handbags for herself, or books and computers for her children. But it could be something more extensive, affecting for example the percentage of children growing up in one-parent vs. two-parent homes or the likelihood that children will be abused or end up turning to drugs or criminal activity.

Economists routinely talk about the importance of technology to growth, but it is hard to imagine that beliefs which infuse inspirational thoughts, comforting love, or praiseworthy actions into families and a society would not be every bit as important to economic development.

This is especially true in free societies. When people are free they tend to do what they believe most strongly in, which is good if they have well-thought-out and ordered moral principles, ethics and priorities but not so good if they are either not inclined to examine or have not been held accountable for these things. Religious education is sometime criticized for restricting freedom by way of an excessive focus on morality and ethics, but the possible wisdom of this should not be dismissed too quickly. There are incalculable moral and ethical influences on economic outcomes related to people's core beliefs. For example, how might one's religious commitment affect her willingness to voluntarily pay all taxes owed? How might planting a seed in a child's heart about the nobility of committing one's life to trying to eradicate productivity-sapping diseases compare to permitting him to follow his inclination to play violent video games? Only concentrated moral reflection, and a degree of enlightenment, makes clear that real progress toward peace and prosperity requires that more people spent less time focused on things like comfort and amusement and more time caring more about those who are different from them, learning their languages, understanding their beliefs, meeting their needs, and engaging them for the purpose of learning from them.[18] Vigorous development requires free people who conduct their affairs with a sense of purpose and gravity, and labor to set up the kinds of institutions (such as businesses, governments and NGOs) and systems (in the form of civil society and entrepreneurial activity) that enable people to solve problems and improve their lives. And, in the process, they will create increasingly complex, intangible, and high-value-added products and services, and the jobs that go with them. They are also likely to raise children who will do the same.

Charity and the not-for profit sector

Even more obviously, religious beliefs often drive charitable urges and responses to poverty. They do this in part because of how they influence personal and family financial choices, as noted earlier. For example, some Catholic wedding or fiesta traditions in Latin America or Hindu religious festivals in India may mandate such lavish expenditures that those involved may have to finance them with debt that takes many years to pay off. The burden of this debt often leaves little surplus for charitable endeavors. Other traditions will strongly emphasize both savings and charity, and even build incentives for this into the tax and legal systems. In general, religious traditions that strongly emphasize sharing will tend to downplay wealth accumulation, but this does not necessarily mean they are not involved in wealth creation. Sharing in some religious traditions can involve mandatory sharing, even if recipients take advantage of this generosity to avoid work or consume things that will be damaging to them in the long run; but in others it could and often does focus on financially investing in people so that they too can create wealth and continue this tradition of productive sharing with others.

Differing perspectives on wealth and charity also mean different belief systems will also favor different *solutions* to the poverty problem. Judaism and Islam both assume that all material wealth belongs first of all to God, and both mandate alms, through the Jewish concept of the tithe (often interpreted as 10%) and the Muslim zakat (2.5%). Other belief systems may not address this issue at all, or may sanction or even encourage begging rather than emphasizing the responsibility to engage in productive activity and share surpluses. Along with tithing, many American Christians tend to favor attacking poverty at a local level, and in a way that addresses all of a disadvantaged person's needs, including material/financial, spiritual/moral, intellectual/emotional, social, the need to work, etc. This means they also tend to advocate both limited government involvement and the kind of involvement that does not discriminate against what has come to be known as "faith-based" approaches. Secular groups, on the other hand have generally been more concerned about keeping church and state separate, or with privacy rights, than with accountability or prescriptions for moral behavior. But the views/beliefs of this group must also be parsed. Those on the conservative side of the political spectrum have often favored allowing the poor to fend for themselves, on the assumption that competitive striving is necessary for them to work their way out of poverty, while those on the liberal end have been more inclined to focus on government's responsibility to provide an income stream, with few restrictions on how recipients might use it.

Role of government, laws, and customs

Chapters 5-8 made it abundantly clear that good government is essential to development, and this too is heavily influenced by religious beliefs. Some religious belief systems believe clerics have a divine right to also run the government; others respect the authority of governors in their own right. Some rulers are completely unrestrained by the moral constraints of humility, while others defer to the good advice and judgment of others. Some see a responsibility to promote justice and some do not; those that do often get their ideas about justice from religiously-based sources. These same sources (or lack thereof) will influence whether politicians emphasize personal enrichment, pork barrel payouts to their constituents, or the common good; whether or not they are willing to lie to the public, steal public property, or falsify records; or what kinds of business or personal conduct they encourage or discourage. In Western countries, for example, Christian beliefs have not only influenced laws prohibiting murder and theft, but also how creditors are expected to limit the liability of owners and forgive debts in bankruptcy. In this way, they also influence the incentives and opportunities for people to be able to profit from entrepreneurship and risk-taking.

Religious beliefs also influence many customs with economic impact. For example, people in countries heavily influenced by Christianity have work schedules that reflect Biblical directives for balancing work and rest, and measure their years from a reference point, abbreviated by the letters AD, short for Anno Domini, "the year of our Lord." U.S. calendars include religious holidays like Thanksgiving Day, Christmas, Good Friday, and Easter. But these religious holidays are not simply days off work; they are government-instituted remembrances of significant events or beliefs that undergird the faith of many of its citizens.

Chapter 9: The Economics of Good and Evil

If beliefs were pervasive but relatively benign, we could perhaps stop with a discussion of the logical connections between religious beliefs and the "routine economic understandings" that we discussed in chapters four through seven. But there are a host of other reasons that religious beliefs are important to economic outcomes that, frankly, are more likely to be discovered by philosophers or theologians than economists.

Motivation

One of these, as expressed by John Stuart Mill more than 150 years ago, with only a modicum of hyperbole, involves the fact "that one person with belief is equal to a force of 99 who have only interests."[1] So not only are beliefs widespread, and related to things well known to be important economically, as noted in the previous chapter, but they motivate people in ways that mere preferences or "interests" cannot. They can motivate us to set records, establish foundations, or win Nobel prizes, but they may also cause us to defraud each other and saddle us with abused and permanently damaged children, disease, and terrorism. A careful study of history indicates that beliefs have been at the core of the rise and fall of nations, companies and individuals, in part because they influence a host of important things that many people would initially assume to be unrelated to economic outcomes. This may have been why the widely regarded Russian social philosopher Alexander Solzhenitsyn said, "If you have a religion problem you will have a society problem" (And of course, if you have a society problem you will have an economy problem.) Solzhenitsyn knew this because he had observed, far more than the average person, and was also the victim of what can be best described as the economics of good and evil.

Good and evil

It is not an exaggeration to say that the influences discussed heretofore are really just the tip of the iceberg when it comes to how development is affected by the defining and encouraging of moral behavior, and more broadly by religious beliefs. As the English philosopher Edmund Burke said,

"The only thing necessary for the triumph of evil is for good men to do nothing," and it seems to be the nature of reality that good things are ever and always vulnerable to the forces that many religions would describe as "evil."[2] Perfection, goodness, beauty, purity, and other similarly noble things seem almost always to be in a precarious position, easily capable of being spoiled. It seems to be the nature of reality that destruction is easier than building. Orchards must be carefully tended over many years, but one frost can damage millions of dollars in fruit crops. One tsunami or hurricane can destroy in hours what took people decades and sometimes even centuries to build. With minimal contact, one sick person in a room can infect a dozen others with a cold or flu, but a dozen healthy people are incapable of making the person with the flu healthy (unless they dedicate their lives to and happen to be successful in discovering a cure for the flu). Combating any one of these "evils" requires that difficult and deliberate actions be taken. To minimize the damage from natural disasters and illnesses we need to understand the natural patterns of the world we live in, create insurance mechanisms, and divert resources from other uses to superior construction methods, early warning systems, and elaborate research projects, all difficult and time-consuming activities.

But natural disasters and illnesses are just two flies in the ointment of economic development. People do easily as much or more damage. One misguided parent can ruin a child's life. One killer can terrorize an entire town. One corrupt president can bring his nation's economy to its knees. One misguided but charismatic leader can steer thousands or even millions of people in the wrong direction. Belief systems are capable of rendering their adherents incapable of either defining or confronting evil, or even worse, causing people to conspire and carry out evil acts. Islamic extremists like Osama bin Laden, al Qaeda and others who are consumed with planting bombs and hijacking airplanes in order to kill innocent people give us a highly-publicized and negative example of the importance of beliefs. And, although there are many peace-loving Muslims throughout the world, the actions witnessed that day were not merely the product of angry disenfranchised young Arab men; they were and still are (generally) well-planned "defensive" jihads dependent on a belief that the Qur'an not only justifies these attacks but requires them. And their attacks, including those at the World Trade Center, Pentagon and in the air over Shanksville, Pennsylvania on September 11, 2001, not only took thousands of innocent lives, but they ushered in almost unimaginable inefficiencies into the global economy.

Wrong beliefs the problem, not religious beliefs

We need to be clear that the source of all this damage is *wrong* beliefs.[3] This is not because the beliefs in question were religious beliefs, since religious beliefs, in spite of the fact that they remain mysterious to many people,[4] *may nevertheless square completely with the way things really are*, and even go well beyond this *to light the path to the highest human possibilities*. Rather, the terrorist's beliefs were wrong because they violate immutable laws that govern how people *ought* to treat each other; laws whose immutability depends on something greater than human wisdom and reason: on the kind of religious commitment that is capable of recognizing their fundamental rightness and making them non-negotiable.

Like the many other atrocities cited earlier, the 9/11 attack all but begs us to accept that it is ultimately humankind's inability to win the ongoing battle between good and evil that most jeopardizes the continued economic development of the world economy. Restoring families who lost loved ones in senseless acts of violence, patching up people who've been burned or lost limbs, or suffered traumatic stress because of senseless hatred, repairing a neglected or abused natural environment, and rebuilding crushed spirits and broken relationships are all economically expensive endeavors. Evil is horribly expensive, whether it is these kinds of things or more indirect costs such as those associated with paying more and more people to carry out espionage, screen and search luggage, produce gas masks or stand around with guns protecting the remainder of the population, since we would be considerably better off if these people were able to use their time and talents in more productive ways.

Confronting evil is also an inescapably religious activity. As Solzhenitsyn put it when he edited *From Under the Rubble*, "the universal dividing line between good and evil runs not between countries, not between nations, not between parties, not between classes, not between good and bad men: the dividing line cuts across nations and parties, shifting constantly... It divides the heart of every man." He further explained that real solutions could not be merely political (or technological), but needed to be found in morality and religion, because even something as benign as reaching a consensus opinion on the Golden Rule is an inescapably moral activity that requires a higher frame of reference than people's feelings and preferences. This implies that the ultimate solution to life's most intractable problems is more likely to come primarily from religiously-informed dialog and only secondarily from the kinds of solutions favored by secular thinkers, such as technology or politics.

Technology and politics, although capable of making important contributions to the needed solutions, do not require a broad enough understanding of the nature of people and the world to produce lasting solutions, in and of themselves. Technology has the potential to serve people well by providing structures, processes, and products that are useful for problem solving, but religiously-informed approaches can go well beyond this to the ethics of how these structures and processes are put to use and what people choose to do with them. In addition, by penetrating through myriad layers of symptoms to the root problems, they also have the potential to detach people from many other kinds of things that can divide them, such as ethnicity, national boundaries or social class.

Religious beliefs differ greatly

As readers may have noticed, our discussion has been unable to avoid spilling over into yet another reason religious beliefs greatly impact development - because they vary so much, ranging from horrific and life-taking to loving and life-giving. If we are willing to reflect on the world economy over the past century, it becomes clear that more damage has been done by unethical and morally reprehensible conduct than by anything else. Beliefs about ethnic superiority, the thirst for power, ideological pride, murder and kidnapping (sometimes financed by the sale of diamonds or precious metals), invasions, land grabbing, slavery, rape, other forms of forced sex leading to AIDS, the proliferation of counterfeit drugs, culturally imbedded hierarchies that give men privileged status while women and children go uneducated or hungry, routine corruption (not only by government officials but by other so-called professionals like doctors and lawyers), and the abuse of authority (which permits and even encourages unjust fees, taxes, and other financial burdens on those least able to afford them or on those most capable of creating jobs) have stopped development dead in its tracks in many countries. And the degree to which any or all of these kinds of activities can take place is ultimately couched in what people believe to be right or wrong, good or evil; in what they will tolerate or refuse to tolerate; in short, in the kinds of things they commit to or accept (or *refuse* to commit to or accept) *by faith*, whether that faith is in themselves and their institutions and processes, in a God or gods who may or may not exist behind the scenes, or some combination of these.

Even if one tries to reduce religious beliefs down to rituals (which would be a serious mistake), those rituals can range, on one hand, from an insistence on bathing in a particular river or putting pants on starting with the right foot to, on the other, a substantial commitment by an entire community to support parents in the raising of their children, or public vows to renounce a host of counterproductive behaviors (coupled with a willingness to subject oneself to strict accountability). Likewise some belief systems have no discernible moral code or concept of sin. Some worship gods who are arbitrary and vindictive, or immoral, or distant and unaware of what people are doing, while others worship a "father" God, who is merciful, loving, and just, and who holds people accountable to be and do the same. Some religious beliefs embrace revenge as not only legitimate, but in some cases, required, while others focus on reconciliation and restoration. Some belief systems are action-oriented and others are meditation or chanting- oriented with predictable economic impacts. Some allow participants to be very individualistic and others demand that participants recognize their obligations to others and to live "in community." And the cumulative effect of these differences is significant for economic development.

Beliefs as a form of investment

It should be clear from what we have been saying that we can draw an analogy between variations in belief systems and good and bad investments. Some belief systems represent the accumulation of centuries or millennia of thought and experience; others represent little more than personal preferences. Whether practical ethical systems like Confucianism, perceived direct revelations from God, like the Qur`an, or work believed to be the product of God-inspired human writers, like the Bible, belief systems are much more than just theoretical constructs. Practices laid out in the Ten

Commandments and the Pentateuch protected the Jews from a host of diseases and poor decisions.[5] Confucian teachings have been at the core of the remarkably long Chinese history, and the basis of some remarkable family and social stability. So no thinking person should assume that "religious" writings cannot be historically accurate or without practical wisdom or consequence. When carefully examined, most belief systems end up looking more like ways of living than easily definable sets of rules and rituals. Hinduism for example, has long been understood by its practitioners as much more than a set of beliefs; in fact, most Hindus prefer that scholars of religion recognize them as Hindu people, rather than mere followers of a Hindu religion.

Seeing religion in this way makes it easier to see why healthy beliefs are like investments. Once they have penetrated people hearts, and etched their goals, values, attitudes and priorities there, they will pay life-long "dividends" to individuals and their society in the form of things like honesty, integrity, respect for people and property, work effort, commitment to peaceable change, or a willingness to serve. In doing so, they will function as comprehensive reservoirs of wisdom, capable of addressing many, if not most, of society's most intractable problems. On the other hand, misguided beliefs have great potential for harm and can contribute significantly to driving an economy into the ground. They may address few, if any, of the conundrums of modern life, or may even encourage actions that are counterproductive to development.

The former are like investments, or gifts that keep on giving. Like well-constructed buildings, good books or well written software, healthy religious beliefs take advantage of the wisdom/expertise of others by allowing adherents to stand on the shoulders of those who have gone before them or those who have a better understanding of something than they do. Like all good investments, healthy religious beliefs have relatively high initial "costs" to read, listen, learn, and put religious teachings into practice. But, once a good investment has been made, like a well-built home or a good education or a well-written piece of software, ongoing maintenance or upkeep costs will be small relative to the benefits received. Evidence indicates that these benefits can even persist for so long that people will not only take them for granted but forget their source.

We also note that like a good piece of software, religious beliefs have a distinct economic advantage over other forms of investment like homes or shares of stock. *Habits of the Heart*,[6] to use Bellah's term for these things, can, like DVDs containing millions of lines of software code, be *replicated* at very little cost to the proprietor of the beliefs. One does not have to give up her religious beliefs to make them available to others. Hundreds or thousands of people, or millions in the case of the 20th century's best-known Christian evangelist, Billy Graham,[7] can benefit from what is written on one person's heart, particularly when a person has an "evangelical" bent and a strong desire to give away (replicate) the beliefs and principles which have enriched her life. This is even more so the case when technology (such as the internet or electronic books) makes it possible to spread ideas around the world at light speed. Unfortunately, the same can be said for beliefs that lack integrity. They too have the potential to spread very quickly and do more damage than was possible in the past. So in the same way that physical mobility allows for diverse job opportunities tied to economic prosperity, but also spreads insidious diseases like HIV, the internet that carries the words of Billy Graham and the Dali Lama also multiplies the rewards and incentives for the spam artists, pornographers, sexual predators and terrorists who have very different belief systems. Nevertheless, this supports the underlying premise that belief systems deserve more serious attention, rather than less, of those of us interested in economic outcomes.

God, the game changer

Finally, there is one more reason that religious beliefs could have a significant economic impact, albeit one that is outside the scope of this writing. It seems clear to us that if God exists, it changes everything. Even though we intend here only to report only on the economic significance of such beliefs,[8] rather than argue for the existence or non-existence of God, to say that the kind of God who is routinely described in mono-theistic belief systems, like Islam, Judaism and Christianity would be a game changer, would be the essence of understatement. For example, if there is a God who created, among other things, the laws of logic and proof, those who refuse to consider this possibility logically will, as it turns out, end up thinking somewhat illogically (and in the process close off an important portion of reality) by insisting that the laws and tools of logic and proof are all we need to know or use to prove the existence of something that is above or outside them. In such a situation, the blind belief and blind unbelief in the tails of the human population distribution are probably equally effective in reducing life to something more mundane and predictable than it was intended to be and that most people are willing to accept.

When comparing religions, then, it would be best not to assume in advance that the only way religious beliefs can impact economic development is through the economic activity associated with "religious activities," or their impact on values, attitudes, goals or behaviors. True scholars need to be open to the possibilities that faith, prayer, religiously obedient or disobedient behaviors, or God's will/justice/mercy could have impacts that go well beyond outcomes in the afterlife, or warm fuzzy feelings in the here and now. If there is a God who has a real impact on what happens in the world, whose justice is necessary to rescue the downtrodden, whose anger allows those "who live by the sword to die by the sword" or whose power is essential to "turn a heart of stone into a heart of flesh", there would be fewer bigger mistakes than dismissing this *by assumption*. This is especially true because any God who could bring a universe into being that is bigger than any human can get her mind around, or any God who can create life from dead matter in some mysterious way, or build creatures so complex that even the best medical minds understand only a fraction of the processes that sustain them, could certainly be the source of useful knowledge about how people ought to order their lives or relationships. Such a God could also work behind the scenes to shape processes, people, or even countries, and even the most rational among us would have to admit that this could be done in a way that would be easier for trusting children to discover than overconfident scholars who long ago concluded that the idea of such a Being is preposterous. The first step toward discovering something mysterious is, of course, the ability to believe that *there could possibly be* more than meets the eye. In fact, as we shall see in subsequent chapters, there are many "ways of knowing" available for people to investigate the connections between development outcomes and what people accept by faith (about the existence and nature of God or gods, about the world, the nature of people, relationships, or right or wrong), and as we have seen, there are very tangible differences in outcomes associated with different religious beliefs. So, perhaps it is best for those of us who have the tendency to dismiss most religious beliefs by assumption to take the advice of Jewish scholar Gamaliel. When confronted with those who were unwilling to entertain a new belief system (Christianity), and who thought it best to stamp it out before it had an opportunity to undermine existing views of the world, he convinced those who wanted to intimidate the followers of Jesus shortly after his death that it was better to let Christianity fade away like other religious fads, than to try to violently wipe it out. The story of his speech is recorded in the Bible's New Testament book of Acts:

> A Pharisee named Gamaliel, a teacher of the law, who was honored by all the people, stood up in the Sanhedrin and ordered that the men (Jesus' followers) be put outside for a little while. Then he addressed them: "Men of Israel, consider carefully what you intend to do to these men. Some time ago Theudas appeared, claiming to be somebody, and about four hundred men rallied to him. He was killed, all his followers were dispersed, and it all came to nothing. After him, Judas the Galilean appeared in the days of the census and led a band of people in revolt. He too was killed, and all his followers were scattered. Therefore, in the present case I advise you: Leave these men alone! Let them go! For if their purpose or activity is of human origin, it will fail. But if it is from God, you will not be able to stop these men; you will only find yourselves fighting against God. His speech persuaded them. They called the apostles in and had them flogged. Then they ordered them not to speak in the name of Jesus, and let them go. [9]

This is not to say that government should never interfere with religiously motivated activity. Governments everywhere have important responsibilities to promote justice and protect innocents from harm. Nor should we accept the response of the Jewish leaders – to flog the followers of Jesus and to implement a gag rule – as either well-intentioned or wise. Better (given that had Gamaliel not spoken up or not been heeded, the world and the world economy would both be very different than they are today[10]) to afford religious beliefs the space they need to make their contribution. This also keeps the door open to the kind of life changing experience an encounter with God can be. But the purpose of the present writing is limited to exploring the more mundane impact that different religious beliefs have on economic outcomes. Those who desire to participate in the kinds of things that offer the possibility of a spiritual encounter, such as prayer, worship, readings of sacred texts, or immersion in a community of scholars or believers who embrace and who live out the implications of that encounter, will have to go elsewhere.

Chapter 10: Evidence of the Impact of Beliefs, both Religious and Secular, on Historically Important Individuals and Events

Anecdotal evidence

Given all of the theoretical connections between religious beliefs and economic outcomes uncovered in Chapters Eight and Nine, we ought also to be able to find lots of anecdotal evidence linking religion and economic activity. Anecdotal evidence can be problematic, of course, if relied on exclusively, but it has the advantage of dealing with actual life events, and if we piece together enough accounts of life events, and complement it with research, logic and other ways of understanding, we often pick up more common sense or wisdom than we would have without incorporating the anecdotal. Certainly it is better to pay regular attention to anecdotal evidence than to "only hear what we want to hear."

Lives changed

One powerful piece of anecdotal evidence is that we can observe just about any religious group and see that the lives of people who adhere to that belief system are both oriented around customs related to shared beliefs and different from those who do not share those beliefs. We could also study individuals whose lives have been radically altered by their belief systems. The most obvious of these are people like Mother Teresa, Pope John Paul or Dr. Billy Graham, but there are also myriad lesser-known people whose lives have been radically altered by religious conversion, the study of whom should give pause to anyone inclined to dismiss the motivational potential or importance of religion too quickly. John Newton, for example, the notorious slave trader, gave up this despicable practice and turned, among other things, to hymn-writing when he experienced the "Amazing Grace" of a religious conversion while crossing the ocean in a slave ship. C.S. Lewis, the author of *The Chronicles of Narnia* and a host of other well-known books, is famously known for his description of how he was dragged kicking and screaming into the Christian faith that so radically changed his life and so thoroughly characterized his writings. Norma McCorvey, the "Jane Doe" of the famous (or infamous, depending on one's point of view) 1963 *Roe v. Wade* case that gave American women the right to an abortion later converted to Christianity and founded an anti-abortion organization. Frank Abagnale Jr., the notorious fraudulent check writer and international con artist, and subject of the popular movie "*Catch Me if You Can*," is said to have turned from a life of crime to a life of *fighting* crime in part because of a religious conversion.

Religious beliefs also power far-less-well-known people to do remarkable things. In Africa, churches respond to AIDS and influence family planning; farmers whose religious beliefs change and who no longer fear ancestral disapproval or spirits adopt modern agricultural practices see remarkable increases in yields. [1] Muslims in Northern Africa experience lower AIDS infection rates than animist tribal and Christian groups in Southern Africa.[2] Many low-caste people in India go on to lead remarkably productive lives when religious conversions free them from the shackles of their perceived inadequacy. Many Americans are familiar with the story of an African-American mother of a promising law student who was hanged by three racists, who not only forgave them but visited them in prison, eventually breaking through their hardened hearts, wiping their tears, and helping restore their broken spirits. Fewer have heard about the Native American Christian school in New Mexico that sends an average of 90% of its graduates on to colleges or vocational training schools, at a time when an average of 15% of Native American high school students in the U.S. go on to college. [3] Muslims and Baptists alike are protected from the negative effects of excess alcohol consumption that plague so many other groups because their religious beliefs.[4] Mormons in Utah differ from the rest of the U.S. population in scores of statistical categories, such as fertility rates, out-of-wedlock births, crime rates, business startups, and advanced placement courses taken.[5] Prison inmates who "turn their life over to Christ" have a recidivism rate far below that of other released prisoners.[6]

Countries and people groups

On the global stage, some people groups have been extraordinarily economically successful. For example, it is hard to ignore the economic achievements of the Jewish or Chinese diaspora, Northern European Protestants, or Koreans. It is a historical fact that nations dominated by some belief systems have persistently had larger and healthier economies than nations dominated by other belief systems. Regardless of what one thinks of the state of Israel, or some of their unjust treatment of Palestinians, it cannot be denied that the economic growth of their relatively young oil-poor nation is in sharp contrast to the lackadaisical economic performance of many Middle Eastern oil-rich countries.[7] Likewise, the economic achievements of Protestant "pockets" in Africa and Latin America relative to their Catholic neighbors have been well documented - including persistent differences in the economic performance of former British colonies (influenced by Protestantism) and former French and Spanish colonies (influenced by Catholicism).[8] On the other hand, the predominately-Catholic northern states of the former Yugoslavia (Croatia and Slovenia) have long enjoyed healthier economies than the predominantly-Orthodox Serbs in the south.[9] Likewise, the increasingly-Protestant Christian southern half of Nigeria is characterized by per-capita incomes that are double those of the predominantly-Muslim northern half of the country.[10] There are, of course, many variables that factor into these differences, but it would clearly be a mistake to overlook the critical role of religious differences.

Generally speaking, nations committed to "secular" political and economic policies do very well in GDP-per-capita rankings. And those with predominantly Protestant or Catholic religious influences have long filled many of the top slots on that list. And there have also been some interesting anecdotal developments in nations whose dominant belief systems have been subject to substantial change. South Korea, for example, has experienced remarkable economic growth at the same time it has experienced a remarkable change in the religious beliefs of many of its citizens.[11] The commitment of Taiwanese Christians to the importance of education, coupled with the return to Taiwan of students who adopted evangelical Protestant beliefs while working toward their university degrees in the U.S., has resulted in Taiwanese Christian churches with incomes and education levels well above national averages. But perhaps the most persuasive piece of anecdotal evidence involves the global demise of economies that tried to both implement communism and banish religious belief simultaneously. China experienced economic upheaval after the Cultural Revolution ushered government enforced atheism, and healthy growth during the past several decades as the percentage of the population that identifies as religious has increased.[12] Eastern European countries had varying degrees of economic difficulties under communism, but all eventually fell far behind Western economies. The general assumption is that these nations' problems stemmed from the nature of their collectivistic economies, but that seems an inadequate explanation, since a flourishing form of voluntary communism appears to have existed in the early Christian church and still today in some tightly knit Christian sects. A good case could be made that 70 years of concentrated efforts to destroy religious belief in the former Soviet Union may have been as important to their demise as their misguided economic policies.

Church and theological impacts

For the initiated, there is also ample evidence from earlier centuries on how religious beliefs and organizations have either spurred or impeded economic activity. We will limit our discussion here to some key developments in Western nations, because of their significant role in the spread of capitalism. A good place to start is with recent research that continues to uncover evidence that the Catholic-church-dominated Middle Ages, the so-called Dark Ages, were not nearly as dark economically as they are reputed to be.[13]

Part of the reason for this comes from Western historians who have noted the tie between religious beliefs and two widely-recognized contributors to development, science and technology. The

Catholic Church is often blamed for being anti-science, usually with a reference to the time when it forced Galileo to recant his belief that the earth revolved around the sun. But it is a mistake to more generally paint this kind of picture of the relationship between religion and science. Galileo was a Catholic believer, and in some ways the church's position at the time can be traced more easily to "Scholastics" with ideas grounded in Greek philosophy than to Christian theology.[14] In fact, Galileo was so taken by the evidence of God's work in the majesty of the universe that he even suggested that "if Aristotle were now alive, [Galileo's observations] would make him change his opinion [about the origins of the physical universe]."[15] Galileo's genius lay in part in his understanding that there was an additional valuable way beyond revelation and theology to come to understanding – and that was to relentlessly observe and measure things. In fact, many of Western Civilization's most influential scientists believed in God and saw little need to try to reconcile Aristotle's methods of seeking out truth with Galileo's. Sir Francis Bacon captured their perspective when he said that people had to "render to faith the things that are faith's," and that there were times when people needed "to quit the small vessel of human reason" to allow them to see the true wonders of the natural, or as he would refer to it, "created" world.[16] Interestingly, what may have in part launched the modern miracle of economic growth was, in Galileo's words, a willingness for people to keep their faith *in* reason *at a more modest level* than it had often been prior to that time. The tension between religious beliefs and scientific investigation continues to this day, but it would be a gross simplification to insist that religion and science are at odds while secular belief systems are necessarily pro-science.

Religious beliefs also had a significant impact on the development of legal and judicial structures that were important to the development of the West. The Catholic Church, for example, in order to administer its vast holdings of land in Europe, established a continent-wide system of canon law as well as local administrators, arbitrators and judges. The predictability made possible by this was critical to the growth of trade, which, as we noted in an earlier chapter, is one of the major components of economic development. Already in the 13th century A.D., the thought and writings of Aquinas laid important groundwork for business ethics, and the work in monasteries laid important groundwork for modern business. For example, as Michael Novak's research and writing make clear, monasteries, especially those of the Cistercians, who pioneered cost accounting and entrepreneurship and dominated iron and wool production, were among the first to apply capitalist principles of specialization and production. Organized around the idea of allowing individuals to use their particular gifts, they were in some ways models of the modern corporation. They were also centers of literacy, resulting in the accumulation of the kind of intellectual and/or moral capital that is needed for development.[17]

Proclamations of religious leaders like Thomas Aquinas, Martin Luther, and John Calvin laid important groundwork for private property, business ethics and modern financial markets and institutions, and their admonitions that Christians exercise self-control encouraged the saving and investment that are the lifeblood of these markets. The Puritan work ethic, which is based on the biblical notion that it is evil to be unwilling to work, coupled with strong beliefs among Christians that they must develop their talents and love and serve their neighbors, have affected everything from the goals of Western businesses to our insistence that government officials be public servants and refuse to participate in bribery. The Biblical mandate that Christians care for each other has led to the sharing of burdens through life insurance (the first formal expression of which was designed for Presbyterian ministers), non-profit cooperatives which were the forerunners of some of U.S. corporations (e.g., Sunkist and Amana), and the growth of hundreds of thousands of civil society institutions that were traditionally (prior to governments usurping this task in the latter part of the 20th century) the core of the U.S. "safety net" as well as important leadership and ethics training grounds for workforce participants. Religious beliefs have long been a significant component of what drives people to undertake risky ventures, identify problems, and or start organizations to solve them. The genius of the Reformation lies in part in its ability to free these religiously-based motivators in such a way that they could operate widely throughout the populace.

The impact of Marx and his intellectual heirs

Perhaps the best example of the impact on the global economy of changes in religious beliefs involves well-known atheists and agnostics. Karl Marx, Friedrich Engels, Lenin and Stalin were all notable for having rejected the Christian faith of their childhoods for alternative worldviews that, predictably, had radical effects on the economies of the countries that followed their ideas.

Karl Marx was the son of Jewish convert to Christianity and Friedrich Engels was raised by a Bible-believing (pietist) father, but both rejected Christianity's teachings as they grew older. The roots of their atheism can be traced in part to the influence, at the University of Berlin, of the writings of Charles Darwin, a one-time theology major who had gradually come to reject the authority of the Bible and the idea that God had created the world. Marx at one point wrote to Engels about the usefulness of Darwin's *Origin of Species* "as a basis in natural science for the class struggle in history,"[18] and it was so influential in his thinking that it has been said he even suggested to Darwin at one point that he should dedicate his book *Das Kapital* to him (Darwin reportedly declined at the urging of his wife). Vladimir Lenin, a follower of Marx who had also been raised by Bible-believing parents, and Joseph Stalin (who had been a student at the Gori Divinity School when he became enamored with Darwin's writings) both rejected the Biblical story of creation and the notion of a sovereign God who would someday hold people accountable for their actions in favor of an accidental "survival of the fittest" doctrine of origins and a belief in the sovereignty of communist ideology.

Eastern European economies following the Marxist belief system imploded under the burden of central planning, even as Marx's disciples waited in vain for the proletariat to revolt against the crushing exploitation of labor by greedy capitalists. These things never happened, in part because

Marx had failed to see the potential of religious beliefs to both restrain the worst excesses of capitalism, and to bring out the best in it. Unfortunately, the same could not be said for atheism's effect on communism. As history shows, it neither restrained its worst excesses nor brought out its potential. Neither empirical studies nor historical accounts are timely tools for stopping the damage that the beliefs and actions of these men did to tens of millions of people. But the anecdotal evidence of what they did still horrifies people everywhere who know in their heart of hearts that much of what these men did can only be effectively communicated by using the word "evil." It also reminds us that regardless of whether beliefs can be more easily classified as religious or secular, they are either right, wrong, or a combination of the two,[19] and which of these it is matters immensely. Throughout history people have been collectively hypnotized by leaders like Marx and Lenin with disastrous consequences. And most of this occurred before nearly costless global communication systems could carry an idea or ideology across the world at light speed.

With the benefit of hindsight, it is easy to say that it was pernicious, to say the least, for people like Marx and Lenin to dismiss as divisive or relegate to the backwaters of public life a belief system that started with a few followers but has, after two millennia, become a "major world religion" (subscribed to in some way, shape or form by nearly two billion people). Their attempts to wipe out religious belief in areas under their control can now be safely judged as ill-advised at best and disastrous at worst, and they doomed the countries subjected to their leadership to very different outcomes than those of, for example, Great Britain, The Netherlands, or the U.S., which developed more pluralistic societies (in part because pluralistic approaches - including the economic ways of thinking embedded in them - were more consistent with the predominant religious beliefs in these countries). Some of this can be traced back to Adam Smith's economic thinking, which can now be safely said to have had more influence on the field of economics and the subfield of development than any other way of economic thinking in history. Smith, of course, saw the world very differently from Marx and his compatriots, largely because he was a Scottish Calvinist moral philosopher whose beliefs rested on an entirely different set of assumptions. Although heavily influenced by the Deist ideas of his day, he nevertheless saw the world through the eyes of his Jewish and Christian forebears who believed that people are made in the image of God,[20] which means they have the kind of natural creativity that their Creator exhibited in knitting together and organizing the cosmos.[21] He also likely assumed that "man" rules over and is responsible for the natural world rather than being subject to or fearful of it, that work is a religious requirement, that time is linear and limited, and that certain kinds of "moral sentiments" are essential for an economy to function well.

Smith's particular religious beliefs, and those of his compatriots, it is safe to say, are no longer held by the majority of the populations in the countries that inherited his ways of thinking. But they are (often unknowingly) imbedded in their ideas and institutions, and very helpful in explaining not only differences in economic achievement between formerly communist and enthusiastically capitalist countries, but many other things as well.

Likewise, the atheism of people like Marx and Lenin cannot bear all the blame for the atrocities committed by fascists and communists. Religious leaders have also contributed to severe human and economic dislocations through their misunderstanding of their own religious codes or their inability to live up to them. In Germany, for example, many Protestant church leaders supported or turned a blind eye to the Third Reich, while others, like Dietrich Bonhoeffer and Martin Niemoller, broke early with the Nazi regime and paid a severe price for doing so (prison for both, and death for Bonhoeffer).

U.S. influences

It is also well established that the United States came into existence because of the religious motivations of its earliest settlers.[22] Both the Plymouth and Massachusetts Bay colonies were founded because of a desire to practice religious beliefs freely. For most of its history, the educational institutions of the United States were infused with religious and moral teaching. The First Great Awakening, a religious movement started in 1734 by pastors such as Jonathan Edwards and George Whitefield, led to the founding of distinguished universities like Princeton, Brown and Dartmouth. The first president of the United States, George Washington was a devout Christian, as were many others after him. Many of the other Founding Fathers were either Christians or Deists who believed in a Creator God who had built order into the natural world and moral order into the affairs of humans. It was not uncommon for Washington and his colleagues to hold religious services in the Capitol even though it was public property. Washington's understanding of the importance of religious beliefs to the development of his young country is captured well in his farewell address in 1796:

> Of all the dispositions and habits which lead to political prosperity, religion and morality are indispensable supports… Where is the security for property, for reputation, for life, if the sense of religious obligation deserts the oaths which are the instruments of investigation in courts of justice? And let us with caution indulge the supposition that morality can be maintained without religion. Whatever may be conceded to the influence of refined education on minds of peculiar structure, reason and experience both forbid us to expect that national morality can prevail in exclusion of religious principle.

Christian religious beliefs in particular were also at the root of many major social changes in Europe and the U.S. Two of the great social causes of the Second Great Awakening[23] were women's rights and slavery, both championed, for example, by Timothy Dwight, a Calvinist at Yale. The anti-slavery movements in both England and the U.S. were spearheaded by religious believers (such as William Wilberforce in England and Harriet Beecher Stowe, Henry Ward Beecher, William Lloyd Garrison, and Lewis Tappan in the U.S.), as was the civil rights movement many years later, with the Rev. Dr. Martin Luther King, Rev. Ralph Abernathy, and the Southern Christian Leadership Conference.

All Beliefs are Important, Not Just Religious Beliefs

Although the overview above is brief, the overall evidence for the importance of religion to economic outcomes is apparently convincing enough that even a-religious people like David Landes, the well-known historian, concludes that the primary building blocks which allowed the West to grow economically as it did were religious.[24] But our discussion also makes it clear that when we talk about belief systems, we need to give equal attention to all sorts of belief systems, including those firmly tied to secularism. The examples of Marx and his intellectual heirs points out the negatives of secular belief systems, but there are also elements of secular thinking that have played an important positive role in the nature and pace of development.

Unfortunately, there is a widespread bias toward drawing lines between religious and secular beliefs. A Web search will quickly lead one to scores of definitions for "religion" or "religious belief." Most will refer to a belief in the supernatural, sacred, or divine, and the fact that particular writings, moral codes, practices and institutions may be associated with such belief. But it should be obvious to us by now that it may be a losing battle to try to draw a neat line between "religious" beliefs and "secular" beliefs. Both hold some things "sacred;" both rely on important writings, and on moral codes, practices and institutions to guide people's daily activity. Both "religious and "non-religious" people believe in things they can't see, esteem certain teachers and teachings, and follow certain rituals "religiously." Because of this, separating a continuum of beliefs and belief systems into two camps and labeling some religious and some non-religious is fraught with difficulty. Better, we believe, to simply measure all belief systems by the substance of their assumptions, foundational commitments and practices without either favoring or discriminating against those labeled as "religious." Or, if one prefers, we could simply assume that since all people (including militant atheists) hang their hats on certain fundamental assumptions such as there is a God, many gods, or no God, or that the world we see around us was created, is the product of random events, or is an illusion, all people are therefore believing (or religious) beings at some level. Either way, approaching religion in this way should save us from a host of problems that stem from the current bifurcation of life into religious and secular, the most important of which is making an assumption that religion is irrelevant to economics because economics is *assumed* to be secular.

Unfortunately, we must also live with the fact that many secularists have also felt it necessary to marginalize traditional religious beliefs when it comes to economic development - a tendency which we will argue is neither objective (neutral) nor wise, in part because it runs the same risks that have historically accompanied the unthinking endorsement of a particular ideology or religious belief system. One of these risks is that development strategies that focus inordinately on things deemed to be secular will be favored - to the demise of a host of other things that, although pro-development, look suspiciously like they are tied to religious beliefs. This may in turn (often inadvertently) *decrease* the supply of a host of healthy and productive beliefs, attitudes, values and behaviors that are closely associated with religion while simultaneously elevating some unhealthy beliefs, attitudes, values and behaviors just because they are presumed to be "secular." One example of this is the tendency by some secular thinkers to reject some common religious restraints to freedom simply because they are associated with religious teaching (and/or a religious book) in favor of some potentially unhealthy highly individualistic beliefs and practices that qualify as secular. So things like greed, hording, overconsumption, and other materialistic practices may not only be tolerated but inadvertently favored because there is no secular basis to discourage them, while honesty, self-denial, humility, and a sense of obligation to the poor (which are a significant part of the teachings of many traditional religions) may be downplayed. Or, inordinate attention may be given to decidedly secular goals like winning, fame, or status to the exclusion of religiously-promoted aspirations such as being reflective, humble, or chaste. In effect, the marginalizing of certain important attitudes, values, and behaviors is "the baby that gets thrown out with the bath water" when secularism is elevated to center stage in the educational system or public square and other belief systems become marginalized.

The failure to understand this has unnecessarily polarized the world. Had communists or Western secularists understood that their belief systems are also partially "faith-based, and had they been more open to the possibility that their beliefs could also be based on faulty assumptions, the world would likely be a very different place than it is. For starters, the fascists would have been more likely to try to understand the Jews and less likely to persecute them, and the communists would have been far less likely to persecute the Orthodox Church, misuse their power or use violence to force their ideology on others. It is also likely that Western elites might have refrained from marginalizing religious beliefs from public policy and the public square. This in turn would lead to far more creativity in reaching beyond the beyond military, technological, and secularly-based negotiation strategies that are too often the favored options for resolving global conflict.

This is not to say that these strategies do not have their place, but, rather, that it is important to recognize their weaknesses. All are all capable of being unproductive, depending on the moral and ethical direction of the people employing them. And military action that does not address underlying religious motivations may do little more than both escalate the killing and push a real solution farther into the future. So too with technology: not only must it be compatible with religious beliefs to be accepted, but technologies are nothing more than tools; they can be used for good or evil, to save lives or to kill, to stiffen resentment or to soften it. Likewise, when secular dialog is favored, conversations are often limited to circumventing religious tensions and establishing a secular state with a limited goal of keeping the peace. It would be better to ask whether secular negotiations have any possibility of getting to the root of the problem when peoples' belief systems preclude them from understanding the intended meaning of the word "secular." Expecting secular approaches to be successful in these situations is in some ways analogous to expecting Islamic clerics using Sharia Law to successfully help the West solve its most intractable problems.

Largely unquestioned Western assumptions also contribute to global problems (and underdevelopment) in other ways. Materialism often preoccupies people with accumulation, pleasure, and comfort even as international relations deteriorate or people slaughter each other in other parts of the world. Partly because of this, as evidenced most obviously in places like Cambodia, Bosnia, Rwanda, the DRC and Sudan, Western nations are often unable to summon up the resources, unity or muster needed to turn back evil. In the same way, individualism and autonomy, both widely subscribed to by Western cultural elites, favor giving individuals the right to decide unilaterally, for themselves, what is right and wrong, rather than appealing to principles and/or responsibilities of a higher order. This not only contributes to chaos in some environments, but can allow the killing of innocent civilians and other atrocities to persist for decades, if not centuries.

To take this discussion back to its origins, healthy economic development requires that assumptions behind both religious and secular beliefs that prohibit development be confronted honestly, so people see themselves objectively, and also see the complex way in which values, attitudes, behaviors, and resources must be brought together to optimize the development process. This requires a mental picture, a *worldview* (to be defined more precisely later), which must be open to accommodating most if not all of the things that may be important to development, not just those things that are on the radar screens of some religious or secular elites. In fact, we will argue later that that there are seven unique forms of "capital" that must be accumulated and preserved for healthy development to take place. Not only is one of these seven labeled "spiritual/moral capital," but it turns out that the fundamental beliefs of people (religious or secular) greatly affect the nature and quantity of the other six forms of capital as well, through their influence on the values and attitudes of people and the nature of the society that they construct.

Chapter 11: Connections between Religious Belief and Development: Research and Writing

The last chapter provided a sampling of anecdotal evidence on the importance of religious beliefs to development and an argument for broadening out our understanding of the term "beliefs beyond those traditionally thought of as "religious." But before we respond to this argument, by developing a comprehensive model for differentiating belief systems and incorporating their impact into an economic development model, we need to recognize the labors of those who have devoted their time and efforts into *researching* the relationship between religious beliefs and economic outcomes. Their efforts take a variety of forms as indicated by the headings below:

Books and Papers Dealing With the Importance of Religious Beliefs to Economic Development

Max Weber, the German economist and sociologist, opened the door to the systematic study of the importance of religious beliefs to economic activity more than a century ago with a series of essays that eventually became the book *Die protestantische Ethik und der 'Geist' des Kapitalismus (The Protestant Ethic and the Spirit of Capitalism)*. In his essays and book, he argued that a particular set of beliefs associated with Protestant (particularly Reformed and Calvinistic) Christianity sparked the birth of capitalism. Although Weber was not all that enamored with either Calvinism or capitalism, he took great pains to show how the belief that salvation was a gift, and was not to be earned by exceptional spirituality, good deeds or participation in rituals, spurred development. Coupled with the idea that a Biblically obedient life (e.g., honest, reliable, submissive, thrifty, hardworking, not wasteful) or the accumulation of profit through business activity (which tended to happen when business owners employed workers who exhibited the aforementioned characteristics) could be proof of God's having chosen a person for salvation, Weber concluded that certain belief systems were a recipe for development.

It is worth noting that Weber did not limit this phenomenon to Calvinism. For example, the Methodist Wesley's well-known injunctive to "earn all you can, save all you can, give all you can" is another Protestant example of the encouragement of habits likely to spur the accumulation of worldly wealth. Critics of Weber have rightly noted that capitalistic practices in some cases emerged before the Protestant Reformation or before Calvinistic practices came to an area, (such as some of the highly productive commercial activities that took place in medieval monasteries) but for the most part they have found it difficult to deny Weber's broader thesis that religious beliefs are important to economic outcomes. Critics such as Tawney have also suggested that Weber did not fully understand the breadth and complexity of the Calvinist and Puritan religious beliefs about which he was writing.[1] This was certainly true. For example, most spiritual descendants of the Calvinists and Puritans today would insist that their forebears were living productive lives, not out of a fear that profligate lifestyles could be a sign that they had not received the gift of salvation, but out of joyful thankfulness for the good and free gift of salvation. It is also likely that the Protestant objects of Weber's study did not believe in capitalism as it is commonly understood today, but, rather, in morally-bound business activity as an important component of worshipping God.

Kenneth Boulding extended this discussion to mainstream business periodicals with a 1952 article in the *Harvard Business Review*, titled "Religious Foundations of Economic Progress." He and others who wrote about the subject in subsequent issues (although not uncritical of some strains of capitalism, and recognizing that not all forms of capitalism rewarded the thrift and hard work generally associated with the "Protestant ethic") nevertheless found Christian beliefs to have an overall positive effect on economic activity. Another important contribution was made to the subject six years later when Edward and Laura Banfield published *The Moral Basis of a Backward Society* in 1958. This book was the product of the Banfields' quest to figure out why a small town in southern Italy (Potenza), where they had spent nine months living, was so poor. Eliminating some popular-at-the-time socialist explanations such as class structure and an unwillingness of the national government to effectively redistribute income or properly manage the national economy, the Banfields argued instead that the region's poverty had a "moral basis," particularly the people's inability to trust anyone outside of their immediate families. This conclusion was reached in part by comparing Potenza to a (thriving) small town in Utah (USA) with a different religious tradition and a rich history of voluntary cooperation. Blum and Dudley's (2001) work supported these ideas. They found that wages rose in Protestant cities between 1500 and 1750 but dropped in Catholic cities during this same period. They concluded that differences in trust levels and the ability to cooperate with strangers were keys to explaining the differences in wage growth.

Grier (1997) conducted a cross country study of 63 former British, French and Spanish colonies and found that the former French and Spanish colonies had lower growth rates than the former British colonies. He attributed some of this to the impact of Protestantism. In trying to explain this variation, Putnam argued that trust levels are generally lower in predominately Catholic countries than in predominately Protestant countries. La Porta (1997) and Inglehard's (1999) work supported this observation. Blum and Dudley (2001) offered an additional explanation for higher trust levels in Protestant countries by suggesting that the increased penalty for sin associated with Protestantism (because of the lack of a penance option) improved trust and cooperation.

René M. Stulz and Rohan Williamson suggest another reason altogether in their study of the relationship between creditor rights and religion. They note that the Catholic Church prohibited usury in medieval times, whereas the Reformation (particularly the Calvinists) paved the way for charging of interest. Their study of 49 Catholic and Protestant countries found that creditor rights were better protected in Protestant countries (more specifically, and that creditors in Protestant countries could better access collateral or act on senior claims during bankruptcy proceedings and/or force a reorganization or the ouster of management). They also concluded that these differences were due to religion, not to the differences between common and civil law[2] Nevertheless, as useful as these discussions and findings have been, they have been inordinately focused on Protestantism and remain for the most part generalizations. There are, however, studies that indicate the importance of religious beliefs in other contexts. Wilson (1997) describes how transition difficulties in post-communist countries are related to the failure to account for the interaction between religious beliefs and economic behavior.

Books on the Importance of Cultural Influences

Many other books and articles have approached the subject of the importance of religious beliefs to economic outcomes but do so under the blanket of "cultural influences."[3] Two of the most interesting are Joel Kotkin's *Tribes: How Race, Religion, and Identity Determine Success in the New Global Economy* (1992) and Lawrence Harrison's *Who Prospers? How Cultural Values Shape Economic and Political Success* (1992) which highlight the beliefs, values and habits that are at the root of the unusual accomplishments of communities and subcultures around the world.[4] Cultural influences, including religious beliefs, have also been addressed in the *Civil Society* literature, and most notably by Robert Putnam (Putnam, 2000), who highlighted the importance of churches, synagogues, or temples in forming social networks and incubating values that undergird laws, regulations or habits that are important for economic activity. Others elaborated on these values. Examples include trust relationships (Fukuyama 1995), democracy (Glendon, and Blankenhorn 1995), effective governing (Braithwaite 1994), the rule of law (Coats 1998) and a "good society" (Etzioni 1996). Related to this are writings about how beliefs provide the social cohesion needed for a country to risk the kind of transparency and participation needed for civil society (Eberly 1998; Green 1993), and how they are critical to the economic success of countries and even continents (Ayittey 1998). One of the most comprehensive in this group is Landes's *The Wealth and Poverty of Nations* (1998).

Writings on the Specific Impact of Religious Beliefs on Social and Economic Practices/Outcomes

Another evidence of the significance of religious beliefs to economic behaviors and outcomes is the way in which best-selling "how to" business books in the areas of leadership and management, including some of the best sellers of all time, have focused on the relationship between spirituality and organizational performance.[5] Along a slightly different vein, other writers have focused on the impact of a particular set of beliefs on broader economic and social outcomes. Most of these have been written about Christianity because of its heavy influence on Western Culture and indirectly on other cultures, but books from other religious perspectives are also becoming more common.[6] In addition, a host of writers have written about the influences of religious beliefs on business practices or the commercial enterprises of which they are a part. Once again, most of these are Christian writers, but the number written by people of other faiths is also increasing. Some of these have defined particular aspects of belief systems and how they impact business activity. Others have written about the practical working out of people's beliefs in business, while still others have written autobiographically about the impact of the author's faith on his or her business practices.[7] Yet another genre has attempted to apply leadership lessons from the lives and teachings of well-known "founders" of major religions, like Mohammed or Jesus, or practitioners like Bonhoeffer, Ghandi, or Mother Theresa, to modern economic or social life.[8]

In addition these popular books, in recent decades a few brave scholars have studied how religion influences specific behaviors and outcomes in the areas of social organization, aesthetics, education, and other things of economic significance.[9] In doing so they have established links between external proxies for what people believe and important variables like wages, family stability, poverty, time allocation, school attendance, work success and social deviance among black males, teen pregnancy and suicide, substance abuse, crime, mental and physical health, deviant behavior among teens, and longevity and happiness. For the most part these studies found that religious beliefs positively affect things that most people view as good or healthy for human development, and impede practices that are generally seen as bad or unhealthy.[10]

In 2001, Dr. Lynda Powell headed up a panel of scientists that was asked to look into a host of studies which showed a correlation between religious faith/practice and health benefits. The panel reported in an article in the Wall St. Journal[11] that collectively the studies indicate a 25% lower mortality rate for those attending worship services at least weekly; this difference was still significant when the results were adjusted for the expected social benefits of church attendance. The economic effects of this kind of longevity are significant, as are the likely differences in medical costs experienced by the members of these two groups. Although, the panel was not inclined to attribute the differences to "God," its members did speculate that some religious practices such as the use of prayer or meditation to control anger would likely have positive health effects. One of the studies included in the panel's review (Strawbridge, Shema, Cohen and Kaplan, 2001) also concluded that regular attendees are more successful in overcoming a number of difficulties which have been shown in other studies to have a depressing effect on lifetime productivity - such as smoking, lack of exercise, depression, and loneliness.

Application of Economic Thinking and Methodology to Specific Religious Practices and Beliefs

Empirical researchers are just beginning to try to sort out the complexities of measuring the impact of religious beliefs on economic outcomes. Robert Barro, a Harvard economist, began this quest more than two decades ago when he began studying the links between religion and economic growth. Between 2003 and 2006, he and Rachel McCleary published several papers on the subject.[12] Since there is some overlap in the subject matter of these papers, they will be discussed together here, although an attempt will be made in the process to identify the unique insights of each paper. The first lays out some of the complications involved in investigating the relationship between religious beliefs and economic development. For example, religious beliefs and economic development jointly affect each other. Development raises incomes and life expectancy, lowers fertility rates, and affects a host of other factors that influence religious belief. Likewise, religious beliefs affect a host of things like personal integrity, openness to strangers, desire for education, or work ethic, that affect development. In many cases religious beliefs and economic development are affecting the same things, such as fertility rates, incomes, or trust relationships, to pick just a few from the examples above. In addition to these problems with analysis, it is sometimes difficult to obtain accurate input data. For example, in places where women are not allowed to attend mosques but are allowed to worship privately, it is difficult to know what is meant when they answer questions about the regularity of their "religious participation." Elderly people may attend services less than younger people, not because they don't want to but because they may be physically or mentally unable.

Alternative models

The papers lay out three fundamental ways that economists view the relationship between religion and economic outcomes. According to the "rational-choice approach," pioneered by Azzi and Ehrenberg (1975), people choose their level of religious involvement much like they make other economic choices, with the amount of religious participation and belief ultimately a function of the "costs" and "benefits" of the alternatives offered. According to this model, for example, a promise of salvation that is a function of good works will result in real economic impacts as people respond to a significant incentive to behave in a certain way. Finke and Stark (1992) and Iannaccone and Stark (1994) extended this model to a more comprehensive "market model" which, following time-tested economic principles developed to explain what happens in markets for goods and services, leads to the expectation that, for example, both the level of belief and the amount of attendance at worship services will be higher in situations where there is "religious pluralism" (lots of choices among religions and denominations) than where there is a monopoly (only one church option) because the quality of what the churches, synagogues or mosques are offering will be more suited to the tastes and preferences of the people. This model also predicts that a state establishment of religion will reduce both regular attendance and levels of belief in the same way that business monopolies reduce the overall production and purchase of goods and services because of increased opportunities to be self-serving and unresponsive to their "customers" needs and desires. Although this may sound dreadfully reductionistic to most people of faith, it does reflect how economists tend to think about these issues, and the assumptions that underlie some of their empirical work.

A third model that is explained is the "secularization model," which assumes that the amount of religious belief and practice will gradually diminish as development takes place. Although this model may have its ideological roots in the thinking of people like Hume and Marx who viewed religion as an "opiate," it has also been subscribed to by religious people who know well that the material comforts, reduction in uncertainty, accumulated wealth, and/or preoccupation with "worldly pleasures" that usually accompany economic development can also have a denigrating effect on religious belief.[13]

Barro and McCleary

The primary empirical goal of Barro and McCleary's 2003 paper was to investigate the effects of church attendance and religious beliefs on economic growth using international survey data across 41 countries. In doing so, the authors separated the effects of church attendance or religious belief from other related effects such as the presence of a state religion, government regulation of religion, religious pluralism, or differences in the mix of religions in a country, which, if unaccounted for, could quite easily lead to improper conclusions about the economic impact of religious belief and attendance at worship services. They were also attempting to structure their studies so as not to give religious beliefs or practices credit for economic growth attributable to other factors. For example, in their initial study, they only tested for the impact of religion over and above the impact of average per capita incomes, life expectancy, years of education, fertility rate, ratios of investment and government consumption to GDP, a measure of the openness of the society (based on the amount of international trade relative to GDP), subjective measures of the rule of law and democracy, and the inflation rate. In the study reported in the *Journal of Economic Perspectives* (JEP), they also tried to separate the impact of religion from the impact of climate (which affects health and agricultural productivity), and the fact that a country might be land-locked. The authors also realized that all religions have a rich mix of beliefs, far too many to empirically study, so they focused primarily on several related beliefs that they suspected might have economic consequences – beliefs in an afterlife, heaven, and hell. Interestingly, beliefs in the afterlife (heaven and hell in particular) were strongest among Muslims and a diverse group of non-mainline Christian denominations that included most evangelicals, were next highest among the Catholics and Orthodox, followed by Jews, Mainline Protestants, and finally Hindus (they did not have enough data on Buddhists to include them in this measurement).

Their major finding was that, economic growth responds positively to religious beliefs, particularly a belief in heaven and especially hell, but negatively to church attendance. The first part of this recognizes that if people's beliefs in heaven or hell lead to a commitment to work, integrity, etc., these traits will in turn significantly affect economic performance. The second finding likely reflects the fact that in some fairly wealthy nations like the Scandinavian countries and Japan, beliefs in heaven and hell are still very prevalent even though attendance at churches or temples may be low. But in the process of setting up the study, the authors assume that beliefs are an output of the religious activity and church attendance is an input. Almost by assumption, then, because church attendance is "costly" in terms of time and money, religious activities will be found to be most productive when people are somehow able to adopt healthy beliefs without having to "invest" a lot of time in church or mosque to accomplish this. This is not to say that church attendance necessarily has a negative influence on growth; it will still depend on the effectiveness of attendance on the inculcation of beliefs and the positive and negative economic effects of the particular beliefs being absorbed or reinforced. For example, as Barro and McCleary point out in their JEP paper, several countries, such as the U.S., Singapore, and Poland, have much higher church attendance rates relative to their GDPs (per capita) than would be predicted by the empirical model being used. But across a wide group of religions and nations, the theoretical social benefits of regular church attendance are not what drive the positive impact of religion on economic growth. Rather, it is the beliefs that people hold.

Also interesting is the conclusion that Muslim nations, a group characterized by relatively high rates of beliefs relative to attendance, do not generally have high economic growth although the belief to attendance ratio would predict that they should. The authors speculate that this could be because the rate of attendance could be higher than reported (since women are sometimes prohibited from worshipping in mosques but nevertheless worship privately) or because specific Islamic teachings, such as those which make credit, insurance, corporate ownership, or speculative ventures difficult, are a drag on economic activity. One possibility that they did not speculate about, is the religious teachings/customs in some countries that restrict many Muslim women from participating in measured economic activities such as working outside of the home or driving automobiles.

Equally interesting is the conclusion that religious "adherence" or religious affiliation for Protestants had a marginally negative impact on economic growth (a finding that we could speculate would make Weber roll over in his grave). Likewise, the impact of religious adherence for other religions in the study was never statistically significant. This could be caused by many things, and Barro and

McCleary's general findings seem to point to the fact that adherence and specific beliefs are two different things. We should add to this the possibility that the economic impact of differences in people's religious beliefs, although significant, will only become apparent when the religious pie is sliced into enough pieces to isolate significant differences not only between major religions but within them.

On the way to their overarching conclusions, Barro and McCleary make a number of interesting observations based on their empirical tests and correlations within their data. One is that they find a "professed belief in God" less useful for predicting economic outcomes than a belief in heaven or hell, or attendance at worship services, most likely, as they note, because most people in most countries answer yes to a question about God's existence, but this could mean a variety of things. Another is that people who attend houses of worship more regularly also have higher education levels (stating at one point that a 10% increase in the frequency of attendance correlates with 2.1 additional years of education). Another observation (less surprising to them) is that rural people generally attend church more regularly and have stronger religious beliefs than urban people. They also note that nations with higher numbers of children also have higher church attendance rates.

Barro and McCleary also find that nations with official religions have higher church attendance rates than they would otherwise have (in spite of what the market model described earlier would predict - but they surmise that this is due in part to the fact that states with official religions also often subsidize religion in the process, perhaps by paying pastors, giving tax breaks for contributions to churches, or subsidizing religious schools or the teaching of religion in public schools). They also find that communist atheism, had a significant depressing effect on church attendance but apparently not a permanent one, since the demise of communist governments in the last decade or so of the 20th century led fairly quickly to an increase in religiosity in most of these countries. Other forms of government restrictions on religion (such as government approval of religious leaders) also had a negative effect on beliefs, attendance, and even personal prayer. And although they found that countries with the greatest levels of religious pluralism showed higher levels of participation and belief, the study in the JEP reported no significant effects of religious pluralism on either personal prayer or religious belief being studied (presumably referring to belief in an afterlife). Their studies also found general support for the secularization theory over time. Using the numbers in the JEP paper, they note that an increase in GDP per capita from $7,940 to $20,700 could be expected to correlate with a 17% decrease in attendance at formal religious services, a 23% decrease in weekly prayer, and a 16% decrease in the belief in hell.[14]

Other studies

Two other recent studies deserve attention here. Jonathan Gruber, an economist at MIT, in his *Advances in Economic Policy and Analysis* article "Religious Market Structure, Religious Participation, and the Outcomes: Is Religion Good for You?" (2003) tries to separate the impact of religion and other variables that also affect economic outcomes. In doing so, he found higher church attendance rates, higher income and education levels and lower divorce rates in neighborhoods where people share a religion, relative to what he found in neighborhoods where people shared ethnicity but not religion. A doubling of church attendance, for example, would be expected to correlate with an approximate 10% increase in income. He also found that those who attended church more frequently did not have higher rates of civic participation *outside of the church*, suggesting that it was their religious beliefs that were affecting the differences in income.

One of the most exhaustive empirical studies to date was published in the *Journal of Monetary Economics* in 2003. In it, Guiso, Sapienza and Zingales studied the impact of different belief systems on "economic attitudes." They studied attitudes instead of outcomes in an attempt to remove one of the major sources of uncertainty that plagued previous studies in this area - the problem that economic outcomes are influenced by a host of things besides religious beliefs. This, of course, is also true of *attitudes*, but much less so. Their study used sixteen years of data across 66 countries (from the University of Michigan's World Values Survey) and attempted to separate the effect of religion on people's economic attitudes from other things that also influence these attitudes, like country of origin, health, age, gender, education, income and perceived social status. Overall, they concluded that "religious people trust people more, trust the government and the legal system more, are less willing to break the law, and are more likely to believe that market outcomes are fair."[15] And in spite of their expressed desire to focus on attitudes rather than outcomes, they also concluded that religious beliefs were "conducive to higher income and growth."

Caveats

As useful as these studies are, we caution the reader against putting too much faith in academic research for a number of reasons. Correlation is often not causation, and social science studies are always fraught with difficulty because of the number of variables affecting attitudes, behaviors and outcomes. Secondly, until recently, many (although not all) of the studies in this area focused on religion in the United States and therefore defined religious behavior in terms of activities associated with the dominant belief systems of the West, such as Catholicism, Protestantism, and to a lesser extent Judaism, or Agnosticism. We fear that even the excellent recent work that uses international survey data results could give different results when religious behavior is defined by the activities of other belief systems operating either in the U.S. or in other cultural settings. Thirdly, much of the research cited above, and especially early work in this area, has suffered from the assumption that two groups of people need to be compared, "religious" and "non-religious," when in fact, the most interesting research results will only be uncovered when researchers look much more closely at specific religious systems and well defined subgroups within religions (although some, like Stark (2003) and Guiso, et. al., 2003 have tried to do this). Fourthly, researchers need to capture what people actually believe and key behaviors that tie integrally to those beliefs rather than proxies for this, such as attendance at religious services. Studies that fail to recognize that some belief systems may discourage the earning of profit, the lending of money at interest, or risk taking, while others promote these activities, will by their design lead their authors to misleading conclusions. One reason for this is that from all indications, when intrinsic beliefs are distinguished from extrinsic behavior, the impact of beliefs will become even more evident (Kahoe, 1974; Weibe, and Fleck 1980). Fifthly, it is also quite possible that the economic outcomes in a particular country could be related to a unique combination of different belief systems, which would be difficult if not impossible to replicate. For example, it could be that the economic growth in the U.S. could be the product of a unique combination of Christianity and secular materialism that is also blessed with flavoring from a variety of other belief systems. Perhaps the preoccupation with profit, new technologies and physical capital that accompanies secular materialist beliefs could only have led to good economic results when combined with the moral restraint, justice, and personal integrity emphases that are inimical to a Christian belief system, and vice versa.

Finally, to get a full picture of what determines religiosity or its impact, economists will have to take off their economist glasses and put on another pair that helps them better see what lies beyond the constraints of their discipline. For example, to try to explain people's degree of religiosity by looking at factors that affect the supply and demand for religion is like trying to explain what an elephant looks like by rubbing its leg with a blindfold on. Using economic models when seeking answers to questions related to religious belief is inherently limited because it unwittingly assumes that self-interested people choose religions like they choose restaurants or brands of automobiles, that churches operate along the lines of profit-maximizing institutions, and a host of other assumptions that work fairly well when businesses are assumed to exist to achieve fairly narrow goals, but not well at all when we enter the inner recesses of people's hearts and spirits. This is not to say that economic principles are not useful to explain some religious behaviors; rather, people often believe what they believe and do what they do for religious reasons which cannot necessarily be explained economically. In conclusion, research will always be limited and, realistically may never be more than just one tool among many "ways of knowing." It will always be a useful tool, albeit not a particularly timely or economical one. The best we can hope for is that more robust research results will accumulate as the academic community better understands just how much variation there is in both beliefs and practices within each of the broad classifications of religions typically used in their studies and learns how to isolate and measure the impact of the key differences that distinguish religious subgroups.

Why the Key Role of Religious Beliefs is Often Overlooked

Given what we have discovered in the past four chapters about how wonderfully intertwined belief systems, both religious and secular, are with the causes of and solutions to poverty, it is hard to understand why this is so little discussed. It would be only a slight exaggeration to refer to religious beliefs as the 900 pound gorilla in the (economics class) room that no one dares talk about. Perhaps it is a non-conversation that has been shaped by decades of skillful practice in the art of simultaneously talking about and talking around important subjects. Perhaps the reluctance is part of the vapor trail left by the long-held dogma that people can talk about anything except politics and religion. Perhaps it is a byproduct of ignorance – related to how little time is devoted to the subject of religion in modern secular education systems. Perhaps it is the result of the confusing logic that equates tolerance with a reluctance to speak honestly, or the kind of awkwardness that comes with knowing how radically belief systems differ from each other and that talking about them must eventually lead to questioning their assumptions. Perhaps it is the all-too-common tendency to simply dismiss certain things by assumption – which conveniently permits us to avoid their importance or potentially-complicated impact.

Whatever the reasons, we cannot stop at this point. Rather, we need to recognize that the many paths by which religious beliefs affect economic outcomes, as well as the important differences in the value and attitudes that drive this, owe their existence to something much more fundamental – the way people answer the most fundamental (and unavoidable) questions of life. One of these is "What is religion?" -a question that turns out not to be nearly as easy to answer as some assume. So before we begin to distinguish the core beliefs of differentiate religions and try to bring some order to their divergent impacts on economic outcomes, we need to address the misconceptions and confusion that the word religion evokes.

Chapter 12: Religious Beliefs: Misconceptions and Confusion

We have seen how religious beliefs and the differences among them have been ignored, marginalized and misunderstood - in spite of their importance.   As we go on, it is becoming clearer that many of the most influential differences between belief systems are related to their presuppositions, which in turn influence the answers they come up with to the most fundamental questions of life. We know that eventually we will need to address those questions. But before we do this, we need to examine the source of much of this confusion - some of the commonly held and often unquestioned assumptions about religious beliefs. In this chapter we address nine of the most common and most influential of these assumptions.

Misconception 1: Religion is about God

Religious people are often thought of as those who believe in and have reverence for a supernatural power (or powers) that they believe created and governs the universe. But this idea is problematic as soon as we move away from the three major monotheistic religions, Judaism, Islam, and Christianity. People around the world believe in a variety of spirits and forces, sometimes resident in rocks, trees, or rivers, many of which have little to do with the creation of the world or its governance. Many tribal religions believe that the spirits of deceased ancestors remain in the area and have the potential to do them good or harm, but this too has little to do with the creation of the universe or its governance. Many Chinese people and some well-educated Westerners have a strong belief in luck, but this, too, often has little to do with a supernatural power or the creation of the world. On the other hand, self-described agnostics and atheists often have very strong beliefs about how the world came to be, or the forces that might govern it, but prefer not to consider the possibility of a supernatural power. It is likely that physicists spend as much time on the origin and laws of the universe as theologians, but this is not usually the first group we think of when we think of religion. And many religions (even if we want to limit our definition to belief systems traditionally referred to as religions) spend more time ascertaining how people should live their lives than debating how the universe came into existence. All of these things make it very difficult to easily define religion or religious beliefs and measure the consequences of those beliefs. Depending on the degree to which people associate religion with certain kinds of beliefs, they may or may not be able to see the connections between it and development.

Misconception 2: Religion is about Faith; Science is about Knowledge

The problem with trying to draw a neat line between those who believe in something "divine" and those who do not is that no clear line exists between the visible and invisible, or between faith and knowledge; much that used to be invisible is now visible and much of what we used to accept on the basis of faith we now claim to accept on the basis of knowledge. It would also be fair to say that pretending such a line exists does not accurately reflect how humans come to know things. In reality, we come to know things by observation and reasoning, but also by accepting what is "revealed" to us (by teachers, technological instruments, books, etc.), and by intuition or assumption (faith). We make a serious mistake when we too quickly label some books (like the Bible or the Qur'an) as religious and others (such as the writings of Plato, Aristotle, Locke, Kant, or for that matter, Grisham) as "secular."[1] Nearly all knowledge that comes to us requires some faith to accept, and much faith is based on, or at the very least wrapped up in, knowledge.

It follows then, that some religious beliefs, in spite of the fact that they remain scientifically unverified, may nevertheless square completely with the way things really are or should be, while some "secular" beliefs may be far off the mark. Of course the opposite could also be true. But we should be careful about giving science too much credit over against other "non-scientific" ways of knowing. Many people are certain that they love God, or can trust their spouse or a friend, and that they are loved by God, or trusted by their spouse or friend, even though they have never subjected themselves to any kind of double-blind empirical study to verify it. In this way, they are not all that different from those who declare themselves non-religious but hold unverified or unverifiable beliefs in the power of freedom, money or technology. It is also worth noting that faith in what is seen can be as strong as or stronger than faith in the unseen. There is very little evidence, for example, to suggest that the faith of those who believe in the power of freedom, money, or technology is any weaker than that of those who believe in Buddha, Allah or Christ.

For our purposes this is important because the tendency to relegate faith to the realm of religion and knowledge to the realm of science, *or* to reject knowledge just because it comes in a form traditionally thought of as religious has a serious downside, Not only does this have the potential to squelch the kind of powerful curiosity and exciting pursuit of wisdom that accompanies plumbing the depths of the mind of God, but it could also limit one's practical ability to innovate and solve the problems that often block economic development.

Misconception 3: Religion is Biased; Secular Belief Systems are Not

In reality, all people are biased. It is impossible to function in life without making assumptions or holding presuppositions. These are an important part of what makes us human, and they matter a great deal since our (at least initial) reaction to new ideas depends on the degree to which they fit our preconceived notions about reality. For example, if one assumes that there is no God, or that God is irrelevant, or that people are the evolutionary product of a series of random mutations, or just relatively intelligent animals struggling to survive, he will not be particularly predisposed to accepting a written account that says God exists, has created the universe, and has a revealed purpose and a plan for the world that involves people as key agents of reconciliation. Likewise, someone who already believes that people are created in the image of God and have been entrusted from their beginning with the care and development of the planet, is unlikely to accept that she is ultimately nothing more than the product of random mutations, or is free to do whatever is necessary for her survival. Similarly, one who assumes that truth can only be ascertained through empirical investigation, rationalistic thought processes, or personal experience and encounter will be drawn to different books and teachers than one who believes that God has interacted with and given valuable insights to people throughout history, which have been recorded in a particular sacred book. Furthermore, appeals to reason or rationalism are not likely to result in a convergence in the ideas of these two groups, since rational thinking, at its core, requires mostly that one orders her thinking processes well, relative to her presuppositions. The truth is that rational people can adhere to a variety of religious beliefs, albeit with different presuppositions.

Assuming in advance that religious beliefs are biased not only ignores an important way that knowledge is acquired, formed, and passed on, but also risks ruling out centuries of accumulated wisdom simply because formulators were honest enough to admit their religiosity. It also risks elevating belief systems that are not generally thought of as religious, some of which may have very limited and potentially damaging ideas about right and wrong, to a level well beyond what they deserve,

Misconception 4: Religion Deals Mostly with Rites and Rituals, not with Day-to-Day Life

Being open to the idea that religious beliefs could be a key determinant of economic development and wealth creation will require some of us to let go of some long and tightly held presuppositions. One of these involves our perception of what religious activity is. More pointedly, we need to be open to letting faith and religion out of the little box into which they have been crammed by mostly Western thinkers over the past few centuries. We say "little box because at least since the Enlightenment, religion has often been thought of as primarily relating to the afterlife, or rites, rituals and acts of worship in large magnificent buildings. To many, it has become little more than a mysterious, mystical process unrelated to day-to-day living. Of course, some who feel this way nevertheless find religion useful for helping uncover moral principles, caring for the poor, or performing acts of mercy; but its power is seldom thought to go beyond this.

Of course, religious beliefs and practices do involve some rites and rituals, and have something to say about the possibility of life after death, moral conduct, and acts of mercy, but to stop at this point with regard to any faith system is the intellectual equivalent to describing all Americans as "rich and selfish," or the earth as "big and green." Most faiths are complex and have a long history of influencing behavior and culture. The Christian faith, for example, is in many cases so thoroughly intertwined with Western culture as to be almost inseparable to the untrained eye. It is so pervasive that even people who have not darkened the door of a church for decades still breathe the air of their religious forebears. In the United States or Europe this means even those who seldom open a Bible nevertheless assume as normal and right much of what the Bible teaches about justice, righteousness, obedience to authority, law, property, work, accountability, favoritism, integrity, respect, tolerance, human rights, or compassion.

The tendency to pretend that religious belief can be reduced to rites and rituals and separated from the rest of life has contributed to a host of maladies ranging from gaping holes in the scholarship at universities to predatory behavior in corporations. It has led to the odd practice of social scientists devoting their lives to explaining human behavior while not even thinking about scientifically studying one of the most significant and influential aspects of human behavior — what people believe, and particularly what they believe about God or gods. Even scholars of religion have had a tendency to pay more attention to rites and rituals than probing the source of both things and meaning, often minimizing both the possible importance of a God (or gods), and the impact that religion has on persons and groups. This probably reflects an embedded (though unintentional) bias that many secular scholars have - that relationships between people are important, but not relationships between people and a God or gods. It also likely flows from an assumption on their part that belief in God is an ultimate outcome of participating in rites and rituals, so that if people do rain dances and it rains, or pray for the sick and they get well, they will eventually believe in God. Unfortunately, they are generally much less open to the idea that rites and rituals may stem from the existence of a Divine Being who is involved in the affairs of people and worthy of worship. For our purposes, this means less-than-complete analyses of the potential impact of beliefs on development.

Misconception 5: Using Conventional Wisdom to Judge/Classify Belief Systems (religious stereotyping)

Generally speaking, religious stereotyping allows people to focus on what interests them most without having to do the hard work of getting to know the details of what others believe. But if we stop to think about it even briefly, we will realize that most religious stereotyping is not very different from other forms of stereotyping, e.g., racism. Skin color is a very small part of what constitutes people, and to judge them without knowing what kind of people they are is a grave mistake. Belief systems, like the people holding them, are also rich and complex, but when religious labels such as Buddhist, Christian, Humanist, or Atheist are attached simply because of birth, ethnicity, or tradition these labels may mean something very different than when an intentional and possibly costly faith commitment has been made. Subgroups within Hinduism may worship different deities. Some Buddhists focus primarily on simplicity and enlightenment while others esteem worldly service. In the aftermath of the Gulf Wars, many people know that Sufi, Sunni, and Shiite Muslims see things quite differently from each other and from the radical jihadists that Islam has partially spawned. Some churches although labeled as Christian because of their history or signage may not have had the name of Christ mentioned in them since the janitor fell down the stairs and let loose with a stream of profanities, while in other places groups of Christians who have never been publically identified as such make following Christ their top priority.

The biggest danger of religious stereotyping is that it keeps people from getting to know each other at a level that makes deep friendships and positive change possible. It also robs people of the insights that other perspectives provide and opens up the possibility that false (and damaging) beliefs will persist for centuries or millennia instead of for decades or years. It will certainly lead to culture wars and often far more serious conflicts. It stands to reason, then, that it would be wise to allow broad religious labels to serve primarily as a starting point for conversation and focus most of our efforts on what people actually believe.

Misconception 6: A Little Religion is OK, but People Who Take it too seriously are Misguided at Best and Dangerous at Worst

One logical outgrowth of the marginalization of religion is that people start to feel that religious beliefs are OK and may even be useful in small amounts, but become problematic if taken too seriously. The term *fundamentalist* is a popular term to use when one wants to throw barbs at people who take their beliefs too seriously. Unfortunately, it is sometimes used with reckless abandonment, such as when it is used to imply that a radical Islamist terrorist is really not all that different from a fundamentalist Christian like Pat Robertson. Although we may have serious objections to what both these folks might say and do, we should recognize that their words and actions are radically different from each other and should be judged accordingly.[2] Assuming all fundamentalists are bad (because it is assumed one can't argue with them), is much like other forms of religious stereotyping, almost all of which are employed to save people from having to actually learn about and distinguish between the "fundamental" beliefs of others. The term is seldom if ever used to describe atheists who cannot be argued out of their belief that there is no God, or secular materialists who insist that scientific empiricism is the only way to discover truth, but to be fair, it probably should be applied to some of these folks as well.

The bankruptcy of this kind of blanket use of the term *fundamentalist* becomes readily apparent when we realize that careful people would not ordinarily generalize in this way with respect to most other beliefs that people hold or the practices they engage in. For example, would we say that a game of football is good, as long as the coach and players don't take the strategies and plays too seriously? Or that it is OK for people to believe in democracy as long as they don't insist on voting in every election? Should strongly-held religious beliefs that spur parents to teach children "to treat others as they wish to be treated by them" be rebuffed while weakly-held beliefs that encourage children to seek revenge are embraced?

The truth is that few of us would say that an impassionate manager who treats workers like slaves is better than a passionate one who equips and excites people to work joyfully and feverishly toward the organization's goals. It is not likely that we would admire a government leader who was unwilling to passionately argue for the wisdom or rightness of the path that he believes the country should follow. In fact, we usually hope that those with important information will be eager to share it with us. We fully expect a friend who has seen a good movie to recommend it to us. Is it not reasonable to expect that people who believe they have potentially life-changing religious information to be passionate about sharing it? And is it not possible that some of that information could have a powerful positive effect on the habits (and economic outcomes) of those who hear it? And if not, or if the person dispensing it is up to his eyeballs in arrogance or denial, isn't it better to dialog about these things rather than remain uninformed about what and how he or she thinks?

Perhaps those who issue blanket condemnations of religious fundamentalists are confusing tolerance and apathy. Perhaps they are willing to tolerate weakly held religious beliefs because they themselves are religiously apathetic, or they assume the only way to be tolerant of others' religious beliefs is to be doubtful about one's own beliefs. But it could also be argued that people who strongly dislike fundamentalists have a "fundamental" belief that moderation is always the best approach when it comes to religion, or that religious beliefs are simply not worth the time it takes to understand them well enough to effectively compare them. Would it not be better to discern the wisdom of a particular set of strongly-held beliefs by asking if they could be correct or noble? Or ask whether the attitudes, goals or behaviors that flow from taking these beliefs seriously are healthy or unhealthy?

Misconception 7: Religious Beliefs are O.K. as Long as They are Kept to Oneself

A logical outgrowth of disdain for those who take their religious beliefs too seriously is the insistence that those who hold religious beliefs keep them private. This has led in part to a preference for being viewed as spiritual but not religious, which usually means that although one acknowledges that there is a great deal of mystery in life, and that much that is important is not readily visible or easily understood, he does not regularly attend a house of worship associated with a traditional religion or participate in traditional religious practices or rituals. In this sense, spirituality is viewed as a kind of sixth sense or additional kind of "intelligence" that one can draw on for unconventional wisdom and insight but which is assumed to be isolated from the material world and fundamentally unconnected to social relationships, economic outcomes, or communal activity such as or the development of institutions or systems for solving problems.

But it is ill advised, and frankly impossible, to try to keep people's most deeply held beliefs from infiltrating everything they do, much less from spurring them on to communal activity and problem solving. Trying to privatize spirituality treats it like a kind of useful hobby, when in fact for most people it is much more than this. But privatizing beliefs also has much more insidious effects than this: it effectively neutralizes the most positive contributions that religious beliefs can make to a society by forcing the people who hold them to keep them to themselves and to stay isolated from others who they can help or who can help them. In this way, it keeps us from informing and sharpening each other's points of view, and contributes to the kind of individualism[3] that has increasingly broken down families, neighborhoods, political participation, and civil society in the countries plagued by it. Likewise, it damages belief systems with a strong emphasis on communal activity more than those with an individualistic bent and in the process changes the very nature of what it means to be religious.

Privatizing religious beliefs also marginalizes religious believers of all types and predictably leads to some people publicizing what they believe in less appropriate or effective ways. This could be something as innocuous as insisting on prayer at the beginning of a NASCAR event or football game, or as insidious as planning for years about the best way to terrorize those who have belittled your belief system or dismissed it as irrelevant.

The relegation of religious belief to a dark corner also results in convoluted attempts to explain problems and potential solutions by referencing things far less relevant to economic outcomes. This has led to an excessive focus on race, ethnicity, gender, national boundaries, political parties, or class, when in reality, people who are of different race, gender, country of origin, political party or class often hold remarkably similar views when they share a set of religious beliefs. One would think that academic researchers would be tripping over each other to discover how religious beliefs can be so powerful as to overcome so many potentially divisive differences. But instead, they are more likely to treat them as irrelevant by assumption.

Misconception 8: All Religions are Essentially Similar (all paths lead to the same God)

Without a doubt, the most dangerous of these tendencies is the unwillingness to seriously compare, contrast, and dissect religious beliefs and their impact on people, because of the notion that tolerance requires that we not only accept all belief systems, but commit, in advance, to the position that they are all equally valid. But this is not what tolerance is. By definition, tolerance is the ability to respect and converse civilly with people with whom one has serious disagreements.

This distorted view of tolerance has not only contributed to, but perhaps also caused much of the social upheaval, wars and terrorism that remain as blotches on the history of humankind. It is behind the worldwide spread of the art of "small talk" that focuses on the weather, sports or entertainment preferences rather than serious or difficult issues. It is behind the willingness of enemies to accept decades of uneasy coexistence rather than wrestle with the underlying reasons for hostility. It has led to watered-down educational systems where only a limited group of ideas (sometimes religious and sometimes secular) are open to study, no matter how wrong-headed or indefensible they may have been. The potential damage of this is probably best seen in the results of Hitler or Stalin's reeducation programs. But the promotion of relativism (particularly when it predictably degenerates into a tendency to treat all belief systems as equal, and therefore, by assumption, irrelevant) has also had significant consequences. Rather than vigorous conversations intent on comparing and contrasting belief systems with integrity and those without it, religious beliefs have been shoved off the table in both public schools and the public square in many countries, in spite of their primal importance in shaping human affairs, and clear reminders in the form of the 9/11 attacks, and a host of smaller scale attacks on innocent civilians, that religious beliefs are anything but irrelevant.

Misconception 9: Believing in Freedom of Religion but Implementing Freedom from Religion

Movements to privatize religion and wrongheaded attempts to exclude traditional religious perspectives from public places reflect, at their foundation, an inability to distinguish the need for the freedom to practice one's religion from the desire to force others to adhere to one's religion. Restricting traditional beliefs from the public square unwittingly gives preference to less conventional objects of worship. They may be freedom itself, success or fame, faith in technology, or a preoccupation with material needs, but they are not without religious direction. Freedom, technology, and materialism all have their true believers. And, like traditional belief systems, all have the potential to do harm as well as good. For example, if not checked by fundamental discussions of right and wrong, misguided notions of freedom can lead to disrespectful children, dangerous adults, environmental degradation, or the undermining of legitimate government. Unrestrained technology can lead to family fragmentation (when, for example, each child has his own TV and internet connection), unfair competition (when some athletes use steroids to gain an advantage), or the death of innocent children (when land mines remain in the ground at the cessation of a conflict), and worse. Unrestrained materialism can lead to gross inequities in wealth and income, environmental degradation, or the neglect of important relationships. Although these may not harm economic growth as conventionally measured, as we shall see, they have significant potential to erode our wealth and lower our level of well-being.

Conclusion

The collective result of these misconceptions is that people around the world have misguided ideas about religious beliefs in general, as well as about the content and implications of specific belief systems. But using the word misconception masks the potential damage related to these responses to religious belief. Reducing religion down to God talk, rites, rituals, blind faith or convenient labels, or insisting that all belief systems are essentially equivalent, must not be taken too seriously, or must be kept private, are not just innocent oversights. These misconceptions have had massive effects on the economic well-being of people and nations, and have often been instrumental in keeping them in poverty for decades or centuries. Even more seriously, these misconceptions have shown that they have the ability to contribute to death and destruction on a massive scale, and even alter the course of history. Their impact on leaders, countries, citizens, or employees can range from extremely positive to horrific, depending on the integrity (or lack thereof) of the beliefs. And attempts to meld such a variety of belief systems into a kind of generic and inoffensive spirituality runs a high risk of settling for what could be best described as the lowest common denominator, blinding us to potential solutions to some of the world's most vexing problems, and limiting our reach for the highest human possibilities.

The best way to move ahead in a situation like this is to start with a frank admission about what we know and do not know. If we are honest with ourselves, we will admit that there are often no obvious lines between beliefs that are religious and beliefs that are secular, or faith and knowledge for that matter. All people have things that they must accept on the basis of faith and/or trust, since no one has the time or mental prowess to personally investigate the answers to all of the many things, mysteries or complex problems that are part of life. Likewise, nearly all people naturally desire to connect to something or someone bigger than themselves in the quest for answers to the most important questions in life. The word religion is itself derived from the Latin *re ligare*, which relates to the English word "ligament." It connotes the need that all people have to be connected to something strong but actually comes across even more forcefully than this as the need to be "bound back" to the ultimate source of life and good. This recognizes that all people have things that they believe in, things that are first in priority and power in their lives and that direct their thoughts, words and actions. In the words of Bob Dylan's well-known song, everybody has "gotta serve somebody."

This could be "the devil or the Lord" (as the song goes) or it could be the ego, the almighty dollar, freedom, the downtrodden, or a host of other things or ideals.

This fundamental understanding provides us with an excellent alternative to religious reductionism, stereotyping, privatization, relativism, and coercion – an alternative that is also very good for economic development. We should not view spirituality or, more appropriately, religious beliefs, as a kind of intelligence, like emotional or traditional measures of intelligence, nor as necessarily good or beneficial. We should define it simply as a primary shaper of the lens through which people view the world, radically influencing their answers to basic questions, and therefore, their strategies for making things better. This will enable us to see that all people, whether they consider themselves religious or not, see the world through a set of glasses which can be described as a worldview,[4] which is both strongly influenced by what they believe and a primary shaper of how they develop their economies and societies.

Chapter 13: Worldviews: Introduction and Importance

We need to elaborate on the term *worldview* at this point in part because some readers may be experiencing a fundamental uneasiness with the idea that religious beliefs are critically important when, in fact, they have always thought of themselves as not particularly religious, or, in some cases, as not religious at all. This goes back to a fundamental disagreement about what it means to be religious, which we may never be able to fully resolve. But it also has its roots in how people see the world. In particular, people who consider themselves agnostic, atheist, or Marxist-Leninist prefer not to have their belief systems associated with religion at all. One reason subscribers to secular belief systems don't see their similarity to religious believers may be because they've not yet become comfortable using the word faith to describe the assumptions that underlie their own fundamental commitments. But it is also true that many adherents to traditional religions don't see their similarity to "secularists" because they've been taken captive by one or more of the misconceptions about religion discussed earlier. We believe, however, that there is a way to reach common ground here if we focus on, properly define, and become comfortable using the word *worldview.*

We define a worldview as *a perceptual framework for seeing and understanding one's self and the environment, a guide for determining how things ought to be and how people ought to conduct themselves.* These ways of seeing are passed from generation to generation through child-rearing practices, religious beliefs, educational systems, and other intergenerational interactions and habits, the totality of which, when wrapped up and examined, can be referred to as the out-workings of a worldview. That such a thing exists, although perhaps not self-evident, is nevertheless hard to deny since both our observations and the work of cultural anthropologists and scholars of religion tell us that cultures and people groups who share a common belief system, will generally have far more similarities in the way they see the world than differences.

The Importance of Starting Points

Even people who do not consider themselves religious understand how much one's starting point or vantage point influences both what one sees and where one ends up. One who starts her trek in the middle of Iowa will see rolling hills of corn and soybeans dotted with cattle and hogs regardless of what direction she goes, but this will certainly not be the case for the traveler starting out in Salt Lake City or Miami. The earth looks flat from Nebraska, jagged from Nepal, wet from Hong Kong, and round and smooth from a space shuttle. And although no one would plan a trip without accounting for his starting place, people routinely expect others who are starting out in different places, philosophically, culturally, or religiously, to see what they themselves see and end up where they are. Although this can happen, it will not happen without both an understanding of worldview and some significant interaction between the parties with different worldviews.

In a modern, materialistic, mobile and fast-changing world, many people no longer give much thought to where they are starting from philosophically, and hence cannot know where they will end up, in part because they've become detached from their religious and cultural moorings. Lacking any kind of an anchor, increasing numbers of people seem to chart their position relative to the shifting waves of progress, knowing some things, like their increased wealth, but no longer knowing other important things, such as whether their lives have purpose, just what it is that they need, or how much they should be willing to sacrifice to get it. Others, who may have never ventured more than 500 kilometers from the place of their birth, don't have a particularly good understanding of where they are starting from either. Due to lack of income, opportunity, or contact with the outside world, they remain largely in the dark about how radically different their religious beliefs or cultural habits are from the rest of the people in the world who are increasingly making a significant impact on their lives, albeit from a distance.

As Walsh and Middleton (1984) note in *The Transforming Vision*, worldviews rest ultimately on the answers to life's most fundamental questions - questions such as: Who am I? Why am I here? What is the nature of reality? What's wrong? What should things be like?[1] It should be clear from our discussion up to this point that there is a lot of overlap between the concerns addressed by religious belief systems and Walsh and Middleton's worldview questions. Many of the kinds of questions Walsh and Middleton ask have religious overtones since they deal as much or more with our assumptions as they deal with facts. But using the term worldview is probably superior to using the term religious beliefs, because it allows us to continue our discussion without having to pretend that some beliefs are religious and some are not. It also frees us from the inefficiencies of having to try to find some arbitrary way of putting every belief, value, attitude, and action into either a religious or secular category, which we have already found to be impossible, since there are often no obvious dividing lines between concepts such as knowledge and belief, feelings and reasons, or even attitudes and behaviors.

The Importance of Worldview Illustrated

The importance of worldview on outcomes (including economic outcomes) can perhaps be best illustrated with an example of something that is at the center of both modern market economies and personal preoccupations – competition. One possible starting point would be to assume that individuals are autonomous, accountable only to themselves, and immersed in a cosmos best described by the term "survival of the fittest." Over time, these individuals discover the usefulness of reason, science, and technology, in much the same way football players have discovered the usefulness of helmets, shoulder pads, and game plans, but the object of the game and the rules by which it is played will still be determined primarily by their worldview.

The anonymous players in this "game" of business, sports or life must make a host of assumptions about how the game is to be played. It is fair to assume that those with the worldview described above will not question that the game should be played competitively, that hard work and often pain are to be endured for the hope of a prize at the end, that more points are better than fewer points, and that the unambiguous object of the game is to win. Who in the United States hasn't heard the words, often attributed to Vince Lombardi, that "winning isn't everything, it's the only thing?"[2] The importance of winning is so intricately wrapped up with other goals and assumptions as to be almost inseparable from them. Success/winning allows fame and riches. Riches allow freedom, and freedom allows leisure and ostensibly happiness. More wins, more money, more things, more happiness. That is the context for how the game (of business, sport or life) is played in Western culture, often with little conscious reflection.

Of course neither winning nor competition is value free. Both the goal (winning) and the means (competition) reflect the worldview of the group or society by or in which the game is played. A Darwinian perspective on winning and competition may seem natural and normal to some, but others with a different worldview will be acutely uncomfortable with amount of attention given to these things and will desire a different kind of "game" more consistent with their worldview. For example, the assumption of competition as natural and normal leads to choosing two people or groups of people to be adversaries, as opposed to designing contests that pit people against objects (e.g. a bar to be leapt over), or a clock, which emphasize pure athleticism over against a form of combat. To be sure, competition in the economic area is partially predetermined by scarcity, but our belief systems may also keep us from seeing that the way we have structured our economic pursuits may also reflect our narrowly focused worldviews (and resulting lack of imagination). A different worldview, where freedom and competition are seen as subservient to other loftier goals, might not lead to putting people in opposition to each other, since doing so would seem to be counterproductive. However, this depends both on what people believe is the desired end of human activity and on what they believe about the nature of people. And even among those who see competition as natural and normal, there may be conflicting perspectives on it because it obviously has the potential for both good and bad, depending on the values of the people influencing the competition. Competitive activities can increase one's appreciation for fellow participants, self-discipline and self-control, cooperation among teammates, the ability to handle disappointment as well as the development of leadership skills. They can promote health, respect for authority, patience, humility, courage, and joy (at least for the winners), as well as providing valuable feedback to participants about how well-developed their talents are, and whether their gifts are suited for what they are currently doing or would be better used elsewhere. But competition can also breed pride, resentment, divisiveness, "rule bending", disrespect of authority, hero worship, excessive aggression, stress, lack of joy, a crushed spirit, and even hatred when participants see the world primarily in "survival of the fittest" terms.

In light of all this, it is not difficult to see where radically different perspectives on competitive markets come from, and why attempts to transplant economic structures, institutions and practices often fail. For example, in spite of an increasingly integrated world economy since the collapse of communism, worldview differences and the inability of many globally influential people to recognize the importance of worldview remain a primary source of world tension. Western nations have been almost unanimous in encouraging formerly communist and some Middle Eastern countries to put their faith and hope in concepts like freedom, competition, or democracy. This is not surprising since an assumption of the essentiality of these is a key worldview component of Western-educated opinion leaders. The problem is that these things, although fundamentally good, are not value-free, nor should they be treated as ends in themselves. Freedom can lead to chaos, competition to being crushed, and democracy to the tyranny of the majority depending on the beliefs and values of the people involved.[3] In this sense, freedom is like an empty field on which the members of a society have permission to play a game. Its usefulness depends on how the rest of the components of the predominant worldview will interact to make use of it. It may turn out that players would have been better off not having even taken the field - if fundamental worldview issues have not been resolved first.

Worldviews Unpacked

Worldviews not only shape people and societies but are themselves solidified by people's behaviors over time, and what becomes accepted as normal. For example, if aggression and violence are seen as normal, or at least inevitable, and are regularly observed by children in various settings, the society will likely become more aggressive over time. If "caveat emptor,"[4] rules the day, successive generations will become less trusting of those around them. If government corruption is seen as normal, eventually the number of people attempting to root it out will dwindle. Little development will take place where, for example, people fear the revenge of spirits or witches that oppose change, believe in the fundamental unworthiness of whole groups of people, see no reason to hope, refuse to move to where jobs are, don't trust each other, or choose revenge and retribution over cooperation and compromise. These are all reasons why religious beliefs are so important. Economic development is critically dependent on prevailing ideas about the nature of reality, good, better and best, or right and wrong, all of which can be better understood when viewed from various perspectives, including perspectives informed by religious dialogue and practice. The simple truth is that some understandings of reality or ideas of right and wrong are more accurate or helpful than others. Activities that build people up are simply more useful and praiseworthy than those that tear people down. Football games in which the winning team uses knives or guns to win are not as productive or noble as games which promote fewer injuries and "fair" competition. Athletic competitions that focus inordinately on winning often encourage under-the-counter use of performance-enhancing drugs. They may also require time commitments that jeopardize relationships, learning, or service to community. In doing so, they can damage participants, communities or nations rather than build them up.

In this same way, economic systems which reward effort, quality, cooperation or service are simply better than those that simply reward winners regardless of how they won. A worldview that causes companies to pay attention to the emotional, psychological, spiritual, and social needs of their employees is simply better than one that accepts that employer responsibilities end with the writing of a paycheck. But unless people and societies are willing and able to wrestle with fundamental worldview questions about right and wrong, important and unimportant, true and false, they risk cutting themselves off from the economic outcomes that are best for them.

Worldviews and the Shape of Development

There are clearly many things important to economic development that flow from the basic assumptions that are part of people's worldviews. Unfortunately, however, they may never work their way to the forefront of development policy or even be recognized as critically important until the primacy of worldview is understood. For example, the ideas that wealth consists only of what is "priced" and easily measured, and that per-capita incomes are a proxy for development, spring ultimately from a materialistic and narrowly economic worldview. The idea that people and businesses create wealth and governments destroy it flows in part from an individualistic or libertarian worldview. The failure to care about the costs to future generations associated with massive amounts of waste, pollution, erosion or debt reflects a fundamentally selfish worldview that assumes rights and responsibilities can somehow be separated from each other, and that technological progress allows us to be a little reckless because technology will also likely be part of the solution to many of our most pressing problems. Similarly, the assumption that markets or democracy are the keys to development have their roots in the belief that, since people are basically good, freedom alone will inevitably lead to finding solutions to many of the most vexing problems in life. Furthermore, the pace at which we move ahead to solve these problems will be affected by what our worldviews tell us about what is an acceptable way to proceed with confidence. Some, who have both mind and heart firmly planted in a rationalistic worldview may demand careful, empirical proof of their hunches, whereas others, with worldviews more pragmatic or faith-based may be willing to proceed more rapidly in diagnosing and correcting problems.

Finally, given the remarkable changes that have taken place in the global economy since the fall of communism, we are compelled to offer one more example of the importance of worldview. In contrast to some of the perspectives discussed above, the idea that business is bad and government is needed to fix it is very much residue of a Marxist worldview. Likewise, the idea that one person's gain is automatically another's loss springs in part from a Malthusian worldview. The belief that economies are basically zero sum, or Darwinian jungles where labor, business, and government fight each other, or collections of co-conspirators who feather each other's nests at the expense of the average person are all very different from the belief that organizations can create wealth, that everyone can gain from economic activity, and that progress is ultimately rooted in service, cooperation, and fairness. And these differences will heavily influence whether things like an efficient voluntary tax system, a truly civil society, a just government, pluralistic approaches to building consensus, or hundreds of other ideas and habits that lead to widespread real sustainable development will take root. The Marxist-Leninist-communist worldview that, in spite of noble intentions, had such devastatingly profound economic consequences on the world economy in the 20th century is perhaps the best illustration of this.

An Illustration of the Importance of Worldview: Marxist-Leninism in the Soviet Union

The following discussion, based on the author's eyewitness impressions of the old Soviet Union, illustrates the long-term impact of a worldview based on incorrect assumptions. It also serves to show that it is *the nature of assumptions* that is important, not whether they are artificially classified in some way as religious or not. In the case of the Soviet Union, of course, the assumptions are well known not to have been grounded in religion, but were instead "secular" in that they were officially based on the strong belief that there is no God.

Perhaps the best way to start is to note that by 1991 when a historically important coup took place, almost everything in the CCCP,[5] better known as the Soviet Union, had been touched by its predominant belief system. We are not talking about Russian Orthodoxy here, but rather the (at least initial) victor in the seventy-year long religious war that had so ruthlessly sterilized Orthodoxy: atheistic communism. Marxist-Leninist doctrine had left its mark everywhere, and not just in the obvious ways, such as razed churches, murdered priests, and collectivized agriculture. Single-family homes were nowhere to be seen. Apartment buildings, jammed with pint-sized apartments and claustrophobic elevators, stretched out as far as the eye could see. Abortion helped keep families from outgrowing their apartments, and prices were nicely controlled on everything, so that everyone could afford what they "needed." The architectural uniformity of bland brick or poured concrete buildings nicely complemented the one-color-fits-all overcoats filling the store racks inside; all for the sake of sanctifying their belief in equality and avoiding the carnal sin of individuality. Statues of the saints (Lenin, Stalin, Dresinsky, the Cosmonauts and other communist heroes) stood everywhere, towering over the masses and providing icon-like evidence of the core beliefs of leaders intent on molding the Soviet citizens into their own image.

The beginning of this era can be traced to when Vladimir Lenin seized power and decreed the official *Declaration of the Separation of Church and State*. At first "purely religious" sermons were allowed and registered churches were permitted to remain open, but by the time Stalin was finished interpreting the meaning of "separation," 98% of the Russian Orthodox churches had been closed, Bible printing was prohibited, children were not permitted to attend worship services, attendees of unregistered church services were sometimes given twenty-five year prison sentences, and tens of thousands of priests had been killed. Khrushchev extended this assault to evangelical Protestant churches when he took over in 1959. And once the fundamental philosophical/religious direction had been established, Soviet leaders proceeded to develop the practical aspects of their *doctrine*. One core component of this doctrine was that wealth was created primarily by labor (thereby excusing them from engaging in modern "values based" management techniques, marketing, and financial activities, all of which were assumed to be capitalist tools for appropriating wealth from the people). This belief prevailed right until the end, until the economy finally imploded under the weight of lack of incentives, moral and political corruption, and widespread shortages. It wasn't until March of 1985, when Mikhail Gorbachev ushered in the policies of glasnost and perestroika[6] that culminated, on October 1, 1990, with the Supreme Soviet passing a *Law on Freedom of Conscience and Religious Organizations* that (at least theoretically) religious belief was once again put on an equal footing with atheism. This was done, in the words of the *Freedom of Conscience* legislation, by affirming the legitimacy of religious belief, recognizing the legal "personhood" of churches, and affirming the right of religious education. Although by no means a perfect piece of legislation, it was successful in removing the stranglehold of atheism and opening up the Soviet Union to the possibility of worldview pluralism. And, in spite of the fact that it was a critically important contributor to the continuing change in direction and eventual demise of the economically dying Soviet Union, and to the rebirth of fifteen separate economies whose development would be as diverse as the religious beliefs of the people living in them, it was only lightly covered in the Western press, probably because the Western press lacked a good understanding of the critical importance of subtle shifts in worldview.

It has now been decades since the August, 1991 failed coup that caused the ouster of Mikhail Gorbachev and eventually broke the Soviet Union into fifteen separate countries. But many of these newly birthed nations are still plagued by the vestiges of a misguided Soviet worldview. Sadly, many other countries have also suffered because their leaders have been unable to "see" the source of their problems or learn from their mistakes. For economic development to take place, leaders need worldviews that drive them to want to know what it means for their citizens to have good and meaningful lives, and where goodness and meaning come from -- even if the answers are complex, or counterintuitive, or go against their pre-conceived notions.

As the previous example illustrates, and as noted at the beginning of this chapter, worldviews have their roots in fundamental *starting points*, some of which can easily be labeled as religious and some of which we might be more inclined to label as philosophical. Even the very idea that development is desirable and notions of how development ought to be measured are rooted in people's worldview and beliefs. Contrasting worldviews, in addition to seeing economics and politics differently, will also differ from each other in their conceptions of God, their views of nature, their views of humanness, their views of society, their concepts of time and history, and their views of right and wrong, etc. Together, these dimensions will cause differences in what people value, their concepts of development, and how they live their lives. From an economic development perspective, then, religion is not important primarily because it drives people to construct churches or temples, engage in rituals or worship services, or perform works of charity. As important as these things may be, the real impact of a belief system comes through its potential to transform people's minds and hearts, or more correctly, what it transforms peoples' minds and hearts into, and the impact that this has on their *worldviews*. The Soviet Union purportedly approached economic activity communally. But was the prevailing worldview capable of nurturing true community? If not, what kind of worldview might have made them successful, and what is the role of religious beliefs in this? Do religious beliefs have the potential to transform self-interested, individualists into committed community-minded team members? Do they have the potential to enable people to see that authority, rather than being tantamount to power and privilege, amounts to a sacred trust that must be viewed as service, and delegated to others so they can effectively carry out their responsibilities? These and many more questions must be asked before we can understand the true significance of worldviews and religious beliefs to development.

Conclusion

In conclusion, wrong ideas about what wealth is, how it is created, or how important it is, have their roots in misguided or splintered worldviews; so too, ideas about development, how to achieve it, and how it ought to be measured. Table 1 attempts provide some insight into this by capturing some of the most important dimensions of a worldview, and illustrating, that a worldview encompasses a host of values, attitudes, priorities and behaviors that in turn affect what people do with their time, talents, and money.

In some cases there are relatively straightforward connections between one's worldview and one's assumption, attitudes, values or ideas of what is normal or abnormal, and relatively straightforward connections between these and one's actions (the first twelve major bullet points in Table 1). This means it will also be relatively easy to identify some values, attitudes, and behaviors as more "pro-development" than others. For example, most would agree that honesty, tolerance, a strong work ethic, perseverance, optimism, or a thirst for wisdom are the kinds of things that are pro-development at the personal level.

However, in other cases the impact of one's worldview is considerably more complex, as beliefs can best be described as moderating a tension between a complex soup of values/attitudes/tendencies that both interact with each other and are affected by many other things besides worldview - which makes cause and effect relationships considerably more difficult to sort out (the last major bullet point of Table 1). To illustrate, diversity in ideas and perspectives has great potential to spur economic development, but at some point excessive diversity is likely to strain unity, which is also very important to development. Likewise, humility, motivation, or sacrificial behavior may all be economically productive behaviors, but may be difficult to maintain when people have achieved a great deal of financial security. To further illustrate, stewardship requires accountability, but devoting excessive resources to accountability structures has the potential to impair stewardship. Similarly down the line - productive activity requires that people *value* both freedom and order, courage and patience, and privacy and transparency. So much of the impact of a worldview stems from the way it resolves natural tensions between two or more values, attitudes or priorities. And, in the same way that some belief systems will naturally lead to more tolerance, or a stronger work ethic, some will also be better than others at maintaining unity in the midst of diversity, order in the midst of freedom, humility in the pursuit of wisdom, stewardship in the process of improving productivity, or responsibility when accumulating wealth or benefiting from large amounts of charity.

But the shaping and impact of worldview go much deeper than this, because worldviews are not just individual. One's worldview colors his or her perception of almost everything, and spreads to those with whom he comes into contact. Thus, we can speak of a community's worldview, or a Buddhist worldview, or a Marxist worldview and identify what its members (generally speaking) believe about themselves, the world, what should be, and how things can be made better. The institutions that these worldview clusters create (educational, economic, social, political/legal, religious, etc.) and the structures and processes that characterize those institutions, will look very different from each other. In this way, belief systems exert influence not only over individuals but over entire communities, cultures or nations. Once again, however, some structures and processes will be healthier for development than others. As we know from earlier chapters, private property, peaceful conflict-resolution structures, the rule of law, efficient markets and just regulatory agencies are examples of pro-development structures and institutions which will not be nurtured by all worldviews.

It goes without saying, then, that economic development may not be able to proceed unless fundamental shifts in worldview occur first. Table 1 (following page), in addition to reminding us of the important role that religious beliefs play in the shaping of worldviews - and therefore on wealth creation and economic development, all but begs us to look more deeply into how different belief systems vary with respect to the various categories in the table. It is to this subject that we turn our attention in the next two chapters.

Table 1 - Dimensions of Worldview

- Assumptions about the nature of the universe/reality/God
- Assumptions about the nature and perfectibility of people
- Values/ideas of right/wrong, good/bad, important/unimportant, praiseworthy/lamentable
- Assumptions about truth and how to ascertain it
- Conceptions of justice
- Beliefs about the nature of and what it means to respect authority
- Views of time (e.g., cyclical or straight line)
- Attitudes toward change
- Attitudes toward risk
- Attitudes toward wealth/property, material gain, consumption
- Assumptions about the differences among people
    - Egalitarian or elitist
    - Gender roles/relationships
    - Character ideals
- Ideas of what is normative for interpersonal/intergroup interaction and activities
    - Expectations of others
    - Sense of responsibility for/duty to others
    - Self-interest vs. concern for others
    - Extent of concern for others
        - Inner circle
        - Outside immediate family/friendship circles
        - Unborn/future generations
    - Motivators: guilt, shame, duty …
    - Ideas of what is normative for social, economic or political structures/processes/institutions
        - Family structures and habits
        - Companies/markets/economic institutions
        - Religious structures and habits
        - Government institutions and processes
        - Civil Society institutions and processes
        - Methods for making decisions, reaching agreement, working out differences, compelling behavior
            - Legal systems and processes, authority and responsibility structures
            - Diplomacy/beliefs about the use of force
- Relative emphases/boundaries/ideas of balance/what is most valued (sample tensions):
    - Wholeness/unity/community vs. distinctiveness/diversity/independence
    - Work/knowledge/wisdom vs. leisure/rest/pleasure/entertainment
    - Economic incentives (including risk taking/entrepreneurship) vs. security/equality/safety nets
    - Freedom vs. structure/order

Chapter 13

- Power/authority/control/force vs. submission/service/responsibility
- Justice/voice/participation vs. privilege/influence/power/coercion
- Stewardship/preservation vs. exploitation/development
- Self-control/patience/moral restraint vs. instant gratification/impatience/indulgence/impulsiveness
- Confidence/optimism vs. pessimism/cynicism
- Competition/winning/individualism vs. cooperation/community
- Trust/honesty/sincerity /faith vs. expediency/mistrust/suspicion/skepticism/control
- Transparency/accountability vs. privacy/autonomy/license
- Fame/status/looks/pride vs. humility/reliability/character/morality
- Tolerance/love vs. dogmatism/prejudice
- Wealth/fame/status vs. happiness/relationships

Chapter 14: Critical Differences among Belief Systems I – Beliefs about God and the World

Introduction

Although we have offered ample evidence that nearly all human actions are rooted in beliefs, and that these belief systems lead to very different conclusions on a host of very important issues, these observations will be much more useful if we take one more step and uncover some of the most fundamental ways belief systems differ and develop some measuring sticks for comparing them. Before doing this, we acknowledge up front that all belief systems have some intriguing (and even amazing) components. Most Christians (Orthodox, Catholic and Protestant) believe in a sovereign God, who mysteriously exists in three "persons"[1] and who, although powerful enough to have created the entire universe, cared so much for the human race that he sent his only Son into the world to reveal God's heart, pay the price for human sin, and demonstrate what it means to live an obedient and holy life. Many secular humanists believe that the entire universe (including life) came about by chance and that things as complex as lilies, zebras and human babies are nothing more than the product of unsupervised processes, time and chance. Most followers of Islam believe that the angel Gabriel appeared to an illiterate man named Muhammad in visions and "recited" a book (the Qur`an) to him, and that this book, and the prayers it requires, retain their power only when read or recited in Arabic. Most Hindus venerate cows and many Hindus and Buddhists believe that spirits, perhaps inhabiting humans and perhaps other creatures, need to accumulate good karma as they cycle through multiple earthly lives, in order to reach nirvana (an ethical state marked by the absence of suffering and desire). And tribal religions often fear that ancestral spirits or spirits lurking in the natural world will harm them if they engage in certain behaviors.

Clearly, the minds and hearts of people with differing religious beliefs are wired in very different ways, and no matter how kind and tolerant people want to be, they cannot with integrity say, to paraphrase a well-known expression, that all belief systems are "created equal." Beliefs have consequences every bit as much as ideas have legs, and some of these consequences are very significant for economic development. But, it should not be presumed that most of the beliefs with bad consequences are "religious beliefs" and that most of the beliefs with good consequences have been "enlightened" by secularism. That in itself is a belief that has the potential to bring about some very mixed results.

Most belief systems are complicated combinations of beliefs that maintain specific positions about the existence of a spiritual power or powers, the origin, nature and structure of the universe, rites, rituals, and places of worship, and complex moral and ethical codes. This immediately brings two things to mind: the first is that adequately comparing and contrasting them in a short space is impossible, and the second is that pretending they are more or less the same, and can be divorced from day to day life and/or be privatized, borders on the absurd. Regarding the first, we noted earlier that Oxford's *World Christian Encyclopedia* lists nearly 10,000 distinct belief systems.[2] We make no pretense about our ability to do justice to even one of them, much less all of them. Regarding the second, we conclude it is better to acknowledge the "900 pound gorilla" in the room and strategize about how to live with him or get him out than to pretend he isn't there. Our task is made somewhat (although not a whole lot) easier in that in this particular volume, we will focus primarily on the economic consequences of religious beliefs.

Our task is also complicated by several other problems. There are more similarities between people who adhere to the same religious beliefs than those who bear the same religious label, but data exists at best only for the latter group. And, ordinarily, only a subset of people affiliated with a certain belief system will have studied, evaluated, accepted, and practiced the dominant tenets of the faith. Others may be affiliated only by law, tradition, marriage or birth. Still others may affiliate for cultural reasons or to enjoy the benefits of affiliation. Some will attend religious services faithfully; others will darken the door of a temple or synagogue only on special days. The power of belief, of course, only reaches its full potential in true believers. However, there are spillover effects associated with affiliation and/or regular attendance at worship services, so research that uses religious affiliation or regular church attendance as a proxy for what people believe can still be useful. Indeed many people who believe they have rejected the religious beliefs of their forebears nevertheless live their lives by many of the same principles they claim to be rejecting.

Another complication is that religious beliefs, even for true believers, are often hopelessly intertwined with cultural practices. It is often difficult for newcomers to a country to know if natives think a certain way or engage in a certain behavior because of their religious beliefs, their cultural norms, or even their citizenship. For example, newcomers to the United States who observe the commercial celebrations surrounding Christmas or Easter may assume that these flow logically from the tenets of the Christian faith, when in fact they may be more of a reflection of the influences of secularization or a fondness for capitalism. To further illustrate, those who profess a particular set of religious beliefs will generally not include all of those whose parents professed those beliefs. So, for example, many Christians did not grow up in Christian homes. Nor are those professing a particular belief insulated from the influence of other belief systems. Christian missionaries, for example, will be quick to note that people previously steeped in tribal religions who eventually come to self-identify as Christians nevertheless sometimes return to the witch doctor as a precaution. And even though this kind of behavior is far less likely to occur in subsequent generations, the situation in countries like Haiti makes clear that the pace of change depends on the specific beliefs and practices associated with the missionary message.[3] Many belief systems routinely tolerate far more syncretism than Protestant Christianity – which makes the measurement of the effects of these beliefs even more difficult. Thus, there are at least two other complicating factors for those trying to measure the economic effects of belief changes, that should be highlighted: First, the margins between belief systems are not always clean, and secondly, there may be significant and somewhat unpredictable lags between belief changes and their economic effects.

Measuring Tapes, Scales and IQ Tests

These observations are also a good reminder that little can be accomplished when religious beliefs are amalgamated into such large and broad categories that they tell us almost nothing.[4] Of course eventually we also have to put a stop to the level of differentiation, since time is a scarce commodity and belief systems are complex. The key at this point is to come up with categories that are detailed enough to accomplish the purposes for which they are intended, but not a lot more. In this chapter and the chapter following we will introduce five measures for doing this, each of which is well enough differentiated to allow us to see its economic significance.[5] These categories are framed in this chapter and the next according to five fundamental questions that all belief systems must address and generally address differently.

- Where did all this (and I) come from?
- Where am I? - Beliefs about the world.
- Who am I? What is the nature of humanness?
- How and where do I fit in? How am I to relate to others?
- Where and how do I find truth?

In subsequent chapters we will have the luxury of delving into more specific differences between some of the more economically influential belief systems and their implications.

Where Did All This (and I) Come from? The Importance of Beliefs about God (or gods)

Of course, the most important thing about a God or gods is the truth or falsehood of his (or their) existence. As noted earlier, if God exists and is the creator, ruler, judge and potential savior of all people, everything else that could be said about our subject is little more than background noise. But plumbing the mysteries of how people experience God (or gods), or exploring accounts of divine interactions with people throughout history are outside the scope of this book.[6] On the other hand, exploring the nature of the divine being or other object in which people place their faith and hope is integral to the subject at hand. Is God a personal, informed, powerful, conscious being with desires and concerns, and one who issues commandments or moral judgments, or just some kind of distant deity or vague essence? A sovereign God will have far more impact on people's behaviors than one who is perceived to be relatively benign. If God is omnipotent and omnipresent, so that he will be aware of people's opportunistic, immoral, or unethical behavior, people are much more likely to avoid these behaviors. They will likely be stopped by feelings of guilt, because they will already be conscious, prior to violating one of the precepts of their religious code, of the wrongness of what they are contemplating. This is in stark contrast to a belief system where people are guided more by shame than guilt. The prospect of their actions becoming known publicly could be quite small, certainly much smaller than the 100% probability that a God who is aware of what his creatures are doing at all times. Rodney Stark's study of 34 nations backs this up. He found that

> in each of 27 nations within Christendom, the greater the importance people placed on God, the less likely they were to approve of buying goods they know to be stolen, of someone failing to report that they had accidentally damaged an auto in a parking lot, or of smoking marijuana. These results held up in nations whose primary influence had been Catholic as well as those whose primary influence had been Protestant, and in nations with high average church attendance as well as in nations with low average church attendance. Church attendance still mattered, but nothing like people's perceptions about God.[7]

The nature of the Deity will also make a good deal of difference in which behaviors are promoted.[8] Those who know little about religious beliefs except that they don't generally like them often claim that all religions claim to have gods who reward good behavior or punish bad behavior. But as Rodney Stark's extensive research shows, many scholars have pointed out that this is simply not the case.[9] For example, the founder of British sociology, Herbert Spencer, wrote that the Domras in India celebrated a successful theft by sacrificing to their chief god Gandak. In 1922, J.P.Mills noted that the religion of the Lhotas didn't appear to include any moral code. Peter Lawrence noted that the Garia of New Guinea have no conception of sin or any idea of rewards in the next life for good works in this one. The Tai Dam people who live Viet Nam near the Chinese border had no particularly good word in their language for the English word forgiveness with predictable consequences.[10] And to this day, the Pustanwali tribal codes (encompassing more than 40 million people in Afghanistan and NW Pakistan) accept revenge for the sake of one's honor as a virtue.

Aristotle taught that the gods did not particularly care about humans, so it was unlikely that belief in them was essential to a moral order.[11] Greek and Roman gods were also often morally suspect, reputed at times to have done horrible things to humans or other gods for amusement. Although easily offended, they generally had little interest in what humans were doing to other humans, and could not necessarily be relied on. In contrast, the Judeo-Christian God's desire for a holy people, specific principles and rules for human behavior and high expectations for accountability are recorded in great detail throughout the Bible. But in addition to this, he is also depicted as a warm and loving father, which, when viewed in light of other Biblical accounts, and compared with modern research into the social implications of absent/emotionally distant fathers, carries additional significant implications. People's beliefs about God's approachability not only have direct economic and social effects, but they can also determine the role that religious institutions play in people's lives (e.g., whether the Church plays an important intermediary role or whether people approach God directly), which in turn influences things like their entrepreneurial spirit[12]

This is not to say all mono-theistic religions share this perspective. Islam's Allah is not depicted as either "father" or "love" in the ninety-nine excellent names given to him in the Qur`an. And although he is depicted in the Qur'an as interested in human affairs, it is in a more matter-of-fact way. The Muslim expression "Inshallah," implies considerably less potential to influence God than, for example, most Protestant Christians expect to have when they pray.[13] Nor does the Islamic understanding of Jesus match up with Christian beliefs.[14] Nevertheless, both Islam's Allah and Israel's God are depicted as Promise Keepers, worthy of people's complete reliance. Trustworthiness is also a defining characteristic of the god of science, which is a significant object of faith in most secular belief systems. On the other hand, many tribal gods are presumed to be arbitrary in ways similar to Greco-Roman gods.

Insight into the presumed nature and power of a God or gods can sometimes be gleaned by examining the rituals. If rituals are extremely important in order to avoid bad outcomes, the presumption is that people perceive the gods to be both powerful and punitive. Likewise, a tendency to focus inordinately on the execution of the steps in the ritual as opposed to responding to the broader moral and ethical expectations of the object of worship implies an unspoken assumption that the gods cannot overcome or will not overlook innocent errors. Thus, among some tribal religions, when magic or ritual is unsuccessful there is a tendency to blame the failure to execute the steps in the ritual properly. This is in contrast to most Christians who pray and participate in sacraments like baptism and the Eucharist, but don't believe the activity is any less effectual if a few words get mixed up along the way. It also follows that religions that require their adherents to focus much of their time and energy on precisely executed rites and rituals will leave less time for inculcating the kinds of moral and ethical principles that more broadly apply to human behavior and institutions.

Finally, if God is seen as beyond the constraints of time and matter, infinitely capable of bestowing blessings on people, and otherwise unlimited by the constraints of the material world, his followers will also be less likely to see human activity as "zero-sum," where one person's situation can improve only at the expense of others, one nation can benefit from trade only if others are harmed, or economic development can take place only, say, at the cost of environmental degradation. On the negative side, this belief in God's transcending power could also result in a degree of skepticism or apathy about resource shortages, which could have negative economic consequences. Disruption of the environment, it would seem, would be considered a more serious concern by those who believe that there are spirits in much of the natural world, as well as those who deny the existence of any God or gods and highly value their ability to live in peaceful harmony with the natural world. But apathy toward the environment can also be found among those who, in addition to denying the existence of God, also deny any ownership claims or accountability beyond themselves. And a deep concern for the environment is also widespread among Christians because of Biblical teachings that "the earth is the Lord's" and that people have been entrusted with its care. Once again the actual impact on the environment or economy will depend on the emphases within the belief system.

Other attributes of God could also have significant economic outcomes, but only if people believe that they are connected to God in more than a passing manner. For example, if people believe themselves to be God's children bearing his image, they will seek to pattern in their own lives the attributes associated with God. If God is creative they will see themselves as creative, if he is trustworthy, they will seek to be trustworthy; if he is trusting, they will tend to trust; if he is loving, approachable and forgiving, they will seek to bear his image in those ways. And feeling trusted and knowing that one will be forgiven if mistakes are made will in turn have significant effects on one's willingness to take risks.

In conclusion, the nature of the object of people's worship will have a significant impact on economic development. In the same way that adults often mimic the parenting techniques of their parents (no matter how dysfunctional), humans will be informed by the images of their God or gods in their quest to solve problems and improve their lives. This will cause materialists, for example, to often look first and sometimes only to material and technological solutions to problems, while believers in a God with strong moral and ethical concerns will generally look first to moral and ethical solutions and secondarily to mechanistic or technical solutions.

Where am I? Beliefs about the World

The second measuring stick by which we can compare and contrast religious beliefs involves beliefs about the world as a whole. At many junctures these beliefs tie in with beliefs about God. For example, if God is seen as a creator, then one foundational belief is that the world is the product of this creator's handiwork. Most Muslims, Christians, Orthodox Jews, Mormons, and Sikhs, for example, hold to this view. Some within these groups have adopted a position of theistic evolution, where God creates the original substance of the universe, and the creation process unfolds through evolutionary channels. But even those holding to this view generally assume that this took place under the watchful eye of the Creator God.

Hindus have a variety of creation stories, with two of the most common being that the universe was formed and expands with the breath of the god Vishnu, and declines when he inhales (thus leading to repetitive creations) and that the universe is the product of the sacrifice of the primal man, Parusa, whose body parts formed the earth, its people, and the rest of the universe. Most Buddhists also believe in a creation, and a creation that is part of a cyclical process, but it is less likely to be associated with a particular god, and often quite compatible with the evolutionary theories of origin that are in conflict with most other creation beliefs. These evolutionary theories for the most part stem from Darwin's theory of naturalistic evolution, and its subsequent refinements, where all creatures evolve from lower forms of life *without* any supernatural intervention. Nevertheless, naturalistic evolution, like other beliefs mentioned, also rests on faith at some point, since there is still much that is unknown and perhaps unknowable about our origins, such as where the elements that make up the universe came from, how lifeless matter came to life, and how (beyond our limited understanding of quantum mechanics) time, matter, energy and spiritual forces interact with each other.

As with alternative beliefs about God, we readily admit the impossibility of adequately describing the myriad beliefs about the origin and nature of the world. But we will address four areas that we deem to be important to economic outcomes:

- Beliefs about the goodness or corruption of the world
- Views of the nature and meaning of time
- Views on the destiny of the world and the afterlife, and
- Beliefs about the existence and nature of a spiritual realm.

Beliefs about the Goodness or Corruption of the World

The Judeo-Christian view of the world has also held, throughout history, that the original creation was spoiled as a result of humankind's "fall" into sin, with the result that the world is no longer as it was intended to be. A significant end of economic activity in such a world is the task of repairing what is broken and improving on what the natural or "undeveloped" world has to offer. This urge to improve things often extends beyond the natural world to people, products and services, as well as institutions, and even government. But this response requires an innate belief that one has both the calling and power to change things. Both Christians and Jews view the world as redeemable, but in different ways. Jews (especially orthodox) tend to feel a strong sense of responsibility to correct problems by following the laws that God has instituted to govern relationships between people and the rest of the created world. Christians are more likely to appeal to the importance of the transformation that takes place in individuals as a result of the atoning death of Christ, who "has made all things new." As "new creatures," they sense a strong calling to fix what is broken, i.e., heal sicknesses, mend relationships, or protect crops from weeds. This occurs for a variety of reasons, but it almost always flows, at least in part, out of the motive of wanting to "do for others what has been done for them," which itself flows from a motive of thankfulness for the gift of salvation. More than people of other belief systems, they tend to believe that businesses, markets, and even government can be reformed if peoples' hearts are focused in the right direction. These kinds of connections between people's beliefs and what they did/do with their lives are easy to find. For example, it is clear that Nobel Prize winner and Green Revolution father Norman Borlaug's dedication to improving plant genetics and feeding hungry is related to the influences of the Norwegian-American Lutheran community that shaped him[15] His December 11, 1970 Nobel Lecture starts out with "Adam and Eve's" predicament, and ends with his hope for the fulfillment of Isaiah's prophecy that "the desert shall rejoice, and blossom as a rose…and the parched ground shall become a pool, and the thirsty land springs of water."[16] Many tribal religions, on the other hand, not only see the world as broken, but also as dark, frightening and even overwhelming; so much so that they don't sense an equivalent calling or empowerment to vanquish the darkness.

Beliefs about the relationship between people and the rest of the natural world can have profound economic effects. For example, malaria affects 500 million people per year and kills millions, but the possibility of using DDT to control or eradicate it is not even an option for some people because of its proven environmental dangers. Believing man to be just another animal, or environmental protection as non-negotiable, they have difficulty "seeing" the relationship between protecting animals or the environment and protecting human life.[17] But even if we choose against DDT, which is likely what we should do, economist William Easterly estimates that medicine with the potential to prevent half of all malaria deaths costs only $.12 per dose and bed nets only $4 each to prevent new cases. What has stopped people from making this investment? One thing is the widespread belief that the world's problems are so big and intractable that no one person can make a difference. Another contributing belief, that can be observed in as widely diverse groups as agnostics, inner city Christians living in a culture of poverty, and tribal societies around the world is that there is *limited good* in the world. Where this belief predominates, low levels of trust and a culture of pessimism are also generally found, causing people to wait for outside help to solve their problems and pass up opportunities to solve them themselves.[18] Once again, worldviews matter.

Worldviews that hold that the world that is fundamentally broken can also be differentiated from the teachings of Islam, on the one hand, and those of Hindus and Buddhists on the other. Islam teaches that sin is a serious problem, but rather than emphasizing the original brokenness of the world from the beginning of creation ("original sin"), the focus is on life as a series of choices between right and wrong behavior where individuals must strive (jihad) to stay on the right path. Brokenness is seen primarily as moral degeneracy and the result of arrogance that accompanies distinctions based on class, income, or nationality, and fixing these problems involves calling people back to leading moral lives, and to some Muslims, overcoming these distinctions by propagating the Muslim faith (da`wa) and imposing a moral and egalitarian social order (where individual freedoms are far more restricted than in other belief systems). Many Buddhists, Hindus, and "new age" belief systems see the world in yet another way. A common belief is that the natural world is either good in its original form, or not particularly good or bad, so the task of people is simply to carry out their day-to-day activities as part of that world, doing their best to survive and find happiness. Many Buddhists go beyond this, holding to the "noble truth" that people should not harm any living things, a concept that has profound economic consequences for those who try to follow it strictly, since much of modern economic activity involves harvesting, modifying, experimenting with, and consuming living things. But it should also be noted that most Buddhists and Hindus believe that suffering is an inevitable part of life, and that the absence of suffering (Nirvana) is possible only at the end of a long journey which suppresses desire over many lifetimes.

Most tribal religions do not have a concept of Nirvana or a prohibition against harming "living things," but many do believe that the nature of reality is such that natural objects may contain spirits which have the potential to do harm to those who encroach on them or offend them.[19] Many also believe that ancestral spirits continue to be present in the world after death and may seek to harm those who deviate from traditional behaviors. Both of these beliefs also have the tendency to give rise to various kinds of magic and taboos. And, although these views vary widely from person to person, it is fair to say that these beliefs would make it more likely for their adherents to see relatively low levels of economic development as more normal or acceptable than those whose beliefs allow them to peacefully make use of or improve the natural world, rather than fear it.

Those denying the existence of God and spirits of any kind often derive their views from a strong belief in naturalistic evolution. Not believing that the world is inherently good or bad, but rather an ongoing competitive "jungle," they could have one of several responses. Most seem to see relatively unfettered economic competition as natural or at least necessary. Many in this group would have a difficult time believing that efficient labor, product, or financial markets could exist in the absence of competitive striving, in spite of the fact that they likely believe most people are basically good. But others, especially those who adhere to a humanist belief system, focus on "humanizing the competitive process," rather than allowing their Darwinian bent to infiltrate all areas of life. Hitler, on the other hand, used naturalistic evolution as a justification for killing millions of people, including an estimated six million Jews and even more Russians, and for trying to dominate the world with what he perceived to be a superior race of people. Beliefs about the nature of the world can drive people to protect the rights of the weakest or guarantee the ascendancy of the fittest, to cultivate relationships between nations where the stronger routinely protect the weaker, or exterminate them.

Views of the Nature and Meaning of Time

Based on their beliefs about the origin of the world, many people, including Buddhists, Hindus, and adherents to African tribal religions take a cyclical view of time, while many Christians and secular materialists (such as Marxist-Leninists) take more of a straight-line view. Generally, a cyclical view of time results in a lower sense of urgency, less of a preoccupation with schedules, and a sense that if something doesn't get done, there will always be another opportunity to do it in the future. A straight-line view of time, on the other hand, often goes hand in hand with the feeling that there is never enough time, tight adherence to schedules, and lives that revolve around clocks and smart phones,[20] with predicable economic consequences, both positive and negative.

Patience, on the other hand, is often associated with a cyclical view of time and is a particular strength of Confucian belief systems. The story is told of a Chinese bureaucrat who, when asked about the impact of Napoleon on the world, answered, "It's too early to tell." Although patience can have negative economic effects at times, many of the best economic returns come only after painstakingly patient investment and work.

Religious beliefs also affect the relative amount of attention people give to the past, present and future. Some belief systems are very intentional about connecting successive generations with their history while others focus almost entirely on the present or future. It is likely that economic and social change will be much more rapid in the second group. Whether wealth creation, stewardship or economic development is greater in this second group will depend entirely on the particular values, attitudes and behaviors they are abandoning and what they are replacing them with. As we shall see in subsequent chapters, some traditional values and habits can be remarkably productive and others remarkably counterproductive.

Views on the Destiny of the World and the Afterlife

Most people feel some sort of connection with those who have gone before them and those who will follow them. Some of these people also feel that history has meaning and that world events are progressing toward some particular end. For example, many Christians believe that the inhabitants of the earth are progressing through a series of historical events that could be labeled creation, fall, and redemption, and that time is now moving toward a final consummation when Christ will return to the earth and all people will be judged. This gives many of them a heighted sense of purpose and urgency with respect to their daily actions, but, as we shall see momentarily, can also have the opposite effect by making people fatalistic.

These very different reactions remind us that there is another key belief about the world that has a significant impact on economic outcomes. That belief involves the questions "To what end is the world progressing?" and "What will happen after death?" Most Buddhists, Hindus, and secular materialists expect the world to last a very long time, at least if people take care of it. Some Christians would be inclined to agree with this, since the Bible teaches that God is patient and wants to draw people back to himself, although most of these also believe Christ will suddenly return to usher in a "new heavens and new earth." Because of the Bible's imprecision about the timing of these events and the specifics about what will happen, there is a significant subgroup within Christianity that has come to believe they are called to suffer the evil of this world until Christ comes again, and it is not until this happens that the "good life" will begin. This seemingly minor twist to their understanding of time has the potential to undo much of the sense of purpose and urgency discussed earlier.

Beliefs about life after death also have one other significant impact on economic outcomes. People who believe there is no life after death often have a strong incentive to derive as much pleasure and happiness out of this life as possible, which gives them incentives to work and achieve, and to extend life as much as possible, all of which will affect consumption and savings patterns and the choices of products and services. It is no surprise that increasing secularism is often accompanied by increasing consumption, and especially medical expenditures.[21] In this regard, a person who does not believe in an afterlife may be a good person to share a foxhole with, because he will do everything in his power to stay alive. But a strong belief in life after death, whether out of gratitude for the gift of eternal life, or a striving to achieve it, can have equally significant influences. It can spur people on to heroic acts of service, sacrifice, and risk-taking for the good of others.[22] So if a grenade rolls into the foxhole, one might actually be better off with a comrade who believes in life after death, since he would be more likely to be willing to throw himself on the grenade.[23] Of course, other beliefs, about things like justice, loving one's neighbor, or the morality or immorality of killing are likely more important when it comes to war, influencing decisions to go to war, how to wage war, whether and how to protect or restore innocent victims of war, and the desire to find creative alternatives to war. And few things have greater consequences for the economy of a country or the world than war or the absence of war.

Chapter 14

Beliefs about the Existence and Nature of a Spiritual Realm

Other important aspects of what people believe about the created world are their assumptions about the material world. For example, is there anything beyond what we can see, touch, taste, smell or feel? And, if there is, what is it like, and is it separate from or integrated into the material world? One significant part of this involves whether something called evil exists, and if so, what it looks like. Is it a serious problem, like a cancer that, if undetected and untreated, will grow in insidious ways and eventually bring on death, or a powerful force that is beyond the ability of humans to reckon with, or not really all that big of a deal? Atheists, agnostics, and most secular materialists tend to believe that "what you see is what you get," and generally prefer not to talk about "sin" or "evil" because of the religious overtones associated with these words. On the other hand, religious believers accept that there is much more to the world than meets the eye, but their beliefs about the spiritual world vary widely. When the invisible world is assumed to be a dark and dangerous place, it *can* have a profoundly negative effect on human productivity and economic development. Not only will people refrain from productive activity because of fears about taboos or retribution from ancestral or natural spirits, but they may remain confused for centuries about certain cause and effect relationships. And these tendencies do not just exist among animist religions. In places where versions of Christianity have spread that do not teach "lay" people what the Bible says about the rejection of taboos or magic, or other beliefs that are fundamentally contradictory to Christianity, the effects of these beliefs can persist for centuries. In Haiti, for example, black magic and taboos persist centuries after the first Christian influences arrived. Likewise, it is not uncommon for older Russian Orthodox Church members to believe that the movement of animals has significance for their lives, that a scratch on one's arm or neck is an omen that something bad is likely to happen, or to have a deep sense of pessimism about their eternal destiny.

There is, however, another important belief distinction among those who accept the existence of a spiritual dimension in their lives. Some assume that there is no possible separation between the spiritual and physical worlds and conduct their affairs accordingly, which includes recognizing the relevance of religious beliefs to all of life, and the relevance/importance of the material world to their beliefs; others practice a kind of "spirituality in private" while conducting their "secular lives" much as any agnostic or atheist would. For example, Confucian beliefs assume a fundamental integration between the spiritual and temporal and an underlying order to things which ought not to be violated. They assume, for example, that righteousness in the heart leads to good character which in turn leads to harmony in the home, order in the nation, and peace in the world. Many post modernists and some Christians, on the other hand, buy into a kind of separation between the material and spiritual worlds, which causes them to advocate a kind of private spirituality. However, most Christians believe that there is a "Kingdom of God" which, although largely invisible to the untrained eye, operates concurrently with and in full contact with the material world and represents God's influence on and interaction with the affairs of people and the events of history. The existence of this "kingdom" implies that there are spiritual laws, norms, and boundaries, similar in substance to physical laws like the laws of particle physics, gravity or magnetism, that govern the world and human behavior and are not meant to be violated, or can be violated only at one's risk.[24]

The belief in such laws coupled with the confidence needed to explore them stimulates curiosity in the social sciences in the same way that Michael Faraday's faith drove him to try to uncover principles of electromagnetism in the area of natural science. As Robert Clark has noted, Faraday, a church elder who, like many members of the Royal Society with whom he faithfully met, believed that "since God had created nature, only lazy and unthankful people would be uninterested in that upon which God had lavished so much thought and care." Clark goes on to note that "it was this belief, held with Passion, which enabled the early investigators to overcome the discouragements and difficulties with which the beginnings of science were attended."

Belief in both spiritual and physical laws that are part of the very fabric of reality often go hand in hand with a belief in the existence of boundaries between different spheres of life, such as family, church, school, business, or government that are also not meant to be violated.[25] People of course know instinctively that a family and a school are different and have different tasks to do, but how should we decide when either the parents or the school have overstepped their legitimate authority? Secular individualists, at least those who prefer to relegate values to the "personal preference" corner of people's lives, might be inclined to say that schools and churches ought not to interfere in the private affairs of families.   But others, like Kuyper, who hold religious beliefs that recognize that raising children is an integral task involving parenting, church, and school, have very different ideas of how these different spheres of society ought to interact; likewise with business and government, business and the family, or the church and government. As the Spanish Inquisition or the Soviet Union's seventy year experiment with an overly powerful government made clear, perceptions about such boundaries have massive effects on economic outcomes; so too when businesses attempt to dictate what people should do or not do when they are away from work; or when a state tries to force people to adhere to a favored religion. For better or worse, perceptions about these norms, laws, and boundaries are both important to economic outcomes and inextricably tied up with religious beliefs. Finding the best boundaries between these spheres of life will not be possible in the absence of a religiously informed discussion. Strict separation of church and state where religious voices are stifled in the public square, will not produce a lasting solution to the boundary line problem. It simply elevates one set of beliefs - that religion should be a private matter - above all others without resolving the underlying issues. The only robust solution will be one that recognizes the relevance of differences in belief systems and provides a voice for all.

Chapter 15: Critical Differences among Belief Systems II – Beliefs about People, Relationships, and Sources of Truth

We now examine the answers to the remaining three questions about how belief systems differ. Like the beliefs about God or gods and the world/universe discussed in the last chapter, our third question, dealing with what it means to be human and our fourth, dealing with what it means to be in relationship with other people also profoundly affect economic outcomes. And the fifth question, which deals with how and where we can discover what is true, underlies and in many ways determines the answers to all four of the other questions.

Who am I? What is the Nature of Humanness?

The third fundamental question that distinguishes belief systems involves the nature of what it means to be human. This question has three essential components. The first is an intensely personal component involving the question, "What is my nature?" This may immediately evoke expressions like "he's a chip off the old block," or "the apple doesn't fall far from the tree." The study of self-perception, self-esteem, and self-confidence has always been a popular aspect of the study of psychology, and genetic explanations for behavior have proliferated since the mapping of the human genome. But where does self-esteem or self-confidence come from, or the assumption that these are highly desirable human qualities? Is it possible that those who don't particularly esteem themselves but derive their confidence from other sources could be better off or more productive than those with loads of self-esteem? Is it possible that religious beliefs could have as much or more to do with self-confidence than genetics? Is it possible that even the genetic makeup of a population is affected by religious beliefs - as values about what is desirable in a spouse affect marital choices over successive generations? Unfortunately we cannot investigate all or even many of interesting questions that could shed light on the relationship between religious beliefs and assumptions about what it means to be human or what it means to live in relationship with others. We will however address people's beliefs in three economically significant areas - the degree to which they are what they are because of nature or nurture, their assumptions about the fundamental goodness or badness of their natures, and the degree to which they believe they have been given life for a particular purpose.

Nature, Nurture, or Something Else?

Most religious belief systems begin to answer the "What is my nature?" question in the ordinary way - by tracing human ancestral lines. The degree to which their findings satisfy them depends on whether they believe humans can better be explained by their "nature" or their "nurture." Materialistic belief systems increasingly lean to the nature side, leaning especially heavily in recent years on the advances in genome sequencing in their quest to find genetic causes for almost everything.[1] In communist societies this same line of thinking often resulted in strong efforts to discover unique talents, such as mathematical skill or athleticism, early in life, so that early intervention could take place to develop those talents, and youths could be put on a course where they could best serve their comrades and bring accolades to their mother country. This included channeling students into highly specialized and narrowly focused institutions of higher education at relatively young ages. This overemphasis on genetic predisposition and early specialized training, apparently useful in identifying superior athletes, did not serve communist economies particularly well overall – a fact that became even more noticeable when they attempted near the end of the 20th century to transition to diversified market economies – because dynamic economies require large numbers of people with broad knowledge, diversified skills, and the ability to quickly apply these to new situations.

People committed to materialistic belief systems also look beyond nature to *nurture*, but are more likely to insist that even nurturing habits are genetically based. Increasingly among Western materialists, there is a temptation to reduce almost everything down to biology and chemistry. Why do people commit crimes, fall in love, or believe in God? For increasing numbers, the right answer is that it was not really their choice. They were chemically, biologically, or genetically predisposed for these things. Materialist belief systems also have the often unintended consequence of valuing individuals on the basis of their material wealth or accomplishments, often giving those who produce and/or accumulate the most materially the most attention. All of these beliefs affect the ability to devalue the productive potential of certain groups of people and limit solutions to problems like crime to biological and chemical research, prescription drugs, or expansions of the prison system.

What is perhaps even more striking is how little interest many secular materialists have in looking into possibilities beyond nature and nurture. Ultimately, emphasis on both nature and nurture put people in the straitjacket of being whatever it is that *external* forces have caused them to be, rather than emphasizing the potential for their beliefs or sheer force of will to change this. This bias, however, is not only part of secular belief systems. Traditional Hindu beliefs hold that when the primal man was sacrificed at the creation of the world, the lower parts of the body gave rise to the lower castes of people, while more esteemed parts of the body gave rise to higher castes. A popularly-accepted refinement to this story differentiated four primary castes of people at the time of creation, the Brahmin (priests and teachers), Kshatriya (princes, warriors) *Vaishya* (merchants), and *Shudra* (artisans, masons, and manual laborers, some of whom - the untouchables, or Dalits - could better be described as a fifth caste of laborers assigned to do the most menial and dirty jobs). A series of writings further defined appropriate rules of behavior for each of these castes (Dharma). And, even though the *varna* (caste system) has been technically illegal in India since 1969, many people continue to see themselves along caste lines, with some people still sadly confused as to whether the Dalits are even fully human. There are many other stories that make the same point.[2] Recently Hernando De Soto and others have highlighted the importance of giving the poor property rights, but if bankers believe the poor to be fundamentally unworthy of credit, property cannot be used very productively.[3] Likewise, many conservative Shiites do not permit women to drive or work outside of the home. This requires the hiring of large numbers of foreigners to serve as drivers and to fill jobs that would be performed by women in economies influenced by other belief systems. Clearly the beliefs behind these practices have limited the productivity of large numbers of people and hampered the development of the countries and continents affected by them.

These examples introduce another powerful belief to the mix. Not only does what we believe about our individual nature matter a great deal, but so does our beliefs about the fundamental equality or inequality of all people. If entire segments of the population in a country are not allowed to fully participate in the economy because of what others believe to be inherent in their ethnicity, gender or skin color, the effects on the economy will be enormous.[4] Reaching one's full potential depends as much or more on what others think of a person as it does on his or her nature or nurture. The economic consequences of this are enormous.

Is There Really Anything Wrong With Me?

A second economically significant belief about who we are involves the perceptions we have of our own innate goodness or evil. Beliefs about what people are like "at their core" range from the highly motivating, high responsibility belief that people were created in the very image of an all-powerful God to whom they are accountable, to the highly debilitating and depressing belief that some people were literally formed out of feces and are therefore subhuman or untouchable." If we were to try to create a spectrum for these beliefs, the choices would range from the assumption that all people are bad and essentially unredeemable on one end, to the belief that all people are essentially good and incorruptible on the other end. Most people's beliefs fall somewhere in the middle, with most Christians believing that people were created in the image of God, and even though they "fell" into sin, they are still redeemable; many other religious groups believing that people are basically good, but corruptible. The point to be stressed here is that those who believe that some people are genetically predisposed to incapability or bad behavior will lean toward classifying people, restraining freedom for certain groups and incorporate these biases into activities as diverse as child rearing, business, financial systems, prisons, and government. Those who believe people are eminently capable of change (i.e., they are not destined to be a certain way by genes, biology or chemistry), and perfectible (relatively speaking) when they change their beliefs or receive positive influences, will expend relatively more energy on moral education, positive guidance and correcting misguided beliefs and use external control systems more sparingly. Those who believe, on the other hand, that people are basically good may see less need to emphasize moral education and guidance, or restrict the freedom of subordinates. This affects economic development by affecting things as diverse as educational preparation, ethics, decentralization, delegation of authority, and accountability structures in organizations which in turn have a significant impact on organizational efficiency and competitiveness.

The economic impact of assumptions about sin and evil also depend on the prescription of a particular belief system for addressing these problems. In some Christian churches and denominations today, particularly those that have been infiltrated by individualism, sin is often assumed to be private, pervasive and enduring, whereas in other denominations and churches, people are assumed, through the power of the Holy Spirit and the support of the church community, to have very real power to overcome serious and specific sinful tendencies. The latter belief opens the door to improvements in moral and ethical practices vis-à-vis the former, and overall healthier economic outcomes.

Do I Have Some Kind of Reason for Being Here?

A third aspect of what we believe about ourselves involves our perceptions of *why* we exist. For example, if we exist to survive, to achieve status or superiority, or for happiness or pleasure, there is little incentive for altruistic behavior, since that kind of behavior by definition is not all that helpful to ourselves. In these cases our cooperation with others will tend to be a kind of self-interested cooperation, where we balance our responsibilities to our employer or government with what we get from them. Our time will be our own and entertainment will be deemed as equally valid uses of our time and talents as teaching literacy, feeding the hungry, or sheltering the homeless. Each person may choose what makes him or her happy. In contrast to this, many religions prescribe some attitudes or activities as being morally superior to other attitudes and activities. Both praiseworthy goals for human activity and the methods for accomplishing these things may or may not be prescribed.

One particularly important aspect of this involves what different belief systems teach (or do not teach) about work. Islam, for example, is in many ways a religion of duty. Duty, however, is not defined as a work ethic, but as following strict moral laws (which is also one of the reasons many

Muslims resent the undisciplined *moral* habits of secular materialists and nominal Christians). On the other hand, as noted earlier, many Protestant Christian groups consider idleness to be more sinful than the occasional moral failing, and some Christian denominations (for example, those most heavily influenced by the teachings of John Calvin) have given work a paramount place in the Christian lifestyle by recognizing it as a form of worship. This can be contrasted to many expressions of Buddhism and Hinduism which are more likely to emphasize contemplation as an important component of moving along on the path to Nirvana. But once again, the important differences only emerge when the details are examined. Soka Gakkai International is an expression of Buddhism (that has been influential in Japan and a number of other Asian countries) that holds that working hard to overcome earthly difficulties rather than trying to escape them is one of the best methods of moving along on the path to enlightenment.

In other cases, rites and rituals are what dominate people's ideas about what they are "called" to do. The Five Pillars, consisting of Shahadah (public confession), Salah (prayer, facing Mecca, five times per day at the call of the muezzin/minaret), Sawn (fasting during Ramadan), Zakat (giving alms), and the Hajj (the pilgrimage to Mecca) are extremely important parts of what an observant Muslim would feel is expected of him. Bathing in the Ganges River is believed by millions of Hindus to bring them closer to Nirvana. Equally great importance is attached to the Eucharist and Penance for Catholics, to regular Bible reading and prayer for Evangelical Protestants, to Sabbath observance for Jews, and Icons and lighting candles for Orthodox believers. In addition, it would be plausible to argue that people who do not consider themselves to be "believers" could nonetheless be equally attached to ritual behaviors, whether they be football/soccer games, primetime TV series, casino outings, or rock concerts (although they would be unlikely to recognize them as acts of worship). Our point is not to pass judgment on particular rituals since rituals have very important functions, but rather to recognize that they are not without economic consequences because they require widely varying amounts of resources (time and money) and add widely varying amounts of value to people's lives. For example, some rituals call people to make remarkable commitments or remind them of their high calling while others communicate little to participants (and may not even be understood by them). Some rituals involve something as rote as eating with the right hand or putting pants on starting with the right foot, while others involve life enriching promises of responsibility and accountability. Some rituals require massive church structures with high maintenance and restoration costs that have the potential to sap the resources of parishioners, especially when the ranks of the faithful dwindle. In other cases the sheer numbers of shrines, chedis, temples or wats, although modest in architecture, represents a significant investment. In some large Protestant mega churches the clergy are busy from sun up to sun down with a host of tasks (almost akin to CEOs of major corporations), whereas in some Hindu temples the Sadus (Holy men) spend most of the day sitting around, involved in meditation, smoking and even begging, with predictable economic consequences.

Different religious beliefs also have very different economic effects on all of the other economic activity that takes place in a country. For example, in Sri Lanka, business practices are affected by a host of holidays related to the diverse religious beliefs of the populace and the government's decisions about how to accommodate them. Business and transportation are greatly diminished during Salah (ritual times of prayer) in Muslim shops and neighborhoods, on the Sabbath in observant Jewish neighborhoods, and on Sundays in places where Christian influences have resulted in Blue laws.[5] But belief systems can also increase the likelihood of intentional or unintentional harm. Self-flagellation has been practiced by many sects throughout history and still today. As many as 1,500 people have died in crowd control incidents during the Hajj[6], and scores of people have died during secular rituals like sporting events, or rock concerts as well. But, as tragic as these deaths are, they are the exception. Much more important is whether these rituals are restoring, refreshing, or developing people, or fueling their anger, placing financial strains on them, or exploiting them.

There are many other differences among religious *practices* besides the degree to which they emphasize rituals that have significant implications for economic activity. Some churches, synagogues, or temples are real communities where people develop a host of interpersonal skills; some are not. Some offer people opportunities to contribute their talents, develop as people, and take on significant responsibilities; some do not. Some emphasize rational thinking and/or help their parishioners resolve conflict, resolve intellectual tensions, make concrete applications of teachings and doctrine, etc; some do not. Some hold people accountable for moral and ethical behavior, and beyond this, to lives that reflect the core beliefs of the religion; some do not. Some allow people to retain beliefs and practices that are fundamentally incompatible with the religion; some do not. These differences have a profound influence on people's worldviews, development as people, and expectations and, therefore, on economic outcomes and development.

How and Where Do I Fit in? How am I to Relate to Others?

A fourth economically-significant way we can distinguish belief systems is in how people answer the question "How do I relate to those around me? This deals at a practical level with their perception of norms for social interaction, but more fundamentally with what they believe about how they are connected to each other. Authentic development, in contrast to what we referred to earlier as "smokescreen" development, will always be impeded when, for example, people are incapable of cooperating with each other, believe in the fundamental unworthiness of whole groups of people, don't trust each other, or choose revenge and retribution over cooperation and compromise. These and other problems have their roots in what we believe to be normative when it comes to relationships with others.

Individual first, or Member of a Community?

Secular belief systems with their roots in the Enlightenment for the most part view the individual as the primary building block of society. As such, the individual is relatively autonomous, and it is not particularly important that she consider herself a permanent part of any group larger than herself. Society is structured in such a way that individuals are free to move from place to place, job to job, marriage to singleness, or one sexual partner to another. The number of children a couple has, or how they spend their money, or the values they teach (or fail to teach) their children are generally considered their own business. On the other extreme we find Marxism-Leninism, another secular belief system that has often been accused of deprecating the role of the individual to such a degree that the death or imprisonment of millions of nameless faceless individuals has on more than one occasion been deemed an acceptable price to pay for the maintenance or extension of an ideology.

In the middle we have a variety of more traditional religious beliefs that emphasize the idea of community, but with different structures and meanings.[7] The Jewish Torah puts great emphasis on the fact that the Jewish people stood before their God as *a people*, not just as individuals. They were *collectively* responsible to administer justice, care for aliens and strangers, and purge evil from their midst. Christians too are called to live "in community," as the Biblical New Testament accounts of the early church make clear. The church is often referred to as the "body of Christ," with communal expectations that members "love one another", "pray for one another", "bear one another's burdens", "confess their sins to one another", etc. They are encouraged to give "to the extent they have been blessed," assumed by many to be 10% or more of their income, and to maintain local, national, and international church ministries. Muslims too are asked to give alms of two and one-half percent of their income to meet the needs of the poor within their communities.[8]

What Does it Mean to be "in Relationship" With Other People?

Religious beliefs also affect people's understanding of what it means to be in relationship with other people and their ideas of what it means to live and work together effectively. In some Christian churches, people build deep relationships which extend beyond the church walls into work and business relationships or other areas of life, while in others people worship individualistically, with little knowledge of, or contact with, other believers. Buddhists usually visit temples and perform rituals individually or in small groups rather than gathering for fellowship with other believers at regular times. In general, less attention seems to be given to building relationships in religions that focus more on ritual than on teaching and fellowship (but this is not always the case).

Confucian beliefs in particular give attention to respectful relationships tied to roles. The principle of "Li" lays out how a person filling a particular role should conduct himself. (e.g., a father must be kind, a son obedient, an older brother courteous, a younger brother humble, a ruler just and benevolent, a subject loyal) Every action is assumed to affect others, and an individual is only to be understood as an element of various relationships. The complementary concepts of concepts of *Jen*, *Chun-tzu*, *Te*, and *Wen*[9] reinforce these foundations for human relations. Two economically important outcomes of these beliefs are their impact on the educational discipline of students and the loyalty of employees to companies. Most other belief systems say less about these things, in some cases missing out on the positive effects of the kind of personal discipline that flows from them. On the other hand, the avoidance of conflict and "face saving" associated with Confucian deference to authority also has the potential to lead to miscommunications and economic inefficiencies.

What is the Nature and Proper Exercise of Authority?

On one end of the spectrum people's beliefs about the nature of God (or gods) may lead them to see authority as power, and on the other end they may see it as a heavy responsibility to serve. This has profound effects on economic development by way of gender and interpersonal relationships, the authority structures within organizations (including churches) and the efficiency and effectiveness of government. With respect to gender, some belief systems claim there is no distinction between men and women while others allow multiple wives, forced sexual contact at the behest of the husband, beatings, and/or easy divorce for husbands (but usually not for wives). With respect to the authority of the church, some belief systems (including some expressions of Islam and fundamentalist Christianity) assume that religious leaders have such comprehensive wisdom that they should have veto power over all aspects of culture (including government), whereas other belief systems are more inclined to recognize the limitations of their authority. Islamic teachings for the most part make no distinction between religious and civil law. Because of this, the government is expected to play a very different role in majority Muslim countries than in the West. This is also the reason why, for example, public non-Islamic worship is a crime in Saudi Arabia and some other Islamic countries, and why Muslim clerics in India were able to block government distribution of a polio vaccine because they feared the vaccine might cause impotence, and because they believed it was "for Allah to decide what happens to his children." A variety of sects in other religions have similar impactful suspicions.

Instability, Violence and Political and Social Transitions

Another aspect of the religious understanding of relationships involves perceptions about appropriate ways to interact with people from other traditions. Religious diversity can pose problems when one or more of the religious groups represented are intolerant of other belief systems. Catholic Croats, Orthodox Christian Serbs, and Muslim Bosnians have a long history of struggle in the area of the former Yugoslavia. Another long history of conflict exists between Sunni and Shiite Muslims (which has flared up most recently in Iraq), and Hindus and Muslims continue to kill each other in India. But, as tribal warfare in Africa and atrocities committed by Hitler, Stalin and Mao indicate, both tribal and secular belief systems have precipitated as much if not more violence. In contrast,

Buddhism seldom breeds this kind of conflict, and peaceful communities founded by a host of other religious and secular groups exist worldwide, so there are clearly many things besides beliefs that precipitate violence. Likewise, Western nations did quite better economically when they abandoned imperialism, colonization, and costly church-state battles. They also built more lasting commercial and trust relationships when missionaries like William Carey differentiated themselves from the greedy exploiters with whom they had often shared passage, and encouraged people to voluntarily follow the paths of grace, love and service demonstrated by Jesus.

The peaceful development promoted by people like Carey can be contrasted to the wars waged by scores of secular governments seeking to expand their spheres of influence, to the Jews when they first entered their "promised land," thousands of years ago (and again when reclaiming part of it in 1948), or Islamic radicals who have too often sought both to retain existing believers and capture new ones by means of force.[10] And both of these ways of relating to others (voluntary and forced) can be contrasted to those of other belief systems that, because they capitulate to the cultures in which they are immersed or recede into a small corner of life, have very little positive or negative impact on the nature of people's relationships.

These differences also mean some belief systems are much more capable than others of bringing about peaceful political and social transitions. Christian traditions, for example, generally mandate government to act justly and prohibit revenge by individuals, but otherwise range from complete pacifism to supporters of the "just war theory." Other belief systems range from being pacifist to being silent about government's role in promoting justice, to merely discouraging revenge, or even allowing it. Still other belief systems go beyond revenge, sanctioning the destruction of large groups of people who happen to be of a certain ethnicity or religious persuasion. Hitler's atrocities, the Armenian massacres in the 1890s and during WWI, the slaughter of Tutsis in Rwanda in the 1990s, and most recently the rape, torture, kidnapping and genocide among Nuba Christians and other black Africans in the Darfur region of Sudan are all examples of this. In addition, militants in countries like Indonesia, Nigeria, and Sudan continue to attempt to convert people to Islam by force and threaten to kill those who convert from Islam to other religions, sometimes with the tacit support of the government. This is in part because, although the Qu`ran teaches that war is evil, the prophet Mohammed himself led the first jihad against the pagans in what is now Saudi Arabia. It also teaches that the extinction of Islam would be an even greater evil than war, which makes so-called defensive jihads not only permissible for radicals to engage in but in some cases mandatory. And even though mainstream Islam has always considered suicide a sin leading to eternal punishment, this has not stopped radicals from twisting the concept of defensive jihad in a way that allows them to run websites that promote suicide bombers, urge attacks on Jews or Americans, and offer videos of attacks to satisfy the bloodthirstiness of their followers. It would of course be a grave mistake to imply that most or all Muslims believe in, condone, or even tolerate these practices; in the same way it would be a mistake to insist that Christ would approve of atrocities committed in his name over the centuries.[11]

Those who try to sidestep the critical importance of religious beliefs have said that the real roots of violence lie in poverty or lack of education, but there is plenty of evidence that the followers of Islam who are doing most of the damage to the "infidels," not to mention to innocent women and children, have been anything but poor and uneducated. Princeton economist Alan Kreuger, found that Hezbollah fighters had above average education and financial status (2002). The Palestinian Center for Policy and Survey Research found the same for Pakistani suicide bombers and that educated Pakistanis were more likely to support bomb attacks than the illiterate. At the same time, most victims of injustice and poverty throughout the world suffer quietly or choose peaceful means of calling attention to their plight. The real roots of violence can be found in the beliefs, both secular and religious, of the perpetrators of the violence.

Economic development, then, depends on recognizing differences in specific beliefs (within and between broad religious classifications) and dealing with them. It also requires government to exercise its legitimate right to promote justice and to oppose those who insist on taking it into their own hands. Only if this is done will it be possible to allow the kind of freedom of religion that permits less violent belief systems to freely influence the societies in which they are immersed, bring media attention to them, and find other ways to stop violence and put the communities devastated by it back on the path of uninterrupted economic development.

How Big Are Our Circles?

Violence (and the unwillingness to confront it) is just one manifestation of the difficulty that humans have in recognizing their responsibilities to those who are distant from them philosophically, theologically, geographically, or ethnically. Some belief systems are highly inclusive, racially and ethnically, while others remain suspicious of outsiders and are only too happy to erect both social and economic barriers to interaction and trade. One way of depicting these differences is to envision a series of concentric "circles of concern" emanating out from the individual. Nearly all belief systems feel a strong sense of responsibility to people within their immediate family and friendship circles. Even the members of al Qaeda, who have been condemned around the world for their wanton disregard for the lives of innocent civilians as they pursue their goals, do a good job of helping their own, e.g., in the wake of natural disasters like the Pakistani earthquake of 2005. However, some belief systems draw far larger circles of responsibility, which mean that they are concerned about relatively large numbers of people, including people whom they have never met and have very little in common with. But others, like *militant* Islam and many tribal belief systems not only have very little concern for people outside of their immediate tribe or family, but they fear them and prefer not to cooperate with them. Of course Marxist-Leninists tried to *compel* people to draw very large circles which encompassed all citizens and even citizens of other communist countries, but did so without recognizing the importance of religious beliefs, and with little lasting success. Western secular individualists have been more successful in drawing wide circles than their communist counterparts. Some of them view all people as their brothers and sisters and therefore draw very broad circles. However most have responded to the needs of others through the force of law, *compelling* fellow citizens to share the burden of care by with them by earmarking some of the collective surplus through the vehicles of government taxing and spending. But they can be fairly accused of showing a lukewarm interest at best in voluntary charitable contributions, the idea of a legal "duty to care," and other forms of *personal* sacrifice for the sake of others or the larger community.

Jews and Christians are repeatedly reminded in the Bible that they are expected to be their "brother's keeper" and be hospitable to strangers.[12] These kinds of teachings have not only been influential in the U.S. in establishing whistleblower and sunshine laws that hold both government and corporate officials accountable for the ethics of their actions, but have also contributed to historically favorable attitudes toward economic and cultural openness, international immigration and religious freedom. Coupling these kinds of Biblical encouragements to reach outside of one's social and ethnic group with the call to spread the news of salvation, Christian communities seem particularly suited to establish and extend communities and relationships across economic, racial, ethnic and national boundary lines. These relationships lay the groundwork for the exchange of cultural "best practices"; enhance labor mobility, risk taking, and mutually advantageous international trade; promote cooperative relationships and peace; plant seeds of trust for future business ventures and startups; and a host of other things.

Both Indian and Chinese companies have also been very successful at startup businesses, but, prior to the Western educational and diaspora influences of recent decades, less successful at running large competitive multinationals. This is due in part to the rapidly diminishing trust circles in Confucianism and Hinduism, once we get beyond the family (e.g., *baradari*) relationships, which limits the recruitment of highly-qualified outsiders. Both Hinduism and Confucianism have clear rules for respecting authority in the family but less guidance for how to relate to and work with people or groups who are far away, geographically or religiously.

This discussion calls to attention one other economically-important difference among religious belief systems - some are exclusionary and judgmental, which all but prevents their adherents from making a lasting impact outside of their own circles. That this is true for many tribal religions is evident from centuries of intertribal warfare. But it is also true for some traditional religious and secular belief systems. For example, in Algeria, in 2006, a law was passed stipulating the lengths of prison terms and financial penalties to be levied on those attempting to convert Muslims. Much earlier, when the Turks sacked Constantinople (today's Istanbul) in 1453, they desecrated the famous Hagia Sophia

Cathedral's crosses and icons, and converted it, like hundreds or thousands of other churches in the Byzantine Empire, into a Mosque. Likewise, it was not unusual for Spanish colonizers to forcibly convert the natives in the countries they invaded and destroy their religious symbols. As Protestants gained ground in Northern Europe, their first tendencies were often to confiscate Catholic Church buildings and employ them in the service of the state-declared Protestant religion. To this day, some radical expressions of Islam strongly discourage friendships with non-Muslims.[13]

Militant Hindu nationalists have similar problems accepting Muslim and other religious traditions. In and around Orissa, in east central India, hundreds of Christian churches were burned and thousands of people were killed or displaced in 2008 by militant Hindus seeking revenge for an attack on a prominent Hindu by Marxists. Those who are less militant, although opposed to such violence, will nevertheless be unlikely to invite outsiders into their temples, primarily because they are likely to consider their belief system something one must be born into, rather than a choice. Of course some expressions of secular humanism and Christianity are as exclusionary as Islam, Hinduism, or tribal religions, albeit in different ways. Many secular humanists are radically committed to excluding all religious expressions in public schools and/or public places in general. Even more tragic, during the ascent of Nazism, Ludwig Muller convinced a relatively small minority (but significant number) of German Protestant pastors of the legitimacy of Hitler's model of racist "positive Christianity." And some Christian groups today remain convinced that their way of understanding the Bible is the *only* legitimate way.[14] Although some of these exclusionary communities have other values that permit them to do well economically, all pass up insights that come from the cross-fertilization of perspectives and the creative opportunities that come from this.

Being exclusive and judgmental should not be confused with high expectations or high levels of accountability within religious or secular communities, both of which are essential to healthy development. It takes a profoundly misguided notion of tolerance to believe that all religious communities that have demanding moral and ethical expectations of their followers are therefore exclusionary and judgmental. Quite to the contrary, many of the fastest growing congregations around the world have high moral, ethical and participatory expectations of their followers, usually in conjunction with a genuine concern for and equal acceptance of radically different kinds of people. Likewise, not all kinds of tolerance are good for economic development. For example, some expressions of Buddhism tolerate pickpockets and child prostitution on the assumption that karma will see to it that perpetrators receive their due. Some Christian denominations tolerated racism because they didn't see that sins of omission could be as important as sins of commission. Hinduism has been far too tolerant of caste-related discrimination. Other belief systems seem relatively unconcerned about reconciling logical contradictions, which allows inconsistent beliefs and practices to persist far longer than ought to be the case. Indeed, the secular belief that beliefs themselves are little more than harmless preferences and that all religious philosophies (except theirs) should be kept out of the schools and public square, may be the most blatant example of example of all of misguided "tolerance."

Where and How Do I Find Truth?

The fifth and final area by which we can distinguish belief systems, and one that explains many of the differences between the religious perspectives noted earlier, involves their approach to what they believe to be revealed truth. We address five components:

- The relationship between revealed truth and literacy
- Control of the primary source(s) of the truth
- The integrity of the source(s) used
- Perspectives on how the primary source(s) should be used
- How open people are to alternative ways of uncovering truth.

We must admit from the start that the fundamental question, "Where does one find truth?", evokes a bit of a "chicken and egg" problem. Do people believe in God because a sacred text has convinced them of the truth of God's existence, or do they read the sacred text because God has planted the seeds of belief in their hearts which draws them to the sacred text? Conversely, do atheists refuse to recognize the possibility of a text like the Qur'an or Bible being a legitimate source of authority because of their fundamental commitment against the idea of a God, or because they've read and studied these books carefully and rejected God on that basis? The answer is probably somewhere in between for most people. So in some respects, the question about the extent to which a particular belief system affects economic development is not really a question of revelation vs. scientific methods of uncovering truths, but rather several other things such as the accuracy of its beliefs, the degree to which its adherents long to know what is true, and the openness they have to the many different ways that can be used to find truth.

The Relationship between Revealed Truth and Literacy

It is widely believed that poverty is related to illiteracy, which is true, and that illiteracy is related to lack of education, which is generally also the case. It is also widely accepted that poverty is a primary driver of poor education which makes for a vicious circle that traps people in poverty. What is much less widely understood is the relationship between religious beliefs and literacy. Some belief systems perpetuate poverty, because they are essentially non-literate, being passed on from generation to generation orally, without the need to read or write. Many tribal beliefs fall into this category. Other belief systems, like Confucianism and Christianity require literacy for full participation and give their participants a strong additional motivation (to the usual reasons) for wanting to increase literacy. Islam, too, is built around a sacred book, but with a noticeable and important difference from

Christianity and Confucianism. The emphasis in the latter belief systems is the application of reason to distill principles for living, while the emphasis in Islam is memorization and the avoidance of error. Belief systems with sacred texts also differ in the length and robustness of the texts, and the degree of literacy needed to comprehend and apply them. Belief systems with robust and lengthy texts, which also encourage reading, interpretation and application by large numbers of people are going to have a much greater impact on economic development because of their impact on literacy.

Control of the Primary Source(s) of the Truth

The core teachings or sacred texts of belief systems are sometimes held closely among a relatively small group of clergy or academic elites. However, in other cases they are widely distributed among believers. For example, the Reformation put the Bible and its ethical wisdom in the hands of the common people/masses to a much greater degree than happened either within Catholicism or Eastern Orthodoxy. Protestant readings of the Bible, especially in Northern Europe, eventually led to a belief that the wisdom of God was within the reach of all believers, which freed scholars from always having to practice theology to understand truth.[15] Theology, rather than being above everything, began to be seen more as one important field of investigation among many.

In some cases the state is instrumental in restricting the access of its people to religious information. Sometimes this is intentional as in Islamic states where other religions are illegal, but it can also be unintentional, such as when government controls the educational system. If the government accepts and promotes an official religion and also runs the educational system, that belief system will be given inordinate access to people's minds and hearts. This is also true where secularism is viewed not as one belief system among many but as inherently superior to religious perspectives on learning. It should be noted that this view does not require that, for example, secular humanism or materialism be studied formally (in spite of the fact those who self-identify with these beliefs may have articulated these teachings in books). Rather, they are espoused by default in countries that have tried to separate secular and religious beliefs and keep religious beliefs out of the educational process. In these environments, the secular belief system has come to be widely accepted and practiced among the masses. Of course Christian, Islamic, and other "religious schools" may also have legal rights in these countries. But the favored belief system, in this case secularism, will still have a disproportionate influence on the direction of economic development.

The Integrity of the Primary Source(s) Used

The integrity of the source of the core beliefs varies significantly among belief systems. This involves first of all the particular "source of truth" that is being appealed to, and secondly its trustworthiness. For example, most secular belief systems build on the foundation of "scientific" knowledge. Because of this, their conclusions will suffer if their sources are unqualified, the methods used unreliable, or the results so sketchy that they need to be supported by a host of assumptions and/or speculation.

Likewise, the sources of some oral traditions or sacred writings, or the methods used to pass them on to subsequent generations, may have been unreliable. So in the same way that it would be a mistake to assume all Christians, Muslims, or secular humanists think alike, it would also be a mistake to assume that all of the writings that religious people hold sacred, or scientific studies at the core of secular beliefs will hold up equally well when scrutinized or compared to each other.

It would also be a mistake, however, to judge the veracity of a particular scientific method or sacred text by the misuse of that method or text by a particular individual or group of people. Nevertheless, these kinds of things happen all too often, and are particularly damaging when entire belief systems are stigmatized by the actions of some fringe group. On one hand this has caused secularists to miss out on valuable religiously-informed wisdom and the benefit of the kinds of truths that come mostly by faith. On the other hand it has caused some religious people to close the doors to the benefits of the truths revealed by the work of secular scientists.

Perspectives on How the Source(s) Should be used

Related to this are the significant economic repercussions that come from wrong assumptions routinely made when using scientific methods, on the one hand, or the interpreting of sacred texts, on the other. To simplify, some people refuse to believe anything until it has been proven while others are content to believe almost anything until it has been disproved. This is also true of secular scientists, where, some are quite willing to keep useful products, such as new drugs, off the market until they can be proven safe beyond the shadow of a doubt, while others are very willing to experiment with new things, such as homeopathic drugs, even though they haven't been subjected to so much as a single scientific study. Because of incorrect assumptions about science, some good drugs have been pulled off the market with significant economic consequences, while at other times drugs have been rushed to market at significant risk to some people.

Of course we see the same kind of distinction among religious believers, where some read sacred texts assuming people should not do anything that is not expressly permitted in the text, while others read the text assuming people are free to do whatever is not expressly prohibited. The latter of these "ways of reading" will lead to radically different conclusions than the former.

In Mecca, for example, Muslim clerics initially opposed the installation of telephones because this technological tool was not expressly permitted in the Qur`an, and quite clearly could be used as tool of the devil. Only after hearing passages of the Qur'an read over the telephone were they convinced to allow them to be installed. Some scholars have argued that similar thinking contributed to the demise of the Ottoman Empire centuries earlier when Muslim leaders expressed opposition to the printing press. To this day, the impact of Islam has been muted (relative to, for example, Protestant Christianity) because of the assumption that it can no longer be the word of Allah if translated from Arabic into other languages. This assumption that a language itself is holy (which is also part of the history of the Hindu belief system about Sanskrit) has profound implications for development in that it limits the potential influence of the belief system on people outside of that language group. The Bible, on the other hand, has been translated into hundreds of languages,[16] with the result that its cultural and economic impact is more widespread.

Belief systems that rule out what is not expressly permitted in their oral traditions or sacred texts will experience significantly different economic outcomes than those whose sacred texts are capable of being applied to new situations and technologies as they arise. Those that also restrict access to religious knowledge, either by vesting it primarily with the clergy, or restricting the language or methods for communicating it, also risk the possibility that large numbers of people will conduct themselves in ways very unlike what the sacred texts would require or suggest. Interestingly, then, healthy economic development calls for both scientists and readers of sacred texts to neither rush to judgment (about the wisdom of new technologies, or the usefulness of other languages) nor proceed recklessly (and fail to call others to account). But what is perhaps most interesting and instructive is that the ability to find this middle ground is ultimately rooted in people's willingness to take risks and their sense of calling, which are in turn rooted in their ability to probe what is presently unknown, or perhaps even unknowable, while continuing to step forward in faith.

How Open People are to Alternative Ways of Uncovering Truth

Healthy economic development also requires clarity about what is true and what is false, regardless of the source of this clarity, and belief systems vary in how far afield they will go in their search for truth. For example, some Christians reject the results of particular scientific studies out of hand because they interpret those results as conflicting with wisdom/teachings laid out in the Bible, while others study these results, carefully with the assumption that they could shed light on or deepen their understanding of what the Bible teaches, and reject them only when convinced that they have been poorly constructed or carried out. Some atheists and agnostics reject the authority of the Bible out of hand while others have studied it carefully in the process of developing their beliefs. Some atheists and agnostics blindly trust scientific methods and assumptions and are perfectly content to remain gleefully ignorant about them, while others study them extensively and, in doing so, come to truly believe in them.

Religious believers who refuse to accept what can be learned about God, the world, or people through scientific experimentation and observation are doomed to repeat the mistakes made by the Catholic Church at the time of Galileo. Faith must be applied for people to flourish, or as the Biblical book of James puts it, "faith without works is dead." This could not only be interpreted to mean that the impact of a belief system is undercut when its adherents' actions contradict what they profess to believe, but it could also be interpreted to mean that if people claim to have faith but never take any risks based on that faith, their faith is in danger of atrophying as much as the muscles of a couch potato. This helps explain why many followers of Christ have over the centuries interpreted their call to faith as a call to scientific methods of uncovering truth, exploration and discovery. Likewise, secular humanists who limit their methods to the use of reason and their pursuits to the material world, or who assume science and technology are humankind's only possibility for salvation, risk missing the discovery of important information and the development opportunities that proceed from them. Innovation and discovery require risk taking, and risk taking requires, at least to some degree, the kind of vulnerability that often goes hand in hand with humility and faith. For economic progress to proceed in a healthy way, a balance of faith and prudence is needed, whether one perceives the universe to be like an orchestra playing to the score of a Master Composer or Director or little more than the ongoing momentum of an amalgamation of physical laws and processes.

Values, Goals, Priorities, Normativity, and Practices (things that govern life and dictate behavior)

As noted earlier, the way people answer the fundamental questions addressed in this and the previous chapter will trickle down to their values, goals, priorities, ideas about norms, and everyday actions. Many examples of this were already given in Chapters 10 and 11. In addition, different belief systems will vary in their coverage of and prescription for important attitudes and behaviors. One belief system may either mandate or absolutely prohibit a particular attitude or behavior that could significantly influence development. Another belief system may merely permit or restrict the same attitudes and behaviors, encourage or discourage them, or say nothing about them at all. In still other cases, a belief system may speak clearly to an attitude or behavior, but the message gets lost somewhere between the clergy and laity, or, if the message gets through, it may be distorted because a particular person or group distorts or misapplies it. All of these differences point to the need for a radically new model of how economic development takes place and how wealth is created, nurtured and maintained, and this model needs to properly account for how differences in belief systems affect economic outcomes. It is to precisely such a model that we now turn our attention.

Chapter 16: *Putting it All Together: An Integral Picture of the Wealth Creation and Economic Development Processes*

Introduction

Now that we have seen how the answers people give to the most fundamental questions of life determine their goals, attitudes, values, priorities, and behaviors, and how these in turn coalesce into a worldview that is at the core of the wealth creation and economic development processes, we need a model to illustrate this.[1] As the diagram on the following page indicates, economic development is a productive process, and it is useful to think of this process through the analogy of a rolling wheel. Before any wheel can function properly, "material" must be gathered for the building process. As the diagram illustrates, there are seven types of resources (wheel segments) that must be in place before the Development Wheel can be "rounded out" and function well. And since a round wheel will cover far more distance (more wealth creation and/or development) with less resource waste than a misshapen wheel, this model presumes that development requires incentives to build up, preserve, and replenish all seven of these forms of wealth/capital. A shortage in one or more of the needed inputs will result in something akin to the misshapen inner wheel in the diagram and will appreciably reduce people's standards of living, either in the short run, the long run, or both. A brief glance at the diagram makes it obvious that each country will have a uniquely *misshapen* wheel, primarily because many worldviews are ill suited for the job of building and balancing these seven different kinds of resources. The result may be a wheel that appears to be large and balanced or a wheel that appears to be small and misshapen and actually is. The U.S. is an example of the former, while many underdeveloped countries in Africa, Asia and Latin America are examples of the latter.

The word *capital* is used to describe these wheel segments because people familiar with economics are already accustomed to identifying land, machines, and financial investments as forms of capital. Here, the traditional understanding of capital is broadened to include communal and nonphysical things, such as systems, knowledge, trust relationships, ethics, and the like, that are every bit as important as physical and financial capital for productive activity to take place. The model also illustrates that capital can only be effectively built up in an atmosphere characterized by civil society and entrepreneurial activity. These in turn depend on the values of people, which are ultimately rooted in their view of the world. Both freedom and communication are critical to development, but as it turns out, they are not sufficient. They have the potential to accelerate the rotation of the wheel, but this will only be a good thing if the wheel is smooth, round, and of adequate size.

The Economic Development Wheel

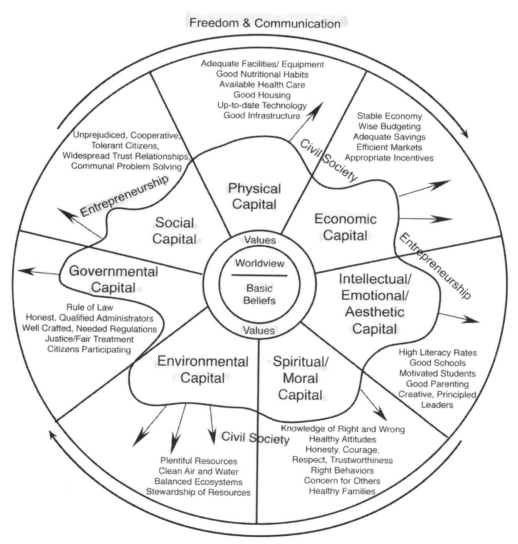

A Broadened Understanding of the Term Capital

Before proceeding, each of these forms of capital needs more explanation. Moving clockwise from the top of the wheel, we provide the following descriptions:

- **Physical capital** refers to assets like land, infrastructure, buildings, machinery, and other forms of applied technology, and also to tangible and intangible things that keep humans alive, safe, and physically productive, like nutritious food, health care, and housing, as well as freedom from violence, sexual assault, or child abuse. The assumption is that people will have enough rights in their property to maintain effective control over it, be secure in it, and be able to use it for their benefit and enjoyment.

- **Economic capital** includes the financial capital needed for companies to operate, such as traditional investments in stocks, bonds, and other financial assets, but also things that must be in place behind the scenes to encourage people and organizations to save and invest and to allow individuals to receive and retain the fruits of their labor. This includes wise macroeconomic and microeconomic decisions, such as those that keep currencies from excessive depreciation or unwarranted fluctuations, incentives for saving and investing, predictability and fairness in economic policies, and efficiency in markets, including financial markets. It also involves wise financial decisions by companies that allow them to create and preserve wealth through their business operations, as well as financial habits by individuals and families that do the same.

Underdeveloped economic capital by itself can nearly destroy the wealth in a society. Inflationary monetary policies cost millions of Russians, Argentines, and people of other countries their life savings when their currencies plunged. Price controls and other ill-advised intrusions into economies have resulted in severe product overuse (such as vodka in Russia), the misallocation of human resources (when people are prevented from taking jobs that remain vacant), waste of natural resources (such as when water rights are misallocated) and even destruction of the environment (such as when communal property rights are poorly defined).

- **Intellectual/emotional/aesthetic capital** includes things such as literacy rates, educational levels, quality of education, and the distribution of needed skills, intelligence, and creativity.

Too often in the past the human contribution to the economic process has been reduced to something vaguely known as "labor." Economists found it far too easy to use well-worn expressions like "land, labor and capital," which not only inadvertently separated the concepts of work and human intellectual development, but also made it sound like there are two fundamentally different kinds of people involved in economic activity – thinkers and doers. In reality, humans are complex creatures whose intellectual/emotional/spiritual/moral dimensions are not clearly separated, and all of these dimensions are of critical importance to the economic development process. More recently the term "human capital" has replaced the term "labor," and this clearly does a better job of incorporating the kinds of things described in the opening sentence of this paragraph. But this too is inadequate to explain the many facets of human activity that contribute to the economic development process.

Hence our term, intellectual/emotional/aesthetic capital, also includes what is often referred to today as "non-traditional intelligences," such as linguistics, logical-mathematical abilities, spatial capacity, physical ability, musical talent, or intrapersonal or interpersonal intelligence, which is particularly important to things like leadership, conflict resolution, social analysis, or the ability to nurture relationships. [2] This expanded definition calls attention to the fact that each book read by a child, each relationship built, each concert completed, or each paper written contributes a tiny amount to an "investment" with economic development consequences. But it is not just intelligence that matters; rather the return on this investment is even more important to economic development. University mathematics graduates who drive taxi cabs will not generate the same positive impact on their economies that those solving complex logistics problems will. Countries with high average levels of educational achievement may nevertheless have impaired intellectual capital if their educational systems focus too much on rote memorization and not enough on critical thinking, the importance of perspective, inference, or implication, or the application of knowledge. Reading may be at the core of the educational system, but if good listening skills or precision, relevance, or logic are not well integrated into the communication skills being taught, intellectual capital will also be impaired. And even if all of this is taught, but the language itself has significant limitations either in vocabulary or breadth of use, educational achievement may once again be an imperfect measure of intellectual capital. And, most of these nuances to intellectual capital will also be missed in empirical studies, which often have little choice but to use education as a proxy for intellectual capital.

The concepts of interpersonal and intrapersonal intelligence mentioned above are also very much interdependent with people's emotions, and for this reason, a lot of attention has been given in recent years to the concept of "emotional intelligence."[3] It has long been recognized that good grades don't always correlate with Nobel prizes or success on the job, and that raw IQ scores by themselves are poor predictors of success, and particularly economic success. [4] It is also becoming more apparent that other things, such as self-awareness, empathy, motivation, or self-regulation, including the ability to handle criticism or calm oneself, may actually play a more significant role in economic achievement. Emotional intelligence, then, represents a particularly important extension of the human capital concept, and one that is essential to a robust understanding of the economic development process. Emotions are wrapped up in one's ability to motivate oneself and others, persistence, the ability to delay gratification, mood regulation, empathy, reading others' emotions, hopefulness, the ability to connect with others, build relationships, etc. All of these are important to the way people function in families, organizations and society and therefore in the economic development process.

This also makes the family, which is the emotional incubator of the next generation, a particularly important cog in the economic development process. If a child watches television or is on the computer playing video games five hours per day (in relative isolation), he will likely be less capable of emotionally vibrant interaction with others than one who plays games, reads aloud, or holds conversations with his parents on a regular basis. Research by Dr. Stanley Greenspan has found that the following six experiences are provided by families to children who are emotionally and intellectually healthy:[5]

- Ongoing, loving, intimate relationships that develop care for others, empathy and trust;
- Lengthy, back-and-forth emotional dialogues to foster the beginnings of a sense of self, logic, and purposefulness;
- Long problem-solving discussions with gestures to foster early types of thinking and social skills;
- Stimulation appropriate to the baby's nervous system: sights, sounds, touches and other sensations to foster learning, language, awareness, attention and self-control;
- Shared use of creative ideas through pretend play in order to foster language and creativity; and
- Logical use of ideas through eliciting opinions and debates to promote logical thinking, planning and readiness for reading and math.

Much more could be said about intellectual/emotional capital, but doing so would immediately translate us into to the next form of critically important capital, spiritual/moral capital, because there is often no clear line between them. For example, emotionally cultivated empathy increases the likelihood of moral behavior. But, conversely, strong beliefs in the immorality of taking advantage of others, physically, sexually, or economically, cultivate empathy. Similarly, if spiritual/moral beliefs impede the desire of parents to educate their children (or, as is too often the case in some cultures, their girls), or encourage children to selfishly accumulate as much as they can for themselves, or make them fearful, or permit them to hate others, no amount of attention to the curriculum or high test scores among those who attend school will be able to counter these negative effects. Likewise, no amount of knowledge gained in school can substitute for the positive effects of children who enter school with beliefs and nurture that enable them to be secure, disciplined, tolerant, respectful, unselfish, or loving.

■ **Spiritual/moral capital**, then, includes things like honesty and integrity, the ability to distinguish right from wrong, moral behavior, limits to selfishness, respect/genuine concern for others, courage, and a host of other "positive values" which flow from people's basic beliefs and commitments and which profoundly affect the structure, direction, and effectiveness of their human activity. In the same way that technologically complex products have many subcomponents that embody engineering principles developed and perfected by previous generations, so too people's goals, attitudes, values, priorities, behaviors and ethical systems have been honed by family traditions, prayer, meditation, reflection, worship services, and/or readings of sacred texts/religious writings over long periods of time.

Spiritual/moral capital is broken out as a separate kind of human capital in part because spirituality is increasingly being recognized as an important force for shaping human thought and behavior *in addition to* intellectual and emotional variables. Additionally, an organization or leader's effectiveness is multiplied many times over when his heart and the hearts of his followers have been set in the right direction and these "habits of the heart" have become so well established as to function reflexively. Spiritual/moral capital does not represent the full impact of religious beliefs in our model, since religious beliefs are inextricably wound up in people's view of the world (which is at the center of the wheel) and in this sense, are more influential than any single form of capital. Religious beliefs, through the prism of our worldviews, color our perceptions of reality and greatly influence how we answer the most fundamental questions of life. In doing so, they also influence our understanding of what the word "civil" means in the expression "civil society," our willingness to take risks (and therefore our propensity for entrepreneurship) and our ability to build up all seven forms of capital.[6] This makes freedom of religion an essential part of development activity.

Spiritual/moral *capital*, on the other hand, represents the visible output of the kind of reflective activities that have traditionally been understood as religious. Like other forms of capital, the nature of the spiritual/moral capital built up will depend on the worldview at the center of the wheel. We should not assume that spirituality is automatically a good thing, just because the word has such a nice ring about it. It can either help or hinder the economic development process. Some forms of spirituality can be quite counterproductive to economic activity as, for example, when they suggest that meditating all day every day is morally superior to working, or that begging is the moral equivalent of working. But other forms can have a very positive effect, such as when belief systems promote healthy child-rearing practices, are education focused, promote significant concern for others, or inculcate attitudes and behaviors such as honesty, courage, respect, or trustworthiness that are essential for healthy economic development.

- **Environmental capital** (often referred to as natural capital) includes such things as raw materials, clean air, pure water, good soil, adequate sunlight, species diversity, intact ecosystems, etc. Some of this capital is renewable (e.g., forests or fisheries) and some is not (e.g., oil, minerals). Understanding the true value of environmental capital is one of the most complex tasks involved in economic development, and for this reason the task is often avoided and resources are simply valued at the cost of extraction, or at the price that equates short term supply and demand. This makes their value very dependent on, for example, the supply of spiritual/moral capital. If people are very self-centered or ignorant of the connections between their actions and the well-being of generations yet to come, environmental capital is likely to be considered free or nearly free and easily depleted. In addition, it is often difficult to know the potential value of environmental capital until it has been depleted. For example, after decades of deforestation, sparrows were at one point declared rural pests in China because they ate the people's grain. Chinese authorities instituted a three day campaign to drive them out of cities by making noise, harassing them, and bludgeoning them to death when they fell to the ground exhausted. Eventually, however, insects (and particularly locusts) multiplied and ravaged the crops, contributing to the deaths of millions of people. At that point sparrows were removed from the list of official pests, but not until after the damage was done. The same is true to some degree for most other resources. Gasoline was once dumped into the ocean when it was viewed as a worthless byproduct of the process used to produce kerosene. With the eventual invention of the automobile, of course, it became clear that this was a mistake.

■ **Governmental capital** includes what is sometimes referred to as "political capital" (the resources available to political leaders to design and carry out policy) but also includes elements such as the "rule of law," fair elections, efficient and effective regulatory agencies, a widespread concern for justice, well-established conflict resolution procedures, widespread political participation, and the capability to deliver needed "public goods."

The rule of law is defined differently by different authors but nearly always includes following careful procedures when making laws, rather than allowing them to be instituted by the whim of those in power. It also includes the effective communication of those laws to those affected by them, consistent application and enforcement of the law to *all* people in the political entity, and an independent judiciary for interpreting the laws. Russ Webster gets even more specific than this when he indicates that the rule of law implies access to government decision makers, as well as *rational* laws governing business, property rights, contracts, anti-monopoly policies, taxation, patent protection, licensing, whistleblower protection, corporate accountability to capital suppliers and government, and financial disclosure for public officials (*Fighting Corruption*, p. 135). Fair elections presume that people will have real candidate choices, will be able to vote their conscience without undue pressure or fear, and they will have good reason to feel confident in the impartiality and integrity of those tallying the vote. Effective regulatory agencies are those that promote fair treatment, see themselves as advocates of those they regulate, and partner with them to find efficient ways to regulate that do not unduly burden law abiding citizens and organizations. Effective conflict resolution procedures limit the number of steps and the economic burden of establishing and enforcing legal rights in areas such as contract disputes, property registration, creditor/debtor relationships, and bankruptcy proceedings. Widespread political participation reflects a sense of governmental "ownership" among the public and a recognition that government exists for the people rather than the other way around. And, finally, the willingness to deliver public goods, like clean water and sanitation, education, adequate ports, pothole free roads, or parks is important because government is often in a position to deliver these goods more efficiently than groups of private organizations or individuals. By providing these goods and doing it efficiently, it will not only make its people more productive, but will also make its organizations more efficient and competitive.

Underdeveloped government capital, on the other hand, in the form of widespread corruption or arbitrary laws and regulations, can undermine physical capital (as infrastructure is ignored), intellectual capital (by neglecting education), economic capital (through disincentives to saving or investing), spiritual/moral capital (by favoring a particular belief system such as secularism), etc. At its worst it leads to a collapse of the public order and long term damage to all of the other forms of wealth.

Government capital, then, is one of the most critical forms of capital, not because it is necessarily more important than the others, but because government carries with it a kind of authority that is unavailable in the other segments of the wheel. This means that bad government decisions have the potential to do extraordinary damage because there are few paths around their authority, other than risking the penalty for breaking the law. This is one reason that widespread corruption has the potential to cause a breakdown in most if not all of these components of governmental capital, as well as do serious damage to most other forms of capital. This can be contrasted to problems in other wheel segments, where people may have other options for obtaining the needed capital when one path is blocked.

■ **Social capital** may be defined as a widely shared commitment to the values of trust and mutual assistance demonstrated by the habits of cooperation. Social capital is best understood by observing the myriad associations that people form in all areas of life, but especially the hundreds of thousands of advocacy groups, church committees, sports clubs, parent-teacher associations, ethnic celebrations, and community service boards, that are voluntary in nature. It also includes the kinds of attitudes that permit people to work well with those who are unlike them. Therefore, a high degree of social capital requires an appreciation for diversity and the ability to achieve unity in spite of diversity. It requires that unjustified discrimination be kept to a minimum so that the rich supply of talent spread around the society can be employed productively. This not only frees people up to take the jobs they are most qualified for, but also increases the likelihood that they will receive equal access to the things they need to apply and develop their talents, such as education, property, raw materials, or credit, as well as the ability to use these things as they see fit. It also requires that all people be given the needed decision making power, negotiating power, opportunities to speak, etc. that are needed for full economic and political participation at the individual, household, business and society levels.

The Importance of Capital

Understanding the full potential of the Economic Development Wheel for illustrating the wealth creation and economic development processes requires a number of clarifications. It must be noted first of all that the process of income generation is essentially a byproduct of the quest to buildup/accumulate the seven different kinds of capital. The model, then, is a much more comprehensive visual picture of an economy's health potential than a simple measure of income like GDP.[7] Income (GDP) is to an economy as a fresh supply of water is to a barrel. But the incoming fresh water, presumably from a faucet, is only part of the picture. The potential good that water can do depends on having the right amount available when it is needed, which in turn depends on three different things: the size of the barrel and the water presently in it, the amount of water coming into it via the faucet (income) and the amount of water leaking or evaporating out of it (depreciation or depletion). Similarly, economic development requires investment, which amounts to building up the seven forms of capital in the wheel. So, no matter how large GDP is, if the income it represents is never used to build up capital or to reduce depreciation and depletion, it is unlikely to end up significantly improving people's lives in the future. Paying attention to the buildup of capital, on the other hand, incorporates not only the important role that income plays, but also other things, such as how the income is used, what is depleted/used up in the process of generating the income, and what may be borrowed in the process of generating income. Accumulated capital is also important because it insures against the vagaries of income by providing a cushion against economic uncertainty, in the same way that water in a bucket remains available for use even when the incoming water supply is shut off. Measurements of accumulated capital also have the ability to incorporate expectations about the future, including the likelihood of sustainability. For example, when a company designs a product that people find useful, its market value increases almost immediately because its current value is based on both its present *and* future prospects. Likewise, a home that is predicted to meet people's needs well into the future will be valued at considerably more than one that is expected to deteriorate or become obsolete. The accumulation of capital then (especially when the term capital is broadly defined to include things like education, health care, ethical systems, etc.), is simply a better measure of the economic health of a community or nation than commonly cited statistics like GDP. And when the word "capital" is used this way, it can be freed of the usual "capitalist" trappings and be viewed as a good thing since it can no longer be reduced to imply an unhealthy preoccupation with the accumulation of money and/or material things.

The Importance of Intangibles

More than half the wheel consists of capital that can best be described as *intangible*. This means that material and non-material, tangible and intangible, market-valued and non-market valued elements are all important to economic development, even though it is only the tangible forms that are routinely measured and targeted. In ancient times, people thought of wealth in terms of natural resources and hoarded things like gold and silver. Later, and especially at the time of the industrial revolution, they began to see the value of transforming these resources into machines and other forms of physical capital. Later the value of exchanging financial, intellectual, and governmental capital moved to the forefront. Some world leaders are beginning to see the potential benefits from the exchange of social and spiritual/moral capital and of facilitating discussions that penetrate to the level of worldview.[8] The stage may finally be set for the value of exchanging the least tangible forms of capital such as beliefs, attitudes, principles or behaviors to be understood. People like Amartya Sen and organizations like the World Bank have captured some, but certainly not all, of this with their emphasis on the importance of mediating institutions.

It can be plausibly argued that the story of modern wealth creation is largely the story of the discovery and accumulation of increasingly intangible forms of capital. It is also arguable that the more intangible forms of capital are the things that give companies and countries their greatest competitive advantage in the global economy - precisely because they are less visible and less transferable than more tangible/traditional forms of capital. Our model suggests that future global increases in economic development will be as dependent on the movement of these intangible forms of capital as the development of the past 50 years was dependent on the movement of physical and financial capital.

The development wheel diagram also points out that the process of wealth creation goes far beyond the success of the business sector or the measurement of its output. Much of what allows a business to effectively create wealth stems from a buildup of capital that occurs outside of the business; non-profit organizations, governments, schools, even churches and stay-at-home moms or dads are integral to the wealth creation and economic development processes, even though they don't show a profit in the same way a company would be expected to.

Building and Retaining Healthy Amounts of Capital

All of the elements that build up or prevent the depletion of financial or physical forms of wealth also apply to each of the five other kinds of capital that make up the wheel.[9] For instance, a portion of each of these seven asset/capital categories can be traced to an endowment or "savings" from the past, each can only be built up gradually over time, each benefits from better methods of multiplying or replenishing it, and each has the potential to either depreciate or be depleted. Many people are quite arbitrary in the attention they give to this. For example, there is widespread concern over the depletion of natural capital, but we ought to be equally concerned about the demise of social or spiritual/moral capital. In the same way that a belief system that is overly materialistic puts the natural environment at risk, a belief system that is overly individualistic or secular can put social capital and spiritual/moral capital at risk, posing a double serious threat to a the idea of "sustainable" economic development. In fact, some social scientists argue that widespread fracturing of families and communities in economically developed countries testifies to the depletion of various aspects of social and spiritual/moral capital almost to the point of no return - in the same way that some natural ecosystems have been disturbed to the point that it is now nearly impossible to reestablish the complex natural interactions necessary for their survival. This has provoked fear that, in the same way that pretending natural laws do not exist can irreparably damage an ecosystem, pretending that all spiritual, moral, or social principles are up for grabs can irreparably damage the social and moral fabric of a society.

Chapter 17: The Development Wheel Continued: Structure and Core

Capital Impairment

The model introduced in the last chapter has applicability to many social units, so it can help us identify and better understand development problem areas at many levels – e.g., countries, regions, subcultures or even organizations. With respect to countries it is equally useful for analyzing problems and finding potential solutions in rich and poor, developing, industrial, and post-industrial service economies. One problem that all countries face is shortages in or impairments to some forms of capital. Referring once again to the diagram, the reality in every society, community or individual life is best represented by the inner distorted circle. As noted earlier, an excessive emphasis on material and financial capital in the U.S. has eroded spiritual/moral and environmental capital, and there is good evidence from the breakdown of the family, the declining quality of K-12 education, and the excessive prison population that intellectual/emotional capital and social capital have suffered significant erosion as well. Fortunately, in a world characterized by relatively open trade and financial flows, the U.S. has been able to secure needed resources from other countries, both natural resources and human resources, so as to maintain a semblance of balance even as these trends persist.

Of course, it is by no means clear that less economically or educationally developed countries are in any better shape when it comes to capital impairment. They struggle with different kinds of capital impairment, but their problems are certainly not less severe. Russia, for example, retains vast quantities of natural resources within its massive geographical area (covering eleven time zones) but is faced with significant shortages of spiritual/moral capital caused by seven decades of systematic attempts to wipe out religious belief, and the endemic corruption related to this. In addition, after the breakup of the Soviet Union, most of the member states also faced acute shortages of financial capital because of the inability of a centrally planned economy based on Marxist principles to create wealth. Although some of this shortage has since been alleviated by the exploitation of its natural resources, some continued (albeit uneven) development of financial markets and businesses, and the import of some foreign capital as its economy has stabilized, many serious problems must still be overcome.

Many countries in sub-Saharan Africa, on the other hand, are rich in both natural resources and some forms of social capital. And although some are in the midst of a spiritual transformation, the impact of which is still unknown, as a group they are plagued by shortages of spiritual/moral and governmental capital, and the scourge of AIDS had decimated their intellectual/emotional and financial capital. Several Middle Eastern countries, although swimming in financial capital because of their oil revenues, lag behind in intellectual capital, in part because financial surpluses make it easy for them to hire foreigners to do much of their work, making education less important to the maintenance of a high standard of living than in most other countries. Additionally, they have traditionally lagged behind in their education of women. However, even though educational activities for women have significantly improved in recent years, (e.g., more than 50% of university grads in Saudi Arabia in recent years have been women), opportunities for women to use their education outside of the home remain scarce. For example, at the time of this writing approximately only 5% of all jobs in Saudi Arabia are held by female workers. The point here is not to deprecate any particular country or region, but to recognize that in an imperfect world every society, community, organization, or individual life requires a unique "development plan" to balance out its wheel, since it has greater or lesser problems in different segments of the wheel.

The Interrelationship between the Forms of Capital

Another reason all countries and societies have development problems is because the contribution of each segment of the wheel to the creation of wealth depends on the health of the other segments. A machine will not just increase in value when moved from a dusty warehouse to a factory where it can be used more intensively. It will also increase in value when it is operated in a responsible manner, by a moral, wise, socially-connected and stable individual who is trusted and valued by a team of solid managers in a financially responsible company operating in a politically and economically stable country. Likewise, a person will command a higher wage because they too are more productive in such an environment. Similarly, the effectiveness and "value" of a government will be greater where it is not saddled with the cost of restoring a natural environment that has been abused or depleted, and where companies and individuals obey the laws and are otherwise honest, productive, and cooperative so the legal system is not forced to resolve frivolous disputes or problems that could have been avoided with a modicum of morality/ethics. In a similar manner, the returns to financial capital are multiplied in an appropriate intellectual and moral climate.

This mutual strengthening of the segments of the wheel occurs in part because each form of capital can be rightly described as both an input and an output with respect to human productive activity.

In addition to being an essential input to the production process, each of the seven segments of the development wheel is also an output of economic activity. For example, synagogues and churches are not thought to carry out economic activity, but they none-the-less have buildings, budgets and paid employees as inputs, and objectives, programs, and activities aimed at "producing" measurable spiritual/moral capital outputs, such as wisdom, character, and healthy interpersonal relationships that are very much needed in the organizations that employ their parishioners. Other not-for-profit organizations, including educational institutions also require inputs in the form of all seven forms of capital in order to "produce" their social or intellectual capital. Further reflection reveals that machines and technology are both inputs and outputs, and that physical items like beds, food, and microwave ovens are both part of measured economic output and inputs that enable people to be well-fed and well-rested enough to be productive at their jobs.

It stands to reason, then, that careful attention to the *interdependence* of the segments is also necessary to build, preserve, or replenish all forms of wealth/capital in a society because the misuse or neglect of one sector of the wheel will eventually lead to problems in the other sectors. For example, material capital, including technological artifacts, although having the potential to build up social capital, can also erode it if people use it imprudently. Examples include using mp3 players, television sets and computers to isolate oneself from friends and families, using an automobile as an excuse to live a great distance from one's workplace, or using text messages as a substitute for face-to-face time with family members. More "toys" than a family can effectively make use of unnecessarily depletes environmental capital. And in the same way that agricultural overproduction can exhaust topsoil, or mining can deplete scarce mineral resources, excessive working hours or an overemphasis on "making money" can exhaust a workforce and damage other forms of capital.[1]

Conversely, when appropriate attention is given to *all* the forms of capital, the opposite can occur. Careful attention to social capital has the potential to build up economic capital as when healthy relationships reduce employee frustration and on-the-job waste, and companies have the freedom to delegate authority or relax internal controls. Technology can preserve environmental capital, such as when consumers demand, and manufacturers produce, more fuel efficient cars (between the oil crises in the mid-1970s and the year 2000 the typical American car was driven 2000 more miles per year but used 200 gallons less gas). Physical and financial capital in the form of adequate buildings, desks, computers and labs on college campuses spur the buildup of intellectual/emotional capital. Workers who regularly replenish their spiritual/moral capital, when given the flexibility and freedom to pray, meditate, or attend worship services, are not only able to build up social capital as they participate in church fellowship and community outreach activities, but they are also less likely to use technology to scam or defraud others and more productive on the job, or generous with their money.

Chapter 17

The Importance of Balance

The ideal healthy state of an economy or society occurs when all sectors are in balance, when the outer rim of the wheel is a perfect circle and people experience wholeness and well-being in every aspect of life. This observation squares with a large amount of research that finds no clear relationship between income and happiness or "subjective well-being" as it is often termed by researchers, once income exceeds a certain amount. Up to some level, money is useful in balancing the wheel since it be helpful in accumulating other needed forms of capital, but beyond a certain point, it does little more than imbalance the wheel rather than add to people's happiness.

David Myers' extensive summary of the research on happiness backs this up. He concludes that hardly any of the things which we generally assume would be related to happiness, such as age, race, location, education, money, economic status, pleasure, possessions, or even physical abilities or disabilities are particularly useful in explaining differences in happiness or hopefulness. He notes that psychologists typically believe that so-called "objective" variables, a category that includes wealth and income, are unlikely to adequately explain more than twenty-five percent of differences in measured happiness among people. Much more important than money, according to Myers, are the difficult-to-measure things like

- whether one sees significant meaning in life - e.g. feels his work is significant, or believes in God
- perceives a good deal of control over her life - e.g. has job security or political influence
- is healthy, has an optimistic personality, or has close supportive relationships, e.g., with friends, family, church and social groups, or
- experiences disciplined renewal - e.g., gets regular sleep, exercise or reflection time. [2]

We are of course interested in development here, rather than happiness, but it is hard to miss the relationship between Myers' list and the Development Wheel. In addition, the research on happiness should be noted by government officials because their policies must generally satisfy people to be successful. So although targeting income level increases may rightfully be a high government priority in the short run, it will likely be ineffective in improving people's sense of wellbeing beyond a certain point. It is better viewed as *one* means to a limited end, and one target among many, which together aim to balance all seven forms of capital.

A less obvious but more important corollary of the happiness research is that satisfaction levels may be as high as possible in highly developed countries only when the worldviews of their citizens become aligned with the things that bring true satisfaction. Once people have a good education, a secure income stream, adequate clothing, a comfortable and safe place to live, and the other necessities of life, they may need to reflect on the meaning of life, see their natural environment cleaned up and protected, or use their wealth to increase opportunities for others before they experience significant increases in happiness. This suggests that rounding out the development wheel is very much dependent on knowing what *should* be done, in addition to what can be done, which is both at the core of the wheel and one of the products of spiritual/moral capital.

Application to Developing Countries

The interdependence between the seven forms of capital creates a particular conundrum in the developing world. Many poor countries are plagued by a shortage of scientists, engineers, and doctors. One reason for this is that the intellectual development of these people depends on the presence of the other six forms of capital. Low wages, poorly equipped labs, too few colleagues, power outages, family issues, disease, lack of job security, the inability to worship freely, corruption, political upheaval, or war all have the potential to temper the optimism of "the best and brightest" for returning or staying in their home countries, and otherwise stifle their contribution to their communities, countries and professions. In the saddest cases it results in decisions to work permanently outside of their home countries. It was reported in 2004 that of 600 doctors trained in Zambia, only 50 were still in the country, and that there were more Malawian doctors in Manchester, England than in Malawi.[3]

Similar challenges exist in developing countries with respect to all forms of capital in the development wheel. For example, development workers have long known that providing essential personal needs such as food, water, shelter or medicine without initiating fundamental changes in what people think and believe may only alleviate an immediate problem without providing long term gain. Most missionaries know that addressing a person's spiritual needs and moral struggles without dealing with basic physical needs, unemployment, deficient infrastructure, or a dangerous environment also falls short of holistic development. When aid came *too quickly* into Malawi in the early 1990s, they were able to eliminate school fees and rapidly increase enrollment, but found themselves unable to come up with enough qualified teachers to handle all of the students who flocked to the schools. Balancing the wheel, then, involves far more than trying to fix a particular problem or promoting "economic activity." It could of course mean things like bringing food to drought-stricken areas, or books to educationally-disadvantaged children, but the wheel analogy makes it clear that the term "needed resources" also includes complex social arrangements, systems, institutions, and beliefs which are encompassed by terms such as social capital, governmental capital, and spiritual/moral capital.

Microfinance serves as a good current example of the economic development potential of fixing a flat spot on the wheel, but it also serves as a reminder that the benefits associated with the provision of one kind of capital are severely limited when other forms of capital are also in short supply. For example, microfinance lenders have focused inordinately on women in their financing activities, in part because of their inferior cultural status in many developing countries, but mostly because of how they tend to use the income generated by the activities that the micro-loans are financing. In particular, they are much more likely than men to use their financial capital to simultaneously build up other forms of capital as they spend it on health, nutrition and education for their children.[4] But even when borrowers use their money in constructive ways, the economic development impact remains small relative to what could happen with radical changes in worldview. Seamstresses and street vendors, working individually, will be unlikely to achieve the productivity gains associated with economies of scale, world class technology, sophisticated organizational communications systems and high value added products. And even the most ambitious microfinance borrowers will be hard pressed to reach anything close to their potential if laws allow others to routinely exploit them, or they are collectively unable to gain or retain access to things like safe food and water supplies.

Developing countries may also, in light of the wheel, want to reexamine conventional wisdom in areas like development aid, population control, wage minimums, or economic stimulus programs. For example, external aid is highly sought after and widely agreed to be helpful, especially when used for things like education. But giving computers to disadvantaged students does little good if they do not also receive the knowledge they need to run them and/or fix them when they malfunction. And educating PhDs is of marginal benefit unless they receive the *right kind* of education, which includes the development of a worldview that motivates them to round out the wheels of their institutions and countries, and the *opportunity* to apply it. In other words, aid will be most productive when it addresses worldview issues, is spread out over the different wheel segments, targets those most in need of being built up, and focuses on equipping people to do this. Likewise, reducing population, or at least its rate of increase, is often cited as an essential step in economic development, but this may *or may not* be a good thing. It depends on the status of the other forms of capital. If talented, energetic, flexible young people are needed to build up and make use of the other forms of capital, policies aimed at population control may not be the best solution. Similarly, the concept of a just wage is nice, but if unemployment is a problem, policies forcing a higher-than-market wage on employers will simply cause them to hire fewer people, substitute other forms of capital for labor, or start employing labor from another location/country, exacerbating the unemployment problem. And finally, government can lower interest rates to try to stimulate development, but if economic/financial capital is already the thing in shortest supply, lower rates will make it even scarcer and will decrease the productivity of each of the other six forms of capital, harming development. Seeing the big picture, then, in particular seeing where the wheel is misshapen and/or the problems at the core, is central to successful development at both the micro and macro level.

The Core

It is for these among many other reasons that values are placed between the hub of the wheel and the capital segments, and worldview is placed at the core. Values critically affect the shape and functioning of the wheel and are themselves shaped by worldviews and foundational commitments. They need a prominent place in our diagram for at least three reasons that flow from our earlier discussions: 1) the minds and hearts of people with differing religious beliefs are wired in very different ways; 2) the power of belief is as pervasive for those who put their faith in money or technology as it is for those who put their faith in Allah or Christ; and 3) these beliefs exert powerful effects on wealth creation and economic development.

It should also be noted that even if having people with good values and attitudes added only a five percent efficiency gain in a business, the businesses that employ these people will still have a continuous competitive advantage in the marketplace. One reason for this is that materials, financial capital, and even technical know-how are much easier to transfer from one organization than beliefs, values and attitudes. The upshot of this is that businesses that hope to compete globally cannot pretend that they are value-free institutions that exist only to make money, and that they have the freedom to relegate values and beliefs to less competitive places like homes and churches. The best companies intentionally choose healthy values and do their best to inculcate them in their employees and infuse them into their organizational policies, procedures, and practices. Countries must do the same. For example, a country cannot be internationally competitive if its people have poor health. But good health won't simply happen in the absence of a public discussion of values and the national will to change things. The tragedy of AIDS, for example, by itself dwarfs all of the positive efforts to help Africa grow. And although AIDS is often thought to be under control in countries like the U.S., it still exacts a heavy human and economic toll around the world. The prevention of and solution to the AIDS epidemic has always been both medical and moral. Although compounded by a lack of medical knowledge, awareness, education, testing, means of protection, and antiviral drugs, AIDS transmission among adults, and consequently transmission from mothers to children, could never have reached epidemic proportions in the absence of two significant moral lapses: widespread sexual contact outside of monogamous marriage relationships, and the willingness of stronger people to impose their sexual will on those weaker than they.[5] The consequences of this for development have been tragic. And the hard-to-hear truth is that money and time spent fighting *preventable* diseases is money and time not spent building infrastructure, preparing the workforce of the future or solving other more intractable problems.[6]

The same line of reasoning extends to the care and maintenance of infrastructure, our political processes, psychological health, moral values, ecosystems, and every other component of the seven segments of our wheel. Problems can always be solved most efficiently when we bring all needed resources to bear on them *before* they get out of hand. But the set of potential solutions that we see and our collective willingness to take the hard medicine that is necessary to attempt these solutions are both dependent on how we see and understand the world. Technological solutions to the AIDS problem, although necessary, should not automatically be presumed superior to moral solutions simply because they are more compatible with the prevailing worldview.

The main reason for this is that all worldviews contain blind spots. A *materialistic worldview* will result in a development wheel that bulges in the areas of financial and physical capital, but is concave in other areas, such as social, intellectual/emotional or spiritual/moral capital. In such a world, houses, cars and people will tend to be bigger than they need to be, storage systems and garage organizers will be big sellers; storage spaces filled with barely used possessions will command premium rents, and education will have to be nearly free for the materially-satisfied majority to take advantage of it. A worldview that elevates fame and success to god-like status will likely be filled with status symbols: cars will be designed as much to evoke envy as to get efficiently from point A to point B, massive "trophy" homes will be filled with empty space or barely used possessions, and entertainment shows following the lifestyles of the rich and famous will clog the TV airwaves.

Strong elements of an *individualistic worldview* will ensure that lavish weddings will be followed up by relatively short marriages, that the number of occupants per square meter in homes will decrease over time, that fences will separate neighbors, and products will be increasingly personalized. Of course none of these worldview elements will be observed in their "pure form," and all will be in some way limited by each other.

A *Darwinian/Malthusian worldview* can serve to limit the excesses of materialistic or individualistic worldview elements because it is strongly rooted in the belief that resources are scarce and difficult if not impossible to replenish, which often translates to an unspoken assumption that the world is zero sum. The economic development wheel recognizes the role of scarcity by noting that *some* resources on the wheel are limited and can be replenished only with great difficulty, but overall it makes it clear that wealth creation is not zero sum game. This is most obvious when we think of the value added to raw materials when they are processed into something more useful. Sand transformed into silicon chips has its value increased thousands of times over in the process. A professor who shares useful ideas with a student has enriched that student's intellectual capital with no appreciable loss of intellectual capital to himself. So, although there are limitations to economic development from a materialistic point of view (since material resources will eventually be depleted where materialistic and individualistic worldviews hold the day), there is no reason that development cannot continue indefinitely if people can be weaned from these kinds of worldviews and find more creative ways to serve each other.[7] The development wheel illustrates that there is no reason that sustainable growth cannot take place, as long as people become increasingly aware of the limited role that material things play in their wellbeing, and choose to invest more of their increasing incomes in the pursuit of wisdom, ethics, community building, or helping others, and less in material self-indulgence. But this can only happen from the core outward.

Chapter 18: The Development Wheel Continued – Essential Catalysts

The Key Role of Entrepreneurs in Development

A closer look at the development wheel reveals that two key elements in the capital building process are civil society and entrepreneurship. They should both be viewed as critical tools that are needed to build all forms of capital and round out the wheel. Both of these activities amount to "bottom up" efforts to build up capital. Civil society depends a great deal on people who have come to be known as "social entrepreneurs," while business requires the more traditional "economic entrepreneurs." Both types of entrepreneurs can be described as people with the vision to see what society needs or wants, and the skills passion and persistence to start an organization capable of channeling the necessary resource inputs (forms of capital) for the purpose of producing and distributing products or services that fulfill these needs and wants. Unfortunately, in materialistic societies, most of the attention often goes to the venture capital firms that fund business startups and to the wealthy individuals who make national headlines for their large contributions to not-for-profit organizations. But the wheel makes clear that for these organizations to thrive; all of the other forms of capital must be put in place as well. In any event, it makes good sense to describe both types of entrepreneurs as "capital gatherers," in the sense that all seven forms of capital must be brought together in proper proportion for not-for-profits (or NGOs) and businesses to thrive and contribute to healthy development.

The level of entrepreneurial activity is very much affected by worldview. It is often stymied by misguided government regulations, which are in turn also rooted in elements of people's worldviews. For example, in many post-communist countries business people are still viewed, at best, with suspicion. In countries where such beliefs are widespread, little attempt is made to distinguish law-abiding, value-creating, socially responsible businesses from scam artists. Assumptions are too often made that all business people are only concerned about profits, themselves, or that they are all too willing to usher in negative cultural change, or exercise undue influence over government. In fact, since worldview is so pervasive, some languages even lack the vocabulary to effectively distinguish business people from speculators, predators, or exploiters.

These negative characterizations about businesses can be accurate about some businesses– but in many poor countries, they are far too often applied to most or all businesses. They may also be exaggerated and perpetuated by political or academic elites, the media, and even the church, mosque or temple. In such an environment, government often feels justified in restricting business startups, controlling prices, interest or exchange rates, or imposing tariffs, quotas or impediments to the free flow of goods and/or movement of capital, and, in the worst case, confiscating assets or entire companies or nationalizing entire industries. A byproduct of this anti-business sentiment is the demise of civil society, since entrepreneurs are also at the core of not-for-profit startups, and these organizations also end up being similarly restricted by cumbersome restrictions on economic activity. One reason for this is that, for the most part, businesses and not-for-profit organizations need the same things to function properly. Not-for-profits need financial capital just like businesses do, with the primary difference being that not-for-profit assets tend to be financed mostly by donations instead of by owners and creditors. Both organizations also need highly qualified workers and managers, sound buildings and equipment, ethical conduct, highly developed trust relationships, and the other things that comprise our seven forms of capital. Both groups can be prevented from accomplishing their missions by a corrupt government, by a shortage of funding, by a shortage of qualified or trustworthy employees, by improperly maintained equipment, or by the absence of any of the other things that make up the seven forms of capital. As noted earlier, serious damage done by the absence of just one capital component, because its absence will lower the productivity of all of the other forms of capital, will make both types of entrepreneurs far less effective in rounding out their organizational wheels and accomplishing their goals. Recent research by the World Bank has made this painfully obvious with respect to business startups, but it is equally true for social entrepreneurs and NGOs.

Because of the critical role that social and economic entrepreneurship play in the development process, countries with grossly underdeveloped businesses and not-for-profit organizations and few entrepreneurs will have either poorly functioning institutions or, in some cases, hardly any well-developed institutions at all. They will have economic activity, but it will often be the type that has limited potential to add value, characterized mostly by the production of subsistence items and traditional cultural artifacts, which tend to be low "value added," and relatively low-productivity trading activity. This paucity of entrepreneurs may also mean that citizens in these countries will wait for their government to do from the top down what small groups working from the bottom up could have accomplished far earlier.

Chapter 18

The Importance of Civil Society

Civil society is not only necessary for entrepreneurs to effectively build up all seven forms of capital in their needed proportions, but it is also important in its own right. We briefly defined the term in Chapter 2, where we first used it, but its importance merits a look at some of its history. Scholars trace the concept of civil society all the way back to the Greeks, but it had a very different meaning at that time than it does today. The term was used by the Greeks to refer to the importance of the state to the development of good people and a good society. The modern use of the term has much less to do with government and much more to do with voluntary communal problem-solving efforts. The most recent spate of attention to the term can perhaps best be traced to December of 1948 when the General Assembly of the United Nations (U.N.) adopted the Universal Declaration of Human Rights with a vote of forty-eight in favor, zero opposed.[1] Human rights, as described in this document and as generally understood by their advocates today, call for the protection of individuals and groups from political oppression, underscore their right to earn a living, and promote the establishment of political and economic conditions that promote dignity for all. Most of the thirty articles in *The Declaration*[2] focused on the least controversial rights such as the right to life; liberty; freedom of religion; freedom from arbitrary arrest, presumed guilt, slavery or torture; equal protection under the law; impartial public hearings; the right to privacy; freedom of movement, association, employment; equal pay for equal work; marriage and family; and property ownership.[3]

It is important to note that the *Universal Declaration* came into existence primarily to address the relationship between a state and its citizens, rather than to articulate the thousands of institutions, laws, processes and values necessary for a truly civil society. In spite of this limited purpose, the term civil society has now become a widely used term for referring to an *independent* sphere of activity or a group of mediating institutions that is not only separate from the state but which provides a buffer between the individual and the state, and guards against the tyranny of the state. Its popularity increased when it became a preferred term for describing the ideals of dissidents struggling against oppressive dictatorships, particularly in Eastern Europe and Latin America. And during the 1990s, when a truly civil society first became an imaginable possibility for many of the newly-free people of the world, the word took on various other shades of meaning as it spread from the pens of academics to the back alleys of world.

We will use the term here to describe *a set of institutions, processes and attitudes that promote cooperation among individuals, private associations and government agencies to produce practical solutions to common problems,* and further note that it commonly assumes the existence of *widespread participation, transparent decision making structures, and a commitment to peaceable change.* But we would like to go beyond this to suggest how we might measure it. Robert Bothwell's summary of the approaches to doing this is helpful in this regard.[4] He groups the many approaches to assessing the degree to which civil society exists in a country into the following four categories.

- Observing behaviors: i.e., do we see much evidence in the society of trust, openness, participation, public debate, etc?
- Inspecting societal foundations: i.e., are freedom of speech, religion, association, the rule of law, educational opportunity, capable government and political processes in place?
- Examining broad outcomes: i.e., is income widely distributed, and literacy rates or life expectancy high?
- Examining institutions: i.e., how many religious organizations, community-based organizations, clubs, voluntary groups, consumer groups, unions, professional associations, etc. are in existence relative to the size of the population?

Bothwell's categories suggest that there is no clear line of demarcation between the idea of civil society as it is currently used and the capital that it is instrumental in building. More civil society means capital will be built up more efficiently and effectively, and more capital means civil society will function better. Unfortunately, the process of building civil society doesn't simply happen because people desire it. It takes a critical mass of people who understand its value and who are also willing to make the sacrifices necessary to implement it. Institutions in both the economic and government sectors must nurture it by removing barriers to its development or, even better, by actively promoting and developing it. Civil society also needs to infiltrate organizations in the private sector. During the past thirty years much has been written in the business management literature about the importance of promoting transparency and participation within companies. A great deal has also been written about promoting civil society outside companies in the "corporate social responsibility" literature. But governments at all levels remain especially important to the development of civil society.

One example of what government can do is embodied in the Civic Index, published by the National Civic League.[5] It suggests government focus community efforts on the following ten objectives if it wants to increase its level of civil society:

- Teaching people the value/benefits of participation and creating avenues for participation.
- Training community leaders to be inclusive, focused on long term results, willing to take risks, be self-critical, etc.
- Promoting communication between diverse racial, economic, ethnic or religious groups.
- Establishing a shared sense of vision and pride which ties the community's past to its future.
- Establishing formal processes for dispute resolution, debate and consensus building.

- Defining and measuring government effectiveness.
- Tracking the breadth and depth of volunteer and philanthropic activity.
- Educating people in order to motivate and enable them to contribute/participate in community activities.
- Sharing valuable and relevant information with the members of the community.
- Planning specific activities that require inter-community cooperation.

These will not only increase the effectiveness of government, but will also spur economic activity among not-for-profit organizations and businesses. This list also provides a good reminder that most forms of capital and the wealth creation process itself have a communal dimension. Social capital is almost by definition about relationships, but it is important to recognize the degree to which all of the other forms of capital also depend on communal activity. Physical and financial forms of capital, for example, are built up through complex *systems* involving markets and institutions. Governments and corporations are each in their own right complex social systems. Educational institutions, support groups, worship services, and other contributors to intellectual/emotional/aesthetic capital and/or spiritual/moral capital are also fundamentally communal activities. So, although individualism may increase consumption and traditional measures of wealth in the short run, it will need to be augmented or replaced by cooperation and community for sustainable long term development.

The Importance of Freedom and Communication

Both civil society and entrepreneurship require that people have a certain amount of freedom to do what needs to be done, and this is why basic freedoms and human rights have been so essential to economic development. If people are not *free* to engage in entrepreneurial activity, the likelihood that adequate amounts of all of the forms of capital will be brought together will be very small, and economic development will be thwarted. Conversely, when people are freer to accumulate needed forms of capital from wherever it may be available around the world, we would expect development to accelerate. This is one reason that so much development has accompanied the modern era globalization process that began after WW II[6] and that accelerated at the end of the 20th and beginning of the 21st centuries with the advent of low-cost global transportation and communication systems. Globalization, at its root, can be viewed as the process of people, organizations, and countries attempting to balance their development wheels. Since land is immobile, and the movement of people is restricted, the early stages of globalization involved people discovering that they could put the output of their land and/or their labor into products that could be traded for either other products or money, both of which are relatively mobile. Trade, in this regard, becomes a way to gain access to needed forms of physical or environmental capital. When borders were open to immigration, companies and individuals were also quick to take advantage of the movements of people to capture or offer needed intellectual/emotional capital. Steady movement toward financial liberalization now allows gaps in financial capital to be easily filled.[7] Diplomacy and academic exchange are slowly facilitating the exchange of governmental capital. And finally, personal interaction and cultural exposure are now chipping away at long held prejudices and other cultural blocks to development, offering great opportunities for the enhancement of social and spiritual/moral capital.[8]

The importance of freedom and advances in communication is illustrated by the arrows placed above and below the wheel. They indicate that the development process can be greatly accelerated in a world where people are free, and where they have access to information about what others believe, how they live, what products and services are available, etc. But although these things can speed the rotation of the development wheel, this will only be a good thing if the wheel is well-constructed and round. Many countries have learned the hard way that when their people see how much better life could be, but "capital" shortages prevent them from achieving their now higher expectations at home, they will use their newfound freedom to seek "greener pastures" elsewhere. This is not necessarily a bad thing, since, if their talents can be better utilized in conjunction with other forms of capital in other countries, they will in fact be more productive there and can send back some of the benefits of that increased productivity to their families back home. But it does not speak well for the future of those countries that allow major barriers to entrepreneurship, civil society and capital accumulation to persist. In the same way that much of Africa lost a lot of potential financial and physical investment to Asia toward the end of the 20th century because of their failure to reform their ways, so too, countries that do not recognize the basic wealth-creation principles enunciated here will continue to lose the battle for other kinds of capital to countries that are more proactive and open. To avoid this, change must first take place at the core of the wheel. The heart of reform is always rooted in the values and attitudes that flow out of the predominant worldviews in a country, which are in turn rooted in basic beliefs.

Ideally, freedom and communication will alter worldviews in ways that lead to increases in entrepreneurship and civil society rather than increases in selfishness, waste, power grabs or violence. If this is the case, people will become less preoccupied with the need to stay alive, not being defrauded, and/or fighting external threats, such as those from wild animals, diseases, or enemies. This in turn should give them the vision, time and energy to devote to the buildup of less tangible but potentially more valuable kinds of capital, such as complex organizations capable of producing higher value-added products, laws that support contracts and provide economic incentives, or the development of healthy religious, social or cultural habits.[9] At this point the predominant worldviews in the society and culture will show themselves for what they are, and will be reflected in the nature of the goods and services produced and the kind of capital accumulated, because development activity will be driven less by necessity and more by intention. It is also at this point that internal threats to development like pride, arrogance, selfishness, jealousy, greed, the desire for revenge, ignorance and other indicators of a shortage of spiritual/moral capital have the most potential to restrain development. So for freedom and communication to have the best possible influence on development, people must be given the opportunity to evaluate the alternatives and be open to changing their ideas about the fundamental questions of life. In the same way that better products, better ways of evaluating the creditworthiness of projects, or better manufacturing methods have spread wealth around the world in the past, so too, better ideas about the nature of reality, methods of distinguishing good from evil, or the purpose of economic activity must have their importance recognized and be free to "move" to wherever they are most needed.

This illustrates once again how the beliefs at the core of the wheel can influence development in unexpected ways. Good attitudes, values and habits will spread most quickly through a society when people are well connected to each other and when they are eager to share good ideas and habits with each other. In this sense, the more *evangelical* people are, that is, the more they want to share good news with others, the faster a society will be built up. The term evangelical is one best known in societies influenced by Protestant Christianity and is often associated with the desire of certain Christian groups to communicate the news of salvation through Jesus Christ to others. But it can also be thought of more broadly as any strong desire to share something with others that the sharer believes has the potential to bring great advantage to the recipient. So, all belief systems have the opportunity to be evangelical. But they vary widely in what they know or believe and in their propensity to share it, and this will have an impact on economic development. Great benefit can come from people who willingly share knowledge that has the potential to build others up. Of course great damage can also ensue if evangelicals are both misguided and successful in carrying their message to large numbers of people. Propaganda machines are perhaps the best example of this, particularly when they have been given monopoly status within the communication networks of a culture or country. So, like many of the other worldview components discussed here, an evangelistic bent may be necessary but not sufficient for rapid and healthy development, and has the potential to be a two-edged sword. Perhaps the most important lesson to take from this is that a particularly important freedom for economic development is freedom of religion – which increases the likelihood that there will be ongoing strengthening at the core of the wheel through regular study and discussion about the meaning of life, integrity, right and wrong-all of which are integral parts of the process of evaluating/adopting/rejecting alternative beliefs and belief systems.

Conclusion

Before proceeding, we judge that it would be good to review where we have been and suggest a list of the attitudes and understandings that are critical to the economic development process. We caution that some understandings might not make the short list of people whose thinking is channeled into "traditional" ways of thinking about these things. By "traditional" we mean for the most part emphasizing GDP as an output measure, and climate and geography, population growth, (tangible) savings and investment, government spending, financial and physical capital (technology), education levels and the like as the relevant inputs. All of these things are important at some level, but they don't shed nearly enough light on the importance of worldviews to development. So alternatively, we propose the following list of values, attitudes and understandings that flow from what we have said so far, and suggest where we need to go from here:

1. That the ultimate purpose of development activity is for people to receive the kinds of goods and services that enable them to flourish (as opposed to whatever they desire) and that these goods and services be provided in the most stewardly way possible.

2. That properly defined, wealth is a good thing; and that the accumulation and preservation of seven different forms of capital are both 1) essential for service and stewardship to take place and 2) evidence that they are taking place.

3. That voluntary, bottom-up, communal construction of institutions (such as businesses, governments and NGOs) and systems (in the form of civil society activity and entrepreneurship) is the most efficient and sustainable path to meeting people's needs, creating wealth, and achieving sustainable development.

4. That the primary *economic development* role of these institutions is to choose projects and activities that promise high returns on the investments made in them.

5. That people are most motivated and productive when they can apply the deepest desires of their hearts toward their personal economic activity and the activities and ends of these institutions.

6. That the deepest desires of people's hearts are rooted in foundational commitments, many of which can be described as religious. These foundational commitments interact with nurturing habits, educational systems, life experiences and other cultural influences to coalesce into a *worldview*.

7. That pretending that there are clear lines between secular and religious beliefs, or classifying people into "religious" of "secular" groups, or demanding that the state limit the public square to only secular beliefs profoundly changes the nature of development, sometimes for the worse.

8. That allowing people the freedom to follow their hearts nevertheless brings with it other challenges that need to be addressed:
    a. That, because of complexities in the wealth creation process and differences in people's worldviews (beliefs, values and habits), the use of incentives for wealth creation will necessarily lead to unequally distributed wealth.
    b. That good things like motivation and freedom only lead to service and stewardship if people's hearts are oriented in the right direction.

c. That people's hearts can only be oriented in the right direction if honest and open conversations, including public conversations, take place about the most basic questions of life.

d. That honest and open conversations require that people be permitted to bring all of their knowledge and beliefs, including religious beliefs, to the table.

e. That for knowledge and beliefs to be given honest consideration in discussions, all participants must accept the fact that some of their knowledge and beliefs may not only be unpersuasive to others, but may be irrelevant, wrong or harmful and in need of changing.

9. That for "misdirected" hearts to reorient (and for people to make wise choices, and for institutions and structures to function well), meaningful dialog must take place at the (deepest) worldview level. For this to happen, government must establish and uphold structural justice. This means they must protect freedom of religion (and other freedoms that are intertwined with it), while simultaneously defining boundaries between the various spheres of society so no group (including government) oversteps the bounds of its authority.

10. That for continuous healthy development to take place, the dialog that occurs must lead to the widespread distribution of pro-development "worldview elements" (beliefs, values, character traits and behaviors). At the broadest level, this will include:

a. A strong sense that things are not as they should be and that it is humankind's responsibility to improve them.

b. Respect for and high expectations of those in authority

c. A stewardship ethic

d. The ability to see oneself objectively and others sympathetically

e. A deep concern for people outside one's family and friendship circles

f. An understanding of high integrity conduct – trustworthiness, honesty and diligence –as not only praiseworthy but mandatory.

g. An understanding of the virtue of humility.

Economic Development: Pulling it All Together

Our summary points, and especially the tenth one, aim us squarely at the philosophical and religious origins of development. This is in keeping with the hints given throughout the book that healthy and lasting development requires the kind of worldview that encourages the buildup and preservation of many forms of capital and also spurs civil society and entrepreneurship. But in succeeding chapters we need to go beyond broad generalizations and "peel the layers off the onion" to better see the core of the wheel. Doing so will help us focus in on what a pro-development worldview looks like by identifying and unpacking the elements identified in point ten that need to flow from it.

Chapter 19: Pro-Development Worldview Element # 1 – A Strong Sense That Things Are Not as They Should Be and That it is Humankind's Responsibility to Improve Them

The next seven chapters represent an attempt to organize scores of pro-development beliefs, attitudes and values into a finite number of key "worldview elements" that need to be at the core of the development wheel. We have chosen of these elements, in part because our model already has seven forms of capital and seven ways of building up and preserving each form of capital. The first of these - a sense that things can and must be improved - is important to development because it is at the root of three other philosophical commitments, each of which, when embedded in people's worldviews, will spur the wealth creation and development.

- The rejection of poverty, and the acceptance of change and economic development as normative (even if it these things bring some inequality[1]).
- A passion for the freedom to take the initiative to diagnose problems and fix them.
- An understanding of civil society as normative, and the desire to nurture it.

Rejection of Poverty

The full-bodied rejection of poverty and the acceptance of wealth and development as normative are critical to a steady stream of improvements in people's lives. The printing press, steam engine, telephone, light bulb, stainless steel, transistor, and silicon chip are products of people who were relentless in their belief that there must be a better way. But all of these inventions depend ultimately on an understanding that the amount of wealth, or goods, or even the amount of "good" in the world is not fixed, but is expandable. It also requires that jealousy and envy be held at bay, and that people see wealth not as an entitlement, but as something that must be earned. And if wealth can be legitimately earned, the fruits of one's labor or ingenuity rightfully accrue to the laborer or entrepreneur, which in turn opens the door to private enterprises, market prices, and meritocracy.[2] Flourishing private enterprises require an understanding that the concept of profit is not the same as, and ought not be confused with, exploitation or stealing. Together these things lead to steadily improving organizations, and a host of other economically productive habits, which in turn permit some to climb out of poverty, even if it is not possible for all to do so simultaneously.

Many belief systems are suspicious of one or more of the critical beliefs/assumptions that underlie a full-bodied rejection of poverty. In the decades following the demise of communism in Eastern Europe, for example, development remained severely hampered by widespread assumptions that one person's wealth is tied to another's poverty, with the result that weak property rights and unjust confiscation of property continued to be serious problems in these countries. Many Russian people still refer to business people as "speculators," a term that implies there is something illegitimate going on wherever business activity is taking place. Privilege and "connections" remain important elements in Russian educational institutions, businesses, and government, in contrast to the meritocracy that (with exceptions) is more prevalent in higher income economies like those of South Korea, Japan, or the U.S., and the fastest growing sectors/industries in rising stars like China and India.

This suspicion of business has been particularly detrimental to development in those countries where it has made inroads into the thinking of professional development workers. Many people go into economic development work because they are concerned about people, and are *not* particularly concerned about creating or accumulating wealth. They often give up the possibility of higher wages in order to help others reach subsistence levels, with little concern for making either themselves or the people they are helping wealthy. But for rapid and lasting development to take place, development workers and those they serve need to see that using the word "wealthy" to describe only the richest of the world's people does a disservice to all. Not only does this disparage the role of asset accumulation in development, but it has also allowed large numbers of people to divide the world into "haves" and "have-nots." This further allows many in the "have-not" group to assume there are few alternatives to living "hand to mouth," or that they are too poor to save money or accumulate "wealth." Fortunately, recent economic improvements in some historically impoverished countries, along with some excellent books that chart the institutions and events that contributed to this, now make it easier than ever to demonstrate that wealth is not and never really was the exclusive province of the rich.[3] Such progress set the state for what we do here – demonstrating how a complex "soup" of beliefs at the core of the Development Wheel, and the values and actions that flow from this, ultimately motivate and enable both rich *and poor* to accumulate the wealth levels needed to take them beyond the subsistence level.

A Passion for the Freedom to Diagnose Problems and Fix Them

Of course, even if property rights are secure, wealth is accepted as legitimate, and some inequality is accepted as natural and possibly even healthy, little development will take place if people do not demand the freedom to act on their inclinations to solve problems or be productive. This is needed not only at the personal level, but also within organizations and political entities. A motivated and productive populace needs to be free to buy things that solve their problems, bring them joy, or give them the best value for their money. This in turn requires that businesses have the freedom to trade with their counterparts in other countries. Voters and organizations need to be free to communicate to or lobby government so that they can solve the problems in their companies and neighborhoods and work cooperatively rather than against each other in accomplishing tasks. People need to be free to read and communicate about problems occurring in their societies in order to form groups, organizations and strategies for dealing with them. Perhaps most importantly, people need to be free to be entrepreneurial - both socially and economically. Because of all these things, development is most likely to take place in an environment where freedom is viewed as *normative*.[4]

One important byproduct of freedom is flexibility. In a modern global economy, the freedom to act quickly and decisively is essential to being competitive in a world where a person or an organization's situation can change hour-to-hour, and be influenced by local competitors, developments on the other side of the world, or upheavals in a completely different industry. Technology, commodity prices, rents, wages, interest rates, exchange rates and many other things change rapidly, and businesses can only continuously source needed inputs at low cost if they have a great deal of freedom. No doubt this is one of the reasons that a study by two Harvard professors that looked at 117 countries found that open economies grew at average rates of 4.5% between 1970 and 1989, while relatively closed economies grew at an average rate of only .6%.[5]

One particularly important example of the importance of freedom, highlighted by The World Bank, is the damage done by barriers that prevent or restrict people from starting businesses. It has long been known that wide gaps exist between the ease of starting a business in the wealthiest and poorest countries, but these gaps have only recently been extensively measured. According to ongoing research by the World Bank throughout the first decade of the 21st Century,[6] there is a strong inverse relationship between the amount of unnecessary business regulation on the one hand, and the number of business startups, ownership diversity, credit availability, employment, GDP/capita and the Human Development Index on the other, *and* that this is not just the result of corruption. Many countries make it nearly impossible for businesses to profitably provide the goods and services that people need by making it prohibitively expensive to register property, get a loan, start a business, meet artificially high capital requirements, enforce a contract, fire an unproductive worker, or recover debts owed in a bankruptcy proceeding. Furthermore, by implementing excessively rigid employment regulations many countries drive workers into the informal sector, increase child labor and otherwise impoverish those on the bottom end of the income spectrum. Although some of these restrictions can be directly tied to corruption, *all* of them can be directly tied to worldview.

According to the *World Bank Business Regulation Survey* based on the *Doing Business* research cited earlier, sixteen of the lowest-ranked countries with respect to the business friendliness of their regulations were in Sub-Saharan Africa, which, not by coincidence, has long been among the most poverty-stricken spots on earth. At the time of the World Bank surveys, it took hundreds of days to start business in some of these countries compared to, only three days in, for example, Canada. The cost of starting a business in Ethiopia was nearly four times the per capita income. It took nearly four months to register property in Malawi compared to just a few days in some other countries, and in Burundi and the Democratic Republic of the Congo it took more than fifty procedures to enforce a contract. At the time of the survey it also took the equivalent of more than three years' salary to fire a worker in Sierra Leone. Faced with such daunting restrictions on the freedom to make wise economic choices, much economic activity moves to the informal sector where it is difficult for government to regulate or tax it, companies will shift some of their hiring from adults to children, and the income share of the poorest drops. Ownership becomes more concentrated and corruption increases as cutting through bureaucratic restrictions on freedom becomes a more essential business skill than innovating, marketing or financing.

But these restrictions on the freedom to start, conduct or liquidate a business were and are by no means limited to Sub-Saharan Africa. They are found wherever poor countries are found. Take for example, the restrictions placed on companies' abilities to enforce contracts, liquidate collateral and collect debts, or creditors' abilities to foreclose on dying companies. In Slovenia it took nearly three years to enforce a contract, and in Argentina it took nearly half a year to liquidate collateral rightfully claimed by a lender. In Serbia, procedures, permissions, legal problems, and inefficiencies together meant it took more than six years for creditors to close a business. Owners and creditors are ill-advised to supply capital to companies under such circumstances because the assets of the company are all but guaranteed to waste away long before any bankruptcy proceedings can be concluded. These inefficiencies also undermine the startup/entry of key service businesses, such as credit bureaus, which in turn restricts the development of financial markets because sellers cannot assess the creditworthiness of buyers. It does not matter that government bureaucrats may have had good intentions when implementing these restrictions. The end result is fewer businesses, less business activity, a larger percentage of businesses moving to the "informal" sector of the economy, fewer jobs, less income equality and less economic development.

Seeing Civil Society as Normative

To prevent these kinds of things from stopping development in its tracks, people need something in their worldviews that make them very uncomfortable when they lack the freedoms needed to conceptualize and build a civil society. The term "civil society" has become quite popular as a shorthand way to describe many of the things *in addition to* the government and businesses that are important for development to occur. Earlier we defined civil society as "a set of institutions, processes, and attitudes that promote cooperation among individuals, private associations and government agencies to produce practical solutions to common problems," and noted that three attitudes or values that are commonly associated with the term are transparency, participation, and a commitment to peaceable change. To elaborate here, the term is also commonly used to refer to mediating institutions that provide a buffer between the individual and the state. Some writers have described civil society as the "third leg" of a three-legged stool upon which society rests. In this way they distinguish civil society from government and markets while simultaneously acknowledging that government and markets depend on civil society, and vice versa. Remove any one of the three legs and the stool cannot stand.

The destruction of civil society, or perhaps more commonly, the existence of beliefs and restrictions that keep it from emerging, are deadly to the wealth creation and economic development processes, whereas literally hundreds of benefits accrue to countries that nurture civil society. We limit our discussion here to how the three aforementioned hallmarks of civil society--participation, transparency, and a commitment to peaceable change--promote development.

Benefits of Widespread Participation

For starters, participation, be it in business, government or civil society organizations (CSOs),[7] prepares people to serve and lead by giving them opportunities to learn and apply important managerial skills, such as planning, organizing, leading, problem solving, conflict resolution, and communicating. Robert Putman's research[8] concluded that the habits formed in civil society organizations promote efficiency in business since the networking and trust relationships they nurture foster the sharing of useful information, services and equipment, faster and sounder strategic alliances, and highly efficient "handshake" business deals. Widespread participation in small groups and institutions also teaches people to see high-trust environments as normal rather than exceptional, enabling both government and business to devote fewer resources to supervision and internal control and more to innovation and production. CSOs in particular provide outlets for people to become an important part of a community, to increase their network of contacts and sources of information, and to enhance their confidence. CSOs also enable people to learn ideas of justice, fairness, and the limits to self-interest, which strengthen interpersonal relationships, keep organizations functioning smoothly, and save countries and markets from becoming bloody competitive battlegrounds.

When people participate, they also begin to take ownership of the activities in which they are involved, increasing commitment to the organization and its goals, and the motivation to see and help the organization succeed. Participation also increases the likelihood that talent will be uncovered and that the best people will rise to positions of significant responsibility – which in turn improves leadership, motivation and productivity – all of which provide important carryover benefits in democratic societies. Businesses have also known for many years that significant employee participation is a key to finding new and better ways to do things. Already in the 1930's U.S. businesses realized that much was to be gained by studying group dynamics and inviting employee participation in management decisions. Massive amounts of management research and entire fields of investigation such as organizational development and organizational behavior grew out of these humble beginnings and have moved the world's leading businesses from the too often inhumane beginnings of the industrial revolution to the now widely-accepted participatory structures of Total Quality Management (TQM), learning organizations, employee stock ownership programs, and broad measurements of organizational development and "human capital."

Increasingly businesses of all types are studying the employee retention and development programs of industry leaders, accounting for a portion of salaries as an asset, measuring the value of brands, teams, or relationships, and adding narrative to previously "black and white" financial statements. As this list implies, "human capital" involves much more than the skills and knowledge individuals bring into a business or the strategies employed by it. It also includes: leadership, character and ethics; relationships built up over time with customers, employees or suppliers; communication patterns, policies and procedures; software code, databases, and networks; and a host of other intangibles, all of which are a function of tapping into the strengths of hundreds or thousands of "participating" employees.

Partly in response to the past over-reliance by businesses on financial measures of success, Harvard professors Robert Kaplan and David Norton laid out a management system in the early 1990s which they termed The Balanced Scorecard. This system retained traditional financial measures but also explicitly recognized the role of organizational learning and growth, external and internal business processes and customer relationships to the development and success of organizations. One of the key insights of this approach was to recognize that modern companies can no longer survive and thrive by investing just in plant, equipment and technology. Rather, they also need to invest in other parts of the business system that are important to their success--customers, suppliers, employees, processes, innovation, and even what has come to be known as spirituality. These "soft science"[9] innovations and a host of offshoots have proven beyond the shadow of a doubt that civil society in the workplace, i.e., the teamwork and trust building that accompany participation, transparency and cooperative, peaceful change on the job, can lead to significant wealth creation.[10] Of course, most of these modern management improvements are better known by names such as "participative management" than as civil society in the workplace. But regardless of what we call them, they serve as a vivid reminder that it is ultimately the "pictures" that people have in their minds of what an organization should be like that are at the core of productivity.

One particularly important reason that widespread participation promotes development is that the authority that accompanies participation *carries with it* a responsibility both to act for the good of fellow participants and to accept the consequences of the decisions one has had a hand in making. In this way, participation clearly stimulates personal growth. Yet it is worth noting that the amount of responsibility people have in businesses sometimes pales in comparison to the responsibility they are given when they participate (i.e. volunteer) in non-profit organizations and/or in their communities. There, they are sometimes given total responsibility for planning, fund raising, operations, and follow-up for a project or even an entire organization. This is also why many corporations, recognizing the employee-training benefits of CSOs, have actively promoted employee volunteerism among other benefits. Highly-respected global-medical-products company Johnson and Johnson's credo, for example, states "we are responsible to the communities in which we live and work, and to the world community as well. We must be good citizens- support good works and charities." Some large corporations even go so far as to financially support employee family volunteering. In a joint survey of the largest public companies in the U.S. by the Conference Board and Points of Light Foundation, 92% of the respondents encouraged their employees to participate in community volunteer activities, 68% made release time available for employees volunteering during working hours, 63% had funds to support such activities, and 50% made community service part of their mission statement.[11] A strong majority of the respondents agreed that the programs not only improved company-community relations, but also built teamwork skills, improved morale, attracted better employees, enhanced training, improved retention, increased employee productivity, and positively affected the corporation's strategic goals and productivity. This survey is supported by work done by UCLA professor David Lewin, whose IBM-commissioned research studies "found employee morale up to three times higher in companies actively involved in the community.....and community involvement positively related to financial performance."[12] These benefits and others have been widely discussed in the "social capital" research and are generally well known. In spite of this, they are virtually ignored in places where the predominant worldview keeps people from "seeing" the need for these kinds of things.

Benefits of Transparency

The same kind of reasoning can be applied to the impact of the closely related civil society concepts of transparency and accountability on wealth creation and economic development. There are many dimensions to these concepts, but at the very least they involve the relatively free flow of information within organizations and society, and the development of widespread reporting and feedback mechanisms for measuring performance. Transparency creates economic efficiencies by lowering the cost of accessing information and ideas, two widely touted engines of economic growth. This in turn makes markets more accessible and prices more accurate, and leads to better economic decisions.[13] Prior to allowing prices to float (so they were free to rise to a point where they reflected the true cost of the time, materials, energy, etc. that went into them), many of the countries of the former Eastern

Block were either producing and selling far fewer products and services than consumers wanted, or they were producing and selling large numbers of products at substantial losses, in essence destroying wealth and in so doing pushing their citizens to the brink of poverty. Governments all over the world are still engaged in these practices to greater or lesser degrees, while their citizen victims remain essentially in the dark because of a lack of transparency and accountability. Of course some of these governments restrict transparency for the very reason that they know it provides an important check on government power, by allowing the sun to shine on government procedures and decisions. In truth, government transparency almost always results in more economically productive projects and fewer "pork barrel" projects--those that enrich government officials or their friends at the expense of taxpayers. Likewise, in a transparent environment, economically productive infrastructure (such as potable water and environmentally healthy sewage systems) will be built up much more quickly since the people who will benefit greatly or be harmed greatly by government decisions will have an opportunity to find out what is actually going on, and influence priorities and programs for the better.

Transparency also makes government more effective by increasing the possibility that wrongdoing such as bribery or extortion will be exposed, because it forces government agencies to hire more people on the basis of merit, and because it makes it easier for the public to scrutinize government decisions. For example, watchdog groups in the U.S. like the Tax Foundation in Washington D.C. help U.S. citizens figure out how much tax they are actually paying and where the money is being spent, so citizens can hold their government accountable. It and other like-minded organizations continue to be very instrumental in the ongoing battle to increase the number of "value added" government services by scrutinizing the allocation of funds and the amount of waste. The same kinds of benefits come with increased transparency in nonprofit organizations. For example, at a local level, civil society organizations like Parent/Teacher Associations (PTAs) provide a forum for holding teachers and schools accountable.

Why do civil society organizations form spontaneously at the local level? Because participation and transparency in business, government, and nonprofit organizations, by their very nature, force decisions down to the level at which they can be made most effectively. The result is less waste and more efficiency as the leaders of these organizations are held accountable for the effective use of the revenues, taxes, or contributions they receive. In fact, it is not unusual for transparency to force some decisions outside of the government altogether ("outsourced" into the private sector) when it is clear that this will result in "more for the money." The result of all this is that the overall size of government tends to stay smaller where civil society organizations are most active. And, over time these benefits multiply as people increasingly look to each other to solve problems first and to government only when it is the best choice for solving a problem.

Finally, it should be noted that in both the public and private sectors transparency also allows people to examine best practices across organizations and even countries. This allows them to find out if they and those around them are employing their time, talents, or financial resources as productively as they could. One example of this involves the 1997-1999 Asian financial crisis that inflicted such heavy financial losses on the citizens of the region. It turns out that investors pulled massive amounts of money out of the region in part because lack of transparency made it difficult for them to assess the value of their investments. A similar crisis occurred ten years later in the U.S. financial markets when holders of so-called mortgage-based securities realized that investment banks and insurance companies had not been as transparent about the risks associated with these assets as they should have been. But these two incidents are just recent reminders that people are reluctant to trust their life's savings to any person, company, or country when they cannot easily uncover the truth about the risks to which they are being subjected.

Business and society also benefit from transparency and accountability. Public[14] businesses, by being accountable through annual reports and disclosure statements, become less risky to investors and attract far more capital at lower costs than they otherwise would. In addition to this, the quality and value of the goods and services provided by trusted companies increases with transparency, thanks to the civil society effects of consumer groups, the news media, and ultimate accountability to the consumer. Society benefits not only from superior products and services but from voluntary organizations that hold businesses accountable for the "external costs" of their products. Without transparency, businesses could sell their products for years or decades below "true cost" by ignoring the detrimental "external" effects of their activities on the public or the environment and, in doing so, deplete the wealth of the society in which they operate with few people even realizing it. Nevertheless, in spite of the increasingly well-known benefits of the kind of capital buildup associated with transparency, it remains an elusive commodity in many places where worldviews seem incapable of recognizing these benefits.

Benefits of a Commitment to Peaceable Change

Finally, a third hallmark of civil society - a widespread commitment to peaceful change - is facilitated by thousands of CSOs ranging from neighborhood associations and arbitration boards aimed at resolving conflicts at the local level, to church denominations and organizations that promote reconciliation and cooperation in their local congregations while sending relief workers or language teachers around the world to build healthy cross-cultural friendships at the international level. The most obvious effect of these kinds of organizations on development comes when their collective influence is successful in preventing injustice and war and the massive destruction of wealth that accompanies it. Although they are less likely to get credit for doing this than the larger formal organizations that they often give birth to or coalesce into (like the United Nations or the Peace Corps), their collective influence is enormous. After decades of working face to face with people who are often very different from them, those who labor in these organizations often understand better than diplomats and presidents that economic prosperity cannot happen unless attitudes and practices like mistrust, corruption, greed and war, can be replaced over time with attitudes and practices like openness, honesty, friendship, and cooperation.

Indirect Benefits of Civil Society Organizations on Economic Development

As valuable as the direct effects of participation, transparency and peaceable change are to individuals, companies and countries, it should also be noted that CSOs and volunteer activities in general also provide *indirect benefits*, such as filling in the cracks through which people have a tendency to fall when they are forced to depend for their welfare only on the economic and government sectors of a society. CSOs do this by, among other things, smoothing out unacceptable economic and social inequities, and providing the kinds of basic services that, from a human rights perspective, are necessary for people to fully participate as productive members of a society. For example, many churches, mosques, or temples minister to the "down and out," tutor struggling students, provide literacy training, and promote the kinds of positive values and character traits such as moderation, honesty, self-discipline, service, and respect that are necessary for businesses, families, governmental organizations, and communities to function effectively or efficiently.[15] They are also often involved and skilled in solving, or at the very least mitigating, a wide variety of social problems. Both the suffrage movement and the battle against racial discrimination in the U.S. have their roots in civil society organizations and especially churches.[16] Imagine how much would have been lost to the U.S. economy if it had continued to marginalize talented women and minority group members! Imagine what is lost to those countries that continue to limit themselves to a small subset of the talent available!

The indirect effects mentioned, however, are just the tip of the iceberg. Consider property rights and their massive impact on wealth and economic development. Are they not also an extension of a belief in the importance of *participation*, unsustainable in the absence of a civil society? What is the economic value of the competitive advantage to an economy that flows from having not-for-profit institutions as alternative service providers to government-run organizations, thereby making the government more efficient and effective? Or the economic benefits (jobs, taxes paid, etc.) of mutual insurance companies or production or agricultural coops like Amana or Sunkist, which started out as non-profits but eventually evolved into industry-leading (and profitable) companies? What too is the value to a country of the larger government surpluses or smaller deficits which flow naturally from all these other positive economic effects?

We could similarly address the *indirect* effects of a civil society concept like *transparency*. Would something as essential to the creation of wealth as the *rule of law* exist in the absence of the kind of commitment to transparency that is part of an open civil society? Would it make any sense to maintain an expensive legal infrastructure including legislative bodies, lawyers, arbitration and mediation agencies, courts, and law enforcement agencies if payments under the table or in the dark of night ultimately determined outcomes? Would businesses even seriously try to compete if they could be kept out of markets or have their competitive bids rejected arbitrarily, with no opportunity to bring the injustice to light? Or, perhaps most importantly, would the fundamental debates about right and wrong that are so essential to the kind of development wheel core that leads to the cultivation, protection and replenishment of moral and spiritual capital ever take place openly?

Examples of the Impact of Civil Society on Economic Development

We have concentrated here on the theoretical evidence of the importance of civil society to development, but documented evidence of its impact is also easy to find. For example, much has been written about the Grameen Bank in Bangladesh and how group decision making, accountability and transparency have allowed a small non-profit micro-lending organization started by Muhammad Yunus in 1976 to grow into a multi-billion dollar financial service provider. Founded as a cooperative to provide poor women small loans to start small agriculturally-oriented businesses, grocery stores, and vegetable gardens, it eventually became a full-fledged, value-creating business with a variety of products and services, including a cellular phone division. Another example of the impact of CSOs on wealth is World Vision's role in the Ansokea Valley in Ethiopia, beginning in 1984. Initially using aid to help with transportation networks and food cultivation, teams of outside volunteers working through and with local people and through churches eventually built medical clinics, terraced hillsides, piped clean water into village reservoirs, taught drought-resistant agricultural techniques, carpentry, and weaving, built schools and improved literacy. Not only was wealth created in the form of physical, intellectual and spiritual/moral capital, but a dust bowl containing 60,000 people on the edge of subsistence was transformed into a self-sustaining exporter of food. And there are not just a few examples of these kinds of things, but thousands!

Increasing Civil Society

Given how civil society is critical to economic development (because it builds and preserves all forms of capital, not just material and financial capital), we would do well to take a few moments to examine how to increase it. As noted in Chapter 18, people must value it enough to sacrifice for it, and institutions in all areas of society must actively promote and nurture it. Government at all levels is especially important in the growth of civil society, because it is uniquely positioned to promote participation, transparency and methods for peaceful cooperation, as well as specific programs, such as those suggested in the *Civic Index*. [17] But, although good, there is no guarantee these top-down approaches will usher in the kind of civil society that can create and sustain wealth, in part because they *presuppose* values which may or may not be widely shared in the society or culture. For example, they may presuppose an accountable, public-spirited government, a well-functioning justice system, or widespread ethical behavior and tolerance when the reality in some countries may be a corrupt government, misguided economic policies, market barriers, unethical behavior, intolerance, foreign predators, or a number of other things that can choke off civil society before its roots ever take hold. Of course even a modicum of civil society significantly reduces the likelihood of these things. But, we must be honest about the fact that civil society, as wonderful as it is, is at best *necessary but not sufficient* for economic development. Its very existence depends, as the Development Wheel illustrates visually, on the beliefs at the core.

Chapter 20: Pro-Development Worldview Element # 2 – Respect for and High Expectations of Authority

The Importance of an Appropriate Understanding of Authority

It should be clear from the last chapter that people need to be very uncomfortable with the *misuse* of authority for healthy economic development to take place. Many of the limitations to freedom discussed earlier that prevent small businesses or NGOs from starting up, or prevent existing businesses and NGOs from operating efficiently, have their roots in the misuse of authority. Most of the time, the damage is done by a single person or a small group of individuals who are in power, and who view authority as *superiority, power and license* rather than as *service and accountability*. A distortion in this dimension of people's worldviews will do much harm at various levels of society. Authority in homes and families that is viewed as power and license has the potential to squash the confidence of spouses and children, and lead, in the worst cases, to various forms of abuse and permanently damaged lives. Authority in organizations including government that is viewed as power and license will often lead to personality cults, "yes men," and an unwillingness to allow the kinds of assessment methods, internal controls and transparency that can effectively limit power, expose wrongdoing, and promote efficiency. When power is viewed as license, people in authority will see themselves as "above" the need to be accountable, which opens the door to a host of shoddy organizational practices. In such an environment, the people at the top can simply ignore the need to set goals and priorities, give attention to efficiency or stewardship, plan for contingencies, or listen to people or treat them justly. These practices can in turn lead to a culture of disrespect for both authority and institutions. People begin telling authorities what they think they want to hear; they hide potentially incriminating information; they begin to cut corners on their obligations, and engage in a host of similar behaviors that damage economic development. In the end, force becomes the method of choice for exacting behavior from others; the assumption that change needs to come from above crystallizes, and creative ideas and spontaneous cooperation dwindle. Local leaders, churches, families, and individuals gradually lose their effectiveness as authority that is legitimately theirs is usurped by those farther up the "food chain." Cooperation, motivation and self-sufficiency are all strangled.

Once again, civil society by itself is no guarantee of good results; even in a democracy the majority can ignore or tyrannize minorities. To wit, the practices uncovered by the World Bank discussed in Chapter 19 that all but strangle small businesses and economic opportunity are in some cultural settings supported by a *misinformed majority* that doesn't understand that they have permitted their government to overreach its authority. Sadly, these practices are often misdiagnosed as little more than a misunderstanding or ignorance of economic principles by those in authority. This kind of misunderstanding can cause plenty of damage, but history shows that markets have a way of fixing most of their own problems in the absence of more deeply-seated problems - like sustained interference of entrenched interests directed by a misguided and ultimately damaging worldview. The real problem here is an inability to understand that holding an office amounts to a sacred trust, that those under authority deserve to be treated with respect, and that it is never morally permissible to divorce authority from either responsibility or accountability.

Corruption and Development

Unfortunately, misguided worldviews will result in government officials who remain impervious to correction over long periods of time. George B.N. Ayittey illustrates this well in *Africa in Chaos,[1]* where he describes how international organizations and Western countries spent hundreds of millions of dollars in Africa trying to establish democracy and healthy economies before recognizing that these kinds of things might never take root in countries run by people with misguided notions of authority.[2] Without leadership capable of ushering in a civil society, there simply was not enough incentive, for example, for central banks to refrain from creating money for politicians' pet projects, for judges to risk their jobs and financial security by insisting that the powerful and politically well-connected be subject to the law, or for autocrats to allow a free press or install qualified civil servants in their governments instead of unqualified friends and relatives. Ayittey notes that even in fairly large countries with solid natural resource endowments like Nigeria, foreign investors exited through much of the 1990s, tired of bribes, extortion, permission fees, confiscatory exchange rates, petty and not so petty crime, and the threat of serious conflict. Much of Sub-Saharan Africa became a textbook illustration for the mantra that in a global free market economy, countries with leaders unwilling or unable to serve or be held accountable would not be able to compete.

An illustration of the damage caused by corruption serves to enlighten our understanding of the importance of a country leader's perspective on authority. Corruption is multi-faceted, but often includes bribery, extortion, nepotism, favoritism, black market activities, patronage, conflicts of interest, official theft, falsification of records, and the widespread expectation of excessive and often illegal "service fees" to get things done. It is clear from the data of organizations like Transparency

International, Political Risk Services, and Economist Intelligence Unit that there is a strong inverse relationship between the amount of corruption in a country and the health of its economy. There are many reasons for this, the most commonly cited of which are the following:

- Corruption makes economic activity less efficient because of delays associated with receiving permits, permissions, access, etc.
- Corruption greatly reduces the ability of government to carry out its objectives by increasing, for example, the nonpayment of taxes, rent seeking, theft, and other economically damaging behaviors among citizens, because society-wide trust levels drop when citizens come to see government not as a servant, but as a predator.
- Corruption lowers the return on investment for government projects because there is a tendency for officials to choose projects/expenditures that benefit them personally or consolidate their power rather than those with widespread and public benefits.[3]
- Corrupt countries attract the least efficient and least reputable foreign companies, since companies that would otherwise have trouble competing have the most to gain by paying bribes.[4]
- Corruption slows the growth of small businesses, which are the primary engine of job creation, since the cost of extortion, delays and unaffordable fees represent a larger percentage of their total costs.[5]
- Corruption causes talented people and ethical, efficient companies to become frustrated and seek to locate outside of the country.
- Corruption results in inefficient resource allocation since arbitrary choices by government distort prices and economic decisions throughout the society.

An Example of the Destructive Nature of Corruption: Mugabe's Zimbabwe

The damage done by Robert Mugabe to Zimbabwe is a textbook example of the damage a misguided worldview can to do a country.[6] By the first decade of the 21st century, life expectancy in Zimbabwe had slipped to thirty-five years from fifty-six years thirty years earlier, and humanitarian agencies were feeding millions of people, sometimes more than half of the population. A decade earlier the country had been exporting copious amounts of grain to feed people outside their country. To be sure, a serious drought had contributed to Zimbabwe's problems, HIV had infected more than a quarter of its adults, and many trading partners had imposed sanctions. But the "Jewel of Africa," as Zimbabwe had been known, had (and still has) excellent soil, natural beauty, good infrastructure, and a literacy rate of nearly ninety percent. What Zimbabwe did not have was a leader who understood that leadership is about service and accountability rather than power and license, and it was this that was at the root of the implosion of the country. Under Mugabe's leadership, more than 5,000 farms were confiscated and turned over to his political supporters. By the end of 2003, fewer than three percent of these were still functioning fully, by 2009 the annual inflation rate was more than a billion percent, unemployment was approaching ninety percent, and large numbers of desperate citizens had left the country.

On the surface, Mugabe's most obvious mistake was to take land away from the people who had learned over decades and even generations how to farm it. But his fundamental mistake was to use his authority to run roughshod over justice, since two-thirds of these farmers had titles that had been issued not by some colonial repressor, but by Mugabe's government itself. Then, alarmed at the inflation rate caused by shortages of his own making, he used his authority to fix grain prices at a fraction of the market-clearing price, causing farmers to choose not to grow grain at a loss, making the problem even worse. By 2003 corn production was down by two-thirds and wheat by nearly ninety percent compared to 2000. If farmers attempted to export to avoid a loss, Mugabe used his authority to force them to convert their foreign money to Zimbabwean dollars at an exchange rate that left them with pennies on the dollar. To make matters worse, a culture of disrespect emerged: roving bands of thugs tore down fencing, and equipment was stolen, dismantled, or sold as scrap, all but ensuring that there would be no quick recovery in the country's food production capability.

Rejecting the humility and honesty that would characterize a servant leader, Mugabe hid the truth about the shortages, rigged the election, shut down opposition newspapers, kept foreign journalists from exposing the truth, and jailed and abused opponents. As his power slipped, he indoctrinated the youth of the country through his National Youth Service Training Program, and gave preferential treatment in civil service jobs and university admissions to loyal followers. Amazingly, he "saw" the need for this beehive of unproductive government abuse of authority but was unable to "see" how he could have used his authority to implement justice or economic incentives, or inspire the citizenry to help the nearly ten percent of the county's population that had become orphaned because of his unwillingness to deal seriously with his country's AIDS epidemic. And by peeling off the layers of his worldview we are also able to see the other stultifying beliefs that contributed to the crisis - beliefs such as "the ends justify the means," "my needs and wants come first," or "it's only a problem if it is exposed," all of which tend to perpetuate corruption and inefficiency.

Time and money spent on destructive or unproductive activity, or damage control is time and money not spent solving more perplexing problems and/or building and growing an economy. So in addition to the direct damage resulting from Mugabe's misuse of authority were the lost opportunities to build and maintain infrastructure, or improve political processes, or replenish moral capital or any of the other forms of capital so badly damaged during his thirty years of mismanagement – all because of his perceptions of authority as license (rather than an obligation to serve), of accountability as optional, of people as expendable (rather than priceless), and of public property as his treasure trove (rather than a sacred trust) were the primary causes of the demise of his country. In short, Mugabe and his cohorts' misguided understanding of authority, their wanton disregard for civil society, and their inability to recognize what ultimately creates wealth and development were at the core of the implosion of an entire country.

Why Corruption Persists

As the earlier list of the damage done by corruption illustrates, corruption is widely understood in the academic and business communities to be strongly negatively correlated with job creation, incomes, and economic growth.[7] But where does corruption *ultimately* come from, and why does it persist for decades or centuries in some places while posing little or no problem in others, especially when most religions and secular belief systems teach, and most people believe, that stealing is wrong? Part of the answer is that there is a difference between believing something is wrong and tolerating it. But this is just one of many worldview nuances that contribute to corruption. A brief example, where we dissect some of the other worldview components that allow government corruption to persist will be helpful in making the point. We will do this by comparing the worldviews of two hypothetical officials in "Country A" and "Country B."

Assume first of all that a political official in Country A has no religious beliefs that tell him corruption is wrong; in this case his decision whether or not to engage in it will be based on other practical decisions, such as the potential rewards, the likelihood of being caught, and the penalties associated with being caught. This can be contrasted to an official in Country B who, by following an uncomplicated religious teaching that says *corruption is stealing and stealing is wrong*, chooses not to engage in it, and perhaps even does everything in his power to root it out. No expensive studies or lengthy discussions will be necessary to precipitate this action, but, unfortunately, in the real world things are seldom either this simple or clear cut.

Now assume that the official in Country A believes that corruption is wrong but his willingness to engage in it depends primarily on the likelihood that he will be shamed if it is revealed (rather than experiencing guilt even when there is no possibility that it will be revealed). In this case, he may be inclined to engage in it anyway. Conversely, an official in country B, who is uncertain about the teachings of his belief system on corruption, but who, nevertheless, has been *conditioned to feel guilty for sinful behavior*, will be more inclined to shy away from it or at least commission a study on the effects of corruption before engaging in it. Similarly, if the official in Country A is not compelled by his belief system to seek wisdom by consulting advisors, he may be perfectly content to remain ignorant about economic studies that expose the damaging nature of corruption. On the other hand, an official in Country B who has been indoctrinated by religious teachings that place a high *premium on seeking advice or attaining wisdo*m would be much more likely to commission a study that would reveal the benefits of instituting laws or regulations to limit corruption.

But even if the official in Country A decides to commission a study, if his belief system has little appreciation for the value of diversity he may ask for an opinion on the impact of corruption from a like-minded friend or "yes-man" in his bureaucracy, but little more. On the other hand, an official in Country B whose belief system has trained him to *respect and appreciate* (and appoint to his government) *people who may be unlike him* may commission a study that looks at the impact of corruption from many perspectives (e.g., ethical/moral, legal, economic, long term, short term), even though he might not have strict control over those chosen to serve on the commission.

But even if a commission reports that corruption is exceptionally harmful to the economy, if the official in Country A believes that authority begets power and privilege he may choose to simply ignore this advice. In contrast, an official in Country B, whose worldview insists that *authority is ultimately a call to service*, and who believes that laws apply equally to all people and are needed to curb people in authority from abusing their privileged positions, will, if laws against corruption exist, subject himself and other officials to them, and, if not, work toward instituting them.

To take the example even farther, we note that even if the official in Country A is persuaded to pass legislation against corruption, if he does not believe that it is a *fundamental responsibility of the government to expose the truth*, he may continue to engage in corrupt activities but carefully conceal his actions. And, if his staff members do not *value honesty more than financial security*, he will simply keep their wages low and share some of the bribe and extortion money with them, or use the threat of job loss to minimize the likelihood that his actions will be revealed.

And finally, even if the official in Country A is coerced into accepting legislative constraints that make government more transparent, if he is fundamentally *unconcerned about stewardship*, he may still find ways to engage in a very small number of highly-profitable well-concealed transactions with trusted partners.

The purpose of this illustration is to reinforce, once again, that economic outcomes are the product of many different values, attitudes and behaviors that are in turn influenced by belief systems. In this case corruption will persist as long as any one of a number of different values is relatively unimportant to the official. And although we have used a government official in our example, we could relay stories of the differing impacts of alternative worldviews at all levels and sectors of the economy.

The Importance of Justice

Our discussions about the need for a proper understating of authority, and the damage related to corruption, lead naturally to a discussion of what should be a primary concern of all political authorities - the widespread implementation of justice. As the debilitating effects of corruption, favoritism, and discrimination make clear, injustice will eventually undermine all but the strongest commitments to motivation, and, consequently, economic development. There is very little incentive, for example, for businesses to go through the trouble to make the best products and services if unfair laws or regulations, or behind the scenes shenanigans make it unlikely that their permits will be granted or their bids taken seriously. In education there is little incentive for students to work hard if the best jobs or college or grad school admissions go primarily to people with connections, rather than those most qualified. In politics there is little incentive for honest, hardworking people to run for public office if the vote count will always, inexplicitly, come out against them. But these kinds of things are just the tip of the iceberg.

Justice in the taxation and regulatory systems is particularly important. People who are able to keep a significant component of the fruits of their labor will be more highly motivated in their work than those who have been demoralized by the vagaries of arbitrary tax laws. In contrast, taxation practices that fall unjustly on those least able to pay can cause financial stress and a host of expensive social problems. As noted in Chapters 20 and 21, unjust regulations that prevent people from starting businesses have many documented negative effects on economic development. Government interference with market-determined interest rates or prices can also wreak havoc on economies. Ceilings on interest rates penalize savers and reduce the overall amount of savings. In doing so, they deny needed capital to those unable to get loans while favoring the select group of borrowers who are given loans at below market rates. Shortages caused by price freezes or ceilings penalize producers and consumers who are unable to obtain the goods, while favoring the select group of consumers who are able to obtain them. Price supports enrich producers at the expense of consumers. Tariffs enrich domestic producers at the expense of foreign producers and domestic consumers. All of these injustices have been widely shown by economists to create economic inefficiencies and to be a drag on economic development.

Inadequate protection of, or unreasonable restrictions on, private property have been particularly damaging to economic development. It has long been known that standards of living are substantially higher in countries that have secure private property rights. There are many reasons for this, some of which have been mentioned earlier. One way that private property benefits an economy is by encouraging stewardship. For example, if one does not properly maintain his vehicle or paint his house, he will bear the entire burden of this poor stewardship; the resultant costs will not be absorbed by the government or other joint owners. Private property also encourages use, but not overuse. If one owns a building or a piece of machinery but does not efficiently use that asset in some way, she bears the full opportunity cost associated with the asset's idleness. With adequate property rights she will have an incentive to use the property but not overuse it, since overuse will cause the property to lose value. Common property, on the other hand, will tend to be overused by individuals when they are able to profit from that overuse. This is in part why government officials in countries with weak private property rights have had a long history of abuse and looting of public assets. Most importantly, however, is the fact that private property gives people tangible ways to store wealth, and thereby protect the fruits of their labor, making their labor more worthwhile. This is true for individuals, but it is also true for groups of people with a shared vision; hence private property rights are also a critical requirement for the establishment of productive businesses and not-for-profit organizations.

It should also be noted that private property works in tandem with other manifestations of justice to create additional positive economic effects. The relative ease with which businesses and not-for-profits are able to start up determines available alternatives to government services. In many cases justice can be served by allowing citizen/consumers to choose the best service providers, whether private and public. This is likely why structures such as voucher systems, which provide government financing but allow people to freely choose the best hospital, school, or other service provider, typically result in efficient economic outcomes.[8]

One kind of property that provides a particularly important example of the benefits of justice to economic development is intangible or intellectual property.[9] Appropriate intellectual property protection plays a very important role in providing incentives for economic activity. The implementation of patent, copyright, and trademark protection requires the ability to walk a fine line between bringing justice to innovators, inventors or producers, on the one hand, *and* to the buyers, users or potential beneficiaries of innovation, on the other. Too much protection for innovators has the potential to put them on "easy street," thus removing financial incentives for additional innovation, and may also keep innovations from spreading quickly to new applications that can benefit large numbers of people. Too little protection, on the other hand, rewards copycats and thieves (and sometimes the consumers who get dirt cheap knockoff products) to the detriment of hard-working but undercompensated innovators.

But intellectual property justice does not only promote development because of the incentives it provides. It also permits so-called "highly developed" nations to continue to trade with developing nations because it allows them to receive some compensation for risk taking and innovation, two of the most significant products/services they can exchange for the labor and commodity-intensive products that they import from poorer countries. Without intellectual property protection, they gain little from interacting with developing nations, since they must pay for what they import, but may not be paid for much of what they export because the product of their work can be easily stolen. Eventually this will cause them to withhold their most innovative products and services from developing countries to protect their own interests and because of their inability to ever achieve a "balance of trade."[10]

Intellectual property protection provides justice to companies and their customers but economic development also requires justice to be practiced within and by companies. In the same way that companies have little incentive to work hard when the fruits of their labor go to others, there is little incentive for workers to work hard if they are being exploited. Employees who are being treated unjustly in the workplace are seldom able to productively contribute to an economy to the degree that they could if they were treated fairly. If promotions and raises go primarily to relatives or people with connections, there is little incentive for employees to work hard. Likewise, if excessive work hours or odd-hour shifts prevent people from having the time to properly care for and nurture their families, or excessively low pay makes it impossible for them to afford the medicines and other necessities that sustain the health and strength needed to work effectively, they and their families will be caught in a cycle of low productivity and poverty. Failing to see and treat employees as valuable resources may also mean that companies fail to share important information with them or solicit their ideas, further impeding economic output.

Companies may also treat customers unjustly, to the detriment of economic output. By deceiving people about the value of products and services, overcharging, or otherwise exploiting them, companies deprive customers of money that could have been used for more important things. Making them feel insecure so that they can be returned to a position of security only by purchasing the company's product or service is another type of injustice that wastes resources and robs customers of better opportunities for their money. Colluding, fixing prices or divvying up markets may enrich companies but only at the expense of customers. The same could be said when a particularly powerful company unjustly runs its competition out of business and then raises prices – it gains, but only at the expense of competitors and customers.

Injustice at the macroeconomic level can also sweep large amounts of wealth away in a very short period of time. Inflating a currency, which results in a significant depreciation of its value relative to other currencies effectively impoverishes those who have accumulated financial assets over time, as these assets will no longer buy much either at home or abroad. Rational responses to this include saving less in the future or moving savings offshore, both of which have serious effects on the long term health of an economy. A currency that retains its value, on the other hand, makes business less risky and more efficient. It enhances competition, because new companies entering a market aren't at a significant disadvantage to existing firms who made all their investments before prices went up so much. It also attracts foreign capital, which lowers the cost of borrowing for the people and companies of a country. Likewise, large fiscal deficits put upward pressure on interest rates and deprive private sector borrowers of funds that might have been used for expansion and job creation, with similarly negative effects. Low deficits, on the other hand, coupled with integrity in monetary policy, dampen the business cycle, make doing business less risky, and in the process make companies and other assets more valuable.

In conclusion, respect for, and high expectations of, authority, and the efficiency, peace and justice that flow from these things, are at the foundation of continued economic success. The U.S., in spite of its flaws - and especially after realizing the profoundly-damaging error of its mistreatment of Native Americans and slaves, has become one of the world's most resilient economies - in part because a critical mass of its citizens has been comparatively vigilant about rooting out corruption and injustice. This is no doubt related to the fact that a significant percentage of its population had either experienced injustice in the country from which they emigrated, or are descendants of those who did. At its birth it was dominated by immigrants from Europe, many of whom had come to escape the limitations of old world class structures and hierarchies. More recently it has benefitted from immigrants from nearly every country on earth, many of whom entered their adopted country with little more than the clothes on their backs. These people have blessed the U.S. not only with their willingness to work and diverse talents; they have also helped it stay focused on one of the basic principles of wealth creation: the need to continue writing laws and regulations with the golden rule in mind – that we should always treat others in the same way we would want to be treated by them. The golden rule, of course, reminds us once again of the importance of beliefs and values to economic development. Treating others fairly, especially those unlike us, is not necessarily an instinctive human reaction. Some people experience pangs of conscience if they don't do it; others are unlikely to do it unless motivated by shame; a small minority may feel no compulsion whatsoever. Healthy economic development needs as many people as possible in the first group, and fewer of those in the latter groups.

Chapter 21: Pro-Development Worldview Element # 3 – A Stewardship Ethic

A Stewardship Ethic

Although markets have some built in mechanisms for promoting stewardship (like the high prices that accompany supply shortages or demand increases), these pale in comparison to the ways in which a deeply imbedded stewardship ethic can promote healthy economic development. As implied in Chapter 6, there are many activities that members of a society can engage in that amount to little more than treading water. This was also one of the reasons we distinguished wealth from income, and expenditures from expenses, when we introduced the importance of wealth to development in Chapter 4, since these distinctions help us see that some uses of money have far more lasting value than others. Stewardship involves many things, but it has four primary elements:

- To do what is most beneficial in the long run, rather than anything/everything possible.
- To accomplish needed tasks with the fewest resources possible.
- To minimize the depreciation and depletion of existing assets, and
- To use resources to address fundamental problems rather than just symptoms of problems.

Doing what is Most Beneficial

The idea of doing what is most beneficial rather than everything possible could be easily misinterpreted. This is not to say that only work with immediate practical application should be undertaken. Such a view would result, for example, in far fewer scientific discoveries and technological improvements than we have had in the past. Rather, applied to this situation, it means we should focus on research into diseases like malaria, AIDS, cancer and diabetes, rather than on tummy tucks, face lifts, and elective breast augmentation. It also means that when behavioral changes can stop a disease or detrimental activity dead in its tracks, we should change our behavior so that we can use our organizations and productive time to fight seemingly intractable problems that stalk completely innocent victims, regardless of their behavior. This still leaves the dilemma of whether we should put lots of resources into trying to solve problems that affect a large number of people, to the exclusion of putting them into research that holds the promise of greatly helping a small number of sufferers. Helping large numbers of people with particularly difficult problems should guide our decisions, but perhaps to play these two groups against each other is really a false dilemma. A better option would be to divert resources from producing things like vanity products and services, lavish forms of entertainment, or luxury pet products, to give just a few examples, and apply them to research into rare diseases, rather than diverting basic-disease research funds from other needy people to help these victims.

Of course "doing what is most beneficial" means that economic policy will need to factor in priorities and values instead of purporting to be value-neutral. But how can this not be done? When a man leaves work with his paycheck, he may choose to stop at the bar and spend some of it on his wants instead of on his family's needs. Recognizing this simple fact, and being willing to say that bringing money home to share with family members is a better choice than leaving it at a bar, is the kind of moral stand that is essential to economic development.[1] This is obvious when we see the benefits of this kind of simple commitment in some of the micro-credit lending programs that have contributed so much to the development in the poorest countries of the world. By targeting mostly women with their loans, because in many subcultures women have different values than men (and are, for example, more likely to spend extra income on health, nutrition, education and children's needs, and less on alcohol, cigarettes or gambling), these programs have lifted millions of children out of poverty throughout the developing world. But, of course it is not the focus on women that is the key in situations like this. It is the focus on particular people (in this case poor women) *with particular values*. To illustrate this point, we will contrast what these women do with their small surpluses, for example, with what young women in Japan might do with theirs. A marketing survey several years ago indicated that 94% of all twenty-something women in Japan carry a Louis Vuitton handbag. Assuming they each paid tens of thousands of yen for these bags, one can conclude that this use of income would have a decidedly different effect on the Japanese economy than that of the microfinance recipients on theirs. The same could be said for Americans who spend lavishly on diamond-studded collars, braces and plastic surgery for their pets, or a Brit who buys Almas caviar at $25,000 per (gold-plated) tin. It is difficult to see how these things could multiply the productivity of people in the same way that nutritious food, medicine or business investment might.[2]

Focusing on needs rather than wants also helps sustainability, since satisfying the consumer's every whim often means using too much of the world's limited supply of resources too quickly, sometimes on products with grotesquely short lives, only to have these resources get scattered about in landfills a short time later, never again to see the light of day. Interestingly, even a tree is capable of matching its growth to its environment, to drop and recycle its leaves to nurture its future growth, and to bear fruit for the benefit of others with its excess resources. In this same way, any measure of development that does not factor in the sustainability of the economic activity taking place ought not to be termed "development."

The idea of sustainability can also be illustrated in a less obvious way by looking at what was happening in the United States shortly before the end of the 20th century. Just prior to the stock market doldrums, recession and terrorist attacks that ushered in the twenty-first century, the U.S had gone through one of the most amazing growth spurts in economic history. During the 1990s it seemed like nearly everything that could boost an economy had happened. Billions of new buyers entered the markets as communist countries opened up, and developing countries liberalized their economies. Trade barriers were reduced throughout the world. Americans spent with abandon, aided by large government fiscal deficits (initially) and large trade deficits throughout the decade. Computer chip technology, which could be applied to nearly every product and service imaginable, gave a substantial boost to the innovation, automation and productivity of business and industry. It also gave consumers a good excuse to go out and buy new, more-technologically-sophisticated things to replace their old things. Meanwhile, the internet multiplied the availability of information, so buyers and sellers found each other more quickly and more often. Businesses multiplied these communications advantages with steady increases in advertising. And, on the production side, producers achieved efficiencies by running additional shifts, staying open longer hours or more days each week. Business profits bolstered financial markets, and they engaged in a frenzy of mergers to achieve economies of scale. The result was a steady increase in the amount of economic activity both on and off the job. People routinely engaged in overtime on the job, but also held phone conversations while they drove, composed email messages at home or on airplanes, and responded to pagers as they strolled through the park. Further spurred by a large crop of baby boomers nearing its peak productivity and earning years, productivity, consumption and investment all increased and helped drive the stock markets to new heights. An additional boost came from a significant increase in the numbers of highly qualified women and members of minority groups entering the work force. And if labor shortages even remotely threatened this prosperity, waves of wealthy and educated immigrants were welcomed into the front door, and poorer, less educated, and often undocumented into the back (to fill unskilled and lesser skilled positions). [This list, of course, could be even longer, but it should already be clear that there was a remarkable confluence of positive factors that contributed to the growth that the U.S. and many other parts of the global economy experienced in the 1990s.[3]

But there was also a troubling thread that ran through these developments. Many of them were simply not sustainable.[4] The reason for this is that there are fundamentally three ways to develop: sustainably, temporarily, or at the expense of future development. Even if we ignore the depletion of natural resources, too much of the growth in the 1990s was not sustainable. The transition of the formerly communist economies to markets could only occur once. This also meant that the real decreases in defense spending at the cessation of the Cold War, which led to easy budget surpluses for a while, would also likely be a one-time shot in the arm. Trade barriers can only be reduced so far, and then there are no longer tariffs and quotas to eliminate. Hence foreign capital could not continue to flow into the U.S. at the rate of 400-700 billion dollars per year indefinitely (the range of the U.S.'s trade deficits and capital inflows between 2000 and 2008). In fact, the flow could even be reversed. Foreign investors are free to pull their money from the U.S. (or any other country) at any time, which could cause a significant decline in the stock market and the international value of the dollar, an increase in interest rates, and a slowdown in the economy. Likewise, increases in time devoted to economic activity cannot continue indefinitely. There are only twenty four hours in a day and seven days in a week, and it seems clear that by the end of the 20th century not much more time could be squeezed out by either producers or consumers for economic activity. To be sure, even in the U.S. there are still opportunities for members of some disadvantaged minority groups to increase their contribution to the economy, but studies at the beginning of the new century indicated that most women in the U.S. were already working as many hours and sometimes more hours than they desired, so little additional stimulus was likely to come from increased participation rates in this group. Many teenagers were also working so many hours that they were on the brink of compromising their education, if they had not already done so.

The demographic boost to the U.S. economy was also diminishing. With the age distribution of the U.S. population about ten to fifteen years behind Japan's, the U.S. was vulnerable to some of the same problems Japan struggled through in the 1990s - as the ratio of retirees to workers increased.[5] By the time of the recession that began in 2008, the baby boomers were beginning to retire with an anticipated strain on the Social Security and Medicare systems. The flow of immigrants into the U.S. was also slowing, partly because of security-related bureaucracy, and a rebound was by no means assured, because decades of economic improvement in post-communist and other "developing" countries had provided many new opportunities for educated potential immigrants or foreign-born residents of the U.S. to stay at home or return home. Of course, these potential difficulties were not unique to the U.S. Many other countries of the world have far lower birth rates than the U.S and less immigration as well. And, although we believe it is ill-advised to overact to these birth-rate declines, it seems fair to say that these demographic trends would make it challenging for many of the wealthy countries to sustain the growth rates they had experienced in the latter half of the 20th century.

One thing the "Great Recession"[6] made clear is that measures designed to stimulate an economy in the short run may do little more than shift economic activity from the future to the present. The same could be said for global stock markets which can sometimes be "juiced" by policies that cannot be repeated. For example, decreases in capital gains taxes and taxes on dividends, deferred taxes on capital gains, the implementation of tax-free retirement-savings vehicles, incentives for rewarding employees with stock options in lieu of wages, discussions about privatizing social security and investing social security surpluses in the stock market, and the elimination of the estate tax all helped the U.S. stock market defy gravity prior to the Great Recession. In addition, when greed kept some well-known companies' bottom lines from increasing as fast as investors had come to expect, they boosted current income and cannibalized future income by levering their balance sheets with debt and playing short-lived marketing and accounting games. U.S. Legislation had already reversed some of these accounting games prior to the Great Recession, but the battle between the government and a new crop of companies was rejoined when government missteps and corporate ethical breaches combined to deepen the U.S. recession and exacerbate the already severe problems in the financial markets. The result of all this was fatigue in the markets and the impression that future stimulus policy options were limited. Since many of the best policy "cards" had been (over)played already in the 1990s, they were no longer available to be used again. And with politicians mulling the withdrawal of some longstanding economic incentives, the prospects for a significant reversal of the stock market's dismal performance during the first decade of the 21st century remained dim.

All this suggests that sustainable economic development also depends on another dimension of stewardship – that of being prepared for the inevitable reversals in the domestic and global economies. Unfortunately, one of the best methods for surviving a reversal, that of building surpluses during times of prosperity that can be used during lean years, is not an option for many Americans, because they had saved too little during the prosperous years at the end of the 20th and beginning of the 21st centuries - choosing instead to raise their debt levels to historically high levels. High debt levels are not necessarily a problem, especially if income streams are secure and assets constitute good collateral. Unfortunately, this was not the case, since over time consumer spending had gradually shifted toward things people wanted, rather than things they needed, and things that don't last as opposed to things that last. By the time the bubble burst in 2008, even many *asset* purchases including homes were for speculative reasons rather than for meeting needs. These trends, coupled with the fact that an increasing share of the developed world's economies were devoted to producing and selling things that people could easily do without made the entire global economy more vulnerable to an economic downturn. People simply stopped purchasing some non-necessities when resource shortages drove up prices or when they became more fearful about the future.

The best way to protect the global economy from such vulnerabilities is for companies to concentrate on the long run, by producing and promoting goods, services and assets that people really need, and for governments to encourage ongoing generosity rather than implementing a treadmill of politically popular policies that do little more than encourage people to accelerate or increase their purchases because of government subsidies. Of course, transforming the global economy from what increasing looks like a resource-consuming hamster wheel that people dare not get off to something more sustainable requires returning to some time-honored values such as honesty, patience, service and generosity - which in turn suggest a worldview reorientation.

Accomplishing Needed Tasks with as Few Resources as Possible

Conserving resources, since resources are "costs" in the production of goods and services, both create wealth and stimulate economic development. As Adam Smith noted, competition is a great vehicle for encouraging producers to keep costs to a minimum, and the intelligent use of technology has also been very important. New communications technologies have allowed people to work and interact in significant ways with people thousands of miles away without having to fly or drive long distances; LED technologies now provide light at a fraction of the cost of conventional bulbs; computers and printers now accomplish what once required massive offset presses, pocket-sized MP3 players can play thousands of songs with impeccable sound quality; and hybrid vehicles now carry passengers while consuming as little as 1/3 as much gas as other vehicles. Social cooperation, as noted earlier, is also a valuable method of conserving resources, as carpooling, shared delivery systems, and many highly efficient and reliable public transportation systems around the world illustrate. But what is often overlooked is that a widely-shared stewardship ethic can spur these efficiencies even when competition and social cooperation are imperfect.

Almost everything a business does internally to improve its profits could be viewed as part of a stewardship ethic. In order to keep costs to a minimum, businesses have instituted just-in-time inventory systems, quality control systems, asset management systems, safety systems, recycling programs, and logistics systems, all of which are tracked by elaborate accounting programs. To maintain stewardship on the revenue side they have designed elaborate credit analysis and collections systems. Of course a danger in the relentless push to do more with less is that at times organizations will take steps to cut their own costs that will simultaneously raise costs to others, a phenomenon that economists refer to as an "externality." A stewardship ethic, however, will spur governments and private organizations to work together to maximize the likelihood that both private and public decisions actually minimize *overall* costs. This requires that businesses be transparent about what they are doing and that governments both measure stealth costs (externalities) and assign property rights in such a way that those benefitting from externalities compensate those damaged by them.

It is also important to remember that costs are not only a concern to producers of goods and services; goods and services may also "cost" consumers far more than the price being charged. The reason for this is that people pay for the products and services they purchase with their time and energy as well as with money. In other words, even when the prices of products and services do not increase and GDP stays flat, the value people receive from them could be reduced by things statistics can't easily capture. For example, even when prices have not gone up, consumers could find that they are devoting more time, energy, and frustration to the products and services they use, by, e.g., being stuck in traffic, crowded public places or voice-mail "black holes." In Bangkok, people spend the equivalent of 35 days per year stopped or crawling in traffic, and there are around

300 births per year in automobiles, neither of which is effectively factored into their economic statistics. Likewise, gas or grocery prices may not rise, but people may be asked to pump the gas or bag the groceries themselves. Or, prices may not rise, but products received may be of poorer quality or people may enjoy what they buy less because they are forced to waste time wading through junk mail, having their meals interrupted by telemarketers, or dealing with the effects of spam or viruses on their computers. U.S. households, for example, receive an average of two-three pieces of junk mail every day and by some estimates nearly half the email messages sent in the U.S. are classified as spam. Clearly, lots of resources are being misused or wasted.

These situations underscore the degree to which efficient and healthy economic activity depends as much on beliefs, values, morality and ethics as on technology and brainpower. This is most obvious when we observe people who come to work well rested every morning because their commitment to stewardship also carries over into their private lives. It is perhaps less obvious when many of these same people work hard day in and day out without supervision, refuse to pilfer company supplies or misuse company property, or contribute cost-cutting ideas to their organizations even when there is no financial incentive to do so. Even if having people with these kinds of values and attitudes added only a five percent efficiency gain to a business's bottom line, the organization that employs them would still have a continuous competitive advantage in the marketplace. This kind of competitive advantage will also often persist for long periods of time because values and attitudes, unlike materials, financial capital and know-how, which can be transferred relatively easily from one organization to another, are the unique product of a particular group of people who are knit together in a unique way. Because of this, the best businesses know that they cannot pretend to be value-free institutions that exist only to make money or allow values and ethics to be relegated to the private domain of families and churches. The best companies publicize their values and ethics, do their best to attract people who subscribe to them, and find creative ways to imbed them throughout their organizations.

Countries must do the same. A country cannot be competitive if its people have poor ethics any more than if its people have poor health. But neither good health nor good ethics will happen in the absence of a public discussion of values. Part of the reason for this is that the market only functions as well as the values in which it is immersed. The fast food and auto industries will give us fast food and fast cars if we value speed, and rich food or luxurious cars if we value pleasure, but they will not give us healthy food or efficient and effective cars unless we value stewardship. To be competitive, a country must not only have healthy citizens who drive carefully, it must have citizens who stay healthy and drive carefully *in a manner that best conserves resources*.[7] This is equally true of hundreds of other behaviors that also contribute to productivity, many of which are public rather than private. If people believe their political leaders are trustworthy, they are more likely to pay their taxes. Even a custom as expensive and seemingly unnecessary as having a royal family could have a positive effect on an economy.[8] If the queen and her family inspire widespread civic participation, or volunteerism, or if they are helpful in raising the integrity level of citizens, or in maintaining unity and peace, they could actually contribute to a healthier economy. It all depends on the values espoused and their impact on people's behavior.

Minimizing Waste and the Depreciation and Depletion of Existing Assets

Anything that is produced and wasted is a drag on economic development and growth. Examples include the unusual quantity of used goods trashed in Japan because of the taboo against using other people's things, or the approximately $30 billion in food that is estimated to end up in landfills in the U.S. in a typical year.[9] Depreciation and depletion, on the other hand, require a bit more discussion. Depreciation involves the rate at which the things we have and use wear out, whereas depletion is related to the rate at which people tap the earth's limited resources to make new things and replace old ones. The two are clearly related since minimizing depreciation with technologies like vinyl or cement siding, brick and mortar, or stainless steel, each of which has a significantly longer life than the older technology it replaced, vastly increases the life of whatever these materials are being used for and consequently reduces the amount of extraction necessary.

But minimizing depreciation and depletion means far more than using good technologies. It means understanding the difference between renewable and nonrenewable resources and recognizing that non-renewable resources are a type of wealth, whereas renewable resources are more like income. Liquidating wealth makes sense on occasion, when doing so allows us to create things that are much more valuable than what we are using up in the process. It also helps if what we are producing is exceptionally long lasting, or appreciates in value over time. But worldviews that do a poor job of factoring in their responsibilities to future generations will often unthinkingly accept the valuation of non-renewable resources at extraction cost. This ignores their true potential value since we do not know what other valuable uses they could have now or in the future, and often leads to using them without care, for anything or everything. [10] The financial equivalent of this would be pulling our savings out of the bank, because we do not realize its value, spending it, and then pretending that the only cost to us is the bank's transaction fee. It would be better to view non-renewable sources of energy such as oil, coal or natural gas as energy wealth that is available to sustain our energy needs during times when our energy income, e.g., solar, tidal, hydroelectric power, is inadequate. A stewardship ethic also mandates recognizing that if we use a resource like oil in a way that prevents it from ever being reused, the true cost to us is greater than if we use it, for example, to manufacture a plastic which can be recycled and/or be reused by future generations.   Competition and markets by themselves to do not make these things obvious, but a commitment to stewardship does.

We are not suggesting here that we gradually withdraw from all the technologies that have allowed us to substitute other forms of power for human effort. Nevertheless, if we are serious about wanting

Chapter 21

our descendants to "stand on our shoulders," as it were, rather than pay for our sins, we need to pay attention to all of the different kinds of wealth that we are using up in addition to those we are creating.   We also need to look seriously at substitutes for non-renewable forms of energy, be responsible with the resources we remove from the earth (reusing them whenever possible) and find ways to control energy-wasting whims.[11]   As noted earlier, minimizing depletion and depreciation also means caring for the things we already have.   Much could be said about the unthinking behaviors that contribute to the excessive wear out and too-frequent replacement of the many things that are part of our lives.   But since these kinds of excesses and abuses have been talked about in many other books, and most people are already aware of the problem, we will devote our remaining time here to other forms of depreciation and depletion that often go unnoticed.

The depletion of common property often goes unnoticed.   For example, in Bangkok the air quality has been depleted, as has both the quality of water and the water table itself.   Only a small percentage of the population has adequate sewage disposal, which contributes to the water and perhaps air quality problems.   Problems like these diminish the health of large numbers of people, affect productivity and absenteeism, and reduce possibilities for true/sustainable development.   Although the official statistics will not capture it, the country is taking one step back for every two steps forward.   Another example of depletion and depreciation is poor stewardship over more visible communal assets such as public parks, lakes, rivers, public buildings and common areas.   Anyone who traveled into the Soviet Union prior to its demise in 1991, or to some of the other Eastern-European communist countries prior to their restructurings, will have vivid pictures in her mind of the neglect of some government-owned or communal property.   Parks and playground equipment were often run down.   Apartment buildings with nicely kept individual apartments nevertheless had filthy common areas, dark elevators and hallways - because the common property, light bulbs in this case, was often diverted to private use.   But the most serious depreciation of environmental capital in the former Soviet Union wase the result of seventy years of lax environmental standards that resulted in radiation damage, polluted rivers, and dirty air.   In one particularly graphic example of this, the Soviet authorities, in an attempt to be self-sufficient in the production of cotton and rice, pumped so much water out of the rivers flowing into the Aral Sea, and the sea itself, that by the late 1980s this body of water, once larger than any of the Great Lakes except Lake Superior, had to be declared off limits to all commercial fishing and shipping, and towns once on the water's edge were by then as far as forty miles from it.

Many of the poorest countries in the world also have large strips of land that have become greatly devalued, in this case because nearly all the trees were cut down without regard to the long term effects of erosion and the failure to reforest.   We recognize in some cases this was done out of desperation as the firewood was necessary to protect people on the brink of existence from cold or to enable them to cook a daily meal – our purpose here is not to fix blame.[12]   But these problems are not limited to communist and poor countries, or to public property.   The earth is abused wherever there is an insufficient stewardship ethic. For example, graffiti damage to public and private property is probably a bigger problem in radically-individualistic countries than in communist ones. Neither are these problems limited to tangible property. Recalling our development wheel discussions of spiritual/moral, intellectual/emotional or social capital, three of the most serious kinds of depletion and depreciation stem from people's unwillingness to care for their heritage, their health and/or their relationships. In some cultures, for example, young people glibly throw away the wisdom that their ancestors accumulated and passed on over decades and centuries, such as the importance of hard work, or the essentiality of marriage fidelity, honesty and integrity to a cohesive society, preferring only to focus on their immediate concerns and pleasures.[13]

Our basic point is that excessive depreciation and depletion of all forms of capital costs an economy a great deal.[14] The failure to care for the human body represents the depletion/depreciation of one kind of physical capital and extorts a heavy cost from the medical system. Broken marriages and family relationships represent the depletion/depreciation of spiritual/moral capital and exact a heavy toll on children. The breakdown of trust in communities is an example of the depreciation/depletion of emotional or social capital and exacerbates many other kinds of health problems. And, finally, of course, war, particularly when being used for purposes other than stopping the spread of evil, is the ultimate form of brokenness, depleting and depreciating almost everything.

In conclusion, it is fair to say that allowing or causing both public and private resources to depreciate unnecessarily, and thereby wasting funds to repair or restore things that could have been preserved with little more than a worldview adjustment, is a significant impediment to economic development in nearly every corner of the world. But these things are only manifestations of an even more significant dimension of poor stewardship, and one that is even less obvious to most people. This is the problem of wasting resources by addressing *symptoms* of problems, rather than the underlying problems themselves – the subject of the final section of this chapter.

The Importance of Addressing Fundamental Problems Rather Than Just Symptoms of Problems

Although seldom written about, the importance of addressing problems rather than symptoms may be the most important component of stewardship. Many books, studies, and organizations, chief among them the group Redefining Progress, have demonstrated that the quality of life *in wealthy countries* is also not nearly as good as their national income statistics such as Gross Domestic Product (GDP) indicate. Of course many aspects of life are much better in relatively-wealthy countries now than has ever been the case in the history of the world, but as Easterbrook demonstrates in *The Progress Paradox* even though people are making and spending more money and have more stuff than ever before, they aren't necessarily pleased with the status of their lives. Why does so much money often buy so little satisfaction? Easterbrook offers a panoply of reasons, but the one most relevant to this discussion is the tendency for too large a percentage of our private and public expenditures (all of which count equally economic statistics), to be spent on symptoms of problems, rather than on eliminating underlying problems. This means, in effect, that money is spent over and over again on the same problem, and although this may boost GDP, it is costly to the wealth creation process because funds wasted on symptoms are unavailable for solving other more important or pressing problems. In general terms, the most significant example of this is when resources must be diverted to combating the effects of irresponsible behavior, making these same resources unavailable to create products and services that could greatly improve the lives of the people of the world.

To make this point clearer we will examine the U.S., which has one of the highest official standards of living in the world. Starting, for example, with crime and terrorism, at the time of this writing, citizens of the U.S. spent between $50 and 100 billion a year purchasing locks for cars, offices, desks, homes, etc. and over 100 billion a year on business security systems, bank guards, software protection, etc. Through government they spend tens of billions more on police, judicial systems, corrections, drug enforcement agencies, library surveillance systems, and white-collar crime prevention.[15] U.S. citizens also pay too-high insurance premiums to protect their property because of insurance fraud, unscrupulous liability claims, and, more recently, billions more to protect people from terrorism. In some cases fear forces people (and especially victims to alter everyday behaviors, and in some cases even uproot their families from their communities. Altogether, these costs, all of which have their roots in misguided worldviews, amount to thousands of dollars for every adult. Although difficult to measure, World Bank estimates have put the cost of crime at as much as 25% of GDP in some countries. And money spent combating crime directly reduces the production and enjoyment of other products and services that could make people's lives more joyful and meaningful.

The examples above however are just the tip of the iceberg. Consider further the billions of dollars spent annually on replacing things, cleaning up the environment, or patching up relationships that were not properly cared for in the first place. According to the Redefining Progress, car crashes - many related to inebriated or distracted driving - cost U.S. inhabitants between 100 and 200 billion dollars per year. Costly attempts are made to restore health lost to cigarettes, alcohol and drug abuse. Sales of bottled water have skyrocketed around the world wherever confidence in public water supplies is low. Ecologists tell us that as much as 200 million tons of topsoil slide off the U.S. continental shelf yearly without a single debit to our national accounts. Pollution, like many of the other things mentioned above, is an especially "good" deal for official statistics, since it has the possibility of being counted in GDP twice. This is because the cost of polluting is initially treated as productive economic activity since it is not an explicit cost and therefore allows the profits of polluters to be overstated. Then, later, when someone pays to clean things up, it gets counted a second time and usually at a much higher value since cleanup costs are invariably greater than the cost savings associated with the original polluting.

Our inability to distinguish symptoms from problems in the area of social capital is equally costly. Imagine the expenses borne by millions of divorced or separated people who are saddled with two sets of rent or mortgage payments, or lawyers' fees, because they need two houses or apartments, or two lawyers rather than one. Unmeasured stresses and broken relationships also increasingly diminish modern life, with nothing subtracted from GDP, but the sales of antidepressants contribute billions to GDP. Unbridled sexual activity requires large amounts to be spent on researching, diagnosing, medicating and curing sexually transmitted diseases and sexual addictions in order to restore people to the level of health and protection they could have had by engaging responsibly in sexual activity and restricting access to pornography. Additional billions are spent on airbrushing, editing, body doubles, and the like to create unrealistic images of physically perfect people and billions more are spent on therapy or plastic surgery aimed at building people's self-esteem back up. U.S. citizens also spend around 100 billion dollars annually on diet plans and products, and obesity-related health care services attempting to get back to the level of health they would have had if they hadn't routinely overeaten. One can only guess how much more money was wasted purchasing the excessive amounts of food that brought them to the point where they needed these diet and health plans. Likewise, the amount of money spent on casino gambling - which has risen substantially in its contribution to GDP in recent decades - has also brought gambling addictions and family struggles along with it, creating additional demand for social services but certainly not adding to the quality of people's lives.

This general and gradual increase in spending on fundamentally unnecessary or even harmful behaviors means far less of people's incomes and wealth is available to be saved and invested in other things that could make their lives and the lives of their children and grandchildren better. This is also true of the shift to the purchase of disposable products, the use of non-recyclable packaging, unconcern for maintaining and prolonging the lives of existing assets, and the frequent disposal of goods before the end of their useful life. Each of these activities forces people to work many more hours than necessary to attain a particular standard of living. It's as if they are pouring water into a leaky bucket. Does it make sense to measure our accomplishment by the amount of water we have poured into the bucket (GDP), or the amount that is actually in the bucket when it comes time to use it? Unfortunately, once a nation settles comfortably into a materialistic worldview, chooses, tracks and sets policy by a statistic that is consistent with that worldview (like GDP, which makes no distinction between wise and unwise spending), it will eventually lose sight of the fact that the quality of its citizens lives may well be dropping even as its measured output soars.

But even when it appears that problems, rather than symptoms, are being directly addressed, such as when women receiving micro-credit loans use their surplus funds for the good of their children, or when well-off people divert their funds from capricious consumption to NGOs that save the lives of starving people, this is no guarantee of an optimal solution. How much better would it be if the hearts and minds of the husbands of the microloan recipients were changed so that they derived their greatest joy from spending their time, energy and money on the development of their children? How much better if NGO donors and farmers had been unwilling to rest until a combination of drought-resistant or nutritious plants, irrigation, fertilizers, training, or even migration had made death by famine a thing of the past.[16] Clearly, the ultimate solution to these problems, and others like them, is as much philosophical and religious as it is social or economic.[17]

Chapter 22: Pro-Development Worldview Element # 4 – The Ability to See Oneself Objectively and Others Sympathetically

Introduction

One thing that is likely to make a powerful person more committed to identifying and fixing problems, and more oriented to service and stewardship, would be for him to see himself objectively and others sympathetically.   It would also be good for development if this trait were widely distributed throughout the population. Seeing ourselves objectively means we are able to see our own limitations and flaws, which in turn allows us to see our need for both outside wisdom and other people. Those who are unable to see their own flaws also usually have difficulty relating well to and bringing out the best in others. Seeing ourselves objectively requires that we value having others "hold up a mirror" to us as often and for as long as is necessary for us to get an accurate picture of ourselves.   Seeing others sympathetically requires that in addition to seeing ourselves objectively, something motivates us to be able to overcome the natural human tendency to be primarily self-interested. It also means we become capable of doing this not just for those in our immediate family and friendship circles, but for those with whom we do not have regular contact and who may be very unlike us.

The ability to see others sympathetically is something that we could probably best describe as a continuum. At one end of the continuum are those who, for whatever reason, mistrust, fear, and sometimes even hate almost everyone. On the other end of the spectrum are those who are legitimately interested in, have a deep concern for, and may even be willing to selflessly risk their time, energy, and personal comfort for the sake of those who not only have no familial or friendship connection with them, but may also be very unlike them. Between these extremes are people who show concern for others mainly when it is to their advantage, those who are committed to be generally tolerant of different kinds of people, and those who respect and even appreciate different kinds of people, but stop short of regularly inconveniencing themselves on their behalf.   These categories, of course, are arbitrary, but hopefully helpful in describing the spectrum of perspectives in this area.

Mistrust and Fear

Little needs to be said about the economic impact of widespread mistrust, fear and/or hatred for others. At best this stifles economic exchanges or increases the transactions costs associated with them; at worst it will destroy both productive capacity and people. Francis Fukuyama's book *Trust* does an excellent job of describing how trust relationships are at the core of both the development of markets and democracy. He does this in part by showing the importance of having organizations that are glued together by solid lasting bonds that have their roots in shared norms and values, as opposed to those held together by autocratic or charismatic leaders or patronage relationships. The ability to form these kinds of organizations, according to Fukuyama, is itself a function of the amount of trust in a culture or subculture. Fukuyama does not say economic activity cannot be organized and stimulated through restrictive or intimidating policies or government action, only that it will be inherently less efficient.

It is a sad fact that people who tend to mistrust, fear and even hate large numbers of people are more often than not both motivated by these emotions and inclined to use them to try to motivate others. It is not unusual for them to exploit the need to confront a common enemy to achieve motivation or group cohesiveness. But the need for a common enemy, though sometimes motivating, is not usually healthy for economic development because it pushes people in the direction of destructive competition, and success becomes more closely tied to beating an opponent than providing the best quality service at the best price. This worldview element is especially destructive when one or both of the parties that reflect it has destructive weapons and technologies at their disposal. The history books are full of accounts of the economic and human damage done by people with more than a trace of this perspective in their worldviews: the Spanish in Mexico, European settlers in the Americas, the Voortrekkers in South Africa, the Germans in WW II, the Japanese in China, and the Hutus in Rwanda, just to name a small sample. Much of this damage can be traced to an assumed inequality of people and the legitimacy of the pursuit of self-interest even when others are harmed in the process. It opens the door to greed, exploitation, slavery, and even murder.

Although less damaging then war, mistrust and fear among business competitors also has the ability to introduce inefficiencies into the economy. Competition, of course, has the potential to either increase or decrease business and economic efficiency, depending on the worldview of the participants. Competitive activities have great potential for good. At an individual level, they can, for example, increase one's appreciation for fellow competitors, spur the development of self-discipline and self-control, increase levels of enthusiasm, cooperation, or creativity within a group or organization, and teach virtues such as patience, humility, courage, and the ability to handle disappointment. On the other hand, an atmosphere of fear and mistrust among competitors can foster pride, resentment, divisiveness, "rule bending", excessive aggression, stress, and an unhealthy emphasis on winning to the detriment of an emphasis on service.

Tolerance

Tolerance greatly reduces the possibility of war and other similarly destructive activity, permits routine arm's length transactions, and opens up at least the possibility that people with different norms and values can develop trust relationships and work well together. But there is nothing inherent in a tolerance-oriented worldview that will spur people beyond the postponement of judgment toward the highest human possibilities. For example, there is nothing inherent in tolerance that will foster exceptional group cohesiveness, or give its adherents any special advantage in their ability to build highly productive social and economic organizations or alliances. Nor does tolerance evoke a passion to redress the inequities that freedom and markets inevitably bring with them, or encourage the conservation of resources for the benefit of others who could productively use them, or for future generations - things that would make economic growth more sustainable. Tolerance is also not a strong enough virtue to keep people from erecting trade or other barriers to improve their competitive position vis-à-vis others, or spur them to look out for the interest or actively work to improve the position of others up who have no particular connection to them.

Another big problem with the sense that our obligations to others stops at the level of tolerance is that it allows those who are tolerating to maintain an air of superiority over those with whom they come into contact. A manager or bureaucrat who tolerates his workers but doesn't truly care about them, or who tolerates people of a particular skin color, but doesn't see their unlimited potential, effectively blocks the development of the kind of relationships that motivate people to do their best. People who are made to feel inferior seldom participate or work up to their potential. Even worse, such an attitude allows the person who believes that tolerance is all that he owes to others to take advantage of others when the opportunity arises - which opens the door to all kinds of counter-productive economic activity. In the best-case scenario, this kind of activity simply redistributes wealth from the exploited to the exploiter, but even in this case it usually results in giving people far too little for their money, leaving them either a bit worse off or perhaps seriously damaged. It is not unusual for people who are flamboyant with their wealth to be people who value tolerance, but feel little obligation to go beyond this. Comfortably spending large quantities of money indulging themselves, their families and their close friends, they effectively use up more than their share of resources and compel (with their expenditures) large numbers of people to serve them (which also keeps these resources and people from being employed for the benefit of others). Although they may not actually control servants or slaves, they nevertheless have hundreds or thousands of "freemen" at their beck-and-call wherever they flash their stashes of currency or travel and entertainment cards. If we add to this the "energy slaves" they command (discussed in a Chapter 21 footnote), there are many thousands of little-known people globally who in effect have entourages that rival those of the kings, czars or emperors of yesteryear.

Tolerance can also dampen economic activity by allowing unhealthy misconceptions to last much longer and do more damage than they should. Increasingly, commitments to tolerance are coupled with an unwillingness to engage others about fundamental ideas of right and wrong, leaving people far too much wiggle room to make and persist in unwise thinking patterns and unhelpful behaviors. Surprisingly large numbers of people in the U.S. are becoming comfortable with tolerating disrespect for authority, selfishness, crude language and behavior, mediocrity, and sometimes even insolence and laziness in the interest of not being critical.[1]

Finally, excessive tolerance also opens the door to both small problems and unimaginable evil. Recent research on bullying, and more specifically on school shootings, has uncovered some of the long-term damage that has its origins on school playgrounds. Joseph Stalin, to cite an extreme example, is said to have suffered schoolyard taunting about his weak arm as well as abuse by his father. Although this can hardly explain the millions of innocent people who suffered and/or died at his hands, or the accompanying damage done to the Soviet economy and society, it is plausibly a contributing factor. A case could also be made that Stalin's WW II problems (more accurately, the problems of the Soviet citizens who suffered almost unimaginable hardship during WW II) were at least partly the result of his own inappropriate willingness to tolerate evil. Rather than recognize the Nazi regime for what it was, he was all too willing, as long as Hitler's victims were nameless, faceless and far enough away, to cavort with evil via the Nazi-Soviet pact, rather than sharing the outrage that others expressed for what Hitler was doing. More recently, the tolerance of evil and/or incompetence has had similarly disastrous consequences in, among other places, Cambodia (Kampuchea), Rwanda, Liberia, Sierra Leone, the Democratic Republic of the Congo, and Zimbabwe.

Respect and Appreciation

Moving from beliefs that merely encourage tolerance to those that encourage respect and appreciation for all people gives an additional boost to development. True respect and appreciation start with the assumption that all people are worthy and have gifts, talents, and experiences that are valuable not only to themselves but to the groups and organizations in which they participate and society as a whole. This "higher view" of people opens the door to a variety of development-enhancing behaviors such as healthy trust relationships, effective delegation of authority and responsibility, and productivity increases. Respect and appreciation also open the door to appreciation for the elderly, which could result in a greater willingness to tap into the wisdom and capabilities of older members of a society, and less of a tendency to push them aside. It also opens the door for companies to hire members of disadvantaged minority groups, which not only benefits the companies, but allows those hired to learn important employment-related skills. Respect and appreciation for college graduates who don't have Ivy League pedigrees, or even college dropouts (like Bill Gates or Tom Hanks) allows companies to hire strictly on the basis of employee attitudes, skills and potential, again benefiting both the companies and the economy.

Research on the measurements of IQ gives some additional insight on how the appreciation for all kinds of people benefits an economy. Until recently, many people around the world relied heavily on traditional IQ tests that have a tendency to focus disproportionately on cognitive and reasoning skills. Unfortunately, this allowed people with high IQs to think of themselves as superior in spite of the fact that they may have been "all thumbs" when it came to mechanical aptitude, were poor managers or leaders, or were even socially or emotionally inept. In contrast, those whose worldviews give them a keen insight into the diversity of gifts and the inherent worthiness of each and every individual are more likely to be predisposed to "see" the potential in those who, although less gifted academically, have other sensitivities, attitudes and skills that are needed every bit as much as high IQs in the complex social system of the modern organization.

There is also good reason to believe that people whose worldviews permit them to see the fundamental worthiness of all people are more likely to appreciate the things they have, be it their jobs, bosses, paychecks, colleagues or something else. This in turn enables them to understand that the proper response when receiving a paycheck in return for services, or services in return for a paycheck, is gratitude and fair treatment of the other party. This kind of attitude may also make them more likely to "see" things like unemployment, underemployment, or lack of motivation as abnormal and in need of fixing. All of these kinds of heart and/or head responses to others have the potential to take employees, and the businesses, NGOs or government offices they work for, to a higher level of motivation, teamwork and productivity. And when business, NGO or government managers truly respect and appreciate their workers, they are much more likely to come up with creative ways to solicit and reward worker input, and accommodate their desires for more responsibility and authority. In the same way, government officials who respect and appreciate people outside of their immediate family and friendship circles will take the concerns of their citizens and businesses seriously, and do everything in their power to remove regulatory barriers that keep them from accomplishing important goals. And relative to their counterparts whose belief systems do not mandate that they respect the less-privileged or powerful, they will be much less inclined to tolerate or engage in bureaucratic power plays, nepotism, or the kind of bribery, extortion or grease payments that contribute to poverty all around the world.

At an even broader level, respect for and appreciation of all people, including "outsiders," means making a commitment to find as many ways as possible to give people equal treatment - such as removing unnecessary barriers to cross-border trade or starting businesses. This means more job creation and a host of other economic benefits as companies and consumers thrive in an environment where they are free to pursue the capital, products or services they need at the best possible prices. A worldview that reflects respect and appreciation should also make government officials more desirous of making it easier for people to receive the justice due them. In such an environment, creditors could press legitimate claims, and businesses could register property, get credit, protect their investments, fire unproductive workers, or have their contracts enforced as needed - all of which have a profound effect on development.

A final way that respect and appreciation of those who are unlike us benefits an economy is by opening up the door to increased amounts of learning. There is a well-known expression in education that "what one says matters less than who is saying it." Most people have a natural inclination to discount the potential value of the ideas and practices of those who are unlike them, even though these are often the people from whom they could learn the most. The history of the world is replete with examples of both traders and missionaries returning to their home countries with exotic goods and artifacts. But only some of them - generally people who respected and appreciated the ideas of people or cultures very different from their own - returned with the kinds of new ideas that could transform their world. As Nobel Prize winner Amartya Sen noted, a thousand years ago Europe was full of small kingdoms fighting turf wars with each other and many of the technologies that were influential at the time had been developed elsewhere.[2] Part of Europe's "turnaround" and therefore its more rapid development in the subsequent millennium was related to their ability to apply the knowledge of others, and focus on the wisdom and usefulness of ideas in general, without prejudice as to where those ideas originated. Doing this, however, required a worldview transformation, which came to Europe (as elsewhere) in fits and starts, but was largely powered by the sweeping changes ushered in by the Renaissance and Reformation - and the changing beliefs that were at their core.

Benefits of Voluntary Cooperation.

As European history attest, tolerance, respect and appreciation are also essential for both democracy and free markets to work well. Just because people have the freedom and authority to solve their problems is not to imply that they always use that freedom to work well together. Tolerance, respect and appreciation enable people to appreciate the benefits of and give them the capability of working cooperatively with increasingly larger groups of people – many of whom may be unlike them. We briefly addressed the topic of living and working "in community" in Chapter 6, where we noted that the demise of community can masquerade as economic development because the living expenses of a group of isolated individuals is higher than it would be for the same number of people working and living in community. And in our discussion of civil society we spent considerable time addressing the degree to which voluntary participation in CSOs builds productive skills, how the building of civil society is a community activity, and how a commitment to peaceable change leads to significant economic benefits. But we did not adequately address in either of those places what we would like to devote some time to here - the myriad economic benefits that flow from increasingly sophisticated levels of voluntary group efforts. Because not all worldviews seem equally aware of this, it serves us well to be reminded of just how pervasive the opportunities to cooperate are, and how extensive the potential economic benefits of doing so are.

Cooperative ventures come in many forms: economic (e.g. markets, trade, corporations), social (e.g., study groups, housing arrangements, neighborhood watches), and political (coalitions, compromise, bipartisan legislation), but all require tolerance, respect and appreciation to function well. Each form brings efficiency gains, albeit not always of the same nature. Take the financial markets, for instance. The development of markets where people come together to exchange money for promises brings many efficiencies. First of all, resources are preserved when people can carry lightweight paper currency with them instead of cumbersome objects to barter. Secondly, those receiving the money in exchange for their promise to repay will be able to much more productively put their talents and ideas to work to create new wealth than would have been possible without the extension of credit. Thirdly, neither the lenders nor the borrowers need to waste gasoline and time wandering all over the place to find enough people to lend or borrow the amount money they have or need for as long as they think they would like to lend or borrow it. And lastly, lenders also benefit from having experts assuage their worries about the borrowers' creditworthiness.

Corporations, although far from perfect,[3] are excellent examples of cooperative ventures that exist to perform tasks that are too complex for any single individual to perform efficiently or effectively. And we are not talking about minor improvements here, but massive improvements in quality or reductions in cost. Adam Smith's example of the pin factory cited earlier is a simple example of this, but the benefits of producing a pin cooperatively pale in comparison to those associated with producing a jumbo-jet or lap-top computer.

It can be fairly argued that the most successful companies and industries are those that best understand the essentiality of cooperation to economic success. Instead of taking a "winner take all" approach, they often form strategic alliances and industry associations, thereby extending cooperation beyond the organizational level whenever possible. Of course, even for these companies there are still many potential benefits that remain unclaimed. Many companies are still unwilling to work cooperatively *for the sake of third parties* when it will negatively affect their bottom line. Examples include being unwilling to work with competitors when doing so could lower costs for customers, or with the government, even though doing so could benefit taxpayers.

Other examples of cooperative efficiencies include the sharing of one apartment among several friends, college roommates helping each other understand the subject matter of their courses, or neighbors establishing a cooperative security association in place of individually purchasing expensive fences and home protection alarm systems. Political efficiencies are obtained with the passing of legislation that allows states or provinces and governments to divide duties rather than duplicate them, or the provision of roads, clean water, railways, or reliable electricity to people at a fraction of the cost associated with trying to do this independently. Many other partnerships are multifaceted and more difficult to classify, such as when university-student interns serve businesses and community organizations while simultaneously learning on the job.

Countries, too, have experienced massive benefits when governments came to understand the potential benefits of cooperation. Europe benefitted greatly once the church and state stopped fighting for control and implemented pluralistic structures allowing each to serve the people in unique and complementary ways. The business sector flourishes when government recognizes that good, ethical companies provide public benefits, such as job creation and tax revenues; it withers when government views business as an adversary, taxes it punitively, or imposes inefficient regulations or expensive litigation on good and bad companies alike. Cooperative reductions in trade barriers among the nations of the world between WW II and the end of the 20th Century have led to unprecedented increase in global incomes and allowed raw materials, capital, and even immigrants to flow to the places where they can contribute as much as possible to the global economy and help their nations round out their development wheels. A byproduct of this has been a reduction in the number of conflicts between nations, lowered commercial risk, and an increase in the overall level of long-term investment - all of which raise global financial and real asset values over the long run. Here too, of course, there is still much room for improvement. Rogue nations who insist on isolating themselves and their people continue to wallow in poverty. Terrorists and other uncooperative individuals continue to cause a monumental waste of global resources because of the security risks they pose. And greedy investment bankers, relying on opaque institutions and financial assets to lever their personal gains and enrich themselves at the expense of others, have even put the entire global financial system at risk.

Of course, the ability to work cooperatively does not arise in a vacuum. Although there are always economic incentives to do so, many countries, organizations, and people continue to suffer in their isolation from each other because they cannot "see" the importance of widespread cooperation or the possibility of significantly achieving it. Even within otherwise strong communities, relatively homogeneous societies, and strong institutions, durable cooperation is not automatic. It requires that tolerance, respect and appreciation be the norm - widely diffused throughout the community or institution. It also requires that people not be motivated primarily by the sense that they are in competition with each other for grades, food, jobs, promotions, etc.

Community also does not generally come from the top down. It needs to flow up from cooperative voluntary spirits who share goals, values, and beliefs because this results in greater levels of commitment to a group, organization, or country's goals. It also requires both an understanding of the importance of religious beliefs to community formation and the freedom to build "belief communities" from the ground up. This kind of cooperation, the kind that flows from real community, goes well beyond tolerance, and should never be confused with either conformity or uniformity. True communities are often filled with people who rely on their differences but are united in principal and purpose. Achieving them requires a critical mass of people with worldviews capable of appreciating diversity *and* recognizing that true cooperation and unity is possible even in the face of significant differences and diversity. The cultivation of these kinds of worldviews is unlikely to take place unless religious beliefs are taken seriously, rather than dismissed by assumption as unimportant or troublesome.

Increasingly-widespread voluntary cooperation does not necessarily mean increasingly-large homogeneous organizations. Depending on the importance and complexity of the tasks that need to be accomplished, and the differences in worldviews of the participants, it may be a mistake to assume that larger and larger organizations are needed to increase economic efficiency. A large number of small or medium sized businesses may better serve customer, employee and shareholder needs than one too-large one. A large number of small and medium-sized churches, mosques or temples may better serve the worship, fellowship, benevolence, and outreach needs of their parishioners and community than one large one - especially when the members are knit together by strongly held beliefs, goals, and mutual commitments, and the different churches, mosques, temples and denominations also work cooperatively with each other in areas where they have mutual interests and concerns. The same is true in other areas of life were cooperation is critical – for example, as when local and state governments accomplish tasks more efficiently and effectively than a national government could.

Chapter 23: Pro-Development Worldview Element # 5 – A Deep Concern for People outside One's Family and Friendship Circles

Introduction

As critical as tolerance, respect, appreciation and the cooperation that flows from them have been to economic development, the quantum boost that worldview can give to economic development does not occur until we get to another stage - where people have *deep and genuine, even sacrificial concern for people outside of their immediate family and friendship circle, including people who may be different from them.* The best English term to describe the highest stage of this kind of concern, *agapi love*, is derived from the Greek word *ægəpı*, and is defined by the American Heritage Dictionary as

- Love revealed in Jesus, seen as spiritual and selfless and a model for humanity.
- Love that is spiritual, not sexual, in its nature.[1]

Our dictionary definition notwithstanding, John Templeton claims a tradition of agape love is found in at least eight world religions.[2] Henceforward we will simply use the term love, to denote this kind of selfless non-erotic love that extends well beyond family and close friendship circles.

There are many reasons that agapi love is healthy for economic development, but the following will be explored here:

- It spurs positive change, productivity, and productive risk taking
- It unleashes the positive power of self-discipline and self-control
- It spurs generosity
- It moves people's focus from charity to development

- It increases the work force participation rate
- It reduces counterproductive economic activity

Positive Change, Productivity, and Risk Taking

There is a lot of evidence that where the trust that is best engendered by agape love is lacking, development will be impeded, in part because higher levels of insecurity will make it more difficult for people to overcome the fear that often accompanies change. This may cause them, for example, to resist learning new technologies for fear that technology will eliminate their jobs. At a broader level they may resist economic restructuring in their countries when they believe their futures are being manipulated for the benefit of others. In contrast, those who hold worldviews wherein this kind of love is central are likely to look for ways to involve people who are going to be affected by change in the decisions that affect them, and will attempt to minimize the disruptive effects of change on their lives. This decreases anxiety, in part because people are also more inclined to listen to those who care deeply for them, which facilitates organizational change and effectiveness. People's stress levels are also reduced when they know that others are willing to help them with particularly difficult projects or at particularly stressful times. When people care about each other, gossip and the kind of disinformation that damages working relationships is minimized. Organizations with caring people are also less likely to be hurt by employee actions that harm shareholders, other employees or customers.[3] In this way, love can raise the general level of competence, response, and competitiveness in organizations that embrace it.[4]

Some will say that what is being talked about here is simply loyalty. But concern for others has the potential to generate far more positive effects than loyalty. Loyalty can be good or bad depending on what and who is the object of one's loyalty. To be beneficial, loyalty must be given to those *who can be trusted to act in the best interest of others*, and be capable of being extended well beyond one's immediate family and friendship circle.[5] Because of this, the best performing organizations are intentional in their desire to go beyond the achievement of employee loyalty to the active encouragement of teamwork, healthy relationships, profit sharing and benefit plans, and mutual support and care among their employees. What these organizations realize is that a deep and genuine concern for people and relationships initiates a "virtuous circle," increasing employee motivation and productivity and creating new wealth in the process.[6]

Love is also good for development is because it makes it easier for public and private safety nets to be established.[7] In addition to the purchasing power stability and business cycle dampening that safety nets provide to an economy, they also allow people to land on their feet when they suffer temporary setbacks. This could mean many things, such as temporary income if they become ill and can't work, unemployment payments that make it easier for them to make ends meet while they attempt to find another job, or debt forgiveness if they tried to start a business but failed. In all of these cases and more, the presence of safety nets allows people to live with less fear, and take on the kind of risk that could be helpful to overall economic development. Private safety nets likely contribute to the high entrepreneurship rates in some close-knit religious communities. Well-designed public safety nets (neither too stingy, nor too generous) may partially explain the higher entrepreneurship rates in some countries.

The Power of Unleashed Self-Discipline and Self-Control

Few would argue with the proposition that self-discipline and self-control are part of the lifeblood of free societies. Self-discipline and control help economies through their impact on savings rates, productivity, crime rates, social problems, and a host of other things. But most of those who understand this have given little thought to the role that love plays in the development of these traits. Of course, the kind of self-control we are talking about may be of little interest to those who live and die by mantras such as "greed is good," or "whoever dies with the most toys wins." One or another form of self-control may underlie these beliefs, but it will be of a form that is powerless to transform individuals, much less society. For self-control to be powerful it must be exercised for the good of others, which means it needs to be grounded in love.

An excellent example of the economic impact of the power of love-motivated self-control is the willingness of people to forgo immediate pleasures to redirect their income toward the formation and growth of millions of charities and NGOs, many of which are committed to helping people who are unrelated to and highly unlikely to ever be in a position to repay those whose donations support them. In many cases this kind of charity is a private undertaking, but in others, such as in the case of "foreign aid," it represents the collective will and cooperative efforts of the entire population – or at least their representatives. The U.S. leads the world in private charitable contributions, but official foreign aid, expressed as a percentage of GDP, is substantially higher in many other countries - most notably northern European countries.

Another noteworthy historical example of the economic benefits of collective self-control was the way the American people reoriented their lives and factories to support the allied effort in WW II, followed by a contribution of nearly 5% of their incomes in Marshall Plan foreign aid in the years immediately following the war. No one can be sure of how much these efforts may also have benefited the U.S., but scholars agree that the shot in the arm that post-war rebuilding efforts gave to the economies of Europe, and especially Germany, not only reduced the risk of further conflict but significantly accelerated growth in the global economy. A more recent noteworthy example of the economic impact of a high level of concern for others involves the global effort to get critical drugs to places where they are needed to combat the productivity-sapping diseases that have for decades hampered development in many of the poorest countries around the world.

The Global Impact of Generosity

Stories of generosity are not hard to find, and considerable media attention was given at the beginning of the 21st Century to the challenge given by the world's wealthiest couple, Bill and Melinda Gates, to other billionaires to donate the lion's share of their wealth to charity. Considerably less attention has been given to people like Bob Thompson, of the Thompson McCulloh Company, who made a surprise 128 million dollar contribution to his employees' retirement fund and created 77 instant millionaires. The same could be said for Amy Vanderberg, the Iowa mother and businesswomen who donated a kidney to Dea Lieu, an agricultural development specialist in the Ivory coast,[8] and Oral Lee Brown, the Oakland California real estate agent who promised 21 first graders in 1987 that she would pay for their college educations if they would work and graduate from high school, and made regular $10,000 contributions to a college fund from her $45,000 salary to make good on her promise.[9]

Generosity is also spurred by those who have the vision to facilitate the process of connecting donors and worthy recipients. In some cases this is the product of far-sighted public servants who recognized the need for wealthy countries to share their surplus with less fortunate people,[10] but most of the time it is facilitated by visionary social entrepreneurs, driven by their worldviews, of the type who started organizations like Compassion International (CI) and World Vision International (WVI), whose programs link sponsoring families directly with needy children.[11] George and June Bianchi of Colorado, for example, have used CIs services to sponsor, and radically change the lives of, more than 100 children the world over. A number of children sponsored by this family became doctors and other important contributors to their communities. Without the vision of organizations like Compassion International and the strong religious motivation of people like the Bianchis, many of these children may have been relegated to a future of subsistence living, welfare dependence, or even premature lifestyle- or disease-induced death. It is fair to say that there are few, if any, companies in the world that can claim the "return on investment" that this loving couple has achieved. And this takes into account only the immediate and tangible consequences of their generosity. One can only wonder how many additional benefits will accrue to the children and grandchildren of these and other sponsored children because the power of love broke into the Bianchis' hearts and into the hearts of others who established or support millions of other non-profit organizations.[12]

As the Bianchis' lives testify, generosity is often needed for the highest-return development projects to get done. But economies also benefit from altruism in other ways. According to McCloskey (2006), nearly half of the purchases that take place in the U.S. are for the benefit of someone other than the purchaser herself. In addition, foundations, charitable trusts, charitable contributions and government welfare payments not only contribute to economic output, but have the potential to be powerful steadying influences on the economy when consumers or business investors become skittish. This steadies the economy, makes businesses less subject to the ups and downs of the business cycle, and gets more goods and services into the hands of people who need them, rather than excessive goods and services into the hands of people who barely use them. As noted earlier, to the degree that this limits income and wealth inequality, it also has additional indirect positive effects on the economy.

What is it that enables the love of others to progress into generosity, with all its economic consequences? In the past it was not uncommon for wealthy people to "reinvest" their wealth in libraries or hospitals, and, as noted above, in recent years some of the wealthiest people in the world have made commitments to part with astounding sums of money for the purpose of trying to solve some of the most intractable problems related to poverty. Mega-philanthropy, then, is not new, but in the past, attention to these kinds of things was often postponed until advanced age caused people to reflect back on their lives and come to the conclusion that the time had come for them to "give back." Those whose worldviews have been honed by skepticism might insist that such activity is motivated by self-interest or some kind of guilt or shame associated with having so much more than others, but this need not be the case; nor does it explain the millions of other acts of exceptional generosity and kindness by people of ordinary means. People who do these kinds of things are doing more than parting with their money. They are creating a picture of the kind of difference a single person or small group of committed individuals can make in other people's lives, and in the process lifting the spirits and improving the attitudes of millions who hear about what they have done. They are also planting the seeds of future generosity in other hearts, which will continue to pay rich dividends to countless others well into the future.

The Progression from Charity to Development

The story of the Bianchi's illustrates that when the power of love is at work there will be a steady progression from an emphasis on charity to an emphasis on development. Their choice to invest in these children through an accountable organization like CI, one that provides students what they need to become productive citizens (like good nutrition, positive values, education, or job skills) rather than handouts, is at the core of the development process.[13] This same kind of love, one that is willing to invest time, effort and wisdom as well as money, needs to pervade other sectors of society as well (beyond NGOs), such as businesses, government and families, for development to proceed at the fastest possible rate. In business, one would think that the need to build people up would happen with or without any fundamental love motive. But as one examines business habits across industries and cultures, it is clear that many business people could care less about developing their people, unless it is obvious that doing so will immediately help their profits. On the other hand, some other organizations clearly care deeply about their people and want to develop them to the fullest extent possible. They often spend large amounts on training and development, and give them as much authority and responsibility as they are willing to accept, even though they may be employed at will, and are therefore free to leave the organization at any time. Such training and development clearly benefits society, if not always the organization that implements it, because well-trained employees work more skillfully with less supervision and direction. Fortunately, the organizations developing these people also tend to experience high returns on their investment - because well-treated employees exhibit more job satisfaction and productivity, and lower rates of turnover.

Of course most people are uncomfortable with the notion that some of what happens in a business could be motivated by love — they probably find it easier to use the word love to refer to an office tryst than to describe the motivation of managers. On the other hand, nearly all agree that love needs to pervade – and will have motivating and other positive effects within families. But few think beyond this immediate benefit to the impact of this on economic development. Not all families, of course, are infused with love or follow healthy nurturing principles, but there is probably no place where love is more prevalent or necessary, or where the economic consequences are greater.[14] When parents do a good job of raising their children, schools can do a better job educating, businesses can produce products and services more efficiently, and government can govern more effectively. When teachers can teach rather than serving as unofficial counselors, day care providers, social workers, or policemen, students will learn more. When businesses can spend less time on elaborate internal control systems to prevent property theft, poor stewardship, or fraud, or on extensive training systems to promote good employee relations or customer service, they can spend more time on producing goods and services. When government can expend fewer resources on dysfunctional families, police and prisons and more on parks, roads and public welfare, the society will develop more quickly.

Love is essential to healthy child development, and therefore to societal development. Parents who feel and show genuine love for their children and are involved in their children's lives will raise healthier, happier, better-adjusted children.[15] But agape love goes beyond this.

Children raised in a community where adults feel collectively responsible to support other parents in their child-rearing practices have a distinct advantage over those raised in communities infused with individualism. The businesses that hire and continuously develop these healthy children-turned-adults, by putting structures in place for soliciting and sharing information, encouraging them to strengthen each other through team work, or invest in new technologies to make them more productive, will be more effective than those that don't. Political systems in which they participate, and which also give attention to encouraging participation and training future leaders for public service will function more effectively than those that don't.

As with civil society, assessing how widespread agape love is requires measuring one of its proxies. In international development work, annual donation patterns/percentages, or, better yet, the percentage of a population that gives evidence of a long-term commitments to development, could be a proxies.

This is not to say that *relief* work[16] is not motivated by love. But it is possible that both excessive attention to relief vis-à-vis development and "donor fatigue" are symptoms of an agape love deficit. Both guilt and shame can motivate people to respond for a relatively short time to innocent victims forced from their homes by political upheaval, genocide, or famine. But only a persevering kind of love will equip them to make the kinds of sacrificial investment in the lives of victims that have the potential to root out the ultimate causes of their poverty.

Love Increases Worker Participation Rates

It has long been recognized that one significant threat to an otherwise thriving economy comes from the major demographic shifts that occur when both fertility rates and death rates are dropping. One reason for this is that these developments shift the relative percentage of producers and consumers. If people begin their work careers around 20 to 25 years of age, retire at 60, and live to an average age of 85, they will have spent, by the time they die, less than half as many years producing goods and services as consuming them. Fortunately, *agapi* love has significant potential to increase productivity over the demographic lifecycle, as teenagers, fulltime workers, and retirees will all spend less time in self-indulgence, consumption, or leisure, and more time producing or volunteering to do the important (even if unpaid) work that adds to the total goods and services available to improve people's lives.[17]

It is also well recognized that some inequality is unavoidable in market economies because of their built-in tendency to reward productive behavior and penalize unproductive behavior. Unfortunately, in the process, these economies often also penalize people who are less productive than the norm through no fault of their own - such as those who are disabled by their age or by a physical, mental or emotional handicap. Too often, those who are somewhat less disabled forget that people with special needs are also both producers and consumers. One tell-tale sign of a love deficit in a community, society or country is when people with special needs are seldom, if ever, seen in public. This often also means they are not valued by the society or receiving the education or other forms of support and accommodation that they need to develop to their full potential. In other communities or societies, where disadvantaged people are more visible, some attempts, usually through government, will be made to put systems and programs in place to accommodate and financially support them, but even in these situations too little effort may be given to discovering their unique gifts and finding ways to employ their potentially unique contributions to their community. Only in a society infused with love will their gifts be fully utilized.

Much of the same could be said with respect to equipping children without obvious special needs. An ability to be concerned about those outside of one's immediate friendship circles is at the root of the mandatory education systems that have given many nations a competitive advantage in the global economy and penalized those without them. It is often claimed that some societies cannot afford to provide an education to all children, but it is important to recognize that these claims reveal as much about worldviews as about the problem. There are few, if any, societies where adults do not know more than children and where children could not benefit from receiving instruction from adults. Of course if every adult must remain fully employed just to stay at a subsistence level, it would be understandable that mandatory education for children might not be a priority. However, many of the poorest countries in the world also have the highest rates of unemployment. So rather than assuming these nations are too poor to educate their children, we must ask what it is that keeps adults with time on their hands from educating themselves or their children. In some cases repeated crises will be cited, in other cases widespread disease, and in still others misguided government policies that have all but destroyed the economy. But we must also be open to the possibility that, even in these situations, the fundamental problem is rooted in the values and beliefs that underlie cultural practices.

In addition to the rejection of "universal education," in some countries whole groups of people are either not encouraged to, or absolutely restricted from, getting an education. This of course deprives an economy of massive amounts of productive ability. Some proof of this loss is given by studies that indicate that increases in female employment have driven much of the economic expansion in wealthy countries in recent decades. When girls are valued as much as boys, the society will make a large investment in their talents and provide opportunities for them to contribute. For example, Japan, Germany, and Italy, which have all had both shrinking populations and slower-growing economies than the U.S.in recent decades, also have noticeably lower female workforce participation rates than the U.S. In contrast, as noted earlier, many developing nations have recently experienced great success encouraging the productive talents of women through the use of micro-enterprise loans.[18] Similar benefits come from opening up economic opportunities to people traditionally relegated to lower classes. From the antidiscrimination laws in the U.S. and Europe to the gradual loosening of the caste restrictions in India, economic outcomes have improved the world over when people in positions of authority, and therefore in a position to effect change, care enough for others to work with them to peacefully break the chains of discrimination.

Finally, love opens up opportunities for entire groups of people to employ their talents and skills *in places and at times* in which they would be otherwise prevented from contributing, by making it easier for them to move, at least temporarily, to where there are better economic opportunities. In many ways the U.S. is a nation built by immigrants and, in spite of the frustrating bureaucratic maze that prospective immigrants have faced since September 11, 2001, it remains the favored destination for immigrants. Of course, what is a gain to the U.S. is to some extent also a loss for other countries. But this does not imply that the net effect of immigration on global economic outcomes is a wash. When people *voluntarily* move from one location to another it usually means they feel there are more opportunities for them to use their talents, education, and experience in the place to which they are moving. It also means that if a person finds work in her new location that suits her skills, at least one employer also believes its situation has improved because of her change of location. We can assume, then, that if a voluntary move works out, the total wealth producing capacity of the world will have increased, since the transplanted person's gifts are being better complemented by other forms of capital in the new location (per the Development Wheel), which in turn is making her more productive. There is no guarantee this will happen for each and every immigrant, but it is safe to say that, although there is a loss of talent to the country from which the person is emigrating, the overall effect of immigration on the global economy is very beneficial.[19] The important point here is that for people to have opportunities to fully utilize their talents for the good of the global economy, some countries and people must value them enough to give them the freedom to develop and employ these talents without regard to race, religion, gender, social class, geographical location or similar potentially limiting factors.

Love Reduces Counterproductive Economic Activity

Love also minimizes wasteful economic purchases and habits. This is true for both love directed at those closest to us and love that goes well beyond family and friendship circles. For example, loving couples who make a long-term commitment to each other make an unspoken statement to their children that the best things in life are not disposable. They work hard to teach their children not just to clean up after themselves, but not to create unnecessary messes for others. The deep love of close family members for an addicted person and, conversely, her love for them, are both powerful weapons in the fight to escape the damage inflicted by cigarettes, alcohol, or drugs. People are more likely to eat nutritiously, spend less time at the bar, gamble less, drive more carefully, and engage in fewer risky behaviors in general when loved ones are depending on them. Love also prompts honesty which, as we will see in the next chapter, brings with it a whole additional set of efficiencies.

But love for people outside of one's family and friendship circle brings even more economic efficiencies than these. One reason for this is that it has a tendency to check the amount of inequality in a society, which in turn generally improves the utilization of assets. For example, absent a deep concern for others, wealthy people can live grotesquely consumptive lifestyles, the nature of which will often be hidden by the ease with which they can make ends meet using their accumulated capital (or the income from it). This means that they may have extra homes, penthouse apartments, or rooms in their residences which need to be maintained, cooled or heated, even though they are empty much of the time. They may have yachts or swimming pools that are seldom used but have upkeep expenses greater than the entire incomes of several of their middle class neighbors. In contrast, love keeps income inequality from getting out of hand, which increases economic wellbeing because of the time-worn economic principle of "diminishing returns." In this context, diminishing returns implies that since all people are living in a world of 24 hour days and 7 day weeks, more possessions generally means less time spent enjoying each individual possession. So finding ways to reduce hoarding and the selfish use of assets creates more value for more people. Extending this example to the concept of joint ownership, a public lakeshore park that is open to the public has the potential to bring relaxation, joy and re-creation to far more people than a single empty vacation home taking up the same amount of lakeshore. This assumes, of course, that "the public" maintains a stewardship ethic with respect to the park, which may not always be the case, but this is a separate problem and does not negate the principle of diminishing returns.

Love for those outside of our immediate circles also eliminates counterproductive economic activity in business. In the complex impersonal world of global commerce, competition does not always discipline market participants as effectively as economic textbooks indicate it should. For example, a self-interested plumber who installs water heaters has an incentive to sell the product that gives him the highest profit margin, and this will not always be the product that uses the least energy per gallon of hot water delivered. So, if he installs hundreds of inefficient water heaters, some of his gain will be at the expense of his customers. On the other hand if he cares enough for his customers to explain carefully which product will cost them the least in the long run, he can still make a profit, but will also play a part in a reduction in the consumption of natural gas, coal or fuel oil (possibly used to produce electricity) and will have allowed his community to retain more of its wealth and income and be more competitive in its economic activity relative to the rest of the world. Likewise, the lawyer who chases big contingency fees but is blind to the cost to claimants, defendants and the public of an excessively litigious society, and the automobile repairman who performs and charges for unnecessary work, are both engaging in counterproductive economic activity. When hundreds or thousands of these kinds of actions are aggregated it is easy to see why love has a significant positive impact on economic efficiency and development.

The point we are making here is particularly important because a modern complex economy puts producers and consumers in less *direct* contact with each other than ever before, which means that some kind of moral/ethical bond is needed for people to be truly served. Competition may appear to be an adequate substitute for moral behavior in an economics textbook, but the real world is seldom this simple. This is especially true as the goods and services we use become increasingly complex. In the same way that people had to completely trust their doctor a century ago, because the gulf between their knowledge and his was so great, now they must also trust their lawyer, airline, mutual fund manager, financial planner, web page designer, senator, central bank president, etc. In essence, the more "professionals" there are in an economy (meaning people who are highly trained to perform a relatively complex task *and committed to doing (only) what is in the best interest of the people served*), the better that economy will function. We could also ask how much has the productivity of companies increased around the world because agape love influenced managers to pursue voluntary economic relationships rather than play a heavy hand, or the efficiency of government because public servants feel obligated to serve rather than exploit.

Most importantly of all, however, is the potential for love to reduce interpersonal stress, conflicts of various types, and especially all-out war. As noted earlier, a wealth of research into social problems indicates that much crime and antisocial behavior is related to family dysfunction and stresses that make children feel unimportant, unwanted, or unloved. Wars and lesser armed conflicts can perhaps be viewed as family dysfunction on a grand, exceptionally violent and sometimes global scale, with costs that are simply astounding. In addition to the direct damage to people and property, wars also tend to undermine political and financial market stability, which lowers the returns and raise the risk of economic activity, further damaging financial asset valuations, investment, economic growth and development.[20] In addition, they damage the more intangible forms of capital, often almost beyond repair.

Sadly, the World Trade Center and Pentagon attacks of September 11, 2001 are probably the best recent illustration in the U.S. of the counter-productive economic impact that accompanies a lack of love for others.[21] Because of that single event, hundreds of billions of dollars were wiped off the market value of companies, additional billions were "stolen" from the spouses, children and communities of the victims, and massive government infusions of cash were needed to stabilize the U.S. economy. As was only too clear to those who watched the World Trade Towers collapse, evil born and nurtured in the hearts of men is one of the most powerful forces on the face of the earth, with the power to destroy in a matter of minutes what took good people years of teamwork and painstakingly careful work to build. One well-planned hateful act managed to tax people of all ethnicities, skin colors, religious persuasions, and nationalities, and their descendants, for much of the foreseeable future. Time and human energy "wasted" on airport inspections, cargo screenings, and beefed up security budgets are just the tip of the iceberg. A host of other inefficiencies and human difficulties, such as continuous surveillance, resource diversion, traffic snarls, trade and immigration slowdowns, and emotional distress attend a "war" against an enemy who has no regard for either the preciousness of human life or the right of innocent, peace-loving people to conduct their affairs without being torn from their loved ones by senseless acts of violence; all this because nineteen young men and the organizations behind them chose hatred over love.

In addition to the direct costs just mentioned, there is simply no way to accurately measure the long run costs of damaged trust relationships, behaviors altered by fear, post-traumatic stress and other emotional tolls that evil and injustice exact from people. Hatred and other manifestations of evil will always mean fewer and fewer possibilities for using global resources primarily for building people up, rather than protecting them from evil. We can continue to look for technological solutions, but ultimately, ethical codes and changed hearts are our best hope.

This reinforces the need for the kind of agape love that encompasses not only people who we don't know and who are very much unlike us, but also future generations. Only a love that is wide enough to extend to children yet unborn will lead people to choose saving, investing and building others up (allowing future generations to stand "on their shoulders") instead of wasting assets, or borrowing and consuming irresponsibly (leaving their children and grandchildren to pay the price for their shortsightedness). Nor can this love stop at a kind of self-serving tolerance that is unwilling to confront evil. Future generations will have enough of a challenge dealing with our financial shortsightedness; they should not also be asked to pay the price for our unwillingness to confront evil. But even a willingness to combat evil is not enough, because combating evil amounts to damage control rather than dealing with fundamental problems. There are other ways to confront evil before it does its damage, which is why we have insisted from the beginning that there is simply no good way to push conversations about morality, ethics or religion away from the discussion of economic development. Healthy economic development requires agape love, but this is not enough. It also depends very much on the bigger picture we carry around in our minds of what it means to be a praiseworthy person.

Chapter 24: Pro-Development Worldview Element # 6 – High Integrity Conduct as Not Only Praiseworthy but Mandatory

Introduction

Many of the things that we have determined to be important to economic development have their roots in people's mental pictures of what it means to be a praiseworthy person. This is an important component of one's worldview that is shaped primarily by family, education, and religious beliefs, and to a lesser extent by peers, culture and experiences. For example, the Chinese economy has been strongly influenced by the teachings of a scholar and educator by the name of K'ung Fu-tzu (Confucius) who was born in 551 BC. His teachings became particularly influential in China during and after the 13th century, after the scholar Chu Hsi systematized them in his commentaries, which in turn became the basis for the Chinese civil service examination starting in 1315. These teachings have also strongly influenced other economies in the region, such as Singapore, Korea, Viet Nam and Japan. Interestingly, all of these countries have shown a strong cultural predisposition for economic growth, especially when their economies were not repressed by war, or communist anti-religious policies and inefficiencies associated with overly-centralized planning and restricted property rights. Although Confucianism is a belief system with no claim to divine authority, or separate houses of worship, it nevertheless embodies a pervasive ethical code that attaches a sacred character to life that can be compared to that which existed among the Puritans and other historically-influential Protestant groups and denominations in Northern Europe and the U.S.

Although it is always extremely dangerous to try to boil a religion or belief system down to a few key components, we will do this here for the purpose of illustrating how character or a particular picture of what it means to be a praiseworthy person, influences economic outcomes in economies influenced by Confucian teachings. Five key elements of Confucianism are Jen (respect for others and self); Chun-tzu (the picture of a gentleman - assured, a listener, principled); Li (rules for proper conduct – e.g., fathers should be kind; sons obedient, courteous and humble; rulers just and benevolent; and subjects loyal); Te (a recognition of the responsibilities that accompany authority); and Wen (the importance of moral education and peacefully working out differences). Although these kinds of moral principles in some ways give individuals very little status outside of their relationships, and may therefore restrict things like risk taking or rapid change, they nevertheless foster a host of other values that have potentially positive economic consequences, such as discipline, thrift, a willingness to compromise and/or reciprocate, an emphasis on respect/reputation, loyalty, trust; and the expectation of competent but benevolent authority. In short, a Confucian belief system assumes that if people's hearts are oriented correctly, good character will result, which will in turn bring harmony in the home, order in the nation and peace in the world. Given what has been discussed thus far about the roots of wealth creation, the Confucian ethical system and its attendant picture of what it means to be a praiseworthy person can easily be seen to have played an important role in Asia's remarkable economic development during the past half century.[1]

There are many dimensions to the pictures that inform our ideas of what it means to be a praiseworthy person. Ralph Barton Perry gave one picture of the praiseworthy person and its connection to economic outcomes when he said more than a half century ago,

> When an individual possesses the qualities of austerity, reliability, energy, industry, self-control, marital fidelity, frugality, sobriety, thrift, self-reliance, and foresight, the effect is wealth. When, on the other hand, a man is pleasure-loving, untrustworthy, sluggish, idle, dissipated, irregular, extravagant, frivolous, wasteful, dependent, and careless, the effect is poverty.[2]

Many of the other character traits that make up this picture could also be explored, including things that Barton doesn't mention but we have already discussed. For example, a general lack of concern for others also makes it easier to lie. Stealing requires both unconcern for others and lying to keep the theft from being revealed. Murder demonstrates unconcern for others, requires lying to cover it up and tacitly accepts stealing, since it robs not only the victim of her life, but her family, friends, or employer of whatever that person meant to them or did for them. In spite of these examples, we cannot be comprehensive because there are far too many economically-relevant moral and ethical attitudes and behaviors that are encouraged, discouraged, or prohibited by different belief systems to discuss here. So without attempting to cover the waterfront, we will give enough examples to clearly link attitudes and behaviors traditionally focused on by religious writings, creeds, and sermons with economic success or failure. We will limit our discussion here to three aspects that have been somewhat neglected in previous chapters but are especially important to economic development: trustworthiness, honesty, and diligence.

The Importance of Trustworthiness

Many people have written about trust,[3] but one important precondition for trust is trustworthiness. It is also virtually impossible to talk about trust without also talking about accountability, because an unwillingness to be accountable is at fundamental odds with a desire to be trustworthy. Governments, organizations and people must all be willing to be accountable if society-wide trust relationships are to prevail; bosses as well as workers; politicians as well as bureaucrats; teachers as well as truck drivers - all must be both accountable and trustworthy.

By the end of the economically destructive periods of communist rule in 20ᵗʰ century Eastern Europe, neither the governments nor the citizens were particularly interested in being either trusting or accountable, in part because of decades of systematic attempts to destroy the religious core of their citizens.   The extent of the damage done is revealed by an old Russian proverb that goes something like this: "God spare me from my friends. I'll deliver myself from my enemies." It is not necessary to know much about the origin of this proverb to be impressed with the insight it conveys, particularly in the context of the Soviet Union. It reveals what is perhaps the single most important reason that the Soviet/Russian economy got so far off track and had so much difficulty getting on track in the decades following the August 1991 coup that led to the breakup of the Soviet Block: the near total breakdown of trust. By the end of the Soviet era, trust had declined to such an extent that the typical Russian was preoccupied with questions about who could be trusted and how shared information might be used.   Stories abound about how mistrust and suspicion undermined friendships and in some cases destroyed families.   After 74 year of communist overreach, people were even reluctant to linger on the street in groups, for fear of being accused of subversive activities. Many of the most critical sectors of society, including the Russian Orthodox Church, had been infiltrated with KGB informants.

Unfortunately, even after a measure of freedom was ushered in starting in 1991, Russia, by far the largest of the countries birthed from the former Soviet Union, was unable to rebuild trust relationships quickly enough to sustain reform, primarily because the moral fabric of the society (and hence, social capital) had been too badly damaged.   A further erosion of trust occurred during the first stage of economic reforms, due largely to the lack of accountability of the leaders, and this made success at the second stage nearly impossible. In many ways, the rebuilding of trust remains the greatest challenge ahead for the Russian economy. Oil revenues, a degree of freedom, and market activity have already made many people rich, and will continue to do so, but widespread sustainable development will have to wait for the kinds of changes that rebuild and sustain trust relationships. Unfortunately, trust and trustworthiness cannot be quickly reestablished by being taught in schools. They depend on how people see the world, which in turn depends on what is in their hearts, neither of which can be quickly changed, much less manipulated.

Trust and Organizational Efficiency/Information Flow

The benefits of trustworthiness in organizations has been widely written about, hence we will simply list some of the major ways this happens:

- Trustworthiness makes delegation of authority and relatively flat and efficient organizational structures possible.[4]

- It permits flextime and flexplace policies, which enable employees to make important investments in personal, family or community work without shortchanging their employers.

- It allows companies to spend less on security and internal control systems, contracts, litigation, audits, and insurance. [5]

- It improves planning by reducing the uncertainty associated with the information that people provide.

- It lubricates the *flow* of information and the establishment of business-to business (B2B) or outsourcing relationships.

- It allows cost sharing for things like research, lobbying, or the establishment of industrial associations

- It allows for freer markets and less cumbersome regulations.[6]

Many of the most economically successful nations in the world, such as Sweden, Switzerland, The Netherlands, and the United States, are, comparatively speaking, high trust, open societies. These same countries have been at the vanguard of rapidly growing mail order and e-commerce businesses. Interestingly, this kind of activity--i.e., doing business with people one doesn't know, and who are often too far away to make it economically feasible to easily take legal action--depends on healthy trust relationships.[7] The overall level of consumption spending also depends on trust – when people believe the thousands of people preparing their food, medicine, and other necessities in factories and shops all over the world are trustworthy, they will more readily purchase their products and services.

Trust as an Investment

Trust relationships are best viewed as "investments" in social capital, and they generate very significant returns for their "investors." Like an investment in a fiber optic data line, oil drilling rig or software program, once the trustworthiness component of spiritual/moral capital has been built up (in a person or an organization), the income benefits will continue to pour in for years, decades, or possibly centuries. While competitors are wasting money looking over the shoulders of employees, laboring over why their competitive bids are unsuccessful, changing suppliers, losing customers, or paying lawyers, the organization that has a firm network of trust relationships is free to use its resources to enhance quality, service, customer or employee loyalty, or do something else equally productive.[8]

There are many other examples of the bankability of trustworthiness. One example is the use of brands or name association to build relationships and create value at the point of contact between a company and the consumer. In the U.S., historically, nationally-branded products cost approximately 15% more than privately branded products, and 30% more than generic (unbranded) products. In many cases this represents a tremendous investment made by companies to establish their trustworthiness. In one striking example of the bankability of trust, at the end of 1999, George Foreman, a former heavyweight boxing champion, sold his name and likeness to the Salton Corporation for 137.5 million U.S. dollars. Salton was interested in associating Foreman's image and name with their company primarily because consumers want to trust the companies they buy from and the public believed George Foreman to be a trustworthy husband, father, and product endorser. By 2010 the company had sold more than 100 million "George Foreman Grills" worldwide. Popular actors and sports stars, of course, are the people most often used for product endorsements, but they are also very quickly dropped if they do something that demonstrates untrustworthiness. When the infidelity of world's best known golfer, Tiger Woods, was revealed in 2009, he quickly lost tens of millions of dollars in endorsement contracts, demonstrating that the perception of trustworthiness is not nearly as valuable as real trustworthiness. If the companies can convey the same level of trustworthiness to the public without using popular spokespersons, the millions spent could be diverted the stockholders, employees or customers to be used for other things of value. Trustworthiness is clearly valuable.

We have already noted in Chapters 12 and 20 how significant private property is to the creation of wealth. But it needs to be mentioned in this context that private property rights are most easily granted by trusting companies or governments to trustworthy people. Companies routinely withhold valuable technologies and information from the public for fear that untrustworthy individuals will steal it and undermine the companies' extensive investments in research and development.[9] It is similarly difficult for governments that do not trust their citizens to allow them to own private property, "free and clear." Many communist governments retained an iron grip on the land and buildings in their countries. Even in market economies, the government often owns a significant percentage of the land, which in some cases is related to a fear that individual households cannot be trusted to properly manage it. But most of the land is privately owned in these countries, which is a reflection of the level of trust. This is not to say that trusting people will insist that all land be owned privately. *Voluntary* communal ownership, as practiced by the early Christian church and other high-trust communities, is perhaps the highest trust option of all, a reminder of the pervasive influence of beliefs, religious and otherwise.

Trust and Governance

Trustworthiness also makes governing more efficient. When people are trustworthy, governments will collect a larger percentage of taxes due with lower collection costs. When regulators and politicians are trustworthy, people can concentrate on their families and jobs rather than wasting time checking up on those representing them or protecting themselves against the possibility of an unfair or disruptive bureaucratic whim, regulation or piece of legislation. When a legal system and contract enforcement are trustworthy, fewer people and organizations will break contracts and more disputes can be settled efficiently outside of the court system. Fewer high-priced lawyers will be needed and a larger percentage of the society's resources can be devoted to other productive activities.

Trustworthiness also benefits governing because, when it extends to participants in the economic sector, it permits governing "by exception." This allows government to accomplish its task with fewer resources, but it also means it will have a strong incentive to govern in a way that places little or no financial burden on trustworthy people, for example in the way of unnecessary paperwork or similar time or money-wasters. It will instead concentrate on designing laws that inconvenience lawbreakers rather than law abiders, communicating the substance of those laws to people affected by them, instituting severe enough penalties to both deter and punish lawbreakers, and providing incentives for prompt self-reported violations. Government will also institute polices that advance competition in addition to trust, since *trustworthy competitors* are only too glad to work with government to curtail the practices that give law-breaking or untrustworthy competitors an advantage.

Trust also impacts governance efficiency and wealth creation in the way it shapes civil society. A civil society is of course easier to govern than an uncivil one, and as mentioned earlier, a civil society is one characterized by both transparency and participation. Trust is often a prerequisite for people to divulge the information that government needs, and vice versa. People also participate more when they trust the ones soliciting the participation and believe their participation will make a difference, making trust important not only for civil society but for democratic processes in general. And, as noted in Chapter 18, both transparency and participation, in addition to being good for economic activity in general, also bring critical efficiencies to government.

Before moving on, it is important to note that some scholars, in contrast to what we are saying here, have insisted that skepticism and lack of trust are necessary for economic development because it is often prudent to be wary, and because skepticism is the stepparent of dissent - which they argue is an important ingredient in processes that bring about positive change. There may be some truth to this, but it strikes us that this is an example of "letting the good be the enemy of the best." There is no reason why healthy skepticism and dissent cannot exist side by side with trust, as long as it is well understood that a high-trust environment is how things ought to be, and that the need for both wariness and dissent diminish as people increase in trustworthiness. In addition, unhealthy dissent, by which we generally mean violent dissent, is usually economically destructive. This kind of dissent, illustrated by suicide bombers, or the Oklahoma City, Tokyo subway, or World Trade Center attacks, has a tremendously negative effect on the creation of wealth as it forces people and organizations all over the world to waste hundreds of millions of dollars to protect themselves from similar kinds of threats. Constructive dissent, on the other hand, like the non-violent protests led by Dr. Martin Luther King, have had the opposite effect. Those protests not only engendered trust in the African American community, which increased educational and economic opportunities, but also resulted in additional billions of dollars' worth of productive activity as African-American people employed their talents and skills for the benefit of the broader society.[10]

Clearly, trust is much more than just an individual predisposition; rather, like other attitudes and assets, trust is couched in the beliefs, values and practices of a culture or country. Wealth creation and economic development will flourish where a significant percentage of the population and a significant percentage of the leaders are trustworthy. Furthermore, if trust is already the air that the society or subculture breathes, a business or government will have to make very little additional investment in trust-building. Unfortunately, trust can't just be taught in schools. It grows best in a garden where the soil is black with nutriments like justice, transparency, agape love and honesty.

Honesty and Development

The degree to which people revere truth telling affects almost every aspect of economic activity, from educational and workplace efficiency, to selling techniques, to product safety and compensation structures. Truth telling also affects the effectiveness of systems of justice, methods of reaching agreement, business risk and people's willingness to lend or invest.

Honesty is a prerequisite for trust, since trusting people can be easily exploited in the face of dishonesty, and widespread trustworthiness can be viewed as evidence that honesty is bearing its fruit. Honesty, like trustworthiness, has outsized value to economic entities in part because, unlike other inputs to the production process- like raw materials, labor or financial capital - it does not require ongoing expenditures, at least not if there are healthy moral/spiritual capital-replenishing institutions balancing the Development Wheel. Once "installed" in a person's heart, in an organization's practices, or in a country's laws and regulations, it continues to add to the bottom line year after year. A widespread commitment to honesty implies, in the same way that there are two sides to one coin, that a society also has a passion for knowing what is true. This is important, because there are very substantial benefits associated with a passion for the truth that go beyond the benefits of widespread honesty. And it is worth noting that having a passion for the truth is not the same thing as skepticism, which can perhaps best be described as the tendency to routinely require "proof" from others before trusting then. We see no reason that a passion for the truth cannot burn just as brightly in the mind *and heart* of an idealist as in the mind of a skeptic, but without all of the costs that attend skepticism.

The best way to distinguish the importance of truth telling to a belief system is to look at the degree to which violations of this practice are tolerated or ignored. As noted earlier, belief systems differ not only in regard to what they believe are valid sources of truth, but also in the regard to the degree to which they require or revere truth telling. Some religious belief systems hold truth telling to be mandatory; some consider it mandatory in almost all cases other than when protecting innocents from the evil intentions of others, and some consider truth telling to be honorable in some situations, but optional, or even ill-advised in others. These perspectives flow in part from whether the belief system holds to the idea that there is such a thing as absolute truth, or sees truth as something constructed by individuals as they seek to understand the world and their roles in it, and therefore both relative and optional.

Honesty and Market Efficiency

Adam Smith wrote brilliantly about how and why free markets encouraged even self-interested people to be more responsive to the needs of others, but few people know that he also wrote extensively about the role of virtues, such as honesty. Markets may be able to survive without widespread honesty, but it is clear that they will not be nearly as efficient as they would be with it. Purchase decisions depend on an assumption that what will be received is of equivalent or greater value than what is given up. Most market transactions make both parties better off, but only if each knows what she is actually getting, hence the need for both honesty and truth. Financial markets are particularly vulnerable to dishonesty. Financial wealth, at its base, depends on *promises* to pay in the future. Anything that makes it more likely that promises will not be kept can be devastating to both financial markets and the valuation of financial assets. For example, in 1995, Barings, an otherwise healthy company with a more than a three-hundred year history of business dealings, was forced into bankruptcy because a single employee, Nick Leeson, was both willing and able to cover up the truth about his foreign exchange transactions for a time. At this same time and for more than a decade thereafter, Bernie Madoff bilked investors out of tens of billions of dollars, and caused additional billions in losses to financial asset owners all over the world when his Ponzi scheme was uncovered – as investors wondered who else in the financial community might be lying to them.

The Importance of Honesty to Organizations

Dishonesty damages all kinds of businesses and other organizations and dampens overall economic activity whenever it appears. The most obvious example is when people lie to cover up their misdeeds (like Leeson or Madoff). But theft and pilfering are widespread, particularly where religious beliefs have been marginalized and incentives for ethical behavior undermined. For example, the *Global Retail Theft Barometer*, an annual survey conducted by the Centre for Retail Research in Nottingham, UK put the global cost of pilferage at more than 100 billion dollars in 2008.[11] But it is much higher in some places: a student audit of government-owned petrol stations in Cuba revealed that half the gasoline being delivered and sold was unaccounted for.[12]

There are also many less obvious impediments to the efficient production of products or services when rampant dishonesty exists within an organization. For example, internal auditors would be forced to devote time to uncovering a variety of deceptive behaviors in addition to their more traditional focus on the efficiency and effectiveness of processes and systems. Workers would be more likely to call in sick when they are perfectly healthy. Production employees might lie to supervisors to cover up flaws in their work whenever it is clear to them that doing so would be to their personal advantage. Sales people might lie to customers to cover up their own incompetence, or for other reasons that might be to their advantage. Organizations would be willing to tell suppliers that "the check is in the mail" when in fact it is not, or (to protect themselves from potential litigation) tell prospective employers of fired employees that these employees are reputable people and good workers when in fact they were fired precisely because they were not.

Honesty also permits efficiency in an organization by helping its members to confront problems as they arise and make tough decisions when they need to be made. For example, honesty promotes the frank dialog needed to stop counterproductive behaviors, remove troublesome workers from the organization, or resolve interpersonal conflicts. It is needed for job seekers looking for the right job, or companies who need the truth about job seekers, or buyers and sellers who need the truth about each other. Increasingly organizations depend on "knowledge workers," who spend much of their time accumulating information. But more information is only useful when it is accurate. When people use language loosely, filling newspapers, magazines or internet blogs without regard for the truth, knowledge workers will have to pour through myriad sources/sites to obtain accurate information. Many sources of information may be a good thing if one wants to understand an issue from as many perspectives as possible, but having a smaller number of accurate sites that are committed to honing in on the truth by addressing issues from a variety of perspectives is more stewardly than a host of sights that reflect little more than people's opinions.

Honesty also allows organizations to reduce expenses associated with dealing with outside parties. The earnings and stock prices of companies – and especially internet commerce companies - would fall as the costs of dealing with deceptive sellers and buyers rises. In the absence of widespread respect for the truth, banks would be more likely to be tricked into loaning money to unworthy, wealth destroying borrowers, and would have even higher credit checking expenses and bad debts, which would in turn raise interest rates for all borrowers.[13]

In addition, things like negotiation costs, legal fees, time consuming comparison shopping or bid letting expenses can all be reduced when commercial parties can rely on each other's integrity. Business partnerships, strategic alliances, and cross cultural ventures also benefit from the reputational gains that accompany honesty. Similar efficiencies will accrue to relationships among businesses and NGO's. For example, there are many instances where both businesses and environmental groups could have made faster progress in protecting the environment and obtaining needed permits if they had been completely truthful about their perspectives, concerns, agendas, and actual status of the environment, rather than taking exaggerated positions which often later proved to be untenable. This reminds us that NGOs likely have as much to gain as businesses if those with whom they have contact can rely on them to be completely honest. For example, if they have the complete trust of donors, they will be able to spend less time trolling for donations or trying to convince donors that their money is being well spent and more time on the activities needed to reach their goals.

Before moving on, we need to make one final point about the value of honesty to organizations. A well-known quote, attributed to Abraham Lincoln, is "You can fool some of the people all of the time, and all of the people some of the time, but you cannot fool all of the people all of the time." History seems to back this up, as the truth almost always comes out if one is able to wait long enough. Enron's deception was ferreted out in a fairly short time, as were the shenanigans of U.S. Presidents Nixon and Clinton. It took approximately twenty years for Bernie Madoff's Ponzi scheme to fall apart and nearly sixty years for the dirty secrets about Swiss bank accounts amassed in conjunction with the atrocities committed against holocaust victims to see the light of day. However, in the internet age, it is likely that the period of time between deceptive or unscrupulous acts and their coming to light will continue to become shorter and shorter. Although some of Stalin's crimes took decades to come fully to light, the bureaucratic looting of the Russian treasury in the 1990s came to light after only a year or two. The shameful conduct of U.S. soldiers at Abu Graib prison in Iraq became public in a matter of months. Increasingly, telemarketing scams and money laundering activities are being exposed almost as they happen. The increasing difficulty of covering up lies is also likely to mean the damage to individuals, companies, or governments who are dishonest will be even greater than in the past.

Honesty and Consumer Value

The dishonest counterfeiting of products, widespread in countries like Thailand, Turkey, or China, and a variety of other deceptive selling practices rob consumers. The seller may profit, but those buying the sub-par or unneeded products will receive value far below the price paid. Imagine, for example, the wealth and life destroying potential of a single counterfeit bolt in a critical part of an airplane. This single deception means that passengers are receiving considerably less safety than they have the right to expect for the fares they are paying, not to mention the ultimate loss that they could suffer if the bolt failed.[14] On a lesser scale, when governments cajole people into buying lottery tickets that have horrible odds of winning, they are subtly adding to the impoverishment of those people.

These kinds of dishonesty also make an entire society poorer, not just the immediate victims of the deception. For example, the dishonest theft of intellectual property rights slows innovation by removing much of the incentive for inventors to give up rest and leisure and accept the long work days and sacrificial investment that are required for research, experimentation, and invention. Both present and future generations will be poorer for this. The tacit acceptance of dishonesty also lowers the overall honesty quotient in a society, which has the ability to chip away at wealth and wellbeing in a variety of ways over time. Imagine, for example, a society where large numbers of people cheat on their taxes, inflate invoices, falsify financial reports, or deceptively fleece the most vulnerable members of the society, because these practices have become so widespread that they are no longer seem unethical.

Honesty and Government Policy

As implied earlier, for government to do its job effectively it needs large numbers of its citizens to be honest. Imagine the output of an economy where dishonesty was so rampant that justice demanded that every student or worker needed someone to look over his shoulder. This would require half of the population of the country to unproductively follow the other half around, and even this scenario wouldn't solve the problem because even more people would be needed to follow the followers around. No free society has degenerated to the point of having half its population follow the other half around, but there are many where government bureaucracy creates a great deal of unproductive activity. In Eastern-Block nations, prior to their transition to market economies half the population was not charged with following the other half around, but nearly everyone worked for the government, and based on the paucity of output, one could easily argue that there was a great deal of unproductive activity.

The ultimate challenge is that all governments govern flawed human beings. In addition, governments are plagued because people are generally more willing to be deceptive with those who are a greater "personal distance" from them. "Distance" in this context may mean geographically, but people also may feel more "distant" from those who differ from them, for example in terms of income, race, national origin, or interests, or who are simply unknown to them. And organizations are often viewed as the most "distant" of all, simply because they are viewed as impersonal entities. This means that as the honesty quotient goes down in a society, nameless faceless business corporations will be hard hit, but the damage to government, which is the quintessential impersonal organization, will likely be greatest of all. To illustrate, during seven decades of communism, it can be argued that 1) the Soviet government created more and more personal distance between itself and its citizens, and 2) its citizens had an increasingly difficult time distinguishing truth from falsehood. And, since cooperation through government is one of the most efficient ways for an economy to advance, it is not surprising that the Soviet Union's time was marked and that Russia's economic development since its independence has been fitful, delayed, and terribly uneven.

The Soviet experience serves as a good reminder of the damage that can be done when leaders deceive and attempt to cover up the truth, further alienating a citizenry that is already "distant" from them. Even worse is the toll that two other stepchildren of dishonesty, armed conflict and violence, take on individuals and societies. Most violence and injustice around the world requires perpetrators who are comfortable hiding, shading, denying or simply not knowing the truth. But even after the truth has been trampled and the damage done, there is still hope for healing, lasting peace and development *if truth is pursued* in the reconciliation process. Nelson Mandela and Bishop Desmond Tutu understood this far better than most - with the result that South Africa more successfully managed the aftermath of Apartheid than almost anyone could have imagined. The jury is still out, of course, on the eventual outcome in South Africa, and its prospects dim appreciably if and when these two reservoirs of spiritual/moral capital pass on. But the *Truth and Reconciliation Council* they were so instrumental in developing may someday be viewed as a milestone in the history of the world, and a testimony that, especially in the aftermath of violence and injustice, the truth must be pursued and mistakes, weaknesses, and even atrocities admitted before justice can be done and lasting development achieved.

The Soviet Union and South Africa notwithstanding, many of the most subtly damaging examples of dishonesty have been surprisingly mainstream. Widespread apathy has allowed some plants and animals to be taken to near extinction. Unethical companies have ravaged the environment and exploited people while the world looked the other way. But the most insidious example of potential economic damage of dishonesty has probably been the way governments have subtly devalued their currencies over time. This usually occurs when government officials do not have the character to reveal to the public that they are spending far more money than they are collecting in taxes, and deceptively printing money to make up the difference. This new money circulates alongside previously held money, and following laws of supply and demand, each unit of currency becomes worth less and less over time. In the worst case scenario, people try to part with rapidly depreciating money as quickly as possible, which increases its circulation and lowers its value even more; and, if things get bad enough, merchants will lock their doors because they would rather keep the products on their shelves (which are going up in price) than accept money from customers (which is constantly losing value). At this point the economy all but seizes up in the grip of hyperinflation. This of course is precisely the kind of deception that raises the "personal distance" between a government and its taxpayer citizens to new heights, and leads to additional economic problems down the road. In doing so, as with other forms of dishonesty, it will also lower spontaneous cooperation, real economic activity and prospects for development.

It should be clear from what has been said that government can only do its job effectively if it is both truthful with its citizens and encourages its citizens to be truthful with it. Being truthful with citizens means avoiding the kind of deception described above and corruption discussed earlier, as well as encouraging the kind of transparency described in the civil society discussions of Chapters 18 and 19.

Encouraging citizens to be truthful means designing tax systems and other forms of legislation to reward truth telling and penalize deception. One example of this is whistle-blowing legislation. To illustrate, in July of 1999 Donald McLendon received a nearly ten million dollar "whistle-blower fee" as part of a judgment against Kimberly Home Health Care and its parent, the Olsten Corporation (his employer), for exposing an illegal scheme to disguise receipts from the sale of some of Kimberly's Home Health Agencies to Columbia/HCA as government reimbursable fees. Wisely, the U.S. law at the time recognized that encouraging people like McLendon to shine the light of day on such transactions was worthwhile (ten million dollars in his case.

Although the government clearly benefits from exposing lies which might otherwise enable companies to defraud it, whistle-blower legislation makes sense for a more important reason we have been talking about: at every juncture, the pursuit of truth is critical to the very foundations of wealth creation and development. Generic discussions about the importance of freedom, democracy, or markets seldom address this adequately. Hundreds or perhaps thousands of small regulatory, legal, and economic incentives could be put in place to encourage moral and ethical behavior. Even better is government sponsorship of the kind of pluralism that encourages unbiased public discussion of morality and ethics as these apply to communal responsibilities.[15]

A Love for Work

Finally, there is perhaps no more economically important outgrowth of honesty than the commitment to giving "a good day's work for a good day's pay." This does not mean that people work because they must, but that they work because they see it as a moral obligation and have a solid understanding of the relationship between work and living a meaningful life. A love of work makes it possible for people to be productive in many different ways, both on and off the job. It also has a significant spillover effect on society because there are many other things besides "making a living" that requires work, even when there are no economic incentives to do so. Reporting crimes, vandalism, or other destructive activities to authorities, and helping victims, takes more effort than ignoring them. Resolving a dangerous situation or removing a hazard takes more effort than ignoring these things and hoping that no one gets injured. Both the nurture of children and community volunteering depend on people's willingness to work without compensation.

Adults who love work do not need to rely on their leisure, rest or entertainment time for their enjoyment. In fact, they may even choose to accomplish meaningful tasks during their leisure and rest time simply because they receive more joy and satisfaction from being productive than from being indulged.[16] Examples of productive leisure time include volunteer work, restorative hobbies, marriage-building activities or helping children develop important skills and values. In contrast, when people do not love work or, worse yet, believe that work is a necessary evil; they will approach it with a completely different attitude. Many will need supervision to work up to their potential.

They will not be inclined to do work that goes above and beyond their job descriptions, or be eager to take on new responsibilities. All of these will likely lead to productivity stagnation or even less output per worker over time. Worse yet, people who are wealthy enough not to work and choose this option will deplete wealth rather than continuing to produce it, either forcing others to work harder to restore the depleted wealth, or leaving less overall for the others, including future generations.

A poor work ethic also hurts economic development in many other, more direct ways. Lazy and undisciplined children disrupt classroom environments, preventing other students from learning and wasting precious teacher time. A gradual shift from a work ethic to a leisure ethic chips away at the length of school days and school years. Video games erode homework time, or homework is considered an imposition. Students are advanced in school without having mastered the work, and are allowed to drop out, even when they do not intend to engage in productive activity outside of the school. In almost all cases a declining work ethic manifests itself in too few graduates trained in the difficult art of thinking and problem solving. Eventually this leads to social problems and increase of income inequality.

Plenty of international studies have exposed the declining educational achievement of children in Western countries (and especially the U.S.). The hard truth is that some of this can be traced to adults who don't appreciate the fundamental importance of discipline and work, and therefore of education. But a subpar work ethic exists in some groups and subcultures the world over. For example, in some developing countries such as India, Indonesia or Uganda, work ethic problems reveal themselves in excessive absenteeism, even among school teachers.[17] In some cases, of course, this may be related to the prevalence of health problems, or frustration with unpaid wages, but there are many cultural roots of absenteeism as well. In some countries development is also hindered by a general disposition for middle or lower-middle class members to refuse to do work that is "dirty" or "low class." Likewise, a cultural predisposition for large numbers of adults to be content with charity, government aid, or the provision by others of services that they could provide for themselves, will result in many of society's time resources being unnecessarily diverted from more productive uses. In all these cases it takes a worldview that fully appreciates the relationship between work and wellbeing to feel any strong sense of alarm or do anything significant about it.

One problem that has created particular difficulties for developing countries in recent decades is the departure of a disproportionate number of people who have an extraordinary work ethic. Often denied good opportunities to work in their home countries, they nevertheless (or perhaps therefore) have a perspective on work that gives them the potential to be ideal employees, understand that work is a privilege, and conduct themselves accordingly on the job. Of course in this case one country's loss is another's gain. The U.S. in particular has long benefitted from a steady influx of immigrants with good attitudes toward work. During the first decade of the 21st century they played a particularly important role in revitalizing declining "rust belt" towns, increasing agricultural productivity, and spurring innovation and establishing and growing new industries in places like Silicon Valley. The often illegal but almost always productive Hispanic workers who fill many of the lesser skilled positions have also given the U.S. economy a boost, and some journalists have contrasted them to the relatively highly paid European laborers whose long vacations, short work weeks, and significant number of "sick days" have contributed to the European Union's lack of competitiveness relative to its global competitors in recent decades.

Like trustworthiness and honesty, a work ethic is similar to an investment that pays handsome returns both to individuals and society throughout one's life. Few groups know this better, or have benefited more from this kind of investment, than Asian Americans.[18] Of course, examining the values of high-achieving Asian families is not likely to be of significant interest to those who believe values are simply personal preferences that are unrelated to social or economic policy. On the other hand, if more academics understood that values are more important than race and ethnicity, they would spend less time comparing the test score results of black, white, or Asian students, and more time investigating the differences in beliefs and values within the various subgroups in each of these ethnic groups that lead to performance differences in school or on the job. They might just find out that Asian Americans in California, white farmers in Sioux County, Iowa and Black entrepreneurs in Africa have more in common than they think.

We are back once again to the core of the Development Wheel. A work ethic is not only dependent on honesty, but many of other values that need to be at the core. Yes, it is but a small step from a willingness to distort the truth to not giving one's best to his or her employer. But other values are also playing a role. In cultures where women are not treated with the respect due them, and men associate power and privilege with male authority, women are often forced to do the lion's share of the work while men have the privilege of philosophizing or engaging in other more-leisurely activities. Where abusive governments abscond with large percentages of people's paychecks, only those with the strongest work ethics are likely to remain undeterred. And, of course, rooting out these kinds of endemic problems itself requires an outsized work ethic. It also requires humility, another characteristic that needs to be viewed as praiseworthy for development to be sustained, and the subject to which we now turn.

Chapter 25: Pro-Development Worldview Element # 7 – The Importance of Humility

Humility's first cousins

Like all values and virtues, the work ethic and honesty discussed in the last chapter are caught up in a spiritually-informed tension with other values, such as love and humility. Humility contributes to a work ethic by restraining entitlement thinking and reminding people that "there is no such thing as a free lunch." It is also essential to differentiate between the pursuit of truth and the assumption that one has a corner on truth. Likewise, humility is needed to see that the insistence that all truth is relative may be a misguided and damaging conclusion born ultimately of arrogance. Truth, then, is best pursued with humility; to do otherwise would likely lengthen the path to truth or eliminate the possibility of finding it altogether. Humility also suggests that healthy economic development requires both rich and poor countries to begin their interactions with each other with the knowledge that the other party has both seriously good ideas and practices and seriously bad ones.[1]

Knowledge, since it depends on study, experience, or scientific experimentation, also needs humility for maximum positive impact on economic outcomes. Both knowledge and its application flow much more quickly when pride is suppressed. Corrections can be made and damage minimized when mistakes are admitted and learned from - rather than covered up. Even more benefit comes when mistakes are openly shared with others so that they too can avoid making them and learn from them. Humility also helps us distinguish knowledge from wisdom - with wisdom being far more important to development. Wisdom involves understanding what is true, right or important, none of which is necessarily implied by the possession of knowledge. Wisdom, it seems to us, is knowledge in proper moral context. It is knowledge used well, tempered by a respect for the truth and constrained by humility.

Humility is also a prerequisite for both respect and self-esteem. Proudly abusive parents damage their children for life. Prideful gang leaders and (some) rappers use clever words to exploit the insecurities and vulnerabilities of children, and damage the cities and societies in which they are immersed.

Lackadaisical teenagers with too much "attitude" to subject themselves to the authority of their teachers make their schools, cities and nations uncompetitive. It needs to be said, then, that the humility we talk about here is nothing at all like a lack of self-esteem. People who lack self-esteem because they have been beaten down by family, peers, or culture into thinking that they amount to little or nothing are best described by the word broken, rather than the word humble. They are often effectively handicapped by their lack of self-esteem and sometimes spend a lifetime depleting their wealth trying to recover it.[2] Sadly, the simple truth is that had the people in their lives been humble and wise enough to nurture them properly, they most likely would not have become so deeply damaged in the first place. Perhaps, then, humility can best be described by an equation: humility = inner strength - pride.

It should also be noted at this point that because of the dominant position that males have in families (and, indeed, in other sub-sectors of society) in many cultures, male humility may be particularly important to a healthy economy. Imagine the differing economic impacts of a strong young man who chooses to use his strength to build up his girlfriend (or wife if married), mentor other young men, or serve in the community, and another who is fixated on proving how strong, fast, clever or intimidating he can be. Similarly, the difference between a father who is humble enough to sacrificially nurture, invest in, and listen to his children - and another who is more concerned about indulging himself. Only the humble males in these examples will have an outsized positive effect on the self-esteem, health, productivity – and economic impact - of those around them.

Humility and Forgiveness

Another economically significant and religiously influenced attitude that requires humility is people's ability to forgive. Anyone who has had children knows that forgiveness is an essential balm for healing relational wounds. Without this healing, parents would be unable to accomplish the many other complex tasks that together are capable of molding well-adjusted, healthy, productive and cooperative children. Culturally-imbedded forgiveness clearly has economic impacts, and scholars have been noticing these impacts for some time. Much of the formal research has been done in psychology or sociology - looking at the general impact of forgiveness on the health of people who practice forgiveness, or the positive effects of forgiveness on the victims of crime.[3] World-renowned medical facilities have documented these effects and some are overt in their recommendation of the benefits of religious and psychological therapies that improve people's ability to forgive. For example, the Mayo Clinic lists on its web page lower blood pressure and heart rates, and fewer incidences of stress, depression, anxiety, and chronic pain among the benefits of forgiveness.[4]

In the same way that trustworthiness and honesty are inextricably wrapped up with other values, *authentic* forgiveness rests on the twin foundations of honesty and humility. The greatest gains to economic activity occur when these characteristics are widespread in a society - since it will be more likely that both parties to an affront will be involved in the forgiveness process. For this to happen, the offender must be humble enough to admit error or malice; the offended must be honest and humble enough to understand her own weaknesses and empathize with the person who has wronged her. In such an environment, people who have been offended realize that they have an active responsibility to move toward and through both forgiveness and reconciliation - rather than allow resentment to fester for months or years.

Humility as a prerequisite for realizing the positive contributions of religious beliefs to development

Both religion and science lose much of their potential to spur development when their proponents lack humility. Whether we are talking about religious fundamentalists, religious or secular humanists, or scientific atheists, danger signs should flash when people insist that they have cornered the whole truth, or seek to impose their way of thinking on others.

This is most easily seen when examining authoritarian societies. Paul Marshall, in his analysis of data from the *World Values Survey*, has noted that when oil is removed from the equation, many nations in the grip of authoritarian fundamentalist Islam have very poor economic records. The same can be said for particular regions within countries, like Nigeria, where radical Islamists try to effect forced conversions, intimidate fellow Muslims who show an interest in other religions, and do everything within their power to legally repress all belief systems except their version of Islam. And, although we ought not talk about fundamentalist Christians in the same breath - because they are not inclined to use force to spread their religious vision, some members of this group are also well known to resist and deprecate "outside" ideas that could quell their pride or compel modifications of their theology. Religious believers of many other stripes have also been known to negatively affect economic outcomes because of assumed superior knowledge. In some cases this has resulted in an unwillingness to cross sectarian lines and cooperate with people very unlike themselves to accomplish common tasks. In other cases it has involved the wholesale rejection of large-scale economic entities, global trade or even capitalism as an economic system.

Religious governing bodies have also hurt economic development when they have lacked the humility needed to understand the limits of their competence – most frequently by trying to dominate governments, coerce allegiance, or micromanage economies. Europe suffered for centuries as the Catholic Church operated as if it had a corner on the truth. This caused many European clergy to look with indifference, if not contempt, on market activity, until the Protestant Reformation offered a significant alternative, forcing a degree of rethinking on long held positions, and ushering in new churches with fresh perspectives on (and in some cases a significant upturn in) economic activity. One important part of this eventual transformation was the reformers, and particularly John Calvin's elevation of "humble labor" to its rightful role in economic life, and insistence that it was improper for ecclesiastical or political authorities to regulate or restrict every form of economic expansion and technological innovation. This ultimately carved out a sphere of independence and legitimacy for craftsmen, business entrepreneurs and financiers - and the many things they and other members of non-privileged classes of people did that have been so important to economic development. Unfortunately, in spite of these advances, it was not long after the Protestant Reformation that the pride of church and state pushed back - as some Protestant churches also sought and gained official status as state churches. And the history of the Eastern Orthodox Church, although very different from that of the Western church, reflects the same tensions. In Eastern Europe, the Orthodox Church was preeminent until it was crushed by Lenin's communists, who, in a historically well-documented demonstration of even greater arrogance, wiped out a host of important religious traditions, not to mention hundreds of thousands of talented people and their ideas.

In contrast to these kinds of arrogant power grabs, however, some of the most effective religious leaders of all time have been and are both committed to non-negotiable principles and humble enough to be open and interested in others' ideas. William Carey, whose message and ways so radically improved the lives of millions on the Indian sub-continent, saw himself as nothing more than a humble servant of God - in spite of the fact that he was a remarkable lay scientist as well as evangelist. As Carey so elegantly demonstrated, the way of humility seldom allows one to remain firmly planted in just one camp. Desiring to know the whole truth usually means that we need to look at something from as many perspectives as possible. Neither militant atheists nor close-minded religious zealots are usually willing to do this. But many religious people, like Carey, or more recently Dr. Martin Luther King Jr., have been open to new ideas and methods of accomplishing their goals, with remarkable results. Dr. King changed an entire country in part because he was able to maintain both humility and respect for others while suffering many hardships. He correctly understood bigotry and discrimination as a battle to be fought at the level of worldviews, attitudes and person-to-person relations. Just as importantly, he recognized that the willingness to suffer indignity for the sake of achieving justice and improving other people's lives was not only morally superior to the ugly tactics of his opponents, but was the ultimate path to confidence and achievement. In doing so, he demonstrated the path to healthy self-esteem not only for African Americans, but for all Americans. The proof of his effectiveness is in the pudding: a large percentage of both blacks and whites who have embraced attitudes and principles similar to Dr. King's have gravitated into productive and satisfying lifestyles and helped others to do the same. Others, both black and white, whose minds are closed to the irony of humility, service and sacrifice as possible keys to prosperity, relegate themselves to an uncomfortable and sometimes suspicious or outright distrustful attitude toward others. Stymied by their pride from performing useful service to others, they are ensnared in the vicious circle of self-service and/or exploitation of others. Unfortunately, for those starting out in poverty, these kinds of attitudes all but preclude the possibility of escape.

Humbly Enlightened?

Unfortunately, the "religious" orientation of both secularists and scientific atheists leads to as many if not more problems with arrogance than religious leaders. Much has been written, including some here, about the remarkable damage done by the overreach of those committed to secularism. Although the "Enlightenment" may have freed people for a time from the negative effects of the pride of the church, its adherents were anything but enlightened when they assumed a license to dominate education and commerce, and force their secular beliefs on students, business people, and sometimes entire societies (including churches). As we have noted on more than one occasion, even the subtle marginalizing of religious believers eventually cuts off important conversations about what is most important in life, what makes life good, or what makes us truly human. We can only become worse off for doing so. Arrogant atheists like Lenin and Stalin did immeasurable damage to Eastern European economies. Although in the short run, expropriated churches made cheap storage facilities; in the long run these buildings would have been far more economically productive as houses of worship and centers of moral teaching. Mao Zedong made a similarly serious mistake when he gave an uneducated band of ideologues - the Red Guard - the authority to unleash its adolescent fury against intellectuals, religious leaders and the commercially successful. In addition to brutally attacking these repositories of centuries of wisdom, he also initiated a more subtle plan to try to convince the Chinese people that religion was, at best, for the uneducated, rural or elderly.

Although not as aggressively, Western secular elites have also deprecated religious belief, and arrogant secularists still routinely pump degrading forms of popular culture into countries that are deeply offended by it - making the world a much angrier place, and placing large numbers of people (including members of the military) at risk in the process. In all these cases, a lack of humility makes it too easy for people to dismiss the economic and human potential of healthy traditions, and the people and ways of thinking that led to their development.[5] When arrogance or even ignorance encourages the reckless throwing off of traditions (and the political and religious authority wrapped up in them), serious damage can occur, in part because traditions may both reflect truth and embody centuries of practical wisdom that have enabled the societies to coalesce and develop. Countries that have not respected the sacred character of the vast store of knowledge that has been passed from one generation to another have sometimes paid dearly over long periods of time.

In contrast to the approaches above, both good science and good politics - with their relentless observation, experimentation, and reflection, are as much children of our willingness to admit how little we know, as they are children of our desire to know more. They certainly could not flow from the attitude that we "know it all." There are, of course, some arrogant scientists, especially those who chafe at the idea that truth could be revealed by some ancient text, or divine voice. In reality, however, the acceptance of revelation is not only unavoidable; it is also the only appropriate starting point for a scientist. Good scientists start by observing things and trying to figure out what they *reveal*. They generally trust what other scientists have revealed to them through their research and publications, and seldom have time to go back to examine all of their original equipment, samples, data, etc. So, to accept revelation is in some ways the ultimate act of humility. It amounts to an initial declaration that we are incapable in and of ourselves of knowing everything that is important, and that we must be humble enough to accept outside information - including, for religious scientists, information that originates from beyond the puny part of the material universe with which we happen to be in direct contact.

Good science, then, like a host of other things essential for healthy development, requires that we accept the existence, importance and elusiveness of truth, admit that it is bigger and more complex than we can imagine, be humble enough to search for it using all the tools we have, and be patient enough to realize that all of the puzzle pieces needed to reveal it have not yet been and may never be found. Science needs to learn from religion and vice versa; neither should be assumed to be the only path to truth. Both have the potential to reveal truth, albeit it different ways, but also to lead people away from the truth. This is likely why many well-known scientists have also been deeply religious people - and why it is a grave mistake to try to disassociate aspiring scientists from their religious beliefs in the process of their science education. Change needs to be organic, from the ground up, from the inside out, from the heart to the head.

Humility and organizational leadership

Like good scientists, entrepreneurs and inventors must remain humbly inquisitive about the laws of nature, time, space or markets, and go into their ventures with the knowledge that what they think is a great idea could be crushed by market forces far too complex for them to fully anticipate. Soichiro Honda, the founder of one of the most successful companies in the past quarter century, the Honda Motor Corporation, has often been lauded for his insistence that "success is 99% failure." Humility is also crucial to commerce because both specialization and economies of scale are born of a willingness to depend on others, and arrogance undermines the kind of competiveness that comes from being equipped to do the hard work of serving people. Talented team members need to be humble enough to step aside long enough to allow their fellow workers to both contribute and develop. Salesmen must be humble enough to continuously seek feedback about or accept the rejection of the products or services they sell. Managers who are humble enough to see each employees unique gifts and humble enough to seek input about an employee's performance from the employee's peers and subordinates are able to manage their people more effectively. In fact, businesses risk serious damage to themselves if they are arrogant with suppliers, employees, customers, or the law. Recent examples include the destruction of billions of dollars of wealth by CEO's who thought they were above the law, bankers who served themselves instead of their customers, and "quants" who overestimated their risk-modeling skills. So it is not surprising that the best businesses now compete not only for the kind of worker who is willing to do whatever needs to be done without complaining that it is "not my job," or "beneath my dignity," but one who also knows right from wrong.

It should also be noted that the forgiveness that flows from humility and it ability to heal relational wounds is also an important part of smoothly functioning organizations. In normal work environments, people's tasks routinely intersect, and one person's effectiveness is almost always affected by the performance of others. Feelings of superiority, holding grudges and the kind of unwillingness to communicate that accompany a hesitancy to forgive can cause significant inefficiencies. Another often overlooked area where forgiveness affects companies is in the customer service and relations. There are times when companies need the humility to admit their mistakes and ask for forgiveness - and those capable of this are perceived much more positively by the public than those that are not. One study even showed that a significant number of people who sued doctors for malpractice might not have done so had they received a heartfelt apology from the offending doctor. The ability to forgive also keeps companies from destructively competitive activity.

Humility is also exemplified in the successful business people who both serve well and live modest and generous lifestyles, or investment advisors whose advice is far more valuable than their fees are costly. These people create value well beyond their companies, as they build up other forms of essential capital by investing and charitably contributing their surpluses. Even the seeming egomaniacs who are always snooping around looking for companies to acquire realize that respecting the people and culture of the acquired company is essential to a smooth and successful merger. And, at a broader level, the ability to benefit from relatively free markets requires the humility to admit that "everybody knows more than anybody knows" and that no government is wise enough to centrally plan a modern complex global economy. Hayek referred to the inability to understand this as the "fatal conceit" that he correctly predicted would eventually undermine communism. Everything from educational reform to healthy partnerships between businesses, CSOs, and governments works better with a healthy dose of humility.

Humility, leadership, and the rise and fall of nations

Much has been written about the damaging effects of pride on nations, and we have uncovered a number of the examples of this throughout this work. Undoubtedly we could partially trace the demise of most nations to pride, but there is no reason to go back farther than the Roman Empire. From the deification of its emperors, to its inability to tame its expansionary tendencies, to the corruption, mismanagement, and weakening of its army and citizenry related to a culture of assumed superiority and entitlement, Rome in some ways set the standard for the role of arrogance in the rise and fall of nations.

More recently, China's fortunes have risen, fallen, and risen again. We noted earlier how the thinking that coalesced into Confucian values - in spite of some of the criticism it has received from historians (and Chairman Mao) - for the most part laid a strong foundation for economic development in China. So it is not surprising that by most accounts China was economically healthy when Marco Polo visited it in the thirteenth century. From all indications, China had most of the ingredients in place for economic expansion already at the time of the Middle Kingdom, such as businesses, technology, mass production, a monetary system, and commercial infrastructure. But China's economic progress was uneven at best, and certainly slower than Western Europe's until Deng Xiaoping opened his country up during the final quarter of the twentieth century. One explanation for this, as noted by Hugo Restall, is that during the Yong and Song dynasties, a Confucian *elite* emerged because of the restrictive nature of the civil service examinations. Believing they had a corner on the truth, they neglected scientific experimentation in favor of philosophical study and contemplation. They and the neo-Confucianists who followed them had in effect established a state religion that discouraged innovation, grass roots economic initiatives, and investment.[6] Could it be that Chinese progress was impeded by believing that they had a corner on truth (as early as the 13th century), and by detouring from the pursuit of truth (for example during the Cultural Revolution), concluding, therefore, that they couldn't learn very much from the "foreign devils?" To be sure some Westerners justly deserved to be called foreign devils, but the openness needed for development demands that nations effectively distinguish between proud exploiters and humble potential partners.

Of course no nation is more in need of humility at the present time than the U.S. Many influential people have referred to the 20th Century as "The American Century," because of the U.S.'s outsized economic and political impact. However, like China beginning with the 13th century, however, the U.S. has been flirting with and succumbing to the effects of pride. Since the end of the Cold-War period, the U.S. has spent lavishly as the global policeman-in-chief. It has also too often interpreted the ascendancy of markets and democracy as verification of the superiority of its ways of thinking and living. At times is even seems as if the pursuit of wealth, power and pleasure is overtaking the pursuit of truth, humility, and service, and the cost of this is becoming more apparent. The U.S. has already paid dearly for the large-scale jettisoning of the kind of personal responsibility, moral behavior, family stability, and political and economic integrity that contributed to its economic ascendancy. Increasingly-common workplace violence and a record prison population are further evidence of some of these costs. Far-too-frequent incidences of school shootings are a sign that it will likely pay even more dearly in the future for decisions to allow children to come home to empty houses and spend far more hours per week by themselves than with parents or other potentially influential adults.[7] Pride also tends to foster corruption, discrimination and favoritism, all of which, as experience and earlier-cited research show, squelch the development and use of talents, and impede economic growth. Pride has the ability to blind us to many things, not the least of which are our own imperfect nature and our inability, often, to see the long-term consequences of our decisions.

The fact that these kinds of things are happening in a nation known for both its democracy and markets is and will continue to be an important indicator that, when elevated to the level of quasi-ideology, even things as important as democracy and markets are bound to disappoint. This needs saying because there has been an undeniable tendency of late to think that many, if not most, of the world's problems can be fixed by things like freedom, choice, votes or trade. But this too smacks of arrogance. As noted earlier, democratic experiments have failed miserably in places where the worldview foundation they depend on had not been properly laid. All one has to do is look around: internet drug sales, slumlords, externalities and a host of other things make it clear that without a host of "moral sentiments," property rights definitions, and regulatory ground rules, neither markers or democracy will operate properly. Ironically, the most likely outcome of U.S. hubris will be less prosperity – and the very real possibility that it will lose its economic dominance in an even shorter period than China lost hers. So, rather than argue for the infallibility of either markets or democracy, it would be better to humbly recognize that some American values exerted an extremely positive influence on the world during the "American Century," while others exerted a very negative influence - and that much of its ascendancy was also the result of a confluence of good fortune . Not only was it geographically distant from the epicenter of two World Wars, but it was uniquely positioned to sell the goods and services needed to rebuild a twice devastated world economy. So, it is better to classify democracy, markets, and U.S. ascendancy as blessings; and to have the wisdom to recognize that the U.S., like many once-dominant nations, risks rotting from the corrosive internal effects of pride more than succumbing to economic or political pressures from the outside.

It would, however, be a mistake to try to make the case for the importance of humility by focusing primarily on economic giants like the U.S. or China. The comprehensive case for the impact of humility on the global economy comes not from China or the U.S., but from the sheer number of examples in this work alone where by economic ascendance can be linked with humility, economic decline with arrogance. For example, we noted the humble beginnings of many unusually successful ethnic/religious diaspora (such as Jews, Quakers, Puritans and East Asians). Most were oppressed or discriminated against in their home countries - which forced them to and developed an outsized respect for the mutual dependence and the importance of education. Over and over these emigrants made a life for themselves in an adopted country - often by filling a vacuum between elites and the indigenous poor. In England, for example, many white collar "financial types" looked down upon their industrial blue collar compatriots. This created an opportunity for Jews - who parlayed their trading and money lending activities into great wealth throughout Europe, and eventually the U.S. - because elites often considered these activities beneath them. Likewise, India has been plagued by the pride of the upper castes for much of its history, but many Indians who left their native land to indiscriminately serve the masses in cities all over the world flourished. Lower and middle class "overseas Chinese" were equally successful in building wealth as they filled many of these same commercial niches throughout Asia - and eventually throughout the world. It is, of course, tempting to overstate the role of humility – but it would also be easy to oversimplify the activities of these groups as grounded in greed or necessity. These things may also have played a role, but it cannot be denied that it requires a healthy dose of humility to carve out a place for oneself in societies that are inclined to look down on "middlemen," foreigners or particular ethnic groups.

In contrast, arrogant assumptions about racial or ethnic superiority (caste), or male superiority, or the right to demean or harm others because of their religious or ideological beliefs (e.g., *dar-al-harb* or *Boko Haram*[8]) have marginalized millions of people and/or forced individuals and governments to divert massive amounts of resources from productive activities to protection. Arrogance is evident at every stage of Africa's seemingly intractable economic problems. Proud Westerners first colonized and later drew up arbitrary and culturally-indefensible country boundaries in Africa and the Middle East that continue to plague those regions of the world. And, both before and after the colonialists, many tribal leaders (or "big men") parlayed their innate sense of superiority into policies and actions that pushed their tribes and/or countries into abject poverty. Other arrogant leaders, such as the Russian Czars, Saddam Hussein or Kim Jong Il, sated themselves with dozens of gaudy palaces or chalets, even as most of their countrymen wallowed in poverty.[9] Worse yet, are the arrogant leaders who have, throughout history, killed millions of people and destroyed untold amounts of property in the pursuit of power, wealth, or ideological notoriety: Hitler, Lenin, Stalin and Mao, just to name a few.

As these examples make clear, in its rawest application, humility and forgiveness afford the possibility of avoiding the kind of escalating violence and destruction that accompany revenge or war.[10] For example, Germany and Japan were humbled by their defeat in WWII, but they rose quickly from the ashes of war for two important reasons. One is that they were so thoroughly defeated that there was no longer any room for excuses. The bankruptcy of the moral philosophies that had allowed them to commit so many atrocities and destroy massive amounts of wealth had been exposed. They had been humbled, and they were in no position to pretend that what they had been doing could or should be continued; a kind of repentance or turning around, whether voiced or not, was their only option. But secondly, Europe and the United States did not arrogantly insist on humiliating them, as had occurred, and had led to so much resentment in Germany after the end of WWI. Rather, they forced them to rebuild from the ground up – and helped them do so.[11] The result was that during the post-war period, blue collar workers in Germany, where precise, hands-on work had always been especially respected, easily outperformed their counterparts in places like the U.S. or France, where a growing class consciousness was causing blue collar workers to increasingly be viewed and treated as second class citizens. Similarly humbled, Japan set about revolutionizing the industrial world by taking Deming's ideas of "total quality management" to a whole new level, eventually transforming itself into the premier manufacturer in the world.[12]

Humility, then, and the forgiveness it makes possible, are both essential to the restoration process, and restoration greatly increases the likelihood of lasting peace and prosperity. More recently, debt forgiveness, another form of restoration, has also shown some potential to restore economic growth to countries whose citizens were victims of corrupt leaders who had amassed massive amounts of debt but squandered the proceeds.

Humility and the Ability to See Boundaries

Our final foray into the significance of humility to development involves its importance in checking the overreach of some sectors of society into territory rightly the province of others. People, companies, and even governments need to be protected from intrusion into their rightful spheres of authority by other groups. For example, parents cannot properly raise their children if the government forces them to operate like a democracy, or an army disrupts their daily lives. A business cannot properly carry out its economic function if the government provides major subsidies to its competitors. A government cannot properly carry out its role as an arbiter of justice if wealthy individuals or companies exert undue influences on law makers or judges for their benefit (and the detriment of others). In short, individuals, families, religious communities, schools, businesses, and governments each deserve a degree of autonomy as they carry out their tasks.[13]

Unfortunately, the boundaries between these spheres of authority are seldom explicitly determined. They are often simply assumed based on culture, tradition or religious practice. And absent the humility needed to exercise restraint, these boundary markers will often not be well placed, and this can have a substantial negative impact on economic development. For example, in Medieval Europe, the business owner (Lord of the Manor) sometimes dominated the individual, family and church even to the point of dictating when and where people could travel, whether they could marry and how and where they could worship. Today some businesses demand so much from their workers that it makes it very difficult for people to carry out their family and community responsibilities. Likewise, in some places families, via tribal leaders, dominate religious activities, economic activity, and even whole countries. In effect, they have the power to remove almost all meaningful opportunities for individuals to improve their lives by determining who has (or does not have) access to tribal leaders. Churches too have at times tried to dominate countries, businesses and individuals, by, for example, working behind the scenes to determine who would be king (or even appointing them), dictating what could be produced, or limiting people's career options. But none of this should be construed to say that the only proper way to structure a society is to make individual rights absolute. In modern secular societies, individuals sometimes assert their rights to the point of absurdity, refusing to recognize the legitimacy or authority that rightly belongs to families, employers, churches or the government. Only a healthy dose of humility will set people on the path needed to sort this out.

Historically, it has been the dearth of humility in the government sector that has done the most damage. Because little attention has been given to the *appropriate* role of government, many governments have simply used their power to take the authority they wanted, regardless of whether this was good for the economy and society or not. In some cases government has taken parental or school authority by dictating nearly all of what children must or could be taught. In other cases it has seized control of all of the factors of production, usually with disastrous results. In still other cases it has picked official churches, usurped the right to hire and fire pastors, or punished citizens for violation of church doctrine. In the most extreme examples government military officers have pulled children from their homes to turn them into child soldiers, and communist governments have expropriated church buildings, killed thousands of priests, and infiltrated the church with spies.

The primary reason governments have done more damage through overreach is because they, especially when backed by the military, have more power than other institutions in society. Over time, we can see that there is almost nothing that government officials, unconstrained by humility and the common sense that flows from it, have not attempted to do. But this is not limited to tribal or totalitarian thugs. In addition to the relatively benign but important tasks of maintaining order, resisting aggression, enforcing the rule of law, and promoting justice, even democratic governments have tried to control prices and interest rates, or large segments of the economy. They have restricted the movement of goods and services, subsidized favored goods, or producers, or established or marginalized religion - all without a public discussion of the appropriate limits of government authority or the economic effects of usurping the authority of other legitimate spheres of human activity. Although little understood, the arrogant tendency to cross boundaries is an important contributor to uneven development and widely varying degrees of human and institutional flourishing in different countries, cultures and subcultures. As noted in Chapters 14 and 15, the root cause of this is that some religious belief systems, cultures, and worldviews are robust enough to give a reasonable amount of definition and specificity to these boundaries, while others seem barely aware of these issues. This may in fact be the major reason the U.S. - in spite of all of its weaknesses - continues to be one of the most resilient economies in the world. It may just be that the biggest competitive advantage the U.S. has possessed in its short history is its freedom of religion, pluralistic structures and relatively effective way of separating church and state – and the way that these have allowed people to integrate their unique heart commitments into their work, spending, investments and charity. Although under siege, these basic pluralistic structures are still quite alive in the U.S; in fact most are in better shape than in many other countries of the world. And it is the conversations prompted within and around these structures that are essential to not only call attention to the kind of humility that is needed for the building up and maintenance of all seven of the forms of capital, but all other "pro-development worldview elements" as well.

Because of this, we will, in the next several chapters, refocus our attention on the impact that specific belief systems have on these "pro-development world view elements" and other economically important issues. But rather than pick on an easy target, such as a non-literate tribal belief system that leads to strong opposition to change, damaging cultural habits and intertribal conflict, we will instead examine how the two most prominent belief systems in so-called "developed" countries address these and other economically important issues.

Chapter 26: Christianity and Pro-Development Worldview Element # 1 – The Rejection of Human Suffering and Infringements on Human Rights

Introduction

The impact of Christianity on development can only be understood well when we acknowledge that Christians are, first and foremost, "people of the book." The Bible that Protestant Christians read is approximately fourteen hundred pages of historical and poetic writings and letters that, although written by ordinary people in their own languages (Hebrew, Aramaic, and Greek), are widely understood to have been "inspired by God." Catholic and Eastern Orthodox Christians accept the authority of other books not in the Protestant Bible so theirs is longer still. Jewish believers accepted the authority of many of these same (Old Testament) books even earlier, which makes Christianity in some ways an extension of Jewish history and belief. Both the Old and New Testaments of the Bible speak extensively of economic transactions, money and wealth. It is widely accepted that Jesus spoke more about money and wealth than about any other subject but love. And millions of additional pages have been written commenting on the Bible and its application to nearly every dimension of life. The result is that the Christian faith is comprehensive, complex, and thoroughly involved in the economic development of the West.

By influencing people's values and attitudes, biblical principles have directly and indirectly affected the way they structure and carry out economic activity, as well as their social organizations, aesthetics, education, politics, etc. They have also influenced the rules government sets up for business activity, the enforcement of those rules, business structures and management practices, as well as the personal economic decisions of individuals and families. Of course Christian influences have now become so thoroughly intertwined with parallel secular influences in Western Culture as to be almost inseparable to the untrained eye. This is changing and will continue to change the nature and pace of economic activity, and over long periods of time this change is likely to be dramatic. Nevertheless, Christianity, like all belief systems, continues to affect the people, countries and cultures it has been part of, and will continue to do so for decades and centuries, even if formal measures of religiosity continue to erode or formal ties to Christianity are severed.

Goals

At the end of Chapter 18 and our discussion of the Economic Development Wheel, we noted that wealth creation and economic development greatly benefit from ten "understandings." We also noted that it is difficult to know what to include and what not to include when discussing the impact of religious beliefs on wealth creation and economic development because the impact of these beliefs is so pervasive. Rather than try to summarize the massive amount of material contained in the books and articles cited there, we prefer here to focus on only some of the most influential things that the Bible teaches that have direct or indirect impact on the seven worldview elements that we have shown in the previous seven chapters to be important to the creation of wealth and economic development. Some Christians might object to the decision to leave many of the most important tenets of the Christian faith out of this discussion, but the purpose of this book is to examine the impact of religious beliefs on economic development, not on every aspect of life or the way of salvation. This also makes what we are doing more comparable with our efforts in later chapters to represent the foundational beliefs of a "secular" belief system, where we will also try to limit our discussion to those aspects that have *particular relevance for economic development*. In fact, we will not even attempt here to comprehensively explain Christian teachings about many of the things related to economic activity, but will only summarize the most relevant of those teachings for those who are generally unacquainted with them, or who have heretofore assumed that religious beliefs and economic activity are largely unrelated.[1]

Approach

We approach the task of connecting Christian beliefs and economic outcomes with full recognition that people of all philosophies, ideologies and religious persuasions live out their beliefs only imperfectly. For this reason we will rely, whenever helpful, on the original sources (Biblical quotations) when appealing to foundational Christian principles that affect values and behaviors important to economic development. This must be done carefully, since words must always be interpreted within their historical context; hence we will take care to only excise individual verses from the scriptural narrative when they succinctly capture and are consistent with broader Biblical principles. When this is difficult to do, we will paraphrase the Biblical language or summarize the concepts, and invite readers who are not familiar with Christian teachings to verify the integrity of our summary and application of Biblical principles by going to the original source, or to people who have extensively studied the Bible. We make no distinction at this point between Catholic, Orthodox, or Protestant Christians, but note up front that there are *significant* differences, and that, e.g., Christians whose experience has been limited to places where worship is not conducted in a language they understand, or who have seldom read the Bible themselves, will have difficulty corroborating the Biblical foundation of their beliefs and habits. This joint treatment of the different expressions of Christianity is not designed to make light of some important differences between them; rather, we are confident that Biblically-literate Christians from all walks of life, cultures, economic, and social strata will be in agreement on most of the principles summarized here.

Limiting the Scope of the Discussion

Many of the ten "understandings" from Chapter 18 call for structuring institutions and systems so that people can follow their hearts and voluntarily come together to tackle the things (from the bottom up) that their worldviews indicate to them are serious problems. Among other things, the opportunity to do this requires a certain perspective on things like freedom, authority, or service. The implication here is that some worldviews may not even allow institutions and systems to be developed and structured in this way, because their perspective on freedom, authority or service is fundamentally incompatible with voluntary, bottom-up institutions.

In addition, some readers who reflect back to our chapters on how belief systems differ (Chapters 14 and 15), may insist that a thorough job of investigating the impact of Christian beliefs on development requires that we examine all of what is taught about the nature of God, the world, people, what truth is, where it can be found, etc. In fact, all of these are important - since even when healthy systems and institutions are in place, the outcome of the human activity still depends greatly on the myriad goals, attitudes, values, and behaviors that flow from people's worldview. But it is not possible to do justice here to the full range of Biblical teachings or Christian doctrine; hence, we focus only on how Christianity encourages or discourages the seven "pro-development worldview elements" laid out in the previous chapters, revealing in the process some of how Christians answer the basic questions about the nature of God, reality, people, etc.

Christian Perspectives on What Needs to be Improved

As noted in Chapter 19, development is spurred when people have a strong sense that things are not as they should be and that it is humankind's responsibility to improve them. In particular, "poverty-as-normal," the mishandling of wealth, and ill-advised restrictions on the freedoms needed to solve problems and nurture civil society must be rejected.

Rejection of Poverty

The conviction that the world has been tainted by sin and is therefore not as it was intended to be is a core tenet of Christianity. A corollary of this is that Christians have the duty to "subdue the earth," work with God to mitigate the effects of sin, and to "make all things new," a process sometimes referred to as advancing the "kingdom of God." Among other things, this has led to an insatiable march for better ways to do things, as evidenced by the remarkable number of inventions in countries influenced by Judeo-Christian belief systems, more humane working environments, employee benefit plans, world-class medical research, and a host of other similar developments. Poverty is one of many things widely understood to need fixing.[2]

Both the Bible and Christian teaching have a great deal to say about how people should relate to the poor and disenfranchised. God is continually portrayed in the Bible as remembering the poor, caring for them, and hating those who take advantage of them, sometimes even putting their neglect and exploitation on par with adultery, theft, idol worship, and other "detestable things."[3] Oppressors are warned repeatedly throughout the Old and New Testaments against charging the poor excessive interest, permanently disenfranchising them from the land, depriving them of necessities, or taking advantage of them because they lack political power. The Israelites were explicitly called to tithe and otherwise address the concerns of the needy, aliens, widows, orphans, etc., and to use the governing structures to improve social and economic justice.[4] This concern for the poor is reflected with equal vigor in the New Testament. The early Christian church was commended because "there were no needy persons among them," which was the case, we are told, because "from time to time those who owned lands or houses sold them, brought the money from the sales and put it at the apostles' feet, and it was distributed to anyone as he had need."[5] The importance of generosity, then, is a particularly strong theme throughout the Bible; biblical teachings even insist that properly motivated and implemented generosity will increase the wealth and/or wellbeing of both the giver and the receiver.[6]

The economic impact of these kinds of teachings is of course difficult to measure. But in countries heavily influenced by Judeo-Christian beliefs it surely includes, among other things, the extra productivity associated with the education and employment of the poor, the massive economic impact of millions of not-for-profit organizations, the benefits of government safety nets that allow people to be more flexible and take more risks, and even the economic contribution of the insurance industry (which was founded originally by Scottish Presbyterian ministers). Concern for the poor is in many ways also a driving force behind the global civil society movement, and its concern for basic human rights and how we should structure and run the institutions that have been established to promote a civil society (including institutions established to enhance global relations). In its most developed form, the Christian rejection of poverty implies working towards the biblical vision of the ideal, the Jewish concept of *shalom* – which involves bringing balance, wholeness, and well-being into every aspect of life—a concept completely consistent with the framework needed for balancing our Development Wheel.[7]

Acceptance of Wealth

Development also requires that people have an appropriate perspective on wealth. There are four recurring themes in the Bible about wealth:

- That it both comes from and belongs to God [8]
- That it is a good thing, in part because it may be the byproduct of wise decisions, obedience to God's commands, and/or a manifestation of God's blessing [9]
- That it is dangerous if not understood properly or used productively[10]
- That having it entails significant responsibilities [11]

As the brief summary above indicates, the Bible teaches that wealth, rather than being an end in itself, is better viewed as one of many possible benefits of work, and therefore a blessing, albeit not one without its own temptations and potential problems (such as selfishness and laziness). These potential problems were enough to cause some Christians to favor separation from worldly pursuits, and in some cases even to believe the material world to be evil, but today most understand that wealth is good if acquired ethically and used properly (the roots of this debate can be seen as far back as the writings of Augustine, at the end of the 4th century AD). For non "separatist" Christians, however, wealth entails increases in responsibility and accountability, rather than an increase in privilege. Although some Christians engage in charity because they believe doing so will put them in more tenable position at the final judgment, most do so because tithing is widely encouraged in the Bible and because they are thankful for the gifts that have been given to them and want to share them with others ("from those to whom much has been given, much is to be expected").[12] In addition, a deep sense of appreciation related to being beneficiaries of Christ's supreme sacrifice penetrates to the core of sincere Christians, and this, coupled with the belief that they only have one life to live, and this lived in full view of an all-knowing God, adds a sense of urgency and purpose to all of their day-to-day activities, including how they handle their wealth.

Christians and Income Inequality

It should also be noted that because the Bible so heavily emphasizes both charity and the responsible use of money, many Christians will begin to feel guilty if income and wealth are too unequally distributed. Thus it is difficult to divorce even something as seemingly remote as a society's income distribution from their religious beliefs and traditions. Although we have not seen any studies about this, it would be reasonable to expect that, other things held constant, demographic groups that are strongly committed to Protestant Christian beliefs, would tend to have more equal income distributions, as measured by some conventional measure such as a GINI coefficient,[13] and more balanced economic development than societies without that influence. One reason for this is that practicing Protestant Christians give larger percentages of their incomes to charity than others with similar incomes.[14]

The Roots of Wealth

Most Christians' views on investment have been influenced by Jesus' parable on the importance of developing talents. This story, although seemingly couched in monetary terms, extends logically to other kinds of investments as well, since people have talents of many kinds. A general theme that runs throughout the Bible is that surpluses, including financial surpluses, can reasonably be expected as the natural result of obedient living. Obedient living is usually portrayed as not being overly concerned with wealth, but rather focusing on work and moral and ethical living. Although Jesus had a "low impact" lifestyle, compared to many of his contemporaries, he never taught that wealth was evil, and in all of his recorded teachings about wealth, he only suggested the complete divestment of wealth to one person, a "rich young ruler" who was excessively attached to it. This is in contrast to a more persistent Biblical theme that it is God's desire to bless his people, if they are willing to "walk in his ways." This intent, as it applied to the Old testament Israelites, was captured by the prophet Jeremiah in the following words: "For I know the plans I have for you," declares the LORD, "plans to prosper you and not to harm you, plans to give you hope and a future."[15]

These words of hope and comfort, along with others suggesting that the people of God be relatively unconcerned about wealth, also make risk-taking a fairly ordinary part of life for many Christians. In Jesus' parable of the talents, for example, it was the servant who buried the money he had been given, rather than put it to productive use, who was severely chastised. In general, when Christians invest for the future, they are in a good position to take risks, partly because they are part of a religious community in which people care for one another, partly because they have faith in God's promises that he will care for them, and partly because they believe there are many other things far more precious than money.[16]

Nevertheless, a Christian perspective on risk-taking should never be associated with gambling. Although losing money may be considered a normal and necessary part of life, using money irresponsibly is not. In this regard, a Christian understanding of wealth is also influenced by a host of ancillary teachings throughout the Bible. For example, the writer of Proverbs notes that "Dishonest money dwindles away, but he who gathers money little by little makes it grow."[17] Later he says, "He who works his land will have abundant food, but the one who chases fantasies will have his fill of poverty," and, in the very next verse, "A faithful man will be richly blessed, but one eager to get rich will not go unpunished."[18] The Apostle Paul, in his New Testament letter to Timothy, hammers this latter point home by warning Timothy and the other Christians with him that "Some people, eager for money, have wandered from the faith and pierced themselves with many griefs." These kinds of passages clearly encourage careful saving and investing over against the reckless pursuit of wealth. The Bible also regularly condemns selfishness, [19]and lack of self-control.[20] Biblical mandates that parents care for and teach their children, and be prepared to help those in need, reinforce these injunctions to handle wealth carefully, since both of these things require Christians to abstain from frivolous consumption and put something away for possible emergencies and future needs. The use of money, then, whether classified as consumption, savings/investment, or charity, cannot be haphazard for Christians. It must be used intentionally, for the things of God (including celebrating his goodness) and/or for the good of people (either to sustain them in their need or to equip them to do meaningful work). Wealth accumulation can be good, but only if wealth is appreciated as God's gift and employed productively for the good of others.

Development as Normative, Even if it Brings Some Inequality

The continued creation of wealth also requires the recognition that *some level* of inequality must be accepted as a byproduct of its creation. Biblical teaching supports this in several ways:

- By stating that it is within God's sovereignty that some become rich and others remain poor.
- By recognizing that in spite of the fact that there are many innocent victims of poverty, there are certain beliefs and behaviors that lead to deserved inequality (such as laziness, lack of discipline, refusal to accept advice, and self-indulgence).
- By teaching that certain attitudes and actions, such as envy or theft, are inappropriate, regardless of the level of inequality.

Although such teachings allow for some inequality to persist, and even some that may be the result of injustice, it also allows those who are most gifted at creating wealth to reinvest their surpluses, and promotes the protection of property rights and other structures that allow wealth to be owned and protected. And these teachings were always to be interpreted by Christians within the context of other Biblical teachings about wealth, usury, and the treatment of the poor that naturally limited both the degree and persistence of the inequality.

Freedom as Normative

The idea of what it means to have the freedom to fix problems will also differ between Christians and those who follow other belief systems. The "freedom to constantly improve things," is of course very different from a simple passion for the freedom to do what one wants. As noted in Chapter 6 and other chapters that describe the wealth creation process, both a lack of freedom and some uses of freedom can be very detrimental to economic development, so we need here to be clear about what a Biblical picture of freedom looks like. Christians may differ from others who do not share their worldview on what "the freedom to fix problems" means in part because 1) they may interpret the word freedom differently, 2) they will have different ideas about what needs to be improved, and 3) they will have different ideas on what improvement looks like. But as a brief look at Biblical teaching makes clear, *responsible* freedom is at the very core of Christianity.

In the Old Testament books of the Bible, the freedom to properly worship and obey God is at the very core of the "exodus" of the Israelites from slavery in Egypt. God routinely proclaimed his desire to "set the captives free,"[21] and chastised the Israelites for keeping fellow Israelites as slaves.[22] In addition, the Israelites are repeatedly called to commemorate special feast days and follow rituals for the purpose of remembering and celebrating their emancipation.[23] In the New Testament, the concept of freedom seems even further elevated and is equated with the pursuit of truth.[24] The apostle Paul takes this even further, when he argues that Christians "may approach God with freedom and confidence,[25] that "where the Spirit of the Lord is, there is freedom,"[26] and that "it is for freedom that Christ has set us free. Stand firm, then, and do not let yourselves be burdened again by a yoke of slavery."[27] He also tells those who were slaves when they became Christians "if you can gain your freedom, do so."[28] But both Jesus and Paul also clarify what true freedom is by noting, in Jesus' words, that "everyone who sins is a slave to sin,"[29] and in Paul's, that "a man is a slave to whatever has mastered him."[30] Paul further defines what freedom should mean to Christians when he says, for example, to the Galatians, "You…were called to be free. But do not use your freedom to indulge the sinful nature; rather, serve one another in love,"[31] and to the Corinthians, 'Everything is permissible'—but not everything is beneficial. 'Everything is permissible'—but not everything is constructive."[32] The apostle Peter also reinforces the central role of responsible freedom to the Christian church when he says, "Live as free men, but do not use your freedom as a cover-up for evil; live as servants of God."[33]

The Biblical concept of freedom also goes well beyond people. The apostle Paul states in Romans 8:21-22 that the whole creation groans under the weight of sin and that it is God's purpose in Christ that "the creation itself will be liberated from its bondage to decay and brought into the glorious freedom of the children of God." The implication here is that the "children of God" will use their freedom to engage in responsible economic activity for the purpose of restoring the proper order of things. Since risk taking is often required for this kind of activity, Christians have yet another reason to take financial risks with a degree of enthusiasm, which perhaps explains why some researchers have found Christians to be particularly entrepreneurial.[34] Of course entrepreneurs come from many religious and secular belief systems, so we want to be clear that although some Christian beliefs about freedom may encourage entrepreneurial activity, they are not sufficient to ensure it. Nevertheless, and more importantly, the net effect of these Biblical teachings about freedom goes well beyond an impact on risk taking and entrepreneurship. They also filter into commitments to democracy, free enterprise, civil society, limited government, and a host of other concepts that undergird healthy economic development. And, judging from the number of universities started by Christians, these beliefs have apparently also been a significant contributor to the idea that having the freedom to pursue truth should be a hallmark of the educational process.

An Understanding of Civil Society, and the Desire to Nurture it

As the previous section has already implied, Biblical teachings about freedom have played an important role in the conceptualization of the idea of civil society. But it is not just freedom that undergirds civil society. Civil society also involves a host of concepts that we addressed individually in the chapters dealing with wealth creation, such as perspectives on authority, proclivities toward voluntary cooperation, commitments to justice and the like. Since we addressed these topics separately in our wealth creation chapters, we will briefly address a Christian perspective on them here as well - but first we will briefly address biblical tie-ins to the concept of civil society.

Biblical Tie-Ins to Civil Society

People's concern for, ideas about, and understanding of civil society flow from their worldviews, which are in turn repositories of their most deeply held beliefs and convictions. Christians are naturally drawn to notions of civil society, in part because Christ advocated and demonstrated a concern for the marginalized and a habit of calling people to improve their treatment of others rather than using power to coerce it. That said, it is unlikely that Christians will take kindly to the idea that all notions of civil society are equally valid, or that the nations of the world should settle for a "lowest common denominator" definition of the word "civil" in order to get broad buy-in.

Most Christians would agree that civil society principles like participation, accountability, and an insistence on peaceable change are best viewed as necessary means to achieve obviously lofty ends, but that without appropriate values, such principles in and of themselves will not be capable of ushering in a truly civil society.[35] This prompts Christians to focus on underlying values, like love or humility, upon which a civil society ultimately rests. And, rather than merely supporting civil society as an abstract concept, Christians will be led to build the kind of civil society *structures* that not only allow, but encourage people to do what the God of the Bible calls them to do - such as work hard, speak out against injustice, help others, mold ethical institutions and communities, enable people to develop their talents, seek the truth, etc. In this sense, when Christians ask if a civil society allows markets to function in a way that healthy economic development can take place, they are ultimately less concerned about markets than about people. This requires values that go well beyond the protection of individual liberties; they must be capable of actually building up the kind of "healthy soil" in which a civil society can grow and thrive.

From a Christian perspective, then, a truly-civil society requires a progression toward a consensus about the nature of people, their calling or task in the world, and how to discern right from wrong before turning to a discussion of basic human rights. For example, since the Bible teaches clearly that extortion or bribe taking is harmful to both the immediate victims and the society,[36] Christians are called to reject so-called "enlightened" or "tolerant" views of civil society which result in bribery being accepted as a cultural given rather than as something to be changed. This does not necessarily mean, however that because Christians take a strong position against bribery *on religious grounds* that they are necessarily intolerant of other points of view. Nor does such a position imply that they believe people of diverse faiths and cultures cannot share many common values or work well in the public square - rather, it underscores the importance of dealing with fundamental worldview questions before attempting to implement some sort of generic policies or programs aimed at increasing "civil society." To Christians, the very essence of a civil society involves learning how to "decently disagree," with those holding opposing worldviews. To pick two examples - both ethical relativism's unspoken assumptions that man is effectively at the center of the universe, master of his destiny, and fully capable of solving his own problems without any divine guidance, and radical Islamists' ideas about enforcing faith through exercising power or inciting fear, would be considered ill advised by most Christians. But, based on Christ's example, they would still insist that personal contact, careful listening, reasoned argumentation, tolerance for opposing points and even love for those with whom they disagree are essential for any possibility of achieving a truly civil society.

Both Christ and his apostles preached and practiced the kind of responsible activity and attention to duty that treat human rights and civility as not only normative, but logical outgrowths of Biblical ideas about right and wrong. Perhaps we can illustrate this best by applying Christian thinking to one of the most longstanding, and depressing challenges facing human kind —war. War is recorded throughout history and is also part of the Biblical record.[37] It, along with universal accounts of conflict, deception, injustice, neglect and a host of other maladies throughout history, implies that abstract concepts about things like participation or transparency will not by themselves lead to civil behavior. Nor will education and high-mindedness by themselves usher in a civil society. Every supposedly "civil" nation in the world sat on its hands while between one and two million people were slaughtered in Cambodia in the late 1970s, while more than 700,000 people were slaughtered in Rwanda in the early 1990s, and again while more than four million were killed in fighting in the Democratic Republic of the Congo at the intersection of the 20th and 21st centuries.[38]

These events were an affront to all people, but especially to Christians because the Bible teaches that Jesus came to earth to reconcile God to people and people to each other. In fact, Jesus is often referred to as the *Prince of Peace.* He didn't organize an army to force peace, but, as the Bible records it, came with and as the Word of God, which is "living and active. Sharper than any double-edged sword, it penetrates even to dividing soul and spirit, joints and marrow; it judges the thoughts and attitudes of the heart."[39] For Christians, then, a truly civil society requires that hearts be oriented in the right direction. But since most Christians believe it would be inappropriate for diplomats to elevate one set of religious beliefs above others, the real seeds of civil society must be sown from the bottom up, through the face-to-face interactions between NGO workers, business people, missionaries, or cultural ambassadors and those with whom they come into contact. For the most part, these interactions will lead to the peaceful transformation of societies. At times, however, as Jesus' life and death illustrated, it may require the courage to put oneself at risk for the sake of others.

Ending the economically-destructive power of war also likely requires that significant numbers of people feel a deep sense of guilt (i.e. remorse when they have done something evil, or failed to stop others from doing evil when it was in their power to prevent it) when others - including those far away - are harmed. Christianity, unlike many belief systems, mandates its adherents to accept and admit their guilt, regardless of whether their sins of commission or omission are known to others. This can be contrasted to shame-based belief systems, where one tends to feel remorse only when the evil activity has been discovered or made public. The entire fabric of the Christian scriptures encourages people to bring evil deeds "into the light" so that they can be dealt with appropriately, and evil can be kept at bay.[40] This obviously encourages the institutionalization of civil society concepts such as transparency and accountability.

It is also no surprise, then, that Christian churches have often been at the core of efforts to build, rebuild, or reclaim civil society. As has been documented in many ways, and as a host of publications make abundantly clear,[41] churches and synagogues have long been at the core of community renewal projects in the U.S. This is because, as longstanding local institutions that reflect people's deepest motivations (or heart commitments), churches are logical partners with individuals, the private sector, public institutions, and community associations. Churches open their doors to clubs, neighborhood watch groups, and a host of community associations whose goals include building their communities up and rolling up their sleeves to fight urban injustice and rot, which includes things like unemployment, the demise of good businesses, and spread of unhealthy products and services. They start, develop directories of, and/or steer people to human service agencies, credit unions, day care centers, or YMCAs. They work with other churches to feed the hungry, provide shelter for the homeless, sponsor refugees, and promote development. They complement government by helping to clean up parks and roadsides, funding scholarships and school trips, by sending out work teams (locally, nationally, and internationally), promoting literacy, teaching ESL, promoting good health habits, and working out joint-use agreements with schools. They complement the private sector by providing facilities for business association meetings, encouraging business ethics, soliciting funds for community activities and scholarships, and working with businesses in job placement and improving job skills. They help individuals through after school programs, home building and repair, emergency response, budgeting and nutrition training, abuse prevention, "senior adoption" programs, and training in the arts. Of course not every church does all these things, but the collective impact on development of a religiously-motivated "thousand of points of light" should not be underestimated, nor should the impact of bringing people with widely varying educational, ethnic, social, or political backgrounds together and commanding them to love one another.

It is similarly not surprising, that so many charities have been started by Christians - including those that try to shine a light on far-away atrocities - such as *Voice of the Martyrs* and *Amnesty International*.[42] And, given Biblical reminders of God's love for "the World," it is also not surprising that thousands of other charities inspired by Christian principles have blossomed into national and international charities. Christian charities have also evolved into cooperative and mutual for-profit companies over time, as they became large and successful when the markets for their products and services grew and the economies in which they were immersed became highly monetized.

In conclusion, Christians are called to be passionate about combatting the effects of sin and changing things that must be changed to improve people's lives. Their views on poverty, wealth, inequality and freedom are of the sort needed to promote both civil society and development. But a Biblically-literate Christian perspective would argue that progress toward civil society is unlikely without addressing the heart commitments that guide people's beliefs about right and wrong and the actions that flow from these beliefs. This must be done in an integrated way – because all of the influences of Christianity discussed here relate in one way or another to civil society's development. In the case of developing countries, this means values that tolerate theft of public property, corruption, nepotism, abuse of power, revenge, etc. must be replaced with values like love, joy, peace, patience, kindness, gentleness, self-control, and institutions and structures that formalize the importance of these things. In more economically-developed countries it may mean that the depth of civil society people depends ultimately on what people care about. For civil society to advance, people need to spend less time and fewer resources on material things, entertainment, recreation or status-seeking, and more on heart-to-heart dialogue about what concepts like love, peace, or joy, or freedom, authority, rights, or justice mean to Muslims, Hindu's, Christians, or atheists - and the implications of these shades of meaning for things like politics, economics, or social policy and development.

Chapter 27: Christianity and Pro-Development Worldview Elements #2 and #3 – Perspectives on Authority and Stewardship

A Correct Understanding of Authority

At the beginning of our Chapter 26 discussion of Christian perspectives on civil society, we noted that Biblical teaching has much to say about some of the things that undergird civil society - such as views on authority, ideas about cooperation, and concerns about justice - hence we will also investigate the roots of Christian perspectives on these things. In the area of *authority*, the Bible teaches Christians (and Jews, based on Old Testament injunctions) to submit to authority, that rulers have been established by God and are ultimately accountable to him, and that government authorities are called to be both "God's servant to do [people] good", and "an agent of wrath to bring punishment on the wrongdoer."[1] From the very beginning of Israel's existence as a people, the primary qualifications for rulers and judges were capability and integrity. For example, when Jethro, the father-in-law of the revered Jewish emancipator Moses, advised his son-in-law on the task of governing/judging an increasingly large number of people, he suggested that Moses "select *capable* men from all the people—men who *fear God, trustworthy* men who *hate dishonest gain*—and appoint them as officials.[2] And, although there are many teachings directed toward ruling authorities, and scores of personal examples of rulers who were commended for doing what was right - or chastised or punished for doing what was wrong - the idea that those in authority are accountable permeates the entire Old and New Testaments. To illustrate briefly, at the very beginning of the Bible, God calls Adam and Eve to account for their disobedience (eating from the tree of knowledge of good and evil) in the Garden of Eden;[3] one chapter later, Cain is called to account for killing his brother Abel, whose blood, metaphorically speaking, is said to cry out to God from the ground.[4] A few chapters later Noah is reminded that God will demand "from each man…an accounting for the life of his fellow man."[5] And so it goes throughout the Bible, accountability not just for murder but for theft, adultery, envy, the behavior of one's children, and the entire host of human failings - ending finally with a description of the final accounting in the last book of the Bible, Revelation, as people find out if their "names are written in Jesus' book of life."

Much of what the New Testament has to say about how Christians are to view *government* authority is captured in Paul's letter to the Romans (Chapter 13) where he says:

> Everyone must submit himself to the governing authorities, for there is no authority except that which God has established. The authorities that exist have been established by God. Consequently, he who rebels against the authority is rebelling against what God has instituted, and those who do so will bring judgment on themselves. For rulers hold no terror for those who do right, but for those who do wrong. Do you want to be free from fear of the one in authority? Then do what is right and he will commend you. For he is God's servant to do you good. But if you do wrong, be afraid, for he does not bear the sword for nothing. He is God's servant, an agent of wrath to bring punishment on the wrongdoer. Therefore, it is necessary to submit to the authorities, not only because of possible punishment but also because of conscience. This is also why you pay taxes, for the authorities are God's servants, who give their full time to governing. Give everyone what you owe him: If you owe taxes, pay taxes; if revenue, then revenue; if respect, then respect; if honor, then honor.[6]

The reason Christians continue to subjugate themselves to governments that they consider immoral or unethical is found elsewhere in the Bible. The short summary of why this occurs is that Jesus' followers assumed that because Jesus was God, "all things…in heaven and on earth, visible and invisible, whether thrones or powers or rulers or authorities…were created by him and for him[7] and that "having disarmed the powers and authorities, he made a public spectacle of them, triumphing over them by the cross."[8] Therefore there was no need or permission for Christians to engage in violent revolutions, especially since they had been told by one of their most courageous leaders (the apostle Paul), "if it is possible, as far as it depends on you, live at peace with everyone."[9] The assumption was and is that good will triumph over evil, if not always in the short run, then most assuredly in the long run. These teachings have been very important to economic development, not only because they promote civil society and peaceful political transitions, but because they underlie commitments to freedom of religion, and to the strong understanding that government has an important and legitimate, albeit limited, role to play in the social order.

Biblical teachings related to authority, then, which tie into concepts like God's sovereignty, the responsible use of freedom, conviction about the seriousness of both personal and corporate sin, and accountability for making things better have contributed to a host of positive effects on development - from employees who do a good job even when no one is looking over their shoulder, to whistleblowers who expose the corporate fleecing of government and taxpayers, to high rates of voluntary compliance in tax payments, to the quest of products and services like security systems or genetic testing. Biblical teachings about authority also make Christians uncomfortable when their leaders are less than transparent, and lead to the development of structures and institutions that exist for the purpose of discouraging and exposing fraud, dishonesty, bribery, and dangerous products. They help government define its role in the economy, promote honesty, integrity and trustworthiness in business and government, give guidance on an appropriate balance between rights and responsibilities, and help government leaders understand what it means to be "public servants." Perhaps most importantly, however, they provide a framework for the kind of justice that makes economic activity worth engaging in.

Biblical Teaching about Justice

If justice is as important to development as we concluded in Chapter 20, it is no surprise that nations that have been historically influenced by Biblical teaching have developed relatively healthy economies. The word justice is mentioned hundreds of times in the Biblical Old Testament and is a rich term that encompasses a wide variety of activities that are necessary for a well-ordered and fair society. The God of the Old Testament is revealed to be relentless in his pursuit of both justice and righteousness among his people, and both are well defined in the Old Testament - as these nine brief passages from nine different books of the Bible illustrate:

- Do not pervert justice; do not show partiality to the poor or favoritism to the great, but judge your neighbor fairly.[10]
- By justice a king gives a country stability, but one who is greedy for bribes tears it down. [11]
- He who walks righteously and speaks what is right, who rejects gain from extortion and keeps his hand from accepting bribes…his bread will be supplied, and water will not fail him.[12]
- But let justice roll on like a river, righteousness like a never-failing stream![13]
- These are the things you are to do: Speak the truth to each other, and render true and sound judgment in your courts.[14]
- He has showed you, O man, what is good. And what does the Lord require of you? To act justly and to love mercy and to walk humbly with your God."[15]
- "Woe to him who builds his palace by unrighteousness, his upper rooms by injustice, making his countrymen work for nothing, not paying them for their labor…..Does it make you a king to have more and more cedar? Did not your father have food and drink? He did what was right and just, so all went well

with him. He defended the cause of the poor and needy, and so all went well. Is that not what it means to know me?" declares the Lord.[16]

- Do not oppress an alien; you yourselves know how it feels to be aliens, because you were aliens in Egypt.[17]
- Hear the disputes between your brothers and judge fairly, whether the case is between brother Israelites or between one of them and an alien.[18]

Righteousness is also clearly defined, as in the Ten Commandments where people were told simply and clearly "You shall not kill," or "You shall not steal." An overriding theme of the Old Testament is that justice is not possible without righteousness - i.e., if the rulers and people ignore God's moral laws, injustice will be the result. Israel, for example, was not to shed innocent blood and had elaborate rituals for atoning for it when it happened.[19] Nevertheless, already in the Old Testament - in spite of the fact that the Israelites often demanded "an eye for an eye and a tooth for a tooth"[20] - *individuals* were not allowed to decide who was innocent or guilty and to mete out justice, and they were called to a degree of concern for both prisoners and enemies. God is recorded there as saying "It is mine to avenge; I will repay,"[21] and telling the Israelites, "Do not say, 'I'll do to him as he has done to me; I'll pay that man back for what he did,"[22] and "If your enemy is hungry, give him food to eat; if he is thirsty, give him water to drink."[23]

This theme continues in the New Testament, and is strengthened by Jesus in particular, who says in Matthew 5: 43-48:

> You have heard that it was said, 'Love your neighbor and hate your enemy.' But I tell you: Love your enemies and pray for those who persecute you, that you may be sons of your Father in heaven. He causes his sun to rise on the evil and the good, and sends rain on the righteous and the unrighteous. If you love those who love you, what reward will you get? Are not even the tax collectors doing that? And if you greet only your brothers, what are you doing more than others? Do not even pagans do that? Be perfect, therefore, as your heavenly Father is perfect.

The apostles consistently reinforced these principles, sometimes quoting Jesus or the Old Testament teachings in the process. Paul, for example, says to the Romans (and makes a similar point when writing his letter to the Hebrews), "Do not take revenge, my friends, but leave room for God's wrath, for it is written: 'It is mine to avenge; I will repay,' says the Lord. On the contrary 'If your enemy is hungry, feed him; if he is thirsty, give him something to drink. Do not be overcome by evil, but overcome evil with good.'"[24] In the context of the rest of the Bible, it is clear that it is the government alone - and not revolutionaries or self-appointed zealots - that is ultimately responsible and accountable for meting out justice.

Equally important is the assertion that God does not show favoritism,[25] and the corollary principle that "if [people] show favoritism, [they] sin and are convicted by the law as lawbreakers."[26] These principles are merely an extension of Old Testament Jewish law that repeatedly warned rulers about God's abhorrence of rulers and judges who showed partiality, accepted bribes, preyed on the weak or otherwise perverted justice.

Christian Perspective on Government

The end result of this is that most Christians do not see government as an adversary to be thwarted, or as a powerful friend who may be able to help secure an advantage, but as a partner for doing good - called to a kind of public justice that is consistent with the order God has established for human activity. Promoting justice has traditionally focused on establishing the rule of law maintaining a level playing field ("no favoritism"), and protecting the weak from the powerful people who would take advantage of them. It therefore involves clear laws, consistent enforcement, impartiality, promises kept, and the efficient operation of government. Nowhere is this more important than in a market economy — and this explains at least in part why most Christians support market economies where all competitors are given an equal chance to compete. This perspective also assumes that when the state needs to use its coercive powers to, for example, tax, punish evildoers, or prevent economic entities from to gaining so much power that they can take advantage of competitors or customers, it will always do so using just processes aimed at just ends.

In addition, since the teachings of Christ give no hints of the concept of forced religious observance or conversions, most Christians do not feel it is appropriate for government to force adherence to specific religious beliefs or behaviors. But neither do they believe that government should discourage religious activity by either secularizing the provision of cultural, economic or social resources, or making itself the *primary* provider of these things. This is one reason that many Christian teachers, parents, and students in the U.S. believe the government's provision of educational services under the umbrella of a secular humanist belief system is ill-advised. They might argue - based on government's responsibility to maintain a level playing field and promote justice - that all children have a right to education, but most would argue against giving monopoly rights to a secular worldview within that educational system.[27]

Biblically speaking, the concept of justice is always joined at the hip to mercy. Although there are many Biblical prohibitions against punishing people more severely than they deserve, there is no prohibition against treating people better than they deserve. In fact, two things at the core of the Biblical story - redemption and grace - center on people being treated better than they deserve. This kind of over-the-top love that is characterized not only by forgiveness, but by a willingness to forget that an offense was even committed, and even a willingness to bear the punishment due another, is not considered a travesty of justice, in part because true justice requires both adequate punishment and restoration. As we will note in our discussion about the wealth-creating impact of love, this extension to the concept of justice - taught and embodied by Jesus - may well have been even more important to human development than the sum total of Biblical teachings about justice.

In addition to the practical impacts of Biblical teachings about justice discussed earlier, these teachings have also contributed much toward elevating the rule of law to a prominent place in Western societies, and the corresponding positive effects of this on economic development. They have also spurred efforts to reduce fraud, clean up government, and ensure that monetary and fiscal policies are carried out with integrity. Combined with the Biblical teaching about the ultimate accountability of people to God, these beliefs about justice cause people to promote human rights[28] and speak out against deception, dishonesty, bribery, or dangerous products, even when there is money to be made from such activity and the likelihood of being caught is low. This has also led to a willingness to help define, accept and even promote appropriate and impartial government involvement in economic activities by both individuals and businesses. This means that just taxes will be paid willingly and attempts to gain special privileges will be deemed inappropriate. Businesses will be expected to pay attention to the spirit of the law over against the letter of the law, and be willing to inform government about legal loopholes, and lawbreakers. Even actions which may be costly to businesses in the short run (e.g., pollution regulations, health care regulation, or support for education) may nevertheless be supported by business if these actions reflect attempts to use the authority of government in appropriate ways to accomplish its mandate of promoting justice. And, since a healthy competitive atmosphere results in better products and services, business owners should be supportive of government efforts to promote competition as well.

Prohibitions against showing favoritism have also had a significant impact - contributing to the widespread use of meritocracy in hiring, and the war against prejudice and discrimination - both of which encourage people to develop their talents and free them up to use these talents for the benefit of others. The recognition of envy as a sin has made it easier for people with different incomes and wealth to live and work peaceably together. As noted earlier, the Judeo-Christian belief that every person is created in the image of God has contributed throughout history to emphases on respect, tolerance, and human rights, all of which have in turn contributed to the economic benefits associated with democracy, relatively open borders and markets, and immigration policies. The last of these has had a particularly positive effect on development in the U.S., attracting people from a wide variety of backgrounds, and unleashing the productive resources of women, minorities, and many others who would have remained disenfranchised in other places.

Christianity and Stewardship

Biblical teachings also contain a strong stewardship ethic. As noted in Chapter 21, stewardship involves doing what is most needed, and what is sustainable, accomplishing needed tasks with the fewest resources possible, minimizing depreciation and depletion, and using resources to address fundamental problems rather than just symptoms of problems.

Doing What is Most Needed, and What is Sustainable, Rather Than Anything/Everything That May be Desired

Decisions about what is most needed clearly flow from people's worldviews and religious beliefs. As noted earlier, Christians are mandated by God to love and serve each other and others outside of their immediate family and friendship circles, and told that they will someday give an account of how they carried out these mandates. Taking this accounting seriously leads to stewardship of action - to careful analyses of contemplated actions prior to committing to them, to assess whether or not they will truly serve and benefit others. But figuring out what is most needed, and the impact of one's actions, also means uncovering the truth about reality. For Christians, this means searching for abstract principles and basic laws (physical and/or spiritual) and embracing science and technology as tools for figuring out how things work. In doing this they are following the path of the many great scientists whose faith spurred their interest in science, such as Copernicus, Galileo, Descartes, Kepler, Bacon, Newton, Boyle, Mendel, Kelvin, Pasteur and Lister or contemporaries like Francis Collins (who headed up the human genome project).

Accomplishing Tasks with the Fewest Resources Possible

Biblical teachings about God's claim to all resources, and people's accountability for what they do with them, also foster attempts to accomplish tasks with the fewest resources possible. It is not surprising, then that much of the science of double entry accounting can be traced back to the writings of Luca Pacioli, a 15th century Franciscan friar. But stewardship is to be viewed as broadly as possible, and will always include the stewardship of time. So it is also no accident that clocks were invented and first used in Christian monasteries. Later, clocks became closely associated with the Protestant work ethic as clock production shifted from Catholic southern Europe to places like Switzerland, Germany, England, and the Netherlands, and large numbers of people began to conduct their affairs and gauge their productivity, not by natural rhythms, but by the clock. Clocks have since so transformed the lives of many people in "highly-developed" economies that they feel guilty about arriving late for appointments, and go to great pains to accomplish tasks in the time allotted for them.[29]

Stewardship has also come to be associated among Christians with minimizing waste in their personal activities. Many Christians draw a kind of collective conclusion from 1) Biblical mandates to "take care of" the earth,[30] 2) mandates to care for the poor, 3) "warnings against luxurious living,[31] 4) mandates to use and develop talents, 5) frequent exhortations to maintain self-control,[32] and 6) other passages dealing with financial and other kinds of accountability, that they ought to distinguish between wants and needs, focus primarily on needs, and share the resulting surplus with others. In some cases this has also led Christians to share possessions with each other and their neighbors – with the result that material things are used more efficiently and resources that would otherwise be tied up in excessive property accumulation are freed up for more productive uses (monasteries were early examples of this). These inclinations have also reduced the amount of resources tied up in church property over time, particularly for Protestant Christians. In contrast to long stretches of human history where massive church structures requiring thousands of "man years" of labor were the norm, most Protestant churches today elevate function over form, with the result that that fewer resources are tied up in buildings, grandiose religious artifacts and maintenance, and more resources are devoted to preaching, teaching, value inculcation, building community, promoting ethical behavior, and the like. Christian belief systems also do not generally require church members to participate in lavish consumptive celebrations, unlike some belief systems that require long journeys to sacred locations, massive week-long celebrations or expensive rituals. All of these things free up resources for activities that are more likely to spur development.

The theological shift within Christendom from form to function has also had another profound effect on economic activity. By emphasizing Biblical passages that indicate that God can be worshipped anywhere [33] and that he prefers obedience to his moral and ethical laws over/against elaborate structures and rituals,[34] there is little reason for Protestant Christians (and others who have also embraced this theology) to engage in fighting over a particular holy temple, mosque, shrine, or location, with the resultant destruction of life, property and capital associated with these conflicts. This can be contrasted, for example, to the importance of holy sites to the Catholic Church at the time of the Reformation, the continuing tension and violence associated with competing claims to the temple mount in Jerusalem, or the thousands killed and arrested over the years in the towns of Northern India) where both Hindus and Muslims lay claim to particular sacred sites.

Christian Perspectives on Depletion and Depreciation

Other Biblical themes encourage Christians to conduct their affairs in ways that minimize the depletion and depreciation of all assets, broadly defined, that comprise wealth. One reason for this is that most Christians believe the earth and everything in it is a divine gift from the Creator, that people have been given authority over the physical world, and that both the physical world and the physical state of human beings matter to God. In fact, the Bible portrays a God who expects his followers to both care for the needs of others and take care of their own bodies. The apostle Paul likens the care and feeding of relationships in the family and church to the care and feeding of the body,[35] and at one point says "Do you not know that your body is a temple of the Holy Spirit, who is in you, whom you have received from God? You are not your own; you were bought at a price. Therefore honor God with your body."[36] The Bible also espouses a consistently high view of children as gifts from God, deserving of nurture and education, and worthy recipients of and participants in the kingdom of God. Because of this, in addition to holding education in high regard, many Christians are repulsed by the idea that parents would thoughtlessly damage their children's future opportunities by engaging in selfish behavior and excessive and material consumption.

In spite of these inclinations toward stewardship, a Christian worldview views the natural world as a gift *to be used*, not an object of worship. Hence, unlike with some other belief systems, Christians and Jews have been free from the beginning to cut down trees, crush rocks, use plants and animals, and otherwise "subdue" the natural world by building homes, roads, dams, or airports, or developing food products or medicines without worrying that powerful, easily-offended, retaliatory spirits inhabit these natural resources.[37] They are also free to innovate without fear of ancestral spirits cursing them because they are not following traditional ways, and carry out economic activity without superstition or the fear that something bad will happen because of magic or the possibility that they have violated a taboo. On the demand side of the economic exchange, Christians believe humans ("consumers") have been given the privilege of responsibly enjoying the fruits of the earth. Unlike Jews, Hindus, or Muslims, they are free to kill all non-human living things for food in the most efficient way possible, subject only to good animal husbandry practices (although some Christians nevertheless choose to be vegetarians). But consumption is not a particularly good word to describe a Christian perspective on economic activity. Consuming goods and services are not mindless activities that spontaneously flow from personal preferences; rather, they are to be viewed as opportunities to build people up for service in God's kingdom.[38]

Guidance in these areas comes not only from the Bible but also from the writings of Christian scholars who have interpreted the Bible for the benefit of Christians throughout the centuries. Their writings have repeatedly reigned in abuses, by reminding Christians that the natural world is claimed by God,[39] and that they are free to use it only in the sense that they would tend, keep and cultivate a garden - in a sustainable way, making sure that they don't compromise its future productivity future generations for the lure of easy riches.[40] Property ownership laws set up in the Old Testament are consistent with this perspective. People could own land, but had the responsibility to be stewardly with it and its produce and its creatures, not exploitative or mean-spirited. The Biblical principle of Sabbath rest was instituted in part to keep people from abusing the land, and Biblical accounts convey that the Israelites were punished by God on more than one occasion for abusing the land.[41]

Christians are also called to contentment, which means they must try seriously to distinguish between needs and wants, and be willing to subject their personal wants to the needs of others, both inside and outside of their families and friendship circles, and especially to the needs of the poor. They are also called to distinguish between "goods" and "bads," and avoid products, services, and behaviors that are unhealthy or destructive. In light of these teachings, most Christians believe thrift to be good, and conspicuous consumption to be both unnecessary and unhealthy. The Bible also teaches (in Proverbs) that "the borrower is the servant of the lender," and that failing to repay debts is a serious matter,[42] so many Christians believe the use of debt should be limited to the financing of productive activities (including businesses) that allow for self-liquidation of the debt, or at the very least for the purchase of assets that have lasting value (like homes) rather than for consumptive binges. The sum total of all these slightly modified behaviors has been and continues to be a significant influence on economic development in localities and countries heavily influenced by Christian beliefs.

Dealing With Fundamental Problems, Rather Than With Symptoms of Problems

Christian beliefs and doctrine also deal with the last dimension of stewardship, that of dealing with fundamental problems, rather than with symptoms of problems. A continuous theme throughout the Bible is that problems (including economic problems) are largely the result of people's inability or unwillingness to follow the laws and guidelines that God has revealed *for people's good/protection*. Whether it be overusing the land, playing fast and loose with the truth, turning a blind eye to injustice, sexual immorality, abuse of power, or any other of the hundreds of issues dealt with throughout the Bible, the assumption is always that it is not only more responsible but also more efficient to refrain from harmful behaviors in the first place than to have to fix the damage that they do later on. This means that Christians would prefer vaccines to medicines or surgical fixes, but if behavioral changes have the potential to stop the spread of disease without any medical intervention at all (including vaccines), this will be the favored solution. Likewise, poverty alleviation programs that address the moral and ethical roots of poverty are to be preferred to those that simply provide a minimum level of income. Emphasizing things like healthy marriages or good parenting (via church and school education programs that hold adults accountable) is to be preferred to allowing systemic family problems to develop for the sake of protecting people's privacy or autonomy. Restricting sexual activity to committed marriage relationships is to be preferred to random sexual trysts, dishonestly covering them up, and the high costs of dealing with the sexually transmitted diseases or juvenile delinquents and adult criminals that these relationships and families too often spawn. In short, a Christian perspective on stewardship is that it is inseparable from the values and attitudes that people hold. This also means that one of the most important things government can do to promote stewardship is to not marginalize people's most deeply held beliefs from the public square. Rather, they should create structures, processes and institutions that ensure that each and every perspective has an equal shot at penetrating people's minds and hearts, whether secular or religious. This means allowing faith communities to actively live out their perspectives on marriage, health care, poverty alleviation, etc., rather than undermining these efforts by unthinkingly redirecting community resources to secular government programs. In short they should never inadvertently block the best solutions to a nation or community's most persistent problems by allowing "freedom of religion" to degenerate into "freedom from religion."

Chapter 28: Christianity and Pro-Development Worldview Elements #4 and #5 – Perspectives on Objectivity and the Journey from Mistrust and Fear to Sincere Concern and Love

The Ability to See Oneself Objectively and Others Sympathetically

As noted when we introduced the fourth and fifth pro-development worldview elements in Chapters 22 and 23, the widespread ability of people to see themselves objectively and others sympathetically is very healthy for development. We indicated that this involves replacing mistrust, fear and hatred with tolerance, respect, and appreciation, and then moving beyond this to the kind of love that begets self-discipline, a widespread concern for others, and generosity, and, finally, even beyond this, to a passion for building others up, and an ability to care deeply about even those who are very unlike us or who may even dislike us or oppose us, even to the point of being willing to suffer for or sacrifice for them.

Seeing Oneself Objectively

The Bible's take on "seeing objectively" focuses on the need for people to understand that there is an endemic "sin problem." It insists that all people are "sinful at birth,"[1] and by doing so rules out any myopic assumptions that just because one is a Christian he or she will not have to struggle with sin. Nor are the effects of sin confined to individuals and families. It does damage to the natural world and infiltrates the institutions, policies, procedures and societies that people build. The Christian scriptures even teach that sin has undermined the very notion of law or norms (i.e., that God has very specific intentions for human conduct that need to be followed), and people's ability to decipher them. But humankind is not without hope. The insidious effects of sin can be dealt with, but only when people understand that it exists, and that dealing with it requires a kind of new start or "rebirth" that requires no less than the power of God. So the story turns out to be one of hope and the potential for human flourishing. As the apostle John put it, "No one who is born of God will continue to [intend to] sin, because God's seed remains in him; he cannot go on sinning, because he has been born of God."[2]

But the Christian scriptures also teach that honesty, self-examination, sorrow for sin, and repentance must precede the "turning around" associated with rebirth. Rather than buying into "watered down," individualistic or humanistic principles which allow everyone to do pretty much what they want, it calls followers of Christ to put his claims up against those of other belief systems (in a loving manner), in the hope of shaping a society where the damaging effects of sin can be minimized, and all people can reach their highest human potential, not just materially, but in every other way as well.

Seeing Others Sympathetically

For Christians, seeing others sympathetically means much more than tolerance, or thinking fondly of one's children or close friends. It means seeing the good in all people and being genuinely concerned for people with whom one has little in common and with which one has had no prior relationship. Christianity has a very strong undercurrent of doctrine dealing with this, which is likely one of the reasons it has had so much impact globally. From its birth, Christianity strongly emphasized the importance of bridging gaps between diverse people groups. As Jesus' disciples preached the amazing news of his resurrection, a new religion was launched, not among a few like-minded people, but among people of every tongue and nation. This launching of the Christian church is recorded in Acts 2:

> Now there were staying in Jerusalem God-fearing Jews from every nation under heaven. When they heard this sound, a crowd came together in bewilderment, because each one heard them speaking in his own language. Utterly amazed, they asked: "Are not all these men who are speaking Galileans? Then how is it that each of us hears them in his own native language? Parthians, Medes and Elamites; residents of Mesopotamia, Judea and Cappadocia, Pontus and Asia, Phrygia and Pamphylia, Egypt and the parts of Libya near Cyrene; visitors from Rome (both Jews and converts to Judaism), Cretans and Arabs—we hear them declaring the wonders of God in our own tongues!" Amazed and perplexed, they asked one another, "What does this mean?"

Although the Bible records that some of the bystanders were convinced that these new Christians had had too much wine, the words recorded in the book of Acts indicate that the apostle Peter tried to correct this misconception by indicating that the event they were witnessing was in fact God's calling all people to be bound back to him through the power of the Holy Spirit, as foretold in the Old Testament. Peter said "These men are not drunk, as you suppose. It's only nine in the morning! No, this is what was spoken by the prophet Joel: 'In the last days, God says, I will pour out my Spirit on all people … and everyone who calls on the name of the Lord will be saved.'"[3] Later on in the same chapter of the Book of Acts, Peter reiterates that this religion is wide open, that its "promise is for you and your children and for all who are far off—for all whom the Lord our God will call." This inclusiveness is underscored in the Apostle John's vision of "the new heavens and the new earth" where he writes, "Before me was a great multitude that no one could count, from every nation, tribe, people and language standing before the throne and in front of the lamb."[4] For Christians, then, religious beliefs are a choice; they are not the equivalent of fate or predetermined by birth, ethnicity or family origin. This both invites considerable interaction with others and opens the door to significant transformations in worldview, and, of course, the significant impact that these transformations can have on development.

The Importance of Jesus

Given the primacy of worldview, as we have unpacked it here, one must be open to the possibility that the teachings of Christ may have been more influential on Western economies than almost anything else   This of course is not because Christ would have championed consumer-driven booms or the lavish parties of billionaires, but because he preached an ethic of tolerance, forgiveness, love and openness that was unusual, to say the least, for both his time and most of human history. Historical records indicate that he entered a largely pagan world that had little regard for slaves, women, the disabled and weak, and outsiders in general, and transformed it, first through the lives of his followers, and eventually, through them, to nearly every nook and cranny of the globe. Today, large numbers of people who have been affected either directly or indirectly by what he taught, see love as mandatory and believe that building others up is part of their calling in life. And this includes not only a select few who have received extensive theological education, but people from all walks of life and all income and education levels. They include not only people who profess to be his followers, but even unbelievers whose great or great-great grandparents were believers, and who still carry in them the residual effects of their forbearers' worldviews. This is not to say that the influence of secular thinkers or other belief systems has not contributed to these ideas. There have of course been many other important philosophers and peacemakers in the past two thousand years, but arguably none with anywhere near Jesus's impact.

Much of this impact is the result of the kind of person Jesus is depicted as being. Biblical accounts indicate that he left his lofty heavenly position at God's "right hand" to come to earth as a helpless baby, born in what amounted to a feeding trough in an animal barn. During his ministry he routinely talked to people who the religious leaders of his day thought were beneath them. He treated women, who were often viewed as little more than property by the more powerful men, as not only worthy of respect, but as equal partners in his ministry.

One of his disciples, the apostle John, records that Jesus even washed his followers feet and, when he had finished, said, "You call me 'Teacher' and 'Lord,' and rightly so, for that is what I am. Now that I, your Lord and Teacher, have washed your feet, you also should wash one another's feet. I have set you an example that you should do as I have done for you".[5] Jesus repeatedly explained and demonstrated what he meant by this, saying at one point that "You have heard that it was said, 'Love your neighbor and hate your enemy.' But I tell you: Love your enemies and pray for those who persecute you."[6]

Beyond Love to Service and Sacrifice

Jesus also lived out his words about loving enemies. Described in the Bible as a suffering servant of God, he preached and illustrated by his life and death that not only should one not kill, but she should even be willing to give up her life for the sake of others. After his death, the apostle Paul describes Jesus' ultimate sacrifice in these words: "He humbled himself and became obedient to death— even death on a cross."[7] Accounts in the gospel writings also indicate that he was mocked, scourged, and killed without a hint of retaliation. Known by Christians worldwide as the Prince of Peace, he taught that people - and by extension nations - should follow the "Golden Rule" and treat others as they would like to be treated by them. But perhaps the most remarkable thing, at least for Christians, who believe he was (and is) the son of God, is that the most powerful person in the history of the world, who hates sin more than any other person could, would choose to accomplish his purposes not through force but through the patient teaching and sacrificial love of sinners.

This emphasis on service and sacrifice in Christian theology coalesces with the belief that all people are created in the image of God and makes it mandatory for Christians to be significantly concerned about all people, including those who are powerless, uneducated, and/or not Christians. One inevitable consequence of these teachings was the Protestant Reformation and its insistence on translating the Bible into the languages of the common people. This in turn had a remarkable influence on literacy, and because, as Benson Bobrick put it in his book *Wide as the Waters*, it led large numbers of formerly marginalized people to "think for themselves," it was a critical building block for modern conceptions of individual rights, civil society, and the establishment of democracy and freedom. The de-emphasis on class associated with this opened the door to the idea that people from the humblest beginnings can go on to do amazing things. One such person from humble beginnings was Billy Graham, whose inclusive style (working with Christians of all denominations and refusal to allow racial barriers to segregate people attending his evangelistic meetings) set the tone for much of what is good about the modern evangelical movement. His tireless work to replace a kind of closed fundamentalism with open international evangelicalism spawned a host of other influential events. Examples from the latter half of the 20th century include the advent of influential Christian periodicals and new Bible translations more accessible to younger people, people with less education, and those without access to it in their primary language. During this same period, Christians who had been pushed to the edge of an increasingly secularized culture and public square began the reentry procedure, and issues of concern to Christians began to be increasingly addressed in American politics. Perhaps most importantly, Christians reconnected globally (through events like the Lausanne Covenant) highlighting the sea change that had taken place as the epicenter of the Christian faith shifted from Europe and North America, to the South (Latin America and Africa) and the East (Asia). As R. Stephen Warner notes, this even affected immigration patterns, as the immigration wave into the U.S. that started following The Immigration and Nationality Act of 1965 was overwhelmingly Christian (and Evangelical and often Pentecostal). This not only led, as Warner put it, to the "de-Europeanization of American Christianity," but it invigorated the U.S. economy as well.

Even the Christian emphasis on evangelism, which has often been narrowly construed as an attempt to "save souls," can be fairly interpreted as a deeply felt concern for other people. Evangelism also goes well beyond a concern for the after-life because it flows from Christ's teaching that Christians ought to "go and make disciples of all nations, baptizing them in the name of the Father and of the Son and of the Holy Spirit, *and teaching them* to obey everything [Jesus] commanded."[8] The last part of this command is conveniently ignored both by those who misunderstand Christianity and by reductionist Christian evangelists who assume their job is finished when they get an apparent commitment to Christ from the (sometimes unsuspecting) object of their evangelistic attention. The last part of Christ's command - that evangelists ought to be "teaching [converts] to obey everything [Christ commanded]" - is very telling. Although religious conversions are thought by many to deal mostly with people's ultimate destiny ("salvation" in the afterlife), they are likely not authentic unless they also change people's worldviews and the way they live the rest of their earthly lives. As millions of converts to Christianity will attest to, one of the most significant influences of Christianity on their lives (and, therefore, on the development process) is its ability help them overcome the values and attitudes that enslaved them to bad ideas and bad habits. Of course the development impact of dropping a few bad habits pales in comparison to the impact of large numbers of people beginning to see the world differently, or key decision makers being transformed from being insecure, selfish, unjust, or power hungry to being selfless servants, intent on building others up. Together these kinds of changes have had a powerful historical influence not only on individuals and families, but on communities and many entire countries, including, at various times, most of the countries of Europe and the United States. The impact of these changed beliefs (which are compared in the Bible to what yeast does in a loaf of bread) is more recently becoming visible in many parts of Asia, Africa and South America, and is certain to continue as the global religious and economic scenes are reshaped throughout the 21st century.

Voluntary Cooperation as Normative

Another aspect of Christianity that impacts economic development every bit as much as its Pentecost-inspired outward focus is its ability to demand high levels of voluntary cooperation without undercutting individual responsibility. The Bible gives Jews and Christians little choice but to consider voluntary cooperation as normal and to seek ways to accomplish tasks communally. The distinguishing mark of the Jews - from the beginning - is that they were called not to be a collection of individuals, or loose knit tribes, but a *people*.[9] A series of covenants laid out in the Old Testament called for the Israelites to live in community with each other and their God and to accept the individual and collective responsibilities that were laid out as part of these covenants.[10] In order to live in community, they were given strict rules for interpersonal relationships, including rules for resolving conflicts, dealing with those who had offended them and the treatment of gentiles (non-Jews) and aliens (foreigners).

In the New Testament, the concept of a "people" was expanded to include the entire Christian church, which quickly came to encompass people of many races, languages, and cultures. The apostle Peter put it this way: "You are a chosen people, a royal priesthood, a holy nation, a people belonging to God, that you may declare the praises of him who called you out of darkness into his wonderful light. Once you were not a people, but now you are the people of God."[11]

Castes, classes, rankings, discrimination, favoritism, and arrogance had no place in the early Christian church. Christians are to avoid status consciousness, or as the apostle Paul bluntly puts it in his letter to the Romans, they must "be willing to associate with people of low position."[12] In dealing with others, Christians are also repeatedly commanded in the Bible to be governed by so-called "fruits of the spirit," like "love, joy, peace, patience, kindness, goodness, faithfulness, gentleness, and self-control."[13] These virtues are not simply interpersonal; rather they are designed to govern the way all conflict is resolved, whether personal, in business, or in the political arena. More specifically, Christ's teachings urge face-to-face dialog, and if necessary, the use of an unbiased, wise third party authority in the resolution of conflict. In the book of Matthew Christians are told, for all practical purposes, not even to come with a gift to their house of worship unless they've first tried to resolve the conflict that they have with one another. They were warned repeatedly about the kinds of things that would break down a community: Paul told the Galatians, "If you keep on biting and devouring each other, watch out or you will be destroyed by each other,"[14] and the Ephesians "Do not let any unwholesome talk come out of your mouths, but only that which is helpful for building others up according to their needs, that it might benefit those who listen."[15] James told the early Christians that "Everyone should be quick to listen, [and] slow to speak,"[16] and Paul warns his apprentice Timothy about "gossips and busybodies, saying things they ought not to."[17] The clear message is that interpersonal problems need to be fixed, and there are right and wrong ways to fix them.

Living in community also requires that selfishness be held at bay, which in turn requires that people get their sense of self-worth from something greater than individualistic achievement. Individual effort and achievement are still important, but Biblical teaching instructs Christians not to allow their sense of self-worth to be dependent on their being successful *relative to* others. Rather than be enamored by the status, fame or riches that attend the kind of individual success associated with "climbing the ladder," they are called to see achievement as an opportunity to be a blessing to others. Jesus insisted that "Whoever would be great among you must be your servant," and that "Bearing each other's burdens "fulfills the law of Christ." The implications were and are that true community cannot develop without an honest respect, appreciation and ongoing concern for the needs of others. Even when Jesus taught Christians how to pray, using words that have come to be known as The Lord's Prayer," he used plural pronouns (e.g., "give *us*," "lead *us*," "deliver *us*").

The remainder of the New Testament supports the idea that the expectations for voluntary cooperation and unity in the early Christian church were every bit as high, if not higher than they were for the Old Testament Jews. A repeated theme is that Christians must live peacefully with and love all people, even including enemies, but the *church* is called to an especially stringent standard of care relative to those in its midst. It is described as a *body* composed of many parts, each of which is *essential* to its smooth functioning.[18] It clearly teaches that all members, regardless of their wealth, education or social status, have been given gifts by God that are not ends in themselves or to be used for personal gain, but which must be used in conjunction with the talents of others to serve/benefit the entire church. One who selfishly focuses on her own needs, ignoring the needs of those around her, is sometimes compared to a tree that is growing but never bears fruit. Specific rules are also given for conflict resolution within the church, and believers are repeatedly commanded to "build one another up," in a host of ways, through their words and actions. This theme is so strong that the Greek word *allelon*, which means "one another" (in the sense of mutual, reciprocal obligation), is used nearly 100 times in the New Testament. In addition to its use to call Christians to build each other up, this word is also used in passages that call Christians to greet one another, be hospitable to one another, encourage one another, accept one another, love one another, admonish one another, forgive one another, pray for one another, be devoted to one another, be at peace with one another, be patient with one another, confess their sins to one another, spur one another to good deeds, and even wash one another's feet.

The net effect of these repeated positive "one another" urgings, coupled with nearly as many warnings about not doing specific things that would be detrimental to others, has shaped the Christian church in many ways, as well as the organizations and institutions that Christians influence. It is not hard to see how careful speech, forbearance, the recognition of other's needs, and an eagerness to serve others can foster healthy interpersonal relationships, conflict resolution, smooth functioning organizations, and peaceful coexistence. And, although difficult to measure, there can be little doubt that these teachings have had an extremely positive effect on the development of societies that have large numbers of Christians and/or people who have been or continue to be heavily influenced by Biblical teachings. The U.S. founding fathers, for example, are well known to have sprinkled their written exchanges with Bible passages when they were discussing the structure and shape of the constitution and their vision for their new country.

It is also clear from the writings of historians that these teachings have since significantly influenced things as diverse as anti-discrimination laws, the promotion of meritocracies, civil society organizations, prisoner rehabilitation, pacifist movements, ideas about "just war," and community development efforts. Perhaps most importantly, people who live "in community" experience routine social encouragement to do many good things that need doing - such as volunteer work, charity, investing, skill-building hobbies, worship, nurture, relationship building, socializing, teaching, learning, practicing, etc. These things, although healthy for the community and essential for economic development, are unlikely to be captured by official statistics.

Christian thought also calls for people to live in community and work in community to create and reform processes and structures so that these will provide checks and balances on the people involved in them, and lead to as much moral, ethical and productive behavior as possible.

In countries strongly influenced by Christian beliefs, this has affected a wide range of structures and processes. Examples include bicameral legislatures and the separation of legislative and judicial branches; products and services aimed at deterring criminal activity or encouraging moral development; ethics education and internal control systems in schools, corporations, and NGOs; and laws and regulations designed to expose corruption and increase accountability.

The Role of Common Grace

One other Christian doctrine that has been important to the building of community is that of "common grace." This teaching stems in part from Jesus' explanation in Matthew 5 and Luke 6 for why Christians should set aside natural human proclivities and thousands of years of history and "love their enemies and pray for those who persecute [them]" He insists they should do so "so that [they] may be sons of [their] Father in heaven…[who] causes his sun to rise on the evil and the good, and sends rain on the righteous and the unrighteous."[19] Immediately after saying this, he chastised his disciples for being unwilling to extend their goodwill beyond their immediate circle when he says, "if you do good to those who are good to you, what credit is that to you? Even 'sinners' do that."[20]

Christian theologians have taken these and other related Biblical teachings and developed them into a doctrine that has come to be widely known as common grace. John Calvin was one of the first reformers to contribute to this discussion when he acknowledged that God dispensed grace "in great variety, and in a certain degree to men that are otherwise profane." The well-known theologian John

Hodge rephrased this when he said, "As God is everywhere present in the material world, guiding its operations according to the laws of nature; so He is everywhere present with the minds of men, as the Spirit of truth and goodness, operating on them according to the laws of their free moral agency, inclining them to good and restraining them from evil." These teachings did two things that had an important effect on both the nature of Christianity and the development of societies heavily influenced by Christianity. They made Christians look for the good (evidences of grace) in all people (including those who did not accept, or in some cases were antagonistic to, their core beliefs) and encouraged them to deeply appreciate and look for ways to cooperate with others who didn't share their faith, at least when others were doing praiseworthy things.

This kind of cross-fertilization that the doctrine of common grace inspires, for example between Christians and secular materialists, has had profound effects on development in the Western world, and indirectly on the entire global economy. While secular materialists may be preoccupied with physical, financial, or intellectual capital, Christians have been equally preoccupied with spiritual/moral, governmental and social capital. It seems likely that neither group - without the contributions of the other and those of people from other religious perspectives and cultural backgrounds - would have been able to round out the Development Wheel and bring about the unique combination of products and services that characterizes the modern global economy. In this way, Christian teaching about how one should relate to those outside of her church or friendship circles has contributed to the inception and growth of large corporations, cooperatives, mutual associations, non-profit organizations, and participatory government structures. Large corporations and governments, in particular, are places where large numbers of people must work well with others who may be very unlike them. The complexity of modern products, markets and economies often demands the cooperation of hundreds of thousands of people. And if people do not feel compelled to cooperate at increasingly complex levels, democracies can quite easily degenerate into partisan bickering, power struggles, or a tyranny of the majority. While these institutions have not always thrived in cultures heavily influenced by Christian teachings, they have fared much better than where religious or cultural principles do not encourage widespread cooperation beyond the family or tribal level. Civil society organizations also flounder when peoples' belief systems do not incline them toward living in community.

Other Impacts of the Christian Journey from Mistrust to Love

We close by noting that even our most astute historians or economists have been slow to recognize the full potential of the movement from fear and mistrust to agape love, in part because Westerners have often done a poor job of following Christ's example. But it is also because even good scholars often do not find what they are not looking for, and because hundreds of small influences are also much more difficult for scholars to see than a few large ones. But Christianity, like other belief systems, has influenced economic activity in hundreds of small ways and the collective impact of this has been substantial. These influences could be visible to scholars who are *looking for* them, but they could also become visible to those who start asking the kinds of questions that assume the relevance of belief systems. The questions needed are of two types: How has a belief system like Christianity affected ....? And how has .... affected economic outcomes? With regard to key worldview elements #s 4 and 5 - that development needs people who care broadly for, and more importantly, love others - we offer, on the following page, a small sample of such questions, choosing also, for purposes of brevity, to frame them strictly from a U.S perspective:

How has Christianity affected?	How has this affected?
Attitudes about love and charity	Vaccines, prescription drugs, foundations, hospitals, libraries or NGOs created
The duties we owe "one another"	The peace benefits linked to soldiers' sacrifices
Attitudes about human rights or equality	Employee profit sharing or benefit plans; meritocracy-related productivity
Ideas about revolution and the use of violence	Political/economic risk, returns on assets, asset preservation
Willingness to take advantage of others	Economic losses related to corruption, fraud, scams, or spam
Commitments to voluntary cooperation	Employee motivation and productivity; democratic functioning
Attitudes toward slavery and discrimination	The economic contributions of minority groups to GDP.
The U.S.'s contribution to rebuilding Japan and Europe after World War II	Post-war global growth and GDP
The U.S.'s willingness to welcome refugees or immigrants	U.S. GDP or income tax revenues
U.S. willingness to give foreign sellers/investors "national" treatment	Trade, innovation or jobs
Family, church, community or government support systems	Risk taking, entrepreneurship; economic stability

None of this is to say that the above questions are either easy to answer or will necessarily be answered in the affirmative. Nor is it to say that many non-Christians have not also made the journey from fear and mistrust to the point where they are broadly concerned about others. But each of these questions, and scores of others like them, are, to say the least, worthy of investigation, as just a little elaboration on a few of the questions will illustrate. For example, it is widely understood that the rejection of slavery in the U.S was precipitated by the slaves understanding of the Christian message of the inherent worth and fundamental equality of all human beings, and that both the anti-slavery and Civil Rights movements were fueled by a commitment to Christian principles. In both Britain and the U.S., slavery was attacked by Quakers, and later Methodists and other Christian denominations as fundamentally evil. Their work continues today - albeit in a different form - as U.S. inner-city pastors attempt to free people and communities from the ravages of sin, one agonizing step and one confused or downtrodden person at a time.

Likewise, it would also be a mistake to disassociate the 19th century proliferation of charities and children's aid societies, YMCAs and character education movements in the U.S. from the spiritual awakenings that took place during those periods. Hospitals, adoption agencies, other charities and non-profit organizations, and the political/legal structure that encourages their birth and proliferation have all been clearly influenced by a Christian worldview. Similar influences can be seen in education and other forms of public infrastructure. Both Calvin's 16th century Geneva and the U.S. ended up with free mandatory public educational systems while many other nations did not. Similarly, U.S. communities routinely provide low cost clean water and sanitation systems to the vast majority of households, and free water and sanitation facilities in public places, but this is not the case in many other places. And since the power of agape love knows no boundaries, evidence of the global impact of Christian these beliefs are becoming increasingly obvious. Chinese CEOs who make a commitment to follow Christ speak out about their obligations to serve, develop, and speak truthfully to the workers in their companies. Korean Christian missionaries give up family, friends, comforts, and safety to minister in underdeveloped and often dangerous locations. South African Christians work to peacefully undo the damage of Apartheid. Christian AIDS workers around the world intervene on behalf of people who may not share their language, customs, skin color, or values. Gifts and charitable foundations dampen the business cycle in any countries by providing purchasing power – even during recessions - for those who would otherwise not have it. The Red Cross, Salvation Army, and a host of relief and development charities stabilize the economies in which they operate by lifting people up in the wake of natural disasters.

The amazing number of not-for-profit institutions started by Christians led Fielding Garrison to claim that the attempt to eliminate human suffering can be largely credited to Christianity. Although this is of course an overstatement, attempts to rewrite history in such a way as to give Christ-inspired love only a minor role in the processes of economic development and human flourishing are simply not credible. So, rather than too quickly attributing the differences that we observe to variations in income and wealth, we would be well advised to research the worldview roots of these kinds of capital, and particularly the role that agape love has played.

Chapter 28

There is clearly enough evidence of the impact of Christian perspectives on what it means to be concerned for others to make these and other economically-relevant questions worth exploring.

Chapter 29: Christianity and Pro-Development Worldview Elements #6 and #7 – Perspectives on What it means to be a Praiseworthy Individual

It was noted in Chapters 24 and 25 that economic development is also dependent on an appropriate societal/cultural understanding of what it means to be a praiseworthy individual, and that what is needed *at the very least* is widespread commitment to trustworthiness/honesty, work/service, and humility.   The Christian understanding of what it means to be a praiseworthy individual is heavily influenced by what the Bible teaches about the *nature* of God (Father, Son, and Holy Spirit), about the *nature* of people, and by specific teachings about what constitutes moral and ethical attitudes and behavior.[1]   The social and economic development implications of this seem to flow primarily through the following four channels:

- Since Christians believe they have been created in the image of God, and are told to "be holy as I am holy," their own character is, to the extent possible for finite creatures, to be patterned after God's character.

- They feel accountable to an all-knowing, all-seeing God for what they do with their time, talents, and resources, regardless of whether or not other people are aware of what they are doing.

- They believe moral and ethical obedience is 1) essential, 2) inextricably bound up in God's willingness to bless people, and 3) more important than ritualistic behavior,[2] and

- They assume large numbers of people are empowered for productive activity because the lowly, uneducated, and unremarkable are as important to, and as empowered by, God as the exceptionally talented, rich, powerful or successful.

Christians believe in one God, who, by operating as three "persons," not only created the world but continues to be actively interested and involved in its development, the salvation of people, and their day-to-day lives. He is called by many names in the Bible, each intended to give insight into his character, such as Almighty, Everlasting Father, Creator, All-sufficient One, the Beginning and the End, the Righteous (or Holy) One, Judge, Provider, Healer, Deliverer, Savior, Redeemer, Lord of lords, King of kings, Prince of Peace, Shepherd, Lamb, Counselor, Comforter, the Word, Wisdom, and Love.

Both Christians and Jews conclude from the *Torah* and elsewhere that they *bear the image* of a holy Trinitarian God, and there is no escaping the fact that this has had and continues to have a profound effect on the mental picture they have of themselves. This means, for example, that if God the Father is creative, busy, discerning (good from evil), just, holy, or loving, then his "children" have the ability (and responsibility) to aspire to the same; and like Jesus, they should, for example, seek to be healing, peace-loving, humble servants; and like the Holy Spirit, they should seek to give counsel and comfort. The Hebrew (and Christian) God's expectations were from the beginning that people would refrain from immoral behavior, as defined in the Ten Commandments and throughout much of the rest of Scripture. In addition, they were severely warned against practicing divination, sorcery, witchcraft, or a number of other activities that have been associated with stunted development (e.g., in countries like Haiti). The Old Testament book of Nahum, Chapter 3, describes these kinds of activities as capable of "enslaving nations," and in other Biblical texts these kinds of activities were castigated because of their association with cruel and inhumane treatment of people (including child sacrifice). One example from Deuteronomy 18 captures the expectations of Jewish and Christian believers very well:

> When you enter the land the LORD your God is giving you, do not learn to imitate the detestable ways of the nations there. Let no one be found among you who sacrifices his son or daughter in the fire, who practices divination or sorcery, interprets omens, engages in witchcraft, or casts spells, or who is a medium or spiritist, or who consults the dead…The nations you will dispossess listen to those who practice sorcery or divination. But as for you, the LORD your God has not permitted you to do so.[3]

In the New Testament witchcraft and the like is again condemned as part of a long list of other socially and economically counterproductive behaviors which are contrasted to the kinds of behaviors that lay the foundation for a civil society and economic development. For example, the Apostle Paul's letter to the Galatians reminds the Christians there that

> The acts of the sinful nature are obvious: sexual immorality, impurity and debauchery; idolatry and *witchcraft*; hatred, discord, jealousy, fits of rage, selfish ambition, dissensions, factions and envy; drunkenness, orgies, and the like. I warn you, as I did before, that those who live like this will not inherit the kingdom of

God. But the fruit of the Spirit is love, joy, peace, patience, kindness, goodness, faithfulness, gentleness and self-control.[4]

It is clear from these passages that what it means to bear the image of God involves restraint, but also much that is positive. In addition to the attributes of God described above, the Bible contains hundreds if not thousands of references to the importance of work, self-control, truth telling, justice, care for the poor, and a variety of other things that have a particularly significant impact on economic activity. In parts of the Bible God even gave explicit instructions to leaders for how to better manage the people, build the walls of the city or the temple, or conduct worship. Omnipotent and omnipresent, he expected his people to be accountable and had the power to back it up. But he is also portrayed throughout the Bible as merciful; hence, there is a strong emphasis in Christian traditions on forgiveness and the need for the kind of humility that begets continuous improvement in character, work and wisdom throughout people's lives.

In addition to explicit teachings about the attributes and character that should accrue to God's children/image bearers, most Christians have been nurtured on the stories in the Bible recounting the extraordinary courage of people like Joshua, David, Daniel, Peter and Paul. One of the most striking patterns in the accounts of Biblical leaders in these stories is the juxtaposition of their absolute ordinariness with their significant accomplishments. Nearly all of the "heroes of the faith" were, in their own right, unremarkable people who did remarkable things. Moses was "slow of speech" and David a mere shepherd boy when chosen for their extraordinary roles; several of Christ's' disciples, from whom extraordinary acts of courage would be expected, were fishermen; even the mother of Jesus was an unremarkable teenage girl. As the apostle Paul said in 1 Corinthians 1:27, the Christian God exhibited a pattern of choosing "the foolish things of the world to shame the wise," and "the weak things of the world to shame the strong." This pattern continues to this day as Christians reach out to people, regardless of education, income level, class or caste. The impact on economic development is twofold: Large numbers of people who saw themselves as incapable, unintelligent, ignorant, or unworthy have been and continue to be "transformed by a renewing of their minds"[5] and begin to see themselves in a very different light; this inevitably leads them to adopt very different attitudes toward others and habits as they learn the expectations of the gospel. Over time, this often involves patterning themselves after Biblical characters who often rejected the status quo in favor of principled living, and who were willing to believe that "the path less taken" might nevertheless be the right way to go. Christ told his followers that "in his name" they would do "even greater things" than they witnessed him doing. The understanding among Christians of what this meant evolved over time and came to include, for example, forming complex universities and hospital systems so that freedom from disease and pain no longer seems so miraculous, banding together in business to make remarkably complex products which improve people's lives, or building institutions and structures so that heavenly ideas of justice take shape here and now.

Another influence of the Biblical picture of what it means to be a praiseworthy person comes from its teaching that Christians are to be known as much by their deeds as by their words (or, as James 2:17 puts it, "faith by itself, if it is not accompanied by action, is dead." This means, for example, that Christian religious activity cannot be confined to prayer, sacraments, and other relatively passive rituals. Rather, it must show itself in the everyday actions of people. The most comprehensive example comes from Jesus' teaching in Matthew 7:12 (repeated in Luke 6:31) where he says, "in everything, do to others what you would have them do to you, for this sums up the Law and the Prophets." This means, for example, that for Christians to truly love people, they must treat them with tolerance, appreciation and respect, regardless of religious persuasion, race, gender, etc. This means that if Christians want to meaningfully participate in government, they would naturally be expected to afford others the same opportunity. If they want enough transparency to know how the government is spending their tax dollars or why it thinks the country should go to war, others deserve the same right to know what they are thinking and doing as well.[6] The Bible also repeatedly urges "righteousness," which is an umbrella term for hearing and doing what is right, and includes scores of attitudes, habits and actions. We have already discussed justice, stewardship and love in the previous two chapters. So we will limit our discussion in the remainder of this chapter to the three key areas mentioned in its initial paragraph – trustworthiness/honesty, work/service, and humility.

Trustworthiness and Honesty in Christian Thought

Trustworthiness - the widespread existence of which is required for people to be trusting of others - depends on a number of other virtues, but none more than honesty. Because of their close relationship, we will discuss them jointly here.

Christians are taught repeatedly in the Bible that God is absolutely trustworthy, as are his laws, statutes/precepts and Word. As the prophet Isaiah puts it, "The grass withers, and the flowers fade, but the word of our God stands forever."[7] In Biblical accounts, when a person is needed for an important job, trustworthiness is often near the front of the line in the job qualifications description.[8] But since the Bible is also in part a historical record of human dealings, it is full of examples of dishonesty. Nevertheless, except in the rare instance when dishonesty is used to protect the innocent, it is soundly condemned. Honesty, on the other hand, is said to be "lifesaving," "better then riches," and it is often tied to positive outcomes such as having a clear conscience, "staying on the right path," or being granted the gift of a "long life." We quote three particularly straightforward passages as illustrations of the Biblical teaching on honesty:

- The LORD detests lying lips, but he delights in men who are truthful.[9]
- Therefore each of you must put off falsehood and speak truthfully to his neighbor, for we are all members of one body.[10]
- Do not lie to each other, since you have taken off your old self with its practices.[11]

Dishonesty is treated with utmost seriousness in the Bible because dishonesty with people is considered also to be dishonesty to God. Expectations for honesty were especially stringent in the church. In the New Testament book of Acts it is recorded that God required the lives of Ananias and Sapphira, as the price of their dishonesty with the elders of the early church.[12] Overall, Biblically speaking, lies are associated with corruption, injustice and slavery, whereas the truth is associated with accountability, justice and freedom.

As noted in Chapter 24, entire books have been written about the economic impact of trustworthiness and honesty. They are at the core of effective leadership, driving leaders to be clear in their expectations, honest in their feedback, accountable to others and effective in their ability to hold others accountable. They are the grease that lubricates workplace efficiency, business partnerships and strategic alliances, internet sales, long-distance relations with customers, and global business. They are essential for policies undergirding macroeconomic stability, accurately valued currencies, efficient financial markets and payments systems, and public service. Without honesty for example, government officials would siphon money from needed projects to fund their personal pleasures. Large numbers of citizens would carry false identities; vital statistics would be inaccurate; people would feel little obligation to "speak the truth, and nothing but the truth, so help me God!" in courts; whistleblowers would not reveal fraud and corruption in government contracts; taxes would be severely underpaid, etc. In short it would be impossible for governments to govern effectively or efficiently. Private life would be equally dysfunctional. As any social scientist worth her salt will admit, lies sustain or, at the very least, are implicated in nearly every social pathology that exists: from racial hatred to broken marriages and families; from alcoholism and drug abuse to fraud, theft, murder and child abuse. Truth-telling is essential to the maintenance of justice and order in a society.[13]

Work and Service

Another aspect of the Christian idea of what it means to be a praiseworthy person involves expectations about work and service. The God of the Bible is portrayed from the very beginning as a worker. In the Biblical creation story (Genesis), the first humans were assigned jobs as part of their responsibility to "rule over" the creation. Later, with the entry of sin into the world, work became more difficult, but remained every bit as important, and maybe even more important - because it remained one of the chief ways to counter the debilitating effects of sinful behavior on people and communities. Because of this, Christians and Jews everywhere view work as fundamentally good, assigned by God from the very beginning of the world as a normal and natural part of an obedient life, even if (as is the case for some in our modern world) one has enough money not to have to work. Work, then, in Christian tradition, is not to be done primarily for money, or begrudgingly, but to use one's talents and gifts to make the world a better place, to bring praise to God, and to be of service to fellow humans. Jesus' "parable of the talents" in particular supports and reinforces these beliefs.

Work as Worship

The early Christians (and by implication, today's Christians) were (are) told "Whatever you do, work at it with all your heart, as working for the Lord, not for men."[14] This implies that pay is a privilege, rather than the primary reason for working, and that the Biblical concept of being "called by God" is much broader than the idea of employment; it encompasses service in all areas of life: on the job, but also in the family, church, community and world. In fact, one aspect of the so-called Protestant work ethic is (particularly in Presbyterian and Reformed expressions of Christianity) the elevation of work to the point where it is considered one component of the *worship* of God. Since the time of Martin Luther and John Calvin, it has been argued by most Protestants that all forms of work, except activities like prostitution or criminality - that are imbibed in their very nature with immoral or unethical conduct - are to be considered "the Lord's work," and Christians were and are encouraged, as with Paul's words to the Corinthians, to "always give [them]selves fully to the work of the Lord, because [they] know that [their] labor in the Lord is not in vain."[15]

Christians are also encouraged repeatedly through Biblical teachings to stand up to difficult circumstances - something that can have a significant effect on productivity in a world where difficulties and problems routinely crop up. For example, the Apostle Paul, the author of many of the New Testament letters, speaking for himself and his fellow Christians, tells the Roman Christians, that "we rejoice in our sufferings, because we know that suffering produces perseverance; perseverance, character; and character, hope."[16] (Paul later reinforces his messages to the Roman Christians by asking them to consider "that our present sufferings are not worth comparing with the glory that will be revealed in us,"[17] and the Apostle Peter adds, when talking about difficult work and harsh masters, "if you suffer for doing good and you endure it, this is commendable before God."[18]) This attitude flows not only out of the many Old and New Testament accounts of people who were commended for doing what was difficult or right at great personal expense, but most of all from the example of Jesus who sacrificed everything (including his life) for the sake of others. Of course it is hard to precisely estimate the impact of a widespread willingness to suffer and sacrifice for the sake of important work, economic outcomes or the good of others, but it would also be absurd to deny its impact.

For Christians for whom work is a form of worship, there are also not to be artificial distinctions between things like "knowing" and "doing," or between high and low status work. Paul the preacher was also a tentmaker, and encouraged the early church to "work, doing something useful with [their] hands."[19] Paul's words and actions, in addition to verifying his lack of status-consciousness, are really just an extension of repeated warnings throughout the Bible about the negatives of being idle, or the sinfulness of being "sluggardly." The writer of Proverbs warns, "Diligent hands will rule, but laziness ends in slave labor,"[20] preferring instead to encourage the people of God to follow the example of the communally productive ant with these words:

> Go to the ant, you sluggard; consider its ways and be wise! It has no commander, no overseer or ruler, yet it stores its provisions in summer and gathers its food at harvest. How long will you lie there, you sluggard? When will you get up from your sleep? A little sleep, a little slumber, a little folding of the hands to rest-
>
> and poverty will come on you like a bandit and scarcity like an armed man.[21]

The apostle Paul, in his letters to the new churches is especially harsh on those who were idle. For example, he says to the Thessalonians:

> In the name of the Lord Jesus Christ, we command you, brothers, to keep away from every brother who is idle and does not live according to the teaching you received from us. For you yourselves know how you ought to follow our example. We were not idle when we were with you, nor did we eat anyone's food without paying for it. On the contrary, we worked night and day, laboring and toiling so that we would not be a burden to any of you. [22]

Because of teachings like these, expectations about "duties" have always played an important role in Christian communities. Monks, for example (both in the Eastern and Western churches), have always been examples of intensity in *both work and prayer*. (Already in the 6th century the Benedictine Monks of Monte Cassino said "to work is to pray."[23]) The clocks and eyeglasses they invented increased the productivity of millions, and their ability to apply and improve other inventions has been important to the evolution of capitalism. Clearly these Catholics were instrumental in planting the seeds that eventually blossomed into what has come to be known as the "Protestant Ethic." Their classical literature preservation, and the pedagogical/study practices they passed down to Protestants were critical to the evolution of modern universities (the earliest and most notable of which were established by Christian traditions). In England, Oxford and Cambridge, and in mainland Europe, Heidelberg and Basil were all established by Christian ministers. In the U.S. Harvard and Yale were started by Congregationalists, Princeton by Presbyterians, and a variety of other schools, including Dartmouth and Brown, were all established with the help of the church. In Korea Ewha University (founded in Seoul in 1880 by American missionaries) is widely accepted as a top academic institution, and many other examples from other countries could also be given.

Another outgrowth of these Biblical teachings is that "providing" has in some ways become not only a virtue but a hallmark of Christian devotion, and not just for one's family, but, as noted earlier, for anyone and everyone in need. As the apostle James put it, "Suppose a brother or sister is without clothes and daily food. If one of you says to him, 'Go, I wish you well; keep warm and well fed,' but does nothing about his physical needs, what good is it?"[24] Combined with the belief that "from everyone who has been given much, much will be demanded; and from the one who has been entrusted with much, much more will be asked,"[25] this kind of teaching has been a very effective motivator, with very significant economic impact in countries heavily influenced by Christianity. As noted earlier, however, these internal "guilt based" motivators, although much more effective in stimulating voluntary productivity than either external "shame based" or "carrot and stick"[26] motivators, may nevertheless still be less effective in stimulating productive activity than the kind of heart motivation that comes from overflowing thankfulness to God and a heartfelt commitment to others. Ultimately it is the latter that needs to be at the very core of economic development for it to be both effective and efficient.

Transmitting wisdom to the next generation

But motivation is only part of the story. Regardless of the motivational level, work will be particularly helpful to development only when motivation and effort is directed toward the kinds of things that build people up and influence them to pass on healthy habits to succeeding generations. Sustainable development requires both right attitudes for wealth creation and the ability to pass on the attitudes that led to wealth creation to succeeding generations. In this area, Christianity as a belief system has two distinct advantages over some other belief systems. The first involves the entire Bible's incessant focus on obtaining *wisdom* (with an entire book, Proverbs, and parts of several others, devoted to this), and the second is its focus on *transmitting* that wisdom to succeeding generations. All of the Old Testament "wisdom literature," and Proverbs in particular, repeatedly warn against the dangers of ignorance and foolishness, and encourages the people of God to "seek wisdom" *with even more energy than they seek after gold or silver.* And wisdom is not just described in generic form, but is parsed out through the rest of the Scriptures, covering a mind-boggling array of details from how to care for the poor, forgive, love, resolve conflict, maintain order in the church, treat workers, etc. Of course there is widespread agreement in many belief systems of the importance of knowledge to economic growth. But knowledge is not the same thing as wisdom, and it is wisdom that is the penultimate wealth creator. Knowledge, as the word implies, involves knowing, usually on the basis of study or experience. Wisdom, on the other hand, involves understanding what is true, right or important, none of which is necessarily implied by the possession of knowledge. Wisdom, then, takes knowledge and makes it more useful by properly couching it in a moral context.

But wisdom is only useful over time when it is effectively passed on to succeeding generations so they are able to "stand on the shoulders" of their forebears. In this regard the Biblical "people of God" were never allowed to be satisfied when they had succeeded in habituating themselves to the pursuit of wisdom. They were also reminded repeatedly of their obligation to *pass on what they had learned* to their children. The words "teach them to your children" are sprinkled throughout the Bible, particularly in the Old Testament, and in many cases the language used to encourage this is anything but subtle. For example, twice within a six chapter segment of the book of Deuteronomy the Jewish people are told in almost identical language not just to teach their children but to:

> Impress [the wisdom/commandments of God] on your children. Talk about them when you sit at home and when you walk along the road, when you lie down and when you get up. Tie them as symbols on your hands and bind them on your foreheads. Write them on the doorframes of your houses and on your gates.[27]

As noted earlier, family, marriage and child-rearing patterns can have a significant effect on development, not only because the family is the incubator for character, but because family beliefs, values and habits tend to get passed on from generation to generation. This includes expectations about self-discipline; attitudes toward outsiders, education, work, right and wrong; and a host of other things that impact economic activity.

This is especially true of the wide acceptance of the concept of *calling* among Christians, which is at the core of the strong improvement orientation and regular building up of all forms of capital in societies influenced by Christian beliefs. Part of the reason for this is these teachings seem to call people to be productive during most of their waking (rather than just working) hours, and not only when on the job (or payroll) but through means as diverse as continuing education, dedicated parenting, volunteer activity, philanthropy, careful investment, or the maintenance of their property. The idea of calling adds greatly to the breadth and significance of work, and the motivation and effort brought to the job. Generally, it raises the relative amount of time that people are willing to devote to their work, and the urgency they give it. It also affects the risks they are willing to take, or the sacrifices they are willing to make for it (such as willingness to travel, relocating away from one's birthplace or family, or in the case of missionaries, giving up much of what is familiar and comfortable). It has this potential because there is a strong undercurrent in Biblical teaching and Christian theology about the presence of an antithesis in the world, which demands a response of righting wrongs, fixing the broken, or restoring the fallen, and, as it happens, these things are potentially more robust motivators than personal satisfaction, selfishness, pleasure or adding a few more toys to an already pleasure saturated and materially prosperous existence.

Humility

As noted earlier, wisdom is knowledge used properly, tempered by a respect for the truth and constrained by humility. This is why we noted the importance of humility in Chapter 25 when dealing with the building blocks of wealth creation. At the very least, humility is (at least when combined with other values that promote determination, confidence and hard work) a valuable contributor to things like understanding what is important, developing healthy interpersonal relations, conflict resolution, and the development of productive work units, all of which are critical to economic development. In contrast, large egos often require expensive pampering, "overhead" in the form of status symbols, toys and income for conspicuous consumption, and a tendency to be associated with personal preoccupation, a reluctance to learn, and narrowly self-interested decisions. In this area as well, Christian teaching serves the economic development process well because from beginning to end, the Bible discourages pride and praises humility. A small sample of verses from Proverbs and the New Testament should be sufficient to make this point.

- When pride comes, then comes disgrace, but with humility comes wisdom.[28]
- The fear of the LORD teaches a man wisdom, and humility comes before honor.[29]
- Humility and the fear of the LORD bring wealth and honor and life.[30]
- Do nothing out of selfish ambition or vain conceit, but in humility consider others better than yourselves.[31]
- Clothe yourselves with humility toward one another, because, "God opposes the proud but gives grace to the humble".[32]

Throughout the Bible people were commended when they demonstrated humility, and many of the unremarkable people God chose to do his important work are also described as humble (Old Testament examples include Moses, Joseph, David, Josiah, and Isaiah, and New Testament examples include Jesus and the apostles Peter, John and Paul). Conversely, pride is routinely condemned as being unbecoming of the people of God. We already gave many examples, when we discussed humility as a building block for economic development in Chapter 25, why adherence to these kinds of teachings is good for economic development. It makes it less likely that leaders will abuse their power, or that courses of action would be pursued without seeking wise counsel. It helps people resist the tendency to "rest on their laurels" or bask in the adulation that accompanies past accomplishments, inclining them more toward how much more could be learned or done. It rightly predisposes people to recognize the human dimension of productive activity, to appreciate those around them - laying a foundation for healthy interpersonal relationships and team efforts. In short, it makes people better spouses, parents, students, workers, and leaders - better all-around people. We also noted how it unleashes the hidden power of forgiveness, which also plays a special role in Christian faith and practice.

Forgiveness

It should perhaps be noted up front, that the term forgiveness, like nearly all linguistic terms, has the potential to take on different meaning for people with different worldviews. In this sense, the term itself may mean different things to Christians than to people with other faith commitments. Indeed, the term is so prevalent in the Bible that it would be hard for its use in Western societies to be uninfluenced by the shades of meaning that the Bible gives it. Without going into excessive detail, it is important for us to say that the Biblical notion of forgiveness is wrapped up in the idea of cancelling a debt - but it does not presume that this cancellation somehow excuses an offender from the need to repent or offer restitution for his or her offense, nor does it eliminate the need for reconciliation between the offender and the offended. Like other attributes discussed earlier, the importance of forgiveness comes first of all from hundreds of Biblical accounts of a forgiving God and the call for people, as his image bearers, to emulate these divine attributes.[33] This is recorded throughout the Old Testament in the very heart of the story of God's interaction with the Jewish people, starting with Israel's near continuous need to repent, receive God's forgiveness and be restored to right relationship with him[34] and receive God's promised blessings.

As suggested in Chapter 25, *pervasive* forgiveness, at least when coupled with repentance and restoration, and widely applied, may actually be a cornerstone of economic development. Not only does it have the potential to thwart war and conflict, but it promotes peaceful changes in leadership and allows one of the most popular forms of government, democracy, to function as intended. Beyond this, Christian teachings about forgiveness lay an important foundation for reasonable contract enforcements and court settlements. In the West, they have also influenced bankruptcy and limited liability laws that allow people to start companies and take substantial risks based on their potentially beneficial ideas and technologies – while still having their losses limited or their debts forgiven when they fail.[35] Perhaps most importantly, the kind of forgiveness that humility makes possible has the potential, over time, to correct a host of unproductive and counterproductive stress-related diseases, parenting practices, attitudes, personal relationships, and behaviors that may exist within the citizenry of a nation, by encouraging victims of cruelty, injustice, or crime to channel their energy away from hatred and revenge toward restoration, education, and enablement.

Balance

Finally, Christian teachings about humility, as noted in Chapter 25 - coupled with a particularly Protestant understanding of the sovereignty of God – have played an important role in Western nations in the kind of understanding and acceptance of one's limitations needed to keep churches, governments, or other institutions from overstepping the bounds of their competence and/or forcing beliefs on people who do not voluntarily accept them. This is just one of many ways that (biblically based) Christian teaching recognizes both the legitimacy and limitations of the different spheres of authority - including government authority. Christian teaching - especially since the time of the Reformation - does not call for the church to dominate the government, but it does recognize the right of religious leaders to call people (including government leaders, business people and others) to recognize the spiritual/moral principles that ought to govern human behavior.[36] This, then, entitles officials to govern without the interference of the church, but also calls them to be willing to take seriously the spiritual/moral wisdom of the church as they carry out their legitimate calling to govern. Over the centuries this has led to increasing attention in Western nations on how to best implement pluralistic structures - and important conversations about the appropriate role of government with respect to policies and actions that are critical to economic development. For now, we note that this includes creating an environment where people are encouraged to engage in civil society and entrepreneurial activities, and the encouragement of the kinds of attitudes, values and behaviors that lead to sustainable economic development - without regard to whether those values are presumed to be religious or secular. As noted earlier, the economic development implications of this are myriad.

The inclination toward pluralism is but one of many aspects of Christian theology that contribute to the balancing of the Economic Development Wheel. Balancing individual initiative and community-mindedness was discussed in Chapter 28. Biblical teaching and Christian doctrine are also able to encourage wealth-building while simultaneously tempering both greed and excess - keeping the physical capital component of the wheel from some unhealthy bulging. Bible passages that both encourage care for the natural world *and* give people permission to fully develop it can temper the depletion of natural capital (for example through low-till farming or recycling), without harming development. And passages that give legitimate authority to government while simultaneously demanding justice and integrity from it promote not only pluralism, but the balanced buildup of governmental capital. And all of these teachings promote the kind of freedom and responsibilities that undergird civil society and entrepreneurship, while also demanding that people build up other critical forms of capital by growing in wisdom, skills, morality, ethics, forgiveness, and love. As such, Christianity weaves together a mosaic of beliefs, values, actions and restraints that provides a particularly fertile environment for sustainable, broadly-defined development. And although this mix is admittedly difficult to model empirically, its effects are observable in the both the research and theoretical evidence that has been gathered over the years about the relationship between religious beliefs and economics, and the economic development experiences of countries that have been heavily influenced by Christianity- particularly the Nordic, Northern Europe, and North American countries influenced by Protestantism.

There are of course many other aspects of Christian belief that have economic impact beyond the honest, work ethic and humility that we have focused on in this chapter, and the attitudes toward improving things, authority, stewardship, and love discussed in the previous three chapters. Bible passages that insist that borrowers have a moral obligation to repay their debts allow for healthier financial institutions and markets. The belief that a Christian's primary allegiance is to Christ - rather than to a particular country - makes it easier to both avoid the excesses of nationalism and reap the benefits of an international orientation. The idea that people are, first of all, part of an inclusive family of God - rather than a particular genetic, geographical, or ethnic group - not only fosters international networks, but allows economy-stimulating labor mobility as people pick up stakes as necessary (by lack of job opportunity) and put them down again in a place where they are able to both find economic opportunity and "a home" with a different part of the (Christian) "family." As such, the existence of a globally connected church community "safety net" allows mobility and exposure to different communities, ideas, products and practices, while also providing valuable security in a fragmented and mobile world. In addition to these macroeconomic benefits, many leadership skills have been honed not only in churches, but in the social service projects, mission work, fundraising, education or not-for-profit institutions that seem to be spawned more frequently in Christian circles than in places influenced by other belief systems.[37] As writers about civil society have long noted, Christian churches can also be schools for political virtue. Still others, as noted in the research summarized in Chapter 11, have shown the ability of religious beliefs (and particularly Christian beliefs) to reduce a host of social maladies including theft, adultery, murder, poverty, social deviance, teen pregnancy, suicide, and substance abuse, and strengthen other development-enhancing traits like mental and physical health, self-discipline, school attendance, work success, longevity and happiness.

Chapter 30: Christianity and Business

Although we have addressed many ways that Biblical teachings underlying Christianity have laid the groundwork for a healthy economy, we have not addressed in any significant detail how Christianity has influenced the particulars of capitalism, markets and more specifically business practice. This is a glaring omission, and one we aim to rectify in this chapter, since businesses ordinarily create the majority of jobs and wealth in an economy. They are also key players in creating the surpluses that fund government services, enlarge and strengthen the middle class, and allow people to pursue the kind of education, spiritual enrichment and civil society pursuits that are so valuable to development. Businesses are also culturally-influential institutions that have great potential for good or - as we saw in the opening chapter – harm, depending on the assumptions made about the nature and purpose of business. In fact, it can be plausibly argued one of communism's most critical errors was its inability to imagine what capitalism could look like when many business owners and employees are guided by religious motives and ethics that go well beyond the desire for power or riches.

Biblical teaching about business

To accomplish our purpose, we once again need to appeal to Biblical/Christian *teaching*, since observing the eclectic version of 21st century capitalism that has evolved over time, would by itself give us little more than a picture of the how the many secular and religious belief systems vying for the hearts and minds of capitalists have worked themselves out in the context of business. However, because Christianity is a belief system that encourages its adherents to read and apply its teachings, much additional insight can be gleaned from specific writings by business scholars and practitioners about what it means to do business according to Christian principles.[1] We will therefore summarize some of these as well.

When examining the Bible, we see much information that speaks to the political authorities about their role in helping all people (including businesses) to thrive - such as the need to clearly define private (and public) property, contract enforcement, public safety, the maintenance of justice, etc. We also see a host of commandments (starting with the Ten Commandments), aimed at keeping people from lying, stealing, killing, envy, revenge, etc., which if adhered to would also be great for business. In addition, a host of other teachings that *indirectly* shape a Biblical worldview - teachings about the nature of God, the state of the world, the nature of people, wealth, profit, equality, freedom, and the nature of calling (including work and service). But the economic benefits of most of these have already been addressed to one degree or another; hence they will not be our focus here. Rather, we aim to address Biblical teaching and commentary that seems particularly addressed to those who own or manage businesses.

No religion known to us has a separate handbook for applying religious principles to business, but the Bible does have some teachings that speak directly to business practices as well as many other teachings that have significant indirect effects on business. Old Testament writings make it clear that commerce was viewed as a natural and normal human activity – but that merchants who withheld grain from people who needed it, or who "stripped the land like locusts," or who otherwise exploited people were violating a sacred trust. Honest weights and measures were required, while deception was expressly forbidden.[2] In fact, people were expected to keep their promises, "even when it hurts."[3] Owners were not to defraud laborers, underpay, or delay the payment of wages, and there were strong warnings that commercial activity should not be carried out in ways that could harm the poor. Early church fathers and theologians elaborated on these texts over many centuries, developing a body of writings on business ethics - with particular emphasis on concepts such as the "fair price," and "just wage." It was further assumed that - if done ethically - commercial activity would ordinarily result in a variety of blessings, such as long life, peace, and the accumulation of wealth. Biblical patriarchs like Abraham, Isaac and Jacob (later given the name Israel) are recorded as having been proprietors of large agricultural ventures, and even Job - whose story includes losing massive amounts of wealth (and family members) in what is sometimes described as the supreme Biblical test of faith - ended up with twice as much wealth as he had before his troubles began. In fact, the Old Testament covenant between God and the Israelites was in some ways both like a contract and an exchange, with God promising to bless them if they would just keep their part of the bargain.

Fortunately for Israel's descendants, the Jews, and eventually for the Christians who followed them, the covenant obligation to obey Old Testament moral laws had the side benefit of stabilizing their society and encouraging economic activity - since people tend to become wealthier when they honestly labor in the production and sale of ethical and useful products and services. In addition, Jews and Christians benefit from Biblical expectations that work be done skillfully, and that they seek to discern the wisdom of God in all that they do. This, combined with an understanding that they are naturally creative - since the Torah makes it clear that they have been made in the image of a Creator and creative God - has not only led to an exceptionally strong emphasis on education, but a history of innovation. Jews in particular get far more education than others, wherever they reside. They have also received an almost unbelievable number of Nobel Prizes, relative to their percentage of the global population. [4] It is no surprise then, that they have been disproportionately engaged (and successful) in commerce wherever they have gone.[5] Nowhere has this been truer than in the U.S. and Israel - since at the time of this writing approximately eighty percent of the world's Jews reside in these two countries.

Since Jesus was a Jew, it is not surprising that he also treated commercial activity as natural and normal. Having grown up with a carpenter father, he made many of his most salient points in stories involving merchants or property owners; he also chose fishermen and tax collectors as disciples - and never discouraged them from continuing to engage in these activities after they began to follow him. Of course he did not particularly encourage wealth accumulation - and in some cases seemed even to discourage it. He accumulated little or no material wealth himself, taught Christians to pray for their daily bread (and little more in terms of material needs) and discouraged any accumulation of wealth that interfered with people's love of God or their identification with and/or concern for the poor.[6] But a careful study of his words makes it clear that what he was really discouraging was things like hoarding, selfishness, self-indulgence, and unconcern for the poor. As it happens, discouraging these kinds of things, along with the encouragement of both moral and productive activity (which Jesus did) provides an excellent foundation for vibrant business activity.

More broadly speaking, business activity in Christian-influenced countries has been seen as a logical outgrowth of what has come to be known as the "cultural mandate" at the beginning of the book of Genesis. In this chapter God indicates that people are created in the image of a *working* God, and were therefore created, among other things, to work. It also indicates that the earth is a gift to humans for their use, albeit with strings attached. They are expected to "be fruitful and multiply," and " to "rule over" and "care for" the "garden" (world) that has been entrusted to them.[7] Business activity from the beginning, then, was to be a stewardship, with frequent reminders that "the earth is the Lord's and everything in it." Beyond this Jesus' *Parable of the Talents*[8] reminded that an *increase* was expected by the one who had entrusted humankind with both the earth and the "talents" to develop it.

In addition to being a stewardship, however, most Christians also see their businesses as normed by service, often citing Jesus' example and his words that he "did not come to be served, but to serve, and to give his life as a ransom for many."[9] Christians in business are also quick to note that they are motivated to accept setbacks, sacrifices and challenges in business in part because of Jesus's sacrificial example. The Apostle Paul reinforced the importance of this and added some additional context when he encouraged Christians to joyfully embrace trials and challenges of all kinds - assuring them that "all things work together for good for those called according to [Christ's] purpose.[10] Faith in Christ, then, serves as an emotional buffer to the ups and downs that accompany business risk/uncertainty in the same way that personal savings are a financial buffer to disruptions in employment, or retained earnings to uncertainties in business revenue. Depending on one's theological leanings, the "good" or "gain" that one might expect from this kind of perseverance could be in the joy that accompanies doing what is right (including generosity), business success and/or a measure of security later in life, or the boundless reward that awaits in the life to come.[11] This reminds us again (as noted earlier at several points), that subgroups within belief systems tend to emphasize different aspects of these belief systems -which can also lead to significant differences in ideas of what it means to do business. Christianity and Christians in business are no exception to this rule.[12]

Christians in business – past and present

Time and space do not allow us to review the many historical and literary connections between Judeo-Christian teachings and business practice, but Western history is full of business people whose actions were driven by their faith, and who - often because of some unique shared beliefs - succeeded disproportionately in business. Max Weber noted the skill of Calvinist business people in Holland, England and Switzerland, as well as the entrepreneurial spirit of American protestant churches. The Anabaptists, perhaps best known for eschewing political and militarily involvement, embraced business activity wherever they went. Some of the best-known British business ventures were started by devout Quakers – such as Cadburys, Rothchilds, Lloyds of London, Barclays, and Price Waterhouse, and in the U.S., of course Quaker Oats. Examples of well-known American corporations founded by committed Christians, in addition to Quaker Oats (Henry Parsons Crowell), include Coca Cola (Asa Candler), J.C. Penny (James Cash Penny), Colgate-Polmolive (William Colgate), Kraft Foods (James Kraft), Hilton Hotels (Conrad Hilton) and, most recently, Walmart (Sam Walton). It is of course much easier to infuse religiously-inspired principles into smaller and medium-sized companies and franchises; so it is no surprise that founders have done so. Recent U.S. examples include Hobby Lobby (David Green), Domino's Pizza (Tom Monaghan), Days Inn (Cecil B. Day), Chick-fil-a (Truett Cathy), Curves (Gary Heavin), ServiceMaster (Marion Wade), Jackson Hewitt (John Hewitt), Tyson Foods (John Tyson) and Herman Miller (D.J.De Pree). Many more companies, such as Yum Brands (David Novak), Mail Boxes, Etc. (Jim Amos), Interstate Batteries (Norm Miller), have had Christian presidents, CEOs or chairpersons who have visibly guided otherwise secular companies to conduct themselves in ways consistent with Christian principles.

The lion's share of the impact of Christianity on business, however, has come from individual Christians quietly influencing their companies - whether those companies consider themselves to be explicitly Christian or secular - people who try to guide their companies to the extent possible down the kind of moral and ethical paths that Christians teachings encourage. Each of these business people - and there are thousands of them that most people have never heard of – has a unique story about how their business ventures are an outgrowth of the commitments to service that are part and parcel of their theology. For example, Milt Kuyers located the Star Sprinkler Corporation in a dangerous neighborhood in Milwaukee so that he could partner with Pastor James Covington and

The Lighthouse Gospel Chapel in their efforts to alleviate poverty. Gary Vermeer (the founder of Vermeer Manufacturing) worked day and night to perfect the round bailer so that farming could be more enjoyable and farmers could use the time that they formerly devoted to "putting up hay" to more productive pursuits. (He also joked to his farmer friends that while they grew crops, he grew manufacturing plants in the fields of Central Iowa.) Bolthouse Farm's wonderfully successful baby carrot business was the result of their Christian passion for stewardship – not wanting anything (including broken carrots) to go to waste. Legend even has it that Guiness Stout was developed by the Christian entrepreneur Arthur Guiness in his quest to find a "healthy" alternative to the whisky that plagued his Irish compatriots.

The Guiness example, reminds us that none of these business people was perfect, and that in some cases even their fellow Christians objected to what they were doing.[13] John D. Rockefeller Sr. is a case in point. It would be impossible to understand (or reconcile) his business tactics and his generosity without an understanding of the religious tension that defined his life.[14] But based on their own writings and the first-hand accounts of others, it is clear that the people mentioned here were/are not just broadly motivated by their broader Christian commitment; in many cases they wrote about specific Bible passages that inspired or motivated their business activity or kept them going during tough times. And without fail, the people we have mentioned gave generously of their wealth. Even Rockefeller, and his compatriots Andrew Carnegie and J.P. Morgan, who have been soundly (and to some degree justifiably) criticized for their business practices, were motivated to make and give away money by their understanding of Jesus' words that "From everyone who has been given much, much will be demanded; and from the one who has been entrusted with much, much more will be asked."[15] Several Christian business people known to the author have even managed to invert the Biblical concept of the tithe, living off less than ten percent of their income while donating more than 90% to charity. But generosity with the wealth accumulated from business activity is only a minor part of the impact Christianity has had on business people. Far greater is how it has shaped the entirety of their worldviews, and the impact of this on all seven forms of capital and the catalysts that build and power our Development Wheel. To see this, we will briefly introduce some Christian writings about business and examine what they say (collectively) about how Christians view their business activity. And, although we will examine how these perspectives on business relate to our seven pro-development worldview elements, we will not reiterate earlier material that addressed how specific Christian teachings reinforce these worldview elements. Rather, we will concentrate on how Christian business owners and managers understand the nature of their calling to business activity and work out their responsibility to the various stakeholder groups with which they interact.

Chapter 30

Writings by Christian business scholars and practitioners

As noted at the beginning of our chapter, in addition to what is directly taught in the Bible, scores of books have been written on the relationship between Christianity and business practice - with titles like *Business for the Glory of God*, *My Business-My Mission*, *The Leadership Lessons of Jesus*, *Succeeding in Business without Selling Your Soul*, *Business through the Eyes of Faith*, *Just Business: Christian Ethics for the Marketplace*, *Believers in Business*, *Business as a Calling*, *Doing Business by the Good Book*, and *Beyond Integrity*.[16] That so many people have taken the time to articulate how their faith has affected how they do business is by itself a testimony to the importance of worldview to economic outcomes.

An overriding theme of these works is that business activity is expected to serve a larger purpose - something beyond being a vehicle for the accomplishment of personal goals. The authors make it clear that they view business, like other areas of life, through the "eyes of faith," and because of this, their commercial activities are both motivated and constrained by the Biblical teachings mentioned at the beginning of this chapter and many others. They write about the need to be guided by the same principles in both their business and personal lives. So, if they are called to, say, integrity, unselfishness, or love of neighbor in their private lives, they are also called to these in their business lives - whether they work in explicitly Christian or secular companies. They assume quite naturally that they are bound by the Apostle Paul's instructions that that followers of Christ have been given freedom not to do whatever they want, but to do *good* works.

Another thing that is obvious from these books is that Christians in organizations see their religious beliefs as not just directing moral and ethical behavior, but as influencing far more than this – things such as the overriding purpose of business activity, the goals and priorities of specific businesses, perspectives on authority, communication strategies, management styles, and organizational structure/culture. It is clear from their writings that they desire to glorify God in whatever aspects of organizational life they are engaged in – whether it be long range planning, building a remarkably cohesive and productive work team, or the mundane work of establishing policies, designing internal control systems, or regulatory adherence. They further assume that owners and managers are called to use their authority and freedom to promote and exercise stewardship, justice and integrity by responsibly serving others, which they acknowledge can only be done well when they spend time in Bible Study and prayer, and seek the wise counsel of mentors. Some describe their business goals as including the cultivation of a community where honesty, humility, forgiveness, trust, love and generosity are not just praiseworthy but strongly encouraged; some give more emphasis to hard work and a willingness to sacrifice for the benefits of others; others give more emphasis to how education, business and family responsibilities are all sacred callings, to be carried out with utmost sincerity and accountability.[17] And, although they have not here-to-fore had the *Development Wheel* at their disposal, it is clear that they would have little difficulty making connections between their desire to view their business obligations through the lens of Biblical authority and the need for the kinds of "pro-development worldview elements" that we have identified.

A passion for solving problems

In ways consistent with our earlier worldview elements discussion, these authors assume that both people and life are deeply flawed, but also have both a God-given mandate and the God-like potential to improve things. In regard to our first worldview element, it is clear that they believe that life would simply not be normal for Christians without the opportunity to form companies for the purpose of making people's lives better, or to manage them in such a way that would allow their employees to "increase their talents" as they had been told God expects of them. They also embrace any kind of change that improves things, often citing the role that faith and their understanding of stewardship play in this.

Authority in business

It is also clear from these writings that Biblical teachings about the need to respect and have high expectations of authority are seen by Christians as extending quite seamlessly into areas of life such as business. Because they believe that their authority has been delegated to them by God (who also holds them accountable for their use of that authority) they understand that the character and operations of the company will differ in some way, shape or form from other companies where authority is equated with, say, power or prestige. They assume that all business functions, such as management, marketing, production, finance, or accounting should glorify God and reflect Christ-like love to the people with whom the business owner or manager interacts. And because these owners and managers accept a powerful, just, and all-knowing God, they feel not only personally but organizationally accountable to him (and to others) for the resources they use, the goods and services they produce and how they go about producing them. These assumptions about accountability also lead to an acceptance that businesses ought to be transparent enough for society members to be able to determine the degree to which they are being served by the business. Concerns of this breadth will also take the purpose of a business far beyond the profit motive,[18] and the concept of business ethics far beyond things like honesty and diligence (which some are inclined to reduce business ethics down to).

Responsibilities to Owners

Most Christians in business also assume that the responsibility of managers to owners must be viewed at least partly in the context of respect for authority in general and respect for government and kinds of laws that are in place to protect owners and other capital providers. Often, in market economies, owner's rights are legally superior to the claims of other stakeholders in the organization. Some Christians feel that this view does not always result in justice in an organization or in a society, but even those who feel this way usually agree that an organization owes a great deal to those who risk their time, life savings or future financial security to build an organization capable of providing both jobs and products or services needed or wanted by society. The responsibility of company employees to respect the legitimate authority of the owners, as given to them by God, is usually assumed - as long as owners operate morally, ethically and legally. And, since owners are also entitled to a fair return for the amount of risk they are taking, Christian managers see their role less as self-interested beneficiaries and more as agents with fiduciary responsibilities to the owners. It would be wrong, therefore, for managers to take advantage of the fact that the owners are not physically on the premises, or engage - without the full knowledge and approval of the owners - in activities that bring about a fundamental change in the nature or riskiness of the business. They should also not engage in activities that present a conflict of interests between personal enrichment and company benefit (such as clandestinely purchasing from suppliers in which they have a financial interest, accepting judgment-influencing gifts, or taking "kickbacks"). And they should also willingly and regularly provide owners with a strict accounting of the stewardship of their funds. These duties should be taken seriously not only because of the legal power owners hold over managers, but out of Biblically-encouraged respect for legitimate authority.

But Christian business owners and managers also understand that their stewardship and service obligations extend well beyond their fiduciary responsibilities to owners.

Based on their writings and actions, it is clear they seek to serve a wide variety of constituent groups - including employees, customers, creditors, suppliers, and their local communities. In addition, their Christian perspective will sometime cause them to serve geographically distant communities through charitable donations and to formally recognize their responsibilities to governments, future generation and even competitors. (Often these diverse groups are referred to as stakeholders in more narrowly focused discussions on business ethics.) We will briefly discuss these obligations in the remainder of this chapter.

Responsibilities to employees

Christian managers for the most part are unwilling to view employees as mere "factor inputs;" rather they are seen as people who, although flawed, still bear God's image, and are endowed with gifts, worthy of love, and capable of remarkable accomplishments - especially when they operate as a unified team. Christian managers, then, attempt to cultivate an employment atmosphere that fosters hard work, the development of talents, excellence, unity, cooperation, contagious enthusiasm for the mission of the company, honesty, respect, and other values that flow from their religious commitments. Policies and procedures are oriented not only toward efficiency, but toward improving the overall moral and ethical climate in the organization. Information is widely disseminated so as to allow employees to make informed judgments about matters relevant to them.

Decentralized and pluralistic decision-making structures in which each employee's authority and responsibilities are both well-defined and coextensive encourage and enable employees to significantly participate in company decisions. Hiring and compensation are based on things like a candidate's knowledge, skills, talents, attitudes, experience, and commitment to the mission of the company, rather than race, color, sex, age, national origin, or some other artificial and inappropriate measure of one's potential contribution to the company. Safety, handicap accessibility, health, performance evaluation, advancement, termination, retirement, and compensation policies reflect an earnest desire to follow Jesus' command "do to others as you would have them do to you." Attention to status is generally played down. When possible, employees are given a stake in the company. Distinctions between skilled and unskilled give way to the more important task of doing every job with excellence. Many also acknowledge the need for workloads to reflect balance between the company's need for competitiveness and the employees' needs for rest, recreation, and family, church and community commitments. The underlying assumption seems to be that if these things are done, the result will be more productivity, lower costs, higher profits and more satisfied customers, employees and investors.

Responsibilities to customers

The Christian commitment to stewardship and service also means that business people are not free to undertake every course of action that could be profitable. This entails being selective about the products and services sold, the quality of these products and services, and the selling methods used. Harmful products like cigarettes or pornography will not be produced and distributed. Products that isolate people, cater to their baser tendencies, promote violence, or cater to selfishness will be discouraged. Products and services that meet needs, alleviate poverty, are more functional or longer lasting, or that bring people together and/or build them up are favored.

A commitment to stewardship and service also means producing things as efficiently as possible, and pricing them fairly. But it does not necessarily mean that either the lowest cost or highest quality products are always best. A $40,000 car that will last for twenty years without a major overhaul appears more stewardly than a $20,000 car that is likely to last only eight years. On the other hand, if one has reason to believe that technological developments could allow the $20,000 car to be replaced in eight years by a much more efficient vehicle, the shorter-lived car (and some judicious recycling) might better serve the customer while also slowing the depletion of natural resources. Even for two equivalent products, a lower price is not necessarily more ethical than a higher price. The former favors the buyer and the latter the seller (and her employees, suppliers, etc.). In spite of this, many Christians - Sam Walton being the best known - have bought into the notion the "the customer is always king," which may not always do justice to other stakeholder groups. Nevertheless, Biblical teaching warns that human nature tends to elevate self over others, and favor insiders over outsiders, so Sam's willingness to see things from the customer's perspective is certainly not a bad thing. The same could be said for his philosophy of "low prices every day." Much time and energy is wasted around the world haggling over prices – most of which is unnecessary when sellers are content to accept the same fair price from all customers.

Of course, even receiving a product for a low/fair price is no guarantee of good service. Some Christians have realized that they don't ultimately sell products; rather they sell service over a specified time period, since it is service, not simply material things, that people need to improve the quality of their lives. (Cyrus McCormick, the devout Christian mid-nineteenth century inventor of the combine is reputed to be among the first, because of this, to offer written product warranties to his customers – along with, training and education.) Giving warranties, of course, makes much more sense when customers use products in the intended manner. So a Christian perspective on business also encourages the provision of education and information along with the products sold - ideally enough to promote both responsible and sustainable purchasing and use. Financing and customer service are also generally part of good service. And, of course, for customers to be truly served, advertising messages, and sales and financing tactics must be truthful, aimed at educating and meeting people's needs, rather than deceptive or aimed at promoting overconsumption.[19] Along the same lines, marketing techniques that deceive, defraud, or take advantage of the weak will be off strictly off limits for Christians in business.

Treatment of suppliers and creditors

Suppliers and creditors are also resource ("capital") providers to a company. Because they are "outside" the company it would be easy for business owners or managers to treat their claims as less important than those of stakeholder groups who are in the company. The rights of creditors, for example, can be transgressed when companies are deceptive about their true financial position or make business decisions that increase the riskiness of the company and undermine the creditor's position after the creditor's money is securely in hand. Creditors can also be hurt when the company pays more of the company profits to owners than is justified - given the riskiness of its business, or the economy, or its financial condition - thus increasing the risk of insolvency and the likelihood of creditor loss. Suppliers' claims are also often treated as if they are less important than the claims of more vocal and/or more powerful groups within the company. Contracts are sometimes cancelled arbitrarily, without concern for the impact on the supplier. In some cases suppliers are not chosen objectively, and information about the selection criteria or process is communicated unevenly. In other cases unjust favors may be requested, and when granted these may be more influential in the purchase decision than objective price and quality information. Christian values, however, rooted as they are in commitments to both respect others and treat them justly, would strongly discourage treating creditors and suppliers in these kinds of ways.

Responsibilities to local (and non-local) communities

Most Christian business people also believe that when a company chooses to draw from the resources of a community in order to reach its goals, it does not merely "purchase labor," but it becomes, or should become, part of the fabric of the community. As such, it needs to recognize the degree to which it benefits from the assets of the community, and should also be willing to maintain and enhance the quality of those assets. For example, if a company benefits from the fact that the people of the community have invested a great deal of their effort and money in the educational system or some other type of infrastructure, the company should feel compelled to contribute to the continued enhancement of this infrastructure. Likewise, if they advertise for workers from outside the community who come into the community and place demands (e.g., language training, medical care, education, etc.) on the social service structures in the community, the company should not assume that it is unobligated to contribute toward the provision of those services. In this regard, it would be inappropriate for a company that identifies stewardship, justice and accountability as key values to take the narrow view that their only community obligation is to pay wages.

Christian owned and influenced companies also understand that taxes are a form of community obligation. Rooted in Jesus' and the Apostle Paul's commands[20] to pay taxes, most companies with strong Christian influences readily pay taxes owed to the various tax authorities - even when these contributions are more than enough to cover the cost of the services provided to them by these political entities. This can be contrasted to companies that have no compunction about doing everything in their power to enhance their bottom line —even if this involves rampant tax evasion or other techniques that damage their local communities. Examples of the latter include negotiating substantial tax privileges and/or financing packages that all but ensure that the company will end up contributing little to the community's infrastructure needs. This is not to say that Christian-influenced companies should blindly pay taxes. They need to hold governments at every level accountable for using taxpayer funds wisely and rooting out any hint of corruption. Christian-influenced companies should also weigh the rights of taxpayers before they extend their hands to accept the benefits of government largess, and abstain from leveraging their economic power to attain special privileges.

Commitments to service and stewardship will also affect other decisions, such as plant closures or pollution. Although companies can and should — indeed must - move at times to remain competitive, these moves should not be made without consideration of the communities they are leaving. A moral case can be made that (public) investments that the community and its members have made in good faith for the benefit of the company must be recognized in this process. And obviously, Christian business people who emphasize stewardship and service cannot be cavalier about resource depletion or ecosystem damage; nor should they allow their communities, rather than their companies, to bear the costs of their environmental pollution. At an individual company level this could mean product redesign or a rethinking of things like packaging and recycling. But it could also mean working actively with other companies, educational institutions, governments, and even competitors to reduce air, water, noise, solid waste or visual pollution, even in situations where there is no pressing financial reason to do so.

Treatment of competitors

We noted back in Chapter 13 how even the nature of competition will be influenced by worldviews. It should come as no surprise then that Christ's words about even loving enemies would affect Christian perspectives on business competition. This is not to say that Christians in business view competitors as enemies – few if any do. Most would argue against characterizing competition as war or even seeing competition and cooperation as mutually exclusive. But in the same way that many people believe a competitive market economy is superior to a command economy, most Christians believe that a competitive economy *guided by healthy religious beliefs* can be superior to other alternatives.

Behind this argument is the idea that religious beliefs that emphasize justice, respect, discipline and service, over against their counterparts can allow businesses to reap the benefits of competition while mitigating its potentially detrimental effects. They do this in part by dampening the emphasis on winning (explicitly or implicitly) as the most important goal of a competitive activity and replacing it with an emphasis on virtuous competition. Cutthroat, bare-knuckled survival-of-the-fittest kind of competition can result in much waste of resources as companies bloody each other. Virtuous competition, on the other hand, by emphasizing how competition need not run contrary to principles of justice, love, and service, calls attention to the detrimental effects of cutthroat competition. These include focusing on eliminating competitors or gaining market strength for the purpose of enhancing the company's position over against its competitors and customers. But this is not to say that virtuous competition is what could be called half-hearted competition. Having a company gain market share by better serving employees, customers, stockholders, etc. is not a bad thing. Nor should virtuous competition be confused with collusion. Rather, it involves promoting cooperation whenever doing so will enhance stewardship and service – such as in shared research, or industrial associations - but not in ways that advance the companies' interests at the expense of any stakeholder groups. In this way, once again, a religiously-grounded worldview demonstrates its ability to make both companies and the economy healthier.

Conclusion

In attempting to summarize Biblical teachings related to business and the perspective of Christian business practitioners, we do not want to imply that Christians in business do not share many perspectives with non-Christians. In fact, we would argue that they have a great deal in common with business people who believe that the primary responsibility of business is creating jobs and value (wealth) while producing needed products and services. In this sense, most Christians, would agree the first line of business continues to be making enough money to be able to continue attracting the revenues and capital needed to pay the expenses and invest in the company at levels needed to keep it strong and competitive. These are undoubtedly reasons that many Christians happily contribute their talents to secular organizations.

In spite of this agreement, however, Christian companies do differ in important ways from secular companies, and significantly different business environments will develop over time in the context of different worldviews. Most notably, businesses will look very different when owners and managers believe their primary responsibilities are service and stewardship, rather than making as much money as they can any way they can. To demonstrate this, we have tried here to faithfully summarize how Biblical teaching and Christian thought have influenced business activity in places where it has been allowed to flourish. In these places, businesses, rather than being seen narrowly as vehicles for enriching owners, are often views as mission-driven engines for creating jobs and wealth - and alleviating poverty - in part because poverty is considered an aberration of the way things are intended to be). It would be difficult to argue, given the writings we have examined, that Christian business owners and managers strive for "success" or "victory" as these terms are generally understood. It would be much easier to argue that they yearn to glorify God, and to receive God's blessing - which flows from a mysterious intermingling of grace, faith and one's desire to do what is right. As we have shown, doing what is right in business, from a Christian perspective, involves producing "goods" and "services," rather than "detrimental things," or "disservices," humbly exercising authority, creating an organizational climate where all people are treated as image bearers of God, and many other things as detailed throughout the chapter. When Christians are not in majority ownership positions, and therefore unable to exercise significant authority over company goals an practices, they nevertheless seek to do these same kinds of things within the sphere of their authority.

One cannot help but see connections between this broad emphasis on stewardship and service to the seven "pro-development worldview elements" we have identified. By being attentive to fairly compensating the providers of all seven kinds of capital for their contributions to the business, and doing their best to nurture civil society on the job and in their communities, it is no surprise that the end result, in places where these Christian values have been especially influential, has been both development and human flourishing.

Chapter 31: When Christianity Impedes Development

Of course not all aspects of Christian theology and not all manifestations of Christian practice are pro-development. One reason for this is the wide variation in focus among different expressions of Christianity which is related to the difficulty of getting one's arms around the whole of Christian teaching. Although its core doctrines, such as the way of salvation and the supremacy of love, are straightforward and relatively well understood, it's teachings are nevertheless based on a large number of books written over a period of approximately two thousand years that ended nearly two thousand years ago, and these books are very much open to interpretation. Biblical revelation did not come as a single unified handbook of policies and procedures, neatly organized, with a Table of Contents and a user-friendly index, but as combination of historical recordings, wisdom literature and personal letters that describe themselves as having been revealed by God through designated individuals over a period of thousands of years, and which were subsequently organized by scholars over additional hundreds of years. Its central figure, Jesus, was born more than two thousand years ago, at a time when the minutia of people's lives were not recorded on videotape or blogs, and, when - in contrast to today's possibilities of cutting and pasting gigabytes of information - the best alternative for recording events was the slow word-for-word hand-copying of documents on scrolls and parchment. One of the most critical series of events to the Christian faith - the appearance of Jesus to his followers after his resurrection - is said to have been witnessed by only a little more than 500 people, and of these, less than a dozen wrote extensively about his life and death, and the events surrounding the birth of the church. Add to this a couple thousand years of interpretation, supplemented with tens of thousands of manuscripts and books written by educated (and sometimes uneducated) people that attempt to draw out and clarify how the Bible can or should be applied to situations and problems that did not exist at the time the Bible was written, and it is easy to see how differing expressions of Christian teaching and practice could have both positive and negative effects on development.

Perspectives on wealth and contentment

Because the Bible warns against the dangers of selfishness, hoarding and loving money, and because it indicates that a willingness to sacrifice and suffer for the good of others it to be commended, some Christians conclude that the accumulation of wealth is to be discouraged. Armed with this kind of thinking, they choose - or at least accept – low levels of work effort and productivity, in direct contrast to the Christian business people described in the previous chapter who have chosen the creation and employment of wealth, not for their selfish indulgence but for the good of others.

Often people who develop this kind of anti-wealth bias also interpret other Bible passages in ways that may not be optimal for development. For example, the Apostle Paul's said, "I know what it is to be in need, and I know what it is to have plenty. I have learned the secret of being content in any and every situation, whether well fed or hungry, whether living in plenty or in want."[1] Most Christians, including the Christian business people described in the previous chapter, take this as a reminder that there are more important things in life than physical comfort, and an encouragement to be strong during difficult economic times as well as self-controlled and generous. Those with an anti-wealth bias, however, are more likely to see it as equating poverty with spirituality, and encouraging a kind of acceptance of the economic status quo that can be a drag on productivity, innovation and development in general. Likewise, when they read that Christians need to "give without expecting return," they may interpret this to mean "without expectations of accountability." This can lead to a kind of blind generosity that contributes to dependency, the development of an underclass, and poor stewardship in general. In international relief and development work, it can result in *relief* lasting months or years longer than it ought to, and the concurrent postponement of needed *development*.

Differing traditions

Some of these differences, of course, are caused or reinforced by differences in the worldviews associated with different Christian traditions. We do not want to reiterate here what we said in Chapters 14 and 15 about the many ways belief systems differ, but it is important to remind ourselves that even the relatively minor differences between some Christian traditions can collectively lead to measurable differences in the economic outcomes experienced by people who are part of these traditions. For example, Eastern Orthodox and Catholic traditions have in general been more accepting of poverty than Protestants.[2] (But this is not say that they have been less responsive to the poor.) They have also focused more on the role of "good works" vis-à-vis Protestant denominations that have been placed a greater focus on the central role of faith. One might expect that an emphasis on "good works" would be healthier for economic development, but this depends on how good works are defined. For example, if good works are defined as vows of poverty, ascetic living or ritualistic behavior that is somewhat detached from day-to-day life (such as long periods of meditation or repetitive chanting), they are likely to have a very different impact on development than if they are defined as moral behavior and applied ethics. There has also been more mysticism and more attention to icons and art in general in the Catholic and Orthodox traditions than in Protestantism. Although there is an inspirational dimension to art, the overall effect of this has been for Catholic and Orthodox traditions to spend more money on large structures, religious artifacts, monasteries and the like than Protestants, and relatively less on Biblical education, evangelism, and/or activities that build relationships among parishioners.

It also appears that activity in Protestant-influenced countries has gotten a boost from less emphasis on official church hierarchy and authority and less emphasis on the distinction between clergy and laity. Catholic and Orthodox Church hierarchies have for the most part been less supportive historically of private property, more suspicious of the processes by which wealth is accumulated, and more aware of the inherent dangers of concentrated wealth - at least of wealth held by private individuals outside of the church. In addition, the very nature of economic activity changes when ordinary people are able to read about and apply Biblical principles to their commercial activities - without fear that they would be violating church teachings on profits, wages, usury, wealth accumulation, and the like. Commerce is also boosted when people widely understand that they are not excused from operating their businesses and financial affairs ethically simply because they are not professional clergymen. So, to the extent that Christians operate their businesses and governments in ignorance of perspectives on authority, honesty, stewardship, or love that we have seen to be some important to development, their actions could have detrimental effects on the economy. In this sense, the more *dualistic* the Christian belief system, i.e. the more people divide reality into sacred and secular realms and live their secular lives as if their Christian beliefs did not matter, the less positive effects on the economy.

As noted earlier, Protestants are also more likely to be emboldened by their understanding that they have direct access to God (rather than through the institutional church as an intermediary) and see wealth as a direct blessing from God, and may therefore give more attention and energy to commercial enterprises and wealth-building activities than Catholics or Orthodox. Protestants have also traditionally given larger percentages of their incomes in the form of charitable contributions than Catholic and Orthodox Christians (at least in the U.S.), a phenomenon that may be related to less emphasis on structure, the additional accountability associated with less emphasis on formality and liturgy and more on fellowship and community, the freedom to start charities, or something else.

These comparisons are, of course, general observations to which there are significant exceptions at various times and places. Some expressions of Protestantism foster economically-detrimental practices that are much rarer in Orthodox and Catholic traditions. For example, the melding of Protestantism and individualism in some denominations has opened the door to the misinterpretation or misapplication of teachings that would otherwise promote healthy development. We are not talking here about minor aberrations of the ordinarily healthy support for individual initiative that is integral to the Protestant work ethic. Rather, we are talking about the subset of Christians that has either been enticed or captured by what has come to be known as the health-wealth gospel. One obvious example of this is when television preachers capitulate to the materialistic culture and preach a kind of easy income and wealth that is not all that different from the "gospel" espoused by gambling casinos, lotteries and snake oil salesmen. Ultimately they promote entertainment and the kind of consumerism that erodes wealth more than the Biblical principles that actually create wealth. By convincing their parishioners that all they need to do is support the TV preacher's grand dreams and lavish lifestyle, and pray hard so that God will also drop a Cadillac or two in their own laps - to the exclusion of emphasizing time-worn Biblical principles like work, the pursuit of wisdom, respect, love or self-control that are the true building blocks of wealth - they are hampering rather than spurring economic development.

Syncretism

A similar tragedy can occur when Christians marry Biblical teaching with secular or tribal beliefs, magic or taboos, and tolerate the kind of evil that is deadly to economic development. One example of this is in Haiti, where it can be argued that the Catholic church - likely for the sake of tolerance - exerted too little effort to root out the tribal beliefs, taboos, and magic, with the result that such beliefs continue to contribute to Haiti's extreme poverty more than two hundred years after its independence. (This observation is emphatically not, however, to minimize the impact of other injustices that have been done to the island country by Europeans and the U.S. over the years. Many of these mistakes, born of misguided worldviews rooted in paternalism, relativism, and "ends justifies means" thinking, have also significantly undermined economic development in other places)[3] Syncretism can also be problematic when Christians meld economically-detrimental secular beliefs with Christian beliefs. For example, ordinarily Christians balance God's call to develop the world and mitigate the effects of sin (what Christians often refer to as the cultural mandate recorded in Genesis 1:28), with God's call to care for "the garden" (described in Genesis 2:15) and the various injunctions about "stewarding the land" that are sprinkled throughout the Old Testament. But some Christians' beliefs are difficult to distinguish from pantheists and radical environmentalists who see almost any exploitation of resources, highly-automated farming methods, or intensive land use as sacrilege.

Of course some other Christians walk the other side of this line, by joining forces with radical individualists – and ignoring much of what the Bible teaches about stewardship and God's concern for the land and all of his creatures. By emphasizing the role that people have as rulers of the natural world and the fact that God expects people to use their creative energies to develop the world and mitigate the effects of sin on a "fallen" creation, they come to the conclusion that natural resources and the environment may be exploited without regard to aesthetics or the need to keep ecosystems balanced. When this is combined with a strong feeling that the earth and its contents will be destroyed (rather than refined and made new) in the final judgment, care for the environment can become an even lower priority.

Otherworldly orientation

This last thought is part of what has sometimes been called an "otherworldly orientation, which means in part that because sin can never be fully eradicated in this world - and the full benefits of Christ's atonement are only available when people are saved from death and hell and enter a new "eternal life" - what is really important is what happens after people die. This orientation can even overcome the usually strong inclinations on the part of Christians to want to mitigate the effects of sin and improve the world, by replacing it with a kind of resignation that the world is corrupt and evil and that Christians must accept disease, evil, and the like until they are freed from it at death and God ushers in a gloriously new heaven and earth. Although Christians who succumb to this kind of thinking usually still feel called to live moral lives, the reduction of their faith to morality, motivation or spirituality - rather than understanding their lives as part of the amazing ongoing story of God's interaction with not only people but the entire cosmos - leads to a general withdrawal from the world and a very negative effect on economic development. This tendency has led to a number of other practices that have not been particularly pro-development and some that have been antidevelopment. One example related to the secular/sacred dualism mentioned earlier is the tendency of some Christians to separate their "material" and "spiritual" lives. This often results in the development of a hierarchy whereby "spiritual" activities are considered to be superior to "worldly" pursuits, which in turn encourages people to shun economic activities like engineering, business, or politics in favor of prayer or scripture reading, rather than seeking a healthy balance between these things. Another problem, not unrelated to this, is the tendency to interpret the day-to-day activities of this life to be "carnal," so that the emphasis shifts to "getting past" the brokenness of this world to the promised eternal life where the Bible promises "there will be no more death or mourning or crying or pain, for the old order of things has passed away." Unfortunately, this can foster a kind of disregard for advancing one's education, or the desire to find new and better ways to do things, or one's responsibility to eliminate waste and/or care for the environment - all of which have a negative impact on the economy. But fortunately, when Christians with this perspective interact over significant periods of time with other Christians — particularly those who uncovered a much bigger picture of God by plumbing the Biblical story from end to end, their otherworldly orientation and the problems associated with it tend to diminish.

Church –State relations

Perhaps no nuance of Christian belief is more important, for good or bad, than the perspective held on the issue of church/state relations. Throughout the history of the Christian church, there has been tension between church and the state, and generally speaking, the countries that have been most successful economically have also been those that were most successful in working through this relationship. Orthodox and Catholic churches have long histories of clashing with czars and monarchs, in part because they have been around for such a long time, but also because they tend to have relatively authoritarian structures and decision making processes when compared to Protestant churches. However, some modern day Protestant church groups have also viewed politics as a battleground for forcing moral behavior through the use of government power. Many Protestants with this view also share an interpretation of history that sees the U.S. founding fathers as having established a "Christian country" - with the implication that today's Christians must work to restore this through the exercise of political power. Of course it cannot be denied that many of the founders of the U.S. were Christians or that even the agnostics and deists among them were heavily influenced by Christian teaching - and that they truly did desire to establish (as they inscribed on their money) a "new order." But they most assuredly did not want to subject the citizens of this new country to the same kind of official religious discrimination that many of the early settlers had been subjected to in their European homelands. This is already evident in the language of the U.S. Declaration of Independence, but it is made especially clear by the speedy passage and wording of the first amendment – which leaves no doubt that the founders believed people were most productive when following the dictates of their hearts, rather than feigning loyalty and marching to the orders of a monarch, pope, or other imposed authority.

Finally - perhaps for some of the reasons discussed earlier - it also appears that Western countries that have found middle ground between the churches dominating the state, and vice versa, have done better economically than those that have not effectively resolved this issue. The likely economic reason for this goes back to Adam Smith's ideas about specialization and the division of labor. No single person or organization can do everything well. From a practical point of view, we could say that churches are more competent to offer spiritual, moral and ethical authority, states are more capable of establishing just legal structures or governing, businesses are more competent to produce goods and services efficiently, etc. But, regardless of the reason that countries do better economically when the church and state respect and accept each other's legitimate authority, it is important to note that the very idea of "spheres of authority" is not just a quaint notion that happens to positively influence development. Rather it grows out of some supportive Biblical teaching that was particularly emphasized by some of the Presbyterian and Reformed churches that - not surprisingly - were also disproportionately influential during the birthing of the United States of America. For example, as noted in Chapter 26, the Christian doctrine of the sovereignty of God insists that" all things were created by and for God (Christ)"[4] and that earthly authorities are accountable to him for the affairs that are within the sphere of their authority. When combined with a host of Biblical directives enjoining parishioners to subject themselves to church elders, employers to pay "fair wages," workers to obey their "masters," children to "obey their parents," parents not to "exasperate their children," subjects to "honor the king," citizens to obey the "governing authorities," taxpayers to "give to Caesar what is Caesar's," etc., the result was the acceptance of an underlying order to and relationship between the various spheres of human activity and the need to differentiate the authority of these spheres. A related Catholic tradition, known as *subsidiarity* also developed. As plagues and poverty created greater and greater needs for intervention at a local level, and Catholic charities responded, the concept of subsidiarity took shape. In contrast to Marxist ideas about using revolution and government power to fix social problems, many Catholics ministered to the needy without reliance on government power or resources. Over time, this led to the principle that larger more powerful institutions ought not usurp power from smaller or weaker institutions – particularly when these latter institutions could minister more effectively than those that would replace them.

For the Christians and countries influenced by these teachings – and particularly those that refined and developed these ideas over time - there was widespread (although perhaps not always explicit) understanding that whenever institutions and authorities overstepped their bounds, they were likely to do damage to other spheres, harm people and slow the development process. This led in turn – particularly in some Northern European nations and the U.S. who were disproportionately influenced by the Presbyterian and Reformed traditions mentioned earlier - to attempts to incorporate the definition, protection and limitation of various authorities – and especially government authority- into the very fabric of the law and national identity. It is our contention that development did not fare quite as well in places where these issues were were sidestepped, or where Christian teaching did not give as much attention to working out the implications of God's sovereignty for organizing human activities.

Chapter 32: Secular Materialism – Basic Doctrine and Positive Economic Effects

Introduction and Caveats

The second of the two major belief systems that have been particularly influential in the development of the global economy - and therefore needing more in-depth analysis - is secular materialism. Although secular materialists and humanists comprise a relatively small percentage of the global population, their beliefs have been disproportionately influential in Western societies, and more recently in other parts of the world that have been heavily influenced by Western education and its related cultural influences. Although there are several reasons for this, the main one is that the followers of secular materialism were successful early on in advancing their belief system as value-neutral and, in so doing, established by assumption that it is fundamentally different from other belief systems - which, being "religious," were known *not* to be value-neutral. This gave secularism a disproportionate influence, particularly in those countries intent on establishing pluralistic structures and institutions. Adherents of secularism were also successful in much of Western Europe and in North America in using the assumption of neutrality to gain near monopoly status in two very influential sectors of society, the public school and the government. And in Eastern Europe, as we noted earlier, secularism manifested itself as a more virulent form of Atheism that sought to influence if not control nearly every sector of society.

Before discussing the impact of secular beliefs on economic activity, it needs to be recognized that, unlike Christianity and some other major world religions, there is no official doctrine that makes it easy to capture the core beliefs of this group - although sub groups committed to important aspects of secularism have tried to capture its defining elements from time to time.[1] There is also no clear line of demarcation that sets secular materialists apart from, say secular-humanists on the one hand or avid Christian church-state separatists on the other. Secular materialists share a commitment to secularity with the former and an interest in limiting the influence of religion with the latter. The reason for this is that in the Western world these groups and their core principles move fairly seamlessly among each other and have significantly influenced each other's belief systems. One could argue that humanists are more concerned with relationships than materialists, or that humanists are generally more open to the kinds of issues that cut across philosophy or religion than dedicated materialists - but those kinds of questions are secondary to our purpose here. To make clear one of the principal points of this book, it is necessary to at least try to isolate the fundamental beliefs of a secular mindset, and to do this in ways that allow it to be contrasted to other belief systems. This is a complicated task for several reasons. We noted earlier how secularism has taken on different functions in Asia, Western Europe, and Eastern Europe. In addition, secular belief systems can also be subdivided according to how much of life they are willing to accede to religion. Most of the secularists in the "Modernist" camp (including many scientific atheists and agnostics) have been willing to tolerate traditional religions as long as people kept their beliefs private – i.e. outside of "public" spheres like business, education or government. But 20th century changes led to an increase in the number of militant secularists (differing strains of which developed in both Communist countries and the West), who has no use for religion at all and has been known to do its best to crush it either intellectually or forcefully, as well as "softer" forms of secularism which encourage peaceful coexistence with a variety of religions. But even most "Modernist" expressions of the latter have never fully conceded a significant role for religious beliefs/teachings in a secular society. Postmodernist secularists, on the other hand, are quite comfortable with the notion of spirituality, but they too are inclined to view spiritual beliefs as so private and individual that the effect is the same —they remain largely separate from and unimportant to other (so-called "secular") aspects of both private and public life.

In spite of these complications, we will attempt to boil down secular materialism's core beliefs, without getting hung up on the many nuances within secularism – in the same way that we focused on Christianity's core beliefs without getting too hung up on denominational differences. This also means some "weeding out" of those aspects of secular thought that come not from the secular beliefs themselves, but from the cultural petri dish where they were nurtured – i.e. Christian-influenced Europe.[2] This must be done - as noted in Chapter 14 - that it is always a dangerous thing to generalize too much when it comes to belief systems. But doing so remains a necessary part of writing a book that seeks to derive wisdom from what is necessarily a limited look at the interaction between human economic and religious activity. We start, then, by trying to capture the essence of a secular belief system, and (as we did for Christianity in the preceding chapters) relating it to the seven pro-development worldview elements previously connected with wealth creation and economic development.

Core Beliefs of Secular Materialism

It was noted in Chapters 14 and 15 – where an attempt was made to uncover "measuring sticks" that could be used to compare and contrast economically-significant aspects of belief systems – that all belief systems rest on foundational commitments or assumptions. These assumptions in turn influence what people voluntarily and involuntarily see or don't see, hear or don't hear, and do or do not do. They influence the conversations, books, media outlets, and web pages people tune into, read or click on, and the ones they stay away from. For this reason, no church, mosque or synagogue is necessary for the assumptions of secular materialists to coalesce into the kind of self-reinforcing core set of beliefs that characterizes traditional religions. And, as with traditional religious belief systems, the assumptions and core beliefs of secularism coalesce into a worldview that is fundamentally different from and quite possibly opposed to - even though it may be outwardly tolerant of - other beliefs systems. That the core beliefs are present is not an issue – the difficult part is that without agreed-upon doctrine one has little choice but to try to distill them from the attitudes, statements and policy recommendations of those publicly committed to secularism. Acknowledging the difficulty of this, we nevertheless suggest the following list of three economically-influential core beliefs that can be historically tied to the advent of secularism and seem least likely to reflect the vestiges of religious beliefs of the cultures in which secularism arose:

- If there is a spiritual/sacred dimension, it is separate from the material/natural world, and not particularly relevant to it. Although some secularists concede that religion can play a role in maintaining a moral order, and a few even recognize the existence of "moral laws," most operate as if religion doesn't or at least shouldn't matter to economic outcomes. Two generally unspoken assumptions of this are that spiritual and moral truths are relative, rather than absolute, and that secularism is a non-religious (and therefore unbiased) worldview. A widely agreed upon consequence is that there should be a strict separation of church and state. In some cases this has developed into practices aimed at minimizing religious influences in schools and other "public" arenas.

- People are autonomous, meaning that the individual is the fundamental unit of society and should be self-governing. To use William Henley's words, a person has the right to declare, "I am the master of my fate; I am the captain of my soul." Typically this belief has come with two additional assumptions: that humans are by nature basically good, and that freedom is a basic right and one of the highest "goods."[3] Freedom and autonomy, then, are often viewed as fundamental rights and ends in themselves, rather than means to accomplish other more important things. Oddly, the "doctrine" of autonomy/freedom is one of the few that secular thinkers on both the extreme right and left of the political spectrum can agree on. The people on the extreme right are sometimes labeled libertarians because they prefer to be free from the laws and taxes restricting their economic or religious choices, while people on the extreme left are equally happy to be free of laws and regulations that would invade their privacy, impose morality, or limit their speech or "expression."

- The world is primarily material, and is on a kind of evolutionary automatic pilot except for the interference of people. Like it or not, the accepted theory is that we are bound up in a competitive system where the fittest survive. In contrast to any reliance on God or revelation, it is assumed that reason applied to this material world is the best hope for improving mankind's condition. Logic and the pursuit of individual and joint interests are by themselves capable of leading people to an understanding of right and wrong and, consequently, to normative behavior. In its strongest form, secularism holds that advances in education and rationality will eventually extinguish the irrationality of religion.

It should be noted before proceeding, that we have chosen to focus on the version of secularism that lives primarily in Western Europe and North America. This is obvious if one notes the role that freedom plays in the second "core belief" above. The versions that arose in Eastern Europe and Asia, although important, have arguably had less influence on the nature of global economic activity than the Enlightenment-generated version that can be directly linked to the expansion of philosophical and scientific thought, the industrial revolution and the advent of global economic activity.

Secularism and the Pro-Development Worldview Elements

We now turn our attention to connections between secularism's key beliefs and the pro-development worldview elements discussed in Chapters 19-25. Our discussion will necessarily be briefer than the discussion of Christian influences, because there is no 1400 page sacred text, nor is there an extensive literature to be examined on the relationship between secularist beliefs and our worldview elements.[4] However, all seven worldview elements will be addressed, at least briefly, and some in considerable detail. In most cases secularism has both positive and negative effects on economic outcomes, but we will concentrate on the positive influences in this chapter and save the negative influences for the following chapters. The last of these chapters will be devoted to a story of how secular thinking can inadvertently contribute to inner-city poverty – in part because this particular path of influence is not generally well understood.

Secularism and pro-development worldview element #1

We begin here with a discussion of the impact of secular thinking on our first pro-development worldview element: the need to have a strong sense that things are not as they should be, and need to be improved – with special focus on the importance to economic development of the need to reject poverty and see freedom and civil society as normative. Believing that the world is primarily material can also have a positive effect on economic development if it frees people from excessive contemplation and gives them more time to get their hands dirty interacting with and transforming the material world into the kinds of products and services that will fix the problems that they see. It also allows people to manipulate the material world without worrying about offending some ancestral spirits or having to account to God for these activities - which frees humankind to use drills, bulldozers, pavers, or cranes to extract things, to build useful structures for moving people and goods around, and to conduct business or facilitate recreational activities without the delays associated with moral or ethical hand-wringing. The assumption that life is short, death is final and only the fittest survive is also a powerful motivator for working hard, largely for the purpose of making life as enjoyable and comfortable as possible, and doing this as quickly as possible.

The assumption of competition as normal further raises the overall level of economic activity by increasing the urgency associated with fixing problems - as people compete more vigorously for what they assume is a limited pool of resources and rewards. Knowing that in order to survive or thrive they will have to come up with and implement creative ideas faster and better than others, they race to improve their products and services and to form the highly productive and fast changing enterprises needed to do this. Perceived and real competitive threats also encourage them to build up their intellectual or physical prowess to increase their chances, not only of surviving, but of making it to the top of the food chain, where they have the eventual possibility of relaxing and enjoying the fruits of their labors. All of this fosters the kind of continuous-improvement mentality that characterizes pro-development worldview element #1.

As noted earlier, an appropriate understanding of the nature and importance of freedom is a key ingredient to continuous development. Several of the basic doctrines of secularism, including the assumption of autonomy/individual self-governance, correctly interpreted, will certainly have positive effects on freedom. For example, when individuals are defined as the basic (autonomous) units of society, they can also be held individually responsible for their behavior. This opens the door for more individual freedom, gives people an incentive to work hard in order to improve their well-being and places much of the burden of unproductive conduct squarely on an individual's shoulders. Hyper-focusing on freedom also gives people the right to design and participate in a variety of economically productive processes and institutions such as markets, democracies, business organizations, or civil society institutions. It promotes the free exchange so essential to healthy market activity. It also increases the total number of economic exchanges and the market value of these exchanges – since it frees people to produce and buy what they are most interested in. Secularism's commitment to keeping spiritual/sacred things separate from the material world, and the moral relativism that flows from this, are also very influential. Together they greatly diminish the need to follow religiously determined distinctions between needs and wants, remove most moral guilt or shame that might otherwise be associated with certain kinds of consumption and accumulation, and give people the freedom to make, sell, and buy almost anything they can imagine. This also has the potential to increase the overall satisfaction associated with purchases, since it increases the likelihood that people will find just what they want when choosing from an almost unlimited number of products and services.

Secularism's preoccupation with freedom also supports the principles of freedom of speech, the press, and religion that are central to civil society. Each of these promotes the flow of ideas and an appreciation of the value of diversity, both of which stimulate innovation and economic activity. By not allowing religious authorities to too-quickly censure technological possibilities and practices beyond the scope of their understanding, each of these has the effect of raising the overall output of goods and services and generic spending-based measures of economic activity like GDP. For example, secular ideas about the goodness of people open the door to decentralized management practices and more flexible and efficient organizational structures. And, since there is little to hide when people are inclined to do the right thing, it can also lead to high trust quotients and transparency in organizations, political processes and government. Secularism's emphasis on the freedom not to be religious can also lead to healthy developments within traditional belief systems — as people are encouraged to examine their religious beliefs relative to the alternatives, and are encouraged to jettison unprincipled or harmful beliefs that are rooted based in little more than custom or superstition.

Secularism and pro-development worldview element #2

Seeing people as autonomous, self-governing and good would certainly seem to give secularism the potential, because it encourages the empowerment of individuals and sees them as worthy recipients of significant authority and responsibility, to foster both high respect for and high expectations of authority. Combined with its focus on freedom this would suggest giving people the authority and responsibility to find innovative ways to solve their problems, including their economic problems.

Secularism's focus on the benefits of Darwinian competition has certainly contributed to the support of market-like striving in education and employment, which advances the kind of meritocracy that increases the chances of capable respect-worthy people rising to positions of authority. The near-worship of logic and reason, coupled with the assumption that if the world is not going to improve unless science and education are advanced, has contributed to the quality of organizational leadership, policies and procedures.

Perhaps most importantly, a high regard for freedom has the potential for limiting the abuse of authority - which we noted to be critically important to development in Chapter 19. This suggests a strong focus on the kind of accountability structures that are needed to keep authorities honest. Combined with secularism's fixation on the material world and suspicion of religious authority, this led predictably to an understanding of the limitations of ecclesiastical authority, the need for constraints on theocratic rule, and a resulting reduction in the potentially negative economic effects of these kinds of arrangements. This eventually led to the idea that church and state should be strictly separated — a concept that is inextricably bound up with the rise of the modern nation state, democracy, the rule of law and even universal public education. The rise of these institutions and political processes has in turn encouraged both the church and state to focus on what they are able to do best. And, the pluralistic structures set up in the name of separation have also been important in supporting freedom of religion and ushering in all of its attendant benefits. Arguably, this increased both the respect for and expectations of government authority by limiting the potential to limit government overreach and the potential negative effects of this. By freeing governments from the authority of the church, it also empowered them better accomplish their tasks, since police power and the use of force is a more universal motivator than excommunication.

Secularism and pro-development worldview element # 3

As secular governments consolidated their authority, this both enabled and forced them to wrestle with stewardship issues. They found themselves with the authority to engage in high return-on-investment legal, economic and social infrastructure projects that we routinely accept as government's responsibility today. The development of crafts, trading, finance and other forms of commercial activity thrived when people were no longer needed restricted by feudal lords or the church from engaging in such activities. This opened up the door to the kind of specialization and economies of scale that spurred both the industrial revolution and globalization that catapulted the world economy into the frenetic beehive of economic activity that we observe today. Secularism's dual emphasis on the material world and freedom also contributed to the need to sort out the limitation of government's authority with respect to property and wealth – leading eventually to critical discussions about and definitions of private property rights, which in turn promote both productivity and stewardship, since it is generally agreed that people are more likely to both use and care for property when they benefit directly from using and caring for it and suffer directly from misusing or abusing it. (History is replete with examples of individuals abusing or neglecting public property, and, although there are many examples of private property abuses, these can generally be traced back to misguided values or poorly defined property rights.)

Secularism's focus on evidence-based skepticism contributed to stewardship by encouraging scientific study and experimentation, and a host of technological advances. In addition, the belief that the world is primarily material has contributed to the desire to conserve, and husband material resources, encouraging things as diverse as continuous-improvement production processes, environmental preservation, recycling and a host of other sustainable production and consumption practices that contribute to healthy economic outcomes. Dedication to the scientific method and the discovery of new technologies that allow people to derive more value from fewer resources are a logical outgrowth of this kind of thinking.

Secularism and pro-development worldview elements #4 and #5

In some sense secularism's commitment to autonomy should also contribute to our fourth pro-development worldview element because it should help people be more objective about who they are

- without regard to the usual cultural markers like family background or religious identity. Likewise, a secular reliance on rational thought processes and the scientific method, properly implemented, has the potential of unmasking a variety of preconceived but fundamentally incorrect notions about people and social dynamics - which should increase people's objectivity. A heavy reliance on science also decreases the likelihood that people will hold onto irrational fears about the forces that govern the natural world or human activity. In this way, secular thought can spur development by transcending the kind of cultural blocks associated with animistic or tribal belief systems and help people understand themselves better and become more sympathetic toward others.

The belief that religion doesn't or shouldn't matter can also improve people's objectivity about themselves and their sympathy toward others by enabling them to approach those who have different belief systems without a particular religiously-based prejudice. This has the potential to effectively move secularists from mistrust and fear to tolerance, even though it is unlikely to be powerful enough to engender respect and appreciation for unapologetically religious people. Tolerance and the desire to deemphasize religious beliefs have in turn motivated secularists to encourage people to step out of their comfort zones and cross religious and ethnic lines to work toward common goals or the development of a common humanistic ethic. By encouraging people to break away from patterns of thinking rooted in a particular culture, tradition, or sacred text, secularism has promoted ways of thinking and working together that might not have been discovered by those who fear going against their ancestors, or who believe their responsibility is limited to unquestioning obedience to a particular set of traditions, customs or doctrines.

Secularism's heavy focus on the material world also offers the possibility of highlighting the commonality of people, deemphasizing sectarian differences, and bringing diverse groups together to address common and decidedly non-sectarian problems like disease, material scarcity, environmental degradation or infrastructure needs. This in turn has the potential of spurring voluntary cooperation and its attendant benefits.

The respect for individual rights that also accompanies assumptions of autonomy has led secularists in business to be active in the development of participatory management systems, and in the stakeholder rights and corporate social responsibility movements. In education, it is hard to imagine, for example, something like a community public school without some of the ground rules established by secular thinking patterns. In public schools, secularists have been active in promoting community mindedness, and the development of programs and structures that not only cognizant of the dangers of divisiveness, but highly focused on dealing with economic, social, racial and ethnic differences. In this sense secular thought brings attention to a number of issues that might be sidestepped in countries with a state church or so much religious homogeneity that minority beliefs and customs are effectively drowned out. Secularism's ability to actively promote the mixing of very different kinds of people has also contributed to the development of large, diverse, complex corporations, global trade, and various forms of international cooperation. The pragmatism inherent in this kind of approach cannot help but lead people to discover what works best in their social and economic transactions, and where trustworthiness and honesty are also operative, economies will expand and flourish.

It has been argued of course, including in this book, that pretending that secular and religious life can be separated ultimately sidesteps many of the worldview issues that must be dealt with for real progress in the public square. Nevertheless, the notion of religion's separateness and secularism's neutrality has been useful in some respects when trying to organize political and economic affairs. Removing religion from the public square is one way of allowing people to practice their religious beliefs - albeit privately - without imposing them on others. It also presents a way of reducing church-state conflict, by assigning these institutions to separate realms, reducing the likelihood of either party making inefficient intrusions into the other's affairs. Separation also permits a kind of cooperation among diverse religious/ethnic groups in the accomplishment of community or even national goals, by focusing everyone's attention on the "secular purpose" to be accomplished, rather than on their differences. This has helped nations influenced by secular thought to achieve levels of political and economic cooperation far beyond what would have been possible for smaller groups working independently.

Secularism and pro-development worldview element # 6

Regarding the sixth pro-development value, there is little doubt that secularism's commitment to individual autonomy and freedom leads to a greater range of ideas about what it means to be praiseworthy, and in some cases, such as with scientific pursuit of the truth, or an objective legal system's pursuit of justice, this has advanced ideas about what it means to be "praiseworthy" in a direction that they need to go. It is also likely that the widespread belief that people are basically good has contributed to the kind of freedoms, encouragements and environment where good, and especially talented people are able to flourish – such as those who are gifted communicators, exceptionally talented in the arts, or entrepreneurial enough to start job-creating companies in their garages, and grow them into multibillion dollar success stories. Secularism's disproportionate emphasis on the material world has certainly contributed to a favorable environment for those who are gifted at creating gadgets and uncovering technological advances that spur the extraction and transformation of material into products that make life easier or more interesting for people. And secularism's assumption that there is nothing beyond this life provides a strong motivation to work hard, and pursue scientific and technological advances that could improve or extend life. Combined with assumptions that the world very much resembles a competitive jungle, this has spurred the kind of rapid technological innovation and inventiveness that are widely viewed as praiseworthy.

Faith in reason as the best and only hope for improving people's condition encourages the establishment of educational institutions that are serious about teaching people to think and apply science and rationality to discovery processes, human behavior and relations, economic activity, and institutions. Many of the world's best universities became increasingly secularized during the same periods (the 19th and 20th centuries) that their reputations were soaring and their societal influence was growing. Focusing less on theology, they often redoubled their efforts in the areas of science, educational methods and new technologies. Undeterred by the thought of either evil spirits or divine intervention in nature, they often worked relentlessly to link cause and effect. Unmotivated by promises of eternal reward for work well done, they nevertheless labored for fame, fortune or the good of humankind. Unencumbered by the potential complication of a God or gods who might interfere with the laws of nature or the affairs of humans, they developed sophisticated empirical methods for understanding reality and measuring cause and effect. In their willingness to find new ways of looking at things, these universities added disciplines and fields of investigation at a remarkable rate, and in the process often transformed the societies and cultures in which they were immersed. Ever practical, they formed research partnerships with businesses and government agencies to apply and advance that knowledge, quickening the pace of innovation and increasing the efficiency of both the production and distribution of goods.

Secularism and pro-development worldview element # 7

It is, admittedly, more difficult to make specific connections between the core beliefs of secularism and pro-development worldview element #7, humility, than with any other - save perhaps the agape love associated with pro-development worldview element #6. Nevertheless, it is worth noting that secular thinking has the potential to free its adherents from the arrogance that sometimes accompanies the assumption by a particular religious group has it has a "corner" on the truth and need not pursue either scientific experimentation or the kind of educational pursuits or cross-cultural interactions that are critical to development. To the degree that secular thinkers can avoid the same trap, they have every reason to demonstrate the kind of honest humility that can lead not only to recognizing one's need for education, but also to the kind of inquisitiveness, good science and cooperative spirit that are essential to material and technological discovery but also to the philosophical and economic discovery that development depends on.

Chapter 33: How Secularist Beliefs about Religion can Hamper Development

Introduction

Our focus in this chapter, in contrast to the previous chapter, is how each of the core beliefs of secular materialism also has the potential to undermine one or more of the development building blocks introduced in Chapters 19-25. In some cases this turns out to be the result of something inherently defective in the belief itself and in other cases it stems from unique ways that a combination of several beliefs coalesce into ways of thinking that in turn leads to unintended consequences. Of course, not all secularists have thought through what they believe about religion, much less secularism, with the result that the negative impact of their ideas on development can range from relatively benign to quite damaging. As with other belief systems, secularism's negative effects depend on the specifics of what its proponents believe and their commitment or lack thereof to spreading these beliefs.

Religious neutrality

One critical area involves whether proponents of secularism think it is possible to be religiously neutral and, if so, what they believe it means to be religiously neutral. If they define religious neutrality as the essential equivalence of all religious beliefs, this spells trouble. Not only does this mean accepting contradictory ideas as equally valid - which is logically inconsistent - but it leads to a host of assumptions, decisions and actions that can hamper development. One problem associated with this is that by being declared equivalent, all religions are simultaneously declared effectively irrelevant, which gives all people carte blanche to ignore or reject good and true religious beliefs - and the ideas and practices they inspire - along with bad and false beliefs. This in turn could allow good religiously-based values, attitudes and practices to fade over time, or false and harmful religious beliefs (and their effects) to persist for decades or centuries. It also makes secularism, by default, the belief system of choice - and perhaps even the only acceptable belief system. This would be fine if secularism could be proven to be the one and only belief system capable of bringing people complete objectivity, truth, nirvana, or salvation – but there is little or no evidence that this is the case.

Tolerance

The potential damage of secular thought also depends on its willingness to recognize healthy religious beliefs and allow them to flourish. Evidence indicates, however, that in spite of secularism's insistence that it holds the moral high ground with respect to tolerance, its proponents have just as many or more axes to grind as proponents of traditional religions. To use the language we used when discussing the "pro-development values," there is little proof that secularism's proponents are any more capable of "seeing themselves objectively and others sympathetically" than those they castigate, and perhaps even less so. This can be seen by reflecting on whether the words and actions of committed and well-regarded secularists show respect to those who disagree with them. In this regard, some of the leading secular voices fail the test. After a columnist at the *Boston Globe* not so subtly revealed his intolerance when discussing the (Christian) religious right's desire for conservative judges by referring to them as "Right wing crackpots – excuse me, 'people of faith,'" Paul Marshall, a senior fellow at Freedom House, compiled a difficult-to-deny array of quotations that makes it clear that the Globe columnist's sentiments are not at all on the fringe of secular thinking.[1] Marshall relays, for example, that starting roughly after the September 11, 2001 attack, a host of influential secular writers revealed their biases by making blanket statements about sincerely religious believers of all kinds. He also notes that, knowingly or not, they in effect put the likes of Osama bin Laden in the company of people like George Washington, James Madison, Trappist nuns, the Dali Lama, and the Amish.[2] To relay just a smattering of Marshall's quotes, one columnist expressed her fears that the U.S. would become "a country rocked by the fundamentalist religious wars we see across the world." Another accused conservative Christian organizations like the Christian Coalition and Moral Majority as having an ideology "essentially identical to that of Muslim extremists." He also quotes a presidential candidate who accused then President Bush of "the same fundamentalist impulse that we see in Saudi Arabia, in Kashmir, and in religions around the world," and a professor, political commentator and former Secretary of Labor's who claimed that the true battle is not with terrorists but with "those who believe that truth is revealed through Scripture and religious dogma." The reelection of George Bush to a second term only intensified the onslaught causing, at one point, three different people to sermonize about the problem of Christian fundamentalists on a single New York Times op. ed. page (including one accusation that President Bush was promoting "a jihad in America so he can fight one in Iraq"). Marshall gave many other examples, and regular readers of the *New York Times* or *Washington Post* know well that the veneer of tolerance that he was pulling back is easily as thin as that of the religious fundamentalists that these writers regularly criticize.[3]

Thankfully, Marshall wittingly and thoughtfully responds to these kinds of remarks by holding up a mirror to the imams of tolerance and exposing their remarkable talent for "denouncing others' faith while attacking those who denounce others' faith." He then describes a panoply of devoutly religious people who are also unflinchingly tolerant and peace loving -including some "fundamentalist" Christians. In conclusion, Marshall notes, since the term fundamentalist has become a buzzword for "someone firmly committed to religious views that I do not like," and therefore includes both the devoutly religious and the devoutly secular, it may be best to stop using it altogether. He suggests, wisely, that secularists need to "stop trying to hitch their postmodern prejudices to the war on Islamist terrorism and instead stoop to learn something of the bewildering variety of committed belief." They need to recognize their own fundamentalist tendencies and begin fairly evaluating all fundamentalists on the basis of what they are committed to, not simply on the strength of their commitment. They should also be as honest as their intellectual forbears - like John Stuart Mill and Rousseau - who in the process of railing against moral standards that were associated with belief systems of which they disapproved, were forthright enough to admit their own commitments by writing about the need for all people to convert to a kind of humanistic "religion."

It is a fact of life that people of all types can be adverse to being questioned about their assumptions. Even highly intelligent people in positions of power can be surprisingly closed to other ideas about what is most important, and what it means to live a responsible life. Even those who fancy themselves as icons of tolerance are not beyond believing that society should be organized according to their views and are often surprisingly willing to exercise their power to make that happen. They are also not beyond penalizing those who do not agree with them by excluding them from equal access. The persecution of religious believers in the Soviet Union and China is one example of this. But the need for Christians in the U.S. to start "faith-based" alternatives to secular government schools and social service agencies - while simultaneously funding their secular counterparts with their tax dollars – is another.

Historical Patterns

The path to officially favoring one belief system over another is well traveled, and proponents of secularism in both the Eastern Block and Western countries have followed it as religiously as the official churches that were their forebears. Generally it requires a degree of elitism, if not authoritarianism, and the use of public policies, rules or laws to promote the favored belief system (in this case, secularism). This includes decisions that favor or restrict the teaching of particular values, attitudes and ideas in government schools, as well as decisions dictating how other "public" institutions such as businesses, social service agencies, or governments conduct their affairs. These decisions tend to increase, over time, the number of people who self-identify with a secular belief system, and cause dissidents - in this case people attempting to consistently apply their religiously-based worldviews - to be marginalized or alienated in free societies, or be persecuted or worse in authoritarian societies.

Chapter 33

As these examples illustrate, the impact on development of favoring a secular belief system depends very much on the specifics of the secular values, attitudes and behaviors being favored, and the religious values, attitudes and behaviors being discriminated against or suppressed. As noted earlier, Western European secularism in many ways rose in opposition to the Catholic (and in some case Protestant) church's overreach. In spite of this, it developed differently in different countries. In some cases it developed pluralistic approaches to religious practice (e.g. the Netherlands) and in other cases it had a strong antireligious - gnostic or atheist - bent (e.g. France). In East Asia (e.g., India) secularism could better be described as a tool for moderating a panoply of beliefs, for the purpose of reducing conflict between them and achieving a degree of social solidarity and national identification. In Communist countries, and particularly in the Soviet Union, secularism was more of a tool for crushing religious "superstition" and achieving communist ideals. In addition to these practical differences are some philosophical differences: Western Enlightenment-influenced democratic expressions of secularism tend to focus on freedom, individualism and science; Communist Marxist-influenced expressions focused on atheism and social and economic reorganization; and East Asia Confucian-influenced expressions on virtue and social harmony. In addition, the specific religious and cultural practices that have been suppressed or replaced have varied from region to region and over time. The impact of secularism is most damaging it pushes out both healthy religious practices and the religious pluralism that allowed them to develop.

For the most part our focus in this and the previous chapter has been on Western expressions of secularism. Although this is largely an attempt not to "bite off more than we can chew," it also reflects the fact that communist expressions of secularism were largely discredited in the closing days of the 20th century, and our feelings (rightly or wrongly) that East Asian expressions of secularism that focus on moderating a panoply of beliefs are less damaging to long-run economic development than Western expressions focused on freedom *from* religion. We briefly restate - in abbreviated form - the three key assumptions of Western secularism articulated in the previous chapter, prior to investigating their economic impact:

- That religion is little more than a private preference (in part because moral truths are relative), and is not particularly relevant to economics or development .
- That autonomous individuals are the fundamental building blocks of a society, and deserve to be largely free to determine what they do with their time and resources.
- That the world is primarily material, a Darwinian jungle where the fittest survive, and where the ability to decipher right and wrong, and humankind's "salvation" rest ultimately in science and reason rather than religion.

We will address the impact of the first of these in the remainder of this chapter, and that of the second and third in the Chapter 34.

The Marginalization of Religious Belief

We start our analysis with the first belief, and one of its strongest expressions – that people have the right to be free from other people's religious expressions and ideas - hence it is government's role to promote secularism. A fundamental problem with this line of thinking is that it is impossible to cleanly separate secular from religious values – making it both unjust and unwise to give preference to secular values or keep religious believers from full participation in public policy debates or the public square. Restricting the free public expression of religiously-based worldviews is damaging on several fronts: it severely limits the available values, goals and priorities that people can draw from when setting public policy; it allows simplistic ideas about "separation of church and state" to substitute for tough decisions about where the legitimate authority of a government, school, church or family begins and ends; it favors policies that strip religion of much of its ability to influence and enrich life, marginalizing, in the process, both healthy and harmful religious beliefs. Not only does this permit people to sidestep much of the hard work of resolving worldview differences, in some cases it causes marginalized religious groups to move to the fringe of society and engage in behaviors that undermine stability and development. Marginalizing religious beliefs also significantly limits the options for deciding among better and worse ideas, behaviors, and solutions to problems, by favoring "watered down" or "lowest common denominator" secular solutions. In a worst case scenario it puts a secular band-aid on deeply-seated religious differences and significantly lengthens the time required to resolve these differences and conflicts.

A commitment to secularity may also inadvertently water down organizational and national goals to the lowest "secular" common denominator. Primary schools and high schools will gravitate over time to the point where they may still be successful in transmitting knowledge and skills but will have little moral influence over the values and character of their students - since morality will be increasingly seen as an individual matter. At best, the subset of values which they can teach with authority will be reduced to those which prevent damage to others or intrude on individual rights to autonomy. University professors will teach concepts and address issues perceived to be secular while avoiding those perceived to be religious. If they talk about religious beliefs, they are most likely to talk about them broadly and generically even though God (or the devil as it may be) is really in the details of the specific belief. The insistence on secularizing the academy has additional implications with respect to research. The study of the impact of religious beliefs on supposedly secular subjects will generally be overlooked. And when religion is researched, the hard work of accounting for the nuances in religious belief will often be sidestepped, as if what it important to know about the impact of religion can be uncovered by aggregating all religious people, or all people who have been given a particular religious label. These oversights, intentional and otherwise, invite considerable skepticism about other empirical work as well. For example, social science researchers may be interested in the impact of education on some social variable such as criminal behavior. But even if a researcher includes an explanatory variable for education in her study, she often has no way of accounting for the fact that the impact of education could range from very positive to very negative depending on the beliefs that underlie or are embedded in that education. And when morality and ethics are seen as relative, the ethical codes of graduating students cannot help but be watered down to prohibiting only practices that are broadly unacceptable. Bankers, lawyers, doctors, and other professionals will be increasingly free to do things that religious codes eschew. Recent damaging corporate scandals and massive investment frauds in the U.S. and the rest of the Western world - most of which were engineered by secular university graduates – support this conclusion.

The long-term marginalization and privatization of religious beliefs, priorities, and values also eventually leaves only smaller, less significant differences to focus on. Therefore, even though a young black female and an older white male may be seriously committed to their faith, and share similar denominational leanings, and see eye-to-eye on most of the important issues in life, the focus will, nevertheless, often be on the less significant things, like gender and race, that make them different. Not only does this tend to heighten perceived differences among gender or racial groups, but it may improperly attribute many differences to gender and race that actually have their origins in differing worldviews. The extreme result is groups like the Klu Klux Klan or Black Panthers who galvanized around race – when the real need is for people of all races to resolve their widely-divergent worldview perspectives on everything from the nature of people to the meaning of justice, restitution, and love. History also suggests that secularists are likely to miss the religious fine points of many conflicts, such as the Arab-Israeli conflict and be relatively impotent in helping bring peace to those parts of the world plagued by these conflicts. This generally comes from too quickly assuming there are secular solutions to fundamentally religious questions - a pattern that has also hampered efforts to solve other problems like global terrorism or even poverty.

The opposite, however, could also happen, when marginalizing religion leads to inappropriately attributing problems and conflict to traditional religious differences. By seeing, for example, the problems in the Middle East as primarily rooted in Jewish/Muslim or Christian/Muslim religious differences, it is easy to miss the role that other factors, including secular beliefs, may have played in the process. For example, many Muslims in Turkey have been frustrated that Western forms of secularism have influenced their schools to teach an evolutionary view of origins - with its focus on the randomness of both the origins and events of life - to the exclusion of the kind of "intelligent design" that would be more consistent with their faith commitments. Furthermore, like people rightfully angry about upstream pollution, these and most other Muslims resent the crime, sexual promiscuity, drug and alcohol abuse, pornography, etc. that permeates Western culture and to an increasing degree, global culture. Although not a direct result of secularism, it is fair to say that these things are more prevalent where secular ideas about censorship and tolerance carry the day. Many around the globe also resent what they perceive as the U.S. assumption that the "American Way" is always best. Some resent its military and economic power. Many resent that the U.S. supplies copious amounts of aid and arms to Israel, while denying aid and even trade to the innocent victims of iron-fisted despots in other parts of the world. In short, secular tendencies to attribute resentment and conflict to religious differences may be obscuring an equally serious problem - that secular Western cultural hegemony is undermining the values and order that people see as essential to their families and social cohesion.

Because of these things, it can be plausibly argued that the extreme levels of resentment and anger seen in militant groups like Hamas or Al Qaeda could not have been sustained in the absence of a steady stream of Westerners who proudly packed their suitcases, products and web pages with an over-commitment to secularism. Had Americans left this bias at home, or discarded it altogether, the global perception of the "American Way" might be very different. At the very least, less of the Western world's pornography, violent music lyrics, and other excesses would have invaded newsstands, movie theatres and homes around the world. The U.S. might also be known less for its pride and more for its humanitarian efforts; less as a nation that cares primarily about wealth, decadence, and "American interests," and more as one that seeks the truth and defends justice. Perhaps too, the U.S. would have armed fewer nations and spent more time intensely studying their cultures and conversing with their citizens (officially and unofficially) at a level that touches people's deepest heart commitments. It is intriguing, to say the least, to consider how different the world might be today if the U.S. and its citizens were perceived around the world as committed to religiously-sensitive conduct and policies.

Increasing Secular Values and Decreasing Religious Values

Over time, accepting secularism as neutral and favoring it leads to the promulgation of values that are at best benignly non-religious and at worst blatantly anti-religious. Intentionally or otherwise, this diminishes values that are overtly religious - no matter how useful and important these values may have been. It also, elevates *desires and preferences* to a privileged position over quaint notions of right and wrong. In the economic sphere this leads to a pretense that the many diverse goals and preferences people bring to their economic activity are equally valid. The preference for accumulating unlimited quantities of money and possessions for selfish consumption is put on a par with using money to create jobs and sharing one's wealth. Products and services that demean people count just as much in official statistics as those that rescue and restore people. This happens in part because economists are encouraged to propose and track secular statistics that measure things like "total spending," as if spending is good in and of itself - without regard to whether it builds people and/or their communities up, disrupts them, or tears them down. GDP, now the most widely used measure of economic progress across the world, is just such a statistic. It measures only "total output" at market prices, so the sale of a pornographic magazine and a children's book - if priced equally - contribute the same amount to measured output, and both are valued more highly (in official terms) than the unpaid time a stay-at home dad or mom spends reading a book to his/her children.[4] And, over time, value-neutral statistics like GDP will come to dominate and sometimes even eclipse other measures that could give insight into the moral or ethical health of a society.

These influences also cause a subtle transformation in the very ideas people hold about what is noble or worth doing. For example, there was a time when an important goal of large numbers of people in the U.S. was the establishment or maintenance of authentic communities where people looked out for and cared for each other and held each other accountable. Too often today that dream has been cut up, individualized, and depreciated as an increasingly larger proportion of economic and human activity conforms to the kind of individualism and materialism that seem to be the unavoidable byproducts of secular belief systems. For example, a public school teacher would be in far less danger of being accused of misconduct if she met with students on school property to run an investment club aimed at helping students get rich than if she conducted a Bible study aimed at increasing love of neighbor.

The desire to be wealthy, famous, physically desirable, or to be entertained, all qualify as decidedly a-religious goals. This qualifies them as eligible and even routine candidates for discussion in secular educational institutions, and in other public settings, such as the media - so that over time, they increasingly become what people strive for and devote their time to. Businesses increasingly focus their attention on products, services and advertising messages that are profitable and entertaining, but religiously neutral. TV talk and variety shows give free publicity to secular authors, movies and sports stars, but do little or none of this for those with religious messages. What emerges over time is a culture with worship-like treatment of rock stars, sports stars and Hollywood celebrities, an amazing number of TV shows patterned after "Who Wants to Be a Millionaire," an equally amazing number of magazines, newspapers and TV shows devoted to the "lifestyles of the rich and famous," massive increases in expenditures related to these things,[5] and decidedly less focus on religious beliefs and habits. This is not to say, of course, that all those who espouse a secular worldview are obsessed with riches, entertainment, physical appearance or fame – only that institutionalized secularism unknowingly encourages these things to the detriment of religiously-inspired goals.

Winning is another highly-valued secular goal, in part, as noted earlier, because of the Darwinian bent of secular education and the increasingly competitive nature of modern acquisitive societies. Winning creates a lot of wealth for winners, as the salaries and endorsement contracts of star athletes, actors, and CEOs attest. Unfortunately, winning also entails losing. Enron's Jeffrey Skilling was intent on turning Enron into a winner. One tool for doing this was the creation of a pressure cooker environment where underperforming employees - in his case the bottom 15% - were "weeded out" approximately every six months. One problem with this kind of highly competitive environment is its inadvertent tendency to give employees incentives to cover up mistakes or misrepresent the truth about what is actually happening in a company. In Enron's case, the survival of the fittest atmosphere eventually led to the implosion of the company, and significant losses for employees, shareholders, customers, suppliers and a host of others. But unhealthy competition also causes more subtle losses. Cutthroat competition has the potential to damage entire industries, or destabilize entire neighborhoods and towns.

A related problem with secular materialist beliefs is that they tend to focus people's attention on religiously neutral *motivators* like self-interest, equality, or the pursuit of fame or wealth. In many cases, these kinds of motivators will be neither as powerful nor as long lasting as the kinds of motivators that might flow from deeply held heart commitments or a religiously inspired sense of thankfulness and/or moral obligation. For example, people who are theoretically committed to equal opportunity may not work as hard at achieving it as those who believe they are obligated to reflect God's grace and mercy, or who believe they will someday stand before a God who "hates injustice" and wants an accounting for any injustice they knowingly participated in. Religious texts, sermons, beliefs in heaven and hell and other aspects of religious practice may in fact be the best possible motivation for getting food to starving people, getting medicine to AIDS victims, or stopping the killing in places like Rwanda, the Democratic Republic of the Congo, or Sudan. Likewise, those who give to charity in order to win affection or praise may not be as dependable in the long run as those who are motivated by bonds of fellowship, love or religious duty. Absent these deeply-seated motivators, and the kinds of discussions about moral absolutes that precede them, people will be left to their own preferences. Some will work tirelessly to "right wrongs" and live productively and generously, but many will choose to ignore injustice, the needs of others and most other social maladies. Worse yet, some, like Stalin, Pol Pot or Joseph Kony, will contribute to the problems rather than the solutions by choosing injustice or violence to get their way.

The long and the short of this is that secularism not only has a particular problem dealing with morality and ethics, but over time, it increases the amount of human activity devoted to secular priorities - changing the fundamental character of a society.[6] As noted earlier, Solzhenitsyn insisted that all people have divided hearts and that it is ultimately the pull of beliefs on their hearts that determines what they do or do not do. This problem becomes all the more serious when we realize that the good and evil in people's hearts gets imbedded in the processes, structures, and institutions they create. Corporations, central banks, prisons, and nursery schools all have the potential to develop in unique ways, and encouraging employees to bring their most deeply-held beliefs "to the table" could lead to higher motivation levels, and/or products and services that are infused with the integrity that can accompany moral and religious commitments. In contrast, routinely playing a secularist trump card in these organizations could squash potentially effective solutions to some of their most intractable problems, simply because these solutions have religious overtones. This may not only keep people from reaching their highest human potential and making the greatest possible positive impact on the world, but in some cases it will mean acceptance and even encouragement of individual behaviors, business practices or government policies that hurt development, just because they are secular.

The Unique Impact on Developing Countries

Unfortunately, the insistence on religious neutrality has been particularly damaging in some developing countries – for at least three additional reasons. The first reason is because the entire system of Western capitalism is couched in a Judeo-Christian cultural/historical soup, which gives shape and meaning to the nature of everything from property rights and freedom to democracy and notions of equality. Absent this framework, capitalism does not always function as planned. For example, as Hernando De Soto has so eloquently illustrated, most small businesses, and the poor as a group, are often forced to operate extra-legally - because the ideas of those controlling the legal system are often very different from what is needed to empower small businesses or the poor. Whereas houses serve as assets and collateral, and an address as an evidence of legal status in countries influenced by Western concepts of freedom and property rights, in developing countries houses may function as little more than temporary shelter. And while Western business people are free to start businesses or buy a thousand head of cattle with the click of a mouse, their counterparts in many parts of the world may not be not even "own" their own persons to the degree that they are able migrate to where a job exists, or improve their skills to get the job of their choice. Many other examples could be given, because, as demonstrated in Chapters 26-30, all seven pro-development worldview elements have been influenced by Judeo-Christian ideas about what needs fixing, the nature of authority, the importance of stewardship, the extent of one's obligations to others and one's ideas about what is or is not praiseworthy.

The second reason ideas about religious neutrality disproportionally hurt developing countries is because the neutral or "value free" notions that the best and brightest young people pick up in secular Western educational institutions stamp a dualistic worldview on them and makes it less likely that they will use their education to the advantage of their countries. For many years people in both wealthy and poor countries have lamented the "brain drain," a situation where those who escape the poverty of their communities or countries settle permanently in the countries where they receive their education (or other so-called developed countries), with the result that their education becomes primarily of benefit to them as individuals or to the countries in which they settle. One reason for this is that the education these students received generally contains some unnecessary baggage in the form of an unhealthy guillotine-like severance of religious beliefs from everything else they are learning about, which splits their world in two: a "modern" world where secular education and complex mechanistic solutions result in development and a "primitive" world where religious beliefs reign and impede the path to modernity and development. After several years of indoctrination into this "modern" belief system, it becomes difficult if not impossible for students to envision taking the giant leap back into their old life, undercutting both their ability to reconnect with their local communities and the dreams of their parents and others in their home communities who made very significant sacrifices in the hope that their children would receive a good education and return home to use it for the benefit of their home community or country.

Thirdly, when they do return, they find themselves ill-equipped by their secular and largely technical education to identify and work to modify those worldview components that must be changed before development can be unleashed.

Of course, none of this needs to happen. In a world where religious beliefs are seen as a normal and natural part of life, students can receive an education that properly recognizes the central role that religious beliefs play in life while also learning everything *else* that is needed to contribute to their countries' development. They can experience the world in all its fullness by being exposed to religious as well as secular perspectives, and evaluate (without indoctrination) the kind of norms, values - and ultimately the kind of world - that flows from particular sets of beliefs, regardless of whether these belief systems have been labeled secular or religious. They are then free to evaluate the predominant belief systems in their family, village or country relative to others to which they have been exposed (including secular belief systems) and begin to form mental pictures of what must be changed for some of the problems in their communities to be solved. They can do all this while still imagining themselves returning to these communities to effect gradual change - without having to jump from one world to another. And they can return home respecting both their parents and the positive aspects of their cultures without feeling that retuning home means repudiating their education and turning their backs on the "modern" world in which they have been immersed. It is difficult to imagine anything that would be more positive for development than having the "best and brightest" return to the communities and countries that need them and respectfully transform them over time from the bottom up - addressing the root causes of their problems while continuing to treat their family, friends, culture, and beliefs with both integrity and affection.

Secularism as a Stand-alone Philosophy

The question that flows naturally from this discussion is whether the limitations placed on human activity by a need to focus on religiously-neutral goals and solutions, and the problems arising from these limitations, are serious enough to warrant a rethinking of the role of predominantly secular approaches to development. The relatively swift demise of atheistic communism following the fall of the Berlin Wall should at the very least make us question secularity's capability, by itself, of accurately describing the human condition or sustaining the key values needed for economic development (i.e., without the benefit of religious belief and teaching). Upon reflection, most secularist dogma arose in settings where the people developing the dogma had the luxury of living securely in a surplus culture where religious people has previously developed laws, regulations, and institutions that actively promoted the kind of moral and ethical behavior that had led to a functioning civil society and a modicum of economic security and surplus. In contrast, as history has shown, communist countries that did their best to squash religious belief and the moral and ethical principles they espoused ended up with corrupt institutions, arbitrary laws and regulations, little or no civil society, and widespread poverty. It appears that, by itself, secular thinking is not only incapable in some cases of allowing people to draw on their noblest instincts, and but insufficient in all cases of motivating people to reach their highest human possibilities.

Chapter 34: The Limited Ability of Secularism's Commitments to Autonomy, Freedom, Reason and Science to Promote Pro-Development Worldview Elements

The Secular Commitment to Autonomy and Freedom

The second core belief of Western secularism, the elevation of autonomy or freedom to the lofty position of being an end in itself - rather than simply a means to an end - has similar potential to impede development. It does this by both magnifying some of the problems associated with marginalizing religion that we discussed in the previous chapter, and creating its own new set of problems. For starters, secular notions of freedom are by definition unconstrained by religious moral and ethical codes. Unfortunately this makes it quite easy for people to use their freedom to adopt attitudes or carry out behaviors that are unhealthy for development — attitudes and behaviors that would otherwise have been restrained by these moral and ethical codes. In fact, the meaning of freedom can change completely, depending on how people define right and wrong, duty, morality, or ethics. Within secular notions of freedom, people may choose to do the good things that are essential to development — such as work honestly, cooperate or promote justice or stewardship, but they are also free to reject these things. In addition, there is very little in the secular conceptions of autonomy or freedom that can *compel* people to make connections with or feel obligated to groups of people beyond their immediate family and friendship circles.

To be more specific, absent moral constraints on freedom, people are free to take unnecessary and even foolish risks, often leaving society or taxpayers with the tab for their medical expenses or unpaid bills. They are free to usurp nearly unlimited resources for selfish purposes, build far more mansions than they could reasonably occupy, and fill them - and eventually landfills - with far more "toys" than they could ever enjoyably use. There is nothing inherent in secular notions of freedom to keep people from obsessing over thinning scalps or smaller-than-average breasts, or spending thousands of dollars a year on their pets, or even a cool twenty million for a private trip into space — all the while ignoring what that same money could have done if earmarked to save people from malnutrition and preventable diseases, or free children from the scourge of forced prostitution or indentured servanthood. Unchecked by religiously-inspired moral principles, autonomy and freedom can even be used to espouse racist or destructive values, promote violence, or allow the powerful or clever to take advantage of the weak. In spite of these risks, fearful of the idea of legislating morality, proponents of secularism have little choice but to accept people's freedom to damage themselves and others, perpetuate evil, and/or thoughtlessly waste the resources so desperately needed by others.

A secular understanding of freedom also gives businesses more leeway to take advantage of people. Absent religiously-based moral constraints on freedom, business people may find themselves "free" to overlook unsafe products or working conditions or environmental damage because rectifying the problem would be costly to them. They are free to decrease product quality without informing customers, use deceptive advertising, or make product claims that cannot be backed up. They can spend money in ways that hurts their creditors, shareholders or both. Investors generally feel free to move their financial capital to wherever it gives them the greatest return, regardless how it is employed, and, if necessary, to snatch it back on a moment's notice regardless of what kind of havoc that could wreak on the community it is being removed from. Hollywood companies — in many ways the high priestesses of secular values - feel free to make movies that glorify the power of weapons, ridiculously-consumptive lifestyles, and recreational sexual activity. Absent the kind of moral mirror that religious communities hold up to their members, they use their freedom to feed their viewers a steady diet of survival-as-entertainment, backstabbing-as-entertainment, even macabre-as-entertainment shows with little thought about their role in cultural formation. And morally uninformed gun and ammunition dealers make it easy for troubled youth to get guns without background checks, and enough ammo via the internet to terrorize an entire neighborhood. It would be a grave mistake to assume that these choices and thousands of others like them are without significant cumulative economic effects.[1] In short, in a world unconstrained by religiously-based moral principles, businesses can do all of these things and more — at least to the point that market transparency reveals what they are doing and their employees, customers, or capital providers can react to it, or government realizes what they are doing and penalizes them for it. But both well-functioning markets and government regulations involve moral and ethical restrictions on freedom that are grounded in a particular worldview. So government ends up doing what people in their worship of freedom refused to do — except with the added inefficiencies of government bureaucracy and regulation. Although this makes it fairly obvious that, sooner or later, secularism needs to make some faith commitments about right and wrong, moral and immoral, ethical and unethical - but it appears that it is very difficult to get agreement on these kinds of things without sacred texts or a degree of moral and ethical consistency.

Chapter 34

The internet is one of the best examples of the downside of the elevation of freedom to god-like status. A wonderful technology that was originally built for a relatively homogeneous and trustworthy community, it was designed with little thought about human nature and little input from religious scholars or ethicists about what could go wrong. Partly because of this it appears that the system was designed to maximize free exchange - with considerably less thought given to preventing evil people from using it in immoral and unethical ways. More specifically, it appears that too little time was devoted to preventing email senders from disguising who a message is from or to whom the reply will actually be going. This kind of freedom, we now know came at a high price, as it opened up a massive global network to virus creators, spammers, and phishers, among others, costing ordinary law-abiding internet users billions in time, frustration, and protective software purchases. According to Nuclease Research of Wellesley, MS, in 2002 spam by itself cost U.S. businesses $874 per year per email-using worker.[2] And those of us who use the internet regularly know that the problem is at least as great today as it was at the time of the study. The anonymity so valued by secular thinkers, and which characterizes so much of the internet, has also made the internet a useful tool for more traditional kinds of criminals. It has become both a preferred communication tool for terrorists, a useful source for ways to break the law without getting caught, and worse yet, a treasure trove of scientific information for making potentially-destructive IEDs and other kinds of weapons. We might well ask, for example, whether the proliferation of bomb-making knowledge or information about the vulnerabilities of major cities to specific types of terrorism would be splashed all over our internet or TV screens if we understood that freedom must necessarily be constrained by religious sensitivities? Or, conversely, would Scotland Yard have been able to foil the London-based terrorist plot to blow up transatlantic flights in August of 2006 if the British government had been unwilling to risk the ire of many of their citizens and infringe on some of the cherished freedoms (and particularly the privacy rights) of it citizens? All these examples underscore the degree to which a healthy economy depends as much on the moral and ethical codes that tell people when and how to limit freedom as on the freedoms that underlie market activity. By marginalizing religious belief and elevating freedom to god-like status, secularism keep the global economy from flourishing as much as it could – by restraining both the positive impact of faith commitments and the myriad benefits that accompany religiously-motivated restrictions on freedoms. Secularism's focus on autonomy also lessens or undermines commitments to economically-healthy communal values like justice and community building. The net effect is a world economy with more economic waste, more risk, and less efficient outcomes than would be possible if religious beliefs were given an equal opportunity to compete for people's hearts and minds.

Secularist Commitments to Materialism and Faith in Science

The problems highlighted above can be magnified by secularism's core assumptions about the world and humankind's responsibility with respect to it. For these purposes, we recap these assumptions here:

- That the world is primarily material - i.e., it is matter that really matters.
- That life can be described as a competitive jungle where people compete for these limited material resources
- That science and reason will provide the solutions to humankind's problems.

Materialism

A preoccupation with the material world means that the benefits of spiritual/moral capital, and to a lesser extent other non-material forms of capital, will tend to be discounted. More importantly, the critical role that beliefs and worldviews play in shaping all seven forms of capital will either be underestimated or overlooked. This hurts development in at least two ways. First of all, the resulting materialism, which has been a distinguishing characteristic of secular societies, works against the kind of stewardship that we identified as an important contributor to development. Secondly, problems that are religiously-based or relationship-based are more likely to be misdiagnosed as materially-based or technology-based. This in turn leads to a tendency to overemphasize material and technical (mechanistic) solutions to problems when morally and ethically-based solutions might be more efficacious.

As both Western history and the experiences of economically-successful non-Western societies increasingly attest, once materialism has taken hold, entire cultures can be preoccupied with the attainment of material success. People are more likely to fill their lives with material things and technological artifacts, often collecting and stockpiling things they seldom use. They live in splendid loneliness in gated mansions. They are so attracted to goods and services that companies can turn healthy profits while relief and development agencies have to beg for donations just to balance their budgets. Over time increasing percentages of people's incomes in secular countries are spent on material things, disproportionately taxing the earth's resources (and particularly those that are non-renewable or renewable but in short supply). The vast majority of this is spent on themselves or their immediate family members. Absent a worldview to constrain this tendency, these trends seem to persist no matter how wealthy a nation becomes and in spite of the fact that redirecting these resources to investments in people who have potential but insufficient resources to develop this potential would be far more productive. And in such an environment, the need to sacrifice or even die for endearing principles or to save far away victims is viewed as a bit odd at best and unnecessary or extreme at worst. Festering injustices are allowed to persist, as long they don't interfere too much with material comforts. So those who insist that education, politics or business be secular *and* lament the fact that society is getting more individualistic, materialistic, or hedonistic need to recognize their own culpability in this matter. Most gods make demands on people, and this is also true of the secular god of progress.

The self-diagnosis of needs as material rather than spiritual or moral also has less visible effects. People who are poor primarily because of their own decisions and actions can easily convince themselves that they are poor because they are materially deprived. This also increases the likelihood that they will see securing of resources as quickly as possible – whether it be through government support, or even crime as a viable solution to their problem. Government's that buy into this kind of thinking are also more likely to try to solve problems of poverty with material fixes like welfare payments or minimum wage legislation. Because they have trouble seeing the spiritual and moral roots of poverty, this aid is also more likely to be given without addressing underlying worldview issues. Governments in materialistic societies are also less likely to focus on the spiritual/moral dimensions of crime - in part because they see their social pathologies as genetic and intractable rather than moral and fixable - effectively warehousing prisoners in an environment where their basic physical needs are met but little or no attempt is made at spiritual/moral rehabilitation,. Eastern Block governments went so far as to try to stamp out religion and structure entire societies around the production of material goods – with disastrous economic consequences. And many secular Western governments have ignored the moral and ethical principles that might have restrained them from going to war, choosing instead to channel societal resources into machines and weapons that improve their ability to forcibly extend their reach over the material resources of others.

These examples are part of a bigger issue: secular approaches to problem solving by definition tend to self-limit themselves to mechanistic solutions rather than spiritual/moral ones. At the very least, they will insist on trying mechanistic solutions prior to being willing to entertain the efficacy of spiritual/moral solutions. Markets, democracy, and technology are all examples of mechanisms that, in and of themselves, are good things with the potential to produce good results. Unfortunately, good mechanisms, although necessary, are never sufficient in and of themselves to do what needs to be accomplished. We can make cars safer, but, if that results in little more than drivers driving faster or more recklessly, we have not solved our problem through technology. We can open and inspect every shipping container that comes into every country for the foreseeable future, or put tamper-proof safety seals on every kind of food and medicine, but these solutions are frustrating and wasteful of resources, compared to spiritual/moral solutions that could change angry and marginalized people from wanting to harm others. Likewise, we can develop mechanisms to encourage people to retrain and move to meet the ever-changing needs of a global economy (a mechanistic solution to the "creative destruction" of a market economy), but other things must be in place for these mechanisms to accomplish their purpose without creating significant social dislocations. Religious communities that enfold and help dislocated workers and their families are another important element of a holistic solution to the need for labor mobility.

Darwinian competition

The unwavering commitment of secular belief systems to Darwinian assumptions about the origins and survival-of-the-fittest nature of the world are also implicated in these problems.

One reason for this is that the Darwinian scheme of things, the object of life is survival, which is not a particularly lofty goal when compared with other possibilities. Christianity, for example, teaches that because people are made in the image of God and because God is perfect, they too should strive for perfection.[3] Survival as a goal, particularly as it plays itself out in the natural world, can mean doing things to others which are certainly not in their best interest. At the very least it allows people to think primarily about relationships in terms of what they will do to enhance survival, comfort or propagation. In addition, it makes it harder for people to see how materialism or technology can undermine relationships and morality, or even change the nature of people and society. In this regard, this aspect of secular thinking works against the kind of widespread concern for others that we noted brings substantial benefits to organizational dynamics and entire societies.

By too easily accepting cutthroat competition and "natural" ways of doing things as best - as opposed to recognizing the need, as some religions do, to some "natural" tendencies - they may be inclined to accept strife and conflict, including expensive legal squabbles or entrenched political positions and infighting as normal. Games and sporting events may also be designed primarily to create winners and losers rather than for education, health improvements, or building community. The natural tendencies for some spouses to be unfaithful will simply have to be accepted, as will the tendency for most people to be selfish. Similarly for people born with a quick temper, or into a dysfunctional family, or with poor resistance to diseases, or into a poor country - the list is endless — too often these things will be seen as natural events which must be accepted.

The assumption that a survival of the fittest atmosphere is natural and normal also deprecates other aspects of life. Schools can turn into places where only the strong survive instead of places where cooperative study habits allow "a rising tide (of knowledge) to lift all the boats." Divorce proceedings can degenerate into battles that leave children and family relationships permanently scarred. Excessive lawsuits add to the costs of insurance policies and the prices of products and services. Negative attack-oriented political advertising creates deep and persistent gulfs between political parties, preventing them from working harmoniously to pass needed legislation.

Science and reason as the answer

The tendency for secular belief systems to look to science and reason alone for the solutions to problems can also be a drag on development. Scientific solutions are possible only with respect to problems science is capable of recognizing and properly defining. And reason, like a road map, is unlikely to lead to the correct destination/conclusion if one is uncertain about the starting point, or is starting with incorrect assumptions. Scientific knowledge is of course extremely useful, but as history shows its accumulation and application are sometimes slow and more uneven than knowledge accumulated via moral intuition, ethical habits or religious heritage. Both science and reason can leave people confused and dejected for decades or centuries when they refuse to supplement their favored "way of knowing" with other paths to knowledge and truth.

And increasingly science finds its ideas and methods bumping up against the dead end of determinism – unable to conclude even that trust, honesty, and virtue, on the one hand, or evil and abhorrent behavior on the other, are anything more than biological or chemical processes; intellectually paralyzed about whether there is such a thing as a "will" or "change of heart" that could govern or radically alter human behavior; incapable (without religion) of explaining why one young man from the ghetto becomes a world-renowned brain surgeon while another becomes a sexual predator; doomed even to championing science methods when they are used by thugs to manipulate and destroy. The damage done by this will depend on how misguided the deterministic diagnoses and solutions turn out to be, and how dogmatic those holding these beliefs are. When they are inclined to use their power and influence to either squash or delay religiously-inspired problem-solving alternatives, development can be slowed appreciably. When science and reason are used to deprecate most other *ways of knowing* it can also be more difficult for people and nations to muster the sense of hopefulness that they need to change the course of their development history.

Combined effects of autonomy, materialism, and faith in science and reason

Although we have been focusing on the impact of individual secular beliefs, it is always a combination of beliefs that jointly determines economic outcomes. Perhaps the most gut wrenching example of this is how several of the core beliefs of secularism have combined to influence the Western world to rely primarily on mechanistic solutions to the AIDS problem. This can be seen best by following the plight of sub-Saharan African children victimized by AIDS. Plagued as much by misinformed parents and the absence of authentic global community as by a viral scourge, tens of millions of children under the age of fifteen had either lost their mothers or both parents to AIDS or were poised to lose them by the time the rest of the world began to pay attention at the beginning of the twenty-first century. In retrospect we can see how all three of the core beliefs of secularism, along with some corollary concepts - such as a propensity to rely on technological solutions, moral relativism, and a fear of being accused of cultural imperialism - contributed to this almost unimaginable AIDS epidemic and huge numbers of orphans. One reason for this is that well-meaning, "enlightened" (or politically correct when viewed from a secular Western perspective) bureaucrats waited far too long for "morally neutral" cures or vaccines to be developed which would fight the disease or allow people to live comfortably with it rather than admit (or better yet, declare) that some behaviors are simply more moral than others. While delays caused by a reliance primarily on technology gave the disease time to spread, weak-kneed relativism and fears of being accused of cultural imperialism simultaneously allowed enough misguided beliefs to persist (like the ideas that women are property, that sleeping with a virgin could cure an HIV infection, or that powerful people deserve special privileges) and the practices that flow from them (like widespread infidelity, the use of prostitutes and rape) to allow what eventually became an African pandemic. In addition to the heart-wrenching stories of suffering and dying people, cold hard numbers tell the truth about the economic effects: millions of orphans, millions of new AIDS cases year after year, and thousands of deaths every single day. Imagine the talent wasted when people die at an average age of forty-five (the U.N. projection for sub-Saharan Africa in 2010) when they should have lived to seventy or eighty or when young orphan girls are forced into prostitution or young boys turn to violence in order to survive. And absent either the religious beliefs or an education which ennobles and equips them to avoid evil, some go well beyond petty crime to engage in gang participation and the kind of child soldiering that has led to the senseless massacres of so many innocent victims that statisticians attempt only to estimate the numbers to the nearest hundred thousand.

How did it happen that educated people in wealthy Western nations were willing to spend 200 billion per year toward finding a scientific antidote to the physical ravages of AIDS and almost nothing on difficult religiously/culturally-based discussions about the communal impact of individual choices, what constitutes appropriate sexual conduct, and the need for moral limits to freedom, which together held the possibility of stopping the scourge in its tracks before it destroyed millions of people and their children and so much of the continent's potential? What kept the world from recognizing ten years earlier that morally-based solutions deserved as much or more funding as empirical studies and scientific/technological solutions? There is no good answer except to admit that a complex confluence of factors allowed this to happen, a number of which can be linked to secular values, attitudes, and beliefs that are in turn linked to each other and other values attitudes and beliefs in ways that no empirical study could ever discover.

One of these factors was secularism's narrow belief that reason and science applied to the material world is our best and perhaps only hope for solving problems. By focusing excessively on only one form of knowing, there will be much about a problem or solution that will be overlooked. Scientific solutions often take years of painstaking research, and there are often many bumps in the road in getting them to work because of the multifaceted nature of people and their behavior. In many cases, a few religious commandments, rigidly adhered to, can save people a world of trouble long before scientific solutions emerge. Scientifically-based treatments for HIV took many years and many billions of dollars to develop, and many more years to work through the difficult political, economic and social issues necessary to get the drugs to those who need them. The result was that twenty-five years after AIDS emerged; most of the victims who needed the drugs still did not have access to them. In the interim, new victims continued to emerge, and, as time went on more and more innocent spouses and children born to HIV infected mothers became victims. And, of course, drug-based solutions are much more expensive than religiously based ones – at this point in time they work only if people continue to take the drugs for the rest of their lives. Clearly secularism must accept its role in this tragedy - securely ensconced among the many other mistaken beliefs that contributed to the severity of the problem.

Unfortunately, the wall that secularism erects between religion and science has done much more than just slow the solution to complex moral/medical problems/diseases. Its full potential is not well understood unless we reflect on the kind of doors that are opened up when people are given free reign when determining what it true or right, or when attempts are made to pit science against religion. The German philosopher, Friedrich Nietzsche, hinted at this when he claimed in the late 19th century that "God is dead," and that "all of us are his murderers." He apparently was not trying to make a statement of fact; rather he is reported as intending to describe Western culture's plight in light of the general decline in the belief in God at the time and the implications of this for the complex system of morality and ethics tied to belief in God. The problem that Nietzsche's words foreshadowed, was perhaps best stated by Ivan, one of Russian novelist Feodor Dostoevsky's famous Karamazov brothers, when he said "if God is dead then everything is permitted." And it seems that already during the increasingly secularized 20th century almost everything - whether permitted or not - had come to pass. Hitler was not uninfluenced by Nietzsche or Ivan's dilemma - or the early 20th century eugenics movement that was spawned in well-regarded secular Western universities - when he experimented on Jews in the name of science and in clear opposition to all religious teachings to which he had been exposed. Nor were Lenin, Stalin and other Eastern Block "scientific socialists" who attempted to solve the problems of poverty and injustice primarily through reason and science - but ended up with societies where the poor were disenfranchised, the bureaucrats privileged, and the technology abysmal. Nor is the supposedly "enlightened" West in a position to claim that science and reason by themselves will make life better. Western science gave us land mines, cluster bombs, atomic bombs, and chemical and biological weapons. More recently our inability to appropriately constrain freedom has allowed the knowledge of these destructive technologies to spread around the world. Eminently capable of destroying in a matter of minutes capital that took decades to build up, it would be difficult to find a better example of the interplay between what people put their faith in and their ability to establish a flourishing economy.

Chapter 35: A Story of Secular Influences Gone Wrong

Shawn Jackson's story

Few people cared about Shawn Jackson, and even fewer purported to understand him. That Shawn had been costly to his family, neighborhood (Englewood), society and economy was a given. At the time of his incarceration, the estimated annual cost of protecting citizens from Shawn was estimated at somewhere between $25,000 and $50,000 per year, and while in prison Shawn did little productive work. But Shawn was certainly not alone. At that time nearly one of every thirty adult residents of the U.S. was either on probation, in jail or prison or on parole, and nearly 2.5 million were incarcerated. Even China, a nation often accused of putting people behind bars for little or no reason, had far fewer inmates, in spite of having a population four times as great.[1]

The mere mention of Shawn's name was as likely as not to cause deep shame to well up in his mother's heart, and tears to her eyes. When asked how Shawn ended up like this, all she could do was look down and shake her head. She had done her best, but it had obviously not been good enough, and sometimes it seemed that at almost every turn, someone or something had been working against her behind the scenes. The term "worldview" was not part of her vocabulary, and as a faithful member of the Apostolic Assembly Church, she was far more likely to attribute Shawn's sordid history to "the devil" than to the subtle influences of secularism. The devil notwithstanding, however, it is instructive to examine how four key tenets of secularism had inadvertently conspired with some of the beliefs of Shawn's ancestors (including his parents), and even his mom's church, to contribute to Shawn's demise and his mother's shame. Hindsight of course is 20/20, but it certainly seems plausible that turned loose from the constraining influences of family and church at an early age, it was the relentless drumbeat of the default beliefs of the 20th Century U.S. culture that had taken an already vulnerable child and both shaped and failed to shape him in ways that had destined him to walk down the paths he had taken. Shaping both his mind and heart, they influenced what he "saw" or didn't "see," heard or didn't hear, did and did not do. They influenced the radio frequencies and TV stations tuned into, the web pages clicked on, the music listened to, and a host of other choices that had made him into the man he had become. Collectively, these things had given Shawn a worldview fundamentally different from (and often opposed to) that of his mother.

How could seemingly reasonable things like a commitment to secularity (including separation of church and state), a life lived freely and autonomously, a not uncommon skepticism about spiritual things, and a faith in science and reason (over against spiritual things and religion) as the tools for solving life's major problems have contributed to making Shawn the person he had become? The answer can only come by noting what each of these had come to mean by the time Shawn was influenced by them, and how Shawn reacted to them. By the time Shawn was old enough to question his mother's values and embark on the process of developing his own, an ongoing march toward secularity in the U.S. had made it more likely that his life would be characterized by "freedom from religion" than "freedom of religion." Secular notions of freedom and autonomy had given Shawn not only the right but the inclination to declare, in William Henley's words, "I am the master of my fate; I am the captain of my soul."

Revelation

Shawn was clearly going to be the captain of his ship, if not his soul. Before his father had disappeared from his life, he had scared Shawn on many occasions and sometimes hurt him. Once Shawn stopped fearing authority, he felt little compulsion to obey it. Although the word autonomy was not part of Shawn's vocabulary, he actually knew more about it than he realized. His father had been aloof, hard to get close to, largely unconnected not only with Shawn, his mom, and the church Shawn's mom faithfully attended, but with extended family as well. When the church's pastor had reminded him of his family responsibilities (and/or asked him if he had ever considered making a marriage commitment to Shawn's mom and their children), he had simply disappeared, sometimes hiding "in plain view" and other times going missing for days or weeks. Although Shawn didn't know it at the time, his dad hadn't "officially" lived in the house Shawn and his mom lived in since Shawn was a baby because doing so would have made Shawn's mom ineligible for government benefits. There was widespread agreement at the time that poverty was an "income problem," related primarily to a lack of material resources, which could be rectified by sending single parents with dependent children regular support checks. Since Shawn's dad was employed most of the time (albeit in not very well-paying jobs), living in the same household with his family would have made them ineligible for support.

And although it had never occurred to Shawn at the time, recent conversations with his prison chaplain/counselor Phillip had made him wonder if his family's real poverty had been more emotional, intellectual (he never saw much use for school), or spiritual than material. It all started when Shawn had told Phillip how a drug dealer had recruited him, at the age of twelve, with a promise of easy money. To Shawn's surprise, this prompted Phillip to draw parallels between the worldviews of slave owners and drug dealers – both, he insisted, assumed "work was for slaves," that they were entitled to make easy money off the sweat of others, and that deception and intimidation were acceptable means of maintaining their way of life! Phillip also noted how large numbers of people - rich and poor, black and white, famous and obscure – seem to be able to live their lives in surprisingly contradictory ways, using as an example the millions of wealthy recreational drug users who express horror at the killing of innocent children in drug-gang crossfire but are incapable of connecting this to their illegal drug consumption. Shawn had never before thought of the people of his neighborhood as "enslaved" by drug dealers, nor had he thought about how drug violence depended on drug users who were capable of turning a "blind eye" to what was happening in the "distribution chain." But over time, Phillip's words enabled Shawn to see a lot of things he had not seen before. Somehow, somewhere, he had become lulled into believing that it was better to be served than to serve, better to be tough than gentle, better to be angry than forgiving. Other false assumptions had also seeped into his worldview, e.g. that the single mothers, absent fathers, high levels of criminal activity and incarceration rates – and the hopelessness to which these contributed – were primarily a function of economic status or skin color. And, because these thought patterns were reinforced by the very real racism Shawn had experienced, he had, over time, come to define himself primarily in terms of his race and economic status. But, most importantly, he was uncovering the connections between his view of the world and the kinds of decisions that had landed him in prison - decisions to take drugs, later to sell them, and eventually violently threaten and harm those who got in his way.

Moreover, the seeds that Phillip had planted and that roiled his thoughts as he lay sleepless on the cot fastened to the wall of his 12' by 6' cell had also sprouted in other ways. They had caused him to also start "seeing" his parents in a completely different light. His parents, he had come to understand, could not help but see the world through lenses partly shaped by those closest to them and their forebears, even forebears who preceded them by centuries. And although there were many wonderful things that had been passed down through his cultural heritage, there were two things he wished had not. Both his parents, he had come to conclude, suffered the ill-effects of intimidation and shame, as had his grandparents and many of those before them. The thinking patterns that had born this fruit, he now believed, had been rooted in the tribal cultures of distant ancestors, been magnified through successive generations by the horrendous experiences of slavery and discrimination, somehow emerging alive as part of his parents' worldview and child-rearing practices. On many occasions over the years he had experienced his father to be aloof (or absent), angry or intimidating. He had heard his mom label him "irresponsible," which seemed to fit well with his spotty work history and tendency to rely on drugs and alcohol. But it had been a revelation to him that his father's problems were most likely rooted in how he and others "saw" the world. Could it be that his actions had been rooted in a kind of fatigue born of a long wrestling match with feelings of inferiority, shame, a perceived inability to make meaningful choices, and ultimately hopelessness? Why not drink too much or do drugs, or otherwise seek immediate gratification if life has little meaning and seems likely to be brutal and short? Shawn had been there. This made some sense to him.

Shawn had also started wondering if his mother's pregnancy (with him) at age sixteen wasn't something more than simply the "mistake" that she had often dismissed it as. (Although in fairness to his mother, she had usually followed that comment up with another about how much she loved him.) How had she "seen" her world as a sixteen year old? Had her "mistake" really been more about an innate human need to feel loved or significant? How could she have not felt inferior with the ambiguous relationship she had had with Shawn's father, not to mention the trips to the "soup kitchen" that had resulted from his unpredictable and often selfish financial behavior? But it was here that Phillip's wisdom had opened up Shawn's mind to the more complicated picture. Could it be, in the same way Shawn's problems were connected to the misguided worldviews of drug users and dealers, that his mom and dad's problems (and economic failures) were as much related to the mistaken worldviews of other people as to their own cultural baggage? Why, for example, had the well-meaning people who drove in from the suburbs to staff the soup kitchen continued to provide meals to his mom and others under the assumption that everyone who came was needy? Why had they done all the cooking, and cleaned the place up without asking for help from the clients? Would his mom have been better served if she had been asked to help cook or clean up, or encouraged to get a job at the local fast food restaurant to earn the money needed to wean her family members from depending on the free meals? Perhaps the well-meaning folks in the soup kitchen saw his mom's material needs but not her need to develop a sense of significance through inclusion, accountability, work or helping others. Or perhaps they saw the world as divided neatly between "haves" and "have-nots," where it is often nearly impossible for the "haves" to see their own spiritual or relational poverty, or how they can perpetuate non-material forms of poverty even as they respond to material poverty.

And why, decades ago, did the government give his mom very little beyond money when Shawn's birth had qualified her for ADC (Aid to Dependent Children) payments? Was it because politicians and bureaucrats "saw" only her material needs and designed programs that reflected their own worldview preoccupations with material things, freedom and autonomy? Or, was it because administering such programs through churches rather than the government (since churches typically want to address character, relational and spiritual issues) would somehow violate separation of church and state? And why did the government penalize his mother and others like her by disqualifying her from assistance when she managed to accumulate a few assets with her meager income when, as Shawn had now come to understand, assets have the potential to improve people's discipline, management skills, and future orientation, while also shielding them from the problems associated with economic uncertainties? Is it because they were able to see her material poverty but not her "poverty of hope"?

It had become increasingly clear to Shawn that his enigmatic father and teenage mother had needed a whole bunch of things as much or more than money - the kind of judgment, discipline, accountability, and meaning in life that can engender hope, a sense of significance, and an orientation toward the future. His whole community had needed far more than welfare checks and high-rise "low-income" housing. They had needed, among other things, a shared moral code, jointly strong enough to turn the tide on family fragmentation and the scourges of drugs, alcohol and crime; to increase the prevalence of healthy work habits, financial management, entrepreneurial and business skills; and restore a sense of community. They had needed a government wise enough to keep the neighborhood safe, allow them to save money without being quickly disqualified from receiving temporary financial assistance, and to earn a paycheck without being quickly penalized with the loss of heath care coverage. In short, they had needed a neighborhood and nation that understood that a shortage of income is just the tip of the iceberg when it comes to poverty, and how the seven forms of capital interact to spur community development and the central role that worldview plays in the process. They had also needed to know that they couldn't afford to wait for government to solve their problems, because government was too impersonal and remote to properly diagnose their problems or know the full extent of their needs. Government had an important role to play, such as keeping the neighborhood safe, providing incentives for those closest to Shawn's family to help them, funding new skills training when the ebb and flow of the global economy causes temporary job loss, or making sure all children have educational opportunities - but it should never have been viewed as (and is incapable of being) the people's savior.

Shawn's education

Of course the seven forms of capital could not have been on Shawn's mother's mind, as she struggled to get by, but her son's education certainly was. She believed education could be Shawn's ticket to a better life, and thankfully the government saw it the same way – and was gracious enough to make one local school, Guggenheim Simon, free to any child in the neighborhood. Shawn had graduated, albeit with a few run-ins with authority. His mom had been hoping that she could send him to the Leo Catholic High School, rather than the local public high school, because it was rumored to do a good job of instilling discipline and good study habits in its students, both of which Shawn needed. But even though it was a reasonably priced private school, it became clear to her long before Shawn made it to the eighth grade that this was not an option. Of course it never occurred to her that the possibility of Shawn attending a Catholic school had been severely limited by innocent but ill-advised bureaucratic commitments to secularism that had been made long before Shawn's birth. The Catholic school was unaffordable, in part because some powerful politically-connected people somewhere had been convinced of the rightness of their idea that government funds should go only to "secular" and not "religious" schools. A whole funding structure had emerged from this which forced parents who wanted religious teachings integrated into their children' education to separately fund private schools even though they were at the same time legally obligated to fund the public schools through their property tax payments. Funding two school systems was simply out of the question for Shawn's mom (and most of her neighbors). This same perspective on religious beliefs carried with it another assumption - that schools should be organized around neighborhoods rather than around shared values, which had another important effect on Shawn's life. This meant the only school Shawn could attend would be funded locally through the assessment of property taxes on structures within the school district. And, as the neighborhood had declined over the years, the school district's finances had also deteriorated. Unfortunately for Shawn, ideas about how religious beliefs should or should not be integrated into education and its financing had, decades earlier, ensured that his only educational option would be a single public high school, and one which would increasingly be plagued by poor performance, pervasive pessimism, and horrendous dropout rates.

But it was not misguided secular beliefs alone that led to this situation. Shawn's mom had moved to Englewood to try to escape the crime and degradation of her previous neighborhood. At the time Englewood was populated by large numbers of Dutch and Polish people, who for whatever reason adhered to religious beliefs and practices that were wrapped up as much in their ethnicity as in the religious doctrines of their churches. Partly because of this, rather than welcome these new immigrants to the neighborhood with open arms, their first inclination was to circle the wagons and their second to exit for the suburbs, taking a large chunk of Englewood's economic activity with them - a migration that left Shawn's mom and dad, and his school, with a significantly reduced set of opportunities. But there were structural injustices working against Shawn as well. By tying property taxes to school funding decisions, bureaucrats had given the descendants of the European immigrants who had settled in Englewood decades earlier three additional reasons for quickly leaving: 1) a critical mass of people would be needed in the suburbs to be able to afford the religiously-based education they desired for their children, while also paying the property taxes that funded public education, 2) it would be best to leave before falling housing prices hurt them financially, and 3) even for those who preferred public education, it was best to leave before falling tax revenues lowered the quality of their children's education.

It would be a mistake, however, to conclude that financial difficulties related to school funding were the major explanation for the problems in Shawn's school. Leo and many other religiously-affiliated schools around the U.S. also experienced serious funding challenges. Many even had smaller per student budgets than Shawn's school - but fewer problems (and significantly higher test scores). What they did have, that Shawn's school did not was the ability to come together around a mission and cohesive set of shared values. In contrast Shawn's school had been surreptitiously bound to assumptions that a public school's goals and priorities be religiously neutral. This also meant it would be inappropriate to discuss spiritual things or permit prayer in the school. Of course those reluctant to part with the notion of a spiritual/sacred dimension to life were often still afforded a small space for their beliefs, but it would have to be a space separate from the material/ natural/practical world, and not particularly relevant to it. In Shawn's school this meant it remained acceptable to believe that religion could play a role in maintaining a moral order, but there was general agreement that spiritual and moral truths were personal, relative, and appropriately kept out of the public school and the public square. And even though some of Shawn's teachers retained personal religious commitments, they necessarily taught that logic and the pursuit of one's interests (individually and jointly), largely through scientific inquiry, were, by themselves, capable of ushering in the good life. This made the material side of life the main focus, and with spiritual forces out of the picture, people were viewed fundamentally as highly evolved animals caught up in a competitive jungle where the fittest survive, in a world that is basically on automatic pilot. Needless to say, this kind of thinking caused little tension with Shawn's view of the world, since he had experienced plenty hostility and insecurity both at home and in the neighborhood.

In the classroom this meant, for example, that it was okay for Shawn's science teacher to describe him as an advanced animal but not as uniquely created in the image of God; his social studies teacher could try to motivate him by linking education with financial success or fame, but could not mandate his best efforts because the Bible required this, or because he would someday have to give account to the God of the universe for his action or inaction. It was ok to teach that a person's self-esteem is a function of what she does (or produces), or has (including how she looks), but not that it comes from emulating the trustworthiness, humility or love of Jesus Christ. Over time, Shawn succumbed to this secular drumbeat, becoming convinced that his success depended not on the honesty, love, humility, or willingness to sacrifice that his mother and church had naively taught, but on a combination of personality, charm, "people" skills and a healthy dose of callous self-interest. Increasingly Shawn defined himself in terms of his color, his poverty and his academic and physical deficiencies, rather than his faith, character or moral code. The unintended effect of this was a gradual erosion in Shawn's morality, ethics and hopefulness; a significant reduction in the set of potential solutions to the problems plaguing his life; and the slow but steady insertion of a wedge between his mom's values and his.

Secular thinking had also contributed to the idea that it was OK for Shawn to be largely excluded from school sports activities because Shawn was not a particularly good athlete, and, after all, the goal of sport was to win. It had not really occurred to the administrators at Shawn's school that the primary purpose of sports might be to develop and care for one's body by getting regular exercise, or "building one another up" though joyful play. And the idea of suggesting that one should "honor God with [his] body because it "is a temple of the Holy Spirit"[2] was certainly not an option at a school committed to not advancing any particular religious teachings. To make matters worse, even the classroom had gradually shifted to a competitive place where the strong survived — in part because no one could come up with a good secular reason for why it needed to reflect the kind of sacred commitment to the children of friends and neighbors that would refuse to leave Shawn behind. In some times and places, of course, churches or other shapers of people's beliefs would have militated against this kind of degraded definition of community. But Shawn's mother's church and many other churches in the neighborhood seemed only too willing to accept the scaled-down role that had been assigned to them – as a refuge from their urban jungle rather than a transformer of it.

As Shawn grew older the emotionalism and insularity of his mother's church seemed more and more at odds with the messages he was getting in school and on the street. Besides, Shawn was free to do what he wanted, and he certainly didn't feel like he should have to cut his Saturday night carousing short so that he could be dragged out of bed to go listen to some pastor on Sunday morning. Occasionally he still felt some guilt when seeing his mother' disappointment, but this usually faded when he remembered how his biology teacher, Mr. Greenbriar, an obviously smart guy, had said that he expected advances in science, education and rationality to eventually extinguish the irrationality of religion. For Shawn, the assumptions of secularism had become a self-fulfilling prophecy. Well-meaning attempts to construct an education system characterized by freedom of religion had effectively melded over successive generations into a system free from many of the religious influences that could have countered the hopelessness that was part of Shawn's life, and offered him an alternative, potentially life-changing paradigm.

The impact of secular ideas about autonomy and freedom

There were many other things, beyond the structure of the educational system that had undermined both Shawn's mother's childrearing efforts and the school's effort to motivate Shawn. The elevation of freedom and autonomy to near-sacred status meant that Shawn's school and teachers could speak more readily to what kinds of behaviors ought not to be *prohibited* than to what behaviors ought or ought not to be practiced. The same was true for others in a position to influence Shawn. Not particularly good at sports, Shawn had learned to escape his world through movies and television at an early age, where powerful secular materialists in the entertainment industry were eager to share their worldview with him. Fixated on freedom and autonomy as morally neutral goals worthy of promulgation, they served up a disproportionate number of movies and television programs which subtly and not so subtly promoted the (perceived) benefits of these things, such as the freedom to shoot up the bad guys, thumb one's nose at authority figures, or have sex with whoever would consent as often as possible. By the time Shawn had become a young adult the seedier side of this industry had also spawned enough horror movies, pornography and violent video games to fill up Shawn's free time for years.

Secular values also influenced the many primetime investigative programs that Shawn has soaked up over the years. A common theme in these programs had been the use of slick technology (and of course intellectual prowess) to solve problems. However, no one seemed to notice, least of all

Shawn, that these programs focused almost exclusively on solving problems rather than how to prevent them in the first place. The worldviews of the producers and writers had simply not permitted them to see, or be interested in, for example, how inner-city Christian pastors were effectively transforming their communities, how conversion experiences had permanently altered the hearts and minds of former criminals, or how religious parents creatively struggled to fight off a cultural preoccupation with greed and violence in their efforts to raise God-fearing, loving, disciplined, and crime-free children. Even the news that Shawn occasionally watched had, over time, increasingly allowed sports, financial updates and sensational stories to crowd out important educational and moral messages without the slightest thought that they might be biased in what they had come to view as news. No stories about the nobility of ordinary, boringly-reliable working people who serve all of us day in and day out by making needed products at nameless, faceless companies around the world; too few stories about the importance of telling the truth, obeying parents, reigning in excesses, or delaying gratification. Other children in other places may have gotten these messages in other ways, but not Shawn. Once again, what was not said was just as influential as what was said.

The secular spin on freedom and autonomy that Shawn was picking up had also infiltrated the thinking of the other people who could have made a difference in Shawn's life. Neighbors and strangers, he had come to understand, were free to sacrifice for the good of the community (or not), to waste precious resource on drugs and alcohol (or not), to build civil society (or not). In the absence of moral accountability they were free to choose pro-development character traits like love, trustworthiness, honesty and humility (or not); free to choose friends, sex partners, and spouses based on what they could get from them rather than seeing these relationships as part of a sacred trust. In the absence of moral judgments about whether children need both a mother and a father, Shawn realized he had come to see himself as an autonomous individual not particularly connected to a tradition much beyond his relationship with his mother, moving fluidly through a jungle where people were free to be reverent or profane, polite or impolite, kind or intimidating, responsible or irresponsible - whatever fit their tastes. At times it had even seemed like the police were free to choose whether or not to risk their safety to protect people like Shawn and his neighbors. In such an environment disappointment and insecurity reigned; Shawn had thought these things had made him tough, but prison had given him a good counselor and a lot of time to reflect, and he now knew otherwise.

It is not difficult to argue that Shawn's life would have been better if there had been regular small constraints to his freedom and the freedoms of those around him early on rather than one big one (prison) later on, but there is little agreement on the best source of these constraints. Efforts to keep people from damaging themselves and those around them are quite quickly colored by religious overtones. For example, it can be argued pragmatically that sexual freedom should be restrained because it can lead to the being at the beck and call of a colicky infant, or being tied down by child support payments or a sexually transmitted disease. But it can also be viewed as a violation of God's principles for human relationships. It is a fair question to ask how religiously-motivated values like chastity, self-control, or the demonstration of Christ-like love might have changed Shawn's life – had they been given an equal opportunity to compete with secular values like success, accumulation, freedom or autonomy. The secular predisposition to relegate religiously based "moral" values to a quiet corner of life (outside of the school, business or government) dismissed this question more than it answered it. The result, for Shawn was a life very different than the life his mother had hoped for him.

The impact of secular ideas about wealth and the material world

Shawn's worldview had also been shaped by another consequence of individual autonomy. People had come to view wealth as the exclusive property of individuals rather than being recognized as something held in trust for the benefits of others. This opened the door to things like greed, poor stewardship and class divisions, with their attendant negative effects on neighborhood development. Some of those who had been financially successful had left the neighborhood for greener pastures; some others lived lavish lifestyles, seemingly oblivious to the possibility of using their assets to reduce their neighbor's poverty. A large segment of the business community had packed up and left with the previous residents of the neighborhood rather than make an effort to tough it out and change with the neighborhood. Those who stayed felt little guilt in doing whatever made them money, regardless of whether it was good for their neighbors, employees, customers or society. They were also all too willing to give people whatever they *wanted* (with little regard to what they needed, or what might be good for them), profiting handsomely from "goods" and "services" like cigarettes, drugs, alcohol, pornography, or prostitution.

Shawn's life and those of his neighbors had also been affected in more subtle ways by an overemphasis on money and material things. By the time he had been born, the government had come to be judged primarily on whether it makes people's lives materially better. Combined with individualism this fundamentally changed the political system to one where representatives were almost forced to do what is best for their local constituents rather than what is best for all of the people in the political unit, and public resources increasingly resembled a jar of Halloween candy where the person who quickly grabs a handful comes out ahead. As Shawn grew up, increasing middle class entitlements and "earmarks" found their way onto government budgets and Shawn's section of the city was not well connected politically. When legislation did get passed it often reflected the dominant worldview, which meant it often focused on providing middle-class secular solutions to perceived middle-class secular problems. Take, for example, the political discussions about minimum wages which took place on several occasions while Shawn was growing up. Worldviews fixated on the material have a tendency to reduce work to something that people do for money (rather than for its own sake). A presumption is made that if one is paid a low wage he or she is necessarily being exploited, even if an employer is spending several hours a day teaching the worker essential job skills and absorbing mistake-related costs during the internship period. The obvious solution is to offer a minimum wage, which may work in the suburbs where education levels and cultural habits allow for a business to continue to make a profit at that wage, but often doesn't work in a neighborhood where profit margins are smaller and potential entrants to the workforce need to be taught a host of job-related skills at the expense of their employers. Worse, such legislation can easily lead to the outsourcing of lesser-skilled jobs to low wage countries, increasing unemployment and underemployment in places like Shawn's neighborhood, making welfare payments and crime even more appealing as means of support.

Another problem with an excessive focus on material progress and material things that affected Shawn without his knowledge was the increasing inclination for people to believe that money and material things are the key to achieving happiness. This in turn caused people to become preoccupied with the kinds of things material objects can satisfy, such as comfort or security and the need to hoard material assets to protect against life's uncertainties and remain relatively oblivious to people's deeper needs. Combined with assumptions about individual autonomy, this lowered both their ability to see non-material needs and their willingness to help those with material needs. Increasingly Shawn's neighbors looked like poorer versions of the rich celebrities whose sordid lives were so famously splashed across both the TV and movie screens – spending their money on things that do not satisfy or improve families or future, often attempting to substitute money for what can only be purchased with love and time. In addition to the money wasted on cigarettes, alcohol or drugs, they unknowingly filled their lives with gadgets that subtly undermined their relationships. Microwave ovens, in spite of being wonderful inventions, made it possible for family members to eat individually and at different times; Multiple TVs not only increasingly isolated Shawn and other family members from each other, but they regularly emanated messages that undermined the values needed to hold the family together. Later on, computers and videogames not only brought destructive values into the privacy of Shawn's bedroom, but invited him into an often violent fantasy world where even his mom's call to dinner was an unwelcome interruption. All-the-while, investments in different kinds of things held great potential for increasing the wealth and wellbeing of Shawn's neighborhood – but those who could afford to make these investments, both rich and poor, were unable to clearly see the value of investing for the sake of others, or why these kinds of investments should be a higher priority for them than their own comfort, security, or entertainment.

Free at last

As time marched on - as it inevitably does in a 6' x 12' cell - Shawn knew that he would never again be able to see the world through the same lens that he had peered through as a young man. Thanks to the many examples Phillip had given Shawn from his own life and family, and the lives and experiences of other African Americans, he could now draw on a deep reservoir of examples of people who had managed to free themselves from the kind of worldview prison that had put him on the wrong path. These insights, coupled with the integrity of Phillip's life and the lives of those whose stories he had related, had changed Shawn's worldview dramatically. Shawn knew this was the case, in part because even though he had had nearly all his assumptions upended by Phillip, and was sitting in a prison cell, he nevertheless felt more in control over his life and freer than he had ever felt before. He still had anger – but it had been appropriately redirected to how and why another generation of young men still outside the prison walls had not been and likely would not be clearly confronted by the life-saving worldview options that had been there all along. But even his anger could never be the same – counterbalanced as it was by a profound sense of peace and the understanding that he was where he was because justice had been done. As he gently grasped the bars of his cell, Shawn wondered how he would explain to his mother how and why he had, in prison, come to feel freer and more appreciative of life than ever before. He decided it would be best to use terms she could understand and to keep it simple – He would simply let her know that he had accepted God's gracious call to be a follower of Jesus, like Phillip - and not just someone who had been "saved," but one who had become a disciple; one whose life would henceforward be devoted to reconciling people to God and to each other. He would work tirelessly to transform worldviews, relationships, structures and institutions - including the prison where he would likely spend the rest of his life – for the purpose of enabling people to flourish.

Chapter 36: Conclusion and Implications for the Future

Conclusion

This book has attempted to break new ground by carefully delineating how differences in inherited or chosen worldviews cannot help but lead people to construct significantly different ways of understanding the world - with profound economic consequences.   It has attempted to look at things that affect economic outcomes from the broadest possible interdisciplinary perspective. As noted in the Foreword, the original purpose of this book was to address the importance of civil society to healthy economic development.   But broad interdisciplinary research can take scholars down paths that are hard to backtrack from, and that has certainly been the case here.   Indeed, evidence of the impact of people's worldviews to economic outcomes seemed to be lurking around every corner.   Nor could the fact that people's worldviews seem to coalesce around fundamental religious or secular beliefs be ignored.   Long story short: healthy economic outcomes require a critical mass of people who believe and live in a way that leads to productive rather than unproductive economic activity.

Because of the complexity of the relationships, it may be best to simplify by comparing development to a meal prepared by a skilled chef.   An optimal outcome requires the correct *ingredients*, such as vegetables, meats, or spices; the best *equipment and techniques*, such as cookware, stirring, or heat; the right mix of *objectives and values*, such as an appreciation for color, taste, and nutrition; and, perhaps most importantly, a love for food, cooking, and bringing joy to hungry people.

Even more so than with cooking, there is much about the art and science of economic development that is neither obvious nor easy to explain.   Navigating the maze of connections between belief systems and economic outcomes often required backing away from "conventional wisdom," putting aside biases and misconceptions (to the degree that this is possible), separating real influences from apparent, major from minor, and being open to new ways of thinking.   Most of all, it required going well beyond the discipline of economics to discover the rich variety of assumptions, attitudes, choices and actions (or inactions) that jointly determine economic outcomes. In this process, we learned that a healthy economy needs lots of people who can sense that things are not as they should be, and passionate about improving things. It needs people who are passionate about uncovering and telling the truth, and willing to take responsibility for their actions. It needs parents who know how to raise productive, ethical, optimistic children, regardless of whether they live in poverty or luxury, aided by a government that knows how to keep kids safe and foster good schools. A healthy economy needs households that borrow and consume wisely, volunteers who serve willingly, and governing officials who are far more interested in justice than personal advancement. It needs investors who are both patient and wise, and willing to risk their wealth for the uncertain and sometimes slow payback associated with turning good ideas into functioning products and services. It needs business people who are more interested in serving their customers, employees and communities than in getting rich quick or profiting at the expense of others. It needs people capable of choosing things like love, patience and humility over revenge, greed and pride. It needs people who can distinguish good from evil, and who accept the fact that the potential for evil lurks not only in those who are unlike them, but also in themselves and the institutions and processes that they design to handle their affairs. And ultimately, it needs people who choose good over evil.

Eventually, we borrowed a term from President George Bush Sr. - "a thousand points of light" - to refer to the innumerable little things that contribute to a healthy economy. We then attempted to bring order to these "points" by constructing a model - the Development Wheel – designed to visually communicate both the big picture of development and the many variables that make up that picture. It was our desire that the model address not only explain differing economic outcomes at the country level, but also at a variety of other levels, such as among individuals, organizations, neighborhoods, or ethnic and religious diaspora. It was also our desire that the model be effective in highlighting impediments to development in all kinds of countries, regardless of income level, history, geographic location, or whether they have traditionally been classified as "developed," "developing," "2/3s world," "emerging," "post-communist," or something else.

The Development Wheel picture that emerged focuses on the need to assemble adequate amounts of seven essential ingredients for development, which we referred to as *seven forms of capital*. We also described *seven techniques* for accumulating each of these forms of capital, two critical catalysts, *civil society and entrepreneurship*, and two things that power the wheel – *freedom and communications systems*. We also attempted to bring order to the impact of worldview by distilling *seven key "pro-development worldview elements,"* that must be at the core of the wheel for healthy capital building to take place. Most importantly, however, we illustrated throughout how the development process is tied to the religious and/or secular attitudes and beliefs that underlie the worldviews at the center of the wheel.

The key role of worldview is easiest to see when reflect on how a wheel ceases to function properly when it has a rotten core. Take, for example, the seven kinds of capital needed for development.

Each has the potential for good, but an equal potential, if misdirected, to do harm. Intellectual capital, for example, can be used positively to invent and build, or negatively to creatively torture people or bilk them out of their life savings. Financial capital can be bequeathed to spoiled children to fund outrageous spending habits and fantasy fulfillments, or entrusted to well-managed, accountable companies or NGOs that are dedicated to producing needed products and services (like computers, libraries or hospitals) or solving difficult problems (like local, regional or world peace). Physical capital (for example, vaccines, dams, weather radar, or computers) can be designed and used to protect or inspire people, preserve property, or enhance productivity. But it can also be employed to take advantage of or even destroy people, or waste their time or resources. And, the impact of a rotten core is perhaps most obvious with government capital. Depending on the predominant worldview, government officials may tolerate bribery, extortion, nepotism, corrupt police forces and judges, or demand meritocracy and justice. They may encourage the wide distribution of accurate information, or impede or distort it. They may protect and empower the innocent and disadvantaged, paving the way for all people to access all forms of needed capital, or erect barriers that allow predators, in both the private and public sectors, to take advantage of the vulnerable. They may provide incentives for healthy risk taking, savings and investment, and wisely steward a public nest egg to protect the citizenry against future downturns, or they can deceptively saddle future generations with debt in order to ensure their reelection and cover up their wanton spending habits. They can use their power to destroy millions of lives, or feel guilty and remorseful for even minor violations of the public's trust.

The Development Wheel's seven techniques for building up capital, its two catalysts - civil society and entrepreneurship, and the two things most responsible for turning the wheel - efficient communication systems and freedom, also depend on worldview. In the absence of appropriate core values, an endowment or inheritance of any kind of capital can degenerate into a license to waste or exploit: savings can degenerate into hoarding; investing into greed and fear; frustrations with environmental depletion into vandalism and sabotage. Similarly, entrepreneurship and innovation are beautiful things, but successfully designing and marketing chemical weapons, cluster bombs, IEDs, or the books, web pages, or movies that inspire their proliferation and use is anything but beautiful. Nor can civil society be achieved in the absence of an appropriate worldview. Transparency can range from a blessing to a curse, depending on who is demanding transparency, why they want it, and what they plan to do with the information gathered. So too with participation: more is not better if it leads, for example, to the kinds of duplication of effort that could be avoided when people can and do routinely trust others to faithfully exercise their agency responsibilities. Even a commitment to peaceable change can be counterproductive if it makes people incapable of identifying, confronting, and stopping evil because they are opposed to the use of force in any and all situations.

Chapter 36

The same could be said for fluid communication systems and freedom that power the wheel. Both can be great for development, when helping a smooth, round wheel to accelerate, but disastrous if the wheel is rough or misshapen. Freedom is essential to a healthy economy, but no economy can afford unlimited freedom to do unproductive things, such as abusing one's body or mind, eschewing savings, spending beyond ones means, wasting resources or taking advantage of others. So too with modern communication systems: smartphones, the internet, Facebook and Twitter are all as capable of facilitating bad ideas, scams, spam, and government overreach as they are good news, life-giving advice, creative thoughts, or collaborative work efforts.

In spite of this overwhelming evidence of the importance of worldview, we recognized that not everyone accepts that religious beliefs significantly influence worldviews. This required that we backtrack a bit to deal with religion as it is, rather than how it is often stereotyped to be. This meant not assuming that the religions of the world are mostly about whether or not there is a God, or primarily about ritual behaviors or the afterlife. It also meant not assuming that they have nothing to learn from or to say to science, that they are interchangeable with each other, or that they ought to be practiced only privately, or can be separated from the more "secular" aspects of life. But it also meant not affording religious beliefs the privilege of being off limits to constructive criticism. Hard questions needed to be asked: Does a particular belief system indoctrinate or transform its adherents? Does it foster ritual obedience, or consumptive activities aimed at placating fickle deities, or deep understanding and literacy? Does it place more emphasis on holy places or transformative ways of thinking? Does it foster escapism or hard work and problem solving? Pessimism or optimism? What does it reject as evil or encourage as good? Does it encourage a thirst for knowledge and wisdom? Does it provide guidance about the ordinary things of life, such as healthy male/female relationships, or healthy parenting? Does it recognize the fundamental value of each person or dismiss large numbers of people as inferior? Does it have the mechanisms needed to replace potentially destructive emotional responses such as jealousy, anger or the desire for revenge with responses like self-control, mercy, forgiveness or reconciliation? Does it have the moral integrity not to look the other way when innocents are slaughtered, parents sell their children into prostitution, people spam and scam the elderly and vulnerable, or pamper themselves with what can only be described as orgies of material and sensual excess? Does it encourage enough sharing to enable all people to have their basic needs met and develop? Does it tolerate or encourage embedded corruption or foster transparency, participation or shared authority? Does it encourage or discourage entrepreneurship, freedom or communication? Does it place appropriate restraints on freedom or authority? Is it static and unchanging, or vibrant and evangelistic?

When attempting to answer these questions it became clear not only that different belief systems differed remarkably, but that some offered very little guidance on questions that are very important to development. It also became clear that the answer to these questions depended on how people answer more fundamental questions such as: Is there a God (or gods), and if so what is He (or they)

374

like? What is the nature of reality? What is the purpose of one's life? How should one relate to the people and things she sees around her? How should one distinguish right from wrong? It also became clear that it should not be assumed that the beliefs associated with organized religions rest only on faith, or that secular belief systems rest only on science and reason. Rather, one needs to investigate the core tenets of both "religious" and "secular" belief systems and their impact on the things that matter to economic development. Ultimately what should matter to those interested in economic outcomes, is whether the object of people's worship, be it Shiva, Jehovah or spirits that lurk in trees or rivers, or rock stars, movie stars, or sports heroes, is truly able to satisfy people's deepest needs and lead them down a path that promotes human flourishing.

To test drive our model, we focused on two particularly economically-influential belief systems, Christianity and secular materialism, and illustrated how their core beliefs affect economic development, both theoretically and through stories illustrating their impact on people's lives. From an economic perspective, both belief systems have positives and negatives, largely because they both represent comprehensive views of the world that are unavoidably subject to differing interpretations. But we also noted that some expressions of Christianity, particularly those that make the holistic Biblical vision for life widely accessible, which includes but it not limited to the Protestant expressions that intrigued Weber and Tocqueville more than a century ago, seem to have more potential to promote human flourishing than secular belief systems. There are many reasons for this, including that their core teachings are easy to understand, widely applicable, widely accepted and shared, and, for the most part, mandates for which one is accountable, rather than mere suggestions. They are also fundamentally optimistic ("good news") and thus spread naturally and voluntarily. Of course, none of these might be an advantage to economic development except for the fact that Bible is infused with commands to "develop talents," "work heartily," "forgive others," "live in unity," "respect government," "refuse bribes," "heal the sick," "love enemies" – and a host of other economically productive attitudes and behaviors that have led to natural risk-taking, ethical behaviors and institutions, global trust networks, peaceful transitions, and a variety of other economically positive outcomes. And although these same kinds of things may be recommended by secularists, they are unlikely to be adhered to or to motivate as broadly or deeply both for the reasons already mentioned and because, to repeat John Stuart Mill's words, "mere preferences" have nowhere near the power of beliefs that carry eternal significance.[1]

This point can be made clearer by making an analogy between healthy development and an excellent orchestra. A group of unconnected musicians, with individually tuned instruments, no particular director, little agreement on the score to be followed, many of whom are also unconvinced of the spiritual potential of beautiful music, and who are performing for people with widely-varying tastes, will find it difficult to make beautiful music or satisfy the audience. On the other hand, a collection of people responding to a Master Director, who together tune their high-quality instruments, practice tirelessly, and work "in concert" because they know they are performing for "the King" have the potential to produce a very different kind of music. In other words, in spite of the imperfections of Christians, it is not hard to see that those with the holistic worldview described above might be far more at home in such an orchestra than most secular materialists. It is also not a stretch to think that they might be more at home in an economy marked by *shalom*. Indeed, this is already well known from the research cited in Chapter 11, the history of economic activity associated with certain Christian traditions, and the remarkably-transformative work done by Christian relief, development and service agencies around the world.

All of this argues not for isolating religious beliefs, but for recognizing that transformative beliefs may be one of the most valuable resources for developmentally deprived areas to import. It also argues not the marginalization of religious beliefs in the public square, but rather for recognizing the fundamental importance of their input for economic thinking, development strategy, and a wide variety of economic, social and public policy decisions. Mostly it means that good long-term sustainable development must be preceded by serious public conversations that penetrate to the worldview level, because people are most motivated and productive when they can act on the deepest desires of their hearts, and because economic outcomes, like political and social outcomes, will be good only when hearts are oriented in the right direction. It is no surprise that there is a strong correlation between the countries that rank high in religious freedom and those that rank high in economic freedom.[2] Of course, bridging the culture gaps between Islam, Christianity, Secular Materialism, Atheism and other belief systems will never be easy. It is far more difficult work than making ourselves comfortable, amusing ourselves, accumulating toys, or pontificating on radio talk shows. But in the same way that a sacrificial investment of time or money in the present can lead to far more valuable future benefits, so too the hard work of studying, understanding, discussing and debating the assumptions and key tenets of both secular and religious belief systems offers the potential of remarkable dividends in the future.

These dividends, however, go well beyond the impact of a worldview reorientation on the many individual "points of light" discussed earlier; they extend to the creation and structuring of institutions, and the methods by which this is done, e.g., communally, from the bottom up, or authoritatively, from the top down. Oddly enough, this may in fact be the area in which the Protestant Reformation has had the most impact on the global economy. By putting the Bible in the hands of the common people, it initiated a centuries-long process wherein people were forced to wrestle, from the bottom up, with the nature and structure of authority within and among the various building blocks of a society – such as the individual, family, church, school, business, or government. And, it was precisely this process that led key theologians, philosophers and politicians in many Northern-European Protestant countries and the U.S. to conclude that each of these different spheres of society was uniquely called and gifted by God to perform certain tasks, and accountable directly to God for performing these well - and therefore ought not to exceed the limits of its authority by dominating or oppressing other spheres. In the ensuing years these countries distinguished themselves economically, but this is not to say that the process of figuring out how to justly apportion and limit authority was not messy. With some European experiments with pluralism, the clergy for all practical purposes became civil servants, controlled by the state. But in the U.S., religious pluralism fared better, even though there was sporadic pressure in the colonies to establish official religions and, later, after constitutional protection of religious freedom was established, regular attempts to elevate secularism to the equivalent of an established religion. In spite of these things, the American experiment radically changed the nature of both the church and the state in ways that were to have dramatic economic consequences. Churches grew, split, reconstituted, and even reversed themselves in an ongoing and endless attempt to better accomplish the primary things that churches are called to do. Government rejected the idea of an official church and concentrated most of its efforts on figuring out its primary function — upholding justice by establishing a rule of law that included protecting freedom of religion (and other freedoms that are intertwined with it) while simultaneously attempting to define and defend the boundaries between the various spheres of society - so that no group (including government) could easily overstep the bounds of its authority. And, although numerous mistakes were and continue to be made, this process eventually led to the establishment of structures, processes, and a version of civil society that for the most part allows people to bring their religious beliefs to bear on the problems they wish to solve, the organizations they create, and the economic decisions they make. And, in spite of the erosion of freedom of religion in recent decades, a significant percentage of the U.S. population has still not lost sight of one very important thing — if governments can figure out how to allow religious and secular beliefs equal access to people's minds and hearts, and to the public square, these beliefs become far more accessible to people whose worldviews could most benefit from an overhaul, and consequently, have far more potential to promote human flourishing.

This accomplishment is far more important than people realize, in part because the history of improvement in the global economy is the story of repeatedly exposing people to new ways of thinking and doing things, and making it possible for best ideas and practices to carry the day. Early on, traders brought natural resources from places where they had less value to places where they had more value. In many cases people also moved freely to improve their economic opportunities. When governments placed barriers to the movement of resources and people, businesspersons found ways to imbed labor and materials into products that could be exported to places where they were valued at significantly more than the cost of these inputs. When the movement of physical goods was hindered, people moved money (financial capital) and know-how (intellectual capital) to profit from the value that these forms of capital brought to others. The final step in this process is for the nations of the world to benefit from the free movement of governmental, social and spiritual capital, the three forms of capital most closely tied to worldview and most heavily dependent on religious beliefs and the ethical systems that flow from them.[3] Globally, this final exchange is in its infancy, but holds at least as much if not more promise to improve human flourishing as the free movement of resources, labor, finished goods, and money combined.

Implications for the future

The real question, then, is not about how to dampen all religious passions, or how to draw lines between secular and religious, or how to deal with religious people in public life, but to recognize the inherent religiosity of people and the impossibility and mistakenness of trying to force them to divorce their beliefs from large swaths of life. It is not government's role to argue whether there is one God, multiple gods or no God, but it is government's job to structure freedom of religion into things like education, politics, business or civil society in a way that gives people the opportunity to see and experience how much of a difference the object of people's worship can make in their lives. This includes structuring the public square in such a way that people with diverse beliefs find themselves welcomed into important conversations, *and* structuring it in a way that effectively mediates these beliefs. This means, for example, structuring an education system that both recognizes the importance of religion but refuses to favor a particular belief system, either religious or secular. This by necessity means giving students and parents choices that go well beyond government-sponsored "secular" schools, since the full impact of religious beliefs on the values, attitudes, goals and behaviors of teachers and students can only be seen when schools to have the freedom to organize around a particular worldview. In the long run, this kind of freedom has the potential to take the focus off of inherent differences among people, like race, gender, nationality, or geography, and put it on differences tied to worldview – which are not only more important but more capable of being bridged over time. This also opens the door to a diminishing focus on rigid demarcations between nations and people groups and an increased focus on how people can cross racial, ethnic and political boundary lines to form true communities from the bottom up. Indeed, some racially or internationally-connected religious communities already give good evidence of this.

It should be clear from the previous discussion that it would be a serious mistake to say that the government has no significant role to play in education. It needs to make it affordable (perhaps by giving parents vouchers to partly or completely cover the cost of education at the school of their choice). It also has the right to influence that part of the curriculum that is essential to equip and motivate the next generation to fully and peacefully participate in the polity. To do this government must also be busy outside of the education system – looking for creative ways to build civil society and preserve the unity of the polity by encouraging frequent interactions among people with diverse worldviews. If it does these things well, people will be more inclined to question the wisdom of their own beliefs, religious or secular, and the temptation to force them on people, and more inclined to engage in the hard work of both listening and clearly communicating their beliefs to others in the hope that they might be absorbed by willing hearts and bring lasting benefits. This will allow fundamental beliefs to be continuously reshaped and will give ideas and beliefs that have integrity the best opportunity to spread from the ground up. It will also allow the citizens of a country (and the world) to increasingly come together to address fundamental problems rather than just the symptoms of these problems, thus removing the most important barrier to development and greatly increasing the prospects for human flourishing.

It should also be noted that with this approach there is no need to deprecate a particular belief system, or give inordinate attention to a belief system that seems to be particularly troublesome, like radical Islam. Rather, we need to simply acknowledge the critical role of religious and secular beliefs, put them front and center, and begin to aggressively seek the truth about the differences these beliefs make in things that are essential to economic outcomes (and pay attention to the research that has already been done in this area - some of which has been cited throughout this work). To do this in a way that will be useful, however, we need to stop stereotyping religious and secular groups, or aggregating nominal believers with true believers. We cannot pretend that the differing beliefs of Sunni or Shiite Muslims, Protestant or Orthodox Christians, or atheists and agnostics are insignificant. Nor can we pretend that one belief system has nothing to learn from the others, or that beliefs can be separated from the rest of life or confined to a dark corner of the academy. Rather, we would have to study them carefully enough to begin to organize them into homogeneous groups and sub groups. Once this is done, there are many useful and interesting questions that can be asked by researchers for the purpose of uncovering the truth about the relationship between religious and/or secular beliefs and economic outcomes. For example,

- How do wealth income levels, or unemployment rates, or rates of change in these measures differ between these groups?

- How do these groups differ in economically-relevant moral behavior? E.g. how do these groups differ in tax evasion, or crime or fraud rates, savings or loan repayment rates? How do they differ in drunk driving or drug use convictions, out-of-wedlock births, divorce rates, or rates of sexually transmitted diseases? In standardized test scores, graduation rates, entrepreneurship, or involvement in civil society organizations?

- How to these groups differ in economically-relevant attitudes? E.g., how do they differ in attitudes toward forgiveness, corruption, or the use of violence; or in their openness to government property monopolies, or the degree to which economies are centrally planned?

- How do various economic measures differ in, e.g., predominantly Catholic, Protestant, Orthodox or Atheistic countries? To what degree does a change in the religious makeup of a country's population correlate with changes in measures of economic outcomes?

- How do economies perform before and after significant changes take place in law or the enforcement of law related to freedom of religion?

Understanding that worldview is at the core of economic wellbeing also means we need to completely rethink where the vulnerabilities in the global economy come from. Could it be that a lack of compassion among the privileged classes had left the poor with insufficient resources or opportunities, causing the economy's actual output to fall well below its potential output? Could it be that greed and a disregard for stewardship are depleting natural capital and compromising the future productivity of the economy? Is impatience causing alternating periods of overspending and deleveraging, or self-centeredness skewing consumption toward non-necessities, causing the business cycle becomes more volatile than it should be? Could it be that hitching our fortunes and economic policies to a "value free" measure of output like GDP, risks missing many of the things that are actually the most essential to a healthy economy?

As this book goes to press, the world stands at both a moral and economic precipice. The global recession that began in 2008 made it clear that both wealth and income are ultimately tied to the promises people make. Trillions of dollars of wealth, and the jobs and income that accompany them, evaporated as it became clear that bankers had come to the point that they were willing to make loans that might not be repaid, as long as they would not have to bear the loss. Additional trillions disappeared when we realized that millions of people could and would walk away from commitments to pay back the money they had borrowed. Trillions more disappeared when we realized that even some of our political representatives had become willing to make promises that would be tough to keep, or worse, might walk away from their obligations to repay because they were unwilling to make the sacrifices necessary to keep their word. The economy, it turned out, was only as strong as the integrity of the commitments and institutions supporting it, and it appeared that those commitments and institutions had changed in fundamental ways. Promise-keeping, it appears, had become optional not to just a few but to many. One conclusion that could be drawn from this is that promise-keeping is not a top priority for the gods that many people are choosing to follow. Not only did these gods fail to save, they led their followers, and many others to the edge of a precipice.

People's values, attitudes, goals and actions, including whether they trip and fall or are able to back away from the edge of the precipice, flow ultimately from the God or gods they choose to follow. These choices influence whether they even notice the problems that needs fixing, whether they recognize their scope and seriousness, and the degree to which they feel compelled to fix them. They influence whether people are inclined to take the easy way out or the hard path of integrity, and whether they are willing to compromise or sacrifice for the well-being of other people or nations or future generations. They influence what people expect from their authorities and their ability to recognize the limits of their capabilities for tinkering with a global economy that affects the lives of billions of people. The God or gods they follow will ultimately determine if they have enough love and patience to risk the time, effort and even danger associated with addressing issues and problems at the worldview level.

Assuming the world learns well that one of the most significant impediments to a healthy economy has been people's inability or unwillingness to recognize the role of worldviews, we need not fear for our economic future. Market economies are resilient. They have the ability to supply what is demanded quite effectively and on fairly short notice. If people develop the moral will to redirect their resources from largely selfish and individualistic pursuits toward doing the hard work of understanding other people's perspectives, defining and combatting evil, protecting the environment, pursuing global justice, and peaceably contending for the kinds of beliefs that call people to their highest human possibilities, the global economy will respond relatively quickly in this direction. It may happen that a heightened focus on interfaith dialog puts a temporary lull in the global economy as it lowers the amount of "toys" and material goods that circulate, but it need not permanently shrink it. Rather, its composition will change, as heightened interaction between people at the educational, philosophical theological, and services level replaces some consumption of material goods. Less time and resources will be devoted to replacing things that are destroyed or discarded for no good reason. People will retrain, schools and factories will retool, money will move, and fundamentally different kinds of goods will be produced and services performed. And regardless of how long it takes or how much it costs, with a healthy dose of agape love and the generosity that it inspires, the global economy should be able to handle the transition. If this process prevents a reoccurrence of the kind of injustices and atrocities that have happened in many if not most of the countries of the world at some point in time, and greatly reduces the number of hungry, thirsty, sick, underemployed and discouraged people, we will not have given up nearly as much as we will have gained. True and sustainable economic development will have been ushered in on an unprecedented scale.

Endnotes

Chapter 1

[1] In this case the word capital is used to indicate the amount of owner money invested, and at risk in the business. However, the word capital has many meanings depending on the context, and most of the time in this book the word will be used in a context that require a broader definition, which, per wordnetweb.prineceton.edu, is "assets used in the production of further assets."

[2] Ponzi schemes refer to a variety of financial scams when promoters use funds from later donors to pay handsome returns to earlier donors, which makes earlier donors, who are usually unaware of the scheme, willing promoters, thus allowing the scheme to perpetuate itself. Often there is no legitimate business activity underlying the scheme.

[3] Proverbs 28:19, Bible, New International Version

[4] I Timothy 6:9, Bible, New International Version

[5] The term wealth (which we will later show to be interchangeable with the term capital) is used throughout this work because it needs to be carefully considered along with traditional forms of income (like GDP) when planning or assessing development, because little or nothing can be produced in the future without some accumulation of wealth in the present (a relationship which will be unpacked throughout the book. For now we will simply define wealth as an accumulation of many different kinds of resources that are needed to engage in productive activity.

Chapter 2

[1] The term civil society will be appropriately unpacked in Chapter 18. For now, we will simply note that the term has become the preferred way of referring to an *independent* sphere of activity or a group of mediating institutions that is not only separate from the government and the economy, but guards against political or economic domination. by serving as a vehicle for bottom up voluntary communal problem-solving efforts.

[2] The Hutu-Tutsi conflict has flared up frequently over the decades, and especially since the 1950s when Belgium lost control of the area in Central Africa that the two ethnic groups come from. Originally come from Ethiopia, the Tutsis had arrived in Rwanda after the Hutu had come from Chad, but ended up with greater wealth and social status, causing class conflict. Eventually Hutu's gained political power in both Burundi and Rwanda, prior to a suspicious plane crash in 1994 that killed the Huto leaders of both countries and triggered the Rwandan genocide.

[3] Transcript of "An Interview with N.R. Narayana Murthy" *YaleGlobal*, 5 June 2006, http://yaleglobal.yale.edu/display.article?id=7509.

[4] As reported by Britain's Department for International Development.

[5] As reported in an interview given to a *World Magazine* reporter in June of 2006.

[6] We use the term secularist at this point to describe people who believe that life can, for the most part, be separated into distinct segments – religious and secular. As such, this group will contain atheists, agnostics and members of a variety of religious groups who are non-the-less comfortable with this kind of perspective on religion. Later we will give due consideration to the varying perspectives within this group.

Chapter 3

[1] This data comes from several articles over a period of years. The first article referenced is "Sioux County Shows the Way," *The Des Moines Register*, July 11, 2004, Sunday Opinion Section, page10. The article cites the source of the statistics as the Iowa Agricultural Statistics Service (2003). The number of farms comes from the 2002 Census of Agriculture.

[2] See "Iowa morality meter," by Mike Kilen, Des Moines Register, February 6, 2005, Sunday Opinion Section, Page 10.

[3] See http://www.countyhealthrankings.org

[4] Christopher J. L. Murray, et;. al., *Eight Americas: Investigating Mortality Disparities across Races, Counties, and Race-Counties in the United States,* PLOS Medicine (2006).

[5] Alexis-Charles-Henri Clérel de Tocqueville was a French historian/writer/political thinker who was sent to the United States in 1831 to study the American prison system. He traveled around the U.S. for nine months observing all aspects of American society, which he eventually published in the book *Democracy in America* in 1835.

[6] But, unfortunately, most of the attention has been given to ethnicity, because Census figures did not record religious or denominational affiliation during the period of time that these religiously-based enclaves would have been easiest to define.

[7] An excellent synopsis of findings related to this subject is available in Robert P. Swierenga's presidential address to the Agricultural Historical Society which is published in *Agricultural History* 71, Fall, 1997.

Chapter 4

[1] http://upload.wikimedia.org/wikipedia/en/d/d5/National_net_worth_per_capita_top100_PPP_2000.gif

[2] Wealth of nations is actually three books combined into a single larger volume. Following the commonly used translations of Smith's work, we will refer to them as "books within a book." For example, in referring to it we will refer to the first part of the book as his "first book," the second part as his "second book," and the last part as his "third book

Chapter 5

[1] As defined by Merriam-Webster.com: An economic system developing during the decay of feudalism to unify and increase the power and especially the monetary wealth of a nation by a strict governmental regulation of the entire national economy usually through policies designed to secure an accumulation of bullion, a favorable balance of trade, the development of agriculture and manufactures, and the establishment of foreign trading monopolies.

[2] See Buchholz, pg. 301.

[3] This is not to say that wealth should not be shared with those in need, but only that some people will do far more productive things with surpluses than others.

[4] Smith's focus on the importance of saving became a lynchpin of economic development research. An early focus was the importance of savings and investment and a nation's ability to finance the buildup of physical capital, research and development, and technology. Capital-to-output ratios were employed on the assumption that putting physical capital in place would fairly directly lead to increases in measures of output and employment in subsequent years. These discussions often assumed that governments were playing a major

role: host (developing country) governments by determining which infrastructure projects received highest priority and by supplying local labor; donor or lender (developed country) governments and international agencies by closing financing gaps and by providing needed expertise. Later, as far too many projects failed to bring about desired results, often because of economic and political instability, more attention was given to governments' ability or inability to "absorb" capital and manage the macro-economy and maintain political stability during the time periods allotted for the development projects.

[5] Laws of *primogeniture* gave extraordinary property inheritance privileges to first-born males, while *entails* insured that these benefits continued indefinitely.

[6] See Sung-wook Nam's "Chronic food shortages and the collective farm system in North Korea" in the Journal of East Asian Studies| January 01, 2007.

[7] The history of modern commercial activity bears this out, since, when buyers are given many merchants to choose from, companies that serve buyers poorly do not thrive.

Chapter 6

[1] We assume, quite reasonably, that the company is competing with other companies and therefore must pay the "going rate" for raw materials and good workers, etc. so that its profit reflects good management. If the company is in reality cutting corners or mistreating suppliers, workers, or customers, it will pay (via a decrease in its business) for these mistakes, its projected future profits will drop, and its stock price will go down.

[2] These fears will drive some people or companies to borrow money in order to make purchases before prices go up, and makes savers more reluctant to tie up (lend) their money. This increase in the demand for funds in the financial markets, coupled with a restriction in the supply, will raise interest rates.

[3] This is not to say that it is only ethics that drive stock prices. U.S. stocks, for example, skyrocketed in the 1990's as inflation and interest rates dropped, and as global competition, improved management techniques, the application of ever-cheaper telecommunications and computer technology, and fortuitous increases in the supply of key raw material inputs, such as oil, kept costs down and improved productivity. These same developments caused companies' profits to go up, which gave them additional opportunities to gain efficiencies and market power by combining with or acquiring other companies. Those that found shopping for other companies unsatisfying could use their cash to buy back their own stock, yet another way to drive up stock prices. If that wasn't enough, stock prices were also helped by legislation that made it very appealing from a tax perspective for U.S. citizens to buy stocks for retirement, and relatively unappealing to sell those after their prices had appreciated substantially. On top of all this, by the end of the 20th century, a communications revolution and a media frenzy focused on overnight millionaires and seemingly non-stop double digit increases in the U.S. stock markets, fueled an unprecedented interest in stocks among a whole new generation of investors who jumped into the fray. The cumulative effect of all this was an unsustainable run-up in the U.S. stock market that carried all the way into the first quarter of the year 2000.

Chapter 7

[1] Some readers will be predisposed to agree that developing countries are more often than not exploited when they trade with wealthier countries. Some of these concerns will be dealt with later in the chapter and the book. But for now, we cite Gary M. Quinlivan, Ph.D., the executive director of the Center for Economic and Policy Education and chair of the economics, political science, and public policy departments at Saint Vincent College. Although acknowledging in his article, "Multinational Corporations: Myths and Facts," that multinational corporations do sometimes act unethically, he also notes that their critics have a strong tendency to ignore the following:

   1.   There are over 60,000 multinational corporations in the world and the vast majority of their dealings are law abiding and ethical.
   2.   As multinational corporations expanded around the globe in the Post WWII period, school enrollment rates rose for all developing countries from 46 percent in 1960 to 57 percent in 1995.

When multinational companies were expanding most aggressively, between 1980 and 1998, world child labor rates fell from 20 to 13 percent, with rates in the regions <u>lacking</u> multinational corporations falling the least.

3. Many of the world's poorest countries (concentrated in sub-Saharan Africa, South Asia, North Africa, and the Middle East) rely heavily on governmental regulations and a disproportionate number of state-operated monopolistic enterprises (and have relatively small number of multinational corporations).

4. Multinational corporations often compete vigorously on a global scale, and the economic benefits of competition to consumers and economies are well documented. They do not sit in the same kind of privileged position as governments, and, in fact, their survival is in no way assured. Interestingly the Wall St. Journal's ranking of the top 100 multinational companies (by market value) has seen as many as 66 names fall off it over a ten year period. Large companies seldom collude or manipulate markets for their advantage. In contrast, governments openly form cartels (e.g., OPEC, The Association of Coffee Producing Countries, The Cocoa Producers' Alliance).

5. Foreign investment seldom harms domestic investment. For example, the United Nations' World Investment Report 1999 cited a study by Eduardo Borensztein, José de Gregorio, and Jong-Wha Lee that found that an additional dollar of foreign direct investment increases.

6. Countries have the authority to restrict set whatever rules they want. For example, from 1991 to 1998, according to the United Nations, there were 895 new foreign direct investment regulations enacted by more than sixty countries.

7. On the average, jobs created by multinationals in developing countries have significantly better pay and benefits than their domestic counterparts. Many studies cited by both the UN and World Bank give multinationals significant credit for developing country economic improvements.

8. The United Nations' World Investment Report 1999 noted the positive effects of multinationals on the environment – foreign-owned companies had higher environmental standards than their domestic counterparts across all manufacturing sectors.

9. Most corruption is initiated by government officials. The UN surveyed multinational and found the main reason multinational corporations <u>do not</u> invest in certain countries is extortion and bribery.

10. Some people have tried to link developing country debt problems with multinational corporations, but multinationals bring jobs, tax revenues, technologies, and exports, and allow the country to import less, all of which should lower the need for external debt.

11. Multinationals have a positive, albeit indirect impact on world peace. The voluntary exchange of goods is superior in every way to armed conflict. Additionally, multinationals are adverse to risk, so countries that fail to address political instability, corruption or civil wars will also miss out on substantial business benefits.

[2] When global wealth increases end up primarily in the hands of the rich, it is not usually because markets have failed. It is more likely that government has intentionally or unintentionally made it difficult for the majority of its citizens to start businesses or access the education, property rights, capital that they need to improve their situation. In many cases the government may also have given preferences to certain individuals, or restricted competition, resulting in extraordinary gains for some at the expense of others. Many of these problems will be discussed in later chapters.

[3] The reasons for this should become increasingly clear as the reader moves progresses through this book.

[4] Measuring the return on investments made by not-for-profit organizations is a tricky business to say the least, since many not-for-profits are not sophisticated in their measurement of benefits, and many of the things they offer people are not measured in monetary terms. Nevertheless, there is evidence that relief and development work is some of the highest return investment possible. According to a paper authored by Frank Rijsberman, Director-General of the International Water Management Institute in Colombo, Sri Lanka, and published by the Copenhagen Consensus Project, even if we conservatively value a year of life at the typical wage a poor person in a poor country earns, the payback to a global-scale project providing sanitation to everyone who

currently lacks it is about 600% per year. Similarly, because of medical advances, some forms of night blindness can now be cured with oral doses of Vitamin A, a capsule of which cost as little as U.S. $.02 as of the time of this writing. It is hard to imagine that the payback to preventing blindness wouldn't be even higher than the payback on good sanitation. Hundreds of other examples could be given related to clean water, electric power, the eradication of malaria, or the treatment of AIDS.

But work in not-for-profits and volunteering do not just pay pack to the communities in which the volunteers and not-for-profits operate. According to the Conference Board, a well-known New York based corporate research organization, businesses that encourage volunteering are more financially successful. Their publication, Corporate Volunteer programs: Benefits to Business, cites many benefits to businesses from promoting community involvement among their employees. They indicate that "A set of studies… found employee morale up to three times higher in companies actively involved in the community. These studies also found that the level of company community involvement is positively related to financial performance (ROI, ROA, and employee productivity)."

In addition to these benefits, anywhere from 60% to more than 90% of the companies reporting indicated that their programs did all of the following: improved their corporate image, multiplied the value of their financial contributions, improved relations with the community and or government, and built up employee teamwork skills, attracted better employees, improved retention, and benefited the bottom line.

These benefits to business make it clear that charities, in addition to providing direct benefits to users of their services, also provide spillover benefits to their communities and to the volunteers themselves. Benefits to volunteers can be estimated in part by the value of other opportunities they give up to do charitable work. Benefits to donors can be estimated at what they give. And the general public sometimes benefits from products and services produced and sold at or below cost.

[5] Readers are encouraged to read about the economic effects of the Smoot-Hawley Tariff Act and/or refer to the many books written on this subject. See, for example, Barry Eichengreen and Douglas A. Irwin (2009), *The Great Depression and the Protectionist Temptation: Who Succumbed and Why?*

[6] For the initiated reader, a simple example may be helpful. Assume that Thai people can produce shoes for $20 whereas the same shoes will cost Americans $50 to produce. Further assume that Americans can produce wheat for $5 per bushel which would cost Thai people $10 to produce. Clearly if Thai people use, say $100 to produce 5 pairs of shoes and Americans use $100 to produce 20 bushels of wheat the people of both countries will benefit. Americans can trade wheat to get 5 pairs of shoes (3 more pairs than they could produce on their own) and Thais could trade shoes to get 20 bushels of wheat (10 more than they could produce on their own). Interestingly, the same benefit can be achieved if, for example, the U.S. could produce both wheat and shoes more efficiently, although the gains from trading would not be nearly as great. Assume for example that it was the U.S. that could produce shoes at $20 per pair and Thailand at $50 per pair. In this case the U.S. can produce both wheat and shoes more efficiently than the Thais. Nevertheless, without trade, Thais would have to give up ten bushels of wheat to use their $100 of resources to produce two pairs of shoes. If the U.S. produced the two pairs of shoes instead, the cost would only be $40 and they would only have to sacrifice eight bushels of wheat. The Thais would gladly let the Americans produce the two pairs of shoes and trade nine bushels of wheat for them because it would give them the shoes they need and leave them with an extra bushel of wheat. Both nations would end up with an extra bushel of wheat from this arrangement (minus shipping costs). If the gains exceed the shipping costs, both parties (nations in this case) gain from trade. Of course, shipping costs may exceed the value of the extra two bushels of wheat gained, in which case the trade would not take place.

[7] For example, few if any Americans would deny that Japanese automakers, such as Toyota and Honda, have been instrumental in forcing American automakers to produce higher quality vehicles for less money than they would have, absent these competitors.

[8] Business activity, when not distorted by misguided worldviews or government-induced special privileges (which means we are talking about voluntary exchanges when both parties have real choices and access to

important information) is simply superior to most other methods of redistributing goods and property. These kinds of voluntary exchanges benefit both parties, something that can seldom be said for most of the other methods of obtaining goods or property (such as acquisition through inheritance, perceived superiority (race, beauty, class gender), military superiority, theft, bribes or extortion). Cajoling encouraging or serving people to get them to accept your offer are simply morally superior ways to get what one would like compared to heavy handedness. They encourage productive rather than destructive behaviors; they build bridges between parties rather than raising frustration levels, promoting envy, or prompting revenge.

9 For example, when cheaper imported products for playing video or music become available, producers of movies and music benefit indirectly from this.

Chapter 8

1 In spite of its name, the *World Christian Encyclopedia* gathers statistical data and reports on trends among a wide variety of religions.

2 David Barrett et al, "*World Christian Encyclopedia: A comparative survey of churches and religions - AD 30 to 2200*," Oxford University Press, (2001). See also ReligiousTolerance.org for regular updates on these statistics.

3 Gallup Poll, 2008.

4 To some degree they can be forgiven for this, since these nations have tended to keep the best statistics about religiosity, while many less developed nations have much less accurate data about the religiosity of their people.

5 According the McCreary and Barro (JEP, 2006), belief and religious participation have increased in nearly all the post-communist countries since 1990, and the share of people in these countries identified as "non-religious" dropped from 64% in 1970 to 50% in 2000.

6 Balkanization: A term that has come to popularly describe situations where differing worldviews and conflicts cause near-continuous fragmentation of people and/or geo-political boundaries.

7 As reported in a May 14, 2007 article in Foreign Policy magazine.

8 A well-known South African philosopher/theologian/author

9 Estimates reported in a speech on the campus of Dordt College, September, 2004.

10 As reported in the article "Oh, Gods!," by Toby Lester in *The Atlantic Monthly*, February, 2002).

11 The primary assumption (usually unstated) of zero-sum economics is that because the resources of the world are fixed, one person's wealth is necessarily tied to the poverty of others. This ignores much of the economic history of the world, where resources have often been transformed or enhanced, and goods traded, to improve the wealth and well being of people on both sides of a transaction.

12 Western concepts of eminent domain and some aspects of Islamic property law are, for example, carryovers from these ideas.

13 He also insisted that when God distributed excess goods and property to some they were called to be instruments of justice by using and or distributing this surplus for the benefit of others. This may partly explain how the St. Basil cathedral was given its prominent position in Moscow's Red Square.

14 And partly because of England's global influence, these developments have had an inordinate effect on views of property in many other countries and on the global economy.

15 Sunnah refers to recorded words, actions and habits of the prophet Muhammad.

16 See Jomo, 1992

17 For evidence of this, see Freedom House's statistics on the number of countries classified as free, partly free or unfree and related articles on their web site.

18 Oddly, some hints of this kind of spiritual sensitivity surfaced in the U.S. immediately after 9/11. Prior to this, Western culture, with essential assistance from Hollywood, had demoted the phrase "Oh my God," to little more than an overused and flippant expression of surprise, in spite of the fact that such a demotion was highly offensive to devout Muslims and Christians around the world. But immediately after 9/11, the same expression was suddenly transformed into an acknowledgment of the gut-wrenching sickness of evil and a plea for mercy. New Yorkers and many others came together to weep, reflect, and help each other out without regard to personal differences, self-interest, race, religion or class. Fiercely competitive companies also helped

each other out, and millions of dollars in aid flowed in from strangers. The city had, at least for a short time, become a community, a place of widespread prayer and soul searching, a place where the mingling of sorrow and love replaced expressions of pride and bravado. It is precisely this kind of response that holds the seeds of real peace and prosperity at the global level.

Chapter 9

[1] As quoted in Economist, July 22-28, 2006, pg. 56.

[2] We understand that people will vary greatly in their notions of good and evil, but this is precisely our point: that because economic outcomes are so heavily dependent on ideas of and responses to good and evil, it is incumbent on serious students of the economy to wrestle with and try to reach agreement on these things.

[3] Our insistence here that the Al Queda suicide bombers' beliefs were *just wrong* reflects a foundational commitment to a particular frame of reference for evaluating such things. For many in Western cultures, including many who don't realize it, this involves a (past, if not present) commitment to the authority of the teachings of the Bible, including the 6th of the 10 Commandments which specifically prohibits the shedding of innocent blood. Of course, for those Muslims, Buddhists, and agnostics who were equally outraged by these vicious attacks, the underlying basis for their condemnation of these acts may have been different but the conclusion was the same. But, as difficult as it is to believe, for literally millions of others, and particularly for those radical Muslims who viewed the innocent people in the World Trade Center towers (and Pentagon) as infidels and worthy objects of a "defensive" jihad, the killings were not only justified but laudable.

[4] The mystery of religious beliefs is due in part to the fact that they encompass far more than can be verified by popularly accepted "ways of knowing," such as simple observation or empirical investigation.

[5] For example, it has been estimated that well over two hundred health and hygiene laws and regulations are contained in the books of the Torah.

[6] *Habits of the heart: individualism and commitment in American life* / Robert N. Bellah ... [et al.] Berkeley : University of California Press, c1996. xlvii, 355 p. : ill. ; 21 cm.

[7] Perhaps the most famous Christian evangelist of all time, and a prolific author; According to the Billy Graham Evangelistic Association he gave testimony to the life-changing power of Jesus Christ to as many as 215 million people in 185 countries during his lifetime and authored 26 books.

[8] The purpose of the present writing is limited to exploring the very real impact that different religious beliefs have on the economic outcomes of those who hold them, regardless of the kind of life changing experience that an encounter with God can be. To explore the latter, the interested reader will have to participate in things that offer the possibility of this experience, such as prayer, worship, readings of sacred texts, or immersion in a community of scholars or believers who embrace and who live out the implications of that encounter.

[9] Acts 5:34-40, Bible, New International Version, Zondervan Publishing Company.

[10] Whether they would be better or worse ought not to be assumed too quickly without an honest attempt to study the matter, including consideration of the issues we raise in subsequent chapters.

Chapter 10

[1] Sara E. Yeatman and Jenny Trinitapoli. Beyond denomination: The relationship between religion and family planning in rural Malawi. Demographic Research, Volume 19, Article 55, pages 1851-1882. Published 24 October 2008; http://www.demographic-research.org/volumes/vol19/55/.

[2] "Religious and Cultural Traits in HIV/AIDS Epidemics in Sub-Saharan Africa" by Ali-Akbar Velayati MD*, Valerii Bakayev PhD•*, Moslem Bahadori MD*, Seyed-Javad Tabatabaei MD*, Arash Alaei MD*, Amir Farahbood MD*, Mohammad-Reza Masjedi MD* in the *Archives of Iranian Medicine*, Volume 10, Number 4, October 2007, pp. 486-497.

[3] Per fundraising documents, Rehoboth Christian School, Rehoboth, New Mexico.

[4] Of course, based on some studies they may also be missing out on the benefits associated with the occasional glass of red wine.

[5] James T. Duke: *What We Have Learned About Latter-day Saints from Social Research*

Endnotes

[6]The term recidivism refers to the percentage of released prisoners who reoffend and must return to prison within a specified period of time. The lower rate has been documented in many publications over many years, including in the article "Faith-based prison programs cut costs and recidivism," by Robert L. Maginnis, accessed on July 7, 2010 at http://www.conquesthouse.org/is96j2cr.html.

[7] Guido Tabellini, in his paper for the April, 2004 Middle East and North Africa Region (IMF) Conference on the Challenges of Growth and Globalization noted that productivity had fallen in the Middle East over the preceding twenty year period by 0.7 percent per year, in contrast to what had been happening in many other parts of the world.

[8] Grier (1997) conducted a cross country study of 63 former British, French and Spanish colonies and found that the former French and Spanish colonies had lower growth rates than the former British colonies. He attributed some of this to the impact of Protestantism. In trying to explain this variation, Putnam argued that trust levels are generally lower in predominately Catholic countries than in predominately Protestant countries. La Porta (1997) and Inglehard's (1999) work supported this observation. René M. Stulz and Rohan Williamson suggest another reason altogether in their study of the relationship between creditor rights and religion. They note that the Catholic Church prohibited usury in medieval times, whereas the Reformation (particularly the Calvinists) paved the way for charging of interest. Their study of 49 Catholic and Protestant countries found that creditor rights were better protected in Protestant countries (more specifically, and that creditors in Protestant countries could better access collateral or act on senior claims during bankruptcy proceedings and/or force a reorganization or the ouster of management). They also concluded that these differences were due to religion, not to the differences between common and civil law   ("Culture, Openness, and Finance." Journal of Financial Economics 70 (2003): 313-349).

[9] See *World on Fire: How Exporting Free Market Democracy Breeds Ethnic Hatred and Global Instability* by Amy Chua, 170-175.

[10] Data from the Lagos Business School as reported in "New Attacks Threaten Nigeria's Future," Drew Hinshaw, *Wall St. Journal*, February 17, 2012.

[11] Source: Korea Overseas Information Service. According to Andrew E. Kim *in A History of Christianity in Korea: From Its Troubled Beginning to Its Contemporary Success,* South Korea has witnessed a spectacular and historically significant Christian expansion during the last few decades of the 20th century, which was also a period of remarkable modernization. The number of Christians went from less than one million in the early 1960s to approximately 1/3 of the country's population at the time of this writing.

[12] Information based on the article "Religion in China," by Jeffrey Hays, retrieved, July 8, 2010 from http://factsanddetails.com/china.php?itemid=86&catid=3.

[13] See Jean Gimpel's *The Industrial Revolution of the Middle Ages* (1976) and Rodney Stark's *The Victory of Reason: How Christianity Led to Freedom, Capitalism, and Western Success* (2005).

[14] For example, The Scholastics, a group of intellectuals who spent their time trying to explain why things were the way they were by starting with the truths they already had in their possession and using the tool of logical deduction from that point on, had heavily influenced the Catholic Church at that time. But many of Scholasticism's roots were in the teachings of the ancient Greeks and Aristotle, whose belief system was quite in opposition to the beliefs of the Judeo-Christian tradition.

[15] The Norman Podhoretz reader, pg. 458.

[16] Francis Bacon, Novum Organum 1620 Basil Montague, ed. and trans. The Works, 3 vols. (Philadelphia: Parry & MacMillan, 1854), 3: 343-71.   Hanover Historical Texts Project Scanned by Alison Waugh and proofread by Monica Banas in 1996. Proofread and page numbers added by Jonathan Perry, March 2001. Accessed on July 7, 2010 at http://www.scrollpublishing.com/store/Francis-Bacon.html.

[17] As summarized in Michael Novak's article, "How Christianity Created Capitalism," in the December 23, 1999, Wall Street Journal.

[18] From a letter written to Ferdinand Lassalle (1825 - 1864), London, 16 January, 1861; Published by Gesamtausgabe, International Publishers, 1942; transcribed by Sally Ryan; retrieved July, 6, 2010 from http://www.marxists.org/archive/marx/works/1861/letters/61_01_16-abs.htm.

[19] Even people who are squeamish about using terms like right and wrong will admit that when people hold contradictory beliefs, they cannot both be correct.

[20] With the attendant creativity that this implies.

[21] Some scholars conjecture that even the cloud on the ceiling of the Sistine Chapel that surrounds God's head as he gives life to Adam with the tip of his finger was painted by Michelangelo in the shape of a human brain to depict that the very nature of God's creativity is implanted in each person.

[22] This is not to imply that the U.S. was founded as a Christian nation or that it ever had or intended to have an official "state" church.

[23] A second major religious movement that began around 1801.

[24] Landes, *Wealth and Poverty*, 1998.

Chapter 11

[1] In particular, Tawney argued that Calvin's Geneva was more authoritarian and collectivistic than England's Puritan communities, which seemed to be Weber's main focus. See R.H. Tawney's *Religion and the Rise of Capitalism*. New York: Harcourt, Brace and World, Inc., 1926.

[2] See "Culture, Openness, and Finance." *Journal of Financial Economics* 70 (2003): 313-349.

[3] This has sometimes been a byproduct of attempts to keep the academy secular, which by some interpretations, requires that religious beliefs be privatized to homes, churches, or perhaps theology departments.

[4] Kotkin highlights how mobile global tribes, like the Jew, Calvinists, Japanese, and "offshore" Chinese or Indians seem to fare well economically, nearly everywhere they go, largely because of strong ethnic, cultural and/or religious identities and the values that flow from them. Harrison highlights immigrant success stories in a variety of countries, the entrepreneurial power of Confucianism in Asia, and the disparate fortunes of various ethnic groups in America.

[5] One common theme of these books is that inner change drives external improvements, and principles and conscience are far more important for achieving results than the power of coercion. Many different terms are used for the disciplines, core values and sense of purpose that are part of effective leadership, but a common theme is that achieving these requires a recognition that there is much more to life than just making money, including what is referred to quite explicitly in some books as the spiritual dimension of life. Well know examples examples include Covey's *Habits of Highly Effective People* (1989) and *Principle Centered Leadership* (1992), Senge's *The Fifth Discipline* (1994), and Collins' *Good to Great* (2001

[6] Recent examples include, Kennedy's *What if Jesus Had Never Been Born? (1994)*, Schmidt's *Under the Influence: How Christianity Transformed Civilization* (2001), Stark's *For the Glory of God: How Monotheism Led to Reformations, Science, Witch Hunts and the End of Slavery* (2003), and *The Victory of Reason: How Christianity Led to Freedom, Capitalism, and Western Success* (2005), and Aikman's *Jesus in Beijing: How Christianity is Transforming China and Changing the Global Balance of Power* (2003). But people of other faiths are also beginning to recognize and write about the relevance of their beliefs to economic outcomes in general and to business ethics in particular. Examples include P.A. Payutto's, *Buddhist Economics - A Middle Way for the Marketplace* (1994), R.Wilson's *Economics, Ethics, and Religion: Jewish, Christian, and Muslim Economic Thought* (1997), Chen Huan-Chang's *The Economic Principles of Confucius and His School* (2003), and Muhammad Akram Khan's *Islamic Economics and Finance* (2007).

[7] For example: Books defining particular aspects of belief systems and how they impact business activity (Novak's *Business as a Calling* (1996); Stackhouse, McCann, and Roels' *On Moral Business* (1995); Hill's *Just Business* (1997); and Chewning, Eby, and Roels' *Business through the Eyes of Faith* (1990)); books about the practical working out of people's beliefs in business (Nash's *Believers in Business* (1994)); autobiographical books about the impact of faith on business practices (DePree's *Leadership is An Art* (1989), *Leadership Jazz* (1992), and *Leading Without Power* (1997); Blanchard, Hybels, and Hodges' *Leadership by the Book: Tools to Transform Your Workplace* (1999); *and* Dennis Bakke's *Joy at Work* (2005)).

[8] Examples of books attempting to draw leadership lessons from the lives and teachings of well-known founders of major religions: (Kelly, Nelson, and Bethge's *The Cost of Moral Leadership: The Spirituality of Dietrich Bonhoeffer* (2003), Nair's *Higher Standard of Leadership : Lessons From the Life of Gandhi* (1994), Mukhtar's *Genesis of a New American Leadership: A Muslim Commentary* (2000), Briner and Prichard's *The Leadership Lessons of Jesus* (1997), Manz's *Leadership Wisdom of Jesus—Practical Lessons for Today* (1998) and Jones' *Jesus, CEO* (1995)).

[9] We use the term brave because empirical studies on the importance of religious beliefs to the economy are relatively rare for good reasons. Two examples are the complexity of the relationships and the tendency by social scientists to privatize religion.

[10] For more information, consult the original research on wages (Chiswick, 1983), family stability (Bergin 1991), poverty (Freeman 1985), time allocation, school attendance, work success and social deviance among black males (Freeman, 1986), teen pregnancy and suicide (Larson, Larson and Gartner 1990), substance abuse (Daum and Lavenhar, 1980; National Center on Addiction and Substance Abuse, 2001), crime (Rohrbaugh and Jessor ,1975; Evans et al, 1995; Hull and Bold, 1995), mental and physical health (Comstock and Partridge, 1972; Levin and Vander Pol, 1987), deviant behavior among teens (Wallace and Williams, 1987; Bachman et al, 2002), and longevity and happiness (Beit-Hallami 1974).

[11] May 16, 2005.

[12] Barro and McCleary (2003); McCleary and Barro (2006); Barro and McCleary (2006).

[13] One of the main themes of this work is that what appears to be a decline in religiosity is better viewed as a change in the nature of religiosity, with changes in objects of worship, rituals, and beliefs, rather than the demise of these things.

[14] In their JEP paper, Barro and McCleary deal with the complexities of sorting out the effects of the dual influence that religion and what economists generally refer to as "political economy" have on each other. For researchers to accurately measure the impact of religious beliefs on economic activity, they need to figure out how to measure just that, without simultaneously picking up the effects that improvements in an economy have on religious beliefs. As noted earlier, an example of this reverse impact would be the possibly detrimental impact of wealth and prosperity on religious belief or attendance. So, for example, if excessive wealth lowers the level of religious commitment in a society because people increasingly substitute reliance on wealth or income for reliance on God, these effects will skew the results. Their *Journal for the Scientific Study of Religion* article, Barro and McCleary (2006) investigates two different theories of religiosity. The first, as we noted, focuses on the (generally negative) impact of the economic growth on religious belief and practice, and the second assumes that religious beliefs and practices are determined more by things such as the existence of a state religion and government control over religion (such as has happened in small ways in many countries and in severe ways in many communist countries) or its promotion of freedom of religion (more precisely religious pluralism). Using survey information for 68 countries over 20 years, they find support for the eroding power of income (measured as per capita GDP) on religious beliefs. They find that the presence of an official state religion tends to increase religiosity (which they point out is to be expected when anything, including organized religion, is subsidized), and, as expected, religiosity falls with government regulation of the religion market and Communist suppression. Surprisingly, although they find that greater religious pluralism raises attendance at formal services, it had no significant effect on "religious beliefs" (it is not obvious exactly what is meant by this) or the number of people who identify themselves as religious. They also find several other effects of religion on the economy, some hinted at in their earlier work, noting that religiosity is higher among educated people, those who care for children, and those in smaller towns and rural areas.

[15] Although less directly related to our topic, on the negative side, they also found that people who were "raised religiously" were "more intolerant" (although this was not true for a group that consisted only of active "churchgoers") and "less sympathetic to women's rights" (this was also true of active churchgoers). Unfortunately the terms in quote marks here were not as clearly defined as we would like.

Chapter 12

[1] This is not, of course, to suggest that all writings be accepted as having equal authority. Rather it is to suggest only that secular writings not be favored in public settings just because they are secular.

[2] As two "world wars" and hundreds or thousands of other battles and skirmishes around the world have made plain over time, sometimes the supreme sacrifice must be made to counter the effects of evil. Combating this evil requires the ability to differentiate good from evil, and a sober-minded understanding that people who are willing to die in the process of committing evil acts know only too well that the only ones who can effectively stop them are those who are also willing to give up their lives to prevent these acts. The imperfections of the Western world, and of its individual soldiers, notwithstanding, the moral gulf between a terrorist and a sacrificial peace maker/protector could not be greater. A commitment that motivates a person to risk his life to secure a stranger's future, whether spawned by religious or secular motives, is so morally superior to what a suicide bomber does that anyone suggesting some kind of moral equivalence between them ought to be ashamed of himself.

[3] By individualism, we are not referring to the kind of individual initiative and responsibility that fosters human productivity and accountability, but rather the kind that allows individuals to believe that they can get along fine without each other, or isolates individuals from one other.

[4] The meaning of this term will be unpacked in the next chapter.

Chapter 13

[1] Walsh and Middleton, *The Transforming Vision*, pg. 35.

[2] Although Lombardi is on record as having said this, it is likely that it was not original with him, since the same quote is attributed to another football coach, Red Sanders, of UCLA many years earlier.

[3] It should also be noted that this depends on the structures that flow from these beliefs and values. The U.S. for example is a democratic "republic' (representative democracy) which makes tyranny of the majority more difficult to carry out than might be the case elsewhere.

[4] Latin for "let the buyer beware."

[5] A transliteration of a Cyrillic character acronym for the USSR, equivalent to Union of Soviet Socialist Republics in English.

[6] The concepts of 'openness' and 'restructuring' introduced by President Mikhail Gorbachev shortly after he became the Soviet leader in 1985. Together they were intended to increase Soviet contact with the Western world, create a more open society, and reduce inefficiency and corruption.

Chapter 14

[1] Although the Orthodox view of this three-fold nature differs from the Catholic and Protestant views with respect to the nature of the relationship between the third of the three "persons" of God, the Holy Spirit, and the other two, the Father and the Son. But all major expressions of Christianity are in fundamental agreement concerning the work of the Holy Spirit – that of convicting people of their sin, revealing God to them and enabling them to live obedient lives.

[2] In spite of the name, *World Christian Encyclopedia*, this includes permutations of all major religions and "secular" belief systems.

[3] These observations reflect anecdotal reports from long-term Protestant missionaries. Haiti is well known for the amount of syncretism that exists between tribal beliefs and the Catholicism introduced centuries ago.

[4] Most of us would be deeply offended if someone tried to give other people a picture of who we are simply by describing our weight or skin color. It would be much more useful if they also included something about, for example, our marital status, educational background, church affiliation, or political leanings. Similarly, not breaking major belief systems down into subgroups is a lot like referring to both internet scam artists and CEOs of highly reputable blue chip companies as "business people" and teaching the management techniques

of both as if they were equivalent. Even worse, associating terrorists with peaceful Muslims, or Klu Klux Klan members with people who study and practice the teachings of Christ, are not just errors that will lead to wrong conclusions – they are a dangerous form of bigotry. So when we develop yardsticks for comparing and contrasting belief systems in the next section, the reader is cautioned against thinking only in terms of widely-held beliefs or broad religious classifications.

[5] I am indebted to B.J. Vander Walt of South Africa for the insights that his writings, which elaborate on H. Richard Niebuhr's *Christ and Culture*, have provided related to this subject.

[6]

[7] From an article by Rodney Stark, adapted from *For the Glory of God: How Monotheism Led to Reformations, Science, Witch-Hunts, and the End of Slavery*, Princeton University Press, 2003.

[8] If God is omnipotent and omnipresent, he is also aware of the good and right things that his servants are involved in. This should spur people on to good deeds, and doubly so if their religious beliefs promise blessings of one sort or another for engaging in these kinds of activities.

[9] See, for example, Rodney Stark, "Why Gods should matter in Social Science" from The Chronicle of Higher Education, 6/6/2003 or his books, *For the Glory of God: How Monotheism led to Reformations, Science, Witch Hunts, and the End of Slavery, or The Victory of Reason: How Christianity Led to Freedom, Capitalism and Western Success*, Random House, New York, (2005).

[10] Based on the authors conversations with many of the Tai Dam people who immigrated to the U.S. following the Viet Nam war.

[11] It also does not appear that those who frequented temples in Greek or Roman times lived appreciably more moral lives than those who didn't frequent them. Scholars, such as the founder of British anthropology Edward Burnett Tylor, as well as Reo Franklin Fortune, Ruth Benedict, and Mary Douglas all note that there are moral people who are not particularly religious and religious people who are not particularly moral – but this is useful information only if what they mean by the word "religious" is examined. Stark, for example, finds that in Japan, because gods are conceived as numerous, relatively limited in scope, and generally uninterested in human morality, there is no correlation between visits to temples, prayer or meditation and morality. This situation, where multiple gods with limited power are revered, is also common in Buddhism, Daoism, and Hinduism. In some parts of China, Stark even found increased prayer correlating with more immorality, perhaps because it reflects self-serving attempts to manipulate relatively limited-scope deities for one's personal benefit (a religious system that would also be more likely to appeal to the kind of self-centered people who would engage in immoral behavior for their own pleasure). But as other scholars such as Ralph Barton have pointed out, this may be related to the fact that some religions assume their gods are as unscrupulous as they are, with predicable consequences, rather than reform their behavior to meet a difficult-to-achieve divine standard.

[12] Part of Weber's original thesis that the Protestant work ethic, which stresses the importance of work, self-discipline, and individual responsibility, would encourage entrepreneurial activity; also the subject of many other studies since. See for example, Audretsch, David B., Bönte, Werner and Tamvada, Jagannadha Pawan, Religion and Entrepreneurship (July 2007). , Vol. , pp. -, 2007. Available at SSRN: http://ssrn.com/abstract=1136703

[13] This is, of course, not to say that Muslims do not believe that prayer matters, or that all Muslims are fatalistic, but only to call attention to these differences and their importance.

[14] Islamic belief does not assume Jesus to be either part of the Godhead or God's gift whose sacrificial death lifted the burden of sin off the shoulders of believers and brought salvation. Rather, most Muslims believe that Jesus, although untouched by sin, was merely a messenger of God, like other prophets.

[15] Borlaug is best known for his work with Mexican scientists on problems of wheat improvement; and his collaboration with scientists from other parts of the world, especially from India and Pakistan, in producing and adapting new varieties of wheat. His grandfather, Nels Olson Borlaug, was one of the founders of the Norwegian Evangelical Lutheran Congregation near Cresco, Iowa, where Borlaug was raised. An examination of the Bible verses referenced in his Nobel Lecture seem to indicate that Borlaug assumed that, as recorded in Genesis, the first book of the Bible, that when the creation was spoiled by sin, and the "garden" spoiled by

weeds, the production of food became difficult and uncertain, and it was the part of the calling of humans, like Borlaug , to use their time, talents and resources to mitigate these effects of sin, try to fix the problem, and "reclaim" the garden.

[16]Nobel Lecture, December 11, 1970: The Green Revolution, Peace, and Humanity. From *Nobel Lectures, Peace 1951-1970*, Editor Frederick W. Haberman, Elsevier Publishing Company, Amsterdam, 1972. Borlaug delivered this lecture in the auditorium of the Nobel Institute. The text, which in actual delivery was shortened, is taken from *Les Prix Nobel en 1970*. Retrieved on July 13, 2010, http://nobelprize.org/nobel_prizes/peace/laureates/1970/borlaug-lecture.html

[17] These dangers are real, and we are not recommending widespread use of DDT; rather our purpose is to highlight how answers to these basic questions affect the potential solutions to problems that have massive and widespread economic effects.

[18] We do not want to leave the reader with the impression that we are unaware of the complex array of things that contributes to the problems that plague many inner city neighborhoods or tribal societies, but do want to call attention to the role that beliefs play in this.

[19] For example, by cutting down a tree, moving a rock, or refusing to make sacrifices before digging.

[20] We use smartphones as a catch all term for a host of electronic gadgets aimed at providing information, keeping schedules, and connecting people with their work and each other.

[21] Of course some would argue that these tendencies can become economically counterproductive, e.g., with the conspicuous depletion of wealth that so often characterizes the lives of children who inherit fortunes, or the large percentage of total medical expenditures spent in the last year of people's lives, or the oddly massive expenditures some are willing to make to have their bodies preserved in liquid nitrogen in the hopes of someday being brought back to life; all of which seem more prominent in increasingly secular countries.

[22] The list of responses is limited only by the creativity of people. Examples include donating organs, adopting special needs children, risking one's wealth on risky business ventures or not-for-profit startups, or sacrificing one's life for the benefit of total strangers.

[23] On the other hand, it is also possible that the person who threw the grenade into the foxhole did so in part because he believes that if he dies in a holy war, he will live on blissfully with a healthy helping of virgins. Once again, God (or the devil) is in the details, but clearly, beliefs are anything but irrelevant.

[24] The implications of this are that it is incumbent on people to discover, accept, or adhere to spiritual laws in the same sense that they need to do this with respect to physical laws. In other words, in the same way someone who doesn't believe in (or know) about the force of gravity will die if he jumps off a cliff or tall building, people can do sever damage to themselves and others by remaining ignorant about the spiritual dimensions of life.

[25] This concept spurred 19th and early 20th century Christian politicians like Abraham Kuyper, the Prime Minister of The Netherlands to develop the kinds of pluralistic political structures which became an important part of European development, and somewhat influential in the U.S.

Chapter 15

[1] This is not to disparage the ongoing highly important work surrounding the sequencing of various genomes, but to call attention to the danger of overlooking the importance of the human will and freedom of choice to decisions with significant consequences for development.

[2] Some Christians, convinced that dark-skinned people were under the "curse of Ham," created dual societies that separated people by skin color, greatly restricted opportunities for dark-skinned people, and severely restricted the development of their societies for decades (the best known and last dismantled of these was the apartheid system of South Africa). Some secularists at the center of the global slave trade had little or no difficulty convincing themselves of the inferiority of African slaves they were "sacrificing" to their gods of money and power.

[3] Interestingly, not-for-profit organizations, which as a group seem much more likely to "see" the potential of the poor than bankers, were very important in extending credit to the poor through microfinance programs.

Interestingly, the success of these programs caught he eyes of bankers, and helped change their perception of the poor, leading eventually to the replication of these programs by banks.

[4] In contrast, Christians and Jews, for the most part, although paying attention to both nature and nurture, also see themselves as *children of God*, a designation that add an additional layer of definition to their connection to their physical forbears, and makes them (and others) the equivalent of royalty (since they bear the "image" of the almighty God). This means that, in spite of their genes and their parents, they (and others) have the potential to become something quite different from what their parents were or are. For the Jews this often entailed a focus on the attributes of Yahweh. Recognizing that they are called to be holy, because their "father" God is holy, they intentionally focus on Biblical accounts of Yahweh and the characteristics of God that should be sought by his image bearers, such as creativity, a passion for justice, patience, etc. For Christians the concept of image bearing evokes something in addition to this, the New Testament expectation of being "transformed" by the Holy Spirit over time to become more and more like Christ. Together, these beliefs offer a powerful incentive for people to envision what they should be in the future, rather than settle for what they are or have been. And given the sheer volume of innovation, medical cures, creative management techniques, etc. that have been spawned in Western nations, it is clear that Marx was particularly mistaken about at least one thing: Far from being the opiate of the people, some religious beliefs have apparently fueled passionate investigation, or at the very least, laid the groundwork for the explosion of Western-led innovation and growth that not only contributed to the demise of Marxist-Leninism but is increasingly changing the rest of the world.

[5] The common term for laws restricting one or another form of business on religiously-prescribed days of rest (primarily Sunday in nations influenced by Christianity). The laws are said to have originated among the 17th century Puritans, but no record of the referring to them as Blue Laws exists from that period. The first recorded use of the term Blue Law is in the Reverend Samuel Peters 1781 book, *The General History of Connecticut*, where he also referred to them as "bloody" laws because of the harsh penalties sometimes associated with violating them.

[6] The largest annual pilgrimage in the world; a Muslim religious duty to journey to Mecca, Saudi Arabia, that is to be carried out by able-bodied Muslims who can afford to do so at least once in their lifetime

[7] We caution again at this point, as we did earlier, that beliefs and practices in these areas are *jointly* determined by religious beliefs and cultural practices.

[8] And, in all Christian churches, individuals are subject to one degree or another to church authorities, whether that be to the leadership hierarchy (as in the Catholic or Orthodox churches) or to the board of elders (as in most Protestant churches). Muslims too gather at mosques at regular times, and for the most part are under the strict authority of the imams or mullahs.

[9] These terms roughly correspond, respectively, to the concepts of respect, gentlemanliness, the appropriate use of authority, and peace.

[10] Although some consider this little more than a strategy that reflects an error of judgment on the part of Islamic fringe groups, others insist that the problem is more endemic - a Qur`an-encouraged struggle to conquer the world for Islam.

[11] Unfortunately, most scholars conclude that, in contrast to Christ's teachings, there is ample wiggle room in the Qu`ran and Sharia law for those who wish to use violence to accomplish their purposes.

[12]. In addition, Christian groups have also been strongly influenced by Christ's command to "love your enemies, and do good to those who persecute you," and the Apostle Paul's urgings to "do good to *all* people, and especially to members of the household of faith." This has led, for example, to relatively high adoption rates, NGO establishment rates, development work, and child sponsorship levels among certain Protestant and Catholic Christian groups. These Biblical teachings have also influenced them to be relatively unwilling to allow orphans and other disadvantaged children to live on the streets or miss getting an education, all of which has significant long term economic effects..

[13] For the radical members of Hamas, Islamic law divides the world into two groups: dar al-Islam (territory ruled by Muslims) and dar al-harb (the rest). This in effect prevents them from ever signing a peace treaty

(hudna) with Israel because doing so would be tantamount to recognizing Israeli occupied territory as a legitimate part of dar al-Islam.

[14] In many, if not most, of these cases, exclusivity appears to be the result of an inability to separate out religious and ethnic identities.

[15] There are, of course, also drawbacks to this, as poorly educated sects or fringe groups can take sacred writings out of context and apply them in ways that are inconsistent with the overarching intent of the texts.

[16] …with some Christian groups dedicated to translating it into every language group, no matter how few people speak it.

Chapter 16

[1] To that end we introduce an economic development wheel, a simpler version of which was first laid out by Bill Essig, Steve Hoffman and this author in the first chapter of the book *Civil Society: A Foundation for Sustainable Economic Development*, a joint publication of the Coalition of Christian Colleges and Universities and Mercy Corps (Rose 1998).

[2] Popularized by Howard Gardner, among others. Increasing use of the term can be traced to his first book on the subject, *Frames of Mind: The theory of multiple intelligences*, New York: Basic Books, 1983.

[3] A term popularized by Daniel Goleman, among others, in his book, *Emotional Intelligence*.

[4] Goleman estimated that they explain less than 25% of these.

[5] From "The Reasons Why We Need to Rely Less on Day Care," published in The Washington Post, 10/19/97) More information is available in his book *Building Healthy Minds: The Six Experiences that Create Intelligence and Emotional Growth in Babies and Young Children* by Stanley Greenspan, M.D. with Nancy Breslau Lewis (1999).

[6] Although, as the Development Wheel illustrates, both civil society and entrepreneurship are integral parts of the development process, we will wait until Chapter 18 to unpack these concepts.

[7] Although we defined income and wealth and noted the differences between them in Chapter 4, we judge that a more detailed picture of the interrelationship between them will be useful at this point, in the context of the Development Wheel and its use of the term capital.

[8] Interestingly, it is not only economic development specialists that are discovering the importance of these things. Groups as diverse as Russian Orthodox Patriarchs (like the late Alexander Men), inner-city pastors in the U.S. (e.g., the Ten-Point Coalition), and communist bureaucrats in China have all recognized that misdirected beliefs and misguided worldviews can damage nearly all other forms of capital and, therefore, almost any meaningful progress toward economic development. At the same time, hundreds of creative ideas, ranging from church-led inner-city renewal projects to NGO sponsored micro-finance institutions to socially responsible businesses, have shown the power of enabling people to solve their own problems from the bottom up.

[9] We remind the reader of the discussion at the beginning of Chapter 5. In addition to seven different kinds of capital, illustrated in the wheel diagram, there are also seven different *sources* of capital, by which we mean seve different ways of building each kind of capital up and/or minimizing the amount by which each kind of capital depreciates or is depleted..

Chapter 17

[1] One good example of this is the practice of using swing shifts, which require workers to continually reorient their biological clocks as they move from working days to working nights. If these workers are too exhausted to teach their children, interact with their neighbors, participate in the political process, or attend a church or synagogue, then social, governmental, or spiritual/moral capital will be eroded even as physical and financial capital may be built up.

[2] Myers, D.G. 1992. The Pursuit of Happiness: Who Is Happy and Why. New York: William Morrow.

[3] The Economist, November 27, 2004

[4] See the Mott Foundation's Pathways Out of Poverty Program publications for more information about this.

[5] In Africa the primary mechanism of AIDS transmission is unprotected heterosexual contact. In the U.S. the primary transmission mechanisms for AIDS involve sexual intercourse with an infected partner, injecting drugs using a needle or syringe that has been used by someone who is infected,, babies being infected by their mothers during pregnancy, labor or delivery, or through breastfeeding. CDC statistics show that in the U.S. in 2007, 73% of persons living with a diagnosis of HIV infection were male adults or adolescents. Just over half of men diagnosed with HIV in 2008 became infected through male-to-male sexual contact, around 30% of those diagnosed were infected through heterosexual contact, and 10.5% through injecting drug use. Accessed, July 20, 2010 at http://www.avert.org/usa-transmission-gender.htm

[6] For example, as the well-known actor Michael J. Fox's testimony before the U.S. Congress in the fall of 1999 made clear, the U.S. was spending nearly fifty times more per patient to fight AIDS than to fight Parkinson's disease, a disease for which there is no behavioral cure.

[7] Indeed, this is exactly what has started to happen in many "developed" economies in recent years as the bankruptcy of rampant materialism has become apparent. The material weight of everything produced relative to the market value of everything purchased has continued to decline over time, which gives us a glimpse of what sustainable growth could look like.

Chapter 18

[1] This also shows, based on the number of countries now in the U.N., how much the world has changed since 1948.

[2] See Brownlie, 1992.

[3] Toward the end of the Declaration some even more ambitious (but also more difficult to define) rights were touched on, like the right to a "standard of living adequate for the health and well-being of self and of family," the right "to choose the kind of education that shall be given to (one's) children," and the right to "participate in the cultural life of the community." The U.N. later tried to become more specific about many of these rights via a host of "standards," the best known of which are the *International Covenant on Civil and Political Rights* and the *International Covenant on Economic, Social and Cultural Rights*. But it is fair to say that none of these latter documents enjoys as much support, or has been as influential as the *Universal Declaration*.

[4] See Bothwell, "Indicators of a Healthy Civil Society," in *Community Works*, John Burbidge, ed., 1997, pp. 249-262.

[5] See www.NCL.org

[6] The significant uptick in globalization following WW II can be traced to many things, but the Bretton Woods Conference, where politicians laid down a framework for international commerce and finance and the founding of international institutions such as the World Bank, the International Monetary Fund and the General Agreement on Tariffs and Trade (GATT), is often cited as one of the keys.

[7] The wheel also helps us understand other seemingly contradictory aspects of the global economy, such as the capital flows *from* lesser developed *to* highly developed countries. One would expect that the wealthiest countries would regularly funnel their savings to financially poorer developing countries; however, it is common for people in relatively poor countries like China to have higher savings rates than people in relatively rich countries like the U.S. (and to lend these savings to developed countries). In addition, this suggests the possibility that better developed financial markets in wealthy countries, in conjunction with deeper civil societies and greater opportunities for entrepreneurial activities, may in fact better match financial capital with the other six forms of capital that it depends on, making this capital more productive with less risk than it would be in many developing countries. The end result is that highly developed countries serve as a useful repository for the savings of the world's poor, until such time as they are able to balance their wheels and make equally productive use of their capital at home.

[8] This is not to say that one homogeneous global culture is either desirable or a likely end result of globalization; rather that the mixing of cultures will allow distinct cultures to adopt things that the deem to be culturally appropriate improvements, and jettison cultural traditions that they no longer see as beneficial.

[9] There should be no presumption that these are necessarily the same values that are widely held in wealthy countries.

Chapter 19

[1] It is well established that market economies where people are free to offer and act on economic incentives will lead to varying degrees of inequality. This is especially the case when generosity is not particularly valued or encouraged in the culture. Thus, societies or cultures which tend to associate inequality with injustice, such as such as was the case in many communist countries, were often willing to trade off lower standards of living for higher degrees of equality. It is also important to note at this point that the values described in this and the next chapter are part of an integrated worldview, which can never be fully disentangled. For example, market economies also assume that people have the right to be secure in their persons and their property (a function of a correct understanding of justice – the subject of Chapter 20), which in turn requires that government accept as one of its primary roles the protection of individuals and property rights, and that people accept the legitimacy of government (which require a correct understanding of authority-the subject of Chapter 20). The legitimacy of property ownership in turn presupposes the legitimacy of business organizations, and healthy business activity requires both a "passion for solving problems" and a "stewardship ethic" (the subject of Chapter 21).

[2] The practice of rewarding people for productivity rather than status or birthright.

[3] Stanley and Danko's *The Millionaire Next Door: The Surprising Secrets of America's Wealthy*, C.L. Pravalad's *The Fortune at the Bottom of the Pyramid* and Nobel Prize winner Muhammad Yunus' *Banker To The Poor: Micro-Lending and the Battle Against World Poverty*, among other books, make it clear that the surpluses needed to finance economic development need not come only from the rich (or the government)

[4] This is of course not to equate the idea of "freedom as normative" with the idea of "unlimited freedom."

[5] Jeffrey Sachs and Andrew Warner, "Economic Reform and the Process of Global Integration, Brookings Papers on Economic Activity 1 (1995). The OECD has concluded similarly, concluding that a one percent increase in the ration of trade to GDP can be expected to lead to between a .5% and 2% increase in per capita income. See Organization for Economic Cooperation and Development, Open Markets Matter: The Benefits of Trade and Investment Liberalization, 1998, 10.

[6] See especially, the World Bank's *Doing Business in 2004: Understanding Regulation*, and *Doing Business in 2005: Removing Obstacles to Growth*, and the ongoing *Ease of Doing Business* country rankings that grew out of these reports.

[7] Although some people make minor distinctions between non-government organizations (NGOs) and Civil Society Organizations (CSOs) we will not so here. Generally speaking, the term CSO is broader than the term NGO and includes a variety of unstructured and unregistered social groups, such as the Bowling Leagues made famous by Robert Putnam, which would ordinarily not be referred to as NGO's.

[8] Putnam, Robert D. *Making Democracy Work: Civic Traditions in Modern Italy.* Princeton: Princeton University Press, 1993.

[9] In the early days of management professionalism, the emphasis was often on quantifying productivity, output and performance. As the profession evolved there has been a much greater understanding of the importance of things that are less easy to quantify, such as leadership, interpersonal dynamics, teamwork, etc. It is these later things that are sometime referred to as "soft science."

[10] See, for example, Deming (1982), and Osborne and Gaebler, 1992)

[11] See *Corporate Volunteer Programs: Benefits to Business*, 1992, pg. 35.

[12] Studies performed in 1989 and 1992. *Corporate Volunteer Programs;* See also David Lewin, *Community Involvement, Employee Morale, and Business Performance*.

[13] It is worth noting here that although transparency brings efficiencies, it is, as will be discussed later, considerably less efficient than trustworthiness and ethics. An illustration of this is the additional time, paper and audit fees associated with Sarbanes Oxley legislation aimed at reducing corporate financial fraud. Although

perhaps necessary to reign in questionable accounting practices, it added little more than paperwork costs and wasted time to ethical companies and their investors.

[14] The term "public" here refers to publically traded companies who must meet reporting and ethics requirements to maintain their status.

[15] Many, of these services are provided free of charge, but is clear that value of the social problems solved and products and services provided by CSOs is substantial. Some attempts have been made to value the time spent in volunteering, but the benefits go far beyond this. For example, how many young people have been nurtured toward productive adulthood with the help of service opportunities and training provided by civil society organizations? What is the value to society of people who have become skilled, via their immersion in a civil society, at diagnosing and taking the initiative to solve problems before they get out of hand? What is the value of the economic output of the socially or medically "down and out" people saved or restored by non-profit hospitals and other charities?

[16] Therefore, before relegating civil society to a third place position, behind government and business, with respect to its impact on the economy, it would be well for economic policy makers to reflect on all the contributions made by women and/or people of color, and the degree to which these opportunities might not have been possible without the civil society organizations that were involved in securing the rights that led to these contributions and the worldviews that led to the development of these organizations.

[17] See the discussion of the Civic Index in Chapter 18.

Chapter 20

[1] Ayittey, George N. (1998). *Africa in Chaos*. New York, NY: St Martin's Press.

[2] William Easterly corroborates Ayittey's research, noting how "the West spent $2.3 trillion on foreign aid over the last five decades and still had not managed to get 12-cent medicine to children to prevent half of all malaria deaths. The West spend $2.3 trillion and still had not managed to get $4 bed nets to poor families. The West spent $2.3 trillion and still had not managed to get $3 to each new mother to prevent five million child deaths." Easterly, W. (2006). *'The White Man's Burden: Why the West's Efforts to Aid the Rest Have Done so Much Ill and So Little Good'*. New York, NY: The Penguin Press.

[3] Such projects are almost always lower quality or provide lower return than would otherwise be available. Corruption results in a society-wide focus on short-term gains since a corrupt environment is one in which the future is often unpredictable. This impedes the kind of long-term investing and risk taking that is associated with the development of Overall, foreign investment is reduced because costs associated with corruption function like a tax, uncertainty causes domestic new industries and the economy as a whole. See, for example, Rose-Ackerman's 1999 research on the quality of public services for evidence of this.

[4] capital flee (since people are concerned that their savings/investments will be jeopardized by arbitrary actions), and less private and public foreign aid flows in, creating a depressing effect on the country's currency.

[5] See De Soto, 2001.

[6] See Power, 2003 for an abbreviated account of Mugabe's misguided policies.

[7] See, for example, the work of Paolo Mauro (*Corruption and Growth*, Quarterly Journal of Economics, 1995, p. 681-712, or *The Effects of Corruption on Growth, Investment, and Government Expenditure: A Cross-Country Analysis*, Institute for International Economics [IIE: www. iie.org] p. 83-107); or the comprehensive study done by Jakob Svensson using a large cross section of data on the countries of the world from the IIE and the World Bank.

[8] Both the high quality of U.S. private K-12 schools and the existence of a world class private/public college and university structure in the U.S., in spite of an overall poor quality K-12 public education system, are evidence of the benefits of these kinds of choices. Experiments in the U.S. with vouchers, beginning in the 1980s in places like Milwaukee, Cleveland and Washington, D.C. as well as the success of charter schools, are additional evidence of how recognizing the fundamental justice issue of allowing parents to choose the kind of school they send their children improves educational achievement.

[9] As defined by the World Intellectual Property Organization (WIPO), Intellectual property (IP) refers to creations of the mind: inventions, literary and artistic works, and symbols, names, images, and designs used in commerce.

IP is divided into two categories: Industrial property, which includes inventions (patents), trademarks, industrial designs, and geographic indications of source; and Copyright, which includes literary and artistic works such as novels, poems and plays, films, musical works, artistic works such as drawings, paintings, photographs and sculptures, and architectural designs. Rights related to copyright include those of performing artists in their performances, producers of phonograms in their recordings, and those of broadcasters in their radio and television programs. Se e www.WIPO.int for additional detail.

[10] In the meantime subpar counterfeit products will proliferate, transferring wealth from consumers to con artists, or, even worse, posing serious safety risks to both people and the economy. But the benefits of justly protecting intellectual property are not limited to wealthy countries and consumers. Most recently, India had become a world leader in software development after revamping their intellectual property laws and both Brazil and China have seen significant increases in their pharmaceutical industries after strengthening their patent laws. These nations are also increasingly giving foreigners "national treatment" with respect to prices, taxes, and regulatory restrictions, which is another way that attention to justice issues spurs economic development.

Chapter 21

[1] Problems with liquor are part of the folklore of nearly every culture, because they can have a serious impact on individuals, families and societies. See, for example, Harvey's *Feast of Fools*. But there is also solid research that indicates that in some countries, people spend considerable amounts on liquor, even as their children receive inadequate nutrition or education. For one of the most thorough accounts of this, see [insert paper by two MIT professors]. Our intent here is not to particularly highlight consumption decisions involving liquor, but to note how consumption choices in general can greatly affect economic outcomes. There is along legacy of poverty in countries where leaders build lavish palaces while their people suffer (Iraq's Saddam Hussein) or massive wine collections while millions of people starve to death (North Korea's Kim Jung Il) or who steal people life savings by printing massive quantities of money to fund their personal wants (Zimbabwe's Robert Mugabe).

[2] This is not to argue that so-called luxury goods are never acceptable, but that they have less potential to improve an economy than goods which meet subsistence needs. Eventually, as people's subsistence needs are met, luxury goods and services may a useful option for continuing economic activity, since higher "return on investment" options may no longer be plentiful.

[3] It should be clear from this overview of events that neither Republicans nor Democrats have very much right to claim responsibility for the positive developments that took place during this period.

[4] This is not to say, as has often been suggested in the past, that the pace of innovation must necessarily slow to a trickle because almost everything that can be invented has been invented. No, we should fully expect that the pace of innovation will be continuous and rapid for some time. But there were not very many good reasons to expect the U.S. growth rates of the 1990s in revenue, profit, productivity, or GDP to continue at those rates well into the 21st century. Nor could investors value shares of stock for the long run using growth projections tainted by the rose-colored glasses of the 1990s.

[5] One evidence of this was the low average unemployment rates between the late 1980s and 2008 and the continued reliance on immigrants to fill many positions, which would be expected we a productive but aging populations moves into its pre-retirement years.

[6] The Great Recession, related to the global financial crisis that began in 2008 should not be confused with the Great Depression of the 1930s. The U.S. portion of what is now often called the Great Recession occurred, technically speaking, between the very end of 2007 and the middle of 2009, but the entire global economy was still very fragile at the time of this writing (2012).

[7] In other words, although a country can spend billions on diet plans and research into preventable health problems to keep medical costs down, even though such activity counts in its official measured output (e.g.

GDP), it will be the country whose values allow it to eat lightly and wisely in the first place that will have the competitive advantage. Likewise money spent on new cars, the gasoline to power them and insurance policies to replace them in the event of an accident all contribute to GDP but it is the nation that gets the most benefit from its vehicles, i.e. that moves the most people per vehicle mile or gets the best average fuel efficiency, and has the lowest vehicle depreciation from unnecessary wear and tear or accidents that will have the competitive advantage.

[8] By popular estimates, the British Royal Family costs British taxpayers approximately 100 million per year.

[9] As reported on the website pathtofreedom.com

[10] This illustrates another less recognized but important kind of "externality," where private producers can impose costs on the public - in this case on future generations. One poignant example of this was the practice, near the end of the 19th century, of dumping gasoline, which is now highly valued, into the ocean because it was thought to be a relatively useless by-product of kerosene. Since the automobile had not yet been invented, kerosene was the primary product that gave oil value at that time.

[11] Scientists tell us that the consumption of energy by the average American amounts to the equivalent of about 10,000 watts per day. So given that the unaided human is capable of generating about 100 watts of power a day, the typical American would need an additional 99 people working for her full time if she wasn't using "energy slaves" to power her car, hair dryer, light bulbs, etc. Interestingly, since we use roughly a third of our energy to power vehicles of various types we are commanding the equivalent of between thirty and forty "slaves," just to move us around. Perhaps even more interesting, Southern Californians, who generally pride themselves on their environmental consciousness, use water that comes from as far as six hundred miles away. When the pumping stations that are needed to pump this water over a mountain pass are running at full capacity, the city is using the equivalent of over 2,000,000 energy slaves just for their water needs. Since the population of Los Angeles is approximately four million, this means about half of the people in the city would be needed at certain times just to supply water to them and their neighbors.

[12] The desertification of large parts of Africa and the island of Haiti are two well-known examples of this.

[13] It has been argued that this is one lasting advantage that many Asian cultures have, which partly explains their rapid growth in the second half of the 20th century, in spite of sometimes lukewarm reception for democracy and completely free markets. It should also be noted, however, that in some cases development improves when young people avoid their ancestors *mistakes* by listening to wise mentors, learning from good books and making wiser choices than their parents. Once again, worldview matters.

[14] Drug and alcohol abuse, cigarette smoking, and overeating, are all examples of activities immensely expensive activities that deplete human capital. This is especially obvious when all of the direct and indirect expenses are added up. For example, cigarette smoking alone is responsible for 25% of the house fires in the U.S. What is less obvious is the cost of excessive/extreme sports and so-called recreational activities that break down bodies rather than build them up, and are also unnecessary for health and sometimes costly and harmful to their participants. In many cases these activities also involve the taking of completely unnecessary risks for little more than an adrenaline rush, money, or the notoriety that accompanies fame. Evel Knievel and his son Robbie, two often-injured daredevil motorcycle riders, may be best-known examples of this kind of activity in the U.S., but there are an increasing number of mini-Knievels engaging in extreme sports all over the world.

[15] The prison industry in the U.S. grew nearly 30% per year between 1990 and 2000, and has led the world in the number of prisoners per capita since that time.

[16] Oxfam International estimates that saving lives through emergency food relief during a crisis costs approximately seven times more over time than preventing severe famines through a combination of improved plant genetics, and changes in farming practices.

[17] Interestingly, these problems may not even only primarily be the fault of the men of the culture. Perhaps some of the blame should be shared by the academically and politically influential, whose worldviews led to policies that assumed discussions of personal morality and ethics must be kept private, and out of the public square. Regardless of how well-intentioned the idea that there must be a wall of separation between personal behavior and public policy, a holistic look at economic development demands that it be reconsidered.

Chapter 22

[1]Many people seem to assume they should have the right to determine what others should think and say of them, as if this can be separated from the reality of their attitudes and actions. In reality unchecked arrogance, unwarranted self-esteem, and various other forms of self-delusion can be seriously detrimental to both people's achievement and their contribution to economic development. This kind of attitude is in contrast to many great leaders who were influential in shaping the course of history in spite of their doubts, struggles and humility. Abraham Lincoln, to give one well-known example, suffered from deep self-doubt but is nevertheless listed on almost every American's list of greatest presidents. This is no surprise to an increasing number of researchers who have come to the conclusion that the correlation between self-esteem and achievement is tenuous at best, and that the small amount of positive correlation that does exist between self-esteem and achievement is most likely because self-esteem *results from* effort and academic achievement rather causing it. Researchers have concluded that high self-esteem is not by itself effective in preventing teen pregnancy, crime, alcohol or drug use (although students who have been nurtured to avoid these things should certainly be expected to end up feeling better about themselves, which could lead to self-esteem). Many other things which also create a drag on economic development - such as many of the pathologies in the U.S. education – are also the result of a willingness to tolerate bad ideas, some of which involve the assumption that widespread self-esteem as a panacea. For more information on this topic, see David Myers' *The Pursuit of Happiness*, or Neil J. Smelser's *Self-Esteem and Social Problems*. An excellent summary of the research as well as a clear description of the problems underlying this debate can be found in "The Truth about Self-Esteem" by Alfie Kohn, retrieved from http://www.alfiekohn.org/teaching/tase.htm on October 24, 2012.

[2] Examples include gun powder, clocks, paper and printing, developed in China, and the decimal system, developed in India.

[3] Many will argue that corporations too often have disproportionate power and have damaged people and nations because of this. It is not our intent to go into a lengthy academic debate about how cooperative ventures can be used for good or ill here; rather we want to note the remarkable efficiencies that are possible through voluntary cooperation.

Chapter 23

[1] Taken from *The American Heritage® Dictionary of the English Language*, Fourth Edition copyright ©2000 by Houghton Mifflin Company. Updated in 2009. Published by Houghton Mifflin Company.

[2] Sir John Templeton, *Agape Love: A Tradition Found in Eight World Religions*, Templeton Foundation Press, 1999. This is of course, not to say that this concept is practiced in the same way or to the same degree within these belief systems, or by subgroups within these belief systems.

[3] Enron, for example, was eventually forced into bankruptcy when it became clear that they had attempted to manipulate energy markets to their advantage (and the expense of their customers), and had manipulated their books without regard to the impact of their actions on shareholders, employees or taxpayers. American Home Products was forced to settle for 3.75 billion in damages when internal memos revealed that company employees were cavalier about the dangers of their diet product Fen Phen to overweight people.

[4] This is not say that organizations cannot lay people off, or terminate employees from time to time, but is assumes that because of a previously demonstrated ethic of care, employees will respect the organization's right to do these things, and that they will be done in a way that continues to earn the employees respect and appreciation.

[5] The Cosa Nostra, often simply referred to as "the mob," was filled with loyal people but their loyalty did a lot of damage to the societies in which they operated, and sometimes even to the members of the mob itself.

[6] Management research, for example, shows positive effects on productivity and job satisfaction from teamwork, qualified and congenial coworkers, good management-employee relations, and reductions in on-job status consciousness. A Gallup study of 400 companies indicated that good friendships at work were one of the most powerful indicators (of twelve researched) of productivity in the workplace. Interestingly, the use of

piecework, which relies heavily on individual rather than group effort, has fallen out of favor in many of the highest-productivity workplaces because it has often failed to deliver expected productivity gains.

[7] Once again, public safety nets, because there is a degree of coercion involved in them, may be reflective of an overall lower level of love for those outside of immediate family and friendship circles than private safety nets, but they still reflect far more concern than exists in places where governments do little or nothing, and people do little more than help family and close friends while allowing neighbors and strangers to fend for themselves. Examples of private safety nets include family support for adult children and relatives, intra-family or affinity group loans, private charitable donations, church benevolence funds, soup kitchens, clothing centers, and the like.

[8] http://siouxcityjournal.com/lifestyles/sioux-county-kidney-donor-search-leader-finds-herself-in-giving/article_50e22bd3-ab86-5380-bddc-c5644d955efb.html

[9] As reported by Carolyn Tyler in "Promise of a Free Education Fulfilled," ABC7 Salutes, July 18, 2008. Accessed August 5, 2010 at http://abclocal.go.com/kgo/story?section=news/abc7_salutes&id=6273986. Eventually 19 of the 23 students helped by Ms. Brown and her foundation graduated from college, compared to only four from another first grade class with a similar demographic profile.

[10] Government donations, however have had mixed results, in part because of the great distance between donor-country taxpayers who are funding "foreign aid" and recipient-country beneficiaries, in part because they are generated by involuntary government mandate. Private donations suffer from this problem to a lesser degree and therefore may be a better barometer of true generosity since they are voluntary and generally involve less "distance" between donor and recipient, and therefore more involvement in each other's lives.

[11] They accomplish this by facilitating regular gifts, pictures and correspondence (including translation services). Organizations like these have enabled millions of people of ordinary means to radically change the lives of others, often half a world away.

[12] It should also be noted that since the marginal benefit of receiving something is greatest for those toward the lower end of the income distribution, (because of the principle of diminishing returns which says, for example, that the first cup of clean water, vitamin pill, or job given to someone is of more benefit than the 2nd, 5th or 10th), the highest return public works projects will generally be those that benefit the largest number of people, and especially the largest number of poor people.

[13] Likewise investing it in things that will make them healthier like clean water or sewage treatment, or increasing employment opportunities by giving incentives for business startups, or making neighborhoods safe for shopping, or boosting educational achievement by giving school vouchers to encourage parents to give more attention to their children's education and the values being taught -or not taught - in the schools, can bring excellent paybacks.

[14] As noted in Chapter 11, research shows that healthy, loving family environments have the potential to lower crime, illegitimacy, pregnancy risk (including problems associated with fetal alcohol or drug abuse), welfare dependency, and a host of other social maladies. According to James J. Heckman's January 10, 2006 page A14 Wall St. Journal article, *Catch 'em Young,* the direct and indirect costs of crime alone in the U.S. are estimated to be 1.3 trillion per year ($4,818 per capita) and many career criminals are the products of families with maladjusted ideas about love. Early intervention on behalf of children, then, can have a very high "return on investment." For example, the Perry Preschool program cited in Heckman's article, attaches economic returns of 15-17% per year to intervention in the lives of children ages 4-6. Of course, the desire to intervene and even sacrifice for the good of one's *own* children is widespread, even among parents who are ill equipped to raise them. The kind of love we are referring to, however, is more than this – it involves drawing circles that are much wider than immediate family and friendship groups. So if we are serious about development, we also need to look for ways to assess the extent of this kind of love. One possibility would be to examine the number of community structures or programs focused on helping *any or all* children; another would be to measure how much is "invested" in children vis-a-vis other kinds of expenditures; yet another might be to look at the adoption rates, and especially the adoption rates of "special needs" children.

[15] Parents who see the special gifts and qualities of individual children, and nurture these, will raise emotionally healthier children. Parents who establish, communicate, and consistently and lovingly enforce rules and limits

with have better adjusted children than those who don't. Parents who are able to discern their children's maturity level and give them appropriate amounts of freedom and responsibility as they mature will also see their children develop more quickly than those who don't. And perhaps most importantly, parents who model attitudes and behaviors like respect, gentleness, self-control, a willingness to work and serve, and especially love, will bless their children much more than those who don't.

[16] It is important to distinguish relief work from development work. By relief we are referring primarily to the difficult job of keeping people alive when relatively short term dislocations like drought, famine or war threaten them.

[17] When pervasive, this kind of love may result in more people who desire to "retire late" than desire to "retire early." It is possible that a ratio of the percentages of people in these two groups could even be used as a creative measurement of sustainable development. Even more telling may be a statistic that measures the percentage of retirement-age people are working or volunteering when it is not financially necessary for them to do so.

[18] As alluded to earlier, these programs also found strong evidence that additional income in the hands of women may multiply more productively than the same amount of income in the hands of males, particularly in subcultures where men have a propensity to spend more on alcohol, cigarettes or weapons, and less on education, health or poverty alleviation than women.

[19] This is especially true when the economic impact of remittances (contributions from overseas family members) is factored in. In some countries remittances can make up as much as 25% of the economy.

[20] See Barro (1991) and Alesina and Perotti (1995). Research also indicates that countries untouched by war have better stock market performance.

[21] Although 911 was an act of unspeakable violence, we recognized that it was certainly not the most destructive in terms of human life, as people in Rwanda and The Congo, and many other countries will remind citizens of the U.S.

Chapter 24

[1] The Confucian emphasis on character development in children can be contrasted to examples of dysfunctional trust relationships elsewhere, and the negative economic effect of these. Untrustworthy adults are expensive to employers and society in general. In addition to the direct damage that they cause, the societies in which they are immersed are saddled with a host of laws, government regulations, conflicts, or problems in organizations, (and the bureaucracy that these things spawn). In cultures where entire groups of people are deemed untrustworthy there are additional drags on development. When "untouchables" are deemed too untrustworthy to hire, their problems become compounded, and their untrustworthiness exacerbated. Where women are not trusted enough to leave the home, or men are perceived as so untrustworthy as to be a risk to women who leave the home, women will be undereducated, underrepresented in business, less productive or confident.

[2] Ralph Barton Perry, *Puritanism and Democracy*, New York: The Vanguard Press, 1944, p. 302.

[3] The best known of these is Francis Fukuyama's *Trust*.

[4] The best organizations delegate both authority and responsibility to managers at all levels of the organization so problems can be solved and decisions made as close as possible to where the problems are noticed or the information is received. (Communist central planning was the antithesis of this.) Herb Kelleher, for example, regularly inspired the highly productive employees of Southwest Airlines by reminding them that "there should be as few rules as possible," which of course both assumed and implied a high trust environment. This kind of "decentralized management" is widely agreed to be the best way to operate efficiently in the modern, fast-paced, constantly changing business world, but is impossible in a low trust environment. Low trust levels, on the other hand, fuel the development of bureaucracy, excessive record keeping and multitudes of people looking over other people's shoulders, rather than the productivity and creativity needed by organizations like Southwest.

[5] Multimillion dollar deals can be finalized over the phone or with a handshake following dinner when the parties are trustworthy. Mergers, acquisitions, and joint ventures happen in a timely manner because the parties involved have a degree of trust that the information they have been given is trustworthy, so details can be worked out later.

[6] It has also contributed to increased global trade and investment. The gradual removal of economic barriers between countries since the Second World War, which has spurred so much wealth creation in the countries that have engaged in it, is in some ways an exercise in trust. In contrast, when governments try to block the movement of goods, technologies or capital between countries, or inspect all the containers coming from a particular place, they damage the global economy by their assumption that the leaders of these countries cannot or should not be trusted.

[7] Economies of scale are essential for an economy to achieve the remarkable benefits of specialization, division of labor and exchange – three of Adam Smith's building blocks for economic development.

[8] These examples remind us that trust, like other investments or assets, can also depreciate. In the same way, if a company deceives its supplier or customer or becomes greedy and takes advantage of the supplier or customer's loyalty, the trust relationship will be broken and the investment will soon be lost.

[9] Customarily, low trust relationships impeded economic development, as individuals and companies operated with a "winner take all" mentality with respect to patents and copyrights. This mentality unfortunately meant keeping proprietary information under close wraps until a company's lawyers could make the case for a patent or copyright. This kind of perspective is justified, of course, when competitors are untrustworthy and would gladly steal such information, making it unlikely that the company could ever recoup its investments in research and development. Fortunately, universities followed a different approach to knowledge developed within the academy, treating it as a quasi-public good and sharing it relatively freely. And even though universities and professors have increasingly viewed their research as a vehicle for personal gain rather than for the benefit of others, most still welcome students from around the world and share their knowledge with them. And new computer technology has also providing new opportunities for documenting collaborative creative efforts, which may accelerate the sharing of ideas, since the documented contributions of various parties can be used to establish relative royalty payments. Hopefully these developments will keep the door open to the kind of rapid flow of information needed to spur development while adequately compensating those whose combined efforts helped create something of value. But this too will depend on the trustworthiness of the participants in these collaborative networks.

[10] The economic effects of racism and the benefits of its eradication warrant a brief historical detour. Many people believe, still today, that great wealth was created on the backs of slaves prior to the abolition of slavery. It is true that slave owners robbed slaves of any reasonable share of the wealth created by their labor, the quantity of wealth created by slaves was then and always will be far less than can be created by free people operating in an atmosphere of trust and respect. Many slaves were neither respected nor trusted, and were treated accordingly, with the result that they were actually less productive than they would have been had they been free. Many slave owners did manage to amass wealth, but the total amount of wealth created was surely far less than would have been created under a more trusting and ethical economic arrangement. So in addition to damaging slaves and their descendants, slave owners also damaged themselves and the general level of development in their countries.

[11] http://www.checkpointsystems.com/en/About/press-releases/2008/Global-Theft-Costs-Retailers-and-Consumers-104-Billion-Annually.aspx

[12] According to an endnote on page 656 in *My Life: A Spoken Autobiography* by Fidel Castro and Ignacio Ramonet.

[13] Fortunately, in this kind of environment, deceptive companies would have great difficulty competing with companies whose employees believed *and acted on* the idea that "honesty is the best policy." So, honest companies would gain market share, at least if the truth about their competitors gets out. This depends on their ability to differentiate their message for others – which, once again, depends on *honesty*.

[14] In fact, the July 2000 Concorde crash is thought to have been the result of damage the plane sustained during takeoff when it hit a counterfeit part that had fallen off another aircraft.

[15] Given the importance of widespread honesty to healthy sustainable development, governments should also ask themselves if creating structures which enable their people to be well informed may ultimately be even more important than having a trained military, redistributing income, or a host of other activities in which they have been comfortably engaged in for many years. Governments clearly will receive as much or more benefit from widespread honesty as from any other social incentive; but this is not to say government is the best incubator for honesty. Rather, its appropriate role is to implement laws, policies and regulations that promote and reward honest behavior and support the institutions best equipped to be incubators of honesty - families, schools and civil society institutions.

[16] Interestingly, studies done by psychologists have indicated that work has more potential to satisfy people than, for example, consumption.

[17] According to Esther Bannerjee's research teacher absenteeism can reach as high as 40% in some countries. See http://www.povertyactionlab.org/publication/absenteeism-showing-first-step.

[18] It is well known in the U.S. that the children of Asian immigrants often outperform students from other ethnic groups. What is less well known is that within this subgroup, academic performance is positively correlated with the number of brothers and sisters a student has. This makes it unlikely that the achievement of the highest performing students is a primarily a function of mom and dad helping them with their homework. More likely it is because many of these families (and many families not of Asian ethnicity) have inculcated critical values into all of their children at an early age that make work and self-discipline seems both normal and normative. Since these families are also having *more* children than other families, it is also unlikely they see the world as a zero sum environment where a fixed sized pie necessitates that families be small in order for everyone to get a decent-sized slice.

Chapter 25

[1] The most novel part of this idea is that wealthy countries can and need to be willing to learn from poorer countries. Part of this involves being open to the possibility that wealthy countries are by the very nature of their economic activity compromising not only their own future wealth and wellbeing, but the wealth and wellbeing of other people around the world and generations yet to be born.

[2] There is, it seems, almost no end to how much money people will spend to try to feel better about themselves, or to portray themselves more positively to others. Examples include the purchase of status symbols, elective plastic surgery, therapy, or expensive cosmetics.

[3] A well-known example is Everett Worthington, Jr.'s *Five Steps to Forgiveness: The Art and Science of Forgiving*.

[4] http://www.mayoclinic.com/health/forgiveness/MH00131

[5] One example of this is the remarkable educational achievement and economic productivity of rural religious Midwesterners in the U.S.

[6] Hugo Restall, Asian Wall St. Journal (see article for reference)

[7] Marian Wright Edelman, the director of the Children's Defense Fund, estimates that as many as 16 million children can be classified as "latchkey" kids. A U.S. Department of Education study in the year 2000 estimated that school aged children spent an average of 20-25 hours without parental supervision per week.

[8] *Dar-al-harb* refers to the custom of some Muslims to classify all non-Muslims as the "house of war," which makes meaningful interaction with them all but impossible. Boko Haram is the Nigerian Islamist sect whose name can be translated as *Western education is a sin*.

[9] See Joshua E. Keatings' June 23, 2010 *Foreign Policy* article, "Lifestyles of the Rich and Tyrannical: A tour of dictators' cribs," for more examples. Accessed August 13, 2010 at http://webcache.googleusercontent.com/search?q=cache:BS1mN0ZJ3w0J:www.foreignpolicy.com/articles/2 010/06/23/homes_of_the_rich_and_tyrannical+kim+jong-il's+mansions&cd=6&hl=en&ct=clnk&gl=us.

[10] In many ways the long-standing Arab/Israeli conflict in the Middle East can be traced to the inability to forgive. In contrast, the post-genocide Rwandan government emphasized the importance of forgiveness in its official policies and experienced remarkable growth within a relatively short time of the 1994 genocide.

[11] To paraphrase a well-known commercial created by the financial services firm E.F. Hutton (which incidentally has since crashed and burned because of an internal ethics scandal), these two countries were forced to "make money the old fashioned way- by *earning* it."

[12] All this is not to say that blue-collar workers aren't also subject to the possibility of productivity-sapping pride. Some seem to believe that people who work with their hands are responsible for creating most of a country's wealth and therefore deserve an outsized portion of it. In the U.S. this contributed to unsustainable union-negotiated wage and benefit increases. It also resulted in the development of an underclass that became convinced that those with advanced degrees were somehow engaged in less noble pursuits or less deserving of their salaries. Had this kind of pride carried the day, it could have greatly impeded the growth of many of the "white collar" and "knowledge worker" industries that are now at the core of the global economy. As it was, it contributed to decreasing competitiveness in several major industries and manufacturing in general over several decades. The point here is not to criticize or venerate either blue or white collar workers, but to underscore how important humility is to economic outcomes. Economists have long recognized the importance of a sizeable middle class to economic growth, but it may be that they were overlooking the most important thing about this - that it is actually the values, work ethic, and humility that are typical of those moving from lower to middle classes that are the real engine of economic growth.

[13] Individuals, people would widely agree, are responsible to "earn a living," but should be free to choose where they work, when, where, and what they eat, and many of the other activities needed to sustain their work, as long as their choices do not endanger others. Parents are responsible to care for the children that they brought into the world, but should be relatively free to choose what to put on the dinner table and what their children will wear or get in the way of birthday presents. Religious communities are responsible for enabling worship, and the teaching and practice of the moral and ethical principles of their faith, but should expect significant autonomy in how they plan their worship services, educate their parishioners or carry out their volunteer work in the community. Likewise, schools are responsible for education, and businesses for providing goods and services at reasonable prices, but neither should be so presumptuous as to try to parent children, choose their employee's career path, or equip an army. Likewise, government is responsible to establish laws, maintain order, and protect its citizens from outside threats, but should not be expected to dictate what people eat for dinner, the books that parents read their children, business inventory levels, or whether or not people should pray.

Chapter 26

[1] What we do here can and should be done, and in some cases has been done, with other faith systems as well, but since we have limited space and time, and are less familiar with their teachings, that task will be left to other authors who can describe them and make the necessary connections more accurately than we.

[2] It is sometimes pointed out that Christ, as recorded in Matthew 26:11, said that "the poor you will always have with you," but this was in no way a statement that poverty is an acceptable state for people to be in.

[3] Ezekiel 18:10-13

[4] see, e.g., Leviticus 25, Numbers 16, Deuteronomy 15 & 23

[5] Acts 4:34-35

[6] Proverbs 3:9,10, Proverbs 11:24,25, Malachi 3:7-12

[7] Interestingly, Peter Drucker, the late preeminent management sage, referred to the rise of the large *pastoral* Christian church on the U.S. scene as "the most significant phenomenon in the second half of the 20th century" (He had said the same for the corporation for the first half of the 20th century). Churches bring people together on a regular basis, collect and dispense large amounts of money, solve community problems, encourage political action, and perform a host of other activities beyond the worship activities and rituals that are commonly associated with them. Some U.S. churches have tens of thousands of members, and hundreds of small groups. The caring networks that are part of these churches have a host of economic impacts. After receiving a call from a Thai pastor that had been trained there, Saddleback Church in California, was, by itself, able to warn many people in affiliated churches throughout South East Asia about the impending December

2004 Tsunami in time for them to reach safety (and long before governments were able to). By the next day this church had already mobilized thousands of volunteers and millions of dollars in aid.

[8] see, e.g., Deuteronomy 8:18, I Samuel 2:6-8, Ecclesiastes 5:18-20, Psalm 24:1

[9] see, e.g., Proverbs 8:17-19, Proverbs 10:3-5, Proverbs 10:21-23, , or Isaiah 60:4-6

[10] see, e.g., Proverbs 30:7-9, Psalm 49, Psalm 62: 9-11, I Timothy 6:9,10

[11] see, e.g., Luke 12:48, Luke 16:10-14, II Corinthians 8, I Timothy 6: 17-19

[12] Luke 12:48

[13] The Gini coefficient is a measure of statistical dispersion first published in 1912 by the Italian statistician Corrado Gini. When applied to income, a value of 0 expresses total equality and a value of 1 maximal inequality. Typically the range for countries will be between .2 and .7.

[14] Other belief systems, such as The Church of Jesus Christ – Latter day Saints (Mormons) also accept the Bible as authoritative, although their beliefs on a number of important doctrinal issue differ substantially from those of Protestant, Catholic or Orthodox believers and will be influenced by some of these same principles. They too would be substantially influenced by some of the Biblical principles discussed here, however, the focus will be primarily on Western, and Protestant Christianity.

[15] Jeremiah 29:11

[16] As the writer of the Old Testament book of Ecclesiastes noted, uncertainty needs to be taken in stride since: "As you do not know the path of the wind, or how the body is formed in a mother's womb, so you cannot understand the work of God, the Maker of all things. [Therefore] sow your seed in the morning, and at evening let not your hands be idle, for you do not know which will succeed, whether this or that, or whether both will do equally well." (Ecclesiastes 11:5, 6)

[17] Proverbs 13:11

[18] Proverbs 28:19-20

[19] Luke 16: 19-31; James 5:1-6

[20] Proverbs 25:28, I Thessalonians 5:6-8, I Timothy 3:2, Titus 2:2

[21] e.g., Isaiah 61

[22] e.g., Jeremiah 34

[23] Exodus 12, 13

[24] In Luke 4:18 Jesus says that God "anointed me to preach good news to the poor. He has sent me to proclaim freedom for the prisoners and recovery of sight for the blind, to release the oppressed." In John 8:31-32, he is quoted as saying to the Jews who had believed in him, "If you hold to my teaching, you are really my disciples. Then you will know the truth, and *the truth will set you free*," and again in verse 36, "If the Son sets you free, you will be free indeed."

[25] Ephesians 3:12

[26] 2 Corinthians 3:17

[27] Galatians 5:1

[28] 1 Corinthians 7:21

[29] John 8:34

[30] 2 Peter 2:19

[31] Galatians 5:13

[32] 1 Corinthians 10:23

[33] 1 Peter 2:16

[34] In addition, some writers have suggested that Protestants receive an extra dose of entrepreneurial spirit because of the boldness that accompanies the belief that all people have direct access to God (as opposed to, e.g., looking to a priest as a mediator).

[35] A sports analogy may be helpful here: even thoughtful rules and well-intended enforcement won't necessarily keep participants from injury if the players' attitudes are inappropriate.

[36] see e.g., Exodus 23:6, Deuteronomy 16:19, or Proverbs 17:23

[37] Although the idea of the Israelites slaughtering entire groups of people (which for whatever reason was recorded in the Bible and available for our reading), is repulsive to most people today (and, we should add, repulsive to almost all Christians), much of what the people groups targeted by the Israelites were doing (e.g., raiding cities, killing innocents, sacrificing children, and treating women as property) is equally repulsive. The Biblical explanation for these things is simply that God hates evil and sometimes chooses to remove entire population groups from the earth to rid the earth of evil. See e.g., Genesis 6:13 and Deuteronomy 9:1-6.

[38] Without trivializing the complexity of war, it is instructive to ask what kind of worldview, short of complete pacifism, would minimize it. One can ask, for example, whether it is more civil to use force to restrain and if necessary kill 100,000 killers, or, because of the repulsive nature of getting directly involved in, and the personal sacrifice associated with a war, stand by while they slaughter millions of innocent victims. To some degree this decision reflects whether things like self-preservation or ideas of national sovereignty dominate one's worldview, or whether concepts like justice and mercy hold more sway.

[39] Hebrews 4:11

[40] John 3:19- 21

[41] See for example, *Releasing the Power of Local Associations and Organizations*, and *Economic Home Cookin': An Action Guide for Congregations on Community Economic Development.*

[42] The Voice of the Martyrs was founded in 1967 by Richard and Sabina Wurmbrand, Jewish converts to Christianity, who had suffered mightily at the hand of the Communists in Romania. Amnesty International was founded, in 1961 by Peter Benenson, a recent convert to Catholicism, and his confidant, Eric Baker, a member of the Religious Society of Friends, who had run a Quaker Center in Delhi before becoming General Secretary of the National Peace Council and an anti-nuclear weapons activist.

Chapter 27

[1] Romans 13:4

[2] Exodus 18:21

[3] Genesis 3:11

[4] Genesis 4:8-10

[5] Genesis 9:5

[6] The only exception we know of to this rule is when the government is attempting to force people to commit specific sins or deny their faith. Peter and his fellow apostles set the precedent for this exception when being questioned by the high priest in front of the Sanhedrin (the Jewish court system), as recorded in Acts 5. When told not to preach in Christ's name, they replied "We must obey God rather than men! (vs.29). Interestingly, although members of the Sanhedrin wanted to put them to death for these words, one of their leaders, Gamaliel is recorded in Acts 5:34-40 as convincing them that it was better to leave them alone and let Christianity fade away like other religious fads. The fact that Acts 5 goes on to record that the apostles "never stopped teaching and proclaiming the good news that Jesus is the Christ," testifies both to the importance of this one exception and to the general rule that Christians strongly support the legitimate authority of government, even when government itself is doing things that they disapprove of. This latter point is also evidenced by the fact that Jesus' followers never entertained any sort of insurgency even when the Roman government wrongfully permitted Jesus to be killed.

[7] Colossians 1:16

[8] Colossians 2:15

[9] Romans 12:18

[10] Leviticus 19:15

[11] Proverbs 29:4

[12] Isaiah 33:15-16

[13] Amos 5:24

[14] Zechariah 8:16

[15] Micah 6:8

[16] Jeremiah 22:13,15,16

[17] Exodus 23:9

[18] Deuteronomy 1:16,17

[19] However, as noted earlier, one cannot escape the reality that the Old Testament records that God spoke *directly* to certain individuals during some historical stretches, and there were times he commanded them to violently purge the evil both in their midst and around them-the apparent presumption being that the objects of God's wrath were not really innocent.

[20] Exodus 21:26-27

[21] Deuteronomy 32:35

[22] Proverbs 24:29

[23] Proverbs 25:21

[24] Romans 12:19-21

[25] e.g., Acts 10:34, Romans 2:11

[26] James 2:9

[27] This is not to say that Christians have done a good job of articulating what a normative political order might look like. They generally agree that governments should be vehicles to enable people to act justly, and that individuals are accountable to God for how they treat their fellow humans (implying that both individuals and diverse groups (large and small) must be given the opportunity to effectively participate in the political process). But, there is disagreement on the degree to which governments are to be facilitators of right conduct. Governments, of course will still have to make moral choices, whether or not they feel it is appropriate to attach them to the teachings of a particular religion. But since it is not possible for laws, courts or diplomacy to be completely secular, since they routinely deals with concepts of right and wrong, and good and evil, they too must wrestle with and choose from competing ideas about right, wrong, appropriate punishment, and/or methods of reconciliation, without regard to whether these ideas have secular or religious origins. And there are no easy answers here. Most Christians agree that people deserve the freedom to live out their beliefs (religious, secular, political, etc.) to the extent that these actions don't harm others, or interfere with their rights or the administration of public justice. So although most Christians agree that governments ought to be both a shield (to protect the vulnerable), and a sword (to punish evildoers, provide protection from invaders, and maintain order), and that they ought to promote justice and nurture civil society, there is much less agreement on what they should do beyond this.

[28] Even a cursory glance through the *Universal Declaration of Human Rights* reveals many connections between our discussion points and the 30 articles found there. The same could be said for the less-well-known *Covenant on Civil and Political Rights* and *Covenant on Economic, Social and Cultural Rights*. The major difference is that the Bible talks almost exclusively about *responsibilities* rather than rights. The two of course are integrally connected. Rights mean nothing if no one feels responsible to protect them. So, in a sense, a document focusing on responsibilities evokes higher expectations than documents focusing on rights. This is clear when we look, at the Biblical responsibility to love. The Apostle Paul's first letter to the Corinthians defines love as follows: "Love is patient, love is kind. It does not envy, it does not boast, it is not proud. It is not rude, it is not self-seeking, it is not easily angered, it keeps no record of wrongs. Love does not delight in evil but rejoices with the truth. It always protects, always trusts, always hopes, always perseveres" (I Corinthians 13:4-7). Jesus and the apostle John define it as the willingness to lay down one's life for another (John 15:13, I John 3:16). Clearly these definitions go beyond justice to something much greater, something with the potential to provide the kind of lasting peace and prosperity that most people can only dream about.

[29] This reminds us once again, that there is a difference between measures of economic output, such as gross domestic product, and the broader concept of human flourishing. Being a slave to the clock may boost GDP but also be counterproductive when it leads to other problems in people's lives.

[30] Genesis 2:15

[31] Luke 16: 19-31; James 5:1-6

[32] Proverbs 25:28, I Thessalonians 5:6-8, I Timothy 3:2, Titus 2:2

[33] e.g., John 4:21-24
[34] e.g., I Samuel 15:21-22
[35] Ephesians 5:28-30
[36] I Corinthians 6:19-20
[37] Gen. 1:26-30; Genesis 9:1-3
[38] A similar stewardship governs time and money devoted to leisure activities. The preferred kind of leisure can be described as "re-creation" in the sense that it restores its participants for work and service. This can be contrasted to many other "leisure" activities which are so competitive and stressful that they lead to frequent injury and the need for rehabilitation.
[39] Psalm 24:1; Psalm 50:10-12.
[40] See, for example, Proverbs 13:22 or Leviticus 25:10.
[41] Leviticus 26:33-35
[42] Psalm 37

Chapter 28

[1] Psalm 51:5
[2] 1 John 3:9
[3] Acts 2:15-21
[4] Revelation 7:9
[5] John 13:13-15
[6] Matthew 5:43, 44
[7] Philippians 2:8
[8] Matthew 28:19-20
[9] see, e.g., Deuteronomy 7:6, 14:2, 14:21
[10] Although many people assume there was a single covenant that spelled out the promised made by God and the Israelite people, there were actually a number of different covenants which have come to be referred to by Biblical scholars by various names such as the Adamic, Noahic, Abrahamic or Mosaic covenants.
[11] I Peter 2:9-10
[12] Romans 12:16
[13] Galatians 5:22-23
[14] Galatians 5:15
[15] Ephesians 4:29
[16] James 1:19
[17] I Timothy 5:13
[18] I Corinthians 12
[19] Matthew 5:44-45
[20] Luke 6:33

Chapter 29

[1] As with other subjects addressed in the past few chapters, the primary influences of Christian beliefs on these virtues come from the Bible, but also from sermons and books based on the Bible, the teachings and doctrines of the church (which seek primarily to interpret and apply Biblical teachings), prayer, and the leading of the Holy Spirit in the lives of individuals and church communities.
[2] Based on the teaching that "to obey is better than to sacrifice," from 1 Samuel 15:22)
[3] Deuteronomy 18:9-11, 14; see also the condemnation of King Manasseh, who practiced these things, in II Kings 21
[4] Galatians 5:19-23
[5] Romans 12:2

[6] As noted in Chapter 26, this kind of thinking is very important to what it means to have a civil society. It is simply not possible to have a civil society in a modern diverse world, unless people have the foundational beliefs that they need to reach common ground with people from other religious persuasions, including both those belief systems traditionally labeled as "religious" (e.g., Animistic, Hindu, Buddhist, Islamic, etc.) and other belief systems, generally thought to be secular (such as agnosticism, atheism, materialism or humanism).

[7] Isaiah 40:8

[8] see, e.g., Exodus 18:21 and Nehemiah 13:13

[9] Proverbs 12: 22

[10] Ephesians 4:25

[11] Colossians 3:9

[12] Acts 5

[13] This is perhaps most painfully obvious in countries whose poverty is exacerbated by the untrustworthiness of the police force or military.

[14] Colossians 3:23

[15] I Corinthians 15:58

[16] Romans 5:3-4

[17] Romans 8:18

[18] I Peter 2 20

[19] Ephesians 4:28

[20] Proverbs 12:24

[21] Proverbs 6:6-11

[22] II Thessalonians 3:6-8

[23] See McCloskey's *Bourgeois Virtues,* pg. 461.

[24] James 2:15-16

[25] Luke 12:48

[26] An expression that may not be familiar to all readers, the carrot and stick, often used to motivate horses, represent positive and negative motivators. But both are examples of external, rather than internal motivators.

[27] Deuteronomy 6:6-9; and 11:18-20

[28] Proverbs 11:2

[29] Proverbs 15:33

[30] Proverbs 22:4

[31] Philippians 2:3

[32] I Peter 5:5

[33] In support of this, many of the Old Testament rituals carried out by the priests were for the express purpose of acknowledging the centrality of forgiveness to the wellbeing of the people. Likewise, the core message of the New Testament gospels, is that God forgives people their sins through Christ's atoning sacrifice, but that this act of forgiveness can only be "complete" when it is understood within the context of repentance and restoration.[33] In fact, forgiveness is so wrapped up in the gospel message that Christians have little choice but to accept that in some mysterious way, God's willingness/ability to forgive Christians is tied to Christians' willingness to forgive others.[33] In addition to forgiveness being at the very heart of God's nature, Biblical history and the Christian gospel message, there are many examples throughout the Bible of praiseworthy people who exercised forgiveness (such as Joseph and Jesus) and others who were commended for it. Other verses simply encourage or command people to forgive as necessary and normal for healthy social relationships. For example, the Apostle Paul, in his letter to the Colossian Christians says, "Bear with each other and forgive whatever grievances you may have against one another. Forgive as the Lord forgave you".[33] And when Peter asks Jesus (as recorded in Matthew 18) if he must be willing to forgive his to be willing to forgive his offending "brother" seven times (a number signifying completeness to the Jews), he is told instead to forgive him seventy seven (or as some translators insist, seventy times seven) times.

[34] This idea is central to the very concept of religious belief, since the English word *religion* comes from the Latin *re ligare* which means, literally, to be "bound back."

[35] This is in clear contrast to cultures influenced by religious or secular beliefs that put a great deal of emphasis on not losing face, or otherwise receiving a stain on one's reputation that is almost impossible to overcome.

[36] One of the most important of these principles, which has been referred to as subsidiarity in Catholic teaching, and "sphere sovereignty" in some Protestant circles, holds that decision making power should rest a close to those affected by the decision as possible – which suggests that national governments should vest individuals, families, local churches, civil society organizations, etc. with as the authority to solve their problems to the greatest degree possible.

[37] Hodgkinsin and Weitzman's 1996 study, indicates, e.g., that regular church attendants volunteer more, that sacraments and open membership policies dampen class consciousness, and fellowship activities hone interpersonal and communication skills.

Chapter 30

[1] When we examine these later in the chapter, we will concentrate on writings by Christian business people who have had enough control in their companies to be able to integrate Christian principles into their mission and vision statements and their operations. Many more Christians, of course, work in organizations that make no particular attempt to inculcate Christian principles into their operations. Although many of them will guided by Christian principles in the sphere of their authority, this is by necessity be done in less explicit ways than in Christian owned and operated companies.

[2] See, for example, Leviticus 19:14,35-36, 25:14&17.

[3] Psalm 15:4

[4] At the time of this writing, Jews made up approximately two-tenths of one percent of the global population, but had been involved in approximately 20 % of the research and creative activity that had been deemed worthy of being awarded Nobel Prizes (since the inception of the program).

[5] At the time of this writing, Israel, despite its small population, was among the top twenty-five economies in the world, was ranked near the top in skilled labor. In the U.S., Jews far exceeded national norms in the percentage of high-school graduates going on to college, and entrepreneurship and business ownership rates.

[6] Interestingly, it is neither belief systems that elevate wealth above ethical living nor those communities that deprecate the accumulation of wealth that seem to have the most vibrant business environments.

[7] See, for example, Genesis 1:28 and Genesis 2:15.

[8] Recorded in Matthew 25:14-30 and Luke 19:12-28

[9] See Matthew 20:28 and Mark 10:45.

[10] See, for example, Romans 5:3-5 and 8:28, and the first chapter of the book of James.

[11] In this sense Christianity encourages entrepreneurship. The center of a Christian's faith involves the creator/owner of the entire universe denying himself all of the luxuries of his lofty position, enduring pain and eventually giving up everything, including his life, for his creatures.

[12] Some of these differences, such as the Catholic and Orthodox Churches' historically strong distinction between clergy from laity (over against the Protestant churches' insistence that bakers and butchers also have a sacred calling) and their centralization of authority (compared to the Protestant Church's decentralization and emphasis on personal salvation), or the Calvinist sanctioning of money lending and description of work as a form of worship, or some Pentecostal tendencies to find a stronger connection between wealth and prayer than between wealth and education or work, have profoundly influenced business activity. For long periods of history, at least in Western culture, "elites" found little good to say about business; things like trading, money lending, building cars or selling bread was fine if that was all a person could do, but the general assumption was that these kinds of jobs ought never to be spoken of in the same sentence with professions such as medicine, law or the clergy. Gentlemen either didn't have to work in such lowly professions or would not because they had more important work to do. Interestingly it is only in the past few centuries that business activity has been viewed more favorably in the West by people in the government, academy or church. Although the Catholic Church developed law and administrative procedures to manage its multinational assets and Aquinas laid important groundwork for property law and business ethics, it took reformers like Luther and Calvin to lay the

foundations for widespread acceptance of private property, the crafts, trade, profits, financial markets and institutions and writers like Adam Smith and Max Weber to write about the intersection between religion and economics to jump-start the progression toward the modern global market economy. Not incidentally this period has also included several intervals wherein global growth in economic wellbeing has been quite remarkable.

[13] That none of these people on this list (or any list) were perfect goes without saying. But neither that nor the incomplete caricatures of some of them as "robber barons" can be addressed here. What can be noted is that there is an extremely long history of people motivated by faith who have created a great deal of wealth. In most cases, even those not applauded for their personal generosity have created far more wealth for others than they accumulated themselves. If one looks at the wealth created for the stockholders of the companies headed up by the individuals listed above, or the wealth created for their employees through the salaries received, or for their customers through the usefulness of the products and services received, or for the citizens who benefited from the taxes paid, it does not take a rocket scientist to figure out that they created far more wealth for others than they accumulated for themselves. For example, Carnegie and Rockefeller each managed to lower the price of what they were producing (steel and oil) by around 75% while increasing their employees wages (in spite of the fact that Carnegie was relentless, and ultimately successful in his drive to break the unions) during the last decades of the 19th century. The same is true today for those who, through their entrepreneurial energies, create and distribute innovative products and services today. Every year Microsoft, Dell and other companies deliver hundreds of time more computing power than was possible just a few years earlier for far less money. In addition, most of the people in the list above (and lots of business people since) have given large percentages of their fortunes away, creating wealth in other ways (as noted in previous discussions dealing with the value of intellectual, spiritual, or social capital or on the importance of not-for-profit organizations).

[14] Most interestingly, John grew up in a home with a father who could perhaps best be described as a kind of "snake oil salesmen" and a devoutly religious (Baptist) mother.

[15] These words are from Luke 12:48. Many Christians will argue that some of these capitalists had a very limited understanding of what was "expected" of them - in particular responsibilities that go beyond charitable giving, including care for employees and just pricing for customers. But it cannot be argued that the foundations they started and community infrastructure that they built was motivated by Christian beliefs.

[16] Grudem, Wayne. *Business to the Glory of God*, Crossway Books, 2003; Seebeck, Doug and Timothy Stoner. *My Business My Mission*, Partners Worldwide, Grand Rapids, MI, 2009; Beckett, John D. *Loving Monday: Succeeding in Business Without Selling Your Soul*. Downers Grove: InterVarsity Press, 1998; Briner, Bob and Ray Pritchord. *The Leadership Lessons of Jesus*. Broadman and Holman, Nashville, Tn., 1997; Chewning, Richard; Eby, John; Roels, Shirley. *Business through the Eyes of Faith*. San Francisco: Harper and Row, 1990; Hill, Alexander. *Just Business, Christian Ethics for the Marketplace*. Downers Grove: Intervarsity Press. 1997; Nash, Laura. *Believers in Business*. Thomas Nelson Publishers. 1994; Novak, Michael. *Business as a Calling, Work and the Examined Life*. Free Press. 1996; Rae, Scott and Kenman Wong. *Beyond Integrity: A Judeo-Christian Approach to Business Ethics*. Grand Rapids: Zondervan, 1996.

[17] Historically assumptions that virtues like love, temperance, justice or courage somehow conflicted with "economic prudence" - which was too often viewed as an elevation of self-interest over virtue – were also pervasive. But any careful study of successful companies over a long period of time indicates that these assumptions are misguided. The most successful businesses are those who have been able to identify and inculcate values that serve people well in all areas of life – albeit in a way that recognizes the realities of life in a complex global market economy. It is easy for families and small groups to work out their resource allocation decision without markets, prices or exchanges. But as groups become larger or the number of products and services become more complex, or as relationships between participants become more tenuous, arm's lengths transactions become the next best alternative. This is not to say that the virtues that work well in the family and church have no place in business; only that human nature and social realities do not generally allow for these virtues to work in the same way in large groups (such as corporations) as in small. Nevertheless,

businesses that have enabled thousands of employees to adopt and share important values to the point that they function as one unified whole have become particularly influential in the global economy.

[18] This is not to say of course that profits and religious belief are at loggerheads, or that profit must be seen as unimportant when business activity flows from religious motivation. High profits are often a sign that there are too few businesses supplying products and services that people want. Profit is necessary to attract investment capital to the business (much as wages or salaries are necessary to attract workers), and to treat owners, savers, and other risk-takers justly. In some ways, it can be viewed as a wage – a payment for highly skilled labor – the labor of being alert to people's needs and wants and going through the trouble of risking large amounts of money and figuring out how to bring myriad "factors of production" together to make and deliver these things. So we should not conclude prematurely that religious faith is necessarily at odds with highly rewarding business or economic activity. Faith and obedience can encourage a genuine concern for others, cooperation, a willingness to serve, self-control, patience, hard work, a willingness to take risks, and a host of other potentially (economically) rewarding proclivities. Rather, profits would simply be understood in the context of the responsibilities that business people have to God, his creation, and the many other groups of people (in addition to owners) affected by the activities of the business.

[19] In addition to taking advantage of the consumer, overselling does little more than create artificial buying "booms" interspaced with economic lulls - making the companies' sales, and if practiced widely, the business cycle more pronounced than necessary.

[20] See, for example, Luke 20:25 and Romans 13:6-7.

Chapter 31

[1] Philippians 4:12

[2] http://www.barna.org/barna-update/article/18-congregations/41-new-study-shows-trends-in-tithing-and-donating

[3] Understanding the role of church in relative to Western exploitation and conflict also requires that we recognize that in spite of apparent privilege, many European churches had become little more than historically interesting structures, an ethnic or national designation, representing little more than habitual church attendance or vague moral knowledge rather than a radical life changing virtuous form of existence. How else can we explain a Serbian soldier who trades the peace of Christ for scourge of war, and who is caught on camera flashing three fingers, a symbol of the most holy Trinity, as he departs for his mission to indiscriminately kill Croatian or Albanian enemies? Likewise, Christ's command to love enemies was horribly misapplied by people from nominally Christian countries when they stood idly by when millions of innocent civilians were slaughtered in Kampuchea, Rwanda, or the Democratic Republic of the Congo, rather than risk the possibility of harm. In such cases it can be plausibly argued that their unwillingness to engage in an armed struggle against evil resulted in far more violence, destruction and death than an armed struggle might have. Other examples of this include the watered-down version of German Christianity that is sometime associated with Nazi Anti-Semitism (although many writers have noted that the worldview that allowed Hitler's ascension to power was really neo-pagan and was not a kind of hyper Christianity that some have claimed it to be); as is obvious to anyone with even a passing familiarity with the Biblical New Testament, much of much of what the Nazis did required an almost complete repudiation of the teachings of Jesus.

[4] See, for example, John 1:3 and Colossians 1:15.

Chapter 32

[1] See, for example *The Humanist Manifesto of 1933* and its successor documents available at www.americanhumanist.org/...humanism/Humanist_Manifesto_III and elsewhere.

[2] We also acknowledge that the forms of secular materialism that arose in communist countries are quite different than those that arose in Europe or the U.S. Much of this difference can be attributed to differences in the influences of Christianity, both in terms of the differences between the Orthodox, Catholic and Protestant

churches, and in the degree to which a particular expression of secularism felt the need to crush the church rather than settle for gradually infiltrating and/or marginalizing it over long periods of time.

[3] Although these beliefs are still firmly adhered to, the first lost a significant amount of credibility when the communist utopian dreams unraveled in the 20th century, and the limitations of the second have become more apparent since then, as freedom has increasingly been taken to excess – to the detriment of the broader community.

[4] Additional clarity on connections between secularist beliefs and our pro-development values is welcomed, but this requires that scholars dedicate research efforts to clarifying secular "doctrine" and probing the connections between these doctrines and the many things known to promote development.

Chapter 33

[1] Marshall's article titled, "Fundamentalists and Other Fun People: To Know Them is Not to Despise Them," was published in the November 22, 2004 issue of News Corporation's *Weekly Standard*. Well known secular columnists and public figures quoted in the article include Ellen Goodman, Michael Lind, Al Gore, Robert Reich, and Maureen Dowd.

[2] This kind of generalizing seems especially unwise after observing the concern of the Pennsylvania Amish community for the family of the man who killed their daughters in the 2006 school shooting

[3] Although not discussed directly by Marshall, Richard Dawkins, the outspoken evolutionary biologist, reveals the worst kind of bigotry by referring to the religious teaching of children as "child abuse." Likely because he has been unable to experience in his life what many religious believers have experienced in theirs, he feels justified in insisting that his experience is the norm and his perspective the only valid one. But given the positive contributions of many religious believers, many of whose beliefs were lovingly nurtured by their parents, it is fair to say that if the world were filled with Richard Dawkinses it would be a much darker and narrower place, to say the least, than it is.

[4] A value-neutral measure like GDP will not only go up when good things happen – e.g., when people innovate and create wealth, but also when bad things happen – e.g., when relationships and communities break down and people no longer look out for each other. In these situations, people are often forced to buy goods that might previously have been borrowed or shared, or to buy services that had previously been provided gratis. Likewise, when internet access allows generous people to give away information that would have previously been paid for, GDP will drop, even though people may actually be better off with free information. This is especially true as the 21st Century unfolds and a larger share of the global economy can be characterized as knowledge-based. When amazing personal assistance, problem-solving and enterprise management software can be duplicated with very little cost, in fact so little that individuals and companies can afford to give millions of copies away and still be well compensated, the idea of measuring the health of an economy by some arbitrary measure of total spending seems particularly outdated.

[5] Plastic surgeries in the U.S. went up 400% during the first decade of the 21st century – in spite of difficult economic times.

[6] The ouster of religious beliefs from the public square leaves only one contender — the politically acceptable but ultimately amoral belief system of secularism. This belief system, although having some advantages over radical Islam or fundamentalist Christianity, also has severe weaknesses, especially when given monopoly rights in public schools and the public square. It has contributed to many of the problems discussed earlier by, for example, privatizing important religious beliefs and supplanting time worn ideas about right and wrong with fuzzy relativism. This has also promoted a shift from authority to preference, which although healthy in some respects also opens the door to a variety of opportunities for young people to justify not cooperating with legitimate authorities. It has also replaced the teaching discussion of religion and moral and ethical precepts with an emphasis on spirituality (which can be made to mean almost everything or nothing), and accelerated the degeneration of authentic community into individualism, since one's spirituality is by assumption intensely personal, and therefore unaccompanied by, or subject to, the rigors of community accountability.

Chapter 34

[1] We speculate that few would claim that what happened at the Abu Ghraib prison in Iraq is unrelated to Hollywood films that desensitize the American public to violence and torture; or how the Abu Ghriab videos and pictures made it easier for terrorists group to recruit new members; and added to the number of lost lives and the costs associated with attempts to stabilize the situation in Iraq. But there can be little doubt that the impact, both in human and economic terms, was substantial.

[2] As noted in *Business Week*, August 18-25, 2003 pg. 115.

[3] This is not to say that achieving perfection is in any way related to achieving salvation, Rather that the Bible reports Christ telling his followers in Matthew 5:48 to "Be perfect, therefore, as your heavenly father is perfect," and the apostle Paul encouraging people to be "imitators of the Lord" in I Thessalonians 1:6."

Chapter 35

[1] http://www.nationmaster.com/graph/cri_pri_per_cap-crime-prisoners-per-capita

[2] I Corinthians 6:19-20

Chapter 36

[1] One reason for this is that the primary commitments of secular materialists and humanists, such as individual autonomy and freedom, allow people a great deal of latitude in how they live their lives. When this is combined with atheism or agnosticism, it is hard to decipher the fundamental "doctrines" and implications of these belief systems for the purpose of evaluating their underlying integrity. For example, does a strong belief that there is no God mean each individual can decide for herself what is right and wrong? Does someone who believes life ends with death have the right to maximize his personal pleasure during life, even to the detriment of others? Does a commitment to Darwinian thinking relegate us to also accepting "survival of the fittest" in the arena of human affairs? It appears that the difficulty involved in formalizing these belief systems will continue to make the answers to these and similar questions very had to determine.

[2] It is also noteworthy that the countries with abysmal religious freedom records, unless they also have oil revenues, are also near the bottom in terms of economic performance.

[3] Democracy, of course is already actively promoted around the world, but cultural relativism has significantly impeded the export of social and spiritual capital.

Bibliography

Acemoglu, Daron, and James Robinson. *Why Nations Fail.* New York: Crown Publishering Group, a subsidiary of Random House Inc., 2012.

Acemoglu, Daron, Simon Johnson, and James Robinson. "Reversal of Fortune: Geography and Institutions in the Making of the Modern World Income Distribution." *Quarterly Journal of Economics* 117 (2004): 1231-1294.

Acemoglu, Daron, Simon Johnson, and James Robinson. "The Colonial Origins of Comparative Development: An Empirical Investigation." *American Economic Review*, 2001.

Aikman, David. *Jesus in Beijing: How Christianity is Transforming China and Changing the Global Balance of Power.* Washington D.C.: Regnery Publishing, 2003.

Akram Khan, Muhammed. *Islamic Economics and Finance: A Glossary.* 2nd ed. New York: Routledge, 2007.

Anderson, Gary M. "Mr. Smith and the Preachers: The Economics of Religion in the Wealth of Nations." *Journal of Political Economy* 96, no. 5 (1988): 1066-1088.

Audretsh, David B., ed. *Entrepreneurship and Openness.* Northampton: Edward Elgar Publishing, 2009.

Ayittey, George N. *Africa in Chaos.* New York: St. Martin's Press, 1998.

Bannerjee, Abhijit, and Esther Duflo. *Poor Economics: A Radical Rethinking of the Way to Fight Global Poverty.* New York: PublicAffairs, 2011.

Barro, Robert J. "Economic Growth in a Cross Section of Countries." *Quarterly Journal of Economics*, 1991: 407-443.

Barro, Robert J., and Rachel M. McCleary. "Religion and Economic Growth." *American Sociological Review* 68 (2003): 760-781.

Bibliography

Barro, Robert J., and Rachel M. McCleary. "Religion and Economy." *Journal of Economic Perspectives*, 2006.

Barro, Robert J., and Rachel M. McCleary. "Religion and Political Economy in an International Panel." *Journal for the Scientific Study of Religion*, 2006.

Beckett, John D. *Loving Monday: Succeeding in Business Without Selling Your Soul.* Downers Grove: InterVarsity Press, 1998.

Berger, Peter L., ed. *The Capitalist Spirit: Toward a Religious Ethic of Wealth Creation.* San Francisco: ICS Press/ Institute for Contemporary Studies, 1990.

Bernstein, Peter. *Capital Ideas Evolving.* Hoboken: John Wiley & Sons, Inc., 2007.

—. *Capital Ideas: The Improbable Origins of Modern Wall Street.* New York: The Free Press, A Division of Simon & Schuster Inc., 1993.

Bloom, David E., and Sachs Jeffery. "Geography, Demography, and Economic Growth in Africa." *Brookings Papers on Economic Activity* 2 (1998): 207-295.

Blum, Ulrich, and Leonard Dudley. "Religion and Economic Growth: Was Weber Right?" *Journal of Evolutionary Economics* 22, no. 2 (2001): 207-230.

Bornstein, David, and Susan Davis. *Social Entrpreneurship.* New York: Oxford University Press, 2010.

Braithwaite, Valoerie, and Margaret Levi. *Trust and Governance.* New York: Russel Sage Foundation, 1998.

Brennan, Geoffery H., and A. M. C. Waterman, ed. *Economics and Religion: Are they Distinct?* Dordrecht, Netherlands: Kluwer Academic Publishers, 1994.

Briner, Bob, and Ray Pritchord. *The Leadership Lessons of Jesus.* Nashville: Broadman and Holman, 1997.

Brown, Montague. *Freedom, Philosophy, and Faith: The Transformative Role Of Judeo- Christian Freedom in Western Thought.* Lexington: Lexington Books, 2011.

Brownlie, Ian. *Basic Documents on Human Rights* . 3rd. Oxford, England: Clarendon Press, 1992.

Bruce, Steve. "Religion and Rational Choice: A Critique of Economic Explanations of Religious Behaviour." *Sociology of Religion* 54, no. 2 (1993): 193-205.

Carroll, Vincent. *Christianity on Trial: Arguments Against Anti-Religious Bigotry.* New York: Encounter Books, 2001.

Carson, Ben. *Think Big: Unleashing Your Potential for Excellence.* Grand Rapids: Zondervan, 2006.

Bibliography

Chambers , Simone, and Will Kymlicka, . *Alternative Conceptions of Civil Society.* Princeton, Princeton University Press, 2002.

Chatterji, Saral Kumar. *Religious Values and Economic Development: A Case Study.* Bangalore: Christian Institute for the Study of Religion and Society, 1967.

Chewning, Richard, John Eby, and Shirley Roels. *Business through the Eyes of Faith.* San Francisco: Harper and Row, 1990.

Chua, Amy. *World on Fire: How Exporting Free Market Democracy Breeds Ethnic Hatred and Global Instability.* New York: Anchor Books, 2004.

Clark, Robert Edward David. *Christian Belief and Science.* Philidelphia: Muhlenberg Press, 1961.

Clawson, David L. "Religious Allegiance and Economic Development in Rural Latin America." *Journal of Interamerican Studies and World Affairs* 26, no. 4 (1984): 449-524.

Clouse, Robert, ed. *Wealth and Poverty: Four Christian Views of Economics.* Downers Grove: Inter Varsity, 1984.

Cohen, Jere. *Protestantism and Capitalism: The Mechanisms of Influence.* Piscataway: Transaction Publishers, 2003.

Collier, Paul. *The Bottom Billion.* Oxford; New York: Oxford University Press, 2007.

Collier, Paul, and Jan Willem Gunning. "Explaining African Economic Performance." *Journal of Economic Literature XXXVII,* 1999: 64-111.

Comstock, George W., and K. B. Partridge. "Church Attendance and Health." *Journal of Chronic Disease,* 1972: 665-672.

Corbett, Steve, and Brian Fikkert. *When Helping Hurts.* Chicago: Moody Publishers, 2009.

Covey, Stephen. *Habits of Highly Effective People .* New York: Simon and Schuster, 1989.

—. *Principle Centered Leadership.* New York: Simon and Schuster, 1992.

Coyle, Diane. *The Economics of Enough: How to Run the Economics as if the Future Matters.* Princeton: Princeton University Press, 2011.

Daley- Harris, Sam. *Pathways out of Poverty: Innovations in Microfinance for the Poorest Families.* Bloomfield: Humarian Press Inc., 2002.

Daum, Menachem, and Marvin A. Lavenhar. "Religiosity and Drug Use." *National Institute of Drug Abuse* (DHEW Publication No. (ADM)), 1980.

Bibliography

De Soto, Hernando. *The Mystery of Capital: Why Capitalism Triumps in the West and Fails Everywhere Else.* New York: Basic Books, 2001.

Demerath, N. J., ed. *Sared Companies: Organizational Aspects of Religion and Religious Aspects of Organizations.* New York: Oxford University Press, 1998.

DePree, Max. *Leadership is an Art.* New York: Doubleday and Company, 1989.

—. *Leadership Jazz.* New York: Dell Publishing Company, 1992.

—. *Leading Without Power: Finding Hope in Serving Community.* Holland: Shepherd Foundation, 1997.

Diamond, Jared. *Guns, Germs and Steel: The Fates of Human Societies.* New York: W.W. Norton & Company Inc., 1999.

Diehl, William. *Thank God, It's Monday.* Minneapolis: Fortress Press, 1982.

Diener, Ed, Danie Kahneman, and John Helliwell . *International Differences in Wellbeing.* New York: Oxford University Press, 2010.

Dionne, Eugene Joseph, ed. *Community Works: The Revival of Civil Society in America.* Washingon DC: Brookings Institute Press, 1998.

Dommen, Edward, and James D. Bratt, . *John Calvin Rediscovered: The Impact of His Social and Economic Thought.* Louisville: Westminster John Knox Press, 2007.

Drake, Deborah, and Elisabeth Rhyne. *The Commercialization of Microfinance: Balancing Business and Development.* Bloomfield: Humarian Press Inc., 2003.

Dunning, John, ed. *Globalization Good: The Moral Imperatives of Global Capitalism.* New York: Oxford University Press, 2002.

Easterbrook, Gregg. *The Progress Paradox: How Life Gets Better While People Feel Worse.* New York: Random House Trade Paperbacks, 2003.

Easterly, William, and Ross Levine. "Africa's Growth Tragedy: Policies and Ethnic Divisions." *Quarterly Journal of Economics* 112(4) (1997): 1203-1250.

Easterly, William, and Ross Levine. "Tropics, Germs, and Crops: How Endowments Influence Economic Development." *Journal of Monetary Economics* 50 (2003): 3-39.

Eberly, Don. *The Essential Civil Society Reader.* Lanham: Rowman & Little Field Publishers, Inc., 2000.

Eberyl, Don. *America's Promise: Civil Society and the Renewal of American Culture.* Lanham: Rowman & Littlefield Publishers, 1991.

Eblery, Don. *The Rise of Global Civil Society.* New York: Encounter Books, 2008.

Bibliography

Edin, Per-Anders, Peter Fredriksson, and Olof Aslund. "Ethnic Enclaves and the Economic Success of Immigrants- Evidence from a Natural Experiment." *Quarterly Journal of Economics*, 2003: 329-357.

Edmunds, John C., and John E. Marthinsen. *Wealth by Association: Global Prosperity Through Market Unification.* Westport: Praeger, A Division of Greenwood Publishing Group, 2002.

Etzioni, Amitai. *The New Golden Rule.* New York: Basic Books, 1996.

Finn, Daniel K., ed. *The True Wealth of Nations: Catholic Social Thought and Economic Life.* New York: Oxford University Press, 2010.

Finn, James. "Religion and Economics: Growth is One Thing and Development Quite Another." *Worldview* 24 (1981): 4-6.

Fogel, Robert. *The Fourth Great Awakening and the Future of Egalitarianism.* Chicago: University of Chicago Press, 2000.

Frankel, Jeffery, and David Romer. "Does Trade Cause Growth?" *American Economic Review* 89(3) (1999): 379-399.

Freeman, Richard B. "Who Escapes? The Relation of Church-Going and Other Background Factors to the Socio-Economic Performance of Black Male Youths from Inner-City Poverty Tracts." Cambridge: Working Paper Series No. 1656, National Bureau of Economic Research, 1985.

Fukuyama, Francis. *Trust: The Social Virtues and the Creation of Prosperity.* New York: The Free Press, 1995.

Gallup, John Luke, and Jerffery D. Sachs. "The Economic Burden of Malaria." *The American Journal of Tropical Medicine & Hygiene* 64 (2001).

Glendon, Mary Ann, and David Blackenhorn, . *Seedbeds of Virtue: Sources of Competence, Character, and Citizenship in the American Society.* Lanham: Madison Books, 1995.

Grier, Robin. "The Effect of Religion on Economic Develpment: A Cross National Study of 63 Former Colonies." *Kyklos* 50 (1997): 47-62.

Grier, Robin. "Toothless Tigers? East Asian Economic Performance from 1960-1990." *Review of Development Economics* 7 (2003): 392-405.

Gruber, Jonathan H. "Religious Market Structure, Religious Participation, and Outcomes: Is Religion Good for You?" *Advances in Economic Analysis & Policy* 5, no. 1, Article 5 (2005).

Guiso, Luigi, Paola Sapienza, and Luigi Zingales. "People's Opium? Religion and Economic Attitudes." *Journal of Monetary Economics* 50 (2003): 225-282.

Bibliography

Hamer, Dean H. *The God Gene: How Faith is Hardwired into our Genes.* New York: Random House Inc., 2004.

Harrison, Lawrence E. *Who Prospers? How Cultural Values Shape Economic and Political Success.* New York: Basic Books, 1992.

Hayes, Samuel L., and Frank E Vogel. *Islamic Law and Finance: Religion, Risk and Return.* Vol. 16. Alphen, Netherlands: Kluwer Law International, 1998.

Heclo, Hugh, and Wilfred M. McClay, . *Religion Returns to the Public Square: Faith and Policy in America.* Baltimore: The Johns Hopkins University Press, 2003.

Hill, Alexander. *Just Business, Christian Ethics for the Marketplace.* Downers Grove: InterVaristy Press, 1997.

Hinds, Hilary. *George Fox and Early Quaker Culture.* Manchester: Manchester University Press, 2011.

Hinshaw, Drew. "New Attacks Threaten Nigeria's Future." *Wall St. Journal*, 2012.

Hopper, Kenneth, and William Hopper. *The Puritan Gift: Reclaiming the American Dream Amidst Global Financial Chaos.* New York: I.B.Tauris, 2009.

Houck, John, and Oliver Williams, . *The Judeo-Christian Vision and the Modern Corporation.* Notre Dame: University of Notre Dame, 1982.

Houle, Robert J. *Making African Christianity: Africans Re-Imagining their Faith in Colonial Southern Africa.* Lehigh: Lehigh University Press, 2011.

Huan- Chang, Chen. *The Economic Principles of Confucius and His School.* Honolulu: University Press of the Pacific, 2003.

Iannaccone, Laurence R. "Progress in the Economics of Religion." *Journal of Insititutional and Theoretical Economics* 150, no. 4 (1994): 737-744.

Iannaccone, Laurence R. "The Consequences of Religious Market Structures: Adam Smith and the Economics of Religion." *Rationality and Society*, 1991: 156-177.

Innaccone, Laurence R. "Introduction to the Economics of Religion." *Journal of Economic Literature* 36, no. 3 (1998): 1465-1495.

Jeremy, David, ed. *Religion, Business and Wealth in Modern Britain.* London: Routledge, 1998.

Jonassen, Christen. "Ethical Systems and Economic Development." *Southeast Asian Journal of Social Science* 1, no. 1 (1973): 117-127.

Jonassen, Christen. "The Protestant Ethic and the Spirit of Capitalism in Norway." *American Sociological Review*, 1947.

Bibliography

Jones, Laurie Beth. *Jesus, CEO*. New York: Hyperion Books, 1995.

Kennedy, D. James. *What if Jesus Had Never Been Born?* Nashville: Thomas Nelson Punlishers, 1994.

Kotkin, Joel. *Tribes: How Race, Religion, and Identity Determine Success in the New Global Economy*. New York: Random House , 1992.

Kramer, Hilton, and Roger Kimball, . *The Betrayal of Liberalism: How Disciples of Freedom and Equality Help Foster the Illiberal Politics of Coercion and Control*. Chicago: Ivan R. Dee, 1999.

Krugman, Paul. "The Myth of Asia's Miracle." *Foreign Affairs*, 1994: 62-78.

Kuttner, Robert. *Everything for Sale: The Virtues and Limits of Markets*. Chicago: University of Chicago Press, 1997.

Lal, Deepak. *Unintended Consequences: The Impact of Factor Endowments, Culture, and Politics on the Long Run Economic Performance*. Cambridge: Cambridge University Press, 1998.

Landes, David S. *The Wealth and Poverty of Nations: Why are Some so Rich and Some So Poor*. New York: W. W. Norton & Company Inc., 1998.

Mangalwadi, Vishal, and Ruth Mangalwadi. *The Legacy of William Carey*. Wheaton: Crossway Books, 1999.

Meeter, H. Henry. *The Basic Ideas of Calvinism*. Grand Rapids: Baker Publishing Group, 1990.

Micklethwait, John, and Adrian Wooldridge. *God is Back: How the Global Revival of Faith is Changing the World*. New York: The Penguin Press, 2009.

Muller, Jerry Z. *Adam Smith: His Time and Ours*. Princeton: Princeton University Press, 1993.

Murray, Christopher J. L., et al. "Eight Americas: Investigating Mortality Disparities Across Race, Counties, and Race-Counties in the United States." *PLoS Med* 3(9) (2006).

Myers, Bryant L. *Walking With the Poor: Principles and Practices of Transformational Development*. Maryknoll: Orbis Books, 2011.

Myers, David. *The Pursuit of Happiness: Who is Happy and Why*. New York: William Morrow, 1992.

Nash, Laura. *Believers in Business*. Nashville: Thomas Nelson Publishers, 1994.

Neibuhr, H. Roberts. *Christ and Culture*. New York: Harper & Row, 1956.

Nelson, Richard R., and Howard Pack. "The Asian Miracle and Modern Growth Theory." *The Economic Journal*, 1999: 416-436.

Bibliography

Novak, Michael. "The Millennium That Was: How Christianity Created Capitalism." *The Wall Street Journal*, 1999.

—. *The Spirit of Democratic Capitalism.* New York: Simon & Schuster Publication, 1982.

Novak, William. *Business as a Calling, Work and the Examined Life.* New York: Free Press, 1996.

Palackapilly, George, and T. D. Felix. *Religion and Economics: A World View.* New Delhi: AIDBES, 1998.

Parthasarathi, Prasannan. *Why Europe Grew Rich and Asia did not: Global Economic Divergence.* New York: Cambridge University Press, 2011.

Pearcy, Nancy. *Saving Leonardo: A Call to Resist the Secular Assault on Minds, Morals and Meaning.* Nashville: B&H Publishing Group, 2010.

Pirson, Michael, Wolfgang Amann, Shiban Khan, and Ernst von Kimakowitz, . *Humanism in Business.* New York: Cambridge University Press, 2009.

Putman, Robert D., and David E. Campbell. *American Grace: How Religion Divides and Unites Us.* New York: Simon & Schuster, 2010.

Rae, Scott, and Kenman Wong. *Beyond Integrity: A Judeo-Christian Approach to Business Ethics.* Grand Rapids: Zondervan, 1996.

Rao, Madhugiri Saroja A. "Religon and Economic Development." *Sociological Bulletin* (New Delhi) 18 (1969): 1-15.

Ridley, Matt. *The Rational Optimist: How Prosperity Evolves.* New York: HarperCollins Publishers, 2010.

Roodman, David. *The Natural Wealth of Nations: Harnessing the Market and the Environment.* London: Routledge, 1999.

Rose, David C. *The Moral Foundation of Economic Behavior.* New York: Oxford University Press, 2011.

Sachs, Jeffery D., and Pia Malaney. "The Economic and Social Burden of Malaria." *Nature Insight* 415 (February 2002).

Satz, Debra. *Why Some Things Should not be for Sale: The Moral Limits of Markets.* New York: Oxford University Press, 2010.

Schmidt, Alvin J. *Under the Influence: How Christianity Transformed Civilization.* Grand Rapids: Zondervan Publishing Company, 2001.

Sedlacek, Tomas. *Economics of Good and Evil: The Quest for Economic Meaning from Gilgamesh to Wall Street.* New York: Oxford University Press, 2011.

Bibliography

Shepherd, Frederick M., ed. *Christianity and the Struggle for Human Rights: Christians and the Struggle for Global Justice*. Lanham: Lexington Books, 2009.

Smith, Adam. *An Inquiry Into the Nature and Causes of the Wealth of Nations*. Indianapolis: Hackett Publishing, Inc., 1993.

Sowell, Thomas. *Black Rednecks and White Liberals*. San Francisco: Encounter Books, 2005.

Spector, Bertram I. *Fighting Corruption in Developing Countries: Strategies and Analysis*. Bloomfield: Kumarian Press Inc., 2005.

Stackhouse, Max, Dennis McCann, and Shirley Roels. *On Moral Business, Classical and Contemporary Resources for Ethics in Economic Life*. Grand Rapids: William B. Eerdmans Publishing Company, 1995.

Stark, Rodney. *For the Glory of God: How Monotheism Led to Reformations, Science, Witch-Hunts, and the End of Slavery*. Princeton: Princeton University Press, 2003.

—. *The Victory of Reason: How Christianity Led to Freedom, Capitalism, and Western Success*. New York: Random House, Inc., 2005.

Stearns, Jason K. *Dancing in the Glory of Monsters: The Collapse of the Congo and the Great War of Africa*. New York: PublicAffairs, 2011.

Sweetman, Brendan. *Why Politics Need Religion: The Place of Religious Arguments in the Public Square*. Downers Grover: Intervarsity Press, 2006.

Swierenga, Robert P. "The Little White Church: Historiographical Revisions on Religion in Rural America." *Agricultural History*, 1997.

Thepwethi, Phra, and P. A. Payutto. *Buddhist Economics- A Middle Way for the Market Place*. Bangkok: Buddhadhamma Foundation, 1994.

Thornton, Bruce. *Decline and Fall: Europe's Slow Motion Suicide*. New York: Encounter Books, 2007.

Twitchell, James B. *Lead us into Temptation: The Triumph of American Materialism*. New York: Columbia University Press, 1999.

Tyndale, Wendy. "Faith and Economics in 'Development': A Bridge Across the Chasm?" *Development in Practice* 10, no. 1 (2000): 9-18.

Versluysen, Eugene. *Defying the Odds: Banking for the Poor*. West Hartford: Kumarian Press Inc., 1999.

Warsh, David. *Knowledge and the Wealth of Nations*. New York: W. W. Norton & Company Inc., 2006.

Waterman, Anthony Michael Charles. "In What Sence, If Any, is 'Economics' Distinct from 'Religion', and Why Does it Matter?" *Forum for Social Economics* 25, no. 2 (1996): 1-32.

Bibliography

Wilson, Rodney. "Contemporary Jewish, Christian, and Muslim Economic Thought." *Journal of Interdisciplinary Economics* 8, no. 4 (1997): 307-317.

—. *Economics, Ethics, and Religion: Jewish, Christian, and Muslim Economic Thought.* Basingstroke, U. K.: Macmillian/New York: New York University Press, 1997.

Wilson, Rodney. "Morality in Economics." *Humanomics* 13, no. 3-4 (1997): 1-32.

Witham, Larry. *Marketplace of the Gods: How Economics Explains Religion.* New York: Oxford University Press, 2010.

Witte, John Jr., and M. Christian Green, . *Religion and Human Rights: An Introduction.* New York: Oxford University Printing Press, 2012.

Zweig, Michael, ed. *Religion and Economics.* Philadelphia: Temple University Press, 1991.

Made in the USA
Charleston, SC
21 January 2013